D1092868

Asian Transformations

UNU World Institute for Development Economics Research (UNU-WIDER) was established by the United Nations University as its first research and training centre and started work in Helsinki, Finland, in 1985. The mandate of the institute is to undertake applied research and policy analysis on structural changes affecting developing and transitional economies, to provide a forum for the advocacy of policies leading to robust, equitable, and environmentally sustainable growth, and to promote capacity strengthening and training in the field of economic and social policymaking. Its work is carried out by staff researchers and visiting scholars in Helsinki and via networks of collaborating scholars and institutions around the world.

United Nations University World Institute for
Development Economics Research (UNU-WIDER)
Katajanokanlaituri 6B, 00160 Helsinki, Finland
<www.wider.unu.edu>

Asian Transformations

*An Inquiry into the Development
of Nations*

Edited by

DEEPAK NAYYAR

A study prepared for the United Nations University World Institute
for Development Economics Research (UNU-WIDER)

OXFORD
UNIVERSITY PRESS

OXFORD
UNIVERSITY PRESS

Great Clarendon Street, Oxford, OX2 6DP,
United Kingdom

Oxford University Press is a department of the University of Oxford.
It furthers the University's objective of excellence in research, scholarship,
and education by publishing worldwide. Oxford is a registered trade mark of
Oxford University Press in the UK and in certain other countries

Published in the United States of America by Oxford University Press
198 Madison Avenue, New York, NY 10016, United States of America

British Library Cataloguing in Publication Data
Data available

Library of Congress Control Number: 2019937238

ISBN 978-0-19-884493-8

Printed and bound in Great Britain by
Clays Ltd, Elcograf S.p.A.

Links to third party websites are provided by Oxford in good faith and
for information only. Oxford disclaims any responsibility for the materials
contained in any third party website referenced in this work.

Foreword

Gunnar Myrdal published his magnum opus *Asian Drama: An Inquiry into the Poverty of Nations* in 1968. Described by one of his peers as a cheerful pessimist, Myrdal was deeply negative about Asia's development prospects and this pessimism was manifestly evident across the pages of his tome. However, the half-century since publication has witnessed a most remarkable social and economic transformation in Asia that would have been difficult for Myrdal to imagine, let alone predict, at the time of his writing.

During discussions with Deepak Nayyar—a former Chair of the UNU-WIDER Advisory Board—he proposed an in-depth inquiry into the how and why of the dramatic transformations within Asia since Myrdal's major work, looking at how nations can develop across time given their different national characteristics, political settlements, natural endowments, and starting points of development. As it turned out, that conversation pre-launched the UNU-WIDER research project, Asian Transformations—An Inquiry into the Development of Nations. The project maps and analyses the story of progress and economic development in Asia, with the region's transformed significance in the world economy, and reflects on what future decades might hold.

This book, with its comprehensive chapters by eminent economists and social scientists, is the distillation of the entire academic project, making it essential reading for economists, policymakers, and scholars and students of development. Valuable lessons can be drawn from the research—successes, failures, or mixed outcomes—that will help in thinking about the economic prospects of countries, whether leaders or laggards at the point of departure.

I sincerely thank the contributors for their studies, which share with us their individual expertise, and particularly Deepak Nayyar for bringing this very rich academic inquiry to full fruition.

UNU-WIDER gratefully acknowledges the support and financial contributions to its research programme by the governments of Finland, Sweden, in this case particularly the Swedish International Development Cooperation Agency—Sida, and the United Kingdom. Without this vital funding our research and policy analysis work would be impossible.

Finn Tarp

Director, UNU-WIDER
Helsinki, December 2018

Preface

In early September 2016, I was browsing through the bookshelves in my study, when I spotted the three volumes of Gunnar Myrdal's *Asian Drama*, which I had read as a graduate student in economics at Oxford soon after it was published. I had returned to it off and on while working on development or on India. But this time around, it was after a decade if not longer. I decided to re-read Appendix 3 on economic models, with its critique of capital–output ratios, in the context of development planning. This was, in fact, written by Paul Streeten, who was a part of the Myrdal team for *Asian Drama*. They were close friends for years, as Streeten had translated and edited Myrdal's earlier work on economic theory and on methodological problems. Paul was also my supervisor as a doctoral student at Oxford. It was the beginning of our lifelong friendship. And I met Gunnar Myrdal once with Paul Streeten. The accidental browsing brought back memories from that time. It struck me that, in 2018, it will be fifty years since the book was published. This led me to think that a study, which analyses the story of economic development in Asia, over this span of half a century, would be a wonderful idea.

As it happened, just a week later, I was participating in the WIDER Annual Conference at Helsinki. It occurred to me that UNU-WIDER, located in the Nordic world, with its focus on development would be the perfect institutional base for such a study. And I mentioned this adventurous idea to Finn Tarp, Director of UNU-WIDER. He said that he would think about it and explore possibilities. Barely two months later, he was in touch with me to say that UNU-WIDER would like to collaborate on such a study.

At a first step, I wrote a short concept note setting out the idea. In mid-February 2017, this was discussed in an informal brainstorming meeting with Ernest Aryeteey, Ronald Findlay, Justin Lin, Frances Stewart and Robert Wade, in Helsinki—Finn Tarp and Tony Addison were also present and participated in the discussions. The comments and suggestions from all the participants were most constructive. The study was then conceptualized in terms of structure and contents. The project began life in late March 2017 as authors were commissioned over the next three months. The complete first drafts of the papers written for the project were discussed at a workshop of authors at the Central Institute for Economic Management, in Hanoi, Vietnam, on 9–10 March 2018. The discussions were rich, engaging, and productive. Revised versions of the papers were discussed further at a second workshop of authors at Fudan University, Shanghai, China, on 29–30 June 2017, where Guanghua Wan, a contributor to this volume, was our gracious host. This meeting provided valuable suggestions for the authors and the editor. Selected aspects and highlights of the study were also presented at a plenary session of the WIDER Annual Conference in mid-September 2018, which was followed by a helpful discussion. I would also like to record my appreciation of the work done by referees, who reviewed draft papers at different stages. Their evaluation and comments helped improve the quality of the volume. Above all, I am grateful to the contributors for their patience, understanding, and effort in putting up with my demands for successive rounds of revisions.

This book, and its companion volume, *Resurgent Asia: Diversity in Development*, are the outcome of the UNU-WIDER research project Asian Transformations. I am indebted to Finn Tarp for his acceptance of the idea and his commitment to what seemed an exceedingly difficult task at the time. Somewhat late in the lifecycle of the project, I also persuaded him to write a chapter on Vietnam for the volume. In the journey to completion, the unstinted support from Finn Tarp was invaluable.

I owe a special word of thanks to the staff at UNU-WIDER in Helsinki, who lent wonderful support throughout over two years even though I lived in faraway New Delhi. Tony Addison, with his perceptive and interesting ideas, was a lively participant and discussant at all our meetings and workshops. Paul Silfvenius provided us with quiet, efficient, administrative support. Janis Vehmaan-Kreula, the project secretary, our anchor in Helsinki, was a pillar of support, with tireless effort and complete dedication, for me and for all the contributors spread across the globe. Lorraine Telfer-Taivainen, super efficient at whatever she does, helped us at the Shanghai workshop, and, most importantly, prepared the final manuscript for publication. The authors alone know how hard she worked.

It is difficult for me to find the words to thank Rajeev Malhotra, who worked as my principal assistant on the project with a strong commitment that is worthy of praise. He was conscientious, meticulous, and efficient. It was multi-tasking in every sense of the word. He helped in preparing for our author workshops, making presentations for authors who were unable to come, acting as a discussant, or summing up sessions, and then assisting with follow-up. And he was a careful reader of papers. In fact, Rajeev provided valuable assistance whenever, and in whatever form, it was needed. It was gracious of him to find the time for these tasks, given his own academic obligations—I owe him a debt of gratitude.

The object of this book is to analyse the development experience of Asia over the past five decades. There is no such study yet. And this is new. It should, at the same time, contribute to our understanding of the process of development. There are, perhaps, lessons that can be drawn from the Asian experience—successes, mixed outcomes, failures—which might help in thinking about economic prospects of countries in Asia and elsewhere that are latecomers to, or laggards in, development. In this half-century, the world has witnessed profound changes in economic development, social progress, and living standards. And, contrary to Myrdal's expectations, Asia has been transformed beyond recognition. These transformations have been uneven across countries and unequal among people.

Yet, Asia's remarkable development over the past fifty years has also transformed its significance in the world economy. Thus, how the future unfolds in Asia over the next twenty-five years will have important implications for the world. Given the enormous diversity and massive size of Asia as a continent, this study is obviously an ambitious endeavour. It should come as no surprise that there are unexplored themes, unsettled issues, and unanswered questions. Even so, it is hoped that this book will contribute to our understanding of, and stimulate further thinking on, the subject.

Deepak Nayyar

New Delhi
December 2018

Table of Contents

PART III COUNTRY AND SUB-REGION STUDIES

Country Studies

Sub-Region Studies

List of Figures

List of Tables

List of Tables

List of Abbreviations

ADB	Asian Development Bank
AFTA	ASEAN Free Trade Area
APEC	Asia-Pacific Economic Cooperation
ASEAN	Association of Southeast Asian Nations
ATC	Agreement on Textiles and Clothing
BIMAS	Behavior Intervention Monitoring Assessment System
BJP	Bharatiya Janata Party
BoP	Balance of Payments
BPHS	Basic Package of Hospital Services
BRAC	Bangladesh Rural Advancement Committee
BRIC	Brazil, Russia, India, China
CCP	Chinese Communist Party
CDs	communicable diseases
CDB	China Development Bank
CEXIM	Export–Import Bank of China
CMS	Cooperative Medical System
CPV	Communist Party of Vietnam
DFI	Development Finance Institution
DPP	Democratic Progressive Party
ECE	Economic Commission for Europe
EPB	Economic Planning Board
EPHS	Essential Package of Hospital Services
EPZ	export processing zone
FDI	foreign direct investment
GATT	General Agreement on Tariffs and Trade
GDP	gross domestic product
GER	gross enrolment rate
GFCF	gross fixed capital formation
GNH	gross national happiness
GNI	gross national income
GNP	gross national product
GRI	government research institute
GVCs	global value chains
HIDZ	high-technology industrial development zone
HYVs	high-yielding varieties
ICICI	Industrial Credit and Investment Corporation of India
ICT	Information and Communications Technology
IDBI	Industrial Development Bank of India

IFCI	Industrial Finance Corporation of India
IFI	international financial institution
ILO	International Labour Organization
IMF	International Monetary Fund
IMR	infant mortality rate
IPPG	Index of Pro-Poor Growth
IRRI	International Rice Research Institute
IS	import substitution
ITRI	Industrial Technology Research Institute
IVA	industrial value-added
JKN	*Jaminan Kesehatan Nasional* (Scheme)
Jokowi	Joko Widodo
KMT	Kuomintang
Lao PDR	Lao People's Democratic Republic
LDCs	Least Developed Countries
MDGs	Millennium Development Goals
MEXIM	Export–Import Bank of Malaysia
MFA	multi-fibre arrangement
MMR	maternal mortality rate
MNC	multinational corporation
MVA	manufacturing value-added
NCD	non-communicable disease
NDB	National Development Bank
NER	net enrolment rate
NICs	newly industrializing countries
NIEs	newly industrializing economies
NIF	National Investment Fund
NIP	new industrial policy
NREGA	National Rural Employment Guarantee Act
NU	Nahdlatul Ulama (Indonesia's largest Islamic organization)
ODA	official development assistance
OECD	Organisation for Economic Cooperation and Development
OOP	Out-Of-Pocket (spending)
PAP	People's Action Party
PCR	primary completion rate
PER	primary enrolment rate
PISA	Programme for International Students Assessment
PPP	purchasing power parity
PRC	People's Republic of China
PRSP	Poverty Reduction Strategy Paper
PWT	Penn World Tables
R&D	research and development
ROC	Republic of China (Taiwan)
ROK	Republic of Korea
RRA	relative rate of assistance

SAM	social accounting matrix
SAPs	structural adjustment programmes
SBY	Susilo Bambang Yudhoyono
SDGs	Sustainable Development Goals
SER	secondary enrolment rate
SEZ	special economic zone
SI	social insurance
SLFP	Sri Lanka Freedom Party
SMERU	Social Monitoring and Evaluation Research Unit
SMEs	small and medium-sized enterprises
SOEs	state-owned enterprises
SSA	sub-Saharan Africa
STAG	Science and Technology Advisory Group
SUSENAS	Indonesia National Socio-Economic Survey
TER	tertiary enrolment rate
TFP	total factor productivity
TPP	Trans-Pacific Partnership
TVE	Technical and Vocational Education
UMNO	United Malays National Organisation
UNCTAD	United Nations Conference on Trade and Development
UNP	United National Party
UPFA	United People's Freedom Alliance
VA	value added
VARHS	Vietnam Access to Resources Household Survey
VHLSS	Vietnam Household Living Standard Survey
WDI	World Development Indicators
WID	World Inequality Database
WIID	UNU-WIDER World Income Inequality Database
WTO	World Trade Organization

Notes on Contributors

Kaushik Basu is a professor of economics and Carl Marks Professor of International Studies at Cornell University, Ithaca and New York. He was formerly Chief Economist of the World Bank in Washington. He has published widely in the fields of development economics, game theory, industrial organization, and law and economics. His most recent book is *The Republic of Beliefs: A New Approach to Law and Economics* (Princeton University Press 2018).

Amit Bhaduri is professor emeritus at Jawaharlal Nehru University (JNU), New Delhi. His areas of specialization are macroeconomics and development economics, both aided by appropriate mathematical modelling. He has published widely in these areas.

Ha-Joon Chang teaches economics and is the Director of the Centre of Development Studies at the University of Cambridge. He has published widely on the role of the state, trade and industrial policy, and institutions. By 2018, his writings will have been translated in forty-one languages and forty-four countries. Worldwide, his books have sold around two million copies. He is the winner of the 2003 Gunnar Myrdal Prize and the 2005 Wassily Leontief Prize.

Prasenjit Duara is the Oscar Tang Chair of East Asian Studies at Duke University. He received his PhD in Chinese history from Harvard University. He was Professor of History and East Asian Studies at University of Chicago (1991–2008) and Raffles Professor and Director of Asia Research Institute at the National University of Singapore (2008–2015). His latest book is *The Crisis of Global Modernity: Asian Traditions and a Sustainable Future* (Cambridge 2014). He was awarded an Honorary Doctorate from the University of Oslo in September 2017.

Peter Evans—professor emeritus in the Department of Sociology, University of California, Berkeley, and senior fellow in international studies at the Watson Institute for International Studies, Brown University—is best known for his work on the political economy of national development, as exemplified by his 1995 book *Embedded Autonomy: States and Industrial Transformation* (Princeton University Press 1995). In recent articles he has examined changing state–society relations and the role of labour, as well as transnational social movements.

Ronald Findlay studied at Rangoon University, BA 1954, and MIT, PhD 1960. He taught at Rangoon University during 1954–1957 and again in 1960–1968, and Columbia University during 1969–2014, retiring in 2014 as the Ragnar Nurkse Professor Emeritus of Economics. His fields of interest have been the theory of international trade, economic development, political economy, and the history of the world economy.

Patrick Heller is the Lyn Crost Professor of Social Sciences and professor of sociology and international studies at Brown University. His main area of research is the comparative study of social inequality and democratic deepening. He is the author of *The Labor of*

Development: Workers in the Transformation of Capitalism in Kerala, India (Cornell 1999) and co-author of *Social Democracy and the Global Periphery* (Cambridge 2006), *Bootstrapping Democracy: Transforming Local Governance and Civil Society in Brazil* (Stanford 2011) and most recently, *Deliberation and Development: Rethinking the Role of Voice and Collective Action in Unequal Societies* (World Bank 2015).

Ravi Kanbur is T.H. Lee Professor of World Affairs, International Professor of Applied Economics and Management and Professor of Economics at Cornell University. He is Chair of the Board of United Nations University World Institute for Development Economics Research—UNU-WIDER, Co-Chair of the Scientific Council of the International Panel on Social Progress, member of the OECD High-Level Expert Group on the Measurement of Economic Performance, past-President of the Society for the Study of Economic Inequality, past-President of the Human Development and Capabilities Association, past member of the High-Level Advisory Council of the Climate Justice Dialogue, and past-member of the Core Group of the Commission on Global Poverty.

Mushtaq H. Khan is a professor of economics at SOAS, University of London and Chief Executive Director of the DFID-funded Anti-Corruption Evidence (ACE) Research Partnership Consortium. His research interests are in institutional economics and South Asian development. He has published widely on corruption and rent-seeking, political settlements, industrial policy, and governance reforms in developing countries.

Richard Kozul-Wright is Director of the Globalization and Development Strategies Division in UNCTAD. He has worked at the United Nations in both New York and Geneva. He holds a PhD in economics from the University of Cambridge, UK, and has published widely on a range of economic issues, inter alia, in the *Economic Journal*, the *Cambridge Journal of Economics*, the *Journal of Development Studies*, and the *Oxford Review of Economic Policy*.

Justin Lin Yifu is Dean of Institute of New Structural Economics, and Institute of South–South Cooperation and Development, Peking University. He was the Senior Vice President and Chief Economist of the World Bank, 2008–2012. He has published more than thirty books on development, Chinese economy and agriculture. He is a Corresponding Fellow of the British Academy, and a Fellow of the Academy of Sciences for Developing World.

Manuel F. Montes is Senior Advisor on Finance and Development at the South Centre, Geneva. He was previously chief of the development strategies branch at the UN Department of Economic and Social Affairs, and an associate professor of economics at the University of the Philippines. His publications have been in the areas of development macroeconomics and finance, on industrial development, and on systemic issues.

Sudipto Mundle is Emeritus Professor at the National Institute of Public Finance and Policy. He spent much of his career at the Asian Development Bank, from where he retired as a Director in the Strategy and Policy Department. He has served on the faculty of several research institutions and was also an economic advisor in India's Ministry of Finance. His main research interests include development economics, macroeconomic modelling, fiscal and monetary policy and governance. He has published several books and papers in professional journals in these fields.

Deepak Nayyar is Emeritus Professor of Economics at Jawaharlal Nehru University, New Delhi, and an Honorary Fellow of Balliol College, Oxford. He was Distinguished University Professor of Economics at the New School for Social Research, New York. Earlier, he taught at the University of Oxford, the University of Sussex, and the Indian Institute of Management, Calcutta. He served as Vice Chancellor of the University of Delhi, and as Chief Economic Advisor to the Government of India. He has published widely in academic journals. His books include *Catch Up: Developing Countries in the World Economy* (Oxford University Press 2013).

Siddiqur Rahman Osmani is a professor of development economics at Ulster University, UK. He has published widely on issues related to employment, poverty, inequality, hunger, famine, nutrition, the human rights approach to development, globalization, microcredit, and development problems in general.

Daniel Poon is Economic Affairs Officer in the Division of Globalization and Development Strategies (GDS) in UNCTAD. His research focuses on industrial policy strategy in Asia with a focus on East Asia, and in particular China. He has also published in the area of development finance, and South–South economic co-operation.

Frances Stewart is Emeritus Professor of Development Economics, University of Oxford. Her prime research interests are horizontal inequalities, conflict, and human development. Among many publications, she is leading author of *Horizontal Inequalities and Conflict: Understanding Group Violence in Multiethnic Societies*, and of *Human Development: Theory and Practice*.

Finn Tarp is a professor of development economics, University of Copenhagen, and was Director of UNU-WIDER, Helsinki, 2009–2018. His field experience covers more than two decades of in-country work in thirty-five countries across Africa, and the developing world more generally. Professor Tarp's research focus is on issues of development strategy and foreign aid, with an interest in poverty, income distribution and growth, micro- and macroeconomic policy and modelling, agricultural sector policy and planning, and household and enterprise development. He has published widely and has extensive research and advisory experience in Vietnam. In addition to his university positions, he has held senior posts and advisory positions within governments and with donor organizations, and he is member of a large number of international committees and advisory bodies. In 2015, he was knighted by Queen Margrethe II of Denmark with the Order of the Dannebrog.

C. Peter Timmer is an authority on agricultural development, food security, and the world rice economy, and has published scores of papers and books on these topics. He has served as a professor at Stanford, Cornell, three faculties at Harvard, and the University of California, San Diego. He is currently the Cabot Professor of Development Studies, emeritus, at Harvard University. In 2012 he was awarded the Leontief Prize for advances in economic thought, and in 2014 delivered the 18th Annual WIDER Lecture at the UN in New York.

Rolph van der Hoeven is Professor Emeritus, Employment and Development Economics at the International Institute of Social Studies (ISS), Erasmus University (EUR), The Hague. He is also member of the Committee on Development Cooperation of the International Advisory Council (AIV) of the Dutch Government and of several other

Dutch development organizations. Earlier he was Director Policy Coherence and Manager of the Technical Secretariat of the World Commission on the Social Dimension of Globalization at ILO Geneva. Other positions included Chief Economist of UNICEF in New York and policy analyst for the ILO in Ethiopia and Zambia. He is widely published in the area of employment, inequality, globalization, and global governance.

Rob Vos is Director of Markets, Trade and Institutions at the International Food Policy Research Institute (IFPRI). He is also Professor of Finance and Development at the International Institute of Social Studies, The Hague. Previously, he has held positions at the Food and Agriculture Organization (FAO) as Director of Agricultural Development Economics and at the United Nations as Director of Development Policy Analysis. He has published widely on issues of international trade and finance, poverty, sustainable development, and food security.

Robert H. Wade is a professor of global political economy at the London School of Economics. He is the author of *Irrigation and Agricultural Politics in South Korea* (Westview Press 1982); *Village Republics: Economic Conditions for Collective Action in South India* (Westview Press 1989); and *Governing the Market: Economic Theory and the Role of Government in East Asian Industrialization* (Princeton University Press 2004). The latter was awarded Best Book or Article in Political Economy Prize from the American Political Science Association. He was awarded the Leontief Prize in Economics in 2008.

Guanghua Wan is Director and Professor, Institute of World Economy, Fudan University. Previously, he was Research Director and Head of Poverty and Inequality Group, Asian Development Bank. Prior to ADB, he was a senior economist in the United Nations and has taught in a number of Universities in Australia and China. Trained in development economics and econometrics, he is a multi-award-winning scholar on the Chinese economy and an expert on Asia, with a publication record of more than 100 professional articles and a dozen or so books, including two by Oxford University Press. He is an honorary professor of over ten top institutions in China.

Chen Wang is an associate professor at the Institute of Finance and Economics, Shanghai University of Finance and Economics, and a research fellow at the Department of Economics of Leiden University. Her research interests include income inequality, poverty, consumption, and economics of aging. She has published papers in refereed journals, such as *Journal of Economic Surveys, Cambridge Journal of Economics, Journal of Social Policy, Social Indicators Research, The World Economy, China Economic Review*, and *International Journal of Social Welfare*.

Kiryl Zach is a PhD candidate in the Centre of Development Studies, University of Cambridge. His main research interest is the study of industrial policy of Poland. He is investigating changes and continuities of various policy strategies, principles and driving motives for industrialization in the three seemingly altogether separate periods—inter-war period, post-Second World War communism, and the post-1989 neo-liberal turn.

PART I
SETTING THE STAGE

1

Rethinking *Asian Drama*

Fifty Years Later

Deepak Nayyar

1. Introduction

Gunnar Myrdal published his magnum opus, *Asian Drama: An Inquiry into the Poverty of Nations*, in 1968. The fifty years since then have witnessed a remarkable economic transformation in Asia—even if it has been uneven across countries and unequal between people—that would have been difficult to imagine, let alone predict, when Myrdal and his associates completed their work. The present book analyses the story of economic development in Asia spanning half a century. This chapter explains the conception and design of the study for the reader. It begins with a discussion on Gunnar Myrdal, the author, and *Asian Drama*, the book, as a point of reference. It then sets out the rationale and the object of the study, to outline its structure and framework. This leads into a discussion, illustrative rather than exhaustive, of some important ideas and lessons that emerge, which might serve as a teaser. Thereafter, it provides a brief narrative on the contents and scope of the book, meant as a road map for readers.

2. Gunnar Myrdal and *Asian Drama*

Gunnar Myrdal was a man of many parts. The word polymath is an apt description, which might not suffice to describe a man who was a distinguished academic, policy practitioner, member of parliament, cabinet minister, international civil servant, political actor, public intellectual, and concerned citizen.[1] This diversity of experiences shaped his work and thinking.

In academia, Stockholm University was his institutional home (1933–1950). He started as a brilliant theorist, a brash young academic,[2] who went on to

---

[1] For accounts of Gunnar Myrdal, the person and his life, see Streeten (1990, 1998); Appelqvist and Andersson (2005); Bok (2005); Barber (2008); and Kanbur (Chapter 2, this volume).

[2] Evidently, Gustav Cassel, whom he succeeded as Chair in Political Economy at Stockholm University (1933–1939), once warned him against his brashness, 'Gunnar, you should be more respectful to your elders, because it is we who will determine your promotion'. Yes, the young Myrdal replied, 'but it is we who will write your obituaries'. After Cassel's death, he did indeed write his obituary (Streeten 1990).

question the methodological foundations and ideological underpinnings of economics, returning to his ivory tower at Stockholm University (1962–1967) when he founded the Institute for International Economic Studies, and was awarded the Nobel Prize in Economics in 1974. In professional life outside academia, he turned to political economy and developed the idea of countercyclical macroeconomic policies in the early 1930s. There was an interregnum of four years (1938–1942) when he lived in the United States to study on the 'Negro Problem'. He returned home to political institutions in the 1940s when he chaired a committee that outlined the elements of the post-war Swedish welfare state, to become a member of parliament, Chairman of the Planning Commission in Sweden, and Minister for Trade and Commerce. During the Cold War era, he was appointed Executive Secretary of the United Nations Economic Commission in Europe, where he served from 1947 to 1957. The next ten years were devoted to his study on Asia, of which he spent four years in New Delhi, where his wife, Alva Myrdal (sociologist, diplomat, and politician, who was awarded the Nobel Peace Prize in 1982) served as Sweden's Ambassador in India from 1955 to 1961.

There was also a remarkable intellectual journey that ran in parallel, with many milestones and some landmarks. Three deserve mention for their common purpose—critique of systemic biases and implicit values in economic thinking—and for their diversity of subjects: politics in economics, race in society, and poverty in the world. *The Political Element in the Development of Economic Theory* was published in Swedish in 1930, in German in 1932, and in English, translated by Paul Streeten, in 1953. *An American Dilemma: The Negro Problem and Modern Democracy*, for which he spent four years in the US, was published in 1944.[3] *Asian Drama*, on which he worked in India for four years and in Sweden for six years, was published in 1968. Yet, the book also was influenced by the evolution of Myrdal's thinking in economics and the social sciences over a lifetime.

In this magnum opus, the fundamental point of departure from conventional thinking was the conviction that 'economic problems cannot be studied in isolation but only in their own demographic, social and political setting' (Myrdal 1968: ix). The book and its approach are best described in the author's words from the preface:

> It is not an altogether pretentious metaphor when I describe my endeavour to apply an institutional approach in this study as an attempt to analyse the development problems of South Asia in a manner that Adam Smith studied England's development problems two hundred years ago...The length is abominable. The question can, indeed, be raised why I did not break it up into five or six books...

---

[3] *Economic Theory and Underdeveloped Regions*, published in 1957, was early thinking about development, while *Value in Social Theory*, critical essays on methodology written earlier, translated into English and edited by Paul Streeten, was published in 1958. For a more detailed discussion on Myrdal's academic writings, see Kanbur (Chapter 2, this volume). See also, Streeten (1998) and Barber (2008).

But the central idea in the institutional approach is that history and politics, theories and ideologies, economic structures and levels, social stratification, agriculture and industry, population developments, health and education, and so on, must be studied not in isolation but in their mutual relationships.

(Myrdal 1968: x)

The title, *Asian Drama*, was deceptive in terms of its country coverage. Its focus was on the erstwhile British India, made up of India, Pakistan, and Ceylon, the sub-continent now described as South Asia. Burma and Indonesia were paid some attention. But Malaysia, Philippines, and Thailand were grouped together as the rest of Southeast Asia, while Cambodia, Laos, and South Vietnam were touched upon when some information of interest was available. It is interesting, although somewhat puzzling, to note that Myrdal described all these countries broadly as South Asia even if many of them are now seen as part of Southeast Asia.[4] However, Japan, Korea, China, Formosa (Taiwan), Hong Kong, and Singapore were excluded. So was West Asia. And, it is no surprise that the central Asian economies, then part of the USSR, were also excluded.

Myrdal set out a conceptual framework and an analytical approach to study the constraints on, and possibilities of, development in Asia at an early stage of the postcolonial era when experience in terms of outcomes was limited. Some important points of departure from studies of development at that time, which reflected his methodological concerns, are set out explicitly in the Prologue titled 'The Beam in Our Eyes'. It begins with a plea for the sociology of knowledge, to emphasize the importance of a multidisciplinary approach in social sciences, the recognition of many biases in the study of development, the critical role of institutions, and the necessity of making assumptions, priors and values explicit. The implicit critique of mainstream economics had three dimensions. First, the essence of the institutional approach is to use all relevant knowledge to analyse a problem, unconstrained by the boundaries of disciplines, because in an inter-dependent social system there are only problems that are not simply economic, social, or political. Second, the garb of scientific analysis often conceals or dis-guises values, priors or interests that are political, and the implied objectivity which is spurious must be replaced by explicit valuations. Third, development objectives should be formulated on the basis of the actual needs or valuations of people, instead of the narrow definitions or metaphysical concepts so characteristic of statisticians or economists.

In this worldview, development was a multidimensional process of circular causation and cumulative change in which economy, polity, and society interacted not only with each other but also with technology, history, and culture. Cumulative

---

[4] This description is illustrated by a map of South Asia in Myrdal (1968) which includes all the selected countries (volume 1: 4–5). The scope and coverage of the study is also set out in the text (volume 1: 39–41).

causation could create vicious circles through negative feedbacks or virtuous circles through positive feedbacks. This approach and conceptualization were both perceptive and correct. But his analysis of the prevalent situation in underdeveloped Asia sought to focus on output and incomes, conditions of production, levels of living, attitudes towards life and work, institutions, and policies. Taken together, these constituted a social system that represented a powerful constraint on development, which meant that poor countries and poor people would remain poor.[5] The interaction of these conditions, Myrdal believed, would lead to 'either an unchanged level of underdevelopment, which is to say stagnation, or else development to a higher level or a regression to a lower level' (1968: 1864). The challenge of development, then, was intervention in the form of policies and planning by governments to transform the process of cumulative causation so that it could create virtuous circles through positive feedbacks and spread effects.

In retrospect, it is clear that there were some valuable analytical insights, such as the concept of cumulative causation, that remain just as relevant now for an understanding of development process.[6] The idea of operational controls over the private sector through trade policy, monetary policy, or fiscal policy, which could be positive and uniform (even if selective) or negative and discretionary—and their rational co-ordination—was also perceptive in its thinking about state intervention in markets.[7] These were its strengths. But there were weaknesses too. The role of governments was recognized in the context of planning in market economies, which was also part of the Development Consensus at the time. Yet, this critical importance of governments was diluted by the notion of a 'soft state', where governments did not have the willingness or ability to do what was necessary in the pursuit of development objectives because they could neither resist nor coerce powerful vested interests. Similarly, the possibilities that economic openness could also create development opportunities were simply not recognized, because the belief in export pessimism and the absence of capital movements were accepted as characteristics of the world economy that would remain forever.[8]

For these reasons, perhaps, Myrdal's assessment of the possibilities in the countries studied led him to a deep pessimism about development prospects in Asia.[9] In sum, economic problems were intractable, political problems were formidable, while solutions that could transform the possible into the probable, or the desirable into the feasible, were exceedingly difficult if not elusive. Myrdal's conception of

---

[5] For an elaboration of these ideas, see Myrdal (1968, volume III, appendix 2: 1843–78). For a critical evaluation, see Stewart (Chapter 3, this volume).

[6] On cumulative causation, see Myrdal (1968, volume III, appendix 2: 1870–8).

[7] On operational controls, see Myrdal (1968, volume II, chapter 19 and volume III, appendix 8).

[8] See Myrdal (1968, volume I, chapter 13). Its discussion on foreign trade is based on the premise of export pessimism, while its discussion on capital flows argues that international capital movements could not be a source of investment in Asia.

[9] For a detailed assessment of possibilities and constraints in the countries studied, see Myrdal (1968 volume I: on India, chapter 7; on Pakistan, chapter 8; on Ceylon and Southeast Asia, chapter 9).

drama, speeding towards a climax in which economic, social, and political tensions are mounting, captured the essence of this narrative (1968: 34).

The asymmetry between his optimism in *American Dilemma* and his pessimism in *Asian Drama* is striking indeed. There are three plausible reasons but only conjectures are possible. First, he might have believed that the progressive, liberal and egalitarian values of people and democracy in the US would support progressive change, while the mass of the population in South Asia did not share the modernization values of the elite and democracy could not suffice with a 'soft state'. Second, when he started work on *Asian Drama*, there was an unbounded optimism about India, but a decade later, when he was about to finish the work, the future of India appeared shrouded in uncertainty. Third, in a conversation over dinner, Myrdal told Streeten that when he wrote *American Dilemma* he could identify with American ideals, but when he wrote *Asian Drama*, he saw the half-naked brown bodies in an Indian textile factory, who seemed utterly alien to him, and he could not find anything in common with them.[10]

3. Rationale and Objective

The reality of development that has unfolded in Asia since then has belied such pessimism about its prospects.[11] The significance of Asia in the world economy has witnessed phenomenal change. But that is not all. Asian economies have also undergone a major structural transformation, while development indicators—demographic, social, economic—suggest impressive progress. It is important to note that this transformative change has occurred in just fifty years, which is a relatively short time span in history.[12]

Between 1970 and 2016, the share of Asia in world GDP, in current prices at market exchange rates, more than trebled from less than one-tenth to three-tenths, by as much as 21 percentage points, in almost equal parts at the expense of industrialized countries and transition economies (Eastern Europe and the former USSR). This was attributable to much higher GDP growth rates in Asia as compared with other parts of the world. As population growth rates slowed down, even growth in GDP per capita was significantly higher. Over the same period,

---

[10] The first explanation is put forward by Stewart (Chapter 3, this volume). The second explanation is hinted at by Siegel (2017). And the third explanation is narrated by Streeten (1990). In fairness, it might just have been an affinity with Americans. Streeten continues this story to write, perhaps tongue in cheek, that for Myrdal 'In fact, the Americans came almost as high in the rank order of creation as the Swedes. Then came nothing for a long time; then the English, and only after them the Europeans. He called America his second home' (1990: 1035).

[11] Given the focus on developing countries, in this study, Asia excludes Japan and Israel, which are high-income industrialized countries.

[12] The evidence on Asia, cited in the following paragraphs, draws on the author's work in the companion volume. For a detailed discussion, see Nayyar (2019).

GDP per capita in Asia, as a proportion of GDP per capita in the world economy rose from less than one-sixth to more than one-half, suggesting a significant convergence. But the ratio of GDP per capita in Asia to GDP per capita in industrialized countries, in current prices at market exchange rates, increased far less from 1:20 in 1970 to 1:8 in 2016. The wide gap, which was large to start with, narrowed a little, so that the convergence was at best modest. The catch-up was more impressive in aggregates in the spheres of industrialization and trade. The share of Asia in manufacturing value-added in the world economy soared from 4 per cent in 1970 to 41 per cent in 2016. Over this period, in current prices at market exchange rates, the contribution of Asia to world merchandise trade quadrupled, as its share in world exports rose from 8 per cent to 36 per cent, and in world imports from 8 per cent to 32 per cent. The share of Asia in world exports of manufactured goods almost doubled in just two decades from 21 per cent in 1995 to 39 per cent in 2016.

The structural transformation within Asia was just as striking. During the period 1970–2016, in Asia, the share of the primary sector (agriculture, forestry, animal husbandry, and fishing) in GDP fell from 27 per cent to 8 per cent,[13] while the share of manufacturing value-added in GDP rose from 10 per cent to 22 per cent, and the ratio of merchandise trade (exports plus imports) to GDP increased from 43 per cent to 70 per cent, all measured in current prices at market exchange rates. In 1965, almost four-fifths of the total population of Asia lived in rural areas whereas, by 2016, this proportion was just over one-half, so that urbanization was rapid.

The demographic and social transformation of Asia, during the fifty years from 1965 to 2016, was also remarkable. In terms of demographics, the population of Asia increased from 1.75 billion to 4.24 billion. Consequently, population density in a land-scarce continent almost trebled. Yet, birth rates (per 1000 population) fell from 40 to 17, while fertility rates (births per woman) dropped from 6 to 2. Social development in Asia was also impressive, as life expectancy at birth rose from 49 years to 72 years, literacy rates increased from 43 per cent to 82 per cent, while infant mortality rates dropped 160 to 23 per 1000 live births.

This transformation in terms of aggregates or averages might conceal as much as it reveals. It was characterized by uneven development in Asia. For one, the growth performance and rising shares in output, manufacturing, or trade were concentrated in a few countries. For another, demographic or social indicators are arithmetic averages that cannot measure the well-being of the poor. Development in Asia was most unequal between its constituent sub-regions and among people within countries. Consequently, the rapid economic growth was not always transformed into meaningful development that improved the well-being of

---

[13] For East Asia, Southeast Asia and South Asia, taken together, the share of the primary sector in GDP dropped far more from 42 per cent in 1970 to 9 per cent in 2016 (Nayyar 2019).

people. Of course, there was a significant reduction in absolute poverty that would not have been possible without rapid growth. But sustained rapid growth in Asia did not reduce absolute poverty as much as it could have, in part because the initial income distribution was unequal and in part because of rising income inequality. All the same, it is clear that Asian development in this era was driven by economic growth based on high investment–savings rates, and rapid industrialization, often export-led, associated with structural change in the composition of output and employment, which reinforced the process.[14]

It would seem that, during the past half a century, the Asian continent has witnessed profound transformations, in terms of economic progress and living conditions, even if it has been uneven across countries and unequal between people. Yet, five decades ago, such change would have been thought of as imagination running wild. Indeed, at the time, the economic prospects of Asia were perceived as dim by most observers and analysts. In this sentiment, Myrdal was by no means alone in his pessimism about Asia. Of course, perfect foresight exists only as an abstraction in economic theory. But the benefit of hindsight does provide a good reason for an inquiry into the economic transformation of nations. The story of economic change and social progress in Asia since then deserves exploration. It provides the rationale and the motivation for the present study.

The object of this study is to analyse the development experience of Asia and its associated transformations over the past fifty years. There is no such study yet. And this should be new. It would, at the same time, contribute to our understanding of the process of development. There are, perhaps, lessons that can be drawn from the Asian experience—successes, failures, or mixed outcomes—which might help in thinking about economic prospects of countries in Asia that are latecomers to, or laggards in, development, and suggest possibilities for countries elsewhere in the developing world. In this half-century, the world has changed almost beyond recognition. Thus, it would also be appropriate for the study to reflect, even if briefly, on how the next twenty-five years might unfold in Asia.

It needs to be said that *Asian Drama* is no more than a point of entry or reference for this study. It is not meant to be a sequel. And it is hoped that this work will have an identity of its own. Clearly, a study in three volumes was just not feasible. A stand-alone single book would also have been a difficult if not formidable task, not only because it was bound to have become much too long but also because it could not possibly have had the depth in particular domains that some readers might search for. After much deliberation, I chose the middle path of two companion volumes that complement each other. Given the vast scope of the study, this is perhaps the most appropriate.

---

[14] For a detailed discussion of these issues, with supporting evidence, see Nayyar (2013, 2017). See also, the companion volume, Nayyar (2019).

It is perhaps instructive to invoke a historical fact here. Until around 1750, Asia accounted for almost three-fifths of world population and world income, while China and India together accounted for about one-half of world population and world income. These two Asian giants also contributed 57 per cent of manufacturing production and an even larger proportion of manufactured exports in the world. The Industrial Revolution in Britain brought about a radical transformation of the situation over the next two centuries culminating in the decline and fall of Asia during the period from 1820 to 1950.[15] The solitary exception was Japan after the Meiji Restoration in 1868. The second half of the twentieth century witnessed the beginnings of change once again. It began with South Korea, Taiwan, Hong Kong, and Singapore, often described as the 'East Asian Tigers', in the early 1970s. Some Southeast Asian countries—Malaysia and Thailand—followed in their footsteps in the late 1980s. China and India came next. Rapid economic growth, led by industrialization, has enabled Asia to narrow the gap. This momentous ongoing shift in world economic history has interested me for some time (Nayyar 2013). It needs to be explained and analysed. In this context, I was struck by the pessimism of Myrdal in *Asian Drama*, although he cannot be blamed for not being able to foresee how reality would unfold in Asia over the next fifty years.

Asia is a vast continent, with so many countries distinctly different from each other as economies and societies. Given the enormous diversity, it was clear that such a study was well beyond the expertise of a single individual. This led me to the idea of an edited volume, one which could draw upon distinguished scholars with expertise in subjects, themes, countries, or sub-regions. Once the study was conceptualized, in terms of its approach and framework, I searched and commissioned the authors for this volume. The result is a most valuable set of specialized in-depth studies by economists and social scientists who are among the best in their respective domains. This can, of course, stand by itself as a study. Even so, while necessary, it cannot suffice because it lacks a unified overview and vision. My introductory chapter also cannot provide such an overview.

This is the *raison d'être* for a separate authored book. It uses bold strokes on a wide canvas to sketch a picture of the economic transformation in Asia during the past fifty years and to analyse the underlying factors. It also seeks to highlight the similarities and differences between countries, country-groups or sub-regions, to focus on factors that shaped development outcomes. In this task, the edited book is an intermediate input but the authored book has its own identity, as the whole is sometimes different from the sum total of the parts. More important,

---

[15] For a detailed discussion on this sequence of developments, and on the factors underlying the decline and fall of Asia in the world economy, see Nayyar (2013). For a lucid historical analysis of Asia in the world economy, see Findlay (Chapter 4, this volume). See also, the companion volume (Nayyar 2019).

perhaps, it provides a cohesive analytical narrative of Asian development over five decades to reflect briefly on future prospects. It can also stand by itself as a study. Thus, the two books are best described as companion volumes, which are complements rather than substitutes for each other.

This edited book is divided into three parts. The first part sets the stage before the play begins. It situates the study in a broader context of ideas, space, and time. In doing so, it considers Gunnar Myrdal and *Asian Drama*, to focus on the author's work as a social scientist thinking about development at the time, and revisits his approach to examine the methodology of the book in retrospect fifty years later. And, since Myrdal considered the past only with reference to the closing years of the colonial era, it also provides a much longer-term historical perspective on Asia in the world economy.

The second part comprises cross-country thematic studies. This is necessary because there is enormous diversity among countries in Asia which is embedded in history, geographical size, resource endowments, populations, initial conditions, or income levels. It was so then. It is so now. Growth trajectories and development models have been just as diverse. Outcomes have been different across countries and uneven over time. Therefore, however difficult the task, comparative cross-country studies are essential not only for a continental perspective but also for understanding the story of Asia. In order to reduce the task to manageable proportions, it was clearly necessary to select themes, or subjects, for comparative pan-Asian analysis. In the context of Asia, ten themes in development almost select themselves: the role of governments, economic openness, agricultural and rural transformations, industrialization, macroeconomics, poverty and inequality, education and health, employment and unemployment, institutions, and nationalisms. There are, of course, other themes that could have been interesting, but a choice had to be made. This choice is inevitably based on a judgement about where the important and the feasible coincide.

The third part is constituted by country studies and sub-region studies. The reason is almost obvious. It is necessary but not enough to consider similarities among Asian countries. It is just as important to recognize the differences. Thus, analytical narratives of development experiences that are country-specific or sub-region-specific are essential, as a complement to cross-country thematic studies. The development experiences of countries and of sub-regions differ. And the existing literature is often shaped by the purpose of enquiry. It would be far better if there were some questions, or an analytical approach, in common. Once again, a choice had to be made, where the desirable had to be reduced to the feasible. The three giant economies of Asia—China, India, Indonesia—with a total population of about 3 billion, which is 70 per cent of the total population of Asia, select themselves for country studies. In addition, there is a country study on Vietnam, a country of 100 million people, although medium-sized by Asian standards, which is rather different in both history and trajectory. These are supplemented by country-cluster studies on each of three sub-regions: East Asia, including South Korea, Taiwan, Hong Kong, and Singapore (even though its geographical location is elsewhere, but these four were often studied together and described as the 'East Asian Tigers');[16] Southeast Asia including Malaysia, Philippines, Thailand plus Cambodia, Laos, and Myanmar; South Asia including Bangladesh, Bhutan, Nepal, Pakistan, and Sri Lanka. Japan, a high-income industrialized country, is excluded from the study but is sometimes a point of reference. Even so, two sub-regions—Central Asia and West Asia—are missing from this coverage. Central Asia would have been a very difficult task as its constituent countries were part of the erstwhile USSR for half of the fifty-year period. West Asia is included in the companion book to complete the picture but not studied in depth.

4. Themes, Stylized Facts, and Lessons

This chapter does not even attempt a summary or a synthesis of the following chapters in the book. Given the space constraint, it would be an exceedingly difficult task. It would also serve little purpose as it might detract from the richness and depth of the analysis in the chapters. In any case, the companion volume (Nayyar 2019) seeks to provide a cohesive analytical narrative. Hence, the discussion that follows simply touches upon some important themes to highlight some lessons about Asian development which emerge from the book. This is, at best, selective and illustrative. It cannot claim to be exhaustive.

4.1 Diversity in Development

The diversity of Asia is a recurring theme. There were marked differences between countries in geographical size, embedded histories, colonial legacies, nationalist movements, initial conditions, natural resource endowments, population size, income levels, and political systems. The reliance on markets and the degree of openness in economies varied greatly across space and over time. The politics, too, ranged widely from socialism through state capitalism to capitalism, from authoritarian regimes to political democracies, and from one-party states to multi-party systems. But that is not all. Outcomes in development were also

---

[16] There is an extensive literature and an intensive debate on this subject. For some, their success was attributable to markets and openness (World Bank 1993). But this view was always contested. Lee (1981) was among the first to emphasize the limitations of export-led industrialization. Subsequently, it was argued that their export orientation was not the equivalent of free trade, just as the visible hand of the state was more in evidence than the invisible hand of the market. See, for example, Amsden (1989); Lall (1990); Wade (1990); Chang (1996).

diverse, ranging from success at one end, interspersed with mixed performances or muddling through, to failure at the other, which differed not only between countries at any point in time but also within countries over time. There were different paths to development, simply because there were no unique solutions or magic wands, as one-size-does-not-fit-all. Hence, there were choices to be made, and even the right choices did not guarantee outcomes, which were shaped by a complex mix of economic, social, and political factors in the national context, where history matters.[17] Obviously, generalizations are difficult if not perilous. Even so, some stylized facts do emerge.

4.2 History, Context, and Conjuncture

It is clear that development trajectories of countries in Asia were shaped, in part, by their history, while the context and the conjuncture at the outset made a difference. Initial conditions were, of course, an outcome of history embedded in the past. The legacy of Japanese colonialism in South Korea and Taiwan included high levels of mass education, strong traditions of state intervention, a disciplined workforce and a nationalist zeal.[18] The changed context after the Second World War meant that, in both South Korea and Taiwan, land reform was carried out under the supervision of occupation forces. In fact, the US came to exercise enormous power and influence, not only in South Korea and Taiwan, but also in the other countries such as Indonesia, Malaya (including Singapore), Philippines and Thailand, which were occupied by the Japanese in the war. Soon after, the geopolitics of the Cold War era in Asia brought about a dramatic change in the conjuncture, transforming this into an unequal relationship of dependence on the US for military and economic support. It began with the Korean War followed by the Vietnam War which continued for two decades. The *quid pro quo* for these frontline states, which often had dictatorial or authoritarian regimes with an openly anti-communist stance, was development assistance, military support, and preferential access to US markets. On the other side of the Cold War divide, China and Vietnam carried out land reforms soon after their respective revolutions. Of course, the USSR also provided military and economic support, but communist governments in China and Vietnam were acutely conscious of their geopolitical vulnerabilities, which, together with political ideology, motivated them to address problems in their legacy of initial conditions. It is clear that embedded history, together with the conjuncture in the national and international context,

---

[17] For a lucid exposition of this argument, in a different context, see Kindleberger (1996).
[18] Manchuria in northern China, or Manchukuo as the Japanese described it, experienced the same colonial legacy.

influenced and shaped trajectories of development in many Asian countries during subsequent decades.[19]

4.3 Economic Growth and Structural Change

The transformation of Asia was driven by rapid economic growth. Over a period that spanned almost five decades, 1970–2016, the GDP growth rate in Asia was more than double that in industrialized countries and almost twice that in the world economy. This gap widened progressively after 1990. This was associated with a dramatic change in the composition of output and employment. Economic growth drove structural change from the demand side as the income elasticity of demand for industrial goods was higher than that for agricultural goods, while the income elasticity of demand for services was even higher than that for industrial goods. Structural change drove economic growth from the supply side by transferring surplus labour from low productivity employment in agriculture to higher productivity employment in industry and services. Structural change was a driver of economic growth in Asia, unlike Latin America and Africa where it was not. It was the equivalent of walking on two legs. The transformation was associated with a sharp decline in the share of the agricultural sector in output more than in employment with rising productivity and wages in the agricultural sector, and rapid industrialization with a marked increase in the share of the manufacturing sector, once again more in output than in employment. This was followed by a substantial rise in the share of the services sector in both output and employment in most Asian countries.[20]

4.4 Well-being of People

The rapid economic growth led to a sharp reduction in absolute poverty in Asia, but not as much as it could have, partly because the initial income distribution was unequal and partly because of rising income inequality. And inequality rose almost everywhere in Asia from the 1990s. Consequently, this rapid growth was not always transformed into meaningful development that improved the

---

[19] The importance of these historical and contextual factors in the subsequent development of South Korea and Taiwan is emphasized in this volume by Duara (Chapter 14), Bhaduri (Chapter 9) and Wade (Chapter 19). It is also recognized by Evans and Heller (Chapter 5, this volume) as well as Khan (Chapter 13, this volume). This argument is developed further, in its broader Asian context, by Nayyar (2019).

[20] For a discussion, with supporting evidence, on economic growth in Asia compared with other parts of the world, see Nayyar (2019). For an analysis of structural change in Asia compared with Latin America and Africa, see McMillan and Rodrik (2011), and Nayyar (2013). On rural and agricultural transformations, see Vos (Chapter 7, this volume) and Timmer (2014). For an analysis of industrialization in Asia, see Chang and Zach (Chapter 8, this volume).

well-being of people, particularly in countries where employment creation was slow or where income inequality was high to start with. Economic growth had a greater impact on the living conditions of ordinary people where employment creation was rapid or where initial income distribution was less unequal. The well-being of people was also dependent on the social infrastructure that supported social consumption. The spread of education in society and the delivery of health services to people contributed directly to the well-being of people and were thus constitutive of development. But education and health were also drivers of economic growth insofar as they increased the productivity of the most abundant resource in Asian economies—labour—and were thus instrumental in development. It would seem that employment creation, combined with a public provision of education and healthcare, characterized countries that were success stories in Asian development with sustained growth and better distributional outcomes. In contrast, countries that witnessed slow employment creation or jobless growth, with inadequate or poor public provision of education and healthcare, were laggards in Asian development.[21]

4.5 States, Markets, and Governments

The development experience of Asia during the past fifty years shows that the role of governments was critical everywhere, although this role differed significantly across countries. The developmental states in South Korea and Taiwan, with their embedded autonomy reflected in their capacity to pursue strategic objectives through the use of carrots and sticks, were a special case that could not be reproduced elsewhere with ease. Among other market economies, Singapore came close. But the erstwhile centrally planned economies, China and Vietnam, also evolved similar developmental states which came of age in their transition to market economies. Myrdal would have characterized these as 'hard states'. However, even the 'soft states' in Southeast Asia managed to reach some understanding with business elites in the pursuit of national objectives. Governments in South Asia were, in Myrdal's view, the classic 'soft states' that did not have the willingness or the ability to do what was necessary in the pursuit of development objectives because they could neither resist nor coerce powerful vested interests. Yet, as planning ceded space to markets, even these governments reached some

---

[21] Chapters in this volume provide a detailed discussion of the issues mentioned in this paragraph. On poverty and inequality, see Wan and Wang, Chapter 10. On employment, see Bhaduri and van der Hoeven, Chapters 9 and 12. On education and health, see Mundle, Chapter 11. The sub-region studies also confirm the propositions set out in this paragraph. See Wade, Montes and Osmani, respectively Chapters 19, 20, and 21. On pro-poor growth in Indonesia, see Timmer, Chapter 17.

'political settlements' or 'deals' that were permissive if not causal in development.[22] Ultimately, efficient markets needed effective governments, so that success in development was, in important part, attributable to the effectiveness of state interventions which varied significantly across countries.[23]

In the pursuit of industrialization and development, the role of governments in evolving policies, nurturing institutions and making strategic interventions, whether as a catalyst or a leader, was central to the process everywhere.[24] For countries that relied on markets it was about minimizing market failure and the emphasis was on getting-prices-right. For countries that stressed state intervention, it was about minimizing government failure and getting-institutions-right. But success in this quest was greater in countries that recognized the importance of two propositions.[25] First, the state and the market are complements and not substitutes for each other. Second, the relationship between the state and the market cannot be specified once and for all but must adapt as circumstances and times change. In the earlier stages, it was about reconstructing initial conditions through the creation of a physical infrastructure, the spread of education in society, and institutional reform, particularly in the agricultural sector. In the later stages, there was a change in the nature of this role, which had three dimensions. Functional intervention sought to correct market failure, whether general or specific. Institutional intervention sought to govern the market by setting rules of the game for players in the market, to create frameworks for regulating markets and institutions to monitor the functioning of markets. Strategic intervention sought to guide the market interlinked across sectors to attain the broader long-term objectives of industrialization. Governments also fostered industrialization at the micro-level, through the nurturing of entrepreneurs, or through the creation of managerial capabilities in individuals or technological capabilities in firms in the private sector (Lall 1992; Amsden 2001). Governments often established large public sector firms, in petroleum, steel, telecommunications, or energy, going even further into commercial banks and development banks, which became a strategic form of support for industrialization in the private sector (Nayyar 2013).

---

[22] The notion of 'political settlements' is developed by Khan (Chapter 13, this volume). The idea of 'deals and development', where understandings between governments and business explain the political dynamics underlying episodes of rapid growth in some Asian and African countries, is developed by Pritchett et al. (2018).

[23] Some chapters in this book consider the role of the state in the process of development in Asia directly. See Evans and Heller (Chapter 5), Bhaduri (Chapter 9), Khan (Chapter 13), and Duara (Chapter 14). Some cross-country thematic chapters do so indirectly in relation to their respective themes: Vos (Chapter 7), Chang and Zach (Chapter 8), Mundle (Chapter 11), Kozul-Wright and Poon (Chapter 6), van der Hoeven (Chapter 12), and Wan and Wang (Chapter 10). The country studies and sub-region studies also discuss the role of the state: Lin (Chapter 15), Basu (Chapter 16), Timmer (Chapter 17), Wade (Chapter 19), Montes (Chapter 20), and Osmani (Chapter 21).

[24] See Stiglitz (1989), Shapiro and Taylor (1990), Evans (1995), Lall (1997), Amsden (2001) and Nayyar (2013).

[25] This argument is developed at some length in Bhaduri and Nayyar (1996).

In retrospect, government intervention in the earlier stages turned out to be easier than in the later stages, while functional intervention was easier than the institutional or the strategic. Countries in which states and markets were complements rather than substitutes, and their respective roles vis-à-vis each other were adapted to evolve over time, were the success stories, where the two institutions functioned in a manner that created mutual checks and balances. In this respect, East Asia was the best performer while South Asia was the worst with Southeast Asia in the middle.[26] Yet, all governments in Asia were development oriented.

4.6 Economic Openness

Economic openness also played an important role in Asian development,[27] possibilities of which had not been recognized by Myrdal. The usual characterization of openness is in terms of international trade, international investment, and international finance. In this, there were significant differences between Asian countries,[28] most of which were restrictive in terms of openness until around 1970. Things began to change thereafter. The reality that unfolded since then spanned the entire spectrum from almost unrestricted openness in Singapore, through moderated openness in Indonesia, Malaysia, Philippines, Thailand, and Turkey, or calibrated openness in South Korea and Taiwan, to controlled openness in China, India, and Vietnam. The differences are more than nuances. Unrestricted openness was almost uniform across trade, investment and finance. Moderated openness was largely open economies with selected restrictions but with some differences between trade, investment and finance. Calibrated openness was asymmetries in openness by design manifest in strategic trade policy that was open for the export sector, but restrictive for other sectors, with limits on openness to foreign capital and tight curbs on foreign brand names. Controlled openness was broader and more restrictive, not only in trade but also with respect to foreign investment and technology. Of course, South Korea and Taiwan have changed now, as have China, India, and Vietnam, but openness is not quite unrestricted. For most Asian countries, openness did not mean a passive insertion into the world economy. It was strategic in a few countries and selective in most countries.

There is also a broader characterization of economic openness in terms of the relative importance of the domestic and the foreign in markets, resources, and

---

[26] This geographical classification of sub-regions is useful for analytical purposes. Yet, it is worth noting that, in some important respects, Sri Lanka in South Asia resembled Southeast Asian countries, while Myanmar and Cambodia in Southeast Asia resembled South Asian countries. In some spheres, Philippines, with its Spanish colonial legacy, resembled Latin American countries.

[27] See Kozul-Wright and Poon (Chapter 6, this volume) and Chang and Zach (Chapter 8, this volume).

[28] The following discussion on economic openness draws upon earlier work of the author (Nayyar 2013).

technologies. Some countries relied heavily on foreign capital, foreign technologies, and foreign markets—Indonesia, Malaysia, Philippines, Singapore, and Thailand—where their size ranged from small to large. This is a generalized characterization for there were domestic markets and domestic firms in these countries. South Korea and Taiwan relied on foreign markets but mobilized domestic resources and developed domestic technological capabilities.[29] Turkey sought a blend of domestic and foreign in markets, capital, and technology. China, India, and Vietnam, for quite some time, relied mostly on domestic markets, domestic resources, and domestic technologies, but subsequently these countries joined the quest for external markets with a more open, yet selective, approach to foreign capital and foreign technology. These differences across countries were a function of geographical size or of strategic choice. Small countries sought to internalize external markets, while large countries sought to externalize internal markets, since exports were the beginning of the typical market expansion path for firms in the former, while exports were the end of the typical market expansion path for firms in the latter. Similarly, it was difficult for small countries to mobilize resources on a large-enough scale or develop technologies on their own, while it was easier for large countries. Yet, this was also a matter of strategic choices in the pursuit of development, for South Korea and Taiwan, as also Singapore, were small countries that developed their own technological capabilities.

4.7 Institutions and Policies

In *Asian Drama*, Myrdal stressed the importance of an institutional approach, and he was perhaps the first to provide a systematic analysis of the role of institutions in development with reference to Asia. Yet, for quite some time, orthodox prescriptions sought to harmonize the role as well as form of institutions across the developing world irrespective of space or time. The underlying presumption that one-size-fits-all was wrong. There are specificities in space: institutions are local and cannot be transplanted out of context. There are specificities in time: institutions need time to evolve and cannot be created by a magic wand. Alas, this was not quite recognized. Economic reforms that sought to focus on policies but neglected institutions met with failure. Economic liberalization that moved from over-regulated to under-governed systems led to financial crises. Economic conditionality of lenders or donors who attempted to harmonize institutions across countries ran into difficulties. Since then, there has been considerable work done

---

[29] In developing domestic technological capabilities, these countries imported technology through licensing rather through foreign direct investment an banned the use of foreign brand names to develop their own.

by economists, both orthodox and heterodox.[30] Yet, we do not know exactly what institutions in what forms are necessary, or at least useful for development and in what contexts. Even where we understand what role particular institutions can play in development, we often do not know how to build such institutions. The Asian experience poses a further puzzle. Why did some Asian countries perform so well with unorthodox institutions, and why did other Asian countries with very similar institutions not perform well? The answer might lie in the specific context where the distribution of organizational power affected the operation of these institutions through 'political settlements'.[31] Or why were good performances not sustained over time in countries? The answer might lie in the political dynamics of 'deals' between governments and business.[32] It is clear the institutions were among the important determinants of success, muddling through, or failure at development in Asia.

The puzzle extended beyond institutions to policies. Similar economic reforms did well in some countries and did not perform well in other countries. Experience suggests that countries in Asia that modified, adapted, and contextualized their reform agenda—at the same time calibrating the sequence of, and the speed at which, economic reforms were introduced—did well in terms of outcomes. In sharp contrast, countries that introduced economic reforms without modification, adaptation, or contextualization, and did not pay attention to speed or sequence, often ran into problems. This was also the reason why strategy-based reform with a long-term view of development objectives, emerging from experience or learning within countries rooted in social formations and political processes, did sustain and succeed. But crisis-driven reform, often initiated following an external shock or internal convulsion, or imposed by conditionality of the International Monetary Fund (IMF) and World Bank, was always more difficult to sustain and less likely to succeed because its preordained template was neither contextualized nor sequenced. East Asia and South Asia provide respective examples of this contrast.[33] Reforms apart, there was a critical role for economic policies. Asian countries that were success stories in development used heterodox or unorthodox policies for orthodox objectives, such as strategic trade, industrial, and technology policies in the pursuit of industrialization.[34] Similarly, they used orthodox policies for heterodox or unorthodox objectives, such as interest rates to guide the allocation

---

[30] The original contribution in the orthodox tradition is that of North (1990). See also Acemoglu and Robinson (2012). For the heterodox perspective, see Khan (1995) and Chang (2007). For a discussion on the role of institutions, and States, in development, which also provides a lucid, perceptive, critique of orthodoxy, see Bardhan (2016).

[31] For a detailed discussion on political settlements, see Khan (Chapter 13, this volume).

[32] On deals and development, see Pritchett et al. (2018).

[33] This distinction between strategy-based and crisis-driven economic reforms, is made in Nayyar (1996). For a discussion of its implications and consequences, see Bhaduri and Nayyar (1996).

[34] See Kozul-Wright and Poon, Chang and Zach, and Wade (respectively Chapters 6, 8, and 19, this volume).

of scarce investible resources in a market economy, or exchange rates that were deliberately undervalued over long periods to break into the world market for manufactured goods. And they did not hesitate to use orthodox policies for orthodox objectives, such as expansionary fiscal policies in an economic downturn despite orthodoxy which suggested the opposite in macroeconomic crises.[35]

5. Structure and Contents

The first part of the book, starting with this chapter, sets the stage. It considers Myrdal and *Asian Drama* by discussing their contribution to the debate on development then, and by examining their approach and the methodology in retrospect now. It also situates the present study in its wider context by providing a long-term historical perspective on Asia in the world spanning the last millennium, and outlines the broad contours of the remarkable economic transformation of Asia over the past fifty years.

Chapter 2, by Ravi Kanbur, poses two central questions. How did Myrdal's earlier thinking and experience influence *Asian Drama*? How did *Asian Drama* influence the subsequent development debate? In doing so, he explores how Myrdal's conceptualization of the problems and prospects of development was shaped by his intellectual prowess as a brilliant economic theorist, distinguished social scientist, and philosopher, and his rich professional experience as a policy practitioner and Swedish politician. This discussion is related to the development terrain in the mid-twentieth century and how *Asian Drama* lay on that terrain in the remaining years of Gunnar Myrdal's eventful life.

Chapter 3, by Frances Stewart, highlights the major methodological innovations in *Asian Drama* such as the critical role of values, the necessity of a multidisciplinary approach, the analysis of institutions and attitudes, and the idea that Western economic concepts are mostly inappropriate for an analysis of Asian development, to consider how far Myrdal's perspectives have been adopted since then. Many of his ideas have been accepted by heterodox economics, but mainstream economics has, in general, been the least responsive, particularly on values implicit in their concepts, theories, and policies. It is argued that new thinking is needed to question the appropriateness of some concepts even in advanced countries, and to incorporate environmental considerations into analytical frameworks.

Chapter 4, by Ronald Findlay, studies the political and economic evolution of trade and international relations of countries and regions in Asia between themselves and the rest of the world during the second millennium. The focus is on: the *Pax Mongolica* and overland trade in the Middle Ages; the European

---

[35] For a discussion, see Nayyar (2011, 2013).

intrusion into Asia at the turn of the fifteenth century and the impact of the discovery of the New World; the spread of European imperialism, the rise of nationalisms, and independence from colonial rule. This is followed by a discussion on the comparative evolution of Asia and Europe to consider why the Industrial Revolution did not first occur in Asia.

The second part of the book, on cross-country thematic studies, attempts to include and compare as many countries or sub-regions in Asia as possible, to highlight the similarities and differences between them, in relation to their respective themes. The constituent chapters analyse processes of change, recognize the diversity in paths and outcomes, and wherever possible try to situate their arguments in the context of different theoretical or ideological perspectives. The discussion seeks to focus mostly on the past five decades but also reflects briefly on prospects over the next twenty-five years.

Chapter 5, by Peter Evans and Patrick Heller, explores the changing role of the state in Asia, from Northeast Asia and China through Southeast Asia to India, to discuss how states could promote economic and social transformations. The evolution, emergence, and concept of the 'developmental state' is a central focus. So is the relationship of states to the politics of representation and redistribution. The chapter analyses the ways in which development (well-being of people) and democracy (accountability to society) have been facilitated or frustrated by state structures or state actions. The authors argue that a comparative history of the Asian state offers general lessons for theory and policy in development.

Chapter 6, by Richard Kozul-Wright and Daniel Poon, examines the experiences of increasing economic openness in three Asian countries (China, India, and Malaysia). Its focus is on the orientation of selected policy tools in trade, technology, investment, and finance that shaped the degree of economic openness, combined with the Myrdal idea of the 'rational co-ordination of operational controls', which is interpreted as the strategic use of selected policy tools similar to that in the earlier East Asian success stories (South Korea and Taiwan). The authors argue that the divergence in Asian growth experiences can be explained by differences in institutional capabilities to address market and firm-level (also government) failures in the catch-up process, and the pragmatic experimentation by policymakers in search of more effective institutional mechanisms—carrots, sticks, and competition—in pursuit of desired development outcomes.

Chapter 7, by Rob Vos, considers how rapid agricultural and rural transformations in most Asian countries have helped jumpstart economic development over the past fifty years. But the nature and speed of change differed across sub-regions. In East and Southeast Asia, the Green Revolution led to agricultural productivity growth, facilitating the transfer of labour and savings, to promote industrial growth and foster urbanization, which in turn induced deeper agrarian change and food system transformations. South Asia lagged behind but has now managed to overcome most of the earlier obstacles, though new challenges such as changing dietary patterns and pressing environmental constraints have surfaced. It is argued that, moving forward, the nature of agricultural transformations and structural change in forging economic growth and poverty reduction in the still disadvantaged parts of Asia will need to be different.

Chapter 8, by Ha-Joon Chang and Kiryl Zach, focuses on industrialization and suggests that the industrial transformation of Asia is perhaps the most surprising change in the global economy in the last fifty years. It outlines important trends and analyses selected national industrial policies that promoted this dramatic structural transformation. First, it describes crucial dimensions of industrialization in Asia, to highlight its historical trajectory and the subsequent industrial upgrading. Second, it uses four case studies—South Korea, Malaysia, China, and India—to describe some of the strategies that Asian economies used to induce industrial development. It is argued that the successful cases did not try to implement a golden policy template but pragmatically adapted their policies to overcome specific bottlenecks and meet strategic objectives.

Chapter 9, by Amit Bhaduri, provides a macroeconomic perspective on development in Asia. Although macroeconomic strategies and policies have differed significantly across countries over fifty years, common issues recur despite their immense diversity in initial conditions, political systems, geopolitical situations, and natural resource endowments. The author examines issues such as unemployment, the role of states and markets, domestic and foreign markets, degrees of openness in trade, investment, and finance, industrial and technology policy, and socio-economic inequality, to explain why some countries have been more successful than others in dealing with these issues through innovations in policies and institutions. This comparative perspective presents developmental choices and challenges as moving targets requiring flexible institutional policy responses at each stage of development, which makes uniform guidelines misleadingly oversimplistic.

Chapter 10, by Guanghua Wan and Chen Wang, outlines trends in poverty and inequality in Asia, its sub-regions, and selected countries during the period 1965–2014. It seeks to explain the factors underlying these trends. It also explores the relationship between growth, poverty, and inequality. The evidence and analysis confirm that significant reductions in poverty across the board were due to fast growth, although the positive effect of growth on poverty was partly offset by a worsening income distribution in many countries. Looking ahead, Asia is expected to eradicate poverty but is likely to continue facing high inequality, particularly as technological changes on the horizon, such as artificial intelligence, are likely to displace labour.

Chapter 11, by Sudipto Mundle, analyses the amazing spread of education and healthcare in Asia over fifty years, while recognizing the large variations in this spread between and within countries. The nature of the state has been an important determinant of these variations, because social development has typically been led by governments. But, in most countries, public resource constraints, with growing dependence on private provision and private spending, have generated a pattern of nested disparities in the access to education and healthcare between rich and poor regions, between rural and urban areas within regions, and between rich and poor households within these areas. However, as the better-off regions, areas, and households approach the upper limits of achievable education and health standards, a process of convergence is also underway as those left behind begin to catch up.

Chapter 12, by Rolph van der Hoeven, explores the interaction between employment and development in Asian countries, to argue that while Myrdal rejected the Western concept of employment to emphasize the role of informal employment, he underestimated the effects of the Lewisian development process. In countries that experienced rapid economic growth with better labour market development, initial conditions played some role, but Myrdal's idea of cumulative causation provides a better explanation. Developmental states in these countries used interventionist policies in agriculture and industry, and in the macroeconomic sphere (combined with social policies to strengthen the position of women) making labour markets more conducive to employment creation. Many other countries were less successful despite rapid economic growth. Growing inequality, together with other development challenges are beginning to surface, and if not attended to, could become a problem in the future.

Chapter 13, by Mushtaq Khan, on institutions and development, argues that, while Myrdal emphasized their importance in *Asian Drama*, the role of institutions has been intensely contested ever since with later contributions from institutional economics and writings on the developmental state. Despite much progress in thinking, the dominant approaches do not agree about the institutions that matter nor do they explain why similar institutions delivered such different results across countries. Cultural norms and informal institutions clearly matter but the appropriate norms did not already exist in successful countries—they evolved over time. The author concludes that the distribution of holding power across different types of organizations, the 'political settlement', can explain the diversity of experiences and help to develop more effective policy.

Chapter 14, by Prasenjit Duara, identifies historic patterns in the dialectic between nationalism and development across various East, South, and Southeast Asian countries. Nationalism is used by regimes as the rationale for development to achieve high levels of growth, but it also generates exclusivism and hostilities, often in order to integrate a political core. In fact, popular nationalisms have dialectically reshaped the goals and patterns of development during the post-Second World War period. The Asian continent is divided into regions shaped by twentieth-century historical and geopolitical conditions. Colonial and Cold War conditions were as important as internal political and ethnic circumstances. Turning points in the dialectical relationship were common within a region. More recently, a common trans-regional pattern has emerged with neo-liberal globalization being accompanied by exclusivist nationalism.

The third part of the book is constituted by country studies and sub-region studies. It attempts, as much as possible, to consider initial conditions as a point of reference, highlight turning points in economic performance, assess how processes of change were managed (or mismanaged), discuss the influence of development strategies and economic reform, examine changes in engagement with the world economy, explore the roles of governments and politics, and analyse the factors underlying success or failure at development. The discussion seeks to focus mostly on the past five decades but also reflects briefly on prospects over the next twenty-five years.

Chapter 15, by Justin Lin, begins with the proposition that if Myrdal had studied China, which he did not, he would have been as pessimistic as he was about other Asian countries. But China has witnessed a miraculous transformation since 1978. Six questions are posed to provide an analytical framework. Why was China trapped in poverty before 1978? What explains China's striking performance after 1978? How did China avoid the problems experienced by other transition economies? What price has China paid for its economic success? Can China continue its dynamic performance in the coming decades? What are the lessons other countries can learn from China's development experience? The essential argument is that China exploited its advantage of relative backwardness as a latecomer. In doing so, gradualism and prudence in managing the process of change were the foundations of success.

Chapter 16, by Kaushik Basu, sketches a short history of the economy of India since 1968. India today is a changed country from what it was half a century ago, when Myrdal published *Asian Drama*. The stranglehold of low growth has been broken, its population below the poverty line has fallen markedly, and India has joined the pantheon of major players globally. The author analyses the economic policies and the democratic politics behind this transformation. This provides a backdrop to reflect on the huge challenges that lie ahead.

Chapter 17, by Peter Timmer, addresses the unrelenting pessimism in *Asian Drama* about Indonesia's development prospects. This pessimism was based on two key realities: the poor level of governance demonstrated by the Sukarno regime (partly a heritage of Dutch colonial policies) and the extreme poverty witnessed in rural areas. Using historical and modern data on the Indonesian economy, the chapter explains the policy approach that resulted in three decades of rapid, pro-poor growth during the Suharto regime. The Asian financial crisis in 1998 caused the Suharto regime to fall and introduced democratically elected governments. After a decade of stagnation, economic growth returned to the rapid rate seen during the first three decades of the Suharto regime, but it is no longer pro-poor.

Chapter 18, by Finn Tarp, starts with a historical perspective on Vietnam. It argues that, when the dogged ideological approach to the economy adopted in

1976 did not produce the hoped-for results, in 1986 a radical course correction in the form of a comprehensive reform programme—*Doi Moi*—was introduced. And Vietnam has come a long way since then. The last three decades have witnessed rapid economic growth, impressive poverty reduction, and significant strides in human development. There is a much greater reliance on market forces in resource allocation and price determination. In an economy once completely dominated by the state and co-operative sectors, the private sector and foreign investment both play key dynamic roles. There is a smooth transition from a centrally planned to a market economy, based on institutional reform, without giving up the strategic leadership and influence of the state.

Chapter 19, by Robert Wade, begins with the proposition that few non-Western countries have reached the general prosperity of Western Europe and North America in the past two centuries. The unequal structure of the world economy created after the Industrial Revolution in Britain persists. So does uneven development. The clearest exceptions, which have caught up with the industrialized world, are countries in capitalist East Asia, namely South Korea and Taiwan, to which the island states of Singapore and Hong Kong can also be added. The question posed is: how did they escape? The answer carries lessons for other latecomers to development in Asia in earlier stages of the catching-up process.

Chapter 20, by Manuel Montes, examines Southeast Asia, particularly how Malaysia, Philippines, and Thailand, followed by Cambodia, Laos, and Myanmar, defied the pessimistic prognosis of *Asian Drama* about their prospects for development. In the past half-century, these countries raised agricultural productivity faster than population growth and displayed sufficient state capability to direct change towards a respectable level of industrial development. The contrasts in achievements among the six countries can be understood from the differences in their initial conditions, socio-political contexts, international relations, and economic policies. These contrasts are analysed across four areas: agriculture, industry, foreign trade–investment, and social development. By using an unconventional approach à la Myrdal, it is possible to understand how heterodox economic policies have been effective in overcoming developmental disadvantages. However, shortfalls in social development could make further progress difficult in the future.

Chapter 21, by Siddiqur Osmani, considers South Asia and the topsy-turvy story of Bangladesh, Bhutan, Nepal, Pakistan, and Sri Lanka. Soon after independence from British rule, the region seemed to have a much better prospect than many other Asian countries. The prospects soon dimmed, however, as South Asia crawled while East and Southeast Asia galloped away. But a large part of the region seems finally to have turned a corner and is looking forward to a much better future—in terms of both economic growth and human development—than Myrdal thought possible in *Asian Drama*. The chapter describes and explains this story in terms of the economic strategies and political economy of the sub-region and also looks ahead to identify the major challenges that remain.

Afterword

This book is divided into three parts. It situates the study in a wider context of ideas, space and time. Its cross-country thematic chapters seek to develop an understanding of similarities or patterns across the diversity of Asia. Its country studies and sub-region studies highlight the dissimilarities or differences between countries and among sub-regions. Even so, it cannot possibly cover everything. There are unexplored domains and unasked questions. And the whole might be different from the sum total of the parts. The companion book (Nayyar 2019), which attempts to address some of the issues not considered here, and endeavours to provide a cohesive analytical narrative of the Asian development experience spanning half a century, might thus be of interest to concerned readers.

Both books focus largely on the past fifty years. However, the books also reflect briefly on prospects over the next twenty-five years. Predictions about the future are always difficult if not hazardous. After all, the period 1968 to 2018 turned out to be so different from the expectations in *Asian Drama*. The analysis in this study suggests that Asia will continue to do well in terms of economic growth. There are obvious challenges within Asian countries, such as rising economic inequalities between people, emerging divergences among countries, poor infrastructure, underdeveloped institutions, inadequate education, unstable politics or unsustainable political systems. There are also challenges in the world outside, such as the technological progress on the horizon of which artificial intelligence and robotics are mere examples, environmental consequences of rapid economic growth, the visible discontents with globalization attributable partly to the economic rise of Asia, the populist and nationalist politics that has surfaced in industrialized countries, or major changes in the geopolitical situation which are beginning to surface. The response of Asian countries to these complex challenges will shape their future. Yet, this study suggests reasons for optimism rather than pessimism about Asia.

Gunnar Myrdal described himself as a cheerful pessimist (Streeten 1998), who hoped that Asia might do better but did not think that it was likely. In contrast, given the remarkable economic transformation of the continent over the past five decades, the authors of this study could describe themselves as cautious optimists who believe that an even better world is possible for Asia.

Acknowledgement

The author would like to thank Ronald Findlay, Rajeev Malhotra, Sudipto Mundle, Frances Stewart, and Finn Tarp for helpful comments and suggestions on a preliminary draft of this chapter.

References

Acemoglu, D. and J. Robinson (2012). *Why Nations Fail: The Origins of Power, Prosperity and Poverty*. New York: Crown Business, Random House.

Amsden, A.H. (1989). *Asia's Next Giant: South Korea and Late Industrialization*. New York: Oxford University Press.

Amsden, A.H. (2001). *The Rise of the Rest: Challenges to the West from Late Industrializing Economies*. New York: Oxford University Press.

Appelqvist, O. and S. Andersson (2005). *The Essential Gunnar Myrdal*. New York: The New Press.

Barber, W.J. (2008). *Gunnar Myrdal*. Basingstoke: Palgrave Macmillan.

Bardhan, P. (2016). 'State and Development: The Need for a Reappraisal of the Current Literature', *Journal of Economic Literature*, 54(3): 862–92.

Bhaduri, A. and D. Nayyar (1996). *The Intelligent Person's Guide to Liberalization*. New Delhi: Penguin Books.

Bok, S. (2005). 'Introduction'. In O. Appelqvist and S. Andersson (eds) *The Essential Gunnar Myrdal*. New York: The New Press.

Chang, H.-J. (1996). *The Political Economy of Industrial Policy*. London: Macmillan.

Chang, H.-J. (ed.) (2007). *Institutional Change and Economic Development*. Tokyo: UNU Press, and London: Anthem Press.

Evans, P. (1995). *Embedded Autonomy: States and Industrial Transformation*. Princeton, NJ: Princeton University Press.

Khan, M. (1995). 'State Failure in Weak States: A Critique of New Institutionalist Explanations'. In J. Harriss, J. Hunter, and C.M. Lewis (eds) *The New Institutionalist Economics and Third World Development*. London: Routledge.

Kindleberger, C.P. (1996). *World Economic Primacy: 1500–1990*. New York: Oxford University Press.

Lall, S. (1990). *Building Industrial Competitiveness in Developing Countries*. Paris: OECD Development Centre.

Lall, S. (1992). 'Technological Capabilities and Industrialization', *World Development*, 20: 165–86.

Lall, S. (1997). 'Imperfect Markets and Fallible Governments: The Role of the State in Industrial Development'. In D. Nayyar (ed.) *Trade and Industrialization*. Delhi: Oxford University Press.

Lee, Eddy (ed.) (1981). *Export-Led Industrialization and Development*. Geneva: ILO.

McMillan, M. and D. Rodrik (2011). 'Globalization, Structural Change and Productivity Growth'. In M. Bacchetta and M. Jansen (eds) *Making Globalization Socially Sustainable*. Geneva: ILO and WTO.

Myrdal, G. (1930). *The Political Element in the Development of Economic Theory* (Original Swedish edition. English edition translated by Paul Streeten, 1953). London: Routledge & Kegan Paul.

Myrdal, G. (1944). *An American Dilemma: The Negro Problem and Modern Democracy, Volumes I and II*. New York: Harper and Brothers.

Myrdal, G. (1957). *Economic Theory and Underdeveloped Regions*. New York: Harper and Row.

Myrdal, G. (1958). *Value in Social Theory* (Edited by Paul Streeten). London: Routledge & Kegan Paul.

Myrdal, G. (1968). *Asian Drama: An Inquiry into the Poverty of Nations, Volumes I, II, and III*. London: Penguin Books, Allen Lane.

Nayyar, D. (1996). *Economic Liberalization in India: Analytics, Experience and Lessons*. Calcutta: Orient Longman.

Nayyar, D. (2011). 'Rethinking Macroeconomic Policies for Development', *Brazilian Journal of Political Economy*, 31(3): 339–51.

Nayyar, D. (2013). *Catch Up: Developing Countries in the World Economy*. Oxford: Oxford University Press.

Nayyar, D. (2017). 'Can Catch Up Reduce Inequality?' In P.A.G. van Bergeijk and R. van der Hoeven (eds) *Sustainable Development Goals and Income Inequality*. Cheltenham: Edward Elgar.

Nayyar, D. (2019). *Resurgent Asia: Diversity in Development*. Oxford: Oxford University Press.

North, D.C. (1990). *Institutions, Institutional Change and Economic Performance*. Cambridge: Cambridge University Press.

Pritchett, L., K. Sen, and E. Werker (eds) (2018). *Deals and Development: The Political Dynamics of Growth Episodes*. Oxford: Oxford University Press.

Shapiro, H. and L. Taylor (1990). 'The State and Industrial Strategy', *World Development*, 18: 861–78.

Siegel, B. (2017). 'Asian Drama Revisited', *Humanity: An International Journal of Human Rights, Humanitarianism and Development*, 8(1): 195–205.

Stiglitz, J.E. (1989). 'On the Economic Role of the State'. In A. Heertje (ed.) *The Economic Role of the State*. Oxford: Basil Blackwell.

Streeten, P. (1990). 'Gunnar Myrdal', *World Development*, 18(7): 1031–7.

Streeten, P. (1998). 'The Cheerful Pessimist: Gunnar Myrdal the Dissenter (1898–1987)', *World Development*, 26(3): 539–50.

Timmer, C.P. (2014). 'Managing Structural Transformation: A Political Economy Approach', UNU-WIDER, Helsinki, WIDER Annual Lecture 18.

Wade, R. (1990). *Governing the Market: Economic Theory and the Role of Government in East Asian Industrialization*. Princeton, NJ: Princeton University Press.

World Bank (1993). *The East Asian Miracle*. New York: Oxford University Press.

2

Gunnar Myrdal and *Asian Drama* in Context

Ravi Kanbur

1. Introduction

Some years ago I was in Second Story Books, a well-known second-hand book shop in Washington DC, looking for the three volumes of Gunnar Myrdal's *Asian Drama*. I had been a student in the 1970s, during the decade after its publication, and had read all of the reviews of it and parts of the book itself. It was required reading, or at least required dipping into, for all students interested in development, helped along by the fact that its author won the Nobel Prize in Economics in 1974. A quarter century later, I searched for *Asian Drama* unsuccessfully in the Economics and International Sections, and went up to the desk of Second Story Books for help. The person at the desk looked it up, and led me to the volumes—in the Theatre section of the bookshop.

It was perhaps apocryphal that the volume that had taken the development world by storm in the 1960s and 1970s, and shaped my thinking as a student, now languished in the Theatre section of a second-hand bookshop. The volume is still cited. It shows almost 5,000 cites on Google Scholar, an average of 100 cites for every year of its publication, and there are indeed recent citations. But these, I fear, are more in the nature of obligatory cites to a classic than a deep engagement with the book. Reading recent job market papers for recruitment of young development economists for my university, I do not recall a mention of *Asian Drama* or of Myrdal. This is their loss because, although very much a product of its time, the insights it provides and the questions it raises are perennial in nature and, although they may not know it, the young development economists of today, many of them, are following in his footsteps.

This chapter will attempt to understand *Asian Drama* in the context of the development debates of its time, and in terms of the sensibilities that Gunnar Myrdal—the brilliant economic theorist and philosopher of knowledge, and Swedish politician—brought to the conceptualization of the problems and prospects of development. The next three sections will cover: (i) what Myrdal brought to the analysis of development from his by then long, varied, and distinguished academic and practitioner career; (ii) the development terrain in the mid-twentieth century; and (iii) how *Asian Drama* lay on that terrain and in the remaining years of Myrdal's continued eventful life. The two central questions posed in the chapter are: (i) How did Myrdal's broad experience and perspective influence *Asian Drama*? (ii) How did *Asian Drama* influence the development debate?

2. Gunnar Myrdal Before *Asian Drama*

Gunnar Myrdal was a polymath. He was a brilliant economic theorist in the Swedish tradition, turned iconoclast and questioning the methodological basis of economics; a founder of the Stockholm School with insights (published in Swedish) on macroeconomics which were later to be found in Keynes's *General Theory*; one of the intellectual and political founders of the Swedish welfare state; author of the monumental *An American Dilemma: The Negro Problem and Modern Democracy* (Myrdal 1944), which played its role in laying the foundations of the civil rights struggle in the USA; after the Second World War, tackling economic and political relations across the Iron Curtain as the head of the United Nations Economic Commission for Europe; and of course the author of *Asian Drama*. But *Asian Drama* was by no means his last act. He lived for two decades after the publication of that *magnum opus* and, before his health faded in later years, was fully engaged in the debates on development. Indeed, his Nobel Lecture (Myrdal 1975) was devoted solely to that topic.

Thus, Myrdal brought a fully formed analytical perspective and a sense of political realities to *Asian Drama*. Indeed, more than a decade before, he had already published *Economic Theory and Underdeveloped Regions* (Myrdal 1957; abbreviated from now on to *Underdeveloped Regions*). Although such claims are always problematic for an author as prolific as Myrdal, this is perhaps his first major sustained statement on development, and can be argued to have framed his thinking leading up to *Asian Drama*. I will come to *Underdeveloped Regions* presently as a precursor to *Asian Drama*. However, there were several lifetimes of Myrdal's work before *Underdeveloped Regions* that set the frame for that work and subsequently for *Asian Drama*. I begin with a brief account of Myrdal before *Asian Drama* and before *Underdeveloped Regions*.

There are, of course, several biographies of Myrdal, which give an assessment of the early Myrdal and his contributions. I draw on many of these in shaping my account.[1] Born in 1898 in the Swedish province of Dalarna, he began studying law at the University of Stockholm in 1918. In 1919 was the colourful meeting,

---

[1] The works include Dostaler et al. (1992), Appelqvist and Andersson (2005), Barber (2008), and Etzemuller (2014). There is also a volume of published and previously unpublished papers from before the mid-1970s, put together by Myrdal himself (Myrdal 1973).

recounted many times, with Alva Reimer at her father's farm.[2] She was to become Alva Myrdal, his lifetime companion and in the years to come a powerful presence on the world stage and herself winner of the Nobel Peace Prize. Their early discussions set the frame for the Gunnar Myrdal we came to know, as captured by their daughter Sissela Bok in a later memoir:

> Gunnar also shared with Alva how he wanted to live. He had, first and foremost, a thoroughgoing belief in the value of rationality... Already in his gymnasium, or high school, years, he had decided to choose the Enlightenment thinkers as guides. And the thesis he adopted most unreservedly from some of them was what he would later call his 'development optimism': the belief that human conditions would improve as soon as reason triumphed over misunderstanding and superstition... In Alva, Gunnar found someone with a similar belief that progress was possible but with more clearly delineated ideals and passion to put them into practice.   (Bok 2005: 5)

He graduated in law in 1923 but realized that was not the career for him. Under the influence of Alva, who purchased for him Gustav Cassel's *Theoretische Sozialokonomie*, he immersed himself in economics, reading through all issues of the Swedish economics journal *Ekonomisk tidskrift* since it started in 1899.[3] In his doctoral dissertation Myrdal developed and went beyond Cassel's work on price formation, bringing in expectations in an essential way. The role of expectations was to remain important to him throughout his analytical career, including in the coming decade when he turned to macro-monetary theory and made significant contributions in a vein that led eventually to *Keynes's General Theory*. Interestingly, his biographer, Barber (2008), picks up on his methodological stance in these early years:

> There was innovation in this procedure, but it should be noted that it was embedded in a neoclassical tradition that Myrdal was later to reject forcefully. At this early stage in his career, he was obviously comfortable with—and proficient at—abstract model building. Inherent in his intellectual style was hostility towards the institutionalist approach to the discipline with its suspicions about the usefulness of abstract theorizing.   (Barber 2008: 8)

---

[2] Myrdal and two friends were bicycling in the Swedish countryside and asked to sleep in the hayloft at the farm. Alva, then 17, met him at breakfast and they started talking. Here is how their daughter takes up the story: 'When, summoning up all his courage, Gunnar asked her to do the unthinkable and come along on the bicycle trip, Alva amazed him by saying "yes". She may never have acted so impulsively before. It was as if she knew this chance would never come again. Her mother was in a rest home, temporarily, and she had no trouble in duping her father with a tale of going to visit a friend for a few weeks' (Bok 2005: 3–4).
[3] Velupiilai (1992: 133–4).

All this was to change in the coming decade as he launched a major attack on the core of neoclassical economics, and turned more and more to an institutional perspective. The opening salvo came in his *The Political Element in Development Theory*. It was published in Swedish in 1930 and in German in 1932, and in English only in 1954. So its initial impact was primarily on continental debates, especially within Sweden, where Barber (2008) and others give detailed accounts of the reception by the old guard. Myrdal's central contention was that while the ostensible objective of economics was to be value free, as a matter of fact it was not:

> The task of economic science is to observe and describe empirical reality and to analyse and explain causal relations between economic facts. Our scientific goal is to achieve a knowledge of the world in which we live, sufficiently adequate to enable us to forecast future events and thus to take precautions and to fulfil our wishes rationally. To determine what our fears and wishes ought to be, however, is outside the realm of science... We are only too well aware that throughout the past century economists, speaking in the name of their science, have been airing views on what they consider to be socially imperative... Even when the claim is not explicitly expressed, the conclusions unmistakably imply the notion that economic analysis is capable of yielding laws in the sense of *norms* and not merely laws in the sense of *demonstrable recurrences and regularities of actual and possible events*... Thus the theory of 'free competition' is not intended to be merely a scientific explanation of what course economic relations would take under certain specified assumptions. It simultaneously constitutes a kind of proof that these hypothetical conditions would result in maximum 'total income' or greatest possible 'satisfaction of needs' in society as a whole. 'Free competition' thus on logical and factual grounds becomes more than a set of abstract assumptions, used as a tool in theoretical analysis of the causal relations of facts. It becomes a political *desideratum*.   (Myrdal 1954: 1–4, emphasis in original)

However, Myrdal's conclusion was *not* that value judgements should be excluded, but that they should be made explicit. This is carried through into his *American Dilemma, Underdeveloped Regions*, and *Asian Drama. American Dilemma* famously ends with the word 'enlightenment', deliberately chosen by Myrdal to reflect his value system, about which he was explicit at the start of the volume. In *Asian Drama*, chapter 2 is entitled 'The Value Premises Chosen' and sets them out clearly and explicitly as a list of 'Modernization Ideals': Rationality, Development and Planning for Development, Rise of Productivity, Rise of Levels of Living, Social and Economic Equalization, Improved Institutions and Attitudes, National Consolidation, National Independence, Political Democracy in a Narrow Sense, Democracy at the Grassroots, and Social Discipline versus Democratic Planning.[4]

---

[4] These are laid out with a section devoted to discussion of each, in Myrdal (1968: 57–67).

Myrdal recognizes that these are overlapping and perhaps even nested, but still thinks it important enough to be expansive in the interest of making clear the sweep and spread of value judgements and orientations which will inform and frame the positive economic analysis which will follow. Would that we were all as careful and explicit as this.

In the 1930s, Gunnar, along with Alva, became deeply involved in Swedish politics and economic and social policymaking. From 1933 onwards for a dozen years he served as a member of the commission on social housing. From 1935 to 1938 he served as a member of the population commission in Sweden. He was a member of the Swedish Parliament from 1936 to 1938. The analytical underpinning of much of this policy engagement is to be found in his 1934 book with Alva, *The Population Problem in Crisis* (Myrdal and Myrdal 1934), developed further in various commission reports, and culminating in his Godkin Lectures at Harvard University in 1938, *Population: A Problem for Democracy* (Myrdal 1940). It is remarkable to think that during this same period Gunnar was also engaged in his major contributions to macroeconomics and monetary policy, in analytics and in the policy arena. In 1932, he was the technical architect of the 1933 government budget proposal. He made the case for expansionist fiscal policy in a 45-page appendix to the 1933 budget statement to the Swedish Parliament.[5]

The central role of state intervention came through in this set of engagements, making the bridge between analytical constructs and felt political imperatives. Somewhat paradoxically from the perspective of *Asian Drama*, perhaps, the population-based motivation for intervention in Sweden of the early 1900s was too low a population! The Myrdals' central policy prescription was to support child-bearing and child-rearing among the poorer classes through income transfers, public housing, and the like. The proposals led to a great debate, but the conclusion was clear:

> The bulk of the legislative program was enacted in the 1937 session of the Swedish Parliament which became popularly identified as the 'mothers and babies' session. Most of the proposed benefits were approved with but minor modifications. A sweeping program of highly progressive taxation was also enacted. In addition, the 1910 statute outlawing discussions of contraception was struck down and discriminations against pregnant women in the labor force were banned.   (Barber 2008: 59)

It is widely acknowledged that the modern Swedish welfare state was born out of these interventions in the 1930s, spearheaded by the Myrdals. But there are two elements of these engagements that are worth noting. First, it has to be said that there was a disturbing element of the population discourse, in keeping with the

[5] Barber (2008: 40).

eugenics trend of the times. 'Rational' population policy was the touchstone and the provision and encouragement of the spread of contraception methods was the key instrument. But, unfortunately, the 'rationality' was extended: 'A law enacted in May 1934 mandated compulsory sterilization of persons deemed incapable of consent—that is, the insane and imbecile' (Barber 2008: 60). Secondly, the panoply of interventions relied on the capability of the state to implement them efficiently without, for example, corruption undoing the intent of the policymakers. The issue of whether the state could indeed intervene effectively came to the fore in *Asian Drama*'s discussion of the 'soft state'.

Much else was also going on in the development of Gunnar Myrdal's thinking in the 1930s. One key element of this was the major shift of stance from the hot-shot young neoclassical theorist in the 1920s (and in his own 20s) towards institutional economics, which he had disdained as being too atheoretical. He continued to argue that facts without theory were meaningless, and indeed this was and continued to be his critique of the German Historical School, but he came to have greater appreciation of the role of economic and other institutions in explaining observed phenomena, as opposed to abstract theorizing not rooted in reality.

Myrdal arrived in the US, on a Rockefeller Foundation scholarship, in 1929. It was a momentous time to be in the US, with the onset of the Great Depression. Myrdal's macroeconomic and monetary track of thinking was clearly influenced by these events, but that is not the focus of this chapter. However, he also came into contact with Wesley Mitchell at Columbia and John Commons at Wisconsin, both leading institutionalists. It is perhaps difficult now to appreciate the challenge that the institutionalist school posed to the dominant neoclassical school in the USA—both Mitchell and Commons were former presidents of the American Economic Association. Myrdal could not but be engaged in these debates in his two years in the US.

One can guess at the tugs that Myrdal felt when faced with the challenge of the Institutional School. Adair (1992) sets out the unifying principles of the school as follows:

- Institutions and not value are the object of economics
- The analysis of process and social change requires a dynamic analysis
- To formulate realistic hypotheses, other social sciences (psychology, anthropology) must be involved, and empirical case studies must be undertaken
- The rejection of the 'laissez-faire' policy as a principle of economic coordination and the necessity of social control and State intervention.   (Adair 1992: 165–6)

Clearly, the caution on laissez-faire and the emphasis on dynamic analysis would have sat well with the young Myrdal. But the heavy emphasis on facts and case studies was a barrier to one who had started off as a theorist well versed in abstract models. Even with his iconoclastic *The Political Element in Development Theory*, in which he skewered the unthinking value assumptions of his teachers, he nevertheless worried about the 'facts before theory' line of argument. Indeed, *Political Element* was welcomed by members of the Institutional and German Historical Schools as supportive of their side. However, despite his criticism of orthodoxy for being value laden, and actually because of this, he was critical of these schools as well. As he noted in his preface to the 1954 English translation edition of *Political Element*, his thinking had been evolving:

> The implicit belief in the existence of a body of scientific knowledge acquired independently of all valuations is, as I now see it, naïve empiricism. Facts do not organize themselves into concepts and theories just by being looked at; indeed except within the framework of concepts and theories, there are no scientific facts but only chaos. There is an inescapable *a priori* element in all scientific work. Questions must be asked before answers can be given.   (Myrdal 1954: xli)

And since questions have implicit values, he thus cycles back to his position that the best strategy is to be explicit and upfront about values.

This, then, was the Myrdal who in the 1950s began his deep and sustained engagement with the development discourse, which was to last for the rest of his life. The theoretical and methodological frameworks he took up, discarded, and developed, the cycles in thinking he went through in the eventful 1920s and 1930s, his roles in establishing the Swedish welfare state in the 1930s and 1940s, all of these shaped the man who approached *Asian Drama*. But what was the development terrain he found? The next section takes up that part of the story.

3. The Development Terrain in Mid-twentieth Century

The story of Myrdal's life up to the start of his work on *Asian Drama* is not yet complete. Of course in the late 1930s and early 1940s he worked on the massive project *An American Dilemma*, which helped to frame the civil rights debate in the US for a generation, and in which he displayed the depth and breadth of analytical capacity and moral clarity expected from him. The project also highlighted, and further sharpened, the methodological perspectives we discussed in the previous section. In the mid-1940s he returned to Sweden and served another stint as a member of parliament. But it was starting in 1947 that his engagement with the global economy intensified and his vision can truly be said to have turned to developing countries.[6]

---

[6] Of course, always with Myrdal, there are precursors. Already in a publication in Swedish in 1944 he had begun to discuss international co-operation—see Appelqvist and Andersson (2005: 188).

From 1947 to 1957 Myrdal served as the Executive Secretary of the United Nations Economic Commission for Europe (ECE). Similar Commissions were set up for Latin America and for Asia at about the same time, headed by Raul Prebisch and by P. Lokanathan respectively. Myrdal's institutional focus was of course on the war-torn economies of Europe and, increasingly in the 1950s, the East–West divide across the Iron Curtain. He is well known for having set up an excellent research group. The first director of the Research and Planning Division was none other than Nicholas Kaldor and the group was famously given the freedom to produce research without worrying about its political implications, which Myrdal would, and did, handle.

For our purposes, however, what is interesting is that the ECE period also led to increasing engagement with the problems of development in general, albeit initially in the international context. He gave many lectures on the topic and published widely, including for example *An International Economy: Problems and Prospects* (Myrdal 1956). In 1955, Myrdal delivered the Anniversary Commemoration Lectures at the National Bank of Egypt, entitled *Development and Underdevelopment: A Note on the Mechanism of National and International Economic Inequality*. These Cairo lectures formed the basis of his book, *Economic Theory and Underdeveloped Regions* (Myrdal 1957), which came out as he began his leadership of the team working on *Asian Drama*, a project funded by the Twentieth Century Fund. *Underdeveloped Regions* was thus a precursor to *Asian Drama* and was, in effect, an early statement of the development terrain as Myrdal saw it before embarking on his monumental project.

But the development terrain, and the ideas bubbling in the discourse, had a life of their own before Myrdal shook the ground with *Asian Drama*. What did this terrain look like in the 1940s, 1950s and 1960s? Much, but not all, of the answer is in *Underdeveloped Regions* itself. Since very few people nowadays read Myrdal in the original, I will take the liberty of quoting at length from this volume as necessary, to establish Myrdal's thinking as he approached the writing of *Asian Drama*.

The developing world as seen from the vantage point of the 1950s presented sharp and gloomy contrasts, which coloured the thinking of the development discourse. A very clear statement of this is to be found in *Underdeveloped Regions*:

> ...more than two-thirds of the people in the non-Soviet world live in countries where real income per head is only a very tiny fraction of what it is in the highly developed countries and, indeed, in most cases is much smaller than it was in those countries before they started to develop rapidly a century or more ago.
>
> (Myrdal 1957: 3)

> ...there is a small group of countries which are quite well off and a much larger group of extremely poor countries;...the countries in the former group are on the whole firmly settled in a pattern of continuing economic development, while in the latter group progress is slower, as many countries are in constant danger

of not being able to lift themselves out of stagnation or even of losing ground so far as average income levels are concerned; and...therefore, on the whole, in recent decades the economic inequalities between developed and developing countries have been increasing.   (Myrdal 1957: 6)

These words do not of course fully resonate with the realities of today. The dramatic growth of many Asian economies in the last three decades, led by China and India but also including countries such as Bangladesh and Vietnam, does not sit well with the perspective that *many countries are in constant danger of not being able to lift themselves out of stagnation or even of losing ground so far as average income levels are concerned.* But that was the world that was, and it gave rise to the development doctrines of its time.

These development doctrines were also, of course, creatures of history. The world had just gone through a deep depression in the 1930s, rescued by public expenditures of the war. Faith in the efficacy and effectiveness of public action was strong. Keynesianism ruled the day. Expansion of the welfare state was unquestioned. As Myrdal (1956) said: 'the concept of the welfare state, to which we are now giving reality in all the advanced nations, would have to be widened and changed into a concept of a "welfare world"'.[7] At the same time there were the income realities of the gap between the developed and developing worlds. Analysis and policy discourse naturally ran along two, sometimes related, tracks—a within-country focus and a global cross-country perspective.

The within-country-focused discourse on development in the mid-twentieth century had several strands, including the perennial one of balance between market and state. The need for the state was evidenced by market failures of different types, which held back economic growth. Perhaps the most prominent proponent of this perspective was W. Arthur Lewis, who became a dominant figure in development economics in the 1940s, 1950s and 1960s, and indeed won the Nobel Prize in Economics in 1979, five years after Myrdal. Lewis's contribution to development thinking through his famous surplus labour theory is well known and there is no need for us to rehearse that theory here (Lewis 1954). More important, in the context of *Asian Drama*, is the strong conclusion on the role of state intervention in accelerating industrialization. Throughout the 1940s, Lewis fought a battle with market-oriented development specialists, especially on the Colonial Economic Advisory Committee. Here is how he characterized Sydney Caine, head of the Economic Division of the Colonial Office, in a 1944 memorandum:

...he is a religious devotee of laissez-faire, and his headship of the Economic Department at this juncture is fatal...[his approach] is fatal not only in the decisions he makes, especially on secondary industry, on marketing and on co-operative organisation, but also in the appointments he recommends to

---

[7] Quoted in Barber (2008: 112).

important jobs in the Colonies, for which he chooses almost invariably people as laissez-faire as himself.   (Quoted in Mine 2006: 335)

However, the tension between letting markets be free and an overly interventionist state became clear when Lewis moved in 1957 to be the resident advisor to Kwame Nkrumah, leader of the newly independent Ghana. Lewis's biographer Tignor (2006) quotes the following letter from Lewis in 1958 on the development plan:

> It makes inadequate provision for some essential services while according the highest priority to a number of second importance…Alas, the main reason for this lack of balance is that the plan contains too many schemes on which the Prime Minister is insisting for 'political reasons'…In order to give you these toys, the Development Commission has had to cut down severely on water supplies, health centers, technical schools, roads…It is not easy to make a good development plan for £100 million if the Prime Minister insists on inserting £18 million of his own pet schemes of a sort which neither develop the country nor increase the comfort of the people.   (Tignor 2006: 167)

As argued by Kanbur (2017), the Ghana period in Lewis's life merely revealed his struggles in balancing state and market, cognizant on the one hand of market failures, and on the other of state failures (Lewis 1965). This struggle is also seen in *Underdeveloped Regions* and in *Asian Drama*.

A second, and not unrelated, strand of development thinking in the mid-twentieth century was on the need for a 'big push' for industrialization. Rosenstein-Rodan (1943) is commonly cited as the originator of the idea, but there were others who also espoused it. Here is how it was summarized half a century later in a well-known exposition:

> According to Rosenstein-Rodan, if various sectors of the economy adopted increasing returns technologies simultaneously, they could each create income that becomes a source of demand for goods in other sectors, and so enlarge their markets and make industrialization profitable. In fact, simultaneous industrialization of many sectors can be self-sustaining even if *no* sector could break even industrializing alone. This insight has been developed by Nurkse (1953), Scitovsky (1954), and Fleming (1955) into a doctrine of balanced growth or the big push, with two important elements. First, the same economy must be capable of both the backward preindustrial and the modern industrialized state. No exogenous improvement in endowments or technological opportunities is needed to move to industrialization, only the simultaneous investment by all the sectors using the available technology. Second, industrialization is associated with a better state of affairs. The population of a country benefits from its leap into the industrial state.   (Murphy et al. 1989: 1004)

Thus the idea that growth and industrialization were intimately linked, and that industrialization required significant state intervention, was deeply ingrained in the development discourse of the 1940s and 1950s. It is not surprising then that they were present in Myrdal's *Underdeveloped Regions*, albeit that for him they flowed from a lifetime of thinking about economic processes and in engagement with the creation of the Swedish Welfare State. His thesis of 'circular and cumulative causation' fits in well with arguments for a big push:

> ...my starting point is the assertion that the notion of stable equilibrium is normally a false analogy to choose when constructing a theory to explain the changes in a social system...In the normal case a change does not call forth countervailing changes but, instead, supporting changes, which move the system in the same direction as the first change but much further. Because of such circular causation a social process tends to become cumulative and often to gather speed at an accelerating rate.   (Myrdal 1957: 13)

In keeping with these tenors of the times, and in light of the perceived success of growth in the Soviet Union, planning to accelerate growth was very much in vogue in the 1950s. A leading example is newly independent India, in many ways a crucible of the development discourse at that time. The first five-year plan, for the period 1951–1956, sets out the terms as follows:

> Given these basic conditions of rapid and sustained progress, institutional as well as others, the key to higher productivity and expanding levels of income and employment lies really in stepping up the rate of capital formation. The level of production and the material well-being a community can attain depends, in the main, on the stock of capital at its disposal, i.e., on the amount of land per capita and of productive equipment in the shape of machinery, buildings, tools and implements, factories, locomotives, engines, irrigation facilities, power installations and communications.
>
> (Government of India, Planning Commission 1951: chapter 1, para 15)

This plan, and even more so the second five-year plan for 1956–1961, emphasized the development of heavy industry with state investment. Myrdal in *Underdeveloped Regions* was already a convert to planning, of course:

> ...the matter is sometimes confused by an altogether unfounded counterposition of central state planning and "free enterprise" and by assuming that planning creates rigidities...It should be clear, however, that if an underdeveloped country really succeeds in starting and sustaining by its policy interferences an upward cumulative process of economic development, this will provide more not less space for what private enterprise such a country possesses or is able to foster.   (Myrdal 1957: 81–2)

However, as already alluded to, he was concerned about the nature of the state and what we would now call capture of the state by elite groups: '...most under-developed countries are up against state institutions of social and economic inequality which often cannot easily be broken. Frequently the state is itself initially in the hands of social groups which have an interest in preserving the traditional social chasms' (Myrdal 1957: 83). The failure of state interventions was thus already a theme in his writings in the 1950s, a theme which was to emerge ever more strongly in the decade to come, culminating in the strong positions he took up in *Asian Drama*.

Alongside the country-focused development discourse, which led to discussions of surplus labour and the big push and economic planning, there was a second strand that exercised development thinkers and practitioners in the mid-twentieth century. This was the international dimension of trade between rich and poor countries. As we shall see, there was surprisingly little on this in *Asian Drama* itself, but Myrdal's other writings, before and after, dwelt on this dimension in some detail. It was clear that he was greatly influenced by Raul Prebisch, the head of the sister institution to ECE, CEPAL. In his 1956 book, *An International Economy: Problems and Prospects*, Myrdal quotes Prebisch at length and approv-ingly.[8] Most famously, of course, Prebisch is known for the view that primary commodity-exporting developing countries were at a disadvantage because these commodities would be demanded less in relative terms as world incomes grew, leading to a downward spiral of stagnation for these countries. Here is how Myrdal states this position in *Underdeveloped Regions*:

> The main positive effect of international trade on the underdeveloped countries was in fact to promote the production of primary products; and such production, employing mostly unskilled labor, has come to constitute the bulk of their exports. In these lines, however, they often meet inelastic demands in the export market, often also a demand trend which is not rising very rapidly, and excessive price fluctuations.   (Myrdal 1957: 52)

The way out of this trap for Prebisch was industrialization so these countries could partake of the benefits of growing demand for manufactures as world incomes grew, but the breakthrough into industrialization would in turn need a big push with trade protection and planning.

Such, then, was the development terrain and the development discourse as Myrdal left the ECE in 1957 and began his decade-long engagement in writing *Asian Drama*. The problems of the free market had been laid bare in the Great Depression of the 1930s—high growth rates in the Soviet Union seemed to highlight the benefits of central planning; the 'export pessimism' of Prebisch and

---

[8]   See Barber (2008: 112).

others suggested industrialization as the way out; and central planning with the state directing investment and trade to orchestrate the big push was the instrument at everybody's fingertips. There were concerns about the heavy hand of the state, expressed by Lewis (1965) and to some extent by Myrdal (1957). But these seemed to be secondary to the primary imperative of addressing market failures directly and vigorously, when *Asian Drama* burst upon the scene in 1968.

4. *Asian Drama* and After

Gunnar Myrdal's preface to *Asian Drama* starts with the words 'HABENT SUA FATA LIBELLI—books have their own destiny...', and he added, '...even while they are being written and before they are published'.[9] In fact the full Latin expression 'Pro captu lectoris habent sua fata libelli', 'According to the capabilities of the reader, books have their destiny', may be more appropriate for our purposes since *Asian Drama* has meant many things to many people since it came out more than fifty years ago in 1968. Its full title, *Asian Drama: An Inquiry into the Poverty of Nations*, suggested an epoch-making tome, and it hit the development discourse like a thunderbolt, but not necessarily to universal acclaim. It was reviewed by most of the leading lights of development when it came out, and each saw different elements to praise or criticize. After a brief account of the contents of the volume this section presents a selection of these reviews to start a discussion of the impact of *Asian Drama* in its time and following on to this day.

Asian Drama is famously long, Myrdal himself saying that 'The length is abominable'.[10] It is close to 2,500 pages, spread over three volumes, with seven parts, thirty-three chapters and sixteen appendices. Part of the reason for the length, Myrdal implies, is because of his...

> firm conviction that economic problems cannot be studied in isolation but only in their demographic, social, and political setting...I felt at the outset of the study that only by means of a broad institutional approach could I understand and explain the economic underdevelopment of the region...It is not altogether a pretentious metaphor when I describe my endeavor to apply an institutional approach in this study as an attempt to analyze the development problems of South Asia in the manner that Adam Smith studied England's development problems of two hundred years ago.   (Myrdal 1968: ix–x)

And there you have it. The self-stated scope and ambition of the project to match Adam Smith brought forth reviews that assessed the outcome with a similar standard. But first, briefly, to the contents of the three volumes.

---

[9] Myrdal (1968: vii).   [10] Myrdal (1968: x).

After a long prologue, volume I is in three parts—Introduction, Political Problems, and Economic Realities. Part I sets out the broad scope of the study and, perhaps expectedly from the author of *The Political Element*, a statement in chapter 2 of 'the Value Premises Chosen', whose 'Modernization Ideals' have already been listed in the previous section. Part II sets the stage at the coming of independence, including the partition of India and Pakistan, followed by separate chapters on each of India, Pakistan, and a final chapter on Ceylon and Southeast Asia. A central theme in these chapters, perhaps the dominant theme, was one which Myrdal had presaged in *Underdeveloped Regions*, the disconnect between the ruling elites and the masses:

> In contrast to the poverty-stricken masses, the national political leaders were all members of the privileged upper class, and their new positions of responsibility and power rapidly invested them with still greater privileges...Because of the narrow social base of the elite and the absence of any pressure from the masses, the leaders were under no compulsion to govern vigorously and disinterestedly.
> (Myrdal 1968: 273–5)

Following this discussion of politics, part III of volume I is in many ways a conventional laying out of the economic aggregates on demography, national income, trade, and inequality. Of particular interest is chapter 13 on foreign trade and capital flows, which repeats the analysis and the sentiments of a decade ago from *Underdeveloped Regions*. The existing pattern of trade, with exports of primary commodities dominating, is attributed to the colonial legacy of South Asia, and this pattern is argued to be inimical to future growth and development:

> If development is to occur in the South Asian countries, it will come not as a response to foreign demand for the products in which the region has traditionally had a comparative advantage...Development must be internally based and deliberately prodded and nurtured, since the spontaneous growth-inducing stimulus of a relatively free and expanding international trade is no longer present. This is the main thrust of the present chapter.   (Myrdal 1968: 583)

This line of argument, very much in keeping with the mainstream of the time, is one which stands out as not having stood the test of time in one sense—trade has been the engine of growth for South Asia and Asia as a whole in the last three decades. However, on a more subtle reading, movement from primary commodities to labour-intensive manufacture under initial protection can, in turn, be seen as part of the successful development strategy of Asia to break free from traditional trade patterns.

Volume II has three parts: A Third World of Planning, Problems of Labour Utilization, and Problems of Population Size. The two chapters on population in part VI are perhaps what one might expect from the author of the reports on Swedish population policy three decades previously. Similarly, the themes on planning had already been well signalled in Myrdal's earlier work—on the one hand welcoming it as an appropriate response to market failure in developing countries, but on the other hand expressing significant concern about state failure. The last chapter in this section, 'Corruption—Its Causes and Effects' broke new ground in the development discourse of its time: 'Although corruption is very much an issue in the public debate...it is almost taboo as a research topic and is rarely mentioned in scholarly discussions of the problems of government and planning...Embarrassing questions are avoided by ignoring the problems of attitudes and institutions...' (Myrdal 1968: 938–9).

Myrdal goes on to discuss Facts, Causes, Consequences and Remedies for Corruption. This was indeed a departure from standard development studies of the time and can perhaps be argued to have been one with lasting impact and whose traces can be found in the debates and discourses of the twenty-first century. Part V in volume II also played a role in the discourse of the day by highlighting the role of agriculture and agricultural productivity in raising living standards, tilting the balance away somewhat from the industrialization emphasis to be found in the discourse at that time, as discussed in the previous section.[11] And, although the term 'informality' does not appear in the subject index, chapter 21, on 'Unemployment' and 'Underemployment' can lay claim to have raised the conceptual and statistical issues we are now familiar with, well before the 'discovery' of the informal sector by the development discourse in the 1970s.

Volume III, with only a single part, part VII, is devoted to what we would these days call 'human development'. It has five chapters covering different aspects of health and education. Myrdal built on ongoing development in the 'human capital' approach which was becoming dominant at the time, but went further in expected directions:

> Once economists identified the residual factor in economic growth with investment in man...this approach derived support from various research undertakings that were themselves inspired by it...But the model itself is based on a number of unwarranted assumptions...The model also implies that prevailing attitudes and institutions, items in the level of living other than educational facilities, are of no consequence to the problem... (Myrdal 1968: 1541–6)

How was *Asian Drama* received when it appeared fifty years ago? His biographer, Barber (2008), has compiled an account of the most prominent reviews:

> Thomas Balogh...was lavish in his praise...Kenneth E. Boulding, President of the American Economic Association...spoke approvingly of the 'unsparing... criticism of those Western economists and social scientists who think that development is equivalent to technology and who are unable to recognize the obstacles created by ancient tradition, class structures and especially by the

---

[11] It should be noted, with some surprise perhaps, how little mention is made of Arthur Lewis's surplus labour model of development. Indeed, Lewis is mentioned in this context substantively only in appendix 3 and appendix 6, and that, too, only in footnotes.

existing power structures of society'...Writing in the *American Economic Review*, George Rosen (then with the Asian Development Bank)...thought the prognosis to be 'gloomier...than justified'. He drew attention to prospects for increasing exports and 'increase in farm output with new technologies, especially with new varieties of seed...' and noted that 'some of these technological breakthroughs have only begun to have their effects since the book went to press in 1966'. (Barber 2008: 140–2)

The praise and criticism also reflected the well-worn debates on market versus state, and the position of each reviewer along the spectrum. While Thomas Balogh praised *Asian Drama*, prominent pro-market economist Peter Bauer was equally forthright in criticism:

P.T. Bauer of the London School of Economics spoke for the school of economists suspicious of government interventions and of non-market solutions to economic problems. 'Even more than other writers on development,' he wrote, 'Professor Myrdal regards material progress, including apparently the transformation of values and conduct, as dependent on state action. The defects of this approach are even more pronounced in the underdeveloped world than elsewhere. In these countries, far more than in the West, the government is primarily a section interest.' (Barber 2008: 142)

Of course Myrdal himself would have agreed with the last sentence; after all, he was the one who had written about 'the narrow social base of the elite' and had brought the issue of corruption to the fore in his formulation of the 'soft state', by which he meant 'an unwillingness among the rulers to impose obligations on the governed and corresponding unwillingness on their part to obey rules laid down by democratic procedures' (Myrdal 1968: 277). And yet he recognized the need for state interventions given market failures, thereby restating the eternal question in political economy, of balance between state and market.[12]

How was *Asian Drama* received in India, the dominant focus of the book? In an excellent revisit of *Asian Drama*, Siegel (2017) brings to our attention that Gunnar Myrdal joined Alva Myrdal in Delhi in 1957, where she was working with UNESCO, and was based in Delhi for four years. Here he 'quickly emerged as a visible and voluble presence throughout the city during the heyday of foreign expertise in India's capital' (p. 197) and was 'joined by a rotating cast of junior economists and assistants' (p. 197).[13] Siegel's (2017) review of the reviews of *Asian Drama* in India matches the assessment of Myrdal's biographer, Barber (2008). These were mixed to say the least, with most perhaps being on the negative, or at least the questioning, end of the spectrum. For example, Thapar (1968), Gupta

---

[12] For further discussion of this as the central question in political economy, see Kanbur (2016).

[13] An entire separate chapter could and perhaps should be devoted to this group, whose names are now recognized as stalwarts of the development discourse of the last half-century, among them Ester Boserup, Michael Lipton, and Paul Streeten.

(1968) and Frank (1970) all wrote highly critical reviews, ranging from observations that 'Asian values' had not held up Japan's development, to the fact that Myrdal was not aware of the vigorous and sometimes violent struggles the 'docile' peasantry was fighting against the land-owning class. The doyen of Indian planning P.C. Mahalanobis wrote a respectful, but in parts also highly critical, review. Mahalanobis asked where all the emphasis on politics led to in terms of practical policy (Mahalanobis 1969). Thus, perhaps paradoxically, *Asian Drama* appears to have been received much less warmly in India than in the West.

What is interesting is how little there is in *Asian Drama* on global questions. Sure, in part III of volume I, chapter 13, as its title suggests, addresses 'Foreign Trade and Capital Flows', and makes arguments familiar from *Underdeveloped Regions* and *An International Economy*. And there are, of course, long forays into colonialism and what it wrought. But the inequities of the global system as a whole is not treated at length or systematically in *Asian Drama*, which is more focused on within-country issues, and in making the methodological perspective of institutionalism a centrepiece. But it was an issue to which Myrdal returned with great force and vigour in the rest of his life after *Asian Drama*. In particular, he took up the topic in his Nobel Prize Lecture, 'The Equality Issue in World Development' (Myrdal 1975), which had a central focus on development assistance. In fact, the development assistance issue is an interesting and important lens through which to view changes in Myrdal's thinking, and the evolution of the development discourse, before and after *Asian Drama*.

In his Nobel Lecture, Myrdal began by chiding his former *Underdeveloped Regions'* self for minimizing the role of aid:

> But I must confess that when, twenty years ago in the middle of the Fifties, I delivered a series of lectures in Cairo focused on the same topic as my present lecture (later published in a volume, *Economic Theory and Underdeveloped Regions*), and in spite of my already then having attempted to redirect my thinking in an institutional direction, I could assert: 'What is needed is not primarily a redistribution of wealth and incomes. Indeed, aid can only be a very small part of a rational international equalization program...None of the schemes which have been propounded for capital aid for development of underdeveloped countries has ever amounted to taking away more than a tiny fraction of the yearly increase of national income per head in the richer countries, which implied that no real sacrifice has ever been envisaged...A wholesale income equalization by redistribution between nations is both impossible and, I am inclined to believe, an unimportant objective.' (Myrdal 1975)

He then went on to say why he thought it had become an important issue:

> In recent years there have been sudden, major changes in the world economy. They have radically affected the economic situation of all underdeveloped countries, though in different directions and degrees, and thereby the entire setting of

the equality problem I am discussing in this lecture. For by far the larger part of the peoples in underdeveloped countries, these changes have been worsening their development prospects and in many countries are now threatening the survival of large numbers of their poor masses. The type of marginal foreign aid we have provided, is clearly not enough to meet their barest needs.

(Myrdal 1975)

Among these changes were the rapid growth in population, economic stagnation, and pressures on natural resources—Myrdal was writing then in the aftermath of the OPEC oil prices rises and the global stagflation which followed.

Myrdal became a strong champion of foreign aid in the decade and a half after the publication of *Asian Drama*, influencing Sweden's own strong stance on development assistance. However, in something of a reversal, towards the end of his working life he began to have second thoughts, or at least began to sound cautionary notes. The reasons relate again to the nature of the state and politics in recipient countries. Just as he confessed in the mid-1980s that his views on aid in the mid-1950s were wrong, he confessed in the mid-1980s to 'growing pangs of conscience' (Myrdal 1984) because the aid given was being diverted by the ruling elites. He argued for greater control of the flows and their uses by the donors—conditionality, in other words. One sees again the tensions between market failure, which led to an argument for state intervention and development assistance, and state failure, which subverted the good intentions of the intervention to benefit powerful interests.

Myrdal was thus not at all beyond questioning his premises, sometimes in succession in a long engagement with an issue, and he was known to change his mind. However, perhaps the biggest turnaround, or at least the biggest question-ing of his decade-long project, might have come to him only after his death in 1987, over three decades ago now, and three decades after he started the *Asian Drama* project. As noted in the previous section, he had already signalled what he saw as the dire predicament of the poor countries of the world in *Underdeveloped Regions*, as being 'in constant danger of not being able to lift themselves out of stagnation or even of losing ground so far as average income levels are concerned' (Myrdal 1957: 6), a sensibility and starting point he brought to *Asian Drama*. Much of the thrust of *Asian Drama* was an attempt to answer why this was the case—why these countries, where the bulk of humanity lived, were not able to break out of a low income, low growth, trap—and to do so using an institutional-ist framework which went beyond conventional narrow economic thinking.

But what would now face the Myrdal of *Asian Drama* is the remarkable growth in the very region in which *Asian Drama* was set. There is no need to detail here the historically record-breaking growth performance of China, followed by a slew of countries including India, Vietnam, Bangladesh, Indonesia, Philippines, and even Pakistan and Sri Lanka (Ceylon as it was then). Inequality within these countries has increased along with growth, but income poverty, as conventionally measured, has plummeted in Asia as a whole and, given the relatively anaemic growth of the rich countries, global inequality, as conventionally measured, has also declined.[14]

This growth performance of Asia was not predicted nor expected in *Asian Drama*. The social structures and constraints so emphasized by Myrdal, partly as a rebuke to his own discipline of economics, surely did not undergo a rapid dramatic change in the two decades after the publication of *Asian Drama* and the take-off of Asian economic growth. But, quite contrary to the expectations and predictions of Myrdal and his contemporaries such as Prebisch, openness and trade did explode and Asian countries rode the wave of exporting to the demands of rising global incomes to raise their own levels of living. Rising inequality in these countries is, and was, a reflection of precisely those structural inequalities highlighted by Myrdal in *Asian Drama*. But one feels that the Asian growth turnaround and the role of trade in this turnaround would have to be the centrepiece of an imagined next magnum opus by Myrdal for our time: *Asian Drama in the Twenty-First Century*.

5. Conclusion: *Asian Drama* and the Development Discourse in the Twenty-first Century

To conclude with the beginning of *Asian Drama*, 'HABENT SUA FATA LIBELLI—books have their own destiny…'[15] How much more so with books which are classics, so much so that they are more referred to than read. So far as one can tell, *Asian Drama* has been much cited. At the time of writing this chapter, Google Scholar shows 4,876 cites. This includes citations in such well-known publications as Krueger (1974), Fukuyama (1992) and Acemoglu et al. (2005: 385–472). But, as I note in the Introduction, my anecdotal experience is that young development economists do not cite *Asian Drama* very much, and if they do, they do so in perfunctory fashion. However, strong traces of *Asian Drama*, and of the Myrdal before and after *Asian Drama*, are to be found in the twenty-first-century development discourse. This is because the issues Myrdal raised, throughout his life but also in *Asian Drama*, are fundamental ones, not only for development but also for our discipline of economics and for the broader terrain of political economy in the twenty-first century. I conclude by highlighting three such themes.

---

[14] For Asian growth, poverty, and inequality over this period, see Kanbur and Zhuang (2012).
[15] Myrdal (1968: vii).

The first of these is, of course, the role of values in analysis. Myrdal argued, and on this he never wavered after first staking out his claim in the 1930s, that economics is by necessity value-laden. He argued that although there had been vigorous debate on this in the nineteenth century, the economics of his time had tried to present itself as value free, in an attempt to achieve a status comparable to that of natural science. But this was manifestly not the case, and could not be the case given the nature of the subject. Rather than pretend otherwise, he proposed, and carried out his own proposal very thoroughly in *Asian Drama*, that the values should be made explicit. I think this is a major strand of his thinking and we would do well to take it to heart.

The second theme that emerges from our study of *Asian Drama* in the overall context of Gunnar Myrdal's life work is that of the absolute necessity of going beyond narrow economic principles to understand society, and even to understand the economy itself. Throughout his work Myrdal maintained a healthy respect for the core tenets of economics as a discipline, indeed some of the reviews of *Asian Drama* noted this well.[16] But his main thrust is the need to understand fully the social, cultural and political context when trying to explain economic facts and when developing economic policy prescriptions. This comes through most strongly in his discussions of the roles of the ruling elite, and of the gap between the formulation and implementation of policy in what he called the 'soft state'.

But ruling elites, corruption and soft states bring to the fore what I consider to be the third lasting theme in *Asian Drama* and in Myrdal's life work. This is the constant struggle to find the balance between state and market. The struggle was famously characterized by Edmund Burke as being: 'What the state ought to take upon itself to direct by the public wisdom, and what it ought to leave, with as little interference as possible, to individual discretion' (Burke 1795).

I have argued in Kanbur (2016) that this is, in effect, the eternal question of political economy. Keynes (1926) alluded to this in his equally famous critique of the laissez-faire doctrine.[17] The see-saw between an interventionist stance in the face of manifest market failure, and a pull-back upon realization of state failure, and where the balance is struck, is seen in Arthur Lewis's struggles in Ghana.[18] It is also seen in Gunnar Myrdal's specific struggles with himself and his cycles of thinking on foreign aid, and on the constant back and forth between wanting planning as a way out of an underdevelopment trap, and planning itself as a trap giving hostages to the elites and to the soft state.

---

[16] As Barber (2008: 141) notes, Rosen's (1968) critique in the *American Economic Review* also included the interesting observation that 'in his stress on the need for a more institutional analysis…he himself uses traditional economic concepts centering about the market and the price system as the basis for his own policy suggestions'.

[17] For a detailed discussion, see Kanbur (2016).   [18] Kanbur (2017).

The development vista has changed dramatically over the last half-century. But the fundamental tensions, including the three themes discussed here, are still with us. Myrdal's struggles with these tensions are his ultimate legacy to the development discourse of the twenty-first century.

References

Acemoglu, D., S. Johnson, and J. A. Robinson (2005). 'Institutions as a Fundamental Cause of Long Run Growth'. In P. Aghion and S.N. Durlauf (eds) *Handbook of Economic Growth, Volume I*. Amsterdam: Elsevier.

Adair, P. (1992). 'Myrdal and Institutionalism: From Rejection to Acceptance'. In G. Dostaler, D. Ethier, and L. Lepage (eds) *Gunnar Myrdal and his Works*. Montreal: Harvest House.

Appelqvist, O., and S. Andersson (eds) (2005). *The Essential Gunnar Myrdal*. New York: The New Press.

Barber, W.J. (2008). *Gunnar Myrdal*. New York: Palgrave Macmillan.

Bok, S. (1992). 'Introduction'. In G. Dostaler, D. Ethier, and L. Lepage (eds) *Gunnar Myrdal and his Works* (pp. 3–10). Montreal: Harvest House.

Burke, E. (1795). *Thoughts and Details on Scarcity. Originally Presented to The Right Hon. William Pitt, in the Month of November*. Published in 1990 by Francis Canavan (ed.). Indianapolis, IN: Liberty Fund, Inc.

Dostaler, G., D. Ethier, and L. Lepage (1992). *Gunnar Myrdal and his Works*. Montreal: Harvest House.

Etzemuller, T. (2014). *Alva and Gunnar Myrdal: Social Engineering in the Modern World*. New York: Lexington Books.

Fleming, J.M. (1955). 'External Economies and the Doctrine of Balanced Growth', *Economic Journal*, 65: 241–56.

Frank, A.G. (1970). 'The Wealth and Poverty of Nations: Even Heretics Remain Bound by Traditional Thought', *Economic and Political Weekly*, 5(29/31) (July 1): 1177–84.

Fukuyama. F. (1992). *The End of History and the Last Man*. New York: Free Press.

Government of India, Planning Commission (1951). *1st Five Year Plan*. http://www.planningcommission.nic.in/plans/planrel/fiveyr/welcome.html.

Gupta, K.P. (1968). 'Review of "Asian Drama"', *Commonwealth*, LXXXIX(1) (4 October): 35–6.

Kanbur, R. (2016). 'The End of Laissez Faire, The End of History and The Structure of Scientific Revolutions', *Challenge*, 59(1): 35–46.

Kanbur, R. (2017). 'W. Arthur Lewis and the Roots of Ghanaian Economic Policy'. In E. Aryeetey and R. Kanbur (eds) *The Economy of Ghana Sixty Years after Independence*. Oxford: Oxford University Press.

Kanbur, R., and J. Zhuang. (2012). 'Confronting Rising Inequality in Asia', (with J. Zhuang), Theme Chapter of *Asian Development Outlook 2012*, Asian Development Bank, April.

Keynes, J.M. (1926). 'The End of Laissez-Faire'. In *The Collected Writings of John Maynard Keynes, Volume IX, Essays in Persuasion* (1978). Cambridge: Cambridge University Press.

Krueger, A.O. (1974). 'The Political Economy of a Rent Seeking Society', *American Economic Review*, 64(3): 291–303.

Lewis, W.A. (1954). 'Economic Development with Unlimited Supplies of Labour', *Manchester School*, 22(2): 139–91.

Lewis, W.A. (1965). *Politics in West Africa*. Oxford: Oxford University Press.

Mahalanobis, P.C. (1969). 'The Asian Drama: An Indian View', *Economic and Political Weekly*, 4(28/30) (July 1): 1119–32.

Mine, Y. (2006). 'The Political Element in the Works of W. Arthur Lewis: The 1954 Lewis Model and African Development', *The Developing Economies*, XLIV-3(September): 329–55.

Murphy, K.J., A. Shleifer, and R. Vishny. (1989). 'Industrialization and the Big Push', *Journal of Political Economy*, 97(5): 1003–26.

Myrdal, A., and G. Myrdal (1934). *Kris i befolkningsfragan (Crisis in the Population Question)*. Stockholm: Bonnier.

Myrdal, G. (1940). *Population: A Problem for Democracy. The Godkin Lectures.* Cambridge: Harvard University Press.

Myrdal, G. (1944). *An American Dilemma: The Negro Problem and Modern Democracy: Volumes I and II.* New York: Harper and Row.

Myrdal, G. (1954). *The Political Element in the Development of Economic Theory.* Cambridge: Harvard University Press.

Myrdal, G. (1956). *An International Economy: Problems and Prospects.* New York: Harper and Row.

Myrdal, G. (1957). *Economic Theory and Underdeveloped Regions.* New York: Harper and Row.

Myrdal, G. (1968). *Asian Drama: An Inquiry into the Poverty of Nations. A Twentieth Century Fund Study, Volumes I, II, and III.* New York: Pantheon.

Myrdal, G. (1973). *Against The Stream: Critical Essays on Economics.* New York: Pantheon Books.

Myrdal, G. (1975). 'The Equality Issue in World Development', 1974 Nobel Lecture. https://www.nobelprize.org/nobel_prizes/economic-sciences/laureates/1974/myrdal-lecture.html

Myrdal, G. (1984). 'International Inequality and Foreign Aid in Retrospect'. In G.M. Meier and D. Seers (eds) *Pioneers in Development* (pp. 151–65). New York: Oxford University Press.

Nurkse, R. (1953). *Problems of Capital Formation in Underdeveloped Countries.* New York: Oxford University Press.

Rosen, G. (1968). 'Review of "Asian Drama"', *American Economic Review*, 58(5): 1397–401.

Rosenstein-Rodan, P.N. (1943). 'Problems of Industrialization of Eastern and South-Eastern Europe', *Economic Journal*, 53: 202–11.

Scitovsky, T. (1954). 'Two Concepts of External Economies', *Journal of Political Economy*, 62: 143–51.

Siegel, B. (2017). '*Asian Drama* Revisited', *Humanity: An International Journal of Human Rights, Humanitarianism, and Development*, 8(1, Spring): 195–205.

Thapar, R. (1968). 'Poverty of Nations or Notions?', *Yojana*, 12(9, May): 2–6.

Tignor, R.L. (2006). *W. Arthur Lewis and the Birth of Development Economics.* Princeton, NJ: Princeton University Press.

Velupillai, K. (1992). 'Reflections on Gunnar Myrdal's Contributions to Economic Theory'. In G. Dostaler, D. Ethier, and L. Lepage(eds) *Gunnar Myrdal and his Works* (pp. 128–43). Montreal: Harvest House.

3

Myrdal's Methodology and Approach Revisited

Frances Stewart

'In fact, most writings, particularly in economics,
remain in large part simply ideological'[1]

1. Introduction

I read *Asian Drama* when teaching at the University of Nairobi in 1967–1969, in
my first encounter with development issues. The book made a huge impression,
largely because it made sense of my own early reactions. Rereading it some fifty
years later, I expected to be disappointed; to some extent I am, but in large part I
am not. On rereading, it became clear that the Myrdalian approach has indeed
affected the way I have approached most issues over the past fifty years. Much of
the methodological discussion still seems valid, although no longer so original
since many have caught up with much of what Myrdal said, and wider reading
suggests that others had already come to similar conclusions. Many social scientists take much of what he says for granted. Yet mainstream economists ignore
many of his ideas.

This chapter aims to review the main elements of Myrdal's methodological
innovations; to consider how far they were taken up (or independently developed)
by others and have become accepted over these decades; and to provide an assessment of their validity. Section 2 of the chapter briefly reviews Myrdal's contributions to methodology. The third section discusses how far his perspectives
have been adopted by development analysts, in light of the changes that have
taken place in the last fifty years. Section 4 briefly reviews findings and considers
some limitations of his approach, viewed from a twenty-first-century perspective.
Section 5 concludes.

---

[1] Myrdal (1970: 32).

2. The Main Elements of Myrdal's Methodological Approach

The following lists Myrdal's main methodological preoccupations:

1. the 'beam in our eyes'
2. the political element in analysis
3. the question of values and the definition of development
4. the social system and its five major categories
5. a tentative move towards multidisciplinarity
6. the inapplicability of Western[2] economics.

Myrdal's approach needs to be viewed as a whole rather than in disparate parts, as he reminds us. Yet this makes analysis difficult, so I review his approach bit by bit, though some of the elements are virtually inseparable. The first two elements in the list above—the beam in our eyes and the political element in analysis—are closely interlinked and both relate to distortions and biases that are unavoidably involved in social science. Values and the definition of development are also clearly linked, as values inform how development—as a normative project—is defined; therefore, values and development are discussed together. The issue of values also relates to the beam in our eyes, since the 'beam' means that each social scientist brings their own perceptions and values to their analysis. In contrast to this discussion of influences over social scientists' views, the analysis of the social system with its five-factor approach concerns the nature of developing countries and their economies as Myrdal sees them. Elaboration of the five factors in fact forms the bulk of the analysis in the three volumes of *Asian Drama*, but is treated only briefly here. A need for multidisciplinarity follows from Myrdal's comprehensive analysis of the problems of development.

Section 2.6 of this chapter discusses Myrdal's major methodological conclusion—that is, the inapplicability of Western economics to the economies of developing countries. This conclusion emerges from the discussion in sections 2.1–2.5: on the one hand, the deformed and opportunistic vision of economists explains why Western economists stick to Western economic concepts and theories even when analysing the very different situations to be found in underdeveloped countries; on the other hand, the analysis of values, the definition of development, and the nature of developing economies, including the constraints they face, explain why Myrdal concluded that Western concepts are inapplicable. All these issues, of course, continue to be strongly contested.

---

[2] Myrdal uses 'West' and 'Western' to refer to non-communist, high-income, industrialized countries. Following Myrdal, I use the terms here, but also 'North', to refer to the so-called advanced countries, and 'South' to refer to developing countries.

2.1 The 'Beam in our Eyes'

Here Myrdal disputes the idea that the social scientist can be an impartial, objective observer seeking the truth, someone whose analysis is independent of their own position, history, education, and interests, or, as he puts it, independent of the 'personal and social conditioning of our research activity'. 'The direction of our scientific exertions, particularly in economics, is conditioned by the society in which we live, and most directly by the political climate', he argues (Myrdal 1970: 9), pointing to the myth of 'the "scientific" man, . . . conditioned by nothing except his desire to discover the true nature of things, [which] is still commonly taken for granted' (Myrdal 1970: 7). Yet, according to Myrdal, '[a] "disinterested social scientist" has never existed and never will exist' (Myrdal 1970: 32).

The reasons Myrdal gave for this conclusion lay primarily in the political interests and values that economists bring with them and that inform their selection of topics, concepts, and assumptions. He suggested that, while economists had devoted time to analysing the behaviour of others, '[o]nly about the peculiar behaviour of our own profession do we choose to remain naïve' (Myrdal 1970: 6). One reason that positioning matters, according to Myrdal, is that economic concepts and theories fuse normative and positive elements, with the normative, in particular, reflecting positioning. For Myrdal, this was not a new perspective but had clear origins in *The Political Element in the Development of Economic Theory* (Myrdal 1965, first published in 1930). But there he suggested that, given awareness of the issue, it might be possible to separate the normative and positive in economics. In *Asian Drama*, in contrast, he suggests that such a separation is *not* possible because the normative and positive are intertwined in the conceptual apparatus. The importance of the normative element is brought out in his discussion of the political element and of values.

2.2 The Political Element

Myrdal argues that the political motives of the observer are a major influence on the normative content. When he was writing *Asian Drama*, the Cold War was at its height, and it was mainly this to which he was referring in claiming that political interests were paramount in determining economic analysis. He argued that Western economists aimed to advance the interests of the 'free' world. As he put it: 'A major source of bias in much economic research on poor countries is thus the endeavour to treat their problems from the point of view of the Western political and military interest in saving them from Communism' (Myrdal 1970: 13).

Thirty years after the Cold War ended, it is difficult to remember how deeply it affected international relations and related analysis. There was a war of ideas and of success in promoting development—to which Myrdal was referring—besides many violent proxy wars. This clear political motivation has lessened since the end of the Cold War, although, as argued later, the ideological element has remained strong, but has taken a different form in post-Cold War analysis.

2.3 Values and Concepts

'Valuations enter into the choice of approach, the selection of problems, the definition of concepts and the gathering of data and are by no means confined to the practical or political inferences drawn from theoretical findings [...]. In fact, most writings, particularly in economics, remain in large part simply ideological' (Myrdal 1970: 32). Concerning the choice of approach one major issue is whether the analyst confines their attention to the strictly economic or includes 'non-economic' factors.[3] Myrdal's analysis—to be discussed below—suggests that it is essential to look beyond the strictly economic. He argues that Western economists generally fail to do this, and assume that what can be taken for granted in the West applies equally in developing countries. Moreover, economists tend to use the concepts they have learned in their own (developed) countries, which, for reasons that run through *Asian Drama* to be discussed below, are frequently inappropriate for analysing developing countries. In selecting problems, for example, the major preoccupation of Western economists appears to be the generation of economic growth and the need to raise the investment ratio to do so, neglecting 'non-economic' factors. Myrdal cited, for example, Nurkse, Rosenstein-Rodan, and Hirschman.[4] Similarly, data gathering tends to follow Western concepts and approaches, not taking into account the differences in context, which require different data as well as concepts.

2.3.1 Choice of Values

In the light of his view that the values of the observer are all-important, Myrdal explicitly lays out the values he adopts in *Asian Drama*.[5] As he states, there is a 'need to make explicit the value premises applied in a social study, for both logical clarity of the conceptual apparatus utilized in the research and the avoidance of hidden valuations that lead to biases' (Myrdal 1970: 49). These values should not be selected arbitrarily but should 'reflect actual valuations held by people who are concerned with the problems being studied' and who are 'influential in moulding public policy' (Myrdal 1970: 49). In this he omits the views of the majority of the

---

[3] '[T]he distinction between "economic" and "non-economic" [...] is a useless and meaningless criterion from a logical point of view and should be substituted by the distinction between "relevant" and "non-relevant" factors'(Myrdal 1957: 21–2).

[4] Hirschman did in fact include non-economic factors. For example, Hirschman's work for the World Bank and the Colombian government in the 1950s (Alacevich 2009; Adelman 2013).

[5] These ideas broadly follow his analysis in *An American Dilemma* and *Values in Social Theory* (Myrdal et al. 1944; Myrdal 1958).

population—a point I discuss below. The analysis should be carried out '*not from the viewpoint of* [...] *the foreign observer, but from the viewpoint of those valuations that have relevance and significance in the countries*' (Myrdal 1970: 50, my emphasis).

He notes some difficulties in ascertaining such values. He then proceeds to lay out the values to be adopted in *Asian Drama*, which are summarized as 'modernization ideals', held mainly by 'the politically alert, articulate and active part of the population' (Myrdal 1970: 53).

The modernization ideals include rationality ('Superstitious beliefs and illogical reasoning should be abandoned' (Myrdal 1970: 57)); 'development', which he defines, somewhat tautologically, as 'improvement in the host of undesirable conditions in the social system that have perpetuated a state of underdevelopment' (Myrdal 1970: 58); planning; a rise in productivity and levels of living; social and economic equalization, 'to promote equality in status, opportunities, wealth, incomes and levels of living [...] commonly accepted in public discussion of the goals for planning'(Myrdal 1970: 59); improved institutions and attitudes (including thirteen ideals for changed attitudes, which read very much like the classic Protestant ideals of behaviour);[6] national consolidation and independence; and democracy.

2.4 The Social System and its Five Major Categories

While the previous sections concerned Myrdal's assessment of the way social scientists work, this element relates to the process of development, identifying the major causes of 'underdevelopment'[7] in South Asian economies. He points to five broad categories, together constituting a social system that represents a powerful constraint on development:[8]

1. output and incomes
2. conditions of production
3. levels of living
4. attitudes towards life and work
5. institutions.

The five categories interact with each other, and can result in a vicious cycle of underdevelopment. For example, conditions of production (primitive technology;

---

[6] Efficiency, diligence, orderliness, punctuality, honesty, rationality, preparedness for change, alertness to new opportunities, energetic enterprise, integrity and self-reliance, co-operativeness, and willingness to take the long view.

[7] Myrdal uses 'underdevelopment' to refer to the situation of poor countries.

[8] He adds a sixth category, 'policies'; these act on the other five elements, and may enforce or counteract them.

limited industrialization) lead to low output and incomes and deficient levels of living, which in turn limit productivity, as workers have little education and poor health and are malnourished; this is compounded by prevalent attitudes (towards work, health practices, and so on[9]) and a variety of institutions which are ill-adapted to development (land tenure systems; the caste system; weak government institutions, etc.), all rooted in a highly stratified social system. Viewing the system as an integrated whole means that progress towards development is particularly challenging because operating on just one of the categories will be insufficient, since the system will be held back by limitations in other parts. For example, 'modernization' requires not only investment in new technologies, but also educated and well-nourished workers with 'modern' attitudes to work. According to Myrdal, advancing on one front only—for example, investment— will not produce results in the absence of improvements in the other elements, including education, health, attitudes, and institutions.

The interconnectedness of the five elements led him to quite pessimistic conclusions about the possibility of accelerating progress. Oddly, here he took the opposite view from that in *An American Dilemma*, which was relatively optimistic about progress for the Afro-American population.[10] He also identified the mutually reinforcing factors holding back the progress of Afro-Americans. But in their case he argued that progress on one factor would be likely to stimulate progress on others: 'any change in any one of these factors, independent of the way it is brought about, will, by the aggregate weight of the cumulative effects running back and forth between them all, start the whole system moving in one direction or the other as the case may be' (Myrdal et al. 1944: 1066–7, cited in Barber (2008: 73–4)).

There are, perhaps, two reasons why Myrdal was pessimistic about cumulative causation in South Asia but optimistic for Afro-Americans in the USA: first, in the American case, he believed that the progressive, liberal, and egalitarian values of the American people would support progressive change. In South Asia, he claimed that the mass of the population did not share the 'modernization' values of the elite. Second, he suggested that a 'soft state' was prevalent in South Asia (and, implicitly, not in the USA), which would be unable or unwilling to implement the institutional reforms needed, including tackling corruption.[11]

---

[9] '[L]ow levels of work discipline, punctuality and orderliness; superstitious beliefs and irrational outlook; lack of alertness, adaptability, ambition and general readiness for change and experiment; contempt for manual work; submissiveness to authority and exploitation; low aptitude for co-operation; low standards of personal hygiene and so on' (Myrdal 1970: 226).

[10] He referred to Afro-Americans as 'negroes' but here I use the currently more acceptable term.

[11] 'These countries are all "soft states", both in that policies decided upon are often not enforced, if they are enacted at all, and in that the authorities, even when framing policies, are reluctant to place obligations on people' (Myrdal 1968: 66).

2.5 A Tentative Approach to Multidisciplinarity

In the light of the multi-factored social system constraining development, Myrdal argued for a fundamental change in approach, putting the analysis of institutions, interpreted broadly to include norms and values as well as structures, at the centre—'our approach is broadly "institutional"' (Myrdal 1970: 27). As a consequence of this and his multidimensional account of development, 'in the South Asian countries the "economic" cannot be understood in isolation from other social factors' (Myrdal 1970: 28). This conclusion led him to appreciate the contribution of non-economists. Yet, despite this, he regarded economists as more suited than others to the dynamic and political analysis required, and he was tentative in his attitude towards non-economists: 'If we are correct, there is room for more interdisciplinary research and we should welcome efforts by sociologists and others to improve our system of theories and concepts' (Myrdal 1970: 29). But he saw problems in multidisciplinary work: 'Despite the strivings for "cross-fertilization" and interdisciplinary research, the barriers hampering transmission of ideas among our disciplines remain considerable' (Myrdal 1970: 29). Thus Myrdal did not abandon the imperialism of economics completely, and his own team working on *Asian Drama* consisted mostly of economists.

2.6 The Inappropriateness of Western Economic Concepts

This is his most fundamental conclusion, which follows from the previous points. Indeed, Myrdal states right at the beginning of *Asian Drama*: 'That the use of Western theories, models and concepts in the study of economic problems in the South Asian countries is a cause of bias seriously distorting that study will be the main theme of this book' (Myrdal 1968: 15). The reasons for this view are that Western concepts and models reflect the values of Western economists, implicitly assuming either that Western attitudes and institutions exist, or that attitudes and institutions will adapt automatically. Since Myrdal's fundamental view of development is that attitudes and institutions matter, and that those prevalent in South Asia are very different from those in the West and do not adapt automatically, he concluded that it is wrong to ignore institutions, and that Western economic concepts that do so are generally inappropriate.[12]

A prominent example concerned the concepts of unemployment, under-employment, and disguised employment, which, he argued, assumed a Western labour market, in which almost everyone of working age was either formally employed or formally unemployed and the cause of unemployment and disguised

---

[12] These ideas were evident earlier in his 1955 Cairo lectures, reproduced in Myrdal (1957).

unemployment was demand deficiency (Robinson 1936). Given that people had to survive and unemployment insurance was not available in South Asia, relatively few people were openly unemployed, and the majority of the workforce was working in low-productivity activities. A rise in effective demand would not eliminate low-productivity activities because of a deficiency of capital in modern high-productivity occupations, nor could a Western-style standard working day be assumed, while differences in attitudes had pervasive effects. Hence the concepts had to be radically reinterpreted if used in connection with South Asia. A second example was the distinction between investment and consumption in Western concepts, in particular the classification of expenditure on education, health, and daily essentials such as food, as consumption. Myrdal argued that resources devoted to health, education, and food raised future incomes and should be classified as investment. Arguably, this criticism of the consumption/investment distinction also applied in the West, especially with respect to education. Be that as it may, the use of such clearly inappropriate concepts in developing countries arose from the 'beam in our eyes', or the effects of positioning, education, and culture, as well as the ideological/political element in economics, which led Western economists to adopt the concepts.

3. Has Analysis Changed in a Myrdalian Direction?

In many respects, the analysis of development has changed in a Myrdalian direction, but mostly not among 'mainstream' economists. Here I discuss each of the elements reviewed in the previous section.

3.1 Political Motivation and Ideology

Myrdal's analysis of the Cold War motivation for much development analysis was shared by later political scientists, particularly in relation to aid (for example, Latham 2011). However, as the Cold War waned, the ideological motivation changed from being primarily political to being primarily economic, although economic motives had been present in the Cold War period (largely ignored by Myrdal), and political elements remain in the post-Cold War era. In relation to political motives, for example, during the Cold War, development and foreign aid were regarded as crucial for US national security (McNamara 1968), while in the twenty-first century they are increasingly viewed as a way of countering extremism and migration.[13]

---

[13] See Curtis (2007). In December 2017, London's International Development Centre held a debate entitled: 'Can aid help counter violent extremism and terrorism'.

The development strategy recommended after the Second World War met both the political and economic objectives of the West. The strategy of investment using Western technologies in import-substituting industrialization while maintaining a focus on primary production for export supported the economic interests of the West, by extending their markets and profitable opportunities for their companies, and sustaining supplies of primary products. At the same time, the strategy contributed to the Cold War political objective of promoting development. The strategy recommended broadly reflected the type of Keynesian economics then dominant in the West.

The dramatic turnaround in economics and economic policy in the West in the early 1980s, with the revival of monetarist and neoclassical approaches, which were then incorporated into Western government policies—notably by Thatcher and Reagan—was associated with a similar turnaround in the advice of Western economists and the recommendations of the World Bank concerning developing country policies. (International Monetary Fund (IMF) advice and conditionality had always been monetarist and favoured markets.) This turnaround also served the interests of Western economies, particularly Western banks and companies. Loans from the international financial institutions (IFIs) financed the repayment of some of the debts owed to Western banks, which allowed the banks to survive and indeed prosper.[14] And, the expansion of private markets in developing countries due to trade and capital account liberalization and privatization opened up additional space for Western companies in production and sales.

The economic advice given thus broadly reflected the economic interests of advanced countries—its ideological nature can be seen not only from this perspective but also because the many theoretical and empirical flaws in the system advocated were ignored.[15] Thus the ideological component of Western economic analysis continued, but the underlying motivation tilted towards economic interests rather than largely political considerations. This has persisted, despite increasing focus on social objectives (i.e., on human development, the MDGs, and then the SDGs), as the pro-market approach has continued to form the dominant content of policy advice from Western economists. Similarly, the recent switch to microeconomic randomized experiments, which have come to dominate development economics, leaves the nature of the economy, market approaches, and monetarism untouched.

Regarding economic analysis as ideological has, of course, long traditions in critical analysis, including Marxism, in which theorizing is regarded as

---

[14] We see a similar phenomenon in the case of Greek debt and loans from the EU and IMF in the late 2000s and after (Varoufakis 2017).

[15] For example, the assumption of perfect information (Greenwald and Stiglitz 1986) and the justification for industrial policy and trade interventions (Krugman 1986). Moreover, empirically, it was soon apparent that the policies reduced economic growth and worsened poverty (Cornia et al. 1986; Kakwani 1995).

'superstructure' reflecting the underlying interests of capitalists. Myrdal was a firmly non-Marxist but heterodox economist and, perhaps as a consequence, saw economic analysis not as exclusively reflecting economic interests, but rather as the outcome of a range of circumstances, general as well as personal, political as well as economic. Other non-Marxist heterodox development economists, such as Seers and Hirschman, adopted a similar perspective, agreeing with Myrdal that economists' methods were strongly influenced by their origin, education, and ideology (Seers 1962, 1963, 1983; Hirschman 1969).

Postmodern analysis, which developed from the 1960s, had much in common with Myrdal's views, arguing that there is no single 'objective' truth and that it is necessary to uncover or deconstruct the context and motives underlying any analysis, recognizing the critical role of the observer's positionality (see e.g., Freire 1972; Foucault and Rabinow 1984; Derrida 1997). However, going beyond Myrdal, postmodern thinkers explicitly recognize the role of power in influencing analysis, especially in indigenous postcolonial studies and in feminist literature (Freire 1972; Smith 1999). Yet, despite the prevalence of postmodern analysis throughout most social sciences, mainstream economics has remained broadly untouched: as Myrdal said: 'Only about the peculiar behaviour of our own profession do we choose to remain naïve' (Myrdal 1970: 6).

3.2 The Selection of Values

Given the ideological and value-laden element in economics, Myrdal argued that the values assumed in any study should be presented explicitly and should not be those of the foreign observer.

The idea that values should be locally determined is now almost universally accepted by external development researchers and policy advisors. The IFIs recognize the need for local 'ownership', albeit largely instrumentally, as necessary to get policies implemented. Sen's capability approach regards agency and freedoms as essential components of individual flourishing and of desirable development and hence the values selected must be those of the population where development takes place (Sen 1985).

Yet Myrdal's belief that only the views of the 'politically alert, articulate and active' should be considered is *not* accepted. The presumption is that *all* those affected by policies should be involved—that is, in principle, the mass of the population, who are the agents and intended beneficiaries of development. Moreover, Myrdal's method of arriving at his selected values seems quite amateurish compared with the extensive consultations that are thought appropriate today. He claims that the values he adopts were derived from the national plans and political speeches of the politically active, and 'it turns out that this official creed of the South Asian countries is composed mainly of the ideals long cherished in the

Western world as the heritage of the Enlightenment' (Myrdal 1970: 55)—perhaps not surprising since many of the political leaders were educated in the West and their plans and speeches were often drawn up after consultation with foreign experts. This context, and Myrdal's method of arriving at the selected values, led to a set of values very much in line with the values Myrdal himself held, as he accepts in the quotation above.

Since he wrote, consultations have become more comprehensive and systematic. Yet even these efforts still appear to generate values that largely reflect the perspective of the observer. The IFIs, for example, in drawing up the Poverty Reduction Strategy Papers (PRSPs), had meetings with groups from many classes, regions, and occupations. Yet they ended up with a set of policies that were entirely in line with their own (IFI) perspectives (Bretton Woods Project 2001; Booth 2003; Stewart and Wang 2006). Similarly, Nussbaum produced a 'list' of values and object-ives which, she argues, emerge from an 'overlapping consensus' (Nussbaum 2000). Her list, too, appears to reflect those of a progressive, liberal Westerner.

Robert Chambers has been a powerful critic of the casual consultations typical of most foreign experts and their failure to consult poor people properly. He initiated participatory research involving the poor, and his methodology has been widely taken up (Chambers 1997). Chambers guided the World Bank's Voices of the Poor project, which involved extensive efforts to consult the poor on priorities and seems to have come much closer to getting at actual values held by local non-elites than most attempts (Naraya et al. 2000). Although it, too, can be criticized for assuming an absence of conflict within the groups consulted about priorities, and, once more, as tending to reflect the perspectives of those conducting and interpreting the enquiries (Ruggeri Laderchi 2007), the Chambers approach comes nearest to the ideal of deriving values from the people themselves. But Chambers' approach is poorly suited to ascertaining local priorities on macroeco-nomic policy, and never properly used to do so.

In principle, the SDGs were drawn up after extensive worldwide consultations, many following the Chambers approach. Yet the outcome of these consultations was again totally in line with those of 'enlightened' Westerners, and did not incorporate the opposing views of some in the South, for example with regard to the role of women or child labour. In general, heterogeneity of views makes it easy for those orchestrating the consultations to impose their own values. In any case, Myrdal would not have wanted to adopt Chambers' participatory approach, since an important component of his modernization values is radical *changes* in pre-vailing attitudes. True consultation of the mass of people would thus not have led to modernization values, as interpreted by Myrdal, if his assumption about the prevalence of 'non-modern' attitudes is correct.

In sum, some important subsequent theorizing concurs on the importance of ideology in economics; and the view that the values adopted should be local ones is also accepted. But Myrdal's method of identifying local values—both as to whom to consult and how to consult—no longer appear appropriate. Yet, even with the apparent intent of full consultation and more sophisticated methods of doing so, the perspectives of those orchestrating the consultations (often still the foreign observers) remain highly influential, as they retain power in terms of framing and interpretation, especially where views conflict. And for much policy advice—especially in relation to macro-economic policy—very little genuine consultation takes place.

3.3 The Nature of Development

Myrdal recognized that the concept of 'development' was difficult to define, or 'clearly suffers from indeterminacy' (Myrdal 1968: 1840). He interpreted development as all-encompassing. It involved 'modernization'; a rise in standards of living; social and economic equalization; improved institutions and attitudes; national consolidation and independence; and democracy—most elements being wanted in themselves and likely to promote other elements. It thus goes well beyond the growth-promotion strategy commonly adopted at the time and is in the spirit of the widening of development objectives that has occurred since— from a focus on economic growth to basic needs, human development and capability expansion, poverty reduction, the MDGs, and the SDGs.[16] Myrdal includes some elements that have not been incorporated in the human-oriented objectives that followed: for example, national consolidation and independence, which formed a natural objective in the years immediately following former colonial countries' political independence but has been less emphasized since then although it has much in common with the contemporary objective of promoting 'social cohesion' (de Haan and Webbink 2011; Langer et al. 2017). Institutional improvements are currently accepted as critically important, but instrumentally rather than as a central, intrinsic objective.

The idea that modernization is the overall normative development project truly reflects the 'beam' in Myrdal's eyes. For anthropologists and postmodern analysts this represents an unacceptable imposition of values by the foreigner—just what Myrdal himself criticized, although most contemporary economists implicitly take a 'modernist' perspective. A casual look around the world indicates that many would reject modernization as an ideal, particularly among religious, environmental, and 'indigenist' groups; but that same casual glance would pick up many others who would accept Myrdal's modernization ideals, with growth and Western-type consumerism as their preferred objectives. One thing is sure: in the twenty-first century, it is not possible to be so confident about declarations of objectives, when talking for others.

---

[16] See Seers (1969), Streeten et al. (1981), UNDP (1990), Sen (1999), Stewart et al. (2018).

3.4 The Five Elements of the Social System

Myrdal's five elements were a far cry from the emphasis on physical investment of many economists at the time. He regarded levels of living (including health and education) as essential *inputs* into economic progress and not only desirable *outcomes*. Some contemporary economists agreed that these were important inputs into growth. For example, both Leibenstein and Nurkse recognized that extreme poverty would reduce productivity and could trap countries into a low-level equilibrium (Nurkse 1953; Leibenstein 1957), while Schultz (1963) pointed to the critical importance of investment in education.

Myrdal gave institutions and attitudes paramount importance; indeed an early subsection of the book is entitled 'A plea for an institutional emphasis' (Myrdal 1968: 26). The institutions, which he argued inhibited development, included land tenure systems, caste, some beliefs (such as the Hindu attitudes to cows), a 'soft' state, and corruption. In his emphasis on institutions, he can be seen as a precursor of North, who wrote some twenty years later (North 1986, 1990). Since then, most explanations of patterns of development give institutions (encompassing attitudes) a central role, a view shared by both neoclassical economists and heterodox ones (North 1986; Rutherford 1994), although the neoclassical approach involves a narrower definition of institutions than that of Myrdal. Heterodox analysis of institutions comes much closer to a Myrdalian approach—for example, in Thorp and Paredes' (2010) investigation of the economic history of Peru, or Lall's (1987) examination of factors affecting technological capabilities, and Colclough and Manor's (1991) discussions of states and markets.

Since the publication of *Asian Drama* there has been a vast amount of empirical work on the determinants and consequences of institutions and attitudes—much analysis of agriculture in India has focused on land tenure and alternative contractual arrangements (Mazumdar 1975; Bardhan and Rudra 1980), for example—and there has been extensive research on the role of caste, ethnicity, corruption, 'governance', and 'social capital', among other institutions (Premdas 1993; Easterly and Levine 1997; Khan and Jomo 2000; Harriss-White 2003; Borooah and Iyer 2005; Bangura 2006; Thorat and Newman 2010; Gören 2014).

Myrdal's emphasis on the way the nature of the state influences whether developmental policies are adopted and implemented would now be widely accepted. For several decades, the state was regarded by mainstream economists as the problem rather than the solution to development issues, 'rational' analysis suggesting that states would inevitably be predatory and their role should be minimized (Brennan and Buchanan 1980; Lal 1983); and this remains the view of some economists. But the evidence that some states have clearly effectively promoted development has led to a return to the Myrdalian issue of how and why some states are more developmental than others. Evans' (1995) insightful analysis of states with 'embedded autonomy', which he contrasted with predatory states, is a leading example. However, most analyses do not take a binary view of the state ('soft' or 'hard'), but see a range of state competencies.

Myrdal's belief that 'soft' states prevailed in South Asia, together with his analysis of the interconnected nature of the elements leading to development, led him to take a pessimistic view of development prospects in the region. Yet, in the fifty years that have elapsed since he wrote, there has been substantial economic and social progress in the region (Figures 3.1 and 3.2) despite limited institutional change in terms of the nature of the state, corruption, caste, etc. It has turned out that even 'soft' states can promote, or be consistent with, development. South

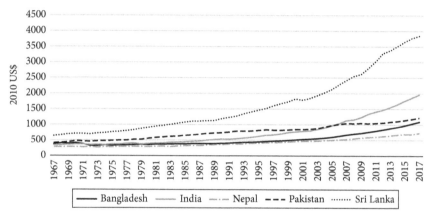

Figure 3.1 GDP per capita, 1967–2017 (constant 2010 US$).

Source: World Bank, World Development Indicators.

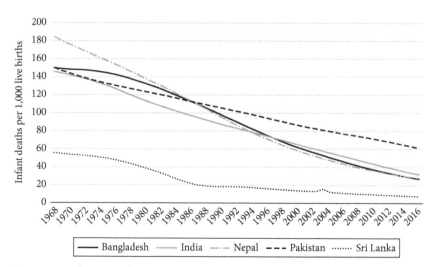

Figure 3.2 Infant mortality rate, 1967–2017.

Source: World Bank, World Development Indicators.

Asian populations appear to be highly adaptable and quick to learn and exploit new opportunities; attitudes, if not institutions, have adapted, contrary to Myrdal's expectation. Institutions of various kinds (including deficiencies in state functioning) have shaped and probably slowed progress, but have not prevented it. While, clearly, Myrdal was right to suggest that more was needed than physical investment alone, progress in education, rising investment, and policy changes have led to accelerating growth and modernization, suggesting that prevailing attitudes and institutions were not insuperable obstacles.

In this respect, developments followed Hirschman's observation:

> our researchers have uncovered a long list of 'prerequisites' for economic development, which range all the way from adequate transportation facilities to basic psychological attitudes, aptitudes and propensities. But many developing countries have a disconcerting habit of disregarding the absence of these and to put them into place a little late.   (Hirschman 1969: 5)

Nonetheless, as the more rapid growth in East Asia suggests,[17] progress could have been faster had more of the institutional deficiencies been overcome,[18] and the non-economic constraints may have slowed progress on some goals, including advancing equality, eliminating malnutrition and ill-health, and reducing insecurities of many kinds.

When Myrdal wrote *Asian Drama*, his comprehensive approach to the causes and constraints on development—embracing education and health, and institutions and attitudes—represented an important advance over the way many development economists approached development issues. Today, such an approach is broadly accepted, even though it is not always apparent in the teaching or practice of economists.

3.5 Multi- and Interdisciplinarity

As noted earlier, Myrdal recognized that a much more comprehensive view of the determinants of development, with non-economic factors as central components, required a broadening of disciplinary approach beyond economics. But he was quite tentative about it, and left the lead role to economics. Since then, there has been wide acceptance of the desirability of multi- and interdisciplinary approaches. Multidisciplinary development journals abound and there are many multidisciplinary university departments of Development Studies and inter- as

---

[17] East Asia had many advantages in 'initial conditions' compared with South Asia, including more homogeneous populations and higher levels of education.

[18] Caste discrimination has seriously impeded efficiency (Thorat and Newman 2010), while the revival of cow-worship in India, with new laws to protect cows and vigilante monitoring, is affecting some industries adversely ('Modi's holy cows disrupt Indian industry', *Financial Times*, 23 November 2017).

well as multidisciplinary courses. Competitions for grants for research on issues of development in the West frequently require a multidisciplinary approach.

The IFIs, however, were slow to accept the need to broaden the disciplinary background of their staff. The World Bank employed its first non-economist professional in 1974. The number of non-economists had risen to almost sixty by 1995, still just a fraction of the economists employed. Michael Cernea, the first sociologist at the World Bank, argued that while he was working there, the view of sociologists 'changed from [the Bank] seeing them as the Bank's own luxury species [...] to treating them as rather respected and desirable' (Cernea 1993). Yet economists continue to be dominant. In 2010, the Bank's 150 non-economists represented about 3 per cent of its professional staff (Cernea 1995; World Bank 2004; Mosse 2006).[19] In an in-depth study of the role of non-economists at the World Bank, Mosse concluded that they are 'a marginal professional group' who 'make the organization work better without changing what it does' (Mosse 2006: 1). The IMF remains substantially monodisciplinary. It began to employ a few non-economists only in 2004, to assist in analysing the social aspects of its programmes (Vetterlein 2010). As Vetterlein (n.d.) states: 'the Fund is very homogenous and made up of macroeconomists and financial experts'. Bilateral development agencies have a stronger non-economist component, and multidisciplinarity has become a genuine feature of teaching and research in Development Studies departments, but rarely in Economics departments. In short, practice tends to reflect Myrdal's somewhat tentative views about the role of non-economists, even as the understanding of the constraints and determinants of development broaden in a Myrdalian direction.

3.6 The Inapplicability of Western Economic Concepts

This was, perhaps, Myrdal's most fundamental methodological conclusion. It arose because of the importance he gave to non-economic factors—especially institutions and attitudes—which, he asserted, were substantially different in South Asia from those in the West, while Western economic concepts were (implicitly) built on the assumed existence of Western institutions and attitudes.

In two classic papers—which predated *Asian Drama*—Seers came to very similar conclusions on most elements of Myrdal's methodological approach, including the inappropriateness of many Western economic concepts, on the basis of similar arguments. 'An economist is by no means immune to chauvinistic or ideological influences, and these are strong today', he stated in 'Why Visiting Economists Fail' (Seers 1962: 326). He argued that visiting economists typically used the models they had been taught, which were suitable for a developed

---

[19] Assuming professional staff are about half the 10,000 employees.

country and underestimated qualitative and non-economic factors. Like Myrdal, he stated that 'even apparently technical questions such as choosing variables considered significant, deciding what ranges for these variables are plausible, and assessing the scope for policy, raise issues which are fundamentally social and political' (Seers 1962: 334).

In 'The Limitations of the Special Case' (Seers 1963), Seers expounded the view that concepts developed for an advanced economy were likely to be inappropriate to less developed countries. He cited earlier analysts who took the same view, including John Neville Keynes (father of J.M. Keynes), and quoted Joan Robinson:

> English economists, from Ricardo to Keynes, [...] have been accustomed to assume as a tacitly accepted background the institutions and problems of the England each of his own day; when their works are studied in other climes and other periods [...] a great deal of confusion and argument at cross-purposes arises.
>
> (Robinson 1960: xvii)

According to Seers, '[a]nalysis focuses on the wrong factor, and the models do not fit at all closely the way in which non-industrial economies operate' (Seers 1963: 83). The Indian economist and sociologist Mukerjee made just the same point: '[T]he postulates of western economics were entirely different from a realistic study of the Indian pattern' (Mukerjee 1955: 9).

Have economists' analyses of developing countries responded to these criticisms? Some have but more have not. With regard to Myrdal's specific examples, there has been a great deal of work on the question of how best to define underemployment in a developing country context, and on the need to analyse work in the 'informal' sector (Turnham 1971; Sen 1975; Stewart 1975; Tokman 1978). Analysis has also focused on the non-marketed production of the household, especially the contribution of women (Evans 1991; Mertz et al. 2005), although national accounts have not been amended accordingly. Myrdal was undoubtedly right that the simple import of Western concepts was inappropriate here. In relation to the investment/consumption distinction, it is widely accepted that much of what is conventionally classified as consumption is in effect investment, raising productivity over time, notably by those who point to the contribution of 'human capital' to economic growth (Dasgupta 1993; Schultz 1993; Psacharopolous 1994). Yet, again, national accounts have not been revised to take this into account.

There has been progress regarding these particular concepts and quite a few others—for example, by structuralists pointing to the problems for theories of inflation raised by structural constraints, as well as the recognition that institutions are an important determinant of development. Nonetheless, macro-economic concepts are generally transferred wholesale by mainstream economists, without regard for their appropriateness (Stiglitz 2006; Nayyar 2007), as is the neoclassical apparatus of market efficiency in resource allocation. The situation in both these areas has worsened since Myrdal was writing. On the macro-front,

Keynesianism—though strictly not applicable to developing countries with limited spare capacity in the formal sector and a high propensity to consume, as pointed out by Rao (1952)—has been discredited in the West, along with most state intervention in the economy. A strict monetarist approach tends to be adopted by the IMF, with a requirement of balanced budgets, often involving cuts in infrastructure and the social sectors, which can severely constrain growth. Moreover, market optimization is assumed, despite its widely acknowledged limitations, which are greater in developing countries where there is a lack of complementary facilities and highly imperfect knowledge. Import liberalization is advocated, despite the learning and scale economies which incipient industrializers experience (Chang 1993). The consequence has been to inhibit industrialization, especially in much of Africa.

In general, most heterodox economists would agree with much of what Myrdal stated about the need to adapt concepts to context. But orthodox economists would not. Indeed, in line with this, the whole idea that development economics should be different from economics in general, requiring different concepts and models, was explicitly challenged by Robbins as early as 1945 (Robbins 1945), by Bauer (Bauer 1957), and later by Lal (1983). As Hirschman noted in 1979, neoclassicals—on the ascendant in the West—claimed their approach was relevant to all types of economy (Hirschman 1979). Implicitly, this view is widely accepted. In practice, most economists working on developing economies continue to adopt the economic concepts and theories accepted in mainstream Economics departments in Western universities.

4. The Relevance and Irrelevance of Myrdal Today

In this section, I discuss three issues: first, areas where Myrdal has influenced the profession, or where it has moved in his direction; second, areas where Myrdal was correct, in my opinion, but his views have rarely been incorporated into analysis, even by heterodox economists; and third, areas where I would depart from Myrdal's methodological analysis, or where developments over the past half-century require new approaches.

4.1 The Acceptance of Myrdal's Ideas

Acceptance is mainly among heterodox economists, but on some issues extends to more orthodox ones:

- Development is recognized as a normative project, and there is now considerable debate about the normative content, although few would accept Myrdal's modernization ideals. Rather, there has been movement towards human-centred and plural objectives, with particular attention to (multidimensional) poverty and the reduction of inequality.

- There is general acceptance of the idea that local people should choose their own priorities, but there remain problems about who and how to consult, and how to deal with diverse views, among other issues.
- There is recognition that the determinants of the state of (under)development are holistic, involving many 'non-economic' factors; most of Myrdal's elements would be agreed on, including the investment aspects of education, health and nutrition, and the critical role of institutions, as well as circular causation among elements.
- There is agreement, especially among heterodox economists, that *context matters*, and considerable efforts are made to identify contextual factors through empirical work. But others take a 'one-size-fits-all' approach.

4.2 The Ideas That Have Not Been Taken Up

Preeminent here is 'the beam in our eyes'. With the major exception of Seers,[20] development economists, whether heterodox or orthodox, rarely analyse or declare how their own positioning, their home society, education, and so on is likely to have affected their analysis. Rather, most economists believe (or at least write as if) there is 'truth' out there, unrelated to their own positioning. Values are typically implicit, not laid down explicitly. On Western concepts, new concepts have emerged in development analysis that are more appropriate to local conditions—such as the informal sector and governance—but mostly this has occurred without discarding the old concepts.

4.3 Moving On...

Several important critiques of Myrdal have emerged from the discussion, pointing to the need to move on. First, despite espousing the need for multidisciplinarity, Myrdal retained a belief in the primacy of economists and suggested only a minor role for other social scientists. Second, while advocating the incorporation of local values, Myrdal deferred to the values of elites, and explicitly rejected those of the masses, even though he firmly favoured democratic institutions. Moreover, while he emphasized the importance of deriving local values (albeit from the elite), in practice the values he put forward were basically those of a progressive Scandinavian (i.e., his own). Third, despite rejecting Western economic concepts as inappropriate, in practice, *Asian Drama* gives little recognition to the contribution of local thinkers. These are all areas where analysis and practice has moved on.

---

[20] In his preface, Seers (1983), for example, gives a potted biography of his life.

Beyond these areas, two other issues relevant to contemporary analysis go beyond Myrdal's approach: first, the inappropriateness of many economics concepts to *developed* as well as developing countries; and second, the increasing convergence between North and South in their economies and the social and economic problems they face. This section briefly discusses these issues.

4.3.1 The Recognition and Practice of Multidisciplinarity

In many cases both recognition and practice go well beyond Myrdal's somewhat tentative bow towards multidisciplinarity. Political scientists, sociologists, anthropologists, and (increasingly) 'hard' scientists contribute to the analysis of development issues, while many individual scholars themselves adopt a multidisciplinary perspective, even if the economist remains 'king', especially in the arena of macro-policies and the work of the IFIs.

4.3.2 The Identification of Local Values

As noted, this has become a much more systematic and sophisticated exercise, no longer confined to capturing the views of the elite, but with attempts to involve the whole population. Yet deficiencies in the identification of local values remain, especially with respect to macroeconomics. In interpreting local values, there is a clear tendency to neglect views that are inconsistent with those prevalent in the West, as indicated by the SDGs, which essentially reflect progressive liberal values—for example, any local questioning of democracy or opposition to gender or other types of equality is ignored. More fundamentally, the difficulty (in part, impossibility) of incorporating the views and interests of future generations raises questions about whether local contemporary values should be supreme.[21]

4.3.3 Recognition of the Contribution of Local Social Scientists

A major defect of *Asian Drama* is the very limited attention paid to South Asian economists, let alone other social scientists. In fact, Indian economists in the 1930s and before had analysed many of the issues that Myrdal discusses, and had come to similar conclusions. Rao, for example, recognized the holistic nature of development constraints, the need to analyse non-economic factors, and the inappropriateness of some Western economic concepts.

Krishnamurty (2017) describes important contributions made by Indian economists in the first half of the twentieth century, as shown in the following quotations from his analysis:

- Radhakamal Mukerjee's (1934) 'highly original paper on the "Broken Balance of Population, Land and Water", dealing with the ecological problems of the

---

[21] See Stewart (2018) for some suggestions about how the interests of future generations might be included in current deliberations.

Gangetic valley [...] long before environment economics became part of professional and popular discourse' (Krishnamurty 2017).[22]

- Gyanchand's 1935 paper 'The Essentials of Economic Planning for India' 'questioned the then current euphoria over economic planning' and the possibility of achieving redistribution with growth in a colonial setting. 'This paper was a precursor to the debates after independence on [...] whether growth by itself would lead to better redistribution.'

- '[P]erhaps the most original paper published in the *IJE* in 1938...was V.K.R.V. Rao's paper "The Problem of Unemployment in India"' in which he adapted Robinson's concept of disguised unemployment to conditions in India, arguing that 'there are on the land a number of people who do not really contribute to the production of agricultural output and that if they give up agriculture output would be much the same. They are the disguised unemployed of India' (Rao 1938: 631).

Other significant Indian contributions included that of B.R. Ambedkar on industrialization as the solution to surplus labour and the Indian agrarian problem, published in 1918, and those of A.K. Dasgupta, including a Lewis-type model, developed earlier in lectures and published in 1954 (Krishnamurty 2008). None of these papers appears in the index of *Asian Drama*. There are many references to Indian economists, but almost entirely to empirical studies, ignoring their methodological contributions.

4.3.4 The Inappropriateness of 'Western' Economic Concepts to the West Itself

In *Asian Drama*, Myrdal rarely challenges the appropriateness of the economic concepts for the West itself, but argues that the concepts become inappropriate when applied to South Asia (although earlier he had questioned the relevance of static equilibrium in analysing Western economies). This may be due to the dominance of Keynesianism when he was writing *Asian Drama*, since Keynesianism did appear to be relevant to the analysis of Western economies, in contrast to the static equilibrium analysis that preceded it (Myrdal 1958).

The inappropriateness of many economic concepts and theories to Western economies has become particularly evident in the post-Keynesian era. For example, Solow's neoclassical growth model 'explains' only a small portion of Western economic growth because it is unrealistic about the nature of technical change, learning economies, and returns to scale (Solow 1956; Balogh and Streeten 1963; Scott 1989). Similarly, neoclassical theories of trade have serious deficiencies,

---

[22] In other work, Mukerjee (1926, 1934, 1939, 1940) emphasizes the need for multidisciplinary work, and the role of institutions in the economy. And already in 1917, he had lectured on the 'incommensurability of the western economic models with the Indian reality' (Thakur 2012: 95).

again largely owing to a failure to incorporate learning and scale economies (Helpman and Krugman 1986; Krugman 1986). Equally, the view that free markets would lead to Pareto optimal equilibria is based on incorrect assumptions about technology and information, whatever the economy (Greenwald and Stiglitz 1986). In addition, the view that the distributional consequences of markets could be corrected by governments ignores universal political constraints. Moreover, the need to broaden objectives beyond growth maximization applies as much in the North as in the South. The need to do so becomes overwhelming once environmental considerations are taken into account. In short, objectives, concepts, models, and policies need to be substantially amended in the North as well as the South, a perspective which I am sure Myrdal would accept, were he around.

4.3.5 A Convergence

Over the last fifty years, there has been considerable convergence between the economies of the North and South, especially among the 'emerging' economies of the South. Many developing economies have grown much faster than developed economies, resulting in a substantial catch-up with the high-income countries and a rising share of the South in the global economy. The structure of many economies has been transformed, moving from heavy reliance on primary production to an increasing share of industry and modern services, becoming much more like that of the high-income economies (Nayyar 2014). Investments and technologies flow from the South to the North as well as from North to South; problems of debt and adjustment are universal; countries everywhere face employment problems and Northern economies, too, have substantial informal sectors; issues of poverty and social protection are universal, as are inequalities and discrimination; governance is a shared problem; political economy is universally relevant, and so on. In every case, context matters. Economic concepts are often inappropriate to a particular context, but this is the case for the North as well as the South. Institutions and attitudes matter everywhere.

Concepts need to be reformulated to fit the context. Some issues and concepts may be applicable in the North and not the South, and conversely. Some may be applicable universally. And some may be inapplicable everywhere. It is no longer correct to differentiate sharply between North and South, as Myrdal did. Rather, we need to revise economic concepts in the light of the best parts of his approach in both North and South.

5. Conclusion

The methodological contributions in *Asian Drama* are of fundamental importance, pushing the economic analysis of development in a holistic and multidisciplinary direction; recognizing how values and politics permeate analysis as well as policy, and how the position of the observer affects the analysis. These ideas all challenged the unthinking transfer of advanced country economic concepts and theories to the analysis of underdevelopment. Myrdal's methodological approach was not entirely original. Others, including Seers, Hirschman, and Rao, had made similar points. Yet put together in *Asian Drama* (and earlier works), they made a major contribution to a radical rethinking of development analysis.

Paradoxically, Myrdal's conclusion from this vision was of deep pessimism about the possibilities of development which subsequent events have shown to be wrong, certainly in the Asian case. Yet the central points he made—on values, on the importance of institutions, on the non-economic determinants of development, and on the need for multidisciplinarity—reflected much of the reality of the situation on the ground, not only in Asia but also beyond, as I found in exploring development issues in the late 1960s in Kenya. His main points remain valid, not only for the South but also for the North. Although some of his ideas seem commonplace now, since they have been widely incorporated into critical analysis, it continues to be important to turn to them, as many economists remain trapped in conventional perspectives.

The world has moved on since *Asian Drama* in one particularly vital respect. Myrdal was writing before environmental considerations became dominant. These require a radically new look at values, objectives, concepts, and theories, which need to be incorporated into any analysis of the development drama today (Gough 2017; Raworth 2017). While this will necessitate substantial revisions of the positive analysis in *Asian Drama*, the work's open and critical methodological approach is well suited to providing guidance for the changes needed.

Acknowledgements

I am grateful to Michele Alacevich, Judith Heyer, Deepak Nayyar, Finn Tarp, and participants at the Hanoi Workshop in March 2018 for extremely helpful comments on an earlier draft.

References

Adelman, J. (2013). *Worldly Philosopher: The Odyssey of Albert O. Hirschman.* Princeton, NJ: Princeton University Press.

Alacevich, M. (2009). *The Political Economy of the World Bank: The Early Years.* Stanford, CA: Stanford University Press.

Balogh, T., and P.P. Streeten (1963). 'The Coefficient of Ignorance', *Bulletin of The Oxford University Institute of Economics & Statistics*, 25(2): 99–107.

Bangura, Y. (2006). *Ethnic Inequalities and Public Sector Governance.* Basingstoke: Palgrave Macmillan.

Barber, W.J. (2008). *Gunnar Myrdal: An Intellectual Biography*. Basingstoke; New York: Palgrave Macmillan.

Bardhan, P., and A. Rudra (1980). 'Terms and Conditions of Sharecropping Contracts: An Analysis of Village Survey Data in India', *Journal of Development Studies*, 16(3): 287–302.

Bauer, P. (1957). *Economic Analysis and Policy in Underdeveloped Countries*. Cambridge: Cambridge University Press.

Booth, D. (2003). 'Introduction and Overview to Special Issue: Are PRSPs Making a Difference? The African Experience', *Development Policy Review*, 21(2): 131–59.

Borooah, V.K., and S. Iyer (2005). 'Vidya, Veda and Varna: The Influence of Religion and Caste on Education in Rural India', *Journal of Development Studies*, 41(8): 1369–404.

Brennan, C., and J.M. Buchanan (1980). *The Power to Tax: Analytical Foundations of a Fiscal Constitution*. New York: Cambridge University Press.

Bretton Woods Project (2001). 'PRSPs Just PR Say Civil Society Groups', available at: https://www.brettonwoodsproject.org/2001/06/art-15999/.

Cernea, M. (1993). *Sociological Work within a Development Agency: Experiences in The World Bank*. Washington, DC: World Bank.

Cernea, M. (1995). 'Social Organisation and Development Anthropology', *Environmentally Sustainable Development Studies and Monograph Series 6*. Washington, DC: World Bank.

Chambers, R. (1997). *Whose Reality Counts? Putting the First Last*. London: Intermediate Technology Publications.

Chang, H.-J. (1993). *The Political Economy of Industrial Policy*. Basingstoke: Macmillan Press.

Colclough, C., and J. Manor (1991). *States or Markets? Neo-Liberalism and the Development Policy Debate*. Oxford: Clarendon Press.

Cornia, G.A., R. Jolly, and F. Stewart (1986). *Adjustment with a Human Face*. Oxford: Oxford University Press.

Curtis, L.A. (2007). 'US Aid to Pakistan: Countering Terrorism through Education Reform', Heritage Lectures 1029. Washington, DC: Heritage Foundation.

Dasgupta, P. (1993). *An Inquiry into Well-Being and Destitution*. Oxford: Clarendon Press.

De Haan, A., and E. Webbink (2011). 'Social Cohesion and Development: Using Cross-Country Data to Understand Social Cohesion and Development', International Conference on Social Cohesion and Development. Paris: OECD.

Derrida, J. (1997). *Of Grammatology*. Baltimore, MD: Johns Hopkins University Press.

Easterly, W., and R. Levine (1997). 'Africa's Growth Tragedy', *Quarterly Journal of Economics*, 112(4): 1203–50.

Evans, A. (1991). 'Gender Issues in Rural Household Economics', *IDS Bulletin*, 22(1): 51–9.

Evans, P. (1995). *Embedded Autonomy: States and Industrial Transformation.* Princeton, NJ: Princeton University Press.

Foucault, M., and P. Rabinow (1984). *The Foucault Reader.* New York: Pantheon Books.

Freire, P. (1972). *Pedagogy of the Oppressed.* Harmondsworth: Penguin Education.

Gören, E. (2014). 'How Ethnic Diversity Affects Economic Growth', *World Development*, 59(Supplement C): 275–97.

Gough, I. (2017). *Heat, Need and Human Greed: Climate Change, Capitalism and Sustainable Wellbeing.* London: Edward Elgar.

Greenwald, B.C., and J.E. Stiglitz (1986). 'Externalities in Economies with Imperfect Information and Incomplete Markets', *Quarterly Journal of Economics*, 90: 229–64.

Gyanchand (1935). 'The Essentials of Economic Planning for India', *Indian Journal of Economics*, 15(59): 409–22, reprinted in Krishnamurty, J. (2009): 169–84.

Harriss-White, B. (2003). *India Working: Essays on Society and Economy.* Cambridge: Cambridge University Press.

Helpman, E., and P.R. Krugman (1986). *Market Structure and Foreign Trade: Increasing Returns, Imperfect Competition and the International Economy.* Cambridge, MA: MIT Press.

Hirschman, A.O. (1969). *Latin American Issues: Essays and Comments.* New York: Twentieth Century Fund.

Hirschman, A.O. (1979). 'The Rise and Decline in Development Economics. The Theory and Experience of Economic Development'. In M. Gersovitz, C. Diaz-Alejandro, G. Ranis, and M. Rosenzweig (eds) *Essays in Honour of Sir W. Arthur Lewis.* London: Routledge: 49–73.

Kakwani, N. (1995). 'Structural Adjustment and Performance in Living Standards in Developing Countries', *Development and Change*, 26(3): 469–502.

Khan, M.H., and K.S. Jomo (2000). *Rents, Rent-Seeking and Economic Development Theory and Evidence in Asia.* Cambridge: Cambridge University Press.

Krishnamurty, J. (2008). 'Indian Antecedents of Disguised Unemployment and Surplus Labour', *Indian Journal of Labour Economics*, 51(1): 53–62.

Krishnamurty, J. (2009). *Towards Development Economics: Indian Contributions 1900–1945.* Delhi: Oxford University Press.

Krishnamurty, J. (2017). 'Looking Back at a Hundred Years of Research in Indian Economics', *The Wire*, 24 February, available at: https://thewire.in/uncategorised/hundred-years-of-research-indian-economics.

Krugman, P.R. (1986). *Strategic Trade Policy and The New International Economics.* Cambridge, MA: MIT Press.

Lal, D. (1983). *Poverty of Development Economics.* London: Institute of Economic Affairs.

Lall, S. (1987). *Learning to Industrialize: The Acquisition of Technological Capability by India.* Basingstoke: Macmillan.

Langer, A., F. Stewart, and K. Smedts (2017). 'Conceptualising and Measuring Social Cohesion in Africa: Towards a Perceptions-Based Index', *Social Indicators Research*, 131(1): 321–43.

Latham, M.E. (2011). *The Right Kind of Revolution: Modernization, Development, and U.S. Foreign Policy from the Cold War to the Present.* Ithaca, NY: Cornell University Press.

Leibenstein, H. (1957). *Economic Backwardness and Economic Growth.* New York: Wiley.

Mazumdar, D. (1975). 'The Theory of Share-Cropping with Labour Market Dualism', *Economica* 42(167): 261–71.

McNamara, R.S. (1968). *The Essence of Security, Reflections in Office.* New York: Harper & Row.

Mertz, O., R.L. Wadley, and A.E. Christensen (2005). 'Local Land Use Strategies in a Globalizing World: Subsistence Farming, Cash Crops and Income Diversification', *Agricultural Systems,* 85(3): 209–15.

Mosse, D. (2006). 'Localized Cosmopolitans: Anthropologists at the World Bank', Paper prepared for 'Cosmopolitanism and Development', Panel 4, ASA Conference, Keele, 10–13 April.

Mukerjee, R. (1926). *Regional Sociology.* New York: Century.

Mukerjee, R. (1934). 'The Broken Balance of Population, Land and Water', *Indian Journal of Economics,* 14(54): 255–66, reprinted in Krishnamurty, J. (2009): 155–68.

Mukerjee, R. (1939). *Economic Problems of Modern India.* Basingstoke: Macmillan.

Mukerjee, R. (1940). *The Institutional Theory of Economics.* Basingstoke: Macmillan.

Mukerjee, R. (1955). 'Faiths and Influences'. In B. Singh (ed.), *The Frontiers of Social Science: In Honour of Radhakamal Mukerjee.* London: Macmillan.

Myrdal, G. (1957). *Economic Theory and Under-Developed Regions.* London: Gerald Duckworth.

Myrdal, G. (1965). *The Political Element in the Development of Economic Theory.* Cambridge, MA: Harvard University Press.

Myrdal, G. (1968). *Asian Drama: An Inquiry into the Poverty of Nations.* London: Allen Lane; The Penguin Press.

Myrdal, G. (1970). *An Approach to the Asian Drama. Methodological and Theoretical.* New York: Random House.

Myrdal, G. (1958). *Value in Social Theory: A Selection of Essays on Methodology.* Edited by P. Streeten. London: Routledge & Kegan Paul.

Myrdal, G., R.M.E. Sterner, and A.M. Rose (1944). *An American Dilemma: The Negro Problem and Modern Democracy.* New York: Harper & Brothers.

Naraya, D., R. Patel, K. Schafft, A. Rademacher, and S. Koch-Schulte (2000). *Voices of the Poor: Can Anyone Hear Us?* Oxford: Oxford University Press.

Nayyar, D. (2007). 'Macroeconomics in Developing Countries', *Banca Nazionale De Lavoro Quarterly Review,* 59(242): 249–69.

Nayyar, D. (2014). *Catch Up: Developing Countries in the World Economy.* Oxford: Oxford University Press.

North, D.C. (1986). 'The New Institutional Economics', *Journal of Institutional and Theoretical Economics,* 142(1): 230–7.

North, D.C. (1990). *Institutions, Institutional Change and Economic Performance.* Cambridge: Cambridge University Press.

Nurkse, R. (1953). *Problems of Capital Formation in Underdeveloped Countries.* Oxford: Blackwell.

Nussbaum, M.C. (2000). *Women and Human Development: The Capabilities Approach.* Cambridge: Cambridge University Press.

Premdas, R.R. (1993). 'Ethnicity and Development: The Case of Fiji', UNRISD Discussion Paper 46. Geneva: UNRISD.

Psacharopolous, G. (1994). 'Returns to Investment in Education: A Global Update', *World Development*, 22(9): 1325–43.

Rao, V.K.R.V. (1938). 'The Problem of Unemployment in India', *The Indian Journal of Economics*, 18(4): 627–34.

Rao, V.K.R.V. (1952). 'Investment, Income and the Multiplier in an Under-Developed Economy', *The Indian Economic Review*, 1(1): 55–67.

Raworth, K. (2017). *Doughnut Economics: Seven Ways to Think Like a 21st-Century Economist.* London: Random House.

Robbins, L.R.B. (1945). *An Essay on The Nature and Significance of Economic Science.* London: Macmillan.

Robinson, J. (1936). 'Disguised Unemployment', *Economic Journal*, 46(182): 225–37.

Robinson, J. (1960). *Exercises in Economic Analysis.* London: Macmillan.

Ruggeri Laderchi, C. (2007). 'Participatory Methods in the Analysis of Poverty: A Critical Review'. In F. Stewart, R. Saith, and B. Harriss-White (eds), *Defining Poverty in the Developing World*. London: Palgrave Macmillan.

Rutherford, M. (1994). *Institutions in Economics: The Old and the New Institutionalism.* Cambridge: Cambridge University Press.

Schultz, T.P. (1993). 'Investments in the Schooling and Health of Women and Men: Quantities and Returns', *Journal of Human Resources*, 28: 694–734.

Schultz, T.W. (1963). *The Economic Value of Education.* New York: Columbia University Press.

Scott, M.F. (1989). *A New View of Economic Growth.* Oxford: Clarendon Press.

Seers, D. (1962). 'Why Visiting Economists Fail', *Journal of Political Economy*, 70(4): 325–38.

Seers, D. (1963). 'The Limitations of the Special Case', *Bulletin of the Oxford University Institute of Economics and Statistics*, 25(2): 77–98.

Seers, D. (1969). 'The Meaning of Development', *International Development Review*, 11(4): 3–4.

Seers, D. (1983). *The Political Economy of Nationalism.* Oxford: Oxford University Press.

Sen, A. (1985). 'Well-Being, Agency and Freedom', *The Journal of Philosophy*, LXXXII: 169–221.

Sen, A.K. (1975). *Employment, Technology and Development.* Oxford: Oxford University Press.

Sen, A.K. (1999). *Development as Freedom*. Oxford: Oxford University Press.

Smith, L.T. (1999). *Decolonizing Methodologies: Research and Indigenous Peoples*. London: Zed Books.

Solow, R.M. (1956). 'A Contribution to the Theory of Economic Growth', *The Quarterly Journal of Economics*, 70(1): 65–94.

Stewart, F. (ed.) (1975). *Employment, Income Distribution and Development*. London: Frank Cass.

Stewart, F. (2018). 'The Double Democratic Deficit: Global Governance and Future Generations'. In L. Keleher and S.J. Kosko (eds) *Agency and Democracy in Development Ethics*. Cambridge: Cambridge University Press.

Stewart, F., G. Ranis, and E. Samman (2018). *Advancing Human Development: Theory and Practice*. Oxford: Oxford University Press.

Stewart, F., and M. Wang (2006). 'Do PRSPs Empower Poor Countries and Disempower The World Bank, or is it the Other Way Round?' In G. Ranis and J.R. Vreeland (eds) *Globalization and the Nation State*. London: Routledge.

Stiglitz, J.E. (2006). *Stability with Growth: Macroeconomics, Liberalization and Development*. Oxford: Oxford University Press.

Streeten, P.P., S.J. Burki, M. Ul Haq, N. Hicks, and F. Stewart (1981). *First Things First: Meeting Basic Human Needs in Developing Countries*. New York: Oxford University Press.

Thakur, M.K. (2012). 'Radhakamal Mukerjee and the Quest for an Indian Sociology', *Sociological Bulletin*, 61(1): 89–108.

Thorat, S., and K.S. Newman (2010). *Blocked by Caste: Economic Discrimination in Modern India*. New Delhi: Oxford University Press.

Thorp, R., and M. Paredes (2010). *Ethnicity and the Persistence of Inequality: The Case of Peru*. Basingstoke: Palgrave Macmillan.

Tokman, V.E. (1978). 'An Exploration into the Nature of Informal—Formal Sector Relationships', *World Development*, 6(9): 1065–75.

Turnham, D. (1971). *The Employment Problem in Less Developed Countries: A Review of the Evidence*. Paris: OECD.

UNDP (1990). *Human Development Report 1990*. Oxford: Oxford University Press.

Varoufakis, Y. (2017). *Adults in the Room*. London: Vintage.

Vetterlein, A. (2010). 'Lacking Ownership: The IMF and its Engagement with Social Development as a Policy Norm. Owning Development Policy: Creating Policy Norms'. In S. Parker and A. Vetterlain (eds) *The IMF and World Bank*. Cambridge: Cambridge University Press.

Vetterlein, A. (n.d.). 'Norm Setting or Following: The World Bank and the IMF in Comparison', Paper. Department of Sociology, University of Essex.

World Bank (2004). *An OED Review of Social Development in Bank Activities*. Washington, DC: World Bank.

4

Asia and the World Economy in Historical Perspective

Ronald Findlay

'History, then, is not taken to be predetermined, but within the power of man to shape. And the drama thus conceived is not necessarily tragedy.'[1]

Gunnar Myrdal, *Asian Drama*

1. Introduction

The Asian world in Myrdal's study essentially begins in the aftermath of the Second World War with the British withdrawal from their empire in Asia and Indian independence. These 'initial conditions' are taken as given without enquiry as to how they came to be what they were. This chapter can be considered as providing the missing historical background to *Asian Drama*, with the advantage of fifty years of hindsight. For convenience Asia will be divided into four regions: South Asia (what is now India, Pakistan, Bangladesh, and Sri Lanka); East Asia (China, Korea, and Japan); Southeast Asia (the members of ASEAN from Myanmar to the Philippines) and Central Asia (the area east of China, west of Russia and Iran and north of India and Pakistan).

The rest of this chapter is divided into six more sections. Section 2 provides the geographic, demographic, cultural, and political background to Asia over the period from 1000 to 1500. Section 3 describes the patterns of trade between the Asian nations and their overseas and overland contacts with the Middle East and Europe over the same period. Section 4 covers the European intrusion into Asia by the Portuguese *Estado da India* and the Dutch, English, and French East India Companies from 1500 to 1650, and the impact of the 'discovery' of the New World on Asian trade flows and economic systems. Section 5 analyses the pressure exerted on the land-based Asian powers by the sea power of the European intruders from 1650 to 1860. Section 6 surveys the imposition of European imperialism on the Asian nations and their resistance to it, resulting in the achievement of political and economic independence by 1968, the year in which *Asian Drama* was

[1] Myrdal (1968: vol. I, p. 35).

published. The final section 7 discusses the differences between the evolutionary paths of European and Asian societies and considers whether the twenty-first will indeed be the 'Asian Century'.

2. Malthus, Muslims, and Mongols, 1000–1500

According to McEvedy and Jones (1978) the population of the world in 1000 was 270 million and of Asia 185 million, with the Indian subcontinent accounting for almost 80 million and China 'proper' for 60 million, substantially higher proportions of both Asia and the world even than they are today. The explanation for the continued dominance of the two Asian giants is, of course, the fertility of the great river valleys of the Ganges and the Indus in India and the Yellow and Yangzi Rivers in China. The underlying economic basis is still best provided by the classical Malthus-Ricardo model, in which long-run equilibrium per capita incomes are determined at the levels which balance the endogenous fertility and mortality rates, while total populations and GDPs are determined by the extent of the land areas and levels of technology in each case.[2] Already accumulated over millennia by 1000, India and China enjoyed not only the advantages of geography but of culture and institutions as well, enabling them to have the two largest and most productive economies in the world at that time.

The sedentary populations of both these civilizations bordered on the steppes of Central Asia. Both were thus natural targets for the predatory inroads of the pastoral nomads, with their mastery of the horse and the bow. The Turko-Afghan warlord Sultan Mahmud of Ghazni (r.998–1030) conducted no less than seventeen deep plundering raids into Northern and Western India, sacking cities and temples and collecting vast amounts of treasure that he took back to his capital in Afghanistan.[3] What John F. Richards (1974) calls the 'Islamic Frontier' had been extending westwards into India since the eighth century when an Arab army crossed the Makran desert and invaded Western India before running out of momentum. It was the conversion to Islam of the Turkish and Afghan warrior tribes that provided the sustained basis for the thrust of that frontier deep into the subcontinent. The systematic conquest and occupation of large parts of India by Muslim rulers, who established a sequence of dynasties collectively known as the Delhi Sultanate that ruled northern and central India from the early thirteenth to the end of the fourteenth century, began in the last quarter of the twelfth century. The Sultanate's rule at its maximum extent ran from Sind and Gujerat in the west to Bengal in the east and deep into the Deccan plateau and parts of the Malabar and Coromandel coasts in the south.

---

[2] See Findlay and Lundahl (2017: chapter 5) for technical details and applications to historical episodes such as the Black Death.
[3] See Thapar (1990: chapter 10).

The Muslim conquests obviously led to the establishment of a new Muslim military and administrative ruling class. By and large the military leaders were Turks and Afghans while the civil administrators tended to be Persian-speaking Tajiks. Both were supported by the rights to rents and taxes on land in return for service held under the familiar Islamic *iqta* system. Despite receiving their incomes from the rural areas, the Muslim ruling class as well as the *ulema* or clergy had a distinct preference for living in cities, leading some historians to speak of a virtual 'urban revolution' as a result of the Muslim conquest. The Hindu caste system had kept most skilled and unskilled workers outside city walls to preserve the ritual purity of the Brahmins within. With this obstacle removed the urban population swelled with a significant boost to economic activity (Habib 1974: 59–80). Many notable technological advances were introduced, such as the production and use of paper, acquired by the Arabs from the Chinese in the eighth century and diffused throughout the Islamic world from Samarkand. Also very important was the introduction of the 'Persian wheel' for lifting water in place of the primitive 'bucket and chain' system which no doubt was a great advantage for irrigation and agriculture. The spinning wheel and carding devices for the cotton textile industry were also major innovations introduced from the Islamic world into India (Digby and Habib 1982).

It would be quite wrong, however, to think of Hindu India as being merely the passive recipient of military, economic, and cultural influences from its Muslim rulers. As we know, the famous 'Arabic numerals' and the crucial concept of zero were actually Indian and had already been transmitted to the Islamic world by the eighth century. While urban life, as we have noted, was strongly influenced by the new ruling class, the countryside where the vast majority of the population lived remained familiarly Hindu, with the caste system still enduring with some adaptations, and even continuing to influence many of those who converted to Islam.

The Muslim population that came in with the invading armies was a miniscule proportion of that of India as a whole. Service in the conquest states was an attractive prospect for the many warriors, clerics, scribes, poets, artists, and scholars from the Middle East and Central Asia, but this immigration still made little difference in the aggregate. There were no forcible conversions and little incentive to do so on a voluntary basis. According to Richards (1974: 104) the Muslim population was estimated at a mere 3–4 million out of a total of 170 million in 1400.

What emerged from the long encounter was in many respects not just a Muslim political superstructure dominating a largely Hindu economic base but a distinctive Indo-Muslim civilization, as can readily be seen in the architectural styles, construction, and workmanship of the many mosques, minarets, palaces, tombs, and fortresses built by the new rulers. Like the British after them, the Muslim conquerors had to rely on the natives to staff their armies and administration, and not always in completely 'subaltern' positions. They also had to rely extensively on the supply of credit from Hindu merchants and brokers, organized collectively into powerful guilds with far-reaching contacts within India and abroad. The 'Hindustani' *lingua franca* that emerged in northern India led to the parallel development of Hindi and Urdu as vernacular languages, while Sanskrit and Persian were the languages of religion and statecraft. India thus proved much more resistant to complete cultural 'Islamicization' than the other ancient civilization of Iran, for example Stein (1998: chapter 3).

During the time that northern India was enduring the depredations of Mahmud of Ghazni, the southern end of the peninsula was blossoming under the rule of the Chola Dynasty. They administered a contiguous, well-organized empire that comprised both the eastern Coromandel and western Malabar coasts but much of the uplands between them. Particularly notable was their command of strong naval forces that enabled them to conquer the Maldive Islands and much of Ceylon as well as to launch successful raiding expeditions into Southeast Asia. This naval power was deployed to support the wide-ranging commercial activities of Tamil merchant guilds that operated not only all over Southeast Asia but also as far as China. When the Sumatran kingdom of Srivijaya attempted to divert the lucrative trade from China to the Middle East to its own advantage, the Cholas sent an expedition in 1025 that forced the local ruler to restore the trading rights of the Tamil merchants. The Cholas ruled until the early fourteenth century, after which power in the south passed to the rising militarized state of Vijayanagar (Thapar 1990: chapters 9 and 14).

While India, as we have seen, had one previously nomadic predatory state on its northern border in the eleventh century, China had two, that of the Khitan Liao Kingdom in the north-east, and that of the Tangut Xi Xia Kingdom in the northwest. The ethnic Chinese Song Dynasty came to power in 960, succeeding the Tang Dynasty after the interregnum known as the 'Five Dynasties' period from 907 to 960, with its capital at Kaifeng. From the beginning it had to confront the problem of how best to deal with its powerful northern neighbours. The option it chose was what Dieter Kuhn (2009: 28) has called 'peaceful coexistence'. In effect it 'bought' peace by sending 300,000 bolts of silk and 200,000 ounces of silver annually to the Liao and 150,000 bolts of silk, 70,000 ounces of silver and 10,000 catties of tea annually to the Xi Xia. With peace thus secured, however humiliatingly, China could proceed with what has rightly been called the 'Song Economic Miracle' with agriculture, manufacturing, and commerce all flourishing as never before under a civil administration of scholar-officials chosen on merit by a rigorous examination system based on the Confucian classics Shiba (1970).

While millet and wheat were the main crops in the north, rice was the mainstay in the Yangzi valley and the south. Production got a huge boost from the introduction of 'early-ripening rice' from Champa, which led to double and sometimes even triple cropping. This stimulated the growth of the population from 60 million in 1000 to 115 million in 1200. By comparison, the population on the Indian subcontinent rose only from 80 million to 86 million over the same two centuries. The population of Kaifeng in 1078 was about 750,000, making it probably the largest city in the world. Iron production at this time was of the order of 150,000 tonnes annually, a level not reached in all of Europe until after 1700 (Hartwell 1966).

The 'peaceful coexistence' that the Song had enjoyed on their north-eastern border came to an end in 1127 when the Khitan state was overthrown by another tribe of warrior nomads, the Jurchen. Not content with simply enjoying the Song tribute the Jurchen invaded North China and drove the Song out of their capital Kaifeng, forcing them to take refuge south of the Yangzi. There they established the Southern Song Dynasty, with its capital at Hangzhou, which soon became even more prosperous than it had been while based in the north. The cultivation of tea and the production of 'true' porcelain were two of the main activities and commerce with Southeast Asia and beyond flourished. The population of Hangzhou was estimated at a staggering 1.5 million and the urban population ratio of the Southern Song was 12 per cent, not exceeded in Europe until 1800, according to Richard von Glahn (2016: 251).

The Southern Song and the Jurchen in the north both fell prey to the rising superpower of the Mongol Empire of Chinggis Khan (r.1206–1227) and his successors. His grandson Khubilai Khan (r.1260–1294) proclaimed himself the first emperor of the Yuan Dynasty in 1271, ruling over a reunified China after the final defeat of the Southern Song in 1279. The regime that he established was on the whole a remarkably enlightened one. The Mongols were clearly the ruling elite but the Chinese people were not subjected to oppression. The Confucian scholar-officials continued to be employed but did not enjoy a monopoly of the higher posts, sharing them with talented individuals from all over the empire and beyond. Agriculture, industry, and commerce were all encouraged and extensive public works undertaken. The famous postal service with riders covering up to 250 miles a day connected all points of the empire. Paper currency was issued, at first excessively but later with more restraint. Foreign trade was actively promoted, both overseas and overland. The borders of China were extended permanently to include the provinces of Yunnan in the southwest and Gansu in the northwest. Inevitably, however, the familiar 'dynastic cycle' of Chinese history took its course. Subsequent rulers had short and troubled reigns, the administration became increasingly corrupt, the hydraulic infrastructure was neglected, leading to disastrous floods and outbreaks of plague that caused severe disruption. Native Chinese dissent multiplied and erupted into fierce rebellion. In 1368, the leader of the rebellion finally drove out the Mongols, proclaiming himself the first emperor of the new Ming Dynasty (Rossabi 1988, 2014).

Korea and Japan had developed autonomously but were recipients of strong cultural influences from China, particularly during the Tang Dynasty. Japan was, in principle, a unified state under an emperor of supposedly divine descent but real power was in the hands of regional feudal lords. One of these lords, Minamoto Yoritomo (1147–1199) acquired the title of *Shogun* ('generalissimo') and established what was known as the Kamakura Shogunate which effectively ruled the country from 1192 to 1333. It was this regime that organized the successful defence against Mongol invasions in 1274 and 1281. The stress caused by these invasions and their aftermath led eventually to the fall of the Kamakura and its replacement by the Ashikaga Shogunate (1338–1573), also known as the Muromachi *Bakufu* ('government') from the location of its headquarters near Kyoto (Hall 1970: chapter 7).

Chinese civilization in the form of Confucianism and Buddhism, as well as the writing system, was diffused to the Korean peninsula where three kingdoms arose: first Koguryo in the north, followed by Paekche in the southwest and Silla in the southeast by the fourth century. All three kingdoms contended for power in the peninsula while also engaging in conflict and co-operation with China, with unification finally being achieved in 1392 by a new state Koryo, renamed Choson by the first ruler of the Yi Dynasty which lasted until 1910 (Lee 1984).

Despite millennia of strong influences from India and China, the mainland states and island polities of Southeast Asia have their own distinct ethnic, linguistic, and cultural identities. Theravada Buddhism in Myanmar and Thailand now exist nowhere else in Asia other than Sri Lanka, and the Islam of Indonesia and Malaysia has a distinctively different social character from that of the Middle East or South Asia. Overland migration routes from China into the great river valleys of the mainland are relatively easy to traverse and there has been traffic on the sea lanes linking the South China Sea, the Indian Ocean, the Red Sea, and the Persian Gulf since time immemorial, with Srivijaya in Sumatra and Melaka on the Malay Peninsula as major *entrepots*. Strong centralized kingdoms on the mainland and the interior of Java like Pagan, Ayuthia, Angkor, Annam, Champa, and Majapahit interacted closely with their coastal regions and with China and India in trade, warfare, and cultural exchange during this period from 1000 to 1500 (D.G.E. Hall 1968: part 1).

3. Silk Roads and Sea Lanes: International Trade, 1000–1500

In the Chinese view of the world order China was the 'central kingdom' from which the emperor ruled 'all under heaven'. All foreign states were thus regarded as vassals and foreign trade was viewed as the payment of 'tribute' to which the 'Son of Heaven' graciously responded with gifts of equal or greater value. Relations with Korea and Japan, in particular, were regulated in this way.[4] Korean exports

---

[4] See Fairbank (1968).

were ginseng, furs, and other natural products while Japan mainly provided raw silk. Paper was imported from China but Japan eventually learned paper-making from the Koreans, attaining quality levels that surpassed that of the Chinese. The Japanese ability to reverse engineer imported products and to improve upon and eventually to export them, so familiar in the twentieth century, was thus evident even from these very early days. Another important example from this early period is the manufacture of the famous *samurai* sword blades that were in great demand all over East and Southeast Asia. Tens of thousands of these swords were exported annually to Japan, in addition to raw materials like sulfur and copper and other manufactured goods such as paper, screens, and decorative folding fans.[5] The Chinese imports most in demand were silk fabrics and books—not only the Chinese classics but also technical works on science and technology. Huge amounts of Chinese copper coins balanced the trade and were increasingly used as a medium of exchange in Japan, an interesting early example of 'dollarization' arising out of spontaneous market forces, even within the archaic framework of the tribute system (Yamamura and Kamiki 1983).

According to von Verschuer (2006: 19), one-third of all the Chinese books in existence at that time were available in Japan as early as 831, showing how successfully Japan was absorbing Chinese culture. China's trade with Korea obviously had lower transport costs and was larger than with Japan. The city of Sakai, near Osaka, became the main centre for trade with Korea and Southeast Asia, particularly Siam. One interesting export item was printed volumes of the Buddhist canon, indicating that Korea was a pioneer in printing even before China and centuries before Gutenberg (von Verschuer (2006: chapter 4–5).

Chinese international trade was particularly active during the period of the Southern Song (1127–1279). With the overland routes to the west cut off, they were obliged to rely on overseas trade, which they did with a vengeance. 'The ocean in Sung times was the front door of China and it was open to all who were interested in commercial relations with China' (Ma 1971: 30). While Canton was the only official port for foreign trade under the Tang, there were nine such port cities under the Song, each under an Office of Maritime Trade. Canton was displaced by Quanzhou in Fujian Province opposite Taiwan as the leading port city. In 1225, the Superintendent of Foreign Trade in this city, Chau Ju-kua, published a remarkable work on the 'Records of Foreign Nations' in which he lists all the nations trading with Quanzhou and the hundreds of commodities they exported and imported, extending from Southeast Asia to India, East Africa and the Middle East, all the way to the Mediterranean (Wheatley 1959; Hirth and Rockhill 1964).

The trade across the Indian Ocean and the South China Sea used to be carried in Arab and Persian vessels but under the Song the large, highly seaworthy

---

[5] See von Verschuer (2006: chapters 4–5) and Kang (2010: chapter 6).

Chinese junks replaced them. With the Middle East enjoying the 'Golden Age of Islam', South India growing vigorously on both the Coromandel and Malabar Coasts under the Chola Dynasty, and strong kingdoms emerging in Southeast Asia, the arc of trade extending from the South China Sea to the Persian Gulf and the Red Sea saw unprecedented prosperity. Silk and porcelain from China, black pepper from the Malabar Coast, cinnamon, nutmeg and cloves from the East Indies, cotton textiles from Bengal and Gujerat, pearls from Ceylon, ivory from East Africa, and the proverbial frankincense and myrrh from Arabia were the main but far from the only goods that entered this commerce. Just to remind us that all commerce is not necessarily peaceful, Simon Digby (1982: 147) notes the continuing significance of the trade in war-animals, cavalry horses from Iran and Arabia and fighting elephants from the jungles of Ceylon and Southeast Asia.

The prospects for overland trade to the Mongol Yuan Dynasty, in contrast to the Southern Song, were virtually unlimited. The Mongol Empire as a whole controlled not only all of China under the Yuan but also the ancestral Mongol lands of Central Asia under the Chagatai Khanate, Iran under the Islamicized Mongol regime known as the Il-Khanate, and most of Russia which owed allegiance to the Golden Horde under the so-called 'Mongol Yoke'. This led to the establishment of what came to be known as the *Pax Mongolica* across the entire extent of Central Asia. The fabled Silk Roads, which had reached their heyday from the seventh to the tenth centuries under the Tang, now enjoyed a great revival under the protection and support of the Great Khans.

It was not only goods that were conveyed in both directions along the Silk Roads and associated sea lanes but, even more importantly, ideas and technical knowledge, as stressed in the seminal work of Joseph Needham (1954). Crucial inventions such as gunpowder, printing, the compass and other navigation aids such as the sternpost rudder and lateen sails, all moved from east to west during this period, stimulating their adoption and improvement in Europe during the Renaissance. Religious ideas propagated by monks and missionaries were written down and influenced scripts adopted by previously unlettered peoples such as the Uighurs and the Mongols (Liu 1988; Millward 2013). Unfortunately, the plague germ that brought the Black Death to Europe and the Middle East in the 1340s also travelled along the Silk Road, wiping out over a third of the population initially but with the associated rise in per capita incomes and wages leading to growth of population and GDP that went well beyond the initial levels in the long run (Findlay and Lundahl 2017: chapters 5, 7).

At the western end the main beneficiaries from the *Pax Mongolica* were the Byzantine Empire, the Mamluk Sultans of Egypt and Syria, and the rising Italian city-states of Venice and Genoa, with their trading stations on the shores of the Black Sea. The fact that all of these states were themselves connected to Europe all the way west to England, Flanders, and France enabled Janet Abu-Lughod (1989) to speak of a 'thirteenth-century world system' from 1250 to 1350, preceding the fully global one established by the European 'voyages of discovery' at the end of the fifteenth century. The Venetian Marco Polo (1254–1324) and the Moroccan Ibn Battuta (1304–1377) were both able to travel from one end of this world to the other and back, one largely by land and the other mainly by sea, without the slightest danger, to bring to the rapt attention of the readers of the accounts of their travels, then and since, the myriad wonders they had witnessed along the way.

After the fall of the Yuan, the first five emperors of the new Ming Dynasty, from 1368 to 1435, maintained a vigorous expansionist policy on both the northern and southern land frontiers and in the South China Sea and the Indian Ocean, switching to a more defensive posture after that date. The celebrated seven voyages from 1405 to 1433 in the Indian Ocean led by the Muslim admiral Zheng He (1371–1433) reflect both the great ambition of the expansionary phase and its abrupt and permanent conclusion.[6] The great armadas of Zheng He displayed the Ming imperial banners to all the mainland and island states of Southeast Asia, Bengal and both coasts of the Indian peninsula, Ceylon, the Horn of Africa, the Red Sea, and the Persian Gulf. After his death and that of the fifth emperor in 1435, the expeditions were discontinued and the resources diverted to frontier defence against a possible return of the Mongols.

A good measure of the rise and fall of Ming China's influence on Southeast Asia is provided by Anthony Reid (1993: table 1) which shows forty-two tribute missions from Java, thirty-seven from the two Malay states of Melaka and Pasai, thirty-three from Champa and thirty-one from Siam, a total of 143 in all over the period 1400 to 1439 of the Zheng He voyages, compared to a total of seventy-three or barely half from these states over the next seventy years from 1440 to 1510. The command of the 'southern ocean' was thus ceded to a small nation on the western edge of Europe that dispatched a flotilla of caravels around Cape Horn, landing at Calicut in 1498 and initiating a new era in Asian and world history, the 'Vasco da Gama Epoch' (Panikkar 1969).

4. The European Intrusion and the Creation of Global Trade, 1500–1650

Lord Acton gave the Portuguese the accolade of being 'the first Europeans to understand that the ocean is not a limit, but the universal waterway that unites mankind' (Acton 1961: 61). In less than two decades after da Gama's historic voyage they captured Goa, Hormuz, and Melaka but failed to take Aden, the entrance to the Red Sea. They thus failed to cut off completely the supply of Eastern spices to Venice through Alexandria, which was the main motivation of their enterprise.

---

[6] See Dreyer (2007) for a detailed account.

Melaka, captured in 1511, commanding the Straits of Malacca, was a fabulously rich port-city-state ruled by a family of Malay sultans since about 1400. It was visited by about a hundred ships a year from the Middle East, both coasts of India, the Bay of Bengal, the Indonesian islands and China, according to the Portuguese traveller Tome Pires. These ships brought an enormous variety of goods: cotton textiles from India, rice from Burma and Siam, Chinese silk, and Indonesian spices that went both east and west. It was Pires who made the famous observation that 'the lord of Melaka has his hand on the throat of Venice', failing to note that Venice could indeed be choked but not strangled if Aden was not also secured (Reid 1993: vol. II).

The Portuguese king Dom Manuel I (r.1495–1521) declared himself 'Lord of the Conquest, Navigation and Commerce of Ethiopia, Arabia, Persia and India' and as such claimed the right to control entry and exit into all ports in the Arabian Sea and the Indian Ocean, in other words issuing a 'license to plunder' by charging 'protection money' from all merchant vessels of any nationality plying these shores (Newitt 1980: 19). The *Estado da India*, as the Portuguese enterprise came to be called, expanded rapidly, settling and fortifying Colombo in 1518, Macao in 1557 and finally Nagasaki in 1571 (Subrahmanyam 1993).

While the Portuguese entered the Pacific from the west, the Spanish crossed it from the east, colonizing the Philippines in the 1540s with Manila as the capital. The arrival there of a galleon from Acapulco, laden with silver from Potosi in Bolivia, returning with an even more precious cargo of Chinese silk, marked the global circuit of trade for the first time in history. The flood of New World silver, brought across the Pacific by the Spaniards and across the Atlantic, Mediterranean, and Indian Ocean by the Portuguese and later the Dutch and the English, transformed the monetary and general economic history of Asia. Silver was basically the only commodity that European traders could offer in exchange for Chinese silk and porcelain, Indonesian cloves and nutmeg, Malabar pepper and the cotton textiles of Bengal and Gujerat, to export back to the markets of Europe, Africa, and the New World. While the silver 'windfall' accrued initially to the Habsburg rulers of Spain and Austria, it increasingly ended up in the hands of the newly established Dutch and English East India Companies that used it for the purchase of the Eastern commodities that they shipped around the world (Findlay and O'Rourke 2007: 212–26).

The period 1500 to 1650 saw a remarkable expansion of the Ming economy, to a considerable extent in response to currents unleashed by the Iberian voyages at the turn of the fifteenth century. Particularly important were the food and other crops from the New World that found their way into China such as maize, sweet potatoes, and peanuts. These were all grown as second or even third crops, boosting rural per capita incomes and stimulating population growth. The population rose from 110 million in 1500 to 160 million in 1600, before falling to 140 million as a consequence of the disturbances associated with the dynastic transition from the Ming to a new Manchu Qing Dynasty in 1644. The influx of silver from the New World and new mines discovered in Japan provided the monetization necessary to lubricate the expansion. Silk and porcelain were exported all over the world and several technical innovations made in transport, manufacturing, and agriculture (Bray 2000; von Glahn 2016: 296–312).

The fall of the Ming was due not to any erosion of the economic base but to problems with the political and administrative superstructure. Corruption and factional disputes within the bureaucracy caused public dissatisfaction, leading to internal disorders and rebellion. This gave an opportunity to the Manchus, a Sinicized nomadic tribe related to the Jurchen, to intervene and oust the Ming, establishing a new Qing Dynasty in 1644 that lasted until 1911 (Rowe 2009: chapter 1).

In Japan, the Ashikaga shoguns based in the capital Kyoto were gradually losing power to a new class of locally based feudal lords, known as the *daimyo*, in the east and the north. Warfare between contending clans and factions, making extensive use of firearms that had been introduced by the Portuguese, became ever more intense leading to the outbreak of a prolonged period of instability known as the *Sengoku Jidai* or 'Warring States Period'. Order was finally restored only after the Battle of Sekigahara in 1600, when Tokugawa Ieyasu defeated a coalition of opposing feudal lords and established the Tokugawa Shogunate that lasted until 1868. To consolidate power the Tokugawa imposed a rigorous policy of *sakoku* or 'seclusion', cutting Japan off from all contact with foreigners, including Christian missionaries, except for official relations with China and a small Dutch trading post in Nagasaki (Hall 1970: chapters 9–10).

India after the fall of the Delhi Sultanate was ruled by a succession of weak regimes until the founding of the Mughal Empire in 1526 by Babur (1483–1530), a Timurid prince from Central Asia. The empire was consolidated and extended over the whole of northern India by his grandson, the great Emperor Akbar (r.1556–1605). The Mughals, like the Ottomans and Safavids, were what Hodgson (1974) called a 'gunpowder empire', one that relied on heavy siege artillery to batter down all opposition into submission. While Akbar began his rule with a succession of hard-fought victories over Hindu Rajput and rival Muslim rulers, his charismatic personality, moral character, and far-sighted vision made the Mughals into what could be called a truly Indian, as opposed to an Indo-Muslim, dynasty (Mukhia 2004).

The population of Mughal India is put at around 115 million in 1600, out of 150 million for the sub-continent as a whole (Streusand 2011: 272), rising to 200 million in 1800. For China, the figures are also 150 million in 1600 but rising to 320 million in 1800. We can thus infer from the Malthus-Ricardo model that technical progress and capital accumulation was much greater in China than in India. The introduction of New World plants, for example seems to have been much less extensive than in China. There is no reason to doubt, however, the contention by Richards (1993: 204) that 'the secular trend for Mughal India was that of economic growth and vitality'. Population growth was slow but steady, indicating no severe squeeze on peasant incomes. The surplus extracted must have been enormous to create such surviving monuments as Fatehpur Sikri, the Taj Mahal, and the great fortresses. The emperor's personal income alone is estimated at one million silver rupees per month, compared to a monthly wage for unskilled workers at 1.5 rupees per month (Moosvi 1987: 284). Cotton cloth, in a very wide range of qualities and styles in the form of calicos, chintzes, taffeta, and the superfine muslins, continued to be the mainstay of manufacturing and international trade, in which the Dutch and English East India Companies were coming to play an increasing role, but without displacing the very active participation of Hindu and Muslim merchants. Indian cotton textiles, together with Chinese silks and porcelain were the main manufactured exports of the world until the rise of Lancashire cotton textiles during the Industrial Revolution (Chaudhuri 1982; Roy 2012: chapter 4).

India's main import was silver, in massive amounts largely to be coined into the silver rupees issued since the time of Akbar at never less than 96 per cent purity. The imports averaged about 100 tonnes annually from about 1590 to 1645, mostly from the Ottoman and Safavid territories and Europe. The silver influx, as in China, did not cause inflation of the price level since it facilitated internal trade and exchange, boosting productivity and output. The two great 'sinks' for the surge of world silver flows from 1500 to 1650 were Ming China and Mughal India, the giant planets of the Asian galaxy, drawing the world's silver into their orbits by the sheer force of gravitational attraction (Findlay and O'Rourke 2007: 212–26).

5. Land Power versus Sea Power, 1650–1860

In 1650, as we have seen in the previous section, Mughal India, Qing China, and Tokugawa Japan were all strong, centralized states in full control of their borders. By 1860, however, the European merchant companies previously confined to the coastal peripheries had succeeded in destabilizing both of the great Asian empires and seriously threatening their sovereignty, while an American commodore was forcing the Tokugawa to breach their seclusion policy and open Japan to free trade. How did all this come about?

The reign of the Emperor Aurangzeb (r.1658–1707), the last of the great Mughal rulers, was most notable for its rejection of Akbar's efforts to rule as an Indian rather than a strictly Muslim monarch. He adopted a narrow and dogmatic Sunni *Sharia* version of Islam and introduced a number of discriminatory measures against his Hindu and Sikh subjects, including the destruction of some temples and shrines. Not surprisingly this led to strong resistance, not only from the previously loyal Rajputs but also particularly from the fierce Maratha warriors of the western Deccan under their great leader Shivaji Bhonsle. After his death in 1707, he was succeeded by a number of mediocre rulers and the empire went into a pronounced decline (Streusand 2011).

Meanwhile, the English East India Company was steadily extending the range and profitability of its operations, acquiring the well-located trading stations of Surat (1607) and Bombay (1661) on the west coast, and Madras (1640) and Calcutta (1690) on the east. Surat was displaced over time by the other three, which became the bases for regional Company 'presidencies'. All three were not only trading stations but fortified city-states,[7] with their own armies of native troops led by European officers, as with the French centre at Pondicherry and the Dutch at Pulicat. With their thriving foreign trade and other commercial opportunities these places attracted many local merchants and others with various skills to offer. With a sort of 'extraterritoriality' in place, they had independent legal systems that many locals must have found more conducive than what the Mughals and other Indian rulers had to offer, on which see (Roy 2012: chapter 4).

From a military standpoint the Company forces of small but well-trained detachments of Indian soldiers with European officers were able to prevail over the much larger but less disciplined armies of the Indian rulers whenever clashes occurred. Thus, the sea power that secured the Europeans in their coastal stations was supplemented by increasingly formidable power on land. This was convincingly demonstrated by the victory of Company forces under Robert Clive at the battle of Plassey in 1757, when it defeated the Nawab of Bengal, and over an even larger Mughal army at the Battle of Buxar in 1764. The prize for these victories was the award to the Company by the Mughal Empire of the *diwani*, the rights to collect the entire revenue of Bihar, Orissa, and the enormously wealthy province of Bengal, rightly called the 'British Bridgehead' to the ultimate conquest of all of India by P.J. Marshall (1987). Subsequent decades saw the consolidation of the Company's hold on India with wars against the Marathas, Sikhs, Afghans, and the Gurkhas of Nepal. The shock of the outbreak of the Sepoy Mutiny in 1857 and its violent suppression finally led to the Crown taking over the administration of India from the Company (Stein 1998: chapters 5–6).

The Manchu Qing Dynasty, which replaced the Ming in 1644, was remarkable in many ways. A branch of the Jurchen tribes of Manchuria, they were not pastoral nomads from the steppes, though their military striking power was also based on mounted archers. They were organized into a very effective military force by two great leaders, Nurhaci (1559–1626) and his son Hong Taiji (1592–1643), divided into what were called the 'Eight Banners', each Banner constituting not just an army unit but the entire households of all the troops within it. The ethnic composition of each Banner was not fixed, consisting not only of Jurchens but

---

[7] See Richards (1993: 240).

also allied Central Asians and ethnic Chinese that had been absorbed into the Manchu orbit (Crossley 1997). Hong Taiji subdued Korea in 1638 but died in 1643, with his infant son becoming the first Qing Emperor Shunzhi (r.1644–1661).

The most urgent problem for the new regime was suppressing multiple rebellions by Ming loyalists. The most important of these was that of the Zheng family, which had been involved in coastal trade and piracy, sometimes in association with, and at others in opposition to, Japanese, Portuguese, Dutch, and other foreign interests. The half-Japanese Zheng Chenggong (1623–1662), known in the west as Coxinga, built up a formidable naval force and mercantile empire, establishing his base in Taiwan after driving out the Dutch, from where the Zhengs conducted lucrative trade with Japan and Southeast Asia, while harassing the Manchu regime until it captured the island in 1683.[8]

The next three Qing emperors Kangxi (r.1662–1722), Yongzheng (r.1723–1735) and Qianlong (r.1736–1795) saw the dynasty reach its zenith during their long and illustrious reigns, with its territorial extent unmatched in Chinese history. They added not only Xinjiang and Tibet but also Manchuria, Inner and Outer Mongolia, and areas of Eastern Turkestan as well. Their forces marched west, armed with cannon and muskets, destroying the threat of the Mongol steppe nomads to China and sedentary civilizations forever. While Qing China was driving through Central Asia from the east, Russia under the Romanovs was already moving vigorously in the opposite direction but further north in Siberia, reaching the Pacific at Okhotsk in the 1640s. The interests of the two empires collided in the fertile valley of the Amur River but were peacefully resolved by the treaties of Nerchinsk (1689) and Kiatkha (1727), leading to considerable trade of Russian furs for Chinese tea and silk (Perdue 2005).

The Manchus accepted Chinese culture and institutions almost entirely, relying on the scholar-gentry officials to administer the country and maintaining the civil service examination system. They also, however, undertook shrewd measure to ensure that their elite position in the society was not threatened. They did this by establishing a sort of parallel administration, pairing Manchu and ethnic Chinese officials at each level below the top, which was solely occupied by Manchus. The Manchu language and script was also used to maintain all confidential records to preserve security. Internally the country continued to thrive economically in the seventeenth and eighteenth centuries, but by the turn of the nineteenth signs of stagnation and decline were becoming evident, as noted by the British ambassador Lord Macartney who observed that Qing China resembled 'an old, crazy man-of-war' that would soon be 'dashed to pieces on the shore' (Spence 1990: 123; Rowe 2009: ch. 2).

---

[8] See Clements (2005).

From about 1800 onwards the Qing regime came under increasing pressure from both internal dissension and external threats. The spread of opium addiction due to the sale of the drug by the East India Company led to a crackdown by Qing officials, in response to which the British launched what came to be known as the First Opium War of 1839–1842, with a small naval force of steam-powered gunboats sailing up the Yangzi, easily defeating the Manchu resistance. The resulting 'unequal' Treaty of Nanjing (1842) saw the ceding of Hong Kong and the opening of five ports, including Shanghai, to free trade. A further dispute led to the Second Opium War of 1856–1860 with the Treaty of Tianjin (1860) opening the Yangzi River to international commerce and adding more ports open to free trade. The crisis created by the Opium Wars was compounded by the outbreak of the devastatingly lethal Taiping Rebellion, in which an estimated 60 million people lost their lives between 1850 and 1864 (Rowe 2009: chapter 7; Rossabi 2014: chapter 9).

Despite the severe political setbacks at the hands of the British and other European interests, the economies of both India and China performed quite well over the 1650 to 1860 period. The population of the Indian subcontinent rose from 145 million in 1650 to 225 million in 1850, while that of China more than trebled from 130 million to 420 million over the same period. While this surge in population undoubtedly contributed to the outbreak of the Taiping Rebellion, it must have been improved economic circumstances that led to the massive rise in the first place. The cultivated area doubled and yields per acre rose as a result of both the continued spread of the New World crops and the boom in tea that was a major driving force of the Qing economy in these decades. Most of the tea was exported from Canton, the sole port officially open to foreign trade before the 'unequal' treaties, and was also the entrance for imports. Naquin and Rawski (1987: table 2) construct an index of the volume of trade passing through Canton that rises from the base of 100 in 1719 to 1338 in 1833, levelling off thereafter up to the 1850s.

The East India Company was the main actor in shaping both intra-Asian trade and the trade of Asia with Europe and the rest of the world. Chaudhuri (1978) calculates that the compound rate of growth of the Company's exports and imports between Asia and England of goods and treasure was 2.2 per cent per annum from when it was founded in 1600 to 1760, a faster rate than that of either population or aggregate output in Asia and Europe between those dates. Initially the Company had to export considerable amounts of treasure, mostly silver, to pay for the purchase of Indian cotton textiles and other goods to be sold in exchange for the spices it acquired in the East Indies for resale in Europe. The proportion of treasure to total exports fell from above 75 per cent for most of the period from 1600 to 1760 to only 30 per cent at the end, reflecting the crucial significance of the acquisition of Bengal. The Company sold Indian raw cotton to China for the manufacture of cheap cotton cloth sold in its home market as well as for export but its exports to China came increasingly to rely on opium, rising from about 2,000 chests a year in the 1790s to 24,000 annually by the 1830s, with which it purchased tea to export to Europe and the rest of the world (Roy 2012: chapter 5). As Tan Chung (1974: 431) wryly observed about the Britain–China–India trade triangle, it worked out as 'Indian opium for the Chinese, Chinese tea for the Britons and the British Raj for the Indians'.

The period 1600 to 1867 that Japan spent under the Tokugawa Shogunate has been widely misunderstood as one of total seclusion from the rest of the world. While most contact with Europeans was cut off, relations with China through Nagasaki, and with Korea through the island of Tsushima and with Southeast Asia through the Ryukyu Islands continued uninterrupted. The tiny Dutch trading post at Deshima was a very narrow 'window to the West' but one through which Japan achieved much greater knowledge of modern science and technology than India or China despite those countries not having anything resembling the *sakoku* policy.[9] In the light of all this it can be argued that the 'seclusion' of Japan under the Tokugawa, giving Japan a century and a half of peace and prosperity, made her better able, not less, to deal with the forced intrusion of the West, when it finally came in the form of Commodore Perry's 'black ships', than the rest of Asia.

6. Imperialism to Independence, 1860–1968

This period begins with Europe at the pinnacle of its global dominance. The Industrial Revolution had spread from Britain to the rest of Western Europe, providing it not only with strong industrial economies but the military power associated with it. India had fallen almost completely under British rule and Qing China was reeling from the shocks of the Opium Wars and the Taiping Rebellion and in no position to resist further European intrusions. Southeast Asia had been opened to European trade and influence for centuries but its traditional kingdoms had started to lose their territorial sovereignty, to Britain in Burma and Malaya, France in Indo-China and to the Netherlands in Indonesia. The opening of the Suez Canal and the substitution of steam for sail saw a drastic reduction in transport costs and the era of the 'Great Specialization' from 1870 to 1914, with Europe providing the manufactured exports and India, China, and Southeast Asia the primary products rice, tea, and industrial raw materials such as rubber, tin, and jute.

Colombo, Calcutta, Rangoon, Saigon, Singapore, and Batavia emerged as the strategic centres of this new pattern of colonial development in Southeast Asia while Hong Kong and Shanghai played the same role on the coast of China.

---

[9] See Keene (1969).

Chinese settlers from the southern provinces of Fujian and Guangdong moved in large numbers into Southeast Asia, expanding the vibrant 'Overseas Chinese' communities in the Dutch East Indies and Malaya, while Indian workers, merchants and moneylenders went to Burma and Malaya. No less than 2.5 million Chinese went to the Dutch East Indies between 1880 and 1922, while 263,000 went to Malaya, bringing the Chinese population residing there to 2.8 million and 433,000 respectively, while the Indian population in Burma in 1930 was 1.3 million and in Malaya 628,000 (Lewis 1978: 185). Capital, and the top layers of the colonial administration, was generally provided by the metropolitan centres in each case. The result was what Furnivall (1948) called the 'plural economy'.

The one Asian country that was not under some sort of colonial or semi-colonial status was of course Japan. The Tokugawa Shogunate, discredited by its humiliations at the hands of Commodore Perry was swept away by the Meiji Restoration of 1868 that launched the country on its then unprecedented course of rapid modernization.[10] The transformation is very evident in terms of foreign trade, brilliantly analysed by Lockwood (1968: chapter 6) on 'Trade as a Highway of Learning'. Japan's exports grew at 7.4 per cent per annum between 1883 and 1913, more than twice as fast as world trade, which grew at 3.4 per cent, with China and India at 3.35 and 3.05 respectively (Lewis 1978: 169). The changing structure of the exports was even more impressive, with the share of manufactures rising from below 60 per cent at the beginning and over 90 per cent at the end (Macpherson 1987: table 3). From 1913 to 1938 Japan's GDP growth rate was 3.9 per cent per annum, compared to 0.7 per cent for Great Britain, 1.1 per cent for the USA and 1.85 for Germany (Nakamura 1997: table 3.2).

It was this very rapid industrialization that enabled Japan to pursue an expansionist foreign policy, defeating China in the Sino-Japanese War of 1894–1895 and annexing Taiwan in 1895 and Korea in 1910. What brought her the most prestige of all, however, was her defeat of Tsarist Russia and the sinking of the Russian fleet at the Battle of Tsushima in the Russo-Japanese War of 1904–1905. While all other Asian nations in one way or another were victims of imperialism, Japan was able not only to avoid that fate but to actively join the imperialist club herself and victimize China and Korea (see Beasley 1987). Further gains at the expense of China were obtained when the German-held 'concessions' in China were given to Japan as reward for her belated entry into the First World War on the Allied side. Finally, it was the Japanese occupation of Manchuria in 1931 followed by the brutal invasion of China in 1937 that led to the outbreak of the Second World War in Asia and the Pacific (Hall 1970: chapters 16–18; Beasley 1987: chapters 12–16).

[10] See Hall (1970: chapters 12–15).

Qing China attempted to recover from the disasters of the Opium Wars and the Taiping Rebellion with some belated reforms, such as the so-called 'self-strengthening' movement to build up her defence capabilities, but after the defeat in the Sino-Japanese War and the Boxer Rebellion of 1900 the position of the regime became increasingly untenable, the six-year-old last emperor abdicated and the Republic of China declared in 1912. The first general election was won by the *Kuomintang* Nationalist Party led by Sun Yatsen but he was soon ousted by a military 'strong man' and the country dominated by a succession of regional war-lords. The Nationalists under Chiang Kaishek and the newly formed Communist Party under Mao Zedong vied for power until they were forced into collaboration by the Japanese invasion of 1937 (Rowe 2009: chapters 8–10); Rossabi (2014: chapters 10–11).

Economic growth in both India and China was dismally poor, both in this period and over the very long run. According to Heston (2005: 379) per capita income growth in India during 1860 to 1920 was under 0.5 per cent per annum and zero from 1920 to 1947. The performance of China was even worse. According to Maddison (2007) real per capita income was constant at US$600 between 1300 and 1820, and then *fell* to US$538 in 1952. In other words, both India and China remained caught in the Malthus–Ricardo 'trap' for the entire millennium (Elvin 1973). Real per capita income in China, in terms of 1990 US dollars, *fell by more than half* from over US$1200 in 1090 under the Northern Song, to under US$600 in 1850, and could not have risen much, if at all, for the rest of the millennium (von Glahn 2016: table 9.4).

It is therefore not surprising that the challenge of economic development confronting the Asian economies, and especially in India and China, should have appeared so daunting to Gunnar Myrdal in *Asian Drama*. With per capita incomes so low, how could a sufficiently high savings rate be attained for GDP to keep pace with population growth, let alone exceed it? How could sufficient 'surplus' resources be squeezed from a desperately poor rural sector to build up infrastructure and manufacturing in the urban areas?

The Southeast Asian export economies all grew fairly rapidly until the onset of the Great Depression, which generally had a devastating effect on all of them when the world prices of rice, rubber, coffee, sugar, and other primary products all collapsed from 50 to 80 per cent, causing great distress to peasant cultivators, smallholders, and agricultural labourers (Elson 1992: 182–7). In Burma this led to the alienation of lands used as collateral for loans taken from the Chettiar moneylenders, leading to riots against urban Indian communities and the Saya San peasant rebellion. The 1930s consequently saw the upsurge of nationalism and demands for independence all over Southeast Asia. Thailand was also hit hard but its political independence enabled it to take more active measures to protect the rural sector than the mostly laissez-faire policies of the colonial regimes (Boomgard and Brown 2000).

The outbreak of the Second World War in the Asia-Pacific region saw Japan in full control of all the colonial parts of Southeast Asia from 1942 until her surrender to the Allied Forces in 1945. By a strange irony it was the Asian country that had turned imperialist itself that 'liberated' the other Asian countries from their colonial oppressors. After their humiliating defeats at the hands of the Japanese there was no way that colonial rule could successfully be restored, despite the futile efforts of the French in Vietnam. The British withdrawal from the Indian subcontinent was tragically accompanied by the calamity of the partition between India and Pakistan. The Southeast Asian former colonies saw hostilities between domestic factions divided along ideological and ethnic lines enduring in Burma to the present day. The fall of Japan brought independence to the Korean people for the first time since 1910 but saw them bitterly divided at the 38th Parallel into a North supported by the USSR and a South by the USA. In China, 1945 saw the end of hostilities with Japan but also the end of the anti-Japanese alliance between the Nationalists and Communists, with the former having to withdraw to Taiwan, leaving Mao Zedong and the Communists in charge of the mainland by 1949. The outbreak of the Korean War in 1950 ended only in 1953 after the entry of China (Spector 2008).

Reshaped by the 'MacArthur Shogunate', Japan launched a sustained drive for development and technological change, powered by manufactured exports of electronics and automobiles. The Japanese model was followed with dazzling success by the 'gang of four' of Korea, Taiwan, Hong Kong, and Singapore (Vogel 1991). Meanwhile China under Mao Zedong was undergoing the pangs of the Cultural Revolution until the situation was transformed by the pragmatic reforms of Deng Xiaoping.

Since then India, China, Korea, and Southeast Asia have all enjoyed sustained and even rapid economic growth, with China and India making vast strides in the eradication of poverty and going a long way to restore their ancient role of being the world's leading manufactured exporters. In terms of the epigraph to this chapter, the Asian 'drama thus conceived' has seen many tragic episodes but on the whole, as viewed in 2018, it certainly has been far from being a tragedy since 'history then is not taken to be predetermined but within the power of man to shape' as the pages of this chapter amply demonstrate.

7. Will this be the Asian Century?

In 1968 the answer to whether the twenty-first would be the 'Asian Century' almost certainly would have been clearly negative. When Myrdal said that the drama need not be 'necessarily tragedy' he was still clearly worried that it was a very real possibility. Today most people would consider the answer to be obviously 'yes'. At this point it would be useful to look back from our millennial perspective into the old question of the differences between Asia and Europe that occupied the greatest minds of Europe from Herodotus and Aristotle to Hegel, Marx, and Weber. Marx envisaged Europe as evolving from primitive communal life through the successive 'modes of production' of slavery, feudalism and capitalism. He specifically excluded Asia from this process, with the important exception of Japan that he unhesitatingly described as 'feudal' (see Marx 1967: vol. I, 718), an opinion confirmed by the complementary authority of Marc Bloch (1961: vol. II, 382) and J.W. Hall (1968: chapter 2).

India and China he designated as instances of an 'Asiatic Mode of Production', characterized by the total dominance of the ruler over the entire society due to the indispensable provision by the state of large-scale irrigation works. Society itself was merely a collection of self-sufficient villages paying tribute to the ruler, with a few cities serving as administrative centres or 'princely camps' rather than independently generating economic activity like the towns of medieval Europe. Here is a complete 'absence of private property in land' and hence no landed aristocracy or self-governing cities and thus no possibility of genuine feudalism. History is merely a succession of different empires changing as a result of internal decay or foreign conquest without any structural evolution. It is apparent, even from the very brief outline presented here, that this is a caricature of Asian history, and its applicability to Asia, or anywhere else for that matter, has been roundly rejected by Marxists and non-Marxists alike, but this brings up the question, plaintively asked by Byres (1985: 13): 'If not feudalism, or the Asiatic Mode, then what?'. Before attempting to provide an answer it will be useful to note that Max Weber also made an unsuccessful attempt to differentiate Europe and Asia on the basis that 'instrumental rationality' was present only in the former, while its absence in the latter made it impossible for the transformation of economy and society to be achieved autonomously.[11]

A very effective answer to the question posed by Byres, provided by John Haldon (1993), and a number of other Marxist writers, is the concept of a 'Tributary Mode of Production' that applies to the Indian and Chinese cases considered here, as well as to the contemporaneous Ottoman, Safavid, and Muscovite empires. The 'ideal type' of this construct is one in which the land is cultivated by peasants, who may be serfs as in the Russian case, but also free to move, as in the Indian and Chinese cases, but who are obliged to pay taxes assessed on the lands they cultivate, collected by local officials designated for that purpose, and then transmitted to a regional headquarters or the capital itself after deducting costs of collection and their own compensation. It is out of this 'surplus' that the ruler has to maintain himself, his court, army, and civil administration. While the bulk of the population will be rural, there will be towns where the officials assigned to the area would live together with merchants, artisans, and other providers of urban services. There

---

[11] See Nayyar (2016: 36–8).

will be markets not only for goods and services but for labour, land, and capital as well, with whatever degree of regulation the ruler deems appropriate. Trade and contact with foreigners would also exist to whatever extent the regime is prepared to permit.

The key tension in the tributary mode is the distribution of the tribute itself, the revenue collected from the peasant producers, between the local elites of landowners and officials on the one hand and the centre on the other. In the early stages of the familiar dynastic cycle, the founder comes to power with a victorious army with all the glory of a conquering hero, local authorities fear his power and transmit as much revenue to the centre as is expected of them. In the later stages the central authority starts to weaken, a smaller fraction of the revenue is transferred, weakening the centre still further until it is overthrown by an external invader or internal rebellions that lead to provinces or regions breaking away and forming independent states until a new unifier arises and starts the cycle all over again. The reader will clearly recognize this pattern repeating itself in the Indian and Chinese cases considered here.

As we have seen, there is no reason why societies operating under this mode of production cannot have thriving and prosperous economies. The frontiers of the empire could also be extended beyond existing borders through both conquest and settlement. The Song clearly had a higher level of development than any contemporary state in feudal Europe and the Mughal Empire at its height was wealthier than any individual state in Europe of its time, though perhaps not of the composite Habsburg Empire with its vast possessions in the New World. All of this raises the questions of why did not capitalism, or more specifically the 'Industrial Revolution', emerge endogenously in either Mughal India or China under the Song or any later dynasty, and why was there a 'Great Divergence' (Pomeranz 2000) between the living standards of Europe and Asia at least by the nineteenth century, if not even earlier.

The answer seems to be that despite the level of prosperity in the aggregate, the tributary states remained parasitic on their rural peasant sectors, precluding any agricultural revolution prior to, or accompanying, an industrial revolution as occurred in Britain. The urban sectors remained self-contained, catering to their elite clientele without any reciprocal interactions with the rural sector beyond the exploitative extraction of land revenue. Irfan Habib (1995: 231) puts this succinctly: 'it must be considered whether the entire commercial system of the Mughal Indian economy was not largely parasitical, depending upon a system of direct agricultural exploitation by a small ruling class'. He goes on to say that capital had tied its fortunes to the Mughal ruling class and failed to develop an independent existence. On China, another distinguished historian Ray Huang (1990: 94) says 'Given the constitutional differences between the Qing Empire and its contemporary nation states in Western Europe, it would have been impossible for the Chinese to follow the path of the latter'.

Joseph Needham (1969, 1981) posed the puzzle of why China failed to follow up on her brilliant early start in science and technology, falling behind the West by the seventeenth century when the Scientific Revolution occurred, failing to endogenously generate an Industrial Revolution. Lin (1995) provides an interesting answer to this 'Needham Puzzle' in terms of the fact that the best intellectual talent in China was channelled into passing the civil service examinations based on mastery of the Chinese classics rather than acquiring the mathematical and scientific knowledge necessary for science-based innovation such as occurred in Britain and Europe. The inventors of the steam engine, Thomas Newcomen and James Watt, were not highly trained scientists themselves but they benefitted greatly from contact with Fellows of the Royal Society with whom they were familiar.[12] The civil service examination itself, however, has to be seen as an integral part of a deeply conservative Confucian 'tributary' society, which could not have been easily replaced or even supplemented by an alternative 'ladder of success'.

We thus see that there was no pathway from the tributary mode to capitalism in either of our two Asian cases, just as there was none with the Ottomans, Safavids, and Romanovs. It was only 'feudal' Japan that was able to make the transition to capitalist modernity before the end of the nineteenth century. The Meiji Restoration accomplished this in the amazingly short period of a single generation. Successful merchants in China bought land and prepared their sons for the civil service examinations so that they could move into the sole prestigious class, that of the scholar-gentry. In Japan, the corresponding *chonin* mercantile group was excluded from entering the ruling *samurai* class and so developed their own independent bourgeois culture in the stimulating environment of the great cities of Tokyo and Osaka, while also building up the great commercial empires of the Matsui, Mitsubishi, and Sumitomo, ready to take full advantage of the vastly greater opportunities that opened up after 1868 (Hall 1970: 226–32).

The two outstanding cases of rapidly catching up to the British lead in the Industrial Revolution were Imperial Germany and Imperial Japan. In both cases, Britain suffered from what Veblen (1966) called the 'penalty of taking the lead' with the follower countries able to take advantage of the mistakes of the pioneer to quicken the pace of catching up. In the 'Opportunity of Japan', Veblen said 'It is this unique combination of feudal fealty and chivalric honor with the material efficiency given by the modern technology that the strength of the Japanese nation lies' (Veblen 1998: 251). The same idea was also advanced by Alexander Gerschenkron (1962) as the 'advantages of backwardness' and applied by his student Henry Rosovsky (1966) to Japan. Gerschenkron noted that as the locus of capitalism and industrialization moved eastward, from Britain to France, Germany and Russia, the state played an increasingly active role in forcing the

---

[12] See Allen (2017).

pace of the catching-up process. The case of Japan, with the Meiji state acting as a very aggressive 'venture capitalist', and also of Korea, Taiwan, and Singapore, only confirms this insight. It is now up to the rest of Asia to catch up with, and perhaps even overtake and surpass, the West.

References

Abu-Lughod, J.L. (1989). *Before European Hegemony.* Oxford: Oxford University Press.

Acton, Lord (1961). *Lectures on Modern History.* New York: Meridian Press.

Allen, R.C. (2017). *The Industrial Revolution.* Oxford: Oxford University Press.

Beasley, W.G. (1987). *Japanese Imperialism 1894–1945.* Oxford: Oxford University Press.

Bloch, M. (1961). *Feudal Society, Volumes I, II.* Chicago, IL: University of Chicago Press.

Boomgard, P., and I. Brown (2000). *Weathering the Storm.* Singapore: Institute of Southeast Asian Studies.

Bray, F. (2000). *Technology and Society in Ming China, 1368–1644.* Washington, DC: American Historical Association.

Byres, T.J. (1985). 'Modes of Production and Pre-Colonial Non-European Societies'. In T.J. Byres and H. Mukhia (eds) *Feudalism and Non-European Societies.* London: Frank Cass.

Chaudhuri, K.N. (1978). *The Trading World of Asia and the English East India Company 1660–1760.* Cambridge: Cambridge University Press.

Chaudhuri, K.N. (1982). 'European Trade with India'. In T. Raychaudhuri and I. Habib (eds) *Cambridge Economic History of India, Volume I.* Cambridge: Cambridge University Press.

Clements, J. (2005). *Coxinga and the Fall of the Ming Dynasty.* Stroud: Sutton Publishing.

Crossley, K. (1997). *The Manchus.* Oxford: Blackwell.

Digby, S. (1982). 'The Maritime Trade of India'. In T. Raychaudhuri and I. Habib (eds) *Cambridge Economic History of India, Volume I, c.1200–1750.* Cambridge: Cambridge University Press.

Digby, S., and I. Habib (1982). 'Northern India under the Sultanate'. In T. Raychaudhuri and I. Habib (eds) *Cambridge Economic History of India, Volume I, c.1200–1750.* Cambridge: Cambridge University Press.

Dreyer, E.L. (2007). *Zheng He.* New York: Pearson Longman.

Elson, R.L. (1992). 'International Commerce, the State and Society'. In N. Tarling (ed.) *Cambridge History of Southeast Asia, Volume III.* Cambridge: Cambridge University Press.

Elvin, M. (1973). *The Pattern of the Chinese Past*. Stanford, CA: Stanford University Press.

Fairbank, J.K. (ed.) (1968). *The Chinese World Order*. Cambridge, MA: Harvard University Press.

Findlay, R., and M. Lundahl (2017). *The Economics of the Frontier*. Basingstoke: Palgrave Macmillan.

Findlay, R., and K.H. O'Rourke (2007). *Power and Plenty*. Princeton, NJ: Princeton University Press.

Furnivall, J.S. (1948). *Colonial Policy and Practice*. Cambridge: Cambridge University Press.

Gerschenkron, A. (1962). *Economic Backwardness in Historical Perspective*. Cambridge, MA: Harvard University Press.

Habib, I. (1995). 'Potentialities of Capitalistic Development in the Economy of Mughal India'. In I. Habib (ed.) *Essays in Indian History*. New Delhi: Tulika.

Habib, M. (1974). 'The Urban Revolution in Northern India'. In *Politics and Society During the Early Medieval Period: Collected Works of Professor Muhammed Habib, Volume I* (pp. 59–80). New Delhi: Tulika.

Haldon, J. (1993). *The State and the Tributary Mode of Production*. London: Verso.

Hall, D.G.E. (1968). *A History of Southeast Asia*. London: Macmillan.

Hall, J.W. (1968). 'Feudalism'. In J.W. Hall and M.B. Jansen (eds) *Studies in the Institutional History of Early Modern Japan*. Princeton, NJ: University Press.

Hall, J.W. (1970). *Japan: From Prehistory to Modern Times*. New York: Dell.

Hartwell, R. (1966). 'Markets, Technology and the Structure of Enterprise in the Development of the Eleventh-century Chinese Iron and Steel Industry', *Journal of Economic History*, 26: 29–58.

Heston, A. (2005). 'National Income'. In D. Kumar (ed.) *Cambridge Economic History of India, Volume III, c.1757–2003*. Cambridge: Cambridge University Press.

Hirth, F., and W.W. Rockhill (1964). *Chau-Ju Kua*. Taipei: Literature House.

Hodgson, M.S. (1974). 'The Gunpowder Empires and Modern Times'. In *The Venture of Islam, Volume III*. Chicago, IL: University of Chicago Press.

Huang, R. (1990). *China: A Macro History*. New York: Sharpe.

Kang, D.C. (2010). *East Asia Before the West*. New York: Columbia University Press.

Keene, D. (1969). *The Japanese Discovery of Europe, 1720–1830*. Stanford, CA: Stanford University Press.

Kuhn, D. (2009). *The Age of Confucian Rule*. Cambridge, MA: Harvard University Press.

Lee, K.B. (1984). *A New History of Korea*. Cambridge, MA: Harvard University Press.

Lewis, W.A. (1978). *Growth and Fluctuations, 1870–1913*. London: George Allen & Unwin.

Lin, J.Y. (1995). 'The Needham Puzzle', *Economic Development and Cultural Change*, 43(2): 269–91.

Liu, X. (1988). *Ancient India and Ancient China*. New Delhi: Oxford University Press.

Lockwood, W.W. (1968). *The Economic Development of Japan*. Princeton, NJ: Princeton University Press.

Ma, L.J.C. (1971). *Commercial Development and Urban Change in Sung China, 960–1279*. Ann Arbor, MI: University of Michigan Press.

Macpherson, W.J. (1987). *The Economic Development of Japan, 1868–1941*. London: Macmillan.

Maddison, A. (2007). *Chinese Economic Performance in the Long Run, 960–2030 AD*. Paris: OECD.

Marshall, P.J. (1987). 'Bengal'. In *New Cambridge History of India, Volume II*. Cambridge: Cambridge University Press.

Marx, K. (1967). *Capital, Volume I*. New York: International Publishers.

McEvedy, C., and R. Jones (1978). *Atlas of World Population History*. London: Penguin Books.

Millward, J.A. (2013). *The Silk Road*. Oxford: Oxford University Press.

Moosvi, S. (1987). *The Economy of the Mughal Empire, c.1595*. New Delhi: Oxford University Press.

Mukhia, H. (2004). *The Mughals of India*. Oxford: Blackwell.

Myrdal, G. (1968). *Asian Drama: An Inquiry into the Poverty of Nations, Volumes I, II, and III*. New York: Pantheon Press.

Nakamura, K. (1997). 'Depression, Recovery and War, 1920–45'. In K. Yamamura (ed.) *The Economic Emergence of Modern Japan*. Cambridge: Cambridge University Press.

Naquin, S., and E.S. Rawski (1987). *Chinese Society in the Eighteenth Century*. New Haven, CT: Yale University Press.

Nayyar, D. (2016). *Catch Up*. Oxford: Oxford University Press.

Needham, J. (1954). *Science and Civilization in China, Volume I*. Cambridge: Cambridge University Press.

Needham, J. (1969). *The Grand Titration*. London: George Allen & Unwin.

Needham, J. (1981). *Science in Traditional China*. Cambridge, MA: Harvard University Press.

Newitt, M. (1980). 'Plunder and the Rewards of Office in the Portuguese Empire'. In M. Duffy (ed.) *The Military Revolution and the State 1500–1800*. Exeter: Exeter University Publications.

Panikkar, K.M. (1969). *Asia and Western Dominance*. London: Collier Books.

Perdue, P. (2005). *China Marches West*. Cambridge, MA: Harvard University Press.

Pomeranz, K. (2000). *The Great Divergence*. Princeton, NJ: Princeton University Press.

Reid, A. (1993). *Southeast Asia in the Age of Commerce 1450–1680, Volume II, Expansion and Crisis*. New Haven, CT: Yale University Press.

Richards, J.F. (1974). 'The Islamic Frontier in the East', *South Asia*, 4(1): 91–109.

Richards, J.F. (1993). *The Mughal Empire, New Cambridge History of India, Volume I*. Cambridge: Cambridge University Press.

Rosovsky, H. (1966). 'Japan's Transition to Modern Economic Growth, 1868–1885'. In H. Rosovsky (ed.) *Industrialization in Two Systems: Essays in Honor of Alexander Gerschenkron*. New York: Wiley.

Rossabi, M. (1988). *Khubilai Khan*. Berkeley and Los Angeles, CA: University of California Press.

Rossabi, M. (2014). *A History of China*. Oxford: Blackwell.

Rowe, W.T. (2009). *China's Last Empire*. Cambridge, MA: Harvard University Press.

Roy, T. (2012). *India in the World Economy*. Cambridge: Cambridge University Press.

Shiba, Y. (1970). *Commerce and Society in Sung China*. Ann Arbor, MI: University of Michigan.

Spector, R.H. (2008). *In the Ruins of Empire*. New York: Random House.

Spence, J.D. (1990). *The Search for Modern China*. New York: Norton.

Stein, B. (1998). *A History of India*. Oxford: Blackwell.

Streusand, D. (2011). *Islamic Gunpowder Empires*. Boulder, CO: Westview Press.

Subrahmanyam, S. (1993). *The Portuguese Empire in Asia 1500–1700*. New York: Longman.

Tan, C. (1974). 'The Britain-India-China Trade Triangle (1771–1840)', *Indian Economic and Social History Review*, 11: 411–31.

Thapar, R. (1990). *A History of India, Volume I*. London: Penguin Books.

Veblen, T. (1966). *Imperial Germany and the Industrial Revolution*. Ann Arbor, MI: University of Michigan Press.

Veblen, T. (1998). 'The Opportunity of Japan'. In *Essays in our Changing Order*. New Brunswick, NJ: Transaction Publishers.

Vogel, E.F. (1991). *The Four Little Dragons*. Cambridge, MA: Harvard University Press.

von Glahn, R. (2016). *The Economic History of China*. Cambridge: Cambridge University Press.

von Verschuer, C. (2006). *Across the Perilous Sea*. Ithaca, NY: East Asia Program, Cornell University.

Wheatley, P. (1959). 'Geographical Notes on Some Commodities Involved in Sung Maritime Trade', *Journal of the Malaysian Branch of the Royal Asiatic Society*, 32: 1–140.

Yamamura, K., and T. Kamiki (1983). 'Silver Mines and Sung Coins'. In J.F. Richards (ed.) *Precious Metals in the Later Medieval and Modern Worlds*. Durham, NC: Carolina Academic Press.

PART II

CROSS-COUNTRY
THEMATIC STUDIES

5

The State and Development

Peter Evans and Patrick Heller

1. Introduction

The 'developmental state' has been Asia's iconic contribution to global theories and empirics of the state over the course of the last half-century, providing both a framework for the comparative examination of Asian states and a global paradigm for how states can play a positive role in social and economic development. Late twentieth-century Asian cases challenged the mid-twentieth-century theoretical paradigm of the Anglo-Saxon 'minimalist' or 'night-watchman' state. The theories of the developmental state that emerged from the analysis of Asia, particularly Northeast Asia, provoked a sea change in global perspectives on the role of the state in development.

We begin our analysis with a review of classic perspectives on the late twentieth-century developmental state in Northeast Asia, followed by a discussion of the evolution of these states to become '21st century developmental states', facilitating the delivery of capability-enhancing collective goods. We then complement this literature by bringing in the case of China, the most important Asian case. The case of China is not only the single most important case for any analysis of the role of the state in the twenty-first century, but also requires new reflections on the political institutions that connect state and society.

Using this East Asian analysis as a foundation, we expand our comparative scope. First, we look briefly at the range of sub-regional outcomes in a selected set of Southeast Asian states: Singapore, Vietnam, the Philippines, and Indonesia. Comparative analysis of Southeast Asia both reinforces the lessons of East and Northeast Asia and makes it clear that Asian states can fail as well as succeed, with colonial histories and national socio-political dynamics undercutting the possibility of states being able to contribute to either development or democracy.

From there we turn to the perplexing case of India, which has enjoyed admirable formal institutions in terms of both a robust bureaucratic structure and systems of political representation that have been successful in uniting a highly pluralistic society, but suffers from both a highly uneven ability to translate local deliberation and mobilization into effective political representation and a disappointing performance at delivering increased well-being in comparison to both China and Northeast Asian. India's inability to build synergistic relations between the central state and local institutions, with results that some have characterized as a 'flailing state' (Pritchett 2009: 4) is particularly striking. Focusing on differences among different scales of governance forces us to argue that Myrdal's original diagnosis of the 'soft state' needs refinement and rethinking.

Recent political shifts have further complicated analysis of the Indian state. Alliances with global capital have transformed what was once comfortable alliance of a dirigiste Nehruvian state and protected local capital. The dominance of social democratic ideology has been replaced by a combination of neo-liberal economic ideology and Hindu nationalism. When these shifts are added to the mix, India's position as the most analytically challenging of the Asian states is reinforced.

To the extent to which it has been instantiated, the developmental state has been effective in Asia, both in its classic form as a strategy of industrial transformation and in its broader form as a strategy for supporting capability expansion. The Northeast Asian developmental state has enjoyed success in promoting societal well-being for over three decades. Yet, despite its apparent efficacy, the political robustness of the developmental state in the coming decades of the twenty-first century cannot be taken for granted.

Will the Asian state continue to be used as a paradigm for general theories of the state as it has been in recent decades? Or, will Asia become yet another instance of the decline of state institutions that has plagued other regions? Based on our analysis, there is unlikely to be a single answer to this question. Amalgamating Northeast Asia, China, the various states of Southeast Asia, and India into a single paradigm did not make sense in the twentieth century. It would be even more clearly a mistake in the twenty-first. The future of the Asian state will involve multiple, often contrasting, trajectories in the twenty-first century, just as it has in the fifty years since *Asian Drama*. The exciting transformations in the role of the state that were emerging in Northeast Asia at the time Myrdal was writing went largely unrecognized in the literature until decades later. We can only hope that contemporary analysis of the Asian state will prove less out of step with empirical realities than they were prior to Myrdal's work.

2. The Northeast Asian Developmental State: Origins and Transformation

Chalmers Johnson's (1982) analysis of Japanese development in the 1970s created the foundations for the model of the developmental state. But it was the small East Asian 'tigers'—Korea, Taiwan, and Singapore—that became the archetypal instantiations of the model (e.g., Amsden 1989; Wade 1990). The East Asian tigers managed to change their position in the world economic hierarchy, moving from 'underdeveloped' to 'developed' in the course of two generations. This kind of shift is unprecedented among twentieth-century developing countries and exceptional even in the broader historical context that includes the historical experience of Europe and the Americas.

To focus on the East Asian developmental states is to focus on the importance of the capacity of public bureaucracies. Nearly everyone agrees that when East Asian public bureaucracies are compared with those of developing countries in other developing countries, they more closely approximate the ideal typical Weberian bureaucracy. Meritocratic recruitment to public service and public service careers offering long-term rewards commensurate with comparable private sector jobs were institutional cornerstones of the East Asian economic miracle. Capable, internally coherent, state bureaucracies were crucial to providing predictability—both the foundational 'rule of law' sort and the more quotidian administrative and policy sort.

The next challenge was connecting the state to key actors in society. At the broadest level, East Asian governments managed to generate a sense of commitment to a collective project of national development. Despite political divisions and governmental missteps, this sense of a national project gained surprisingly widespread credence and constituted one of the most important 'collective goods' provided by the state. The essential complement to this broad ideological connection was a dense set of concrete interpersonal ties that enabled specific agencies and enterprises to construct joint projects at the sectoral level. The 'embeddedness' created by these dense ties is as central to the twentieth-century developmental state as bureaucratic capacity.

Embeddedness was never a tension-free symbiosis. Based on the prior performance of local business, state officials assumed that the private sector's 'natural' strategy was 'rent-seeking', a quest for officially sanctioned niches that would allow local firms to buy cheap and sell dear without having to brave entry into newer, more risky sectors. Therefore, the developmental state had to avoid being politically captured by its partners in order to keep private elites oriented toward national projects of accumulation rather than their own consumption. Maintaining dense ties to entrepreneurial elites, while avoiding capture and being able to discipline these elites, is a defining feature of East Asian development states, distinguishing them from less successful states in Asia and Africa (see Kohli 2004).

East Asian states' crucial ability to maintain autonomy from local industrial elites was not simply the fruit of bureaucratic competency and coherence. The revolutionary violence and chaotic geopolitics of mid-twentieth-century Northeast Asia had the developmentally propitious consequence of wiping out landed elites as politically effective class actors in national politics in East Asia after the Second World War. Local industrial elites were weak, both economically and politically, and transnational capital largely absent from domestic processes of accumulation. Consequently, it was possible to construct a form of embeddedness that facilitated national projects of transformation.

While the twentieth-century developmental states worked to avoid becoming instruments of furthering the particularistic interests of private elites, they did not devote the same effort to counterbalancing elite ties with connections to other social groups. On the contrary, civil society as a whole was excluded from the process of 'state–society synergy'. While private industrial elites were seen as key collaborators, other social groups were seen as peripheral if not threatening to this exclusive state–society partnership.

The basic vision of the twentieth-century developmental state remains compelling. A coherent, capable state apparatus is paired with dense ties to private entrepreneurial elites to produce forward-looking investments that enhance productivity, grow incomes, and lead to increased well-being. This narrative is certainly consistent with the 'institutional turn' in development theory, which emphasizes that functioning markets require a complex of underlying institutional arrangements in which the state is likely to be central (see Rodrik 2000; Evans 2004).

At the same time, the rise of the developmental state in Northeast Asia must be set in its historical and geopolitical context. Korea and Taiwan were miserably poor in the aftermath of colonial domination, the Second World War, and the Korean War and appeared to be institutionally bereft as well. But, they had less obvious key advantages that eventually proved telling. First, Northeast Asia had a thousand-year history of meritocratic state institutions to build on. Second, national projects of development were essential to the political survival of these regimes. Geopolitical uncertainties combined with tiny and unpromising markets meant that global capital found the small, poor countries of Northeast Asia less attractive than larger markets with apparently lower levels of political risk. Consequently, the success of local projects was more dependent on local capitalists, and on their collaboration with the state. Thus, the construction of the Northeast Asian developmental state made sense as the most plausible path to regime survival given where Northeast Asia was situated in the mid-twentieth-century global political economy.

The state capacities exhibited in Korea and Taiwan's successful industrial transformations have been well specified. The coherence and quality of the bureaucratic apparatus, combined with the ability to create dense ties to industrial elites, made it possible for political elites to construct a transformative economic response to their geopolitical vulnerabilities. The power and clarity of the story of the twentieth-century developmental state as an instrument of industrial transformation did, however, have an analytical downside. It created a temptation to overstate the degree to which the Northeast Asian developmental states were institutionally fixed. This, in turn, led to neglect of the transformations that were turning these states into twenty-first-century developmental states with a Senian (1999) agenda of 'capability expansion' (Evans 2010, 2014a, 2014b; Evans and Heller 2015).

By the late 1980s, it was already clear that these developmental states were pursuing an evolving set of political, economic, and social goals on their way to becoming twenty-first-century developmental states. The contribution of capability expansion to the economic success of the East Asian tigers, even in their twentieth-century incarnations, had always been a key feature, always acknowledged, but still not given the centrality it deserved. These states were pioneers in capability expansion, renowned for their levels of investment in human capital. They began their periods of accelerated economic growth with education levels that made them outliers for countries at their income levels, and they continued to invest in the expansion of education throughout the period of their rapid expansion.

If we refocus on these states in the last thirty years, the centrality of capability expansion to their development strategies becomes even more obvious. Over the course of the last thirty years, Korea and Taiwan stand out both for their ability to preserve low levels of inequality and for their continued improvements in terms of the basic indicators of capability expansion, education, and health (Siddiqi and Hertzman 2001). As both Korea and Taiwan moved towards democratization in the 1980s, they began a notable expansion of social protection.[1] The last quarter-century has been a period of socio-political transformation in Northeast Asia that looks, more than anything else, like an effort to construct a twenty-first-century East Asian version of post-Second World War Golden Age European social democracy.

The transformation of Northeast Asian states forced rethinking the meaning of the developmental state (Williams 2014), but the emergence of China as a developmental success story was an equally important stimulus for forcing new theoretical reflections. Adding discussion of China to debates on the origins, structure, and consequences of the developmental state makes these debates more intellectually challenging and productive and results in a more nuanced version of the embedded autonomy framework.

3. China: A Theoretical Challenge to the Analysis of the Asian State

Chalmers Johnson, writing at the beginning of the 1980s, cannot be blamed for leaving China out of his analysis. China was not then a star at industrial transformation. Yet, as the literature on the developmental state burgeoned in the 1990s, China's success at industrialization was clearly extraordinary. Why was China still left out? Probably because the developmental state was implicitly the

[1] See Wong (2004), Peng and Wong (2008), Dostal (2010), McGuire (2010), and Lee (2016).

'developmental *capitalist* state' and China was still seen as a socialist political economy, despite the growing importance of markets and private investment in its development. Nonetheless, leaving China out of the 1990s' developmental state debate was a mistake. Once China is brought into the discussion, its case helps us move towards a more sophisticated understanding of the concept of the developmental state.

Analysis of the long historical process of building the foundations of a coherent and cohesive state apparatus in China would have enriched the 1990s debate on the origins of state capacity. As Zhao's (2015) careful synthesis of the early formation of the organizational and ideological sinews of the Chinese state from the time of the Western Zhou Dynasty (1045 BCE) to the apogee of the Western Han dynasty (50 BCE) shows, Chinese rulers were devising ways to ensure the corporate coherence of the state apparatus long before serious efforts to create state apparatuses in Europe had begun. The most interesting facet of this process of building state capacity was its cultural/ideological dimension. China was too large and variegated for bureaucratic structures in themselves to achieve the scope and penetration necessary to control military and economic elites. The formulation and widespread diffusion of the Confucian–Legalist belief system provided the essential cultural complements. Requiring officials to assimilate and understand the Confucian–Legalist belief system constituted a particular kind of 'meritocratic recruitment'. Shared ideological fundamentals enabled a relatively small, thinly dispersed set of bureaucrats to formulate consistent policy and implement procedures across a domain that would have been otherwise uncontrollable.

The Chinese state has, of course, been implicated in development disasters, but it has also presided over remarkable, indeed globally unprecedented, developmental success. Its surprising degree of coherence in the contemporary period remains one of the prime conundrums to be solved by theorists of the state. The legacies of early cultural and organizational constructions are only part of the story. They must be reinforced by practices that build the contemporary infrastructural power of the state. Nonetheless, their foundational role needs to be acknowledged. There is no comparably compelling Chinese historical narrative regarding embeddedness. From the times of the emperors through most of the communist period, the historical absence of a national capitalist class with an industrial vocation was as much a signal feature of the Chinese political economy as its 'high stateness'.[2] It was only under Deng Xiaoping, that the post-Mao state began building a dense network of ties joining a private entrepreneurial elite together with state officials. The rise of private industrial capital in twenty-first-century China

---

[2] See Nettl's (1968) classic analysis of the concept of 'stateness' and its variations in the North Atlantic. It is interesting to note that Nettl focused on Anglo-Saxon 'low stateness' rather than 'soft' states as the problematic configuration.

could be seen as creating the basis for building the missing embeddedness dimension or as eroding the state's autonomy.

Visions of rising private power overwhelming the control of the state are probably exaggerated. The state's sway appears to remain strong. Zhu (2015: 15) concludes, after an extensive review of the literature, that 'business as a whole has not yet come anywhere close to successfully challenging state power, and government–business relations are still very much dominated by the former'. Yu (2014: 165) puts it even more bluntly, saying: 'The state sector remains the driving force behind economic development in China'.

The analysis of the relation between public and private power in China is further complicated by the fact that in China, unlike the small, compact Northeast Asian countries, public power is constructed around a complex multilevel combination of a national state apparatus interacting with regional, prefect, and county apparatuses (see Chen 2017). According to Zhu (2015: 1), 'Local governments take care of day-to-day business of China's development'. Focusing on any single level is likely to miss the full impact of embedded autonomy in China.

Current strategies in support of a shared project of industrial transformation appear to be articulated via multilevel embeddedness. Anecdotal evidence suggests that the state at various levels is involved in orchestrating a programme of industrial development following the classic developmental state path of encouraging investment in higher-value-added sectors that might otherwise be considered too risky by private investors. For example, Jonas Nahm's (2017a, 2017b) analysis of the role of the state in promoting the solar power industry suggests that a division of labour between national state policies and local implementation has been quite effective. In short, looking at China suggests that a multilevel analysis of embedded autonomy may produce a more sophisticated version of the embedded autonomy framework, one more suited, not just to China, but to larger countries more generally.

Even if China's strategy of industrial transformation continues to be successful, it may not be sufficient to deliver development defined as capability expansion in a twenty-first-century economy where industry is no longer the cornerstone of overall improvements in well-being (Hung 2016). As Drèze and Sen (2002) and Bardhan (2010) among many others have pointed out, the Chinese state was very effective at delivering capability-expanding collective goods as well as structural reforms such as land redistribution in the 1960 to 1980 period, prior to the rise of the market. The question is whether the new 'market-friendly' China will succeed in constructing a robust twenty-first-century version of the developmental state.

Comparison between China and Korea problematizes China's success in becoming a fully-fledged twenty-first-century developmental state (see Drèze and Sen 2002). Starting in the 1980s with levels of life expectancy comparable to China's, Korea ends up at the end of the first decade of the new millennium with levels comparable to the EU and higher than the US. Infant mortality trends provide another window on divergent ability to deliver capability expansion. In the period from 1960 to 1981, China's performance in terms of income growth was significantly inferior to Korea's, yet China outperformed Korea in terms of reductions in infant mortality. In contrast, in the period from 1990 to 1999 improvements in infant mortality collapsed in China, despite spectacular rates of income growth, while Korea's performance in terms of infant mortality accelerated, despite lower rates of economic growth.

In the final decades of the twentieth century, China looked like an example of the negative phase of Polanyi's double movement, the phase in which market forces overpower social protection.[3] Drèze and Sen (2013: 15) argue that the 'huge retreat from the principle of universal health care coverage' that accompanied the 'market reforms' of the 1980s and 1990s 'sharply reduced the progress of longevity in China'. In the early decades of the twenty-first century, however, they underscore the post-millennium return of 'capability-expanding investments' in the Chinese health care system. This early twenty-first-century upsurge may still be followed by another downturn, but regardless of what happens in the future, shifting trends over the course of the last thirty-five years in China do not mirror the clear connections between the evolution of political institutions and shifts in state strategy that characterize the Northeast Asian cases.

Unfortunately, we lack convincing, parsimonious models of China's distinctive forms of embeddedness. Obviously, the superimposition of administrative and party organization is key to structuring state–society relations, but acknowledging this is not the same as understanding the political dynamics at work.[4] Studies at the local level[5] reveal a complex set of dynamics that cannot be reduced to simple imposition by the bureaucratic apparatus of the state, but still reveal only minimal opportunities for bottom-up policy initiatives. In contrast, the politics of increased state involvement in capability expansion in Taiwan and Korea suggest a close connection between the rise of civil society organizations, the emergence of electoral competition, and increasing state receptiveness to a twenty-first-century developmental state agenda (see Peng and Wong 2008; McGuire 2010). Dostal (2010: 165), for example, pinpoints 'democratization and political mobilization' as the most significant factors in expanding social provision in both Korea and Taiwan (see also Wong 2004).

The Northeast Asian cases offer a clear argument that the ability to move to the twenty-first-century developmental state depends on the emergence of a more 'encompassing' form of embeddedness that includes democratization and political mobilization. China suggests that other kinds of political and organizational

---

[3] Wang (2004) exemplifies this position.
[4] One creative, if not fully convincing, effort to understand how party organization might complement administrative hierarchies is Rothstein's (2015) invocation of the model of 'cadre organization'.
[5] For example, Tsai (2007), Birney (2014), Friedman (2014), and Mattingly (2016).

mechanisms may be partial substitutes, even if they are not as efficacious. But, China does not refute the basic proposition that the developmental state as epitomized by Northeast Asian cases offers a credible route, not just to conventional growth but to capability expansion as well.

4. Southeast Asian Counterpoints

If Northeast Asia provided the raw material for what was to become a global template and China complicates the logic of the developmental state, Southeast Asia is the epitome of variation, demonstrating the range of variability that is possible within a single sub-region. We make no claim to be able to fully explore or even catalogue the variegation that might be considered under the rubric of 'Southeast Asia'. We will not venture into the dozen 'Pacific Island Countries'. Among the other eight Southeast Asian countries, we will focus only on a subset of four, hoping to use them to illustrate the range of variation among state structure and, more importantly, offer some clues as to the historical origins and socio-political consequences of that variation. To this end, Singapore, Vietnam, the Philippines, and Indonesia provide a challenging and provocative subset.

As a way of setting the stage for an examination of the range of variation among Southeast Asian states, it is worth noting the positioning of a slightly different set of four Southeast Asian states—Singapore, Malaysia, Thailand, and the Philippines—which were the subject of a quantitative analysis of differences in the quality of state bureaucracies done twenty years ago. These states, among thirty developing countries, were assessed on the dimension of 'Weberianness', which meant primarily assessing the degree to which their bureaucracies were characterized by meritocratic recruitment and predictable career ladders (see Evans and Rauch 1999: figure 1). The degree of 'Weberianess' is a significant feature of states, strongly associated with higher levels of economic growth. The four Southeast Asian states included covered the gamut of results. On one end was Singapore, which was the most Weberian of all the states considered, scoring slightly higher than the Northeast Asian cases (Korea and Taiwan). The Philippines was in the bottom half of the distribution. Malaysia and Thailand sat in between, with Malaysia closer to Singapore and Thailand closer to the Philippines. These results mirror and reinforce the assessments arrived at in qualitative comparative case studies and make the task of exploring the origins and correlates of differences in state structure all the more important.

Singapore is especially interesting in relation to the Northeast Asian developmental states. Two aspects of the comparison are notable. First, Singapore demonstrates that the possibility of the emergence of developmental states is not restricted to the very special geopolitical context of Northeast Asia. Singapore's colonial history bore little resemblance to that of Northeast Asia. Nor was the threat of being overrun militarily an overwhelming variable in the Singaporean regime's quest for survival. In addition, unlike the Northeast Asian cases, but like other cases in South and Southeast Asia, ethnic diversity is a key element in shaping politics. Singapore is therefore a useful case for thinking about the elements that create the conditions for the emergence of developmental states.

The second element that distinguishes Singapore from the Northeast Asian developmental states is that it continues to resist pressures for democratization. Elections are held but the opposition is never allowed to win. While both Korea and Taiwan have succeeded in creating political competition that involves the succession of different parties in power, Singapore has maintained a closely held single party dominance. This contrast makes it clear that the emergence of democratization in Korea and Taiwan cannot be attributed simply to the effects of achieving sufficiently high levels of material prosperity. At the same time, Singapore should serve as a brake on any optimistic readings of the effect of higher income levels on the prospects for democracy in China.[6]

What is perhaps most interesting about the comparison between Singapore (and Malaysia) on the one hand and Taiwan and Korea on the other is the puzzle that it creates for Dan Slater's paradigm of 'strong state democratization' (Slater 2012; Slater and Wong 2013). Slater's formulation is refreshing because it reverses the conventional causal arrow: strong states lead to democratization rather than democratization leading to weak states. Slater argues that Taiwan and Korea were able to allow real competition among political parties in part because of the strength of their state apparatuses. Since 'Korea and Taiwan possess a deeper source for enduring political stability—an inherited strong state' (Slater 2012: 26), political elites were able to make concessions to pressures from below, confident that political change would not derail their developmental success. 'Strong state democratization' is a plausible frame, but it immediately raises the question of why Singapore's elite have been unwilling to accept the same risk.

Vietnam offers a different kind of opportunity for continuing the dialogue with East and Northeast Asian cases, and is particularly interesting in relation to China. While Vietnam fiercely values its autonomy in relation to China, the structure of the Vietnamese state and state–society relations in Vietnam resemble Chinese patterns more than do those of any other Asian case. These similarities are obviously rooted in part in overlapping historical traditions.[7]

Dell et al. (2017) argue that Vietnam offers a fascinating bridge between Northeast Asian models of the state and Southeast Asian patterns of governance. In their view: 'Northern Vietnam (Dai Viet) was ruled by a strong, centralized

[6] Much of this analysis could also be applied to Malaysia. See Doner et al. (2005), Slater (2012), and Slater and Wong (2013). We have foregone introducing the Malaysia–Singapore comparison here in the interests of maintaining minimal levels of parsimony in the overall discussion.

[7] See Montes' (Chapter 20, this volume) reference to Myrdal's (p. 409) invocation of the relevance of East Asian state traditions to the case of Vietnam.

state in which the village was the fundamental administrative unit. Southern Vietnam was a peripheral tributary of the Khmer (Cambodian) Empire, which followed a patron–client model with more informal, personalized power relations and no village intermediation.' They then go on to argue that '... areas exposed to Dai Viet administrative institutions for a longer period prior to French colonization have experienced better economic outcomes over the past 150 years' (Dell et al. 2017).

As in the case of China, Vietnam presents an ambiguous picture of state–society relations. The bureaucratically organized and often repressive party-state dominates civil society. Yet, over decades of resistance to the French and their American successors, the party-state also depended on being able to elicit support from civil society, which suggests again a poorly understood kind of embeddedness. Studies of interactions between party and civil society at the local level find intriguing echoes of this legacy (see O'Rourke 2004). In recent decades, Vietnam has experienced developmental success reminiscent of China's. Having pulled itself out of a tragic history of colonialism and murderous US aggression, it turned its 'Dai Viet' legacies to the task of development with remarkable success. As Stallings and Kim (2017: 172) point out, having emerged from centuries of colonialism and decades of war imposed by Western imperialism, Vietnam enjoyed one of the highest growth rates in the world in the 1990s and 2000s. Stallings and Kim (2017: 174) also point out that Vietnam has had substantial success in the social area. Vietnam's Gini was essentially flat at a low level of 0.36 throughout the period with some small variation, and Vietnam has been extremely successful in lowering poverty, both rural and urban. In rural areas, poverty defined as the share of the population below the national poverty line, fell from 66 per cent in 1993 to 19 per cent in 2008. In urban areas, the figures were 25 and 3 per cent, respectively. Given the economic and political centrality of the state in Vietnam, these results must be attributed in part to the structure and relative efficacy of the state.

Vietnam reinforces yet again the value of strong state institutions for developmental success, including the sort of capability-enhancing success that is central to the twenty-first-century developmental state model. It also reinforces the ambiguous but potentially significant element of an embeddedness with civil society. Nonetheless, Vietnam remains another counter-example to the 'strong state democratization' thesis. China's trajectory is a likely predicator for Vietnam's future political economy with respect to embeddedness and democratic responsiveness. Like the leadership of the Chinese party-state, Vietnam's political leadership has shown little interest in allowing the growth of civil society organizations that might be the basis for democratic politics of the kind that have emerged in Northeast Asia.

Given the similarities in state strength and effectiveness that extend from Korea to Singapore, shifting focus to the Philippines is a startling contrast.

Centuries of Spanish and then American colonial rule appear to have entrenched a powerful, rent-seeking, clientelistic elite whose undermining grip on the state is almost impossible to shake, stifling the possibility of creating a developmentally effective state. The massive land reforms that reshaped the political foundations of the state in Korea and Taiwan were lacking. The Philippines' colonial legacies left it as a case in point for the negative effects of 'non-developmental' political monopoly. Despite powerful and repeated efforts to transform formally demo-cratic institutions into substantive instruments of popular aspirations, elites remain entrenched and development flounders (see Törnquist 2002; Cruz et al. 2017). The overall outcome is a different world from the one that the devel-opmental states, in both Northeast and Southeast Asia, have been able to deliver. Incomes are somewhat higher in the Philippines than in Vietnam, but life expect-ancy is substantially lower and poverty rates are higher.[8]

Indonesia has performed better than the Philippines (see Timmer 2004 and Chapter 17, this volume) but, like the Philippines, it has never had the benefit of the kind of fundamental agrarian reform that was so central to creating the foun-dations for the Northeast Asian developmental states. Despite massive revenues from natural resource exports, Indonesia has not managed to replicate the dyna-mism of the developmental state cases. Income levels are still higher than those in Vietnam but life expectancies are lower. The hopes of global technocrats that sup-porting authoritarian regimes would produce capitalist development, which would in turn lead to democratization, have been only partially realized. At the same time, the powerful 1998 thrust in the direction of more democratic control over the state has also had frustrating results. As in the Philippines, vibrant local efforts aimed at building a more responsive state apparatus have gained only limited traction in relation to the national state apparatus (see Törnquist 2002), though the current regime appears to be making a genuine effort at capability-expanding investments. It is hard to draw cogent analytical lessons from Indonesia's contradictory political economy, but the Indonesian case does serve as good preparation for the even more complex and contradictory case of India.

5. The Contradictory Configuration of the Indian State

The Indian state has been variously described as predatory (Bardhan 1983), semi-developmental (Evans 1995), soft (Myrdal 1968) and exclusionary (Heller and Mukhopadhyay 2015). No state in the global south has so defied clear categorization and prompted so much debate. The best possible generalization is

---

[8] The Philippines' developmental trajectory in the late twentieth century occupied what might be called a 'sour spot' with regard to growth and inequality—that is, high inequality combined with low growth. See Timmer (2004: table 1).

undoubtedly Kohli's: 'India is a well-functioning democracy that delivers a poor quality of government' (Kohli 2012: 225). Kohli's quip immediately draws attention to the central problematic of the Indian state. Unlike its East Asian counterpart, the Indian state in the post-independence period has been democratic, answerable, however imperfectly, to periodic electoral verdicts and to surprisingly robust constitutional powers. The Indian state has always, then, been accountable, if not responsive.

Framed in the developmental state literature, the Indian state appears as a paradox. In formal Weberian terms, it has a robust state machinery dominated by a high-status cadre of high-performing officials (the Indian Administrative Service) and a robust rational–legal governing framework. But in contrast to formal descriptions of the state's properties, most academic accounts of the Indian state paint a picture of a state that has been fully penetrated by particularistic interests and a democratic polity that has served elites more effectively than the people. These accounts of the captured state, more predatory than developmental, take two general forms: Marxist accounts that point to state capture by dominant proprietary groups (Bardhan 1983) or modernization accounts along the lines of Myrdal's 'soft state', a state that fails to impose its institutional rationality over traditional social or individual loyalties.[9]

Even though the Indian state has fallen far short of its East Asian counterpart by any metric, the mid-twentieth-century Nehruvian state saw itself as a developmental state, heavily influenced by the institutionalist perspective (Myrdal) that rejected laissez-faire doctrine in favour of state intervention and planning. The Indian case was, moreover, heavily inflected with a high-modernist vision that vested enormous faith in the central state, technical expertise, and the 'steel frame' of the Indian bureaucracy. This faith was so pronounced that Nehru could confidently emphasize state-led growth over equity-promotion. Investments were accordingly focused on building core industries through state-owned enterprises, infrastructural projects geared to accumulation, and an emphasis on higher education. These investments, and especially the focus on higher education, in part set the stage for the post-1991 take-off, but initially produced low levels of growth (the infamous 'Hindu rate of growth') and very little export dynamism.

The Nehruvian developmental state was much more dirigiste than the East Asian developmental state. The licence-quota-raj, as it became derisively known, micro-managed the economy through both indicative planning and tight regulation of product markets. There was little, if any of the dynamic partnerships with the private sector that characterized the East Asian developmental state.

---

[9] Not coincidentally, the solution invariably takes the form of pleas for 'good governance', precisely what the multilaterals and their armies of consultants (academic and beltway) have to offer. But 'institutional monocropping' (Evans 2004) has never worked and never will because it abstracts from the specific political and institutional conditions under which governance, which is after all a relation of power, takes shape.

State-dominated sectors and the state-protected private monopolies suffered from low levels of productivity and little if any product innovation. Consequently, India missed out on the phase of low-value-added export industrialization that propelled the East Asian states into global markets. Its current growth trajectory began in the 1980s and has been maintained at an impressive rate over the past quarter-century. But the take-off of the much-celebrated Indian tiger has not been as deep, as dynamic, or as inclusive as in East Asia, and much of this can be attributed to failures of the state.

Any positive assessments of the Indian state's performance based on recent high aggregate growth rates must be qualified in at least three respects. First, overall growth rates obscure the regional concentration of growth and the fact that growth has been concentrated in mega-cities. There have been few of the deep backward linkages to rural areas that characterized China's take-off. Agriculture, which still provides the majority of Indians with their livelihoods, has more or less stagnated. Manufacturing growth has been concentrated in a few sectors with little of the widespread diversification and deepening of export sectors witnessed in East Asia. Second, much of the growth has been in rent-thick sectors including land and resource extraction (Heller et al. 2019) rather than in sectors where growth is driven by rising productivity. Third, India's economic growth has been relatively jobless growth, with most of the dynamic sectors concentrated in either capital-intensive manufacturing or high-end IT and business services that only employ highly educated labour. If anything, the divide between the labour-squeezing informal sector and the high-wage, high-productivity formal sector has grown since liberalization, contributing dramatically to India's increasing income inequality. Historically, the Gini coefficient for India has been comparatively low, but it has now reached historically high levels. Using new data sources pioneered by Piketty and Saez, the World Bank reports that in 2016 the share of national income accruing to India's top 1 per cent of earners was 22 per cent, while the share of the top 10 per cent was around 56 per cent, well above China's 41 per cent (World Bank 2018a: 5). The failure to steer the economy into a more dynamic and deeper pattern of economic transformation is also reflected in the social development sector. If the Indian state's performance as a developmental state fails to match Northeast Asian parameters for the classic developmental state, it is equally lacking with respect to the parameters of the twenty-first-century capability-enhancing developmental state.

The Nehruvian state's comparative neglect of social development was well documented. Other than a half-hearted attempt at rural reform through the community development programme, there were few concerted efforts—as Myrdal noted in *Asian Drama*—to invest in social development and rural infrastructure and to implement basic institutional reforms. By the 1980s, India had fallen well behind East Asia in terms of all basic human development indicators. But even more alarming is how little of the growth dividend of the past quarter-century has failed to translate into social development. Indeed, Drèze and Sen (2013) have documented how India has fallen behind both Pakistan and Bangladesh in the past decade, despite having a much more impressive level of growth.

Shortfalls in public investment continue to be a drag on the Indian economy, especially in terms of human capital formation. A range of indicators leave little doubt as to the disconnect between current output growth and capability expansion. For example, despite very significant increases in educational spending and a now near-universal rate of primary school enrolment, teacher absenteeism remains chronic, caste discrimination rampant, and school failure endemic (Ramachandran 2009). The most recent comprehensive national evaluation concluded that by the end of the fifth year of education, more than half of school children have yet to acquire a second-year level of reading (Assessment Survey Evaluation Research Centre 2018). Even as the upper caste/classes of India reap the rewards of the global knowledge economy, World Bank data (World Bank 2018b: 5) show that India continues to be beset by levels of inequality of educational opportunity that surpass almost all Latin American countries and even some African countries. Even more striking is the complete failure to deliver the most basic of capabilities—food and health. A recent assessment found that in 2006, 48 per cent of children under the age of five suffered from stunting (the highest level of malnutrition in the world), a condition that has severe long-term health consequences (Government of India 2009). Annual reports from the National Nutrition Monitoring Bureau actually show a decline in the consumption of calories over the past two decades.

How does one explain the comparative failures of the Indian state? In keeping with the development state literature, we point to the twin analytical variables of autonomy and embeddedness, but with a twist. Autonomy and embeddedness are dynamic only when they are balanced in what is a very delicate equilibrium: co-production (embeddedness) between state and social actors has to be secured without compromising the autonomy of the state to shield itself from particularistic demands and deliver public or social goods. In contrast to the modal East Asian pattern, state formation in India has been less continuous, passing through multiple institutional and territorial configurations. Independent India inherited a mosaic of sovereignties (the 565 princely states) and a myriad of regimes of indirect government bequeathed by layers of Hindu and Moghul empires and multiple British regimes of colonialism.

Continuous stateness provides clear advantages (as per the East Asia argument made above), but lack of historical continuity is not necessarily disqualifying for constructing effective developmental states. Germany and Italy were relative latecomers to European nation building but grew rapidly, and Costa Rica and

Mauritius, the high performers in their respective continents, are both relatively new states (see Sandbrook et al. 2007). But most importantly, within India, as the discussion to follow will indicate, there are sharp differences between states, suggesting that a strict path-dependent view of state formation is not warranted.

Since India is the only continuous post-Second World War democracy in Asia there is a temptation to attribute the problems of the Indian state to its 'prematurely' democratic political foundations. But the premature democratization thesis—which has quite a bit of currency in India—suffers from two glaring flaws. First, recent work on development has reversed the growth–redistribution sequence by making the case that it is investment in social development that drives economic growth and not vice versa (Evans et al. 2017).[10] The capabilities-enhancement path to development popularized by Sen brings us back full circle to Myrdal who dedicated an entire volume of *Asian Drama* to human capital.

Second, the assumption that democracy itself unleashes redistributive demands that undermine growth is clearly false, at least in the Indian case. Six decades of democracy have not produced a welfare state, effective labour market regulation, land reform, or progressive taxation. Indeed, fully 91 per cent of the labour force is mired in the informal sector, wholly lacking in any of the most basic legal and social protections. This is precisely one of the most important institutional hindrances to development that Myrdal identified. The problem, then, is not that there has been too much democracy but that there has not been enough. The problem of democratic deepening is, in turn, inextricably tied to the problem of both the autonomy and embeddedness of the state. Democracy matters for governing large complex societies such as India for two reasons. First, democracy by definition protects and manages pluralism, creating the political underpinnings of recognition in heterogeneous and diverse societies. Second, democracy can, though it does not always, favour encompassing demand making. These two dynamics—recognition and redistribution—are often in tension, and this is where Indian democracy has both succeeded and fallen short.

In the immediate post-independence period, India's first priority was nation building. Having inherited the most diverse and pluralistic society in the world, one that was fragmented into a multiplicity of governance regimes and marked by centrifugal regional forces, and having just lived through a tragic and traumatic partition, India's post-independence leaders were by necessity squarely focused on nation building. In this respect Indian democracy has been a spectacular success, at least until recently. Religious, caste, linguistic, and regional minorities have all developed a stake in the polity precisely because it was democratic. All groups have achieved a modicum of recognition and dignity, even if in some states the process has taken longer than in others. For better or worse,

---

[10]   See also Ranis and Stewart (2006) and Ranis et al. (2000).

India remains the only major nation in Asia, other than Thailand, not to have undergone a violent transition (revolution or war). What had been in fact a multiplicity of nations at the time of Independence has been integrated into a single polity and economy, quite possibly the greatest nation-building effort in human history.

The downside here is that the accommodation of this multiplicity of interests and identities has come, with notable subnational exceptions—at the expense of forging more encompassing interests and interventions. Thus, rather than pursuing broad-based policies and reforms that could secure social and public goods and generally enhance capabilities, the electoral logic of first-past-the-post has prioritized symbolic politics and group patronage. The need to build majoritarian coalitions based on highly complex and localized aggregations of caste and community has resulted in the complete instrumentalization of policies. As Chandra (2007) has wryly noted, Indian elections amount to 'an auction of public assets to the highest bidder'. The autonomy of the state has, in other words, been thoroughly compromised by the political logic of short-term electoral gains in a highly divided and fragmented polity. The institutional boundaries that are meant to separate the roles of representation and bureaucratic implementation, that is, of politics and the state, have been completely blurred. In the absence of autonomy, some commentators have described the Indian state as a form of 'embedded particularism' (Herring 1999).

Attributing the limits of the Indian developmental state to patronage democracy, however, has to be carefully qualified, historicized, and contextualized. First, this is not a story of institutional collapse as in the case of patrimonial or failed states. There are many elements of the Indian state that remain institutionally robust, not least of which are its military and various islands of bureaucratic efficiency (the higher levels of the judiciary, the electoral commission, the Reserve Bank of India, and the armed services). The limits of state autonomy are first and foremost political and emerge from specific state–society relations. Kohli (2004), for example, has carefully documented the historical process of de-institutionalization of Indian politics. Because the Congress Party never developed a mass base it was highly dependent on state-level intermediaries and opportunistic electoral coalitions. This ultimately compromised its capacity to push through the hard reforms—most notably land reform—that development required and made the party increasingly dependent on a heterogeneous coalition of various elite groups competing for scarce state resources.

Second, the problem of stateness in India looks very different depending on what level of the state is under scrutiny. The commanding heights of the Indian state enjoy significant capacity and some autonomy from particularistic interests, particularly in the realm of macro-economic policy. Yet, as one moves downward from the centre through the subnational state and into local government, state capacity deteriorates the more the state directly engages with society. The deterioration is so pronounced that the local state (the municipality and the village panchayat)—with notable exceptions—has almost no developmental capacity.[11]

The ineffectiveness of the Indian state at the local level has earned the Indian state the evocative label of a 'flailing' state, that is one in which the head (national and some state institutions) is highly competent and knows what it is doing, but 'that this head is no longer reliably connected via nerves and sinews to its own limbs' (Pritchett 2009: 4). Indian democracy in other words remains a highly centralized one, and this itself is a specific artefact of the nation-building project. In order to hold the nation together, Nehru devolved significant power to states, which, in turn, developed their own political interests and hoarded power at the state level. Municipalities and village governments (panchayats) have never really developed as a third tier of government. The most important developmental functions at the local level—including land management, planning, housing, basic services, education, health, and policing—are controlled by state-level line departments.

It is tempting, as Myrdal did, to simply argue that the Indian state is 'soft'. Compared to the Chinese state, the Indian state has not penetrated as deeply into society and does not exert as much control over local social forces. But this chain of command problem is less an organizational problem than a political problem. The problem lies more in the chain of *sovereignty* than in the chain of *command* and specifically the limited capacity of democratic citizens to exert binding control over the state. The comparatively top-down and politically instrumentalized manner in which state authority has been constructed has favoured transactional logics of authority over more normatively grounded forms of state legitimacy. In sharp contrast with Tsai's (2007) influential argument that the local rural Chinese state actually enjoys a high degree of embedded legitimacy, the literature on the local state in India paints a relatively unambiguous picture of elite capture.

Given how poorly and selectively the Indian state is actually embedded in society, its developmental limits then become clear. The Indian state is indeed a flailing state: it has few sensors, no effective feedback mechanisms, and no co-producers. It can deliver on macro-economic policy and some mega projects, but it cannot get teachers to teach, nurses to show up, municipalities to make their budgets transparent, or create the kind of stable local institutional environment in which private actors can thrive.

The credibility of this argument is strongly reinforced by the existence of subnational states that have demonstrated a marked capacity for enhancing capabilities, most notably Kerala (Heller 2000) and to a lesser extent Tamil Nadu

---

[11] By 2012, only 19.6 per cent of households in rural India had full basic services (in-house water, toilet, electricity) (Mishra and Shukla 2015: 10). But the variance is enormous across states, from 69.5 per cent in Kerala to 30.7 per cent in Gujarat and 20.4 per cent in Maharashtra, India's most industrialized states.

and Himachel Pradesh. Though all three states share roughly the same resources, institutional forms, and bureaucratic structures of other states, on a wide number of indicators all three are much better governed than other states. Successes at the state and local level are tied, in turn, to patterns of social mobilization. The dramatic progress in social development in the southern states of Kerala and Tamil Nadu can be tied directly to their historical patterns of social mobilization. Broad-based anti-caste movements produced enduring encompassing political formations that not only strengthened the demand-side dynamic of civil society, but also created more competitive, redistributive party politics (Heller 2000; Harriss 2003). This not only secured a greater degree of autonomy for the bureaucracy, but also created far more continuous and effective forms of accountability.

Just as variations across state jurisdictions qualify judgements of the incapacity of Indian state institutions in important ways, developments at the national level in the waning years of the Congress Party domination suggest that significant exceptions to the state's inability to foster transformation are possible. During the two Congress Party-led governments that preceded the current BJP (Bharatiya Janata Party) government, the state adopted more ambitious pro-social development legislation and reforms than in the entire post-independence period. These included legislative projects to universalize education, provide food security, subject the government to greater accountability (the Right to Information), and maybe most significantly guarantee a minimum level of employment to the rural poor (National Rural Employment Guarantee Act—NREGA). It is important to note that these reforms were, in large part, driven by civil society actors. Indeed, it was an alliance between the president of the Congress Party and influential civil society actors that produced the legislation and got it through parliament. This suggests that even when patronage democracy remains well entrenched, other forms of embeddedness can strengthen the state's developmental capacity.

Sadly, the recent re-alignment of Indian political institutions threatens to undercut the momentum of India's exciting experiments in capability expansion. The atrophy of the political foundations of the Nehruvian state, combined with disillusionment created by jobless growth and ineffectual delivery of basic collective goods, lent charisma to a regime that combined the putative economic returns of the 'modern' mystique of neo-liberal capitalism with the traditional identity rewards of Hindu nationalism. The new majoritarianism of upper caste Hindus reinforces traditional exclusions of caste and community and the Modi regime has shown itself to be openly hostile to civil society. The apparent political success of this regime raises the ominous possibility that just as Northeast Asian provided a model of economic efficacy in the decades following *Asian Drama*, South Asia may be offering a new template for the state, combining capture by private capital with political legitimacy based on recognition politics aimed at the majority. If this 'pro-capital populism' proves to be a politically robust model, it will constitute a threatening alternative to the twenty-first-century developmental state.

6. What Lessons from the Transformations of the Asian State?

Over the course of the latter half of the twentieth century, Asia has emerged as the region of the globe that constitutes the most important laboratory for understanding the roots of state effectiveness and the consequences of different modes of state action for delivering enhanced well-being and effective representation of shared societal goals. This role was not anticipated by the main currents of mid-twentieth-century social science research. Mid-twentieth-century social science was still focused on debates between planning and markets. Neo-liberal market worship dominated debate in the later part of the century. Both missed the fact that a new paradigm for state effectiveness—the developmental state—was being incubated in Northeast Asia. By the early twenty-first century times had changed. The centrality of Asian cases to any general theoretical analysis of the state was recognized. Even then continued fascination with the increased output of tangible goods distracted attention from the accomplishments of twenty-first-century developmental states in facilitating the provision of capability-expanding services that enhanced well-being and human flourishing. Can we do better as we look to the future?

Recognition of centrality of the Asian experience does not make it easier to derive clear lessons from the variegated transformations of the Asian state over the period since Myrdal's classic analysis. The lessons of the Asian state are a complex composite created by a mélange of individual national trajectories. We would, nonetheless, like to propose some potential 'lessons'. These are not proven propositions. Some have more evidence behind them than others. But, as the fruits of synoptic reflections on past trajectories, they are hopefully useful starting points for thinking about future transformations.

The most fundamental point to be made is that Asia in the late twentieth and early twenty-first centuries has validated the idea that capable, coherent state bureaucracies are a valuable social asset worth protecting and nurturing. Despite being partially undermined by the encroachments of global capital in Northeast Asia, the original developmental states have continued to perform well. They have managed to incorporate the capability-expanding developmental agenda of the twenty-first-century developmental state into their societal agendas. In addition, they have managed to move from authoritarian politics to competitive democratic politics.

China, Vietnam, and Singapore extend the vindication of the value of state capacity and coherence to East and Southeast Asia, including the idea that such states have been foundational to development in the broader sense of well-being and human flourishing, as well as facilitating industrial growth and rising incomes. At the same time, the range of political configurations that connect these states and their societies cannot be simply summarized. 'Strong state democratization' may be a plausible description for the original Northeast Asia developmental states, but China, Vietnam, and Singapore show that there is no inexorable connection between state capacity and transitions to democratic politics. They leave us with a conundrum: what are the institutional mechanisms that enable these states to remain responsive to social demands in the absence of conventional electoral mechanisms of democratic accountability?

We have suggested that the earlier consolidation of stateness and periods of mass mobilization can, at least in the cases of Vietnam and China, account for a certain degree of general embeddedness of the state in society (if not an independent civil society). This has made these states responsive, if not accountable. We certainly need much more research to identify the specific mechanisms that enable bureaucratically competent states to maintain awareness of demands from below and respond to them, but there is little support for the idea that less powerful state apparatuses facilitate the successful implementation of democratic agendas that reflect popular agendas and aspirations. For example, the clientelistic morass of the Philippine state may have allowed admirable mobilizational upsurges, but none have been able to turn the state into an instrument of their aspirations.

Asian states also contradict another piece of conventional wisdom: the idea that authoritarian state structures produce 'modernizing' economic results which then translate into robust democratic accountability. Reading Myrdal, one might be tempted to conclude that 'soft states' are insufficiently authoritative, prone to an undisciplined sort of democracy. Looking at the Philippines and Indonesia, it is clear that these states are not 'soft' in being excessively responsive to pressures from below; they are 'soft' in relation to privilege from above, unable to resist serving the interests of long-entrenched elites.

Finally, of course, there is India, which is in some ways the richest and most provocative of the Asian cases. The Indian case underscores two central claims of the developmental state literature while raising an additional set of challenges to explaining developmental outcomes. On the one hand, India reinforces the importance of nurturing a coherent Weberian bureaucracy. The rule of law and bureaucratic organization of state authority have secured stability, protected pluralism, and, in the post-liberalization period, have helped create the conditions for sustained growth. At the same time, India is another illustration of the confounding complexities of embeddedness (Veeraraghavan 2017).

The Indian state's embeddedness in society has been doubly compromised. First, in the absence of more genuine decentralization, the efficacy of the state remains highly constrained at the local level. Second, the fragmented nature of representation in the Indian polity has favoured particularistic over more encompassing interests, weakening the bureaucratic autonomy of the state. More than anything else, the limits of embeddedness explain India's dismal performance in social development and its current trajectory of growth without inclusion.

But India also forces introspection. Development academics, multilaterals, and state elites have long harboured explicitly or implicitly the high-modernist fantasy that they have the right tools and policies to get the job done as long as popular demands and pressures can be postponed or kept at bay. It is telling that the current enthusiasm for the elixir of 'good governance' is sanitized of any attention to politics and so allergic to populism.[12]

The first generation of East Asian developmental states and more recently China provide superficial support for this position, until one takes into account the unique histories of these countries, including long histories of state formation and the inevitably violent ruptures (war, revolution, mass famines) that set the stage for the developmental state. This is not a path that India can follow. India demonstrates that 'premature' democracy was not an impediment to development, but was in fact essential to the project of nation building. Variation across Indian states, moreover, shows that where democratic institutions and practices have sunk deeper roots, largely as a result of social mobilization, development has been far more inclusive. India's internal variations show that democratic politics can effectively 'embed the state' and counter its 'flailing' character. This said, the Indian case overall is a sobering reminder that, even fifty years after *Asian Drama*, we have only a limited understanding of how to build and use state apparatuses.

If complex variation defeats efforts at succinct synopsis of the political economy of the Asian state, predicting the trajectories of Asian states over the course of the next twenty-five years would be an even more precarious venture. The analysis of national dynamics, which we have focused on here, is challenging enough, but projecting the future transformations of Asian states requires meshing national dynamics with the evolution of the global political economy, a task that we have prudently avoided. The rise of the Northeast Asian developmental state depended on its ability to engage with global markets without being overrun by the corrosive effects of global neo-liberal capitalism. There is no guarantee that this same ability can be preserved in the coming decades, in Northeast Asia or elsewhere in Asia. At the same time, the global rise of reactionary nationalist populism has already had effects in Asia (for example, in India and the Philippines). This ideological wave could easily undermine the possibility of shifts in the direction of the twenty-first-century developmental state, turning political energies instead towards the exclusion and demonization of the minority 'other'. In short, Asian states must not only deal with internal obstacles and challenges over the course of the next twenty-five years, they must also confront the Scylla and Charybdis of the twenty-first-century global political economy.

The developmental value of competent, coherent state apparatuses remains undeniable. The ability to preserve such states, and create them where they do not

---

[12] Rodrik's (2016) recent work being a notable exception.

yet exist, will be a prime determinant of Asia's future path. At the same time, the quest continues to find ways of replacing control by elites whose narrow short-term interests drown society's developmental agendas, and building institutions that will secure effective delivery of collective goods and enable societies to establish priorities through democratic deliberation. The institutions of democratic accountability remain precarious where they exist and elusive where they have not yet been established. Any teleological vision of the future transformation of the Asian state process must be abandoned in favour of a clear-eyed investigation of political possibilities constrained by historically entrenched circumstances.

References

Amsden, A. (1989). *Asia's Next Giant: South Korea and Late Industrialization*. New York: Oxford University Press.

Assessment Survey Evaluation Research Centre (ASERC) (2018). *Annual Status of Education Report*. New Delhi: ASERC.

Bardhan, P.K. (1983). *The Political Economy of Development in India*. Oxford: Oxford University Press.

Bardhan, P.K. (2010). *Awakening Giants, Feet of Clay: Assessing the Economic Rise of China and India*. Princeton, NJ: Princeton University Press.

Birney, M. (2014). 'Decentralization and Veiled Corruption Under China's "Rule of Mandates"', *World Development*, 53: 55–67.

Chandra, K. (2007). *Why Ethnic Parties Succeed: Patronage and Ethnic Head Counts in India*. New York: Cambridge University Press.

Chen, L. (2017). *Manipulating Globalization: The Influence of Bureaucrats on Business in China*. Stanford, CA: Stanford University Press.

Cruz, C., J. Labonne, and P. Querubin (2017). 'Politician Family Networks and Electoral Outcomes: Evidence from the Philippines', *American Economic Review*, 107(10): 3006–37.

Dell, M., N. Lane, and P. Querubin (2017). 'The Historical State, Local Collective Action and Economic Development in Vietnam', presented at Harvard Conference on Comparative State Capacity, 20 to 21 October.

Doner, R.F., B.K. Ritchie, and D. Slater (2005). 'Systemic Vulnerability and the Origins of Developmental States: Northeast and Southeast Asia in Comparative Perspective', *International Organization*, 59(2): 327–61.

Dostal, J.M. (2010). 'The Developmental Welfare State and Social Policy: Shifting from Basic to Universal Social Protection', *The Korean Journal of Policy Studies*, 25(3): 147–72.

Drèze, J., and A. Sen (2002). *India: Development and Participation*. New Delhi: Oxford University Press.

Drèze, J., and A. Sen (2013). *An Uncertain Glory: India and its Contradictions*. London: Allen Lane.

Evans, P. (1995). *Embedded Autonomy: States and Industrial Transformation*. Princeton, NJ: Princeton University Press.

Evans, P. (2004). 'Development as Institutional Change: The Pitfalls of Monocropping and Potentials of Deliberation', *Studies in Comparative International Development*, 38(4): 30–53.

Evans, P. (2010). 'The Challenge of 21st Century Development: Building Capability Enhancing States', Global Event Working Paper for the United Nations Development Program 2010 'Capacity *is* Development', UNDP, New York.

Evans, P. (2014a). 'The Developmental State: Divergent Responses to Modern Economic Theory and the 21st Century Economy'. In M. Williams (ed.) *The End of the Developmental State?* New York: Routledge.

Evans, P. (2014b). 'The Korean Experience and the 21st Century Transition to a Capability Enhancing Developmental State'. In I. Yi and T. Mkandawire (eds) *Learning from the South Korean Developmental Success: Effective Developmental Cooperation and Synergistic Institutions and Policies*. Basingstoke: Palgrave Macmillan.

Evans, P., and P. Heller. (2015). 'Human Development, State Transformation and the Politics of the Developmental State'. In S. Leibfried, F. Nullmeier, E. Huber, M. Lange, J. Levy, and J.D. Stephens (eds) *The Oxford Handbook of Transformations of the State*. Oxford: Oxford University Press.

Evans, P., and J.E. Rauch (1999). 'Bureaucracy and Growth: A Cross-National Analysis of the Effects of "Weberian" State Structures on Economic Growth', *American Sociological Review*, 64(4): 748–65.

Evans, P., E. Huber, and J. Stephens (2017). 'The Political Foundations of State Effectiveness'. In M. Centeno, A. Kohli, and D. Yashar (eds) *States in the Developing World*. Cambridge: Cambridge University Press.

Friedman, E. (2014). *Insurgency Trap: Labor Politics in Postsocialist China*. Ithaca, NY: Cornell University Press.

Government of India (2009). *National Family Health Survey, 2005–2006*. New Delhi: Ministry of Wealth and Family Welfare.

Harriss, J. (2003). 'Do Political Regimes Matter?'. In P. Houtzager and M. Moore (eds) *Changing Paths: International Development and the New Politics of Inclusion*. Ann Arbor, MI: University of Michigan Press.

Heller, P. (2000). 'Degrees of Democracy: Some Comparative Lessons from India', *World Politics*, 52(4): 484–519.

Heller, P., and P. Mukhopadhyay (2015). 'State-produced Inequality in an Indian City', *Seminar*, 672: 51–5.

Heller, P., P. Mukhopadhyay, and M. Walton (2019). 'Cabal City: India's Urban Regimes and Accumulation without Development'. In K. Murali, A. Kohli, and C. Jaffrelot (eds) *Business and Politics in India*. London: Oxford University Press.

Herring, R. (1999). 'Embedded Particularism: India's Failed Developmental State'. In M. Woo-Cumings (ed.) *The Developmental State*. Ithaca, NY: Cornell University Press.

Hung, H.-F. (2016). *The China Boom: Why China Will Not Rule the World*. New York: Columbia University Press.

Johnson, C. (1982). *MITI and the Japanese Miracle: The Growth of Industrial Policy, 1925–1975*. Stanford, CA: Stanford University Press.

Kohli, A. (2004). *State-directed Development: Political Power and Industrialization in the Global Periphery*. New York: Cambridge University Press.

Kohli, A. (2012). *Poverty Amid Plenty in the New India*. New York: Cambridge University Press.

Lee, C.-S. (2016). *When Solidarity Works: Labor-Civic Networks and Welfare States in the Market Reform Era*. Cambridge: Cambridge University Press.

Mattingly, D. (2016). 'Elite Capture: How Decentralization and Informal Institutions Weaken Property Rights in Rural China', *World Politics*, 68(3): 383–412.

McGuire, J.W. (2010). *Wealth, Health, and Democracy in East Asia and Latin America*. New York: Cambridge University Press.

Mishra, U.S., and V. Shukla (2015). 'Welfare Comparisons with Multidimensional Well-Being Indicators: An Indian Illustration', Centre for Development Studies, Thiruvananthapuram, Working Paper 462.

Myrdal, G. (1968). *Asian Drama: An Inquiry into the Poverty of Nations. A Twentieth Century Fund Study, Volumes I, II, and III*. New York: Pantheon.

Nahm, J. (2017a). 'Renewable Futures and Industrial Legacies: Wind and Solar Sectors in China, Germany, and the United States', *Business and Politics*, 19(1): 68–106.

Nahm, J. (2017b). 'Exploiting the Implementation Gap: Policy Divergence and Industrial Upgrading in China's Wind and Solar Sectors', *The China Quarterly*, 231(September): 705–27.

Nettl, J.P. (1968). 'The State as a Conceptual Variable', *World Politics*, 20(July): 559–92.

O'Rourke, D. (2004). *Community-driven Regulation: Balancing Development and the Environment in Vietnam*. Cambridge, MA: MIT Press.

Peng, I., and J. Wong (2008). 'Institutions and Institutional Purpose: Continuity and Change in East Asian Social Policy', *Politics & Society*, 36(1): 61–88.

Pritchett, L. (2009). 'Is India a Flailing State? Detours on the Four Lane Highway to Modernization', John F. Kennedy School of Government, Harvard University, Cambridge, MA, HKS Faculty Research Working Paper Series RWP09-013.

Ramachandran, V. (2009). 'Systemic Barriers to Equity in Education'. In P. Rustagi (ed.) *Concerns, Conflicts and Cohesions: Universalization of Elementary Education in India*. New Delhi: Oxford University Press.

Ranis, G., and F. Stewart (2006). 'Successful Transition Towards a Virtuous Cycle of Human Development and Economic Growth: Country Studies', Economic Growth Center, Yale University, New Haven, CT, Center Discussion Paper 943.

Ranis, G., F. Stewart, and A. Ramirez (2000). 'Economic Growth and Human Development', *World Development*, 28(2): 197–219.

Rodrik, D. (2000). 'Institutions for High-Quality Growth: What They Are and How to Acquire Them', *Studies in Comparative International Development*, 35(3): 3–31.

Rodrik, D. (2016). 'Is Liberal Democracy Feasible in Developing Countries?', *Studies in Comparative International Development*, 51(May): 1–31.

Rothstein, B. (2015). 'The Chinese Paradox of High Growth and Low Quality of Government: The Cadre Organization Meets Max Weber', *Governance*, 28(4): 533–48.

Sandbrook, R., M. Edelman, P. Heller, and J. Teichman (2007). *Social Democracy in the Global Periphery: Origins and Prospects*. Cambridge: Cambridge University Press.

Sen, A.K. (1999). *Development as Freedom*. New York: Knopf.

Siddiqi, A., and C. Hertzman (2001). 'Economic Growth, Income Equality, and Population Health Among the Asian Tigers', *International Journal of Health Services*, 31(2): 323–33.

Slater, D. (2012). 'Strong-state Democratization in Malaysia and Singapore', *Journal of Democracy*, 23(2): 19–33.

Slater, D., and J. Wong (2013). 'The Strength to Concede: Ruling Parties and Democratization in Developmental Asia', *Perspectives on Politics*, 11(3): 717–33.

Stallings, B., and E.M. Kim (2017). *Promoting Development: The Political Economy of East Asian Foreign Aid*. Singapore: Palgrave-Springer Nature.

Timmer, C.P. (2004). 'The Road to Pro-poor Growth: The Indonesian Experience in Regional Perspective', *Bulletin of Indonesian Economic Studies*, 40(2): 177–207.

Törnquist, O. (2002). 'Popular Development and Democracy: Case Studies with Rural Dimensions in the Philippines, Indonesia, and Kerala', Centre for Development and the Environment (SUM), Oslo, Occasional Paper 3.

Tsai, L.L. (2007). *Accountability Without Democracy: Solidary Groups and Public Goods Provision in Rural China*. Cambridge: Cambridge University Press.

Veeraraghavan, R. (2017). 'Strategies for Synergy in a High Modernist Project: Two Community Responses to India's NREGA Rural Work Program', *World Development*, 99: 203–13.

Wade, R. (1990). *Governing the Market: Economic Theory and the Role of Government in Taiwan's Industrialization*. Princeton, NJ: Princeton University Press.

Wang, S. (2004). 'China's Health System: From Crisis to Opportunity', *Yale-China Health Journal*, 3: 5–49.

Williams, M. (ed.) (2014). *The End of the Developmental State?* New York: Routledge.

Wong, J. (2004). *Healthy Democracies: Welfare Politics in Taiwan and South Korea*. Ithaca, NY: Cornell University Press.

World Bank (2018a). *World Inequality Report*. Washington, DC: World Bank.

World Bank (2018b). *World Development Report.* Washington, DC: World Bank.

Yu, H. (2014). 'The Ascendency of State-owned Enterprises in China: Development, Controversy and Problems', *Journal of Contemporary China*, 23(85): 161–82.

Zhao, D. (2015). *The Confucian-Legalist State: A New Theory of Chinese History.* Oxford: Oxford University Press.

Zhu, T. (2015). 'International Context and China's Government–Business Relations', *Economic and Political Studies*, 3(2): 3–29.

6

Economic Openness and Development

Richard Kozul-Wright and Daniel Poon

1. Introduction: Economic Openness and Asian Divergence

The *Asian Drama* is something of a misnomer; as Gunnar Myrdal himself acknowledged, it was a South Asian drama based, in particular, around the development experiences of India and Pakistan. Myrdal was not optimistic about the region's prospects, in large part because the institutional prerequisites for development were missing and he saw few signs of a break in the class relations that underpinned their soft states, perpetuating a 'fateful development' (Myrdal 1970a: 380) of high, and possibly rising, inequality that would hold back structural transformation and sustained growth.

Myrdal had less to say about Southeast Asia, although Indonesia, Thailand, and others from the region do appear episodically throughout the study (see Myrdal 1968), and there is almost nothing about East Asia. These gaps in the analysis could be overlooked to the extent that these other regions were still largely agricultural with weak industrial sectors, faced much the same external constraints as South Asian economies, and shared similar institutional weaknesses. Moreover, differences in income levels across the region were confined to a relatively narrow band at the time Myrdal was researching his book, annual growth rates were similar in the sub-regions (and too slow to close the income gap with the advanced economies), and manufacturing performance (whether measured in terms of output, jobs, or exports) was weak (UNCTAD 2016a: chapter 3).

In fact, with hindsight, Myrdal was writing on the cusp of a great divergence across the Asia sub-regions: growth accelerated in the East Asian newly industrialized economies (NIEs) as they embarked on catching up with advanced economies; South Asia would continue to stagnate for most of the remainder of the century; and Southeast Asia exhibited a more erratic development path with growth spurts and subsequent setbacks. As an even later latecomer, China's gross domestic product (GDP) per capita level lagged behind through the 1970s, but had surpassed Southeast Asia by the mid-2000s and reached a level of one-quarter the GDP per capita of the United States by 2017 (see Kozul-Wright and Poon 2018: figure 1).

While other contributions in this volume delve into the fine-grained detail and diversity of development processes in Asian countries and sub-regions, this chapter looks in broader terms at approaches to opening up to the global economy, confining the discussion to the experiences of one country per sub-region: China,

India, and Malaysia. These stylized accounts cover the range of approaches to openness, which are often classified as 'high' (Malaysia), 'medium' (China), and 'low' (India). Such a classification by degrees of openness offers a loosely descriptive framework for locating the integration efforts of Asian countries into the global economy, but says little about the mix of different policies used to manage integration and, in particular, the strategic approach to integration adopted by the East Asian NIEs during their formative stages of catch-up development.[1]

Central to our analysis of the direction and impact of the opening-up process in shaping the Asian divergence is whether, and how effectively, state institutions used and co-ordinated 'operational controls' (or policy levers) over the domestic economy, which includes the nature and scope of interactions with foreign economic entities and flows (Myrdal, 1968: 902).

This chapter contends that the Asian divergence can be interpreted in large part by the variations in the institutional capabilities and operational controls to address market (and government) failures encountered in the process of late-comer economic opening, and the pragmatic experimentation of policymakers in search of more effective institutional mechanisms—carrots, sticks, and competitive pressures—in pursuit of desired development outcomes. To set the broad analytical framework used in the remainder of the chapter, section 2 outlines four key concepts closely associated with Myrdal's contributions to the development canon. In section 3, Myrdal's concepts are set in the context of the experience of East Asian NIEs and subsequently contrasted with the three selected Asian countries in relation to policy instruments linked to trade, technology, and global value chains (GVCs) (section 3.1); and foreign and domestic resource mobilization, and development finance (section 3.2). Section 4 summarizes the chapter's policy lessons—particularly the notion of soft states and the rational co-ordination of operational controls—to inform the ongoing and unfinished drama of economic development in Asia.

2. The Abiding Legacy of Myrdal's *Asian Drama*

Myrdal's *Asian Drama: An Inquiry into the Poverty of Nations* was an ambitious project, involving over a decade of research and ranging over three lengthy

---

[1] Despite the repeated assertion by conventional economists and the vast econometric literature testing the links between openness and economic growth, there are plenty of familiar methodological pitfalls in trying to capture a process as complex as economic integration in a linear statistical classification: (i) the often vague definition of openness and the failure to separate episodes of export promotion from those of import liberalization can easily lead to the misrepresentation of trade regimes, making it difficult to draw cross-country comparisons and interpret the findings; (ii) cross-sectional averages hide country-specific differences and breaks in the series; (iii) the failure to present an explicit counterfactual, together with biases in country selection, raises further doubts about the robustness of results; and (iv) the inability of such exercises to analyse non-linear historical processes greatly diminishes their value for guiding policy.

volumes. It not only aimed to discover the constraints on economic and social progress in one of the most populous regions of the world but, as its subtitle suggested, to uncover more broadly the causes of (and remedies for) global poverty. The *Asian Drama* also provided Myrdal with an opportunity to survey the methodological and analytical debates that had accompanied the rise of development economics over the previous two decades, to which he had been a prominent contributor. Four concepts, all closely associated with Myrdal's contribution to the development canon, are key to his analysis of both the regional and global challenges: (i) interdependent development; (ii) circular causation and cumulative change; (iii) spread (and backwash) effects; and (iv) soft states.

For the post-war generation of economists that shaped the classical development canon, and its accompanying policy advice, the interrelationships between economic growth, structural transformation, and institutional conditions took centre stage. Myrdal was no exception, defining development as 'a movement upward of a whole system of interdependent conditions, of which economic growth, assuming that it could be properly defined and measured, is only one of several categories of causally interrelated conditions' (1970a: 391).

The challenge of 'interdependent development' focused on predominantly agrarian economies most of which had recently gained political independence after decades (or longer) of colonial (mis)rule. While there were differences among development scholars and practitioners about where best to begin meeting the challenge and how best to manage it, there was general agreement that shifting resources towards the industrial sector was key to eliminating poverty and catching up with countries higher up the development ladder. Myrdal was in no doubt that 'no substantial development in South Asia is possible over the long run unless the countries can employ a much larger part of their labour force in modern industry or other productive non-agricultural occupations' (1970b: 1185).

The case for industrial development in South Asia—and the South more generally—rested on its capacity to generate and combine a series of linkages and complementarities that together could sustain a virtuous circle of resource mobilization, rising productivity, increasing incomes, and expanding market demand, both at home and abroad (Toner 2000). Moreover, industrialization was closely tied to social and demographic transitions involving a younger, more urban, more educated, and more productive workforce, which would reinforce this virtuous circle. Myrdal associated the spread effects of industrialization with aggregate shifts on both the demand side, operating through higher incomes and investment levels, as well as the supply (or cost) side, operating through scale economies, new skills, and higher productivity. But he also acknowledged the role of Hirschman-type backward and forward linkages within and across sectors of the economy and with external economies in a wider sense associated with changes in the organization of work and attitudes towards it. At the same time, Myrdal recognized that industrialization carried destructive impulses through 'backwash' effects, such as the elimination of labour-intensive jobs in traditional small-scale enterprises unable to compete with larger and more capital-intensive modern firms.

The central role for industry in triggering a circular and cumulative process of self-sustaining development helped frame a policy of planning for development through a series of interrelated investments in infrastructure, skills, and new industries, as well as institutional reforms to help strengthen spread effects. For Myrdal, it also implied a methodological break with the 'biased theoretical approach' of conventional growth models that were guilty not only of abstracting from attitudes and institutions but also of employing unrealistic assumptions that reduced the development process to a series of incremental supply-side adjustments that, guided by price signals, would automatically push a developing economy towards its optimal equilibrium state.

The nature and impact of spread and backwash effects, and the ability of policymakers to manage these in support of a sustained virtuous development circle, were not confined to domestic circumstances and conditions but included the international context. Myrdal believed that while international trade and capital flows had earlier allowed a small group of countries in Western Europe (particularly Sweden) to raise their standard of living at a historically unprecedented rate, episodes of export growth in Asia, linked to commodity production, had failed to produce a cumulative process of development. Rather, these had created (often highly profitable) enclaves with strong links to the developed country from which capital and management had originated, and to where the commodity was often exported, but isolated from the local economy.

As a result, Asian economies found themselves part of an international division of labour dominated by a high-income and technologically sophisticated 'core' that exported mainly manufactured goods, and a low-income and a technologically weak 'periphery' that was largely dependent on primary exports. Under these conditions, the backwash from trade and capital flows would more than likely reinforce a distorted process of development, and which, according to Myrdal, had precluded South Asia from replicating the development path found in Western Europe. Moreover, with their large first-mover advantages, manufacturing firms from advanced countries had established a strong grip on global markets compounding the entry difficulty of potential newcomers into manufacturing sectors.

From this perspective, industrialization would need to be a much more planned process than it had been in the past. By this Myrdal did not have in mind the Soviet model of central planning but, rather, a series of co-ordinated policy initiatives across a broad range of economic and social activities, including concerted measures to raise labour utilization and to improve productivity in all sectors. In particular, following a path well trodden by almost all developed economies, domestic industries needed to be supported and protected in their early stages, until they developed their own capacities to compete. In addition, and more so than for earlier generations of industrial catch-up economies, additional targeted support would be needed to promote manufactured exports from the South, given the first-mover advantages of firms in the leading industrial economies, the productivity and technological gaps this generated, and the size of the domestic market in most developing countries.

In all these respects, Myrdal's approach was in line with conventional development wisdom in the 1950s and 1960s. However, Myrdal insisted that there was no automatic guarantee that state structures would be in place to ensure that virtuous circles would be established. Indeed, central to his *Asian Drama* was a longstanding weakness of South Asian states to manage the policy initiatives he had in mind. In particular, he highlighted a lack of discipline in public institutions (and their officials), which created a 'soft state', too easily captured by special interests and, in turn, promoting a more widespread resistance to public policies and regulations (see Myrdal 1970a: chapter 7).

Myrdal recognized that a harder state would be needed to steer Asian development. Key to moving in this direction would be the application of operational controls over the private sector aimed at influencing its behaviour, both positively and negatively. These could be used in a discretionary or non-discretionary manner by policymakers seeking to align business decisions with wider development goals and targets.[2] But in the absence of an environment that would lend itself to the use of non-discretionary positive control measures (typical of the successful late industrializing states of Northern Europe) and an inability to design effective discretionary negative controls, Myrdal argued that soft states in South Asia had a tendency to resort to overly generous discretionary positive controls to achieve the desired response from business, oftentimes accompanied by an excessive use of broader negative controls that curtailed business development more generally. Myrdal likened this to 'driving a car with the accelerator pushed to the floor but the brakes on' (1968: 925), a combination that favoured incumbent firms and perpetuated vested interests and was more likely to give rise to swerving and skidding in the economy than to producing a sustainable process of catching up.[3]

---

[2] For Myrdal, positive controls are used to stimulate, encourage, facilitate, and induce production or consumption, generally or in a specific sector, and include information support services, technical assistance, fiscal measures, cheap credit, tariff protection, access to foreign exchange, etc.; negative controls are meant to limit production or consumption by means of bullying, administrative restrictions, denial of foreign exchange, and in general raising production and transaction costs. Discretionary use involves a targeted decision by an administrative authority with power to act at its own discretion; non-discretionary use follows a definite rule or induced price change that is not specific to any particular firm.

[3] While Myrdal insisted on the central importance of domestic reforms, he also drew attention to weaknesses in the governance of the international economy that could hinder efforts at catching up. This referred not only to the backwash effects linked to trade and capital flows noted earlier but also to vulnerabilities linked to changes in market conditions and policies in developed countries. Reform of

3. Trade and Investment Patterns in the Asian Divergence

A vast body of literature has described the performance of the East Asian tiger economies, and, in particular, their emergence, as strong manufacturing exporters. However, there is still not agreement about how they did it. A conventional narrative has long argued that rapid opening up to international trade and to foreign firms allowed these countries to fully exploit their comparative advantages with attendant growth impulses (Lal 1985; World Bank 1993). This is, at best, a partial account, recognizing that any poor and predominantly rural country integrating into the global economy can only begin to do so by better mobilizing its existing resources on the basis of inherited institutional conditions. But what distinguished these economies from most other developing countries (including elsewhere in Asia) was not only the pace at which the export of labour-intensive manufactures grew, especially in textiles and clothing, but also their early diversification into other light industry sectors, followed in quick succession by an even more spectacular shift into both capital-intensive and technologically intensive products such as transportation, chemicals, and electronics.

There is no doubt that this success with manufacturing exports demonstrates the potential of outward-oriented catch-up strategies built on the expansion of manufacturing capacity. Given their small domestic markets and the unavoidably heavy demand for imports of intermediate and capital goods, exports were crucial in establishing a virtuous interdependence between structural change, investment, and market expansion. Particularly in the early stages of industrialization, a 'vent for surplus'[4] allowed these countries to meet growing import demand without threatening domestic output growth and, subsequently, to achieve scale economies as they sought to compete internationally, less on the basis of low wages and more through product diversification and rising productivity. In all cases, a very rapid rate of capital formation helped to raise and sustain the rate of economic growth, beginning in the earliest stages of their development, and underpinned by high rates of reinvested profits (UNCTAD 1994, 1996).

In doing so, none of these economies, including the city states of Hong Kong and Singapore, relied only on market forces or on foreign capital, to finance a faster pace of capital accumulation and channel resources into the export

global governance and related efforts to strengthen development co-operation, to ease the balance of payments constraint on faster growth, and to mobilize more (and more predictable) international resources to boost investment, would thus be central to industrialization efforts in developing countries.

---

[4] 'Vent for surplus' differs from conventional trade theory, which assumes full employment of resources, by emphasizing the role of international trade in providing an outlet for domestic productive capacities that would otherwise remain underutilized. This was one of the elements in Adam Smith's attempt to explore the relationship between trade and development (see Myint 1977).

sector.[5] It was the establishment of a nexus between profits, investment and exports, not the simple logic of comparative advantage, which underpinned East Asian success.

Foreign direct investment, which is a hybrid capital flow involving more than new capital in plant and equipment, is only one element of such a nexus,[6] and East Asian economies, contrary to popular perception, exhibit a diversity of experiences with its role in the growth process (see Kozul-Wright and Poon 2018: table 1). FDI did not, in the aggregate, play a prominent role in the industrialization of the two larger economies in the first-tier NIEs, partly because they were very selective in the foreign firms they attracted, and partly because Japan, the obvious source country, had not yet become a major overseas investor.[7] Aggregate figures, such as the share of foreign affiliates in manufacturing sales or the share of FDI in domestic capital formation, do not, however, measure the full importance of international firms in the industrialization process. In the Republic of Korea (ROK), for example, foreign affiliates accounted for a quarter of all manufactured exports, which is many times greater than their small shares of GDP or gross capital formation. In the key electrical and electronics sector, the share of foreign affiliates was between 65 and 73 per cent.[8]

Thus, although development in ROK and Taiwan (Province of China) relied mainly on domestic firms, an important role was, and still is, played by FDI in certain sectors of the economy. However, in all cases, policymakers have used an array of instruments to ensure that FDI complemented wider developmental objectives. The larger economies of the first tier—following the earlier lead of Japan—adopted a more distant and dirigiste approach to FDI with the aim of building domestic technological capabilities. Policymakers in both ROK and Taiwan (Province of China) consciously chose to tap foreign capital in ways other than FDI, while drawing on various other forms of technology transfer to fill gaps in their productive structure. Managerial and technical assistance from Japanese companies played an important role. Thus, with help from companies such as Kawasaki Shipbuilding and Nippon Steel from Japan, world-class industries were created within the space of a decade in ROK. Singapore, which had a much more open policy, also used a variety of measures to direct FDI into strategic sectors.

A defining feature of the successful East Asian development strategies was how business and development interests were 'forcibly aligned' (Studwell 2013: 61)

---

[5] On Singapore's developmental pragmatism, see Low (2001).

[6] This confusion has become commonplace in development policy discussions; for further discussions, see Blanchard and Acalin (2016) and Akyuz (2017).

[7] In this respect, the 'flying geese model of development', which is often used to describe the importance of regional interactions in the East Asian catch-up story, can be misleading (see UNCTAD 1996).

[8] However, these statistics should be treated with caution since many affiliates are part of joint ventures and may include a large domestic contribution. For example, according to some estimates, in 1986 foreign affiliates employed 11.4 per cent of all manufacturing workers in Taiwan, but when the numbers are weighted by equity holdings the foreign share falls to 6.5 per cent (see Tu and Schive 1995).

through the use of effective control mechanisms to both encourage and discipline profits, particularly in an expanding manufacturing sector, as the animus linking a virtuous circle of rising productivity, growing incomes, expanding markets (at home and abroad), and higher investment, feeding back to rising productivity (UNCTAD 1994, 1996, 2003). Just as importantly, those control mechanisms extended to managing their integration into the global economy. From this perspective, integration, through both trade and FDI, was approached from a strategic perspective: in terms of goals to realize scale economies, job creation, technology transfer, and generate foreign exchange, while promoting local linkages and productive capacities, including in favoured sectors, and reducing vulnerability to external shocks. This involved all the East Asian economies adopting a smart and selective combination of policy measures that included trade opening, export promotion, selective attraction of foreign firms, and support for, along with surveillance of, infant industries and domestic content, as part of a broad set of policies to stimulate structural transformation (Thurborn and Weiss 2006).

East Asia's use of special economic zones (SEZs), or export processing zones (EPZs), provides a fitting illustration of the strategic approach to global economic integration. Despite often heralded as having the most successful EPZ cases, the role of EPZs in ROK and Taiwan never gained great significance in terms of respective shares of total exports or employment. Both countries were nonetheless able to deepen their industrial base in diversifying away from low value-added labour-intensive industries, while also building strong input–output linkages between firms located inside the zones and domestic industries located outside the zones (Warr 1984; Madani 1999).

ROK's first EPZ was established in Masan in 1970. The zone granted the 'standard' package of EPZ investor incentives, including preferential access to imports of intermediate goods and raw materials to domestic firms supplying EPZs. Non-fiscal policy tools were also actively deployed (Chang 2009), including domestic content requirements, and the zone proactively provided technical assistance to domestic suppliers and sub-contractors. A key complementary measure was the government's creation in 1973 of the National Investment Fund (NIF) to provide funds to financial institutions, which would extend preferential lending for long-term investment in heavy and chemical industries. From 1974 to 1981, 62 per cent of NIF lending was assigned to the Korean Development Bank, and the NIF accounted for 57 per cent of total manufacturing equipment loans by financial institutions. By the late 1970s, this share rose to 70 per cent, with the creation of large industrial complexes around the country (Sakong and Koh 2010: 22).

With this array of policy tools, domestic content in Masan EPZ rose quickly. In 1971, domestic firms accounted for 3.3 per cent of the materials and intermediate goods used by firms in the zone; by 1975, this rose to 25 per cent and would later reach 44 per cent. Domestic value-added rose steadily from 28 per cent in 1971 to 52 per cent in 1979. In 1976, sub-contractors supplying Masan EPZ firms employed an equivalent of 15 per cent of the zone's workforce; by 1988, this figure grew to half. The use of similar tools in Taiwan saw domestic content increase from 8 per cent of total imports to 46 per cent over 1969 to 1979 (Jenkins et al. 1998: 5–6; Madani 1999: 31–2; Milberg and Winkler 2013: 246–7).[9]

In these cases, EPZs evolved as part of the country's efforts to build an industrial base by fostering domestic capabilities in higher value-added strategic industries, particularly in capital goods sectors and later in high-technology sectors. As ROK's light industry exports began to weaken in the early 1970s, the country also faced persistent trade deficits from the industry's reliance on imports of materials and equipment. To ease this structural trade imbalance, the country switched to promoting heavy and chemical industries and established a host of specialized industrial complexes for specific industries such as steel, refineries and petrochemicals, non-ferrous metals, shipbuilding, and machinery industries. In this way, ROK's industrial complex development is generally associated with the push to establish heavy and chemical industries rather than light industries (Lim 2010; Jo et al. 2012).

Importantly, East Asian countries relied on traditional industrial policy instruments to support domestic capital goods sectors, while other tools were used to promote high-technology sectors in the 1980s, including proactive investments of public research and development (R&D) institutes, strategic spin-offs from research institutes, and conditional subsidies to public and private R&D. In Taiwan, the Industrial Technology Research Institute (ITRI) became the government's premier research centre for high-technology industries. Founded in 1973, ITRI would support strategic industries with key technology projects, such as in semiconductors and personal computers. ITRI also undertook projects with major potential to guide private sector investment and would initiate smaller-scale projects to support the substitution of imports of key components. Thus, the government's efforts to enhance local growth opportunities and local value-added were integral to the process of upgrading domestic technological capabilities (Amsden 2004: 80).

It is often argued that these earlier episodes of East Asian development are not relevant to subsequent development experiences due to changes in international trade rules and production systems organized around GVCs. While such changes have undoubtedly reduced the policy space available to many countries in the era of hyperglobalization, this does not detract from the need for a strategic approach to global engagement, but only reinforces the importance of coherent national

---

[9] In some cases, administrative measures were effectively used to 'promote' linkages between foreign firms operating in EPZs and domestic suppliers. Wade (2010: 156), for example, recounts the case of officials from Taiwan's Industrial Development Bureau delaying approvals for imports of glass needed by a foreign firm producing televisions, while reminding the company of the advantages of switching to domestic suppliers (a proposition the foreign firm had previously refused to consider).

economic planning in the development process (UNCTAD 2014, 2016a). These issues are further explored in the following sub-section.

3.1 Trade and Technology Flows in the Era of Hyperglobalization

As already noted, Southeast and South Asian development paths have exhibited considerable diversity in terms of their reliance on exports and FDI, which has continued albeit with a general rising trend in both elements since the mid-1980s (see Kozul-Wright and Poon 2018: table 1). This trend coincides with the broader consensus of letting international market forces and firms determine the pattern of integration into the global economy. This broad consensus has led to the rise of the era of hyperglobalization characterized by more footloose capital and the pro-liferation of free trade agreements which together have narrowed the options on domestic economic and trade policies. Paradoxically, while this has made it easier to establish a shallow export–investment nexus through participation in GVCs, it has become more challenging for many developing countries to establish a deeper nexus linked to a pattern of diversified development and higher domestic value-added activities (UNCTAD 2014, 2016a).

Some of the diversity in experiences reflects initial conditions and patterns of economic integration inherited from their respective colonial histories, but policy choices continue to matter. Most countries in both regions began their post-inde-pendence development efforts by adopting some form of economic planning, and in pursuit of similar objectives, all pursued industrialization through import sub-stitution. But even as countries in both regions, albeit with differences in timing and degree, shifted towards greater openness, the strategic use of controls, both of a discretionary and non-discretionary nature, such as employed in East Asia to discipline and align the interests of firms with a wider developing strategy, has been elusive. The remainder of this chapter compares the three selected countries with East Asia in the areas of trade, technology, resource mobilization, and devel-opment finance.

At the outset, and albeit with important differences in the commitment to pri-vate property rights and the reach of the price mechanism, policymakers in both post-1947 India and post-1949 China adopted Soviet-inspired five-year central-ized plans that focused on the domestic market, pursued goals of self-sufficiency, and prioritized heavy industries led by the public sector. These development strategies persisted for several decades before decisive market reforms were introduced in the late 1970s in China, and in the early 1990s in India. Both reforms were gradual, but they had important differences: China's began in agriculture and continued sequentially in the industrial and financial sectors, whereas India's reforms stretched, from the outset, across all sectors but were also more piecemeal; China actively promoted FDI inflows from the 1990s as part of its export push, whereas India's reforms also attracted FDI but did not greatly alter the economy's focus towards foreign markets.

Post-1957 Malaysia also initially pursued import substitution through five-year plans, but with a stronger emphasis on private enterprise including a strong presence of foreign investors using foreign technologies in primary sectors and later in manufacturing sectors. Malaysia's first phase of import substitution lasted ten years from 1957 to 1967 before the promotion of export-oriented manufacturing in the 1970s centred on electronics and textiles sectors. A second import substitution phase focusing on heavier industries began in 1981, followed by another export-oriented phase from the mid-1980s onwards that placed greater attention on fostering domestic technologies and know-how.

All countries in the region have used SEZs, or EPZs,[10] as part of their opening-up strategy. In the remainder of this sub-section, each of the three countries' experience with SEZs is briefly examined with emphasis on broad patterns in the application of operational controls to align these policy instruments with wider development strategy.

India was among the first in Asia to establish an EPZ, in the port city of Kandla in 1965, followed by a second EPZ built in a suburb of Mumbai in 1973. Established to foster an electronics manufacturing sector, this second EPZ would later also include firms in the gems and jewellery sector. Unlike Kandla, this EPZ was located in an urbanized area with a history of industrial development and with infrastructure facilities. Four more EPZs were set up in 1984–1986, and a fifth in 1989. At the time, EPZs were owned and managed by the central government with three-tiers of administration; it was only in the 1990s that state governments, autonomous agencies, and the private sector were allowed to develop EPZs (Mukherjee et al. 2016: 53).

Although there were success stories from the first EPZ regime, particularly related to the jewellery sector, these zones had difficulty in attracting firms due to a lack of government commitment, piecemeal reforms and policy reversals, poor site selection and infrastructure provision, weak incentives, and inadequate regulation of the zones. It was not until the mid-2000s that the government introduced a new SEZ regime with added incentives.

Whereas the old EPZ scheme had fostered industrial enclaves, the new regime simplified administrative procedures and promoted an integrated township with fully developed infrastructure (Aggarwal 2006). Exports from SEZs have been growing, but they still accounted for less than a fifth of the total in 2013–2014 and remained heavily focused on the information technology sector (Mukherjee et al. 2016: 69–75). The new scheme has generally failed to achieve its main objectives of increasing manufacturing output, exports, employment, and FDI as

---

[10] Including other related zones such as free trade zones, industrial parks, free ports, and enterprise zones.

well as improving infrastructure. The main problems related to overemphasis on information and communication technology software sectors rather than manufacturing sectors, erosion of incentives through free trade agreements, a lack of supporting infrastructure, particularly transportation, and complications related to land acquisition (Athukorala 2018: 24–5). In response to these challenges, the 'Make in India' initiative seeks to establish five economic corridors to serve as the backbone of a globally competitive manufacturing sector. However, in the absence of clear operational controls to align private and public investment, it remains unclear whether this strategy will be any more successful than past efforts.

In the case of Malaysia, it first established SEZs in 1971 in Penang to attract export-oriented FDI in light manufacturing activities such as textiles and electronics assembly operations. Though generally regarded as successful, the approach did not stimulate a shift from low to high value-added activities in the electronics industry. After a brief interlude, the government began a more successful second round of export orientation in 1986, attracting FDI inflows from Japan and the first-tier NIEs following the Plaza Accord of 1985, which led to appreciations in the currencies of Japan, ROK, Taiwan (Province of China), and Singapore. By the late 1980s, the electronics industry was the largest generator of manufacturing employment, exports, and value-added activities in Malaysia (Rasiah 2015: 9–10).

However, increasing export competition from China and other lower-cost Asian countries, as well as the Asian financial crisis, exposed key structural weaknesses of the Malaysian electronics industry: a heavy import dependence due to weak domestic support industries and undeveloped linkages; a heavy reliance on export markets; a highly concentrated export basket of products, mainly of low-end assembly operations; a declining capacity to generate employment; and a mismatch between the demand and supply for labour skills (Ernst 2002: 38–40; Athukorala 2017: 189–91). Positive operational controls to attract higher value-added activities has had some success but shortcomings in government monitoring and evaluation have reduced the effectiveness of policy tools: for example, it was only in the mid-2000s that the provision of government grants was made conditional on the achievement of upgrading targets and milestones (Rasiah 2015: 12, 16).

China was a relative latecomer in the use of SEZs, with the first four zones—Shantou, Shenzhen, Xiamen, Zhuhai—created in southern coastal areas in 1980. Since then SEZs were scaled up nationwide and their role evolved over time to involve more capital- and technology-intensive activities, including production and services activities aimed at the domestic market. In the latest phase, established zones have adapted to rapid increases in costs by leveraging scale economies, insertion with GVCs, and production clusters to move into higher value-added production and chain functions. In addition to the traditional benefits provided to firms in SEZs, the government also provided measures such as grants, informational and professional platforms, and testing centres, which facilitated links between firms and universities/technical institutions to support the economic upgrading process (Dinh et al. 2013).

Domestic technology-intensive firms generally benefitted from a package of government measures, including imports of foreign technologies, joint venture requirements, and incentives for indigenous R&D—promoted through the next iteration of the SEZ concept, namely, the high-technology industrial development zones (HIDZs). Initiated in 1988 and promoted by China's Torch Program, HIDZs sought to harness the technological capacity and resources of domestic research institutes, universities, and enterprises to foster high-technology products and the commercialization of R&D. HIDZs have subsequently spearheaded China's efforts to move into new sectors, including through co-operation between Chinese and foreign firms (Heilmann et al. 2013) and according to one estimate, by the mid-2000s, the share of HIDZs in China's R&D expenditure reached over one-third (Fu and Gao 2007). Other studies have emphasized China's hands-on approach to raising domestic value-added in GVC-linked exports by enhancing the indigenous R&D capacities of domestic firms (Gallagher and Shafaeddin 2009).

To provide a sense of these trends, Figure 6.1 plots the domestic value-added share of gross exports in the computer, electronics, and optical equipment industry

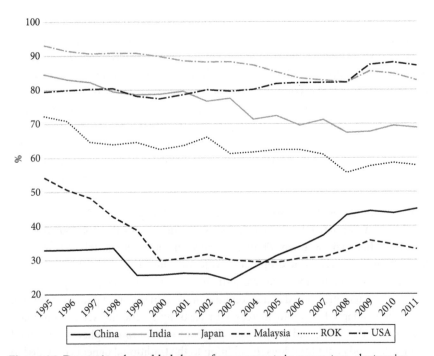

Figure 6.1 Domestic value-added share of gross exports in computers, electronics, and optical equipment for selected countries, 1995–2011.
Source: Authors' elaboration based on OECD (2018).

for selected countries. Countries such as Japan and the United States exhibit high levels of domestic value-added commensurate with their role as core technology suppliers. ROK has relatively high domestic value-added, albeit declining from 72.2 per cent to 57.8 per cent from 1995 to 2011. Over the same period, Malaysia and China had lower respective starting points at 54.2 per cent and 32.9 per cent, but Malaysia's share fell to 33.2 per cent, while China's share rose to 46.2 per cent. India's relatively high level of domestic value-added—declining from 84.6 per cent in 1995 to 68.8 per cent in 2011—can be understood in the context of its relatively lower level of GVC engagement.

Figure 6.2 provides further insight into country-level trends in trade flows and technology structure for the electronics sector—one of the main industries linked to GVCs. Given its relatively early engagement with electronics GVCs, ROK can be used as a rough benchmark as it maintained a net trade surplus over the years even as the share of the electronics sector in total exports has been declining, and its trade structure has shifted from consumer electronic equipment and computer and peripheral equipment to higher value-added communication equipment, and

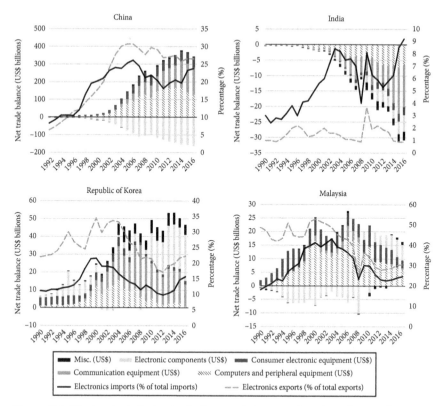

Figure 6.2 Electronics industry trade flows and structure for selected countries, 1990–2016.

Source: Authors' elaboration based on UNCTAD (2018) and United Nations (2018).

Table 6.1 Changes in value-added shares in gross exports, 1995–2014, percentage points

	Foreign	Domestic		
		Agriculture and Extractives	Manufacturing	Services
China	−1.7	−2.8	11.9	−7.4
India	11.6	−3.5	−12.9	4.8
Malaysia	8.7	1.4	−5.8	−4.3
Developing economies	4.2	4.3	−3.5	−5.1
Developed economies	7.2	1.7	−10.1	1.1

Source: Authors' elaboration based on UNCTAD secretariat calculations from OECD (2018).

later in electronic components (such as integrated circuits). By comparison, trade flows and technology structure for the electronics sector in China, India, and Malaysia reveal trends that are reflective of each country's approach to engaging GVCs. The cases of China and Malaysia draw the closest similarities to that of ROK, in terms of maintaining net export surpluses, albeit with qualifications given each country's overall stage of development in general and in the electronics sector in particular.

Beyond the electronics sector, the broader trend appears to be China's steady success in adding more domestic value-added to its manufactured exports while this measure of successful upgrading has declined sharply in the other countries (Table 6.1).

3.2 Foreign and Domestic Resource Mobilization

There is no straightforward way to comprehensively depict the multi-layered policies that comprise a country's macroeconomic framework and its link to sustained resource mobilization, investment, and structural transformation (Ocampo and Vos 2008; UNCTAD 2016a). Much conventional analysis sees financial deepening—understood as the growing use of 'financial instruments, markets, and intermediaries to ameliorate the effects of information, enforcement, and transactions costs by providing broad categories of financial services to the economy' (Loayza et al. 2017: 2) and closely tied to financial liberalization—as the key and links this to a faster pace of investment, particularly by attracting more FDI, growth, and structural transformation.

As noted earlier, the first-tier NIEs adopted a strategic approach to managing foreign capital flows and engaging GVCs with a clear focus on ensuring that spillovers from hosting international firms would enhance productivity in the rest of the economy. Despite receiving different absolute volumes of inward FDI, each country designed policy frameworks to regulate the presence and activities of foreign companies. Each country had its own interpretation of what constitutes a 'strategic sector', but the effectiveness of FDI restrictions to foster national ownership and upgrading of domestic technological capabilities also depended on the management of the underlying growth structure of the sector in question and of the economy as a whole.

Differences in the operational controls used to manage trade, FDI, and technology flows explain much of the Asian divergence. But consideration must also be given to broader controls linked to the macroeconomic policy framework in which trade, FDI, and technology policies operate and which modulate the domestic impact of global financial flows. In particular, the configuration of a country's capital account regime can shape the nature of interaction between monetary and exchange rate policies, which carries significant implications in terms of animating the profit–investment nexus, the strength of domestic resource mobilization, and the structure of domestic growth.

With the proliferation of free trade agreements and bilateral investment treaties, most latecomer countries have not been able to use the same set of policy tools as the earlier cohort of East Asian NIEs and have struggled to adapt to the growing prominence of FDI as the main conduit of international economic, technological, and knowledge flows. China, which has maintained strategic use of operational controls to achieve its rapid catch-up development, appears to be an exception.

In the case of China, rising FDI inflows at the start of the 1990s is associated with the country's encouragement of FDI in SEZs. Since that time, inward FDI flows have climbed steadily, but due to the country's policy framework of maintaining high levels of domestic investment, FDI as a share of gross fixed capital formation (GFCF) has been on the decline since reaching a peak of 17 per cent in 1994. By 2016, gross inward FDI flow was US$133.7 billion but FDI as a share of GFCF was 2.8 per cent. These trends contrast to those of India and Malaysia, which have both received growing FDI inflows over time, particularly since the mid-2000s for India and in the aftermath of the Asian financial crisis for Malaysia. However, because both countries' growth experiences involved lower levels of domestic investment (and higher levels of final consumption), GFCF rates appear more directly influenced by (volatile) FDI inflows (see Kozul-Wright and Poon 2018: figure 4).

The difference, in part, stems from the role of national development banks (NDBs) in supporting national policy goals such as boosting domestic investment, industrial diversification and upgrading, and employment creation. In principle, NDBs are potent policy instruments since they operate in market segments at the core of the process of structural transformation. Their main function is to address imperfect capital markets that are unwilling to bear the risks associated with extending finance to large-scale capital-intensive projects (or new sectors, products) characterized by high degrees of uncertainty, and long gestation and learning periods. As private investors cannot capture the positive externalities often generated from such projects, the result is underinvestment in these areas. NDBs can institutionally bridge asset–liability mismatches between long-term investment in infrastructure projects and short-term deposits in the banking system. NDBs can also play a proactive role by utilizing their accumulation of research, technical support, and institutional capabilities to shape and create markets, in anticipation of demand and in the co-ordination of domestic supply responses (UNCTAD 2016b).

In practice, the effectiveness of NDBs as a policy tool has been uneven and their role remains contested (Studart and Gallagher 2016; Caixin Media 2017). One main lesson from past East Asian experiences with NDBs is the adaptability of government policies to abandon policies that are not functioning and to adjust policies to changing circumstances—that is, adjustments made in the operational controls of these institutions. The design of East Asian development finance institutions (DFIs) included measures to mitigate their susceptibility to political discretion in decision-making and to enhance the likelihood that resources are used effectively. Such measures included the use of performance-based criteria for credit allocation, applying commercial criteria to firms that receive credit and requiring these firms to raise part of their own funds while also contributing their own equity (Stiglitz and Uy 1996: 271–3).

Figure 6.3 shows broad trends in the respective use of NDBs in China, India, and Malaysia, in contributing to growth patterns that gave rise to the Asian divergence. These rough estimates reveal an increasing domestic role of NDB outstanding loans as a share of GDP in China and Malaysia. In contrast, outstanding loans of NDBs in India have stagnated at low levels over the past decade and have fallen dramatically from early 2000 levels. Individual NDB country experiences are examined later to further underscore the different approaches in adjusting the operational controls of these institutions as part of an overall national development strategy. In general terms, trends in Figure 6.3 are consistent with each countries' respective approach to economic (and financial) openness: low for India, medium for China, and high for Malaysia.

In China, three NDBs were created in 1994 as part of overall banking sector reforms, as government authorities sought to better distinguish between commercial-based lending and policy-based lending. The three NDBs were the China Development Bank (CDB), the Export–Import Bank of China (CEXIM), and the Agricultural Development Bank of China, of which CDB has the largest balance sheet and a primary focus on financing large-scale infrastructure and industrial projects. Despite initial difficulties, China's NDBs were backed by state resources and political leadership, which allowed them an increasingly prominent role as providers of long-term financing at the centre of the country's high-investment growth strategy. In terms of its funding sources, CDB is not a deposit-taking institution, but relies on borrowing from domestic capital markets rather than direct government support (UNCTAD 2016b). In 2015, CDB and CEXIM received respective capital injections of US$48 billion and US$45 billion to further bolster their lending capacity.

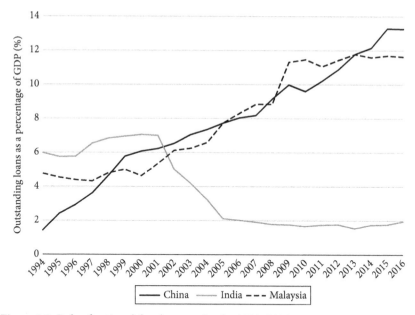

Figure 6.3 Role of national development banks, 1994–2016.

Source: Authors' elaboration based on data from China Development Bank (various years), Xu (2016), Reserve Bank of India (various years), Bank Negara Malaysia (various years), and International Monetary Fund (2018).

Plans to place CDB on a greater commercial footing through measures to bring in an outside strategic investor, take deposits from the public, assume greater responsibility for the risks of its investments, and sell shares in an initial public offering were halted in the advent of the 2008 global financial crisis—an event in which local government financing vehicles, an institutional innovation pioneered by CDB since the late 1990s, played a critical countercyclical role. Since the late 2000s, CDB and CEXIM have also been a major source of China's overseas development finance.

Malaysia's history with NDBs began with the Malaysian Industrial Development Finance, created in 1960 to extend medium- to long-term financing to private industrial enterprises. This was followed by subsequent DFIs: Bank Pertanian (the agricultural sector), Bank Pembangunan (Bumiputera groups in commerce and industry), and Bank Industri (industry and manufacturing sectors), and export-related DFIs such as the Export–Import Bank of Malaysia (MEXIM). From the mid-2000s onwards, Malaysia had thirteen DFIs (Ghani 2005; Islam 2015).

After the Asian financial crisis, Malaysia's fragmented banking sector was consolidated and DFIs were rationalized in the mid-2000s. Aside from concerns over financial sustainability, policymakers wanted to increase DFI financing to priority sectors and reduce overlapping functions. For instance, the formation of a small and medium-sized enterprise bank was the result of restructuring Bank

Pembangunan and Bank Industri. The other major DFI consolidation involved MEXIM and Malaysia's export credit insurance agency. In light of the myriad DFI entities, at the end of 2005, the sectoral allocation of DFI lending (by assets) supported both domestic investment and consumption levels, with the latter accounting for 40 per cent of the total. DFI funding sources can vary, with some mainly drawn from government borrowings and multilateral development agencies and others from bank deposits (Bank Negara Malaysia 2006: 178–9, 183).

In the case of India, it has a longer experience with NDBs that can be divided into three phases: (i) the late 1940s to mid-1960s, (ii) the 1980s, and (iii) the late 1990s to early 2000s. The first phase kick-started industrialization, mainly with the creation of long-term nationwide lending institutions: the Industrial Finance Corporation of India (IFCI) (1948), the Industrial Credit and Investment Corporation of India (ICICI) (1955), and the Industrial Development Bank of India (IDBI) (1964). The 1980s phase featured the creation of refinancing and issue-specific institutions such as the National Bank for Agriculture and Rural Development, the National Housing Bank, and the Small Industries Development Bank of India. In the third phase, however, India's financial sector underwent major reforms that eliminated DFIs' preferential access to concessional government finance and issuance of government-guaranteed bonds (Nayyar 2015; UNCTAD 2016b).

These structural changes reduced the role of development finance in India, as major DFIs were converted into commercial banks (except for IFCI). Over time, the distinction between short-term and long-term finance providers in the Indian banking system was blurred (Reddy 2005), which has led to renewed interest in reviving DFIs for infrastructure sectors (Reddy 2017). India's DFIs have historically played a strong role, but major challenges remain. In particular, they did not focus on infrastructure; and in the sectors in which they did engage, the relationships with firms often did not extend beyond lending. Moreover, there was little co-ordination between DFIs and industrial policy priorities in terms of sectoral focus. This lack of co-ordination has been attributed to weak institutional control mechanisms that (i) adjusted incentives according to performance, and (ii) provided effective checks and balances to prevent and dissuade rent-seeking between governments and firms, or between development banks and firms (Nayyar 2015).

4. Concluding Remarks

In a sense, Myrdal's study of Asia anticipated the Asian divergence even as it missed its genesis; the policy lessons drawn from his work—if broadly implemented—would lead a developing country on a growth path that would separate it from the rest. While Myrdal did not include East Asia, he did so indirectly by outlining the basic institutional, organizational, and policy ingredients needed for sustained development that were already being adopted by East Asian policymakers. As such, *Asian Drama* remains remarkably prescient fifty years after its publication, by still providing core insights to understand (if not predict) the Asian divergence.

The four concepts of Myrdal's analysis have been variously integrated into mainstream development discourse over time, albeit to different extents. Of the four, the soft states concept has arguably received the least attention, but Myrdal's elaboration of operational controls and the need for co-ordination of these controls, predated similar concepts of policy space, reciprocal control mechanisms, and the export–investment nexus that would become essential tenets of heterodox economic policy-thinking.

With the global development discourse gradually progressing from the *why* of conducting industrial policy strategy to the *how* of implementing it, this chapter does not try to comprehensively assess economic openness in the three selected Asian countries, but has sought to advance the discussion by triangulating between (i) the orientation of selected policy tools in trade, technology, investment, and finance in shaping a country's degree of economic openness (low, medium, or high); (ii) the rational co-ordination of operational controls of these policy tools to achieve desired objectives; and (iii) the overall development outcomes observed in the Asian divergence. The rational co-ordination of operational controls is in reference to the strategic use of selected policy tools in the historically successful experiences of the East Asian NIEs.

By this measure, evidence presented in this chapter seems consistent with the idea that China has adopted and adapted the strategic approach to integration from earlier East Asian development strategies. The weakness or absence of similar operational controls in the opening up of both the Indian and Malaysian economy has hampered efforts to diversify and upgrade.

From a wider perspective, in comparing the opening-up experiences of the three Asian countries, each could be considered as separate development pathways based on different approaches to economic reforms. In this respect, these cases provide insights into the application of the theory of the second best, and the likely role of operational controls and their co-ordination, in influencing different reform outcomes. Going forward, it is imperative that the scope of operational controls be calibrated in each country according to the level of openness appropriate for the realization of national objectives at its current stage of development. For China, its transition from medium-income to high-income status entails a continued gradual path towards greater openness with strategic retention of policy space—particularly as it seeks to upgrade its position within existing GVCs and to build its own. At a lower income level, India likely needs more doses of pragmatic openness to spur its manufacturing sector and to better engage with GVCs; while, at a higher income level, Malaysia may need to adopt selective separation from existing GVCs and to generate competitive pressure for upgrading by fostering local value chains.

Perhaps the most striking illustration of a second-best mindset is China's use of DFIs: returned to financial health in the late 1990s without privatization, NDBs were at the heart of China's high-investment industrialization drive. By the mid-2000s, China's DFIs backed the internationalization of Chinese firms, and, more recently, are supporting upgrading efforts in the Made in China 2025 plan. China also led the creation of two new multilateral development banks, which, in conjunction with its NDBs, are spearheading China's Belt and Road initiative—a foreign economic policy focused on building regional infrastructure that could transform development prospects in Asia.

While Myrdal's *Asian Drama* provided a rich portrayal of development prospects in South and Southeast Asia, this chapter also considers the rapid catch-up growth experiences of East Asia, and more recently China, in matching Myrdal's analytical concepts with the few instructive development cases where 'driving a car with the accelerator pushed to the floor' was co-ordinated with use of the brakes. This simple notion goes to the heart of Asian divergence and to ongoing episodes of Asian development drama.

References

Aggarwal, A. (2006). 'Special Economic Zones: Revisiting the Policy Debate', *Economic & Political Weekly*, 41(43–4): 4533–6. Available at: https://www.epw.in/journal/2006/43-44/commentary/special-economic-zones-revisiting-policy-debate.html (accessed 29 April 2019).

Akyuz, Y. (2017). *Playing With Fire*. Oxford: Oxford University Press.

Amsden, A. (2004). 'Import Substitution in High-Tech Industries: Prebisch Lives in Asia!', *CEPAL Review*, 82: 75–89.

Athukorala, P.C. (2017). 'Global Productions Sharing and Local Entrepreneurship in Developing Countries: Evidence from Penang Export Hub, Malaysia', *Asia & The Pacific Policy Studies*, 4(2): 180–94.

Athukorala, P.C. (2018). 'Joining Global Production Networks: Experience and Prospects of India,' Paper presented at the 27the Conference of Asian Economic Policy Review (AEPR), Tokyo, Japan, April, Japan Center for Economic Research (JCER) Working Paper 2018-1-4.

Bank Negara Malaysia (2006). *Annual Report 2005*. Kuala Lumpur: Bank Negara Malaysia.

Bank Negara Malaysia (various years). *Annual Report*. Kuala Lumpur: Bank Negara Malaysia.

Blanchard, O., and J. Acalin (2016). 'What Does FDI Actually Measure?', Policy Brief 16–17, Peterson Institute for International Economics, Washington, DC.

Caixin Media (2017). 'Zhou Xiaochuan: "Belt and Road" Investment Finance should be Market-Oriented' [in Chinese], March.

Chang, H.J. (2009). 'Industrial Policy: Can We Go Beyond an Unproductive Confrontation?'. Paper prepared for Annual World Bank Conference on Development Economics, 22 to 24 June, Seoul, South Korea.

China Development Bank (various years). *Annual Report*. Beijing: CDB.

Dinh, H.T., T.G. Rawski, A. Zafar, L. Wang, and E. Mavroeidi (2013). *Tales from the Development Frontier: How China and Other Countries Harness Light Manufacturing to Create Jobs and Prosperity*. Washington, DC: World Bank.

Ernst, D. (2002). 'Global Production Networks in East Asia's Electronics Industry and Upgrading Perspectives in Malaysia', October, East-West Center, Honolulu, East-West Center Working Papers 44.

Fu, X.L., and Y. Gao (2007). 'Export Processing Zones in China: A Survey', Report submitted to ILO, October.

Gallagher, K.P., and M. Shafaeddin (2009). 'Policies for Industrial Learning in China and Mexico', February, Research and Information System for Developing Countries, New Delhi, RIS Discussion Papers RIS-DP 150.

Ghani, D.Z.A. (2005). 'Role of Development Financial Institutions in the Financial System', Bank of International Settlements, 12 September.

Heilmann, S., L. Shih, and A. Hofem (2013). 'National Planning and Local Technology Zones: Experimental Governance in China's Torch Program', *The China Quarterly*, 216: 896–919.

International Monetary Fund (2018). 'International Financial Statistics'. Available at: https://www.imf.org/en/Data (accessed October 2018).

Islam, M.A. (2015). 'An Empirical Assessment of the Impact of Development Financial Institutions (DFIs) on Malaysian Economy', *International Journal of Financial Economics*, 4(4): 176–84.

Jenkins, M., G. Esquivel, and F. Larraín (1998). 'Export Processing Zones in Central America', Central America Project Series, July, Harvard Institute for International Development, Cambridge, MA, Development Discussion Papers 4.

Jo, J., J. Kim, Y. Lim, C. Chang, D. Kwon, U. Lee, and U. Jung (2012). 'Korea's Development Experience Modularization: Industrial Complex Development Policy in Korea', Korea Research Institute for Human Settlements (KRIHS), Ministry of Land, Transport and Maritime Affairs, Republic of Korea.

Kozul-Wright, R., and D. Poon (2018). 'Asian Development After the Asian Drama', October, WIDER Working Paper 2018/135.

Lal, D. (1985). *The Poverty of Development Economics*. Cambridge, MA: Harvard University Press.

Lim, W. (2010). 'Joint Discovery and Upgrading of Comparative Advantage: Lessons from Korea's Development Experience'. In S. Fardoust, Y. Kim, and C. Sepulveda (eds) *Postcrisis Growth and Development: A Development Agenda for the G20*. Washington, DC: World Bank.

Loayza, N., A. Ouazad, and R. Rancière (2017). 'Financial Development, Growth, and Crisis: Is there a Trade-off?', November, World Bank, Washington, DC, World Bank Policy Research Working Paper Series 8237.

Low, L. (2001). 'The Role of the Government in Singapore's Industrialization'. In K.S. Jomo (ed.) *Southeast Asia's Industrialization: Industrial Policy, Capabilities and Sustainability*. Houndmills: Palgrave.

Madani, D. (1999). 'A Review of the Role and Impact of Export Processing Zones', November, World Bank, Washington, DC, World Bank Policy Research Working Paper 2238.

Milberg, W., and D. Winkler (2013). *Outsourcing Economics: Global Value Chains in Capitalist Development*. Cambridge: Cambridge University Press.

Mukherjee, A., P. Pal, S. Deb, S. Ray, and T.M. Goyal (2016). *Special Economic Zones in India: Status, Issues and Potential*. New Delhi: Indian Council for Research on International Economic Relations.

Myint, M. (1977). 'Adam Smith's Theory of International Trade in the Perspective of Economic Development', *Economica*, 44(175): 231–48.

Myrdal, G. (1968). *Asian Drama: An Inquiry into the Poverty of Nations*. New York: Pantheon.

Myrdal, G. (1970a). *The Challenge of World Poverty: A World Anti-Poverty Programme in Outline*. London: Pelican Books.

Myrdal, G. (1970b). *An Approach to the Asian Drama: Methodological and Theoretical*. New York: Vintage Books.

Nayyar, D. (2015). 'Birth, Life, and Death of Development Finance Institutions in India', *Economic & Political Weekly*, 1(33): 51–60.

Ocampo, J.A., and R. Vos (2008). 'Policy Space and the Changing Paradigm in Conducting Macroeconomic Policies in Developing Countries', February, BIS Papers 36.

OECD (2018). Trade in Value Added (TiVA) Database. Available at: https://stats.oecd.org/ (accessed October 2018).

Rasiah, R. (2015). 'The Industrial Policy Experience of the Electronics Industry in Malaysia', UNU-WIDER, Helsinki, WIDER Working Paper 2015/123.

Reddy, Y.V. (2005). 'Banking Sector Reforms in India—An Overview', May, BIS Review 35/2005.

Reddy, Y.V. (2017). 'Development Banking—Way Forward', NSE-IEA Lecture on Financial Economics, 27 to 30 December.

Reserve Bank of India (various years). *Handbook of Statistics on Indian Economy*.

Sakong, I., and Y. Koh (2010). *The Korean Economy: Six Decades of Growth and Development*. Seoul: Korea Development Institute.

Stiglitz, J.E., and M. Uy (1996). 'Financial Markets, Public Policy, and the East Asian Miracle', *World Bank Research Observer*, 11(2): 249–76.

Studart, R., and K.P. Gallagher (2016). 'Infrastructure for Sustainable Development: The Role of National Development Banks', October, Boston University, Boston, MA, GEGI Policy Brief 007.

Studwell, J. (2013). *How Asia Works: Success and Failure in the World's Most Dynamic Region*. New York: Grove Press.

Thurborn, E., and L. Weiss (2006). 'Investing in Openness: The Evolution of FDI Strategy in South Korea and Taiwan', *New Political Economy*, 11(1): 1–22.

Toner, P. (2000). *Main Currents in Cumulative Causation: The Dynamics of Growth and Development*. London: Palgrave.

Tu, J.H., and C. Schive (1995). 'Determinants of Foreign Direct Investment in Taiwan Province of China: A New Approach and Findings', *Transnational Corporations*, 4(2): 93–103.

United Nations (2018). UN Comtrade Database. Available at: https://comtrade. un.org/ (accessed October 2018).

UNCTAD (1994). *Trade and Development Report, 1994*. New York and Geneva: United Nations.

UNCTAD (1996). *Trade and Development Report, 1996*. New York and Geneva: United Nations.

UNCTAD (2003). *Trade and Development Report, 2003*. New York and Geneva: United Nations.

UNCTAD (2014). *Trade and Development Report, 2014*. New York and Geneva: United Nations.

UNCTAD (2016a). *Structural Transformation for Inclusive and Sustained Growth. Trade and Development Report 2016*. New York and Geneva: United Nations.

UNCTAD (2016b). *The Role of Development Banks in Promoting Growth and Sustainable Development in the South*. UNCTAD Report, December. New York and Geneva: United Nations.

UNCTAD (2018). UNCTADstat. Available at: http://unctadstat.unctad.org/EN/ (accessed October 2018).

Wade, R. (2010). 'After the Crisis: Industrial Policy and the Developmental State in Low-Income Countries', *Global Policy*, 1(2): 150–61.

Warr, P.G. (1984). 'Korea's Masan Free Export Zone: Benefits and Costs', *The Developing Economies*, 22(2): 169–84.

World Bank (1993). *The East Asian Miracle: Economic Growth and Public Policy*. Washington, DC: World Bank.

Xu, Q.Y. (2016). 'CDB: Born Bankrupt, Born Shaper', Presentation to BNDES-CAF-IPD Conference, 15–16 September, Rio de Janeiro.

7

Agriculture, the Rural Sector, and Development

Rob Vos

1. Introduction

Over the past sixty years, most Asian countries have undergone relatively rapid agricultural transformations that helped jump-start broader economic development. However, the changes have differed markedly in nature and speed across countries of the region. In much of East and Southeast Asia, the Green Revolution brought a quantum leap in yields and output of rice and wheat, which boosted smallholder farm productivity and profits. Farms became more commercial and agricultural value-added per worker rose significantly. Public investment and strong support for smallholder agriculture and agrarian reforms through to the late 1990s paved the way for manufacturing industries to develop. Gradually, aggregate economic growth increasingly depended on dynamics in the service and industrial sectors. While the Green Revolution also played an important role in South Asia, the processes of agricultural transformation and structural change have lagged the ones taking place in East Asia. The service sector has become predominant, especially in India, and a mature manufacturing sector has yet to develop. Institutional reforms and public support for rural infrastructure were less pervasive. As a result, South Asia has been slow in making the shift from low- to high-productivity employment, despite the decline in agriculture's share in total gross domestic product (GDP).

These are symptoms of deeper-rooted factors that delayed transformative change, including those that concerned Gunnar Myrdal when he wrote his three-volume *Asian Drama* (Myrdal 1968). At the time of writing, he saw a kind of drama playing out in postcolonial South Asia, and despite the complexities and dissimilarities among the different nations of South Asia there was a clear-cut set of conflicts and a common theme, as in any drama, trapping people into poverty. Myrdal's other seminal contribution (building on ideas of Wicksell and Kaldor) is the concept of circular cumulative causation (Myrdal 1957). From this perspective, he saw that constraints to natural resource availability, historical traditions of production activity, weak institutions, lack of national cohesion, and/or traditional or religious beliefs could conspire to holding back agriculture and broader economic development in cumulative causation.

Myrdal's analysis—and his pessimism—focused mainly on India, but he extended this to Indonesia and other countries as well. He believed that traditional power structures were likely to persist. Unless there was change, the chances of economic take-off were slim. He perceived governments in the region as too 'soft', unable to enforce the discipline needed to implement their development plans. He doubted whether faster agricultural development, crucial for raising living standards in the rural areas and for providing the savings and markets to support industrialization, would take place without either radical land distribution or consolidation into communes, neither of which he believed was politically feasible (Lankester 2004). In such settings, the effect of pushing out labour from traditional activity would initially lead to the reduction of employment, income, and demand. The consequent contraction of the markets would have a depressing effect on new investments, which in turn would cause a further reduction of income and demand and, if nothing happens to modify the trend, there would be a net movement of enterprises and workers towards other areas.

In today's context, the question is how Asian societies managed to break away from this cycle and what type of more benign rural transformation process would be needed to address today's challenges of accelerated urban population growth, rising inequality, unprecedented size of young populations, limited employment prospects, and environmental constraints and threats.

This chapter re-examines Asia's agricultural and rural transformations in the context of economy-wide structural change. It focuses on the different pathways Asian societies have taken in terms of agricultural transitions; transformation of food systems with rising incomes and urbanization; infrastructure development to forge rural–urban linkages; and implications of broader structural economic transformations, with the objective of identifying the factors of cumulative causation explaining why development accelerated in one part of the region and lagged in another. In light of the review of evidence presented in this chapter, lessons will be drawn as to how to address today's challenges for the development of Asia's agriculture and food systems and possible pathways for more inclusive and sustainable rural transformations in the coming decades.

2. Exiting Agriculture, Patterns of Structural Change, and Poverty Reduction

2.1 Agricultural Exit and Structural Change

Economic development has historically been characterized by sustained structural change, typically initiated by a shift of labour out of agriculture into the 'modern' industrial sector. The result of this process is an increased share of non-agricultural sectors in GDP, as well as in employment. The Lewis dual-economy model provided an early theoretical formulation of this process (Lewis 1954).

Investment in modern sector capital would drive economic growth and induce excess labour in agriculture (whose marginal product was assumed to be zero) to move to the modern sector. For most of Asia and Latin America, this modern sector has been industry; rapid growth in Asia has also been spurred by exports of industrial products (especially in China and other parts of East Asia). In India, in contrast, recent structural transformation has been characterized by greater employment in services (both formal and informal), rather than industry (Ashan and Mitra 2016).

The shift from agriculture to non-agriculture has also been a common pattern of growth pathways in Asia. Japan's structural change is most advanced with agriculture shares of GDP of below 2 per cent and agriculture's employment share below 5 per cent (Figure 7.1, upper panel). Structural change in the Republic of Korea started much later, but accelerated from the 1970s to similarly low agricultural shares as prevailing nowadays in Japan. Malaysia's degree of structural change is not far behind. Indonesia, the Philippines, and Thailand still have relatively high shares of agricultural employment at around 30 per cent or more, with the pace of structural change picking up from the 1990s. In these countries, the labour exit from agriculture has lagged the speed in the decline of agriculture's share in GDP. The relative size of Vietnam's agricultural sector was stagnant at around 40 per cent of GDP during the 1970s and 1980s, to start its descent only after the *doi moi* agrarian reform policies of 1987 and 1988 induced a shift away from collective farms to individual private farming (see McCaig and Pavcnik 2016). However, the agricultural employment share remained high at 65 to 70 per cent of the labour force until the early 2000s. Additional domestic and external reforms lifting price controls and restrictions in the mid-1990s induced greater adoption of modern farming practices, pushing up agricultural productivity growth and accelerating the exit of labour from agriculture. Agriculture's employment share dropped from 65 per cent in 2000 to just over 40 per cent in 2016.

In comparison to the other major Asian economies, India's process of structural change appears to be a bit of an outlier, as visible in the lower panel of Figure 7.1. The Green Revolution pushed up agricultural productivity in the country's expanding commercial farm sector. Agriculture's share in GDP declined with the expansion of non-agricultural sectors and, despite the relatively limited labour exit from agriculture, as many (hundreds of millions) smallholders and landless agricultural workers were left behind in the agricultural transformation process. Between 1960 and 1985, agriculture's share in GDP declined from over 60 per cent to about 40 per cent; the sector's employment share remained near stable at around 70 per cent. Agriculture's employment share declined only slowly between 1985 and 2000 to reach 60 per cent at the end of that period. The labour exit from agriculture has accelerated since, as the overall pace of growth of the Indian economy picked up significantly. Nonetheless, in 2016 there was still about

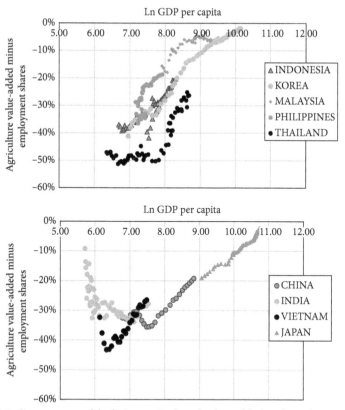

Figure 7.1 Convergence of declining agricultural value-added and employment shares with rising income per capita in China, India, Indonesia, Rep. of Korea, Malaysia, Philippines, Thailand, and Vietnam, 1950–2016.

Note: Period coverage is as follows China (1991–2016); Indonesia (1971–2016); India (1960–2016); Japan (1953–2015); Republic of Korea (1963–2016); Malaysia (1975–2016); Philippines (1971–2016); Thailand (1960–2016); Vietnam (1991–2016).

Source: Author's calculations from sectoral national income and employment data from Groningen Growth and Development Centre (n.d.) database, World Bank (n.d.) World Development Indicators, and ILO (n.d.) ILOSTAT.

45 per cent of the labour force working in agriculture, on a par (also in terms of the degree of structural change) with that of Vietnam. The slow drop in agriculture's employment share signals a decline in agriculture's relative productivity rate. At difference with Vietnam and the rest of the Asian economies, Indian workers leaving agriculture have largely sidestepped manufacturing, whose shares in GDP and employment remain low at around 12 per cent. Instead, the structural change has been towards modern and informal services sectors, with the modern part being a major driver of the recent growth acceleration (Ashan and Mitra 2016).

2.2 Structural Change, Growth, and Poverty Reduction

Economic growth in the developing world has led to substantial reductions in poverty over the last two and a half decades. Much of this success was driven by structural change and associated fast economic growth in Asia. Within the region at large, poverty reduction has been more pronounced in most of East and Southeast Asia, where structural change also has progressed the most. The average poverty headcount for these two regions fell from 60.2 per cent in 1990 to 3.5 per cent in 2013 (World Bank 2017).[1] Around 2015, less than 10 per cent of the world's poor population lived in East and Southeast Asia, down from more than half in 1990. The poverty rate also declined significantly in South Asia over this period (from 44.6 to 15.1 per cent), but not as dramatically as in East Asia and, because of faster population growth in South Asia, the sub-region's share of the world's poor population increased from 27.4 to 33.5 per cent.

Various studies provide evidence showing that, especially in early stages of structural transformation, agricultural productivity growth has a larger poverty-reduction effect than increases in industry or services (World Bank 2008; Ivanic and Martin 2018). While impacts vary across countries, also within South Asia, agricultural growth seems more important to poverty reduction than growth in other sectors. The study by Ivanic and Martin (2018) finds that the impact of productivity improvements in agriculture (equivalent to 1 per cent of GDP) would reduce poverty in India by 1.6 percentage points, more than three times the impact of productivity improvements of the same relative magnitude in industry and services. In Bangladesh, the impact of agricultural productivity growth on poverty reduction would be even greater (2.6 percentage points) and more than six times that of non-agricultural sectors, while, in contrast, in Vietnam, the poverty-reduction impact from agricultural growth would be much smaller and only marginally higher than that of productivity growth in industry or services. This suggests different pathways towards inclusive structural change are possible. To understand those, it is important to look at the key factors that influence sectoral poverty–growth elasticities.

3. Agriculture and Food System Changes as Conditioners of Inclusive and Exclusive Structural Transformation

According to Timmer (2014), three key lessons can be drawn from historical pathways of structural transformation. First, structural transformation has shown to be an important way for people to climb out of poverty, especially when productivity rises in both agricultural and non-agricultural sectors through strong

[1] The poverty headcount is calculated using the World Bank's poverty line of US$1.90 in purchasing power parity (PPP) per person per day.

inter-sectoral linkages (Hirschman 1958; World Bank 2008). Without broad-based productivity growth, labour more likely will be 'pushed' into low-paying informal service jobs, rather than 'pulled' out by highly productive manufacturing and services. Second, even with broad-based productivity growth, structural transformation tends to widen the income gap between agricultural and non-agricultural sectors and between rural and urban areas, putting most of the pressure on rural societies to adjust. Third, in order to catalyse productivity growth and structural change, substantial investments in the agricultural sector are needed despite its declining relative importance.

However, the way in which these factors played out in the past, and should be expected to play out moving forward, is conditioned on five other transformative processes that are taking place in parallel: urbanization, dietary change, agricultural technology and farm size change, food market transformations, and rural labour market changes (Reardon and Timmer 2014). All of these change processes are relevant to structural change in Asia. They should be seen as linked in cumulative causation, as Myrdal would argue. These factors will be discussed in the subsequent sub-sections, starting with the importance of shifting demographics and changing diets, followed by the role of changing farm technologies and farming systems, and the dynamics of rural non-farm activities in driving the nature of agricultural transformations. The role of policies and institutional reforms in all of this will be taken on in section 4.

3.1 Shifting Demographics, Shifting Diets

Myrdal wrote *Asian Drama* against the prevailing economic and social conditions in the 1950s and 1960s. Painted with a broad brush, most Asian economies were still strongly agrarian based, with most people living in rural areas, and population growth driven by high fertility rates. Land was scarce, though generally fertile, such that intensification of staple crop production would be critical to addressing both the challenges of food insecurity and poverty. With economic development, however, demographic pressures have changed, as population growth has decelerated and urbanization rates have gone up. Fertility rates and family sizes have fallen with income levels, altering the underlying drivers of economic growth, as capital accumulation becomes more important than labour supply. Higher average urban incomes and larger city populations have led to expanding urban food markets and have changed the composition of food demand, as higher incomes lead to dietary change: even as food shares tend to fall (Engel's law), total food expenditures typically continue to rise with per capita incomes, as the share of dietary energy that comes from typically cheaper cereals and other starchy food staples falls while consumption of more expensive animal-sourced foods, fruits and vegetables, and processed foods increases (Bennett's law). These changes associated with urbanization have created new opportunities for farmers in terms of larger food markets for products with, generally, higher value-added, meeting the needs of a rising Asian middle class (Tschirley et al. 2015). Meats, dairy products, and fruits and vegetable production require higher input use (land, water, fertilizers, and/or pesticides), inducing changes in land use and requiring farmers to adopt new technologies.

The changing demographics and diets have not only changed agricultural transformation processes, but also created new challenges. Increased resource use may lead to overexploitation of natural resources and accelerate environmental degradation, where land and water resources are already scarce (Vos and Bellù 2019). Where population growth is still strong, expanding rural populations may increase population density and reduce average farm size, especially among smallholders (Masters et al. 2013). This could induce farmers to diversify into off-farm employment, which could help accelerate positive structural change and poverty reduction, if rural non-farm activity expands alongside, and rural–urban linkages are strengthened.

On the Asian continent, urbanization has advanced farthest in East Asia, where 60 per cent of the population lives in cities today and the share is expected to rise to 80 per cent by 2050 (Vos 2018). Importantly, East Asia's rural population started to decrease in absolute terms from around 2005, reflective of advanced structural economic change. The Republic of Korea's rural population started to decrease from 1970 and its urban population share had already surpassed 80 per cent by 2015 and is projected to reach almost 90 per cent by 2050. China's urban share in the population increased from less than 20 per cent at the start of its economic take-off around 1980 to 56 per cent in 2015 and is projected to increase to 75 per cent by 2050. The absolute size of China's rural population has been decreasing since 1995. Korea's and China's populations are ageing rapidly and their total populations are expected to shrink from around 2030 onwards.

In Southeast Asia, Thailand and Malaysia had reached their Lewisian turning points around 2000. Indonesia and Vietnam did so more recently, while the Philippines—where population growth is still high—is not expected to reach its turning point before 2040. South Asia is the least urbanized region (even less so than Sub-Saharan Africa) and its rural population is expected to continue to grow *in absolute terms* until about 2030. This is also the case in India.

Due to restrictive population control policies, East Asia (China in particular) reached its demographic transition point much earlier than countries in South Asia. This is also evident from today's youth dynamics. South Asia's youth population is expanding at a rate close to the total population's growth rate, whereas East Asia's youth population is falling in absolute terms and almost as fast as the rural population (see Vos 2018: figure 4). These trends set different employment challenges across the Asian continent, with those in South Asia being most pressing from a

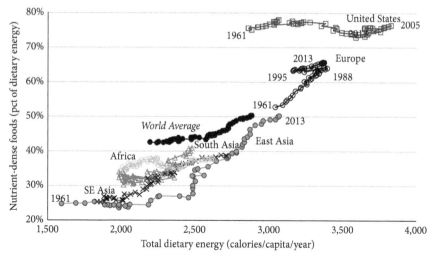

Figure 7.2 From more food to different foods: the dietary transition by Asia in comparison to the rest of the world, 1961–2013.

Note: Europe includes all of the former Soviet Union.

Source: Masters (2018) (with permission), based on FAO food balance sheets data.

structural transformation perspective, as rural populations are still large and rising and vast numbers of young people are entering rural labour markets every year.

Dietary transitions are also taking place at different speeds across the continent. Figure 7.2 shows long-term trends in the per capita quantity of all foods, measured in calories, and a fraction of those calories that come from foods other than starchy staples. Clearly, Asia's sub-regions start at the bottom left of the chart, but, as their incomes have risen, total food energy supply (and apparent consumption) have increased starkly since the 1960s. The share of non-starchy staple crops started to increase markedly from around 1980. This is most visible in East Asia where today over 50 per cent of food energy intake coming from foods other than cereals and starchy roots. In South and Southeast Asia, the dietary transition is clearly less advanced but has also accelerated over the past two decades.

Increased per capita incomes bring not only increased diversity in the types of food, but also the forms in which those foods are consumed (e.g., more processing and packaging). These changes are facilitated by major transformations of agri-food supply chains with increased dominance of modern, large-scale food processing and wholesale and retail distribution. Higher incomes, urbanization, and the structural transformation of the economy have been supported by agricultural productivity increases but impacts on poverty reduction have been influenced by the way in which farm systems have been transformed at the same time through mechanization, changing farm size, and crop and product diversification. We turn to these processes in the next subsection.

3.2   Agricultural Technology Change and Farm Size

Agricultural output growth has been rather robust over the past half-century, especially in East Asia (China in particular), but—from the 1970s—also in Southeast Asia and more recently also in South Asia. As shown in Vos (2018: table 1), in recent decades (from the 1990s), total factor productivity growth has become the main driver of agricultural output growth in Asia, as much as in other parts of the world, whereas output growth in previous decades was mainly driven by increasing the use of inputs (land, labour, fertilizers).[2]

Important changes in Asia's farming systems have underpinned agricultural productivity growth and efficiency gains over the past four to five decades. Reardon and Timmer (2014) summarize the evidence as showing that farms have become commercial, agricultural production has diversified (away from grains, mirroring the dietary change, as discussed later), even as individual farms have become more specialized (into cropping, or livestock, poultry, and aquaculture), and farmers have shifted from non-purchased to purchased input use (i.e., from human to animal to machine power, from manure, by-products, and residues to chemical fertilizer, and to use of more pesticides and herbicides). The degree and speed of these changes has varied across locations. These changes occurred earliest and fastest in the 'classical Green Revolution' zones, particularly lowland rice systems and irrigated wheat areas. During the 2000s, a second wave of intensification and commercialization occurred in areas that were 'catching up' with the initial Green Revolution zones, such as in Uttar Pradesh in India, northern Bangladesh, and northeast China, in rice, potato, and horticulture (Reardon et al. 2012). Gulati et al. (2004) document the diversification of agricultural production in parts of India with the development of horticulture in the 1990s and 2000s.

More recently, capital intensity of Asian agriculture has increased, significantly reflected in increased use of mechanization and less use of labour. Dawe (2015) finds the uptake of machine use in agriculture (for preparing soils and harvesting) among small and larger farms alike. The development of rental markets for agricultural machinery has facilitated this process. These changes have not been across the board and, especially in many parts of South Asia, the process of commercialization-intensification/diversification-mechanization has been slower, explaining in part the slower structural transformation.

The impact on rural wages and off-farm employment of these processes of change in farm systems is relevant to the dynamics of the structural transformation process. Reardon and Timmer (2014) see an important influence running from rural non-farm employment growth and rural wage increases to greater capital intensity. Greater income from off-farm activity allows farmers to buy or

---

[2] See also Alexandratos and Bruinsma (2012), Fuglie (2015), FAO (2017a), and Vos and Bellù (2019) for a corroboration of these trends.

rent machinery. Conversely, mechanization frees labour for both migration to cities and rural non-farm activities.

Improved infrastructure, like rural roads, electricity, irrigation, and communications, has been a critical factor in increasing total factor productivity in China and other parts of Asia over the past three decades (Fan et al. 2004; Fan 2008). Production areas well served by rural roads, and those closer to urban areas, have lower transaction costs of getting inputs, and higher use rates.

These changes (commercialization, modern inputs use, mechanization, improved infrastructure) have helped raise both land and total factor productivity. Growth in labour productivity has been relatively slow in South Asia, as visible from the rather steep upward-sloping land-labour productivity curves in Figure 7.3.

This holds for India, Pakistan, and Nepal, in particular; and to a lesser extent for Bangladesh, where labour and land productivity have moved at a similar pace, albeit both from low levels. Land and labour productivity in Indonesia, Thailand, and the Philippines initially also followed similar growth paths, but giving way for faster agricultural labour productivity and wage growth from the mid-1990s as their industrialization processes further moved up the ladder. In China, land and labour productivity growth have moved in tandem since 1980, as visible in Figure 7.3. The institutional reforms that allowed individual farmers to sell

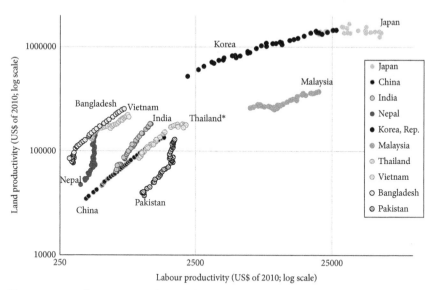

Figure 7.3 Land versus agricultural labour productivity in selected Asian countries, 1980–2015.

Note: * The curves for Indonesia and the Philippines, not shown here, by and large coincide with that for Thailand.

Source: Author's calculations based on FAO (n.d.) FAOSTAT for data on agricultural land, World Bank (n.d.) World Development Indicators for data on agricultural value-added, and ILO (n.d.) ILOSTAT for agricultural employment.

marketable surpluses and labour to move into non-agriculture were instrumental to this development (see section 4). In contrast, the curves are virtually flat for Japan and the Republic of Korea, which had already reached a stage of deep structural change by the beginning of the 1980–2015 period, shown in Figure 7.4. In Malaysia, extensive plantation-based agriculture carries an important weight and its export-orientation provided a push for labour-saving productivity improvements.

Slow agricultural labour productivity growth is likely also associated with insufficient expansion of employment opportunities outside agriculture in low- and lower-middle-income countries, including those in South Asia. Despite the impacts of mechanization in parts of agriculture, on average, labour inputs per unit

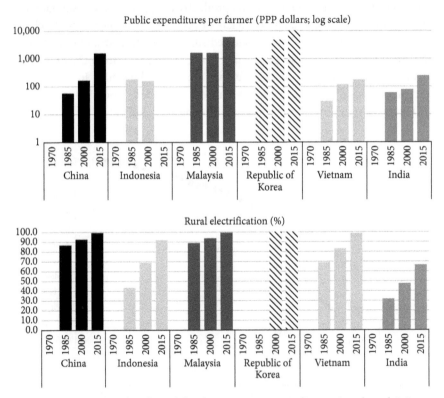

Figure 7.4 Agricultural and rural development support indicators in selected Asian countries, 1970–2015.

Note: The relative rate of assistance (RRA) to agriculture is defined as the percentage by which government policies have raised gross returns to agriculture above what they would be without the government's intervention as a ratio of government support to non-agricultural sectors. A negative RRA means support to non-agriculture is greater than that to agriculture.

Source: Author's calculations based on World Bank (n.d.) World Development Indicators for net enrolment rate and rural electrification, and Laborde et al. (2018) for public expenditures per farmer and estimates of relative rate of assistance to agriculture.

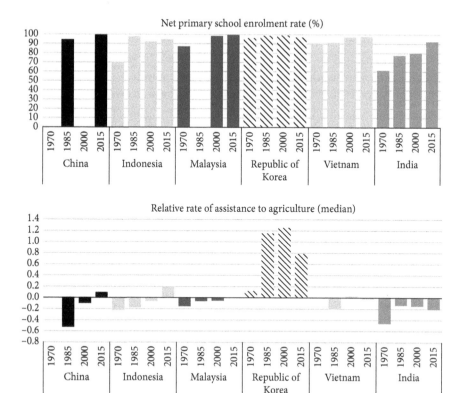

Figure 7.4 Continued

of land have continued to increase in South Asia, which has contributed to higher land productivity while holding back rural wage and labour productivity growth.

Slow agricultural labour productivity growth is further associated with reductions in farm size in Asia. During Europe's earlier stages of structural change, gains in agricultural labour productivity were associated with land consolidation. In South Asia, but also in Southeast Asia, such a process of land consolidation is yet to set in. Instead, the number of landholdings continues to increase resulting in further declines in the average size of landholdings. Vos (2018: figure 8) shows this trend for India, Indonesia, the Philippines, and Thailand. Even in Thailand, the wealthiest of the four, and the more land abundant and advanced in terms of structural transformation, the number of holdings in 2013 was still greater than in 2003. In India, the average size of landholding was cut in half over the past four decades, falling from 2.3 ha in 1970 to 1.15 ha in 2010. In China, in contrast, average farm size has been on the rise since 2002, though only slightly at best: it increased from 0.55 ha in that year to 0.60 ha in 2008, an increase of just 0.05 ha with nearly all of the increase coming from land consolidation in the northeast (Nie and Fang 2013).

The broader trends towards further fragmentation of farm units is taking place in a context of continued unequal land distribution. In South Asia, 60 per cent of farmland is operated by farm units with more than 2 ha of land. In Southeast Asia, the 'larger' farms (those with more than 2 ha) cultivate 77 per cent of farmlands (Eastwood et al. 2009). Most explanations of the persistence and growth of small landholdings point at several factors: continued rural population growth leading farm families to divide up land and distribute among children; the earlier-mentioned lack of non-farm employment opportunities; diversification to higher-value-added crops (e.g., horticulture) allowing even very small farms to be viable; and institutional restrictions on land transactions (see Deininger and Jin 2009; Gulati et al. 2004; Eastwood et al. 2009; Reardon 2013). This is not to deny that large farms are forming as well. Land rentals are contributing to these changes. In China in 1988, just 1 per cent of land was rented in, but this had grown to 18 per cent by 2008 (Jia 2013).

Yet, continued growth in the number of holdings, coupled with ever more pressing land scarcity in much of Asia, suggests that it is unlikely that farm sizes will typically become much larger for the foreseeable future. This could have two key implications. First, as labour shortages increase, mechanization will likely spread more widely, but will need to work at much smaller field scales than in other parts of the world. In addition, given credit market constraints and high fixed costs involved in owning farm machinery, most farmers would need to access machinery through rental markets.

Second, even if the trend towards fragmentation reverses soon, it will be hard to foresee massive increases in farm size to an extent that will make a substantial impact on increasing farm incomes. Thus, to avoid farm income growth from falling further behind non-farm income growth, (smallholder) farmers would need to shift to higher value-added crops (non-staples) and/or diversify their incomes into non-farm sectors (or leave farming entirely).

All of these change processes are already taking place throughout Asia. The spread of rental markets for agricultural equipment was referred to earlier and further documented in Dawe (2015) and FAO (2017b). Crop diversification is also taking place as noted earlier, as visible, for instance, in the rapidly increasing domestic farm supply of non-grains (fruits, vegetables, fish, meat, and dairy) (Pingali 2007). Rao et al. (2006) and Reardon and Timmer (2014) note for the case of India that there is a strong correlation between agricultural diversification, on the one hand, and the urban share and road and population density, on the other. China has also seen substantial crop diversification during the past forty years, much of it in response to changes in dietary patterns. Land use for the cultivation of fruits, vegetables, and pulses has doubled since 1990 and now accounts for more area than any single cereal (although much less than all cereals taken together) (Dawe 2015).

Income diversification has become a more common feature of Asia's rural economies. Haggblade et al. (2010) estimate that rural non-farm employment and remittance income from internal migration could make up as much as 51 per cent of total rural household income, based on survey data for Bangladesh, China, India, Korea, Nepal, Pakistan, Sri Lanka, and Vietnam. According to these estimates, rural non-farm employment is by far the main source of income diversification.

None of these relatively recent transformative changes by themselves are guarantees for broad-based economic growth and accelerated poverty reduction. Where these trends have been slow to develop, major economic and social challenges remain. Declining farm sizes reduce farmers' resource base, limit their access to finance, and prevent investment in new technologies (Jayne et al. 2010), prompting a 'premature' exit from agriculture, where smallholders abandon farming even though profitable technologies and markets exist. Even those who remain in agriculture may not be able to take advantage of rising urban demand, particularly farmers in more remote rural areas or where urban centres have better access to imported food (Hazell 2013). Falling farm sizes and import competition have further weakened agriculture's historically strong linkage to poverty reduction, given that most of the world's rural poor are smallholder farmers. Similarly, where rapid urbanization has outpaced urban economic growth and job creation, this has led to greater pressure on urban infrastructure and services and growing numbers of urban poor. Finally, the influx of young job seekers into the workforce—a 'youth bulge' (as applies to much of South Asia)—could stimulate economic growth, but it also raises concerns about an economy's capacity to create jobs—especially the kinds of jobs that match the aspirations of younger generations. Conversely, countries in developing East Asia have already experienced their demographic transition and now face the prospect of an ageing agricultural and rural workforce.

3.3   Labour Markets and Rural and Agri-Food System Transformations

Not only farm systems have changed in Asia. 'Post farm-gate' parts of food supply chains (wholesale/brokerage/logistics/cold chain, processing, and retail) have undergone major transformations as well, with important implications for employment, income diversification, and poverty reduction among rural households. These agri-food system changes are closely related to urbanization processes, as much of Asia's food supply is already moving from rural to urban. This is creating new income and employment opportunities in wholesale, retail, processing, and the logistics of providing food to growing urban populations. Such opportunities can be critical in defining pathways to climb out of poverty for those exiting agriculture or seeking to diversify incomes during processes of agricultural transformation and structural change. The way rural–urban linkages are shaped is crucial for poverty reduction and broader economic development. Rural–urban linkages have long been recognized as a key aspect of economic development (Lewis 1954; Haggblade et al. 2007). Urban industrial and service sector growth provides employment for workers who exit agriculture, while increases in agricultural production can help avoid an increase in food prices and wages that could slow the pace of industrialization. Agricultural growth can also spur non-agricultural growth in both rural and urban areas through demand for both inputs and intermediation services, as well as consumer goods.

In areas with still widespread low-productivity agriculture, such as in many parts of South Asia, low aggregate demand is likely to generate the development of low-return rural non-farm employment. The low aggregate demand may not only result from poor agriculture, but also growing agriculture with poor links to cities (see e.g., Deichmann et al. 2009, for the case of Bangladesh; Lanjouw and Shariff 2004 and Tiwari 2015, for the case of India) or to export markets so that the farmers cannot 'realize' sufficient profit from agricultural development. Such areas continue to see persistent poverty in a context of increasing shares of low-income non-farm employment and stagnant agricultural production.

Much of rural off-farm employment tends to be generated in the proximity of cities and towns. Recent studies further suggest that dynamic structural change through agri-food system development (characterized by both rapid agricultural productivity growth and rural non-farm wage and employment growth) is more likely to occur when taking place close to smaller towns and intermediate cities (see e.g., FAO 2017b; IFPRI 2017). Based on evidence for Bangladesh, Deichman et al. (2009) similarly find that high-potential agricultural production areas that are near to cities tend to generate more and higher-return rural non-farm employment (both for wage earners and self-employed), while where the high-potential farm area is far from the city, low-return rural non-farm employment predominates, mostly only in informal services. Moreover, most of urban food demand in Asia is concentrated in smaller urban areas: about 60 per cent, according to FAO estimates (FAO 2017b), suggesting there is a large potential for dynamic rural non-farm employment creation through agri-food business development. In fact, during rapid structural transformation in Indonesia, Malaysia, and Vietnam, food processing industries have played an important role in pulling labour into off-farm activity and account for about one-sixth of total manufacturing employment around 2010 (FAO 2017b). In Vietnam, employment in agri-food processing more than doubled between 1999 and 2009. While still most of the employment growth (about 53 per cent) was generated in small, household-based enterprises in rural areas and small towns, employment growth in modern private enterprises was higher in relative terms (McGaig and Pavcnik 2016), reflective of broader changes in agri-food systems taking place in Vietnam as much as elsewhere in Asia.

These transformations involve modernization of the midstream of food supply chains with the emergence of large-scale wholesale and retail food distributors ('supermarket revolution') and vertically integrated food processing companies, and reduced roles for state-operated food distribution networks (Reardon and Timmer 2014). In much of Southeast Asia (outside Vietnam, Cambodia, Laos, and Myanmar), wholesale sector transformation started in the 1970s, while processing transformation took off in the 1980s. Retail transformation (the 'supermarket revolution') did not start until the mid-to-late 1990s. China, India, and Vietnam had their growth and urbanization spurts mainly in the 1990s/2000s or opened up food industries no earlier than during the 1990s.

The massive proliferation of wholesale markets, the extension and improvement of rural roads, and the regulatory liberalization of their operations in most countries opened the door to what Reardon and Timmer (2014) label as 'progressive disintermediation' in the rural areas and in supply chains. This trend is seen to have been driven by two main factors. The first of these is regulatory changes (such as in some states in India and privatization of state-owned businesses in Vietnam) that have freed up wholesale markets and provided incentives to large-scale traders, distributors, and food companies to establish direct links to farmers (e.g., through contract farming or supermarket-led collection centres). The second is the diffusion of wholesale markets in towns near or in rural areas, and the improvement of road systems connecting rural areas to urban wholesale markets. In many locations, however, this has undercut small-scale village traders in diverse settings and further stimulated direct purchase from farmers by wholesale market traders who previously procured via village traders.

The broader agri-food supply chain transformations have been influenced by urbanization and diet change, as discussed earlier. The agri-food system changes themselves, in turn, influence both the change processes taking place downstream (in urban food markets and diets) and upstream (in factor markets and farming). As mentioned, they are bringing sources of new dynamics in the form of off-farm employment demand in processing and distribution services and a source of income diversification for farmers, bringing extra cash for investing in farm productivity and mechanization. However, where rural–urban linkages have remained weak, rural livelihoods have been undermined. Large-scale urban manufacturers catering for mass markets have also displaced (and are displacing) small-scale businesses in food processing and distribution in rural areas and near or in cities, thereby diminishing non-farm rural employment without generating sufficient new jobs for the displaced workers. This problem is particularly pressing in areas with low agricultural potential and poor connectivity to urban markets and is holding back poverty reduction.

4. The Role of Policies

At the time when Myrdal (1968) wrote *Asian Drama*, most of developing Asia faced some similarity in initial conditions in the early stages of their economic lift off, characterized by high birth rates and relatively fertile but scarce agricultural land. The Green Revolution brought new high-yielding varieties for staple crops, facilitating substantial farm productivity increases, even for smallholders, to jump-start agricultural transformations and structural change. While broadly adopted across the region, the speed of adoption of the new technologies and success in 'pushing' broader economic development through agricultural productivity growth has varied depending importantly on policies and institutional reforms. Despite policy differences, a common feature across the region has been the fading of the direct role of Asian governments in agricultural production and other stages of the food chain. The parallel development has been the growth of off-farm, private sector small and medium-sized agri-food businesses and services, which have stepped into the void left by parastatals. Policy reforms further enabled entry of large-scale domestic and foreign firms such as processors and supermarket and fast food chains. Many governments took on another role in supporting transformative change, including through large infrastructure programmes that helped strengthen rural–urban linkages and food supply chain development.

Laborde et al. (2018) and Vos (2018) explain different rates of 'success' with agricultural transformations by key differences in agricultural price incentives, public spending priorities for investing in agricultural research and development (R&D), rural infrastructure, education and health, and reforms of rural institutions (including land reform and credit schemes) across developing-country regions and over different periods of time since 1970. According to Laborde et al. (2018), the more critical factor appears to be the degree of coherence and complementarity across these areas of intervention to promote sufficient agricultural productivity growth to facilitate ('push'), a take-off of non-agricultural sectors by freeing up labour and savings, and by overcoming population pressures on food security.

Based on studies for Asia's major economies, Vos (2018) concludes that institutional reforms were critical in initial stages to unleash farm-level productive forces, while input subsidies (for seeds and fertilizers) and infrastructure development were important to promote the adoption of Green Revolution technologies from the 1970s. The returns to these public support measures have diminished over time and the push for deeper agri-food system transformations was influenced by agricultural price policy reforms and privatization of food distribution and processing networks. These more recent transformations have helped accelerate poverty reduction and underpin broader economic development, where these were supported by public investment in basic services and infrastructure that strengthened rural–urban linkages and enabled non-farm economic development. Agricultural and rural transformations have been slow and have failed to accelerate poverty reduction where policies and institutional reforms, supportive of agricultural productivity growth, fell short on these counts.

Key changes in indicators of public support for agriculture and rural development over 1970–2015 are displayed in Figure 7.4. The Republic of Korea, for instance, maintained a high level of spending, as did China and Malaysia. In all rapidly transforming countries there was a strong focus on complementarity with public investments, including complementary support to agricultural development through public investments in research, extension services, primary education, and rural infrastructure, such as irrigation, electricity, and roads. Direct price interventions also played a key role in the agricultural transformation process for all countries, but the price interventions were first marked by an apparent strong anti-agricultural bias, as indicated by the relative rate of assistance (RRA) in Figure 7.4. Over time, Asian countries saw a strong shift from negative to positive price supports for agriculture. However, as becomes clear from the country narratives below, just looking at the relative price (including support measures) of agriculture vis-à-vis non-agriculture may be misleading if not considering other, complementary forms of support to agricultural development, especially through reforms of agrarian institutions and development of rural infrastructure, as the following country narratives try to make clear.

Institutional reforms in the Republic of Korea, China, and Vietnam, in particular, were critical in unleashing agricultural productive forces and labour for industry in the early stages of their growth accelerations (see also Ocampo and Vos 2008: chapter 5), though the impact of these reforms likely would have been much less if they were not complemented by strong public support for the development of non-agricultural (industrial) sectors.

The land reform introduced by the South Korean government with support of the United States in 1949 led to relatively equitable land distribution (Tsakok 2011). Combined with effective and sustained public support to smallholder agriculture, this proved effective to substantially lift agricultural productivity and develop commercial farming. In the Republic of Korea, significant public rural investments were already made during the Japanese colonial period. Over 1910 through 1945, investments went mostly in support of the development of the rice sector. This was part of a strategy to secure Japan's food self-sufficiency. In the immediate post-Korean war period, public investment prioritized research and extension services leading to the early introduction of new high-yielding varieties and the expanded use of chemical fertilizer and irrigation, compounding the productivity-enhancing effects of the land reform (Tsakok 2011). Korea sustained its relatively strong support to the agricultural sector in subsequent decades (Figure 7.4). After a brief spell of anti-agriculture bias during the initial import-substitution stage of industrial development in the 1960s, price incentives shifted in agriculture's favour with the shift to export-led industrialization in the 1970s, as visible from the strongly positive RRA in Figure 7.4 (Honma and Hayami 2009). The main objective of the Korean government was to keep food prices low and, hence, real urban wages down.

China prioritized import-substituting industrial development until 1979, which proved detrimental to agricultural development. This radically changed with the introduction of the household responsibility system, which entitled farmers and town and village enterprises to manage and commercialize production themselves and earn profits. According to one study, this institutional reform alone would explain 60 per cent of agricultural growth in China between 1978 and 1990 (EIU 2008). The reform was complemented by policies introduced in the 1980s that allowed freer labour mobility and rural–urban migration, facilitating the exit of labour resources out of agriculture and into both rural and urban non-farm employment (Tsakok 2011). During the 1990s and 2000s, China stepped up public expenditures in support of agriculture and rural development, with most of the spending going to rural education (33 per cent), irrigation and water control (30 per cent), and other infrastructure, including power supply and roads (20 per cent). Fan et al. 2004 find a significant impact of public investment on agricultural growth and rural poverty in China either directly by stimulating agricultural production or indirectly by creating improved employment opportunities in the non-farm sector. These support measures were complemented by a gradual build-down of the anti-agriculture bias in price incentives. During the period of the Great Leap Forward, until 1979, agricultural incomes were squeezed through taxes and administered prices, while farmers were not allowed to market their production surpluses (Tsakok 2011). After 1979, purchase prices of most agricultural products were lifted and in-quota and above-quota prices for grains, oil crops, cotton, sugar, and pork were raised. In the 1990s, subsidies on various crops, including soybeans, were introduced. As a result, the RRA moved out of negative territory, turning positive in the 2000s (Figure 7.4).

In Malaysia, government support to large-scale tree-crop plantation agriculture (rubber, palm oil, coconut) has been a critical ingredient of natural resource-led growth and structural transformation. Government policies have underpinned productivity growth on large-scale plantations through significant R&D spending, land development, and infrastructure investment promoting the vertical integration with processing industries. In parallel, however, the Malaysian government also invested heavily in smallholder agriculture through price support schemes, input subsidies, and low-interest rate credits. Between 1971 and 1995, the share of public expenditures allocated to agriculture and rural development averaged 17 per cent. The New Agricultural Policy of 1984 provided a further push to agricultural income growth, commercialization of farming, and overall economic transformation through agricultural market development, R&D, and incentives to diversification from rice to agro-industrial crops, including rubber and palm oil (Tsakok 2011).

In Vietnam, collective farming was replaced with family farming during the period of *doi moi* (the policy of renovation) in the 1980s. Under the new system, farmers were allowed to sign contracts with the government on parcels of land for up to 15 years—in effect, they leased the land—and were given the freedom to sell their products as they wished. As in the case of China, other reforms proceeded at the same time, including domestic market and trade liberalization, allowing for the introduction of market-based transactions in agricultural and non-agricultural products and entry of foreign direct investment. Vietnam's institutional reforms were complemented with significant public investment in rural infrastructure (roads and electrification), as well as in basic social services, including primary education, vocational training, and healthcare. These investments paid off by the 1980s, as visible in accelerated agricultural productivity growth and fast growth of non-agricultural sectors (Van Arkadie and Duc Dinh 2004).

In the case of India, in contrast, land reform was limited to a stricter enforcement of the existing tenancy law. The government had enacted a land reform act in 1955. However, it did not enforce the law largely because of the lack of administrative and legal resources. This, combined with low-level public investment in infrastructure and rural development, was probably a key factor in holding back agricultural productivity growth and rural transformation in most of India until at least the 1990s, after which such investments were stepped up (Ocampo and Vos 2008). Public spending per farmer also increased recently in India, but to levels no higher than those in Vietnam and well below levels spent by faster agricultural transformers in Asia. Spending was stepped up only decades after the land reform of the 1970s and the lack of complementary support through improved rural infrastructure may well have contributed to the failure of that reform to spur agricultural productivity growth. Traditionally most of India's public support to agriculture has been for input subsidies for fertilizers and irrigation water with much less priority for investments in rural infrastructure. More recently, such investments have been stepped up, leading to increased rural road density and access to electricity, helping to accelerate agricultural growth. Yet, at about 60 per cent, rural electrification coverage in India remains well below that in other parts of Asia where agricultural and rural transformations have progressed earlier and at a faster pace (Figure 7.4). Also, the relative rate of agricultural assistance has remained negative to date (Figure 7.4), despite high input subsidies on, especially, fertilizer use. Public procurement of staple crop purchases for food reserve holdings and food distribution schemes tilted agricultural support in favour of consumers.

Regulatory changes to other parts of the agri-food system have been important, too, in facilitating transformative change of agriculture and rural economies. In developing East Asia (other than China), development and opening up of wholesale distribution and food processing came with broader industrial development and urbanization during the 1960s to 1980s. China, India, and Vietnam opened up food industries no earlier than during the 1990s. The bigger changes in most parts of the region took place from the mid-1980s on the wave of economic liberalization and globalization. During these phases, agri-food systems modernized and many parts of supply chains saw the emergence of large-scale operators in retail ('supermarket revolution'), wholesale, and food processing, as well as greater vertical integration of food market value chains, as mentioned in the previous section.

5. The End of the 'Asian Drama'?

Both international experience and economic theory show that structural change is an essential component of long-term economic development. Urbanization and industrial growth are key features of this structural change. Along the way, rural labour and savings are being pulled into higher productivity sectors to underpin broader economic growth. With some variation across countries, this process was key to the remarkable acceleration of economic growth in East Asia over the past half-century or more, belying Gunnar Myrdal's notion of an Asian drama. However, this 'miracle' could not have come about without strong agricultural productivity growth and agrarian change in initial stages of economic take-off. The Green Revolution, reforms of agricultural and rural institutions, and public investment in rural infrastructure have been critical factors in East Asia's take-off. In subsequent stages, industrial and other modern sector development took over as the drivers of economy-wide growth, while at the same time pushing agriculture and rural economies to deeper transformative change, as, inter alia, urbanization and income growth have induced major dietary change and pushed for more industrial organization of food systems at large.

This process is also taking place in South Asia, albeit at a slower and delayed pace. Myrdal's concerns with India's and other South Asian countries' structural impediments to development, including land scarcity, historical traditions of production activity, weak institutions, and a 'soft state', indeed held back agricultural growth and broader economic development in cumulative causation, certainly in comparison with other parts of Asia. Yet, as these constraints were lifted, partially at least, faster growth was unleashed. However, moving forward, fewer of the lessons from East Asia's experience may hold for India and the rest of South Asia.

Some patterns will likely remain the same. All countries will see agricultural employment become less and less important. This decline is consistent with agricultural productivity growth and the wider spread of mechanization, as well as with agri-food transformations and dietary change with increased demand for processed food and importance of off-farm activity related to food chains. But the pace of these changes has been different and will be different across countries (as much as across regions within countries).

Structural transformation is already most advanced in the countries of developing Asia, but pathways have differed starkly. In Malaysia, agricultural export growth and extensive farming have driven the rapid labour exit from agriculture, leading to a faster declining agricultural employment share than the sector's GDP share. Elsewhere, as in India, much of South Asia, and to a lesser extent in Indonesia, Thailand, Vietnam, and the Philippines, the decline of agriculture's employment share has lagged the drop of agriculture's share in GDP. These contexts are further characterized by increased fragmentation of landholdings. Agricultural labour productivity growth has been slower in consequence and could slow down poverty reduction if not offset by other drivers. Employment growth in non-farm (agri-food and other manufacturing) activities as well as agricultural exports have been important other drivers for poverty reduction in the Southeast Asian countries. Such factors have been less dynamic in recent decades in the countries of South Asia, warranting the expectation that poverty among their populations will be far from eradicated in the coming decades.

The ability of small farms to be efficient and dynamic agri-food systems to develop so as to underpin dynamic and inclusive structural change have been strongly conditioned by public investments and policy choices, as discussed in section 4.

Ongoing urbanization and modernization of agri-food systems are changing the nature of rural transformations. Farm efficiency and rural employment opportunities are increasingly influenced by what happens beyond the farm gate and the strength of rural–urban linkages. But this unlikely will suffice to put an end to the Asian drama. Land scarcity combined with continued population pressure has led to further fragmentation of landholdings and to added pressure on already degraded land and water resources (Vos and Bellù 2019). Such constraints imply that continuation along past development pathways will hit on environmental constraints. Likewise, while structural change has dramatically brought down poverty and undernourishment in Asia, dietary and food system changes have brought new malnutrition challenges as overweight and obesity are on the rise.[3]

Finding the appropriate balance between an effective public role and an efficient private role in the modernization of agriculture and the entire food system has always been a difficult challenge. The balance not only needs to focus on underpinning economic growth and development with more productive agriculture and food systems, but also on doing so in a sustainable way and avoiding new burdens of malnutrition and disease to take away from economic progress. The political economy of pathways will be tricky. Myrdal's notion of cumulative

---

[3] While still significantly lower than in high-income countries like the United States, the prevalence of obesity has increased steeply in most Asian countries. It has doubled or tripled in Thailand and Malaysia between 2000 and 2016 to affect well over 10 per cent of adults. Obesity has also (near) tripled in China and Indonesia in the same period. Data based on age-standardized body mass index estimates of the World Health Organization (WHO 2017).

causation remains valid for understanding today's trade-offs, despite the remarkable economic progress made since he wrote *Asian Drama*.

Acknowledgements

I am grateful to Deepak Nayyar, Frances Stewart, Sudipto Mundle, two anonymous referees, as well as to the participants of the project workshop held in Hanoi in March 2018, for helpful comments on earlier drafts. Any possible errors are mine.

References

Alexandratos, N., and J. Bruinsma (2012). 'World Agriculture towards 2030/2050: The 2012 Revision', FAO, Rome, ESA Working Paper 12–03.

Ashan, R.N., and D. Mitra (2016). 'Can the Whole Be Greater Than the Sum of its Parts?'. In M. McMillan, D. Rodrik, and C. Sepúlveda (eds) *Structural Change, Fundamentals, and Growth*. Washington, DC: IFPRI.

Dawe, D. (2015). 'Agricultural Transformation of Middle-income Asian Economies: Diversification, Farm Size and Mechanization', FAO, Rome, ESA Working Paper 15-04.

Deichman, U., F. Shilpi, and R. Vakis (2009). 'Urban Proximity, Agricultural Potential and Rural Non-farm Employment', *World Development*, 37(3): 645–60.

Deininger, K., and S. Jin (2009). 'Securing Property Rights in Transition: Lessons from Implementation of China's Rural Land Contracting Law'. *Journal of Economic Behavior & Organization*, 70(2): 22–8.

Eastwood, R., M. Lipton, and A. Newell (2009). 'Farm Size'. In P. Pingali and R. Evenson (eds) *Handbook of Agricultural Economics*. Amsterdam: Elsevier.

EIU (Economic Intelligence Unit) (2008). 'Lifting African and Asian Farmers out of Poverty', mimeo, research project for the Gates Foundation, Gates Foundation, New York.

Fan, S. (2008). *Public Expenditures, Growth, and Poverty*. Baltimore, MD: Johns Hopkins University Press.

Fan, S., L. Zhan, and X. Zhang (2004). 'Reforms, Investment and Poverty in Rural China', *Economic Development and Cultural Change*, 52(2): 395–421.

FAO (n.d.). 'FAOSTAT'. Available at: http://www.fao.org/faostat/en/#data/RL (accessed 31 January 2018).

FAO (2017a). *The Future of Food and Agriculture*. Rome: FAO.

FAO (2017b). *The State of Food and Agriculture 2017*. Rome: FAO.

Fuglie, K.O. (2015). 'Accounting for Growth in Global Agriculture', *Bio-based and Applied Economics*, 4(3): 221–54.

Groningen Growth and Development Centre (n.d.). 'Groningen Growth and Development Centre Database'. Available at: https://www.rug.nl/ggdc/historicaldevelopment/ (accessed 15 December 2017).

Gulati, A., L. Tewari, P.K. Goshi, and P.S. Birthal (2004). 'Agriculture Diversification in South Asia', *Economic and Political Weekly*, 39(24): 2457–67.

Haggblade, S., P.B.R. Hazell, and P.A. Dorosh (2007). 'Sectoral Growth Linkages Between Agriculture and the Rural Nonfarm Economy'. In S. Haggblade, P.B.R. Hazell, and T. Reardon (eds) *Transforming the Rural Nonfarm Economy*. Baltimore, MD: Johns Hopkins University Press.

Haggblade, S., P. Hazell, and T. Reardon (2010). 'The Rural Non-farm Economy', *World Development*, 38(10): 1429–41.

Hazell, P. (2013). 'Urbanization and Farm Size Changes in Africa and Asia'. Background Paper for the ISPC Foresight Study on Farm Size and Urbanization, Rome. Available at: http://www.sciencecouncil.cgiar.org/sections/strategy-trends (accessed 15 December 2017).

Hirschman, A.O. (1958). *The Strategy of Economic Development*. New Haven, CT: Yale University Press.

Honma, M., and Y. Hayami (2009). 'Japan, Republic of Korea, and Taiwan, China'. In K. Anderson (ed.) *Distortions to Agricultural Incentives*. London: Palgrave Macmillan.

IFPRI (2017). *Global Food Policy Report*. Washington, DC: IFPRI.

ILO (n.d.). 'ILOSTAT: Key Indicators of the Labour Market (KILM)'. Available at: https://www.ilo.org/ilostat/faces/wcnav_defaultSelection;ILOSTATCOOKIE=gM8 ayXNh9D9HNEfSRtphuTIUkb-RKuL-ZKvMGBlIwERmDrmkySl4!351759245?_ afrLoop=806999627626846&_afrWindowMode=0&_afrWindowId=null#!% 40%40%3F_afrWindowId%3Dnull%26_afrLoop%3D806999627626846%26_ afrWindowMode%3D0%26_adf.ctrl-state%3D13a22tcoa6_4 (accessed 31 January 2018).

Ivanic, M., and W. Martin (2018). 'Sectoral Productivity Growth and Poverty Reduction', *World Development*, 109(C): 429–39.

Jayne, T.S., N. Mason, R. Myers, J. Ferris, D. Mather, N. Sitko, M. Beaver, N. Lenski, A. Chapoto, and D. Boughton (2010). 'Patterns and Trends in Food Staples Markets in Eastern and Southern Africa', Ann Arbor, MI, Michigan State University, International Development Working Paper 104. Available at: http://www.aec.msu.edu/fs2/zambia/idwp104.pdf (accessed 3 February 2018).

Jia, X. (2013). 'Transforming Agricultural Production in China: From Smallholders to Pluralistic Large Farms', Presentation at FAO, Rome, 16 December.

Laborde, D., T. Lallemant, K. McDougall, C. Smaller, and F. Traoré (2018). *Transforming Agriculture in Africa and Asia*. Washington, DC and Geneva: IFPRI and IISD.

Lanjouw, P., and A. Shariff (2004). 'Rural Non-farm Employment in India', *Economic and Political Weekly*, 39: 4429–46.

Lankester, T. (2004). '"Asian Drama"': The Pursuit of Modernization in India and Indonesia', *Asian Affairs*, XXXV(III): 291–304.

Lewis, W.A. (1954). 'Economic Development with Unlimited Supplies of Labor', *The Manchester School*, 22(2): 139–91.

Masters, W.A. (2018). 'Rural Transformation and Nutrition Transition', Presentation at PIM Workshop on Rural Transformation in the 21st Century, International Conference of Agricultural Economists, Vancouver, 28 July.

Masters, W.A., A.A. Djurfeldt, C. De Haan, P. Hazell, T. Jayne, M. Jirström, and T. Reardon (2013). 'Urbanization and Farm Size in Asia and Africa', *Global Food Security*, 2(3): 156–65.

McCaig, B., and N. Pavcnik (2016). 'Moving Out of Agriculture: Structural Change in Vietnam'. In M. McMillan, D. Rodrik, and C. Sepúlveda (eds) *Structural Change, Fundamentals, and Growth*. Washington, DC: IFPRI.

Myrdal, G. (1957). *Economic Theory and Underdeveloped Regions*. London: Methuen.

Myrdal, G. (1968). *Asian Drama: An Inquiry into the Poverty of Nations, Volumes I, II, and III*. New York: Pantheon.

Nie, F., and C. Fang (2013). 'Family Farming in China', Seminar Presentation at FAO, Rome, 13 December.

Ocampo, J.A., and R. Vos (2008). *Uneven Economic Development*. London: Zed Books (for United Nations).

Pingali, P. (2007). 'Westernization of Asian Diets and the Transformation of Food Systems', *Food Policy*, 32(3): 281–98.

Rao, P.P., P.S. Birthal, and P.L. Joshi (2006). 'Diversification Towards High Value Agriculture', *Economic and Political Weekly*, 41(26): 2747–53.

Reardon, T. (2013). 'Asia Agrifood System's 5 Linked Transformations: Implications for Agricultural Research and Development Strategies', A Foresight Study of the Independent Science and Partnership Council (ISPC/CGIAR), Rome.

Reardon, T., and C.P. Timmer (2014). 'Five Inter-linked Transformations in the Asian Agrifood Economy', *Global Food Security*, 3: 108–17.

Reardon, T., K. Chen, B. Minten, and L. Adriano (2012). *The Quiet Revolution in Staple Food Value Chains in Asia*. Washington, DC: IFPRI and Asian Development Bank.

Timmer, C.P. (2014). 'Managing Structural Transformation: A Political Economy Approach', UNU-WIDER, Helsinki, UNU-WIDER Annual Lecture 18.

Tiwari, S. (2015). 'Managing Transformation of Rural India Through Rural Non-farm Economy', *Journal of Rural and Industrial Development*, 3(2): 37–47.

Tsakok, I. (2011). *Success in Agricultural Transformation*. Cambridge: Cambridge University Press.

Tschirley, D., T. Reardon, M. Dolislager, and J. Snyder (2015). 'The Rise of a Middle Class in East and Southern Africa', *Journal of International Development*, 27(5): 628–46.

Van Arkadie, B., and D. Duc Dinh (2004). 'Economic Reform in Tanzania and Vietnam', University of Michigan, Ann Arbor, MI, William Davidson Institute Working Paper 706.

Vos, R. (2018). 'Agricultural and Rural Transformations in Asian Development', UNU-WIDER, Helsinki, WIDER Working Paper 2018/87.

Vos, R., and L. Bellù (2019). 'Global Trends and Challenges to Food and Agriculture into the Twenty-First Century'. In C. Campanhola and S. Pandey (eds) *Sustainable Food and Agriculture: An Integrated Approach*. London: Elsevier/Academic Press.

WHO (2017). 'Global Health Observatory Data Respository: Prevalence of Obesity among Adults, BMI ≥ 30, Age-standardized Estimates by Country'. Available at: http://apps.who.int/gho/data/node.main.A900A?lang=en (accessed 3 March 2018).

World Bank (2008). *World Development Report: Agriculture for Development*. Washington, DC: World Bank.

World Bank (2017). 'PovcalNet: An Online Analysis Tool for Global Poverty Monitoring', World Bank, Washington, DC. Available at: http://iresearch.worldbank.org/PovcalNet (accessed August 2018).

World Bank (n.d.). 'DataBank: World Development Indicators'. Available at: http://databank.worldbank.org/data/reports.aspx?source=world-development-indicators (accessed 15 December 2017).

8

Industrialization and Development

Ha-Joon Chang and Kiryl Zach

1. Introduction

Fifty years ago, in the freshly published *Asian Drama*, Gunnar Myrdal was cautious, if not outright sceptical, about the industrialization prospects of the Asian economies in the upcoming decades, pointing to the many institutional, social, political, and economic barriers they faced. In this light, it is fitting to call the industrialization successes in a number of Asian economies in the last five decades 'development miracles'. From today's vantage point of view, the phenomenal growth of China or the industrial prowess of the East Asian 'tigers' may appear as a natural, or even inevitable, outcome of the region's culture or other uniquely favourable initial conditions. Yet this had not been so when South Korea (henceforth Korea), fresh from the destructions of the Korean War (1950–1953), was denounced as a 'bottomless pit' in an internal memo of the United States Agency for International Development (Chang 2007). Taiwan faced the threat of military intervention from China, which itself was often politically isolated by the Western powers, and its gross domestic product (GDP) per capita was barely half that of India. None of these, or other 'developing' Asian economies in South or Southeast Asia, had any significant industrial capacity at the time.

It was a tall order to achieve this success. The developing economies of Asia[1] had aspirations of seemingly Icarian heights: to close, in a single generation, the huge gap in industrial development that separated them from their old colonial masters. This feat was to be achieved against the tides of rapid population growth and persistent trade deficits without the benefits provided to the earlier industrializers by colonial possessions.

Even though not all odds were stacked against them, we cannot explain the industrialization achievements of the more successful developing Asian economies only by structural factors.[2] Likewise, it is just as inadequate to credit structural

---

[1] The 'developing Asia' category excludes Japan and Israel, as well as the Asian part of the USSR due to a lack of reliable data for the period. The 'developing economies' are defined following the definition by UNCTAD (2017).

[2] For a rebuttal of the 'cultural' arguments, see Chang (2007: chapter 9) and Chang (2011a), which also discusses 'institutional' arguments. For a rebuttal of explanations involving other types of initial conditions (e.g., natural resources, human resources, infrastructure, geopolitical factors), see Chang (2006: chapter 4).

barriers and conditions as the only causes of relatively less successful industrialization of other Asian economies. To understand the differences in the structural trans-formation[3] of different Asian countries (as well as the differences between the Asian and other developing countries), one needs to look at the differences in their choices of overall development strategy and industrial policy.

In section 2,we provide a bird's-eye view of Asia's industrial transformation in the last five decades. We explore: (i) the progress of industrialization, measured by value-added (henceforth VA) indicators; (ii) the changes in employment patterns and manufacturing VA (henceforth MVA) indicators; and (iii) industrial upgrad-ing, with the use of export indicators. In section 3,drawing on insights from Myrdal's work, we discuss the role played by industrial policy in industrialization, outline experiences of four notable cases—Korea, Malaysia, China, and India—and discuss some of the general factors behind a successful industrial policy.

2. Asian Industrial Development in Numbers

2.1 The Extent of Industrialization in Developing Asia

In the last five decades, the manufacturing sector in Asia has become the largest in the world, which happened in tandem with other important developments, including the continent's increasing share in global trade and rapid urbanization. All Asian regions have industrialized faster than the global average during that period, but most startlingly the 'developing' East Asian region, while being mar-ginal in terms of industrial development in 1970, became the world's largest 'core' industrial region by 2015.

These changes were by no means predestined. Asia of the 1960s was a continent of subsistent farming with a few 'enclaves' of modern industry. In 1970, the devel-oping Asian economies produced around 32.98 per cent of their VA in agriculture, compared to the world average of 9.46 per cent,[4] while the share of their MVA in GDP was lower than that of Africa (10.57 per cent vs. 12.89 per cent). MVA con-stituted less than a third of Asia's total industrial VA (henceforth IVA), typically for extractive-industries-dominated postcolonial economies (see Table 8.1; also see UNCTAD (2017) for data on Africa). In 1970, developing Asia accounted for only 4.15 per cent of the world's MVA, despite holding over half the world's population (Table 8.1).

---

[3] Structural transformation is defined in this chapter as the series of economic and social changes resulting from changes in the production structure. These involve notably transition in employment towards manufacturing and modern industries, new organization of production, technological upgrading, and related changes in social conditions, such as urbanization. For discussion of industrial transformation in Asia, see ADB (2013).

[4] Compared to 22.26 per cent for Africa or 11.25 per cent for 'developing' Latin America (UNCTAD 2017).

Table 8.1 Comparing developing Asia in 1970 and 2015

Indicator		Value in 1970	Value in 2015	% increase $\left(\dfrac{\text{Value in 2015}}{\text{Value in 1970}}-100\%\right)$
Average GDP per capita (constant 2005 US$)	Developing Asia	501	3,272	553%
	World	4,283	8,178	91%
Total IVA (constant 2005 US$)	Developing Asia	400,769	5,615,672	1,301%
	World	5,361,309	16,453,140	207%
Total MVA in constant 2005 US$	Developing Asia	109,433	3,567,380	3,160%
	World	2,634,860	10,174,996	286%
Developing Asia's share of global total	IVA	7.48%	34.13%	356%
	MVA	4.15%	35.06%	745%
Developing Asia's share of global GDP		6.2%	22.7%	264%
Developing Asia's share of global exports		8.42%	35.87%[a]	326%
Developing Asia's inward FDI flows as a % of global total[b]	Developing Asia	7.1%	29.2%	310%
	World	20.7%	46.7%	126%
Share of urban population	Developing Asia	36.7%	53.8%	47%
Population in millions	Developing Asia	1,971	4,173	112%
	World	3,683	7,350	100%

Notes: (a) For 2016; (b) Asia's FDI flows numbers are 1970–1974 and 2010–2015 averages.

Source: Authors' calculations based on data from UNCTADstat (UNCTAD 2017) and WDI Database Archives (World Bank 2017).

In the five decades that followed, Asia experienced rapid industrialization, outpacing every other continent by a big margin. From 1970 to 2015, while the world's MVA grew by 286 per cent, Asia's grew by a staggering 3,160 per cent. The bulk of this came from developing Asia, which expanded its share in global MVA from 4.15 per cent to 35.06 per cent, pulling ahead of both Europe and the Americas (26.35 per cent and 25.81 per cent respectively). In doing so, it also became the only 'developing' continent whose share in global MVA outgrew its share in IVA (35.06 per cent to 34.13 per cent, with 1.80 per cent to 3.02 per cent for Africa, and 5.01 per cent to 6.42 per cent for developing Americas (UNCTAD 2017)). This means a transition away from dependence on extractive industries to manufacturing as the engine of development.

Most of the expansion in Asia's share of global MVA was concentrated in developing East Asia. From 1970 to 2015, the region expanded its share in global MVA from a mere 1.60 per cent to 25.30 per cent. Although other Asian regions have also expanded their global share of MVA their increases were much less dramatic by comparison. In South Asia it grew from 0.97 per cent to 3.83 per cent, in South-Eastern Asia from 0.75 per cent to 3.56 per cent, and for Western Asia from 0.88 per cent to 2.37 per cent (for more detail see Chang and Zach 2018: table A1).

The importance of these facts cannot be overemphasized. In less than five decades, developing East Asia has gone from having a globally marginal manufacturing base to eclipsing the industrial capacity of other Asian regions and rising above the world average in per capita terms. It has also pulled ahead of the old industrial centres of the world economy—Europe and the Americas—in terms of total MVA. In other words, East Asia has emerged as the largest industrial 'core' region in the world. In contrast, Southeast Asia is at best halfway towards that goal, and South Asia is just beyond the starting line.

In 1970, there was nothing in East Asia's 'initial conditions' that would have allowed us to predict such a dramatic industrial expansion in the subsequent fifty years. Their comparative advantages were in products using cheap labour. Given the low levels of GDP per capita, there was also little potential to generate capital from savings. A sharp ideological divide, military tensions, and low share in international exports at that time made the region uninviting for foreign investors. Heavy state involvement in the economies in the region (and not just in centrally planned China) was seen by many as being inimical to the growth of domestic private capital. By any conventional economic standards the region in 1970 was destined to stay at a low level of development for the foreseeable future.

Table 8.2 shows the industrialization trends in the selected Asian countries. Between 1950 and 2005, agriculture's share of output in all Asian countries fell by more than it did in Africa, despite the fact that in the 1950s and the 1960s Asia was the most 'agricultural' continent (measured by agriculture's share in total output). Furthermore, Asia is the only continent in which the share of

Table 8.2 Structure of production in selected Asian countries, 1950–2005 (gross value-added in main sectors of the economy as % of GDP at current prices)

	1950				1980				2005				Per capita GDP 1970–2015, %		
	agr	ind	mf	sv	agr	ind	mf	sv	agr	ind	mf	sv	1970	2015	growth
South Korea	47	13	9	41	16	37	24	47	3	40	28	56	1,869	25,280	6.0
Taiwan	34	22	15	45	8	46	36	46	2	26	22	72	1,862	22,481	5.7
Turkey	49	16	11	35	27	20	17	54	11	27	22	63	3,124	8,943	2.4
Malaysia	40	19	11	41	23	41	22	36	8	50	30	42	1,201	7,622	4.2
China	51	21	14	29	30	49	40	21	13	48	34	40	150	4,187	7.7
Thailand	48	15	12	37	23	29	22	48	10	44	35	46	616	3,853	4.2
Sri Lanka	46	12	4	42	28	30	18	43	17	27	15	56	477	2,470	3.7
Indonesia	58	9	7	33	24	42	13	34	13	47	28	40	349	2,043	4.0
Philippines	42	17	8	41	25	39	26	36	14	32	23	54	826	1,734	1.7
India	55	14	10	31	36	25	17	40	18	28	16	54	259	1,279	3.6
Pakistan	61	7	7	32	30	25	16	46	21	27	19	51	371	904	2.0
Bangladesh	61	7	7	32	32	21	14	48	20	27	17	53	271	653	2.0
World													4,283	8,178	1.4
Averages:															
Asia	49	14	10	36	25	33	22	42	13	35	24	52			
Latin America	22	28	16	50	10	40	24	50	7	37	18	56			
Africa	44	19	9	36	25	32	14	43	26	30	12	45			
Developing countries	41	19	11	40	21	35	20	44	16	34	18	51			
16 OECD countries	15	42	31	43	4	36	24	59	2	28	17	70			

Notes: (a) Agr—agriculture, ind—industry, mf—manufacturing, sv—services; (b) earliest year for which data are available: 1950; except for Taiwan and Thailand, 1951; Japan and China, 1952; South Korea, 1953; Malaysia, 1955; (c) Bangladesh 1950–1959, same data as Pakistan; (d) the countries are arranged by their 2015 per capita incomes.

Source: Adapted from Szirmai (2009) and authors' calculations based on data for GDP per capita at constant 2005 US\$ are from UNCTADstat (UNCTAD 2017).

manufacturing in GDP increased continuously between 1950 and 2005. Thus, in 2005, the share of non-manufacturing industry in GDP in Asia was similar to that of the OECD (both 11 per cent), whereas those in Latin America and Africa were much higher (19 per cent and 18 per cent respectively), suggesting the dominance of extractive industries.

All in all, at the continental, the regional, and the country levels, the Asian experience shows that the most rapid per capita growth is associated with the highest degree of industrialization. This is both consistent with the historical record of currently rich countries (Chang 2002; Szirmai 2009) and with the arguments that manufacturing serves as an engine of growth for the rest of the economy, which we discuss in the next section.

2.2 The Trajectory of Industrialization Among the Asian Economies

The main impact of industrialization on economic development comes, in the classical formulation, from the transfer of labour from sectors with low and slowly growing productivity to the industrial (and especially manufacturing) sector, as discussed by Myrdal (1968: chapter 24). Most notably, this was formulated as Kaldor's (1966) first growth law, positing that GDP growth is positively correlated with manufacturing growth, owing to such transfer. This is supported by two other propositions—second and third laws—which state, in turn, that the productivity of the manufacturing sector is positively related to manufacturing output growth (due to static scale economies and learning-by-doing) and that the productivities of other sectors are positively related to the size of the manufacturing sector (due to technological spillovers). This would suggest that the richest and the fastest-growing economies would be the ones with the largest manufacturing sectors.

In this section, we look at how far and how fast different Asian economies have increased their manufacturing employment (see Table 8.3) and manufacturing value-added (see Figure 8.1). We find that the experience of the major Asian economies is in line with Kaldor's prediction; the currently richest major Asian economies (Japan and the first-tier Newly Industrialized Countries—NICs[5]) are the ones that have increased the most their manufacturing employment share relative to total employment and population. We find that the key to their success lies in the ability to sustain the growth of manufacturing production.

In Table 8.3, we see that the peak of per capita employment in manufacturing is an accurate predictor of income levels of that country in line with Kaldor's first

---

[5] In the chapter we mention first-tier NICs—South Korea, Taiwan, Singapore, and Hong Kong—and second-tier NICs—Malaysia, Indonesia, and Thailand.

Table 8.3 Peaks in manufacturing employment share in total employment and in total population in selected Asian economies (employment, population, and MVA growth prior to and after reaching the manufacturing employment 'peak' relative to total population)

	Data entries	'Peak' in mf share in total employment		'Peak' in mf empl as a proportion of total population		Pre-peak growth rates (regards the 'population' peak, %)			Post-peak growth rates (regards the 'population' peak, %)		
		year	%	year	per 1,000	empl	pop	MVA	empl	pop	MVA
Japan	1953–2012	1969	24.5	1969	135.2	4.6	1.1	13.0	-1.2	0.5	2.6
Singapore	1970–2011	1981	30.4	1982	142.8	8.0	1.6	9.5	1.4	2.5	6.3
Hong Kong	1974–2011	1976	45.3	1981	197.3	6.1	2.8	12.5	-6.4	1.1	0.4
South Korea	1963–2010	1988	28.1	1991	116.4	7.8	1.6	14.6	-0.8	0.7	6.7
Taiwan	1963–2012	1987	33.7	1987	144.1	7.4	2.1	13.8	0.2	0.7	3.1
Malaysia	1975–2011	1997	24.9	1997	100.5	7.4	2.5	10.5	0.2	2.0	3.7
China	1952–2011	2010	**<u>19.2</u>**	2010	**<u>107.3</u>**	4.5	1.5	14.4	n/a	n/a	n/a
Thailand	1960–2011	2007	<u>15.1</u>	2007	**<u>84.5</u>**	5.1	1.9	8.9	n/a	n/a	n/a
Indonesia	1971–2012	1994	13.5	1994	62.5	6.1	2.2	12.1	1.2	1.4	3.3
Philippines	1971–2012	1971	<u>12.0</u>	1975	<u>40.6</u>	n/a	n/a	n/a	1.6	2.3	3.1
India	1960–2010	2002	12.5	2003	49.7	2.8	2.1	5.5	-0.2	1.5	8.7
US	1950–2010	1953	<u>25.6</u>	1953	<u>106.0</u>	n/a	n/a	n/a	-0.7	1.3	2.8

Notes: (a) mf—manufacturing, empl—employment, pop—population; (b) **Bold Underlined numbers** indicate that the 'peak' is within the last 5 years of the period covered, and therefore that it could go higher. Double-underlined numbers indicate that the 'peak' is within the first 5 years of the period covered and therefore that it might have been higher before. The growth rates prior to 'bold underlined' peaks, as well as after 'double-underlined' peaks, are omitted (marked n/a), either due to lack of data or because they may be reflecting short-term fluctuations rather than longer-term trends in growth; (c) The MVA growth rates and the employment growth rates are calculated for the same years, except for Japan (whose post-peak MVA growth rate is for 1969–2011) due to data availability; (d) Countries are ranked according to their per capita GDP in 2015 from the richest to the poorest (UNCTADstat 2017 database), except for the US, which serves as a reference.

Source: Authors' calculations based on employment and MVA at constant 2005 national prices data from GGDC 10-Sector Database, Timmer et al. (2015); population data from UN DESA Population Division (2017) database.

proposition. This applies to Japan and the first-tier NICs, but also to the richest second-tier NIC, Malaysia.

Relatively rapid rates of employment and output growth in the manufacturing sector were significant in the rise of the currently industrialized East Asian countries to their 'peak' industrializations. This is consistent with Myrdal's (1968: appendix 2) assertion that, in order to achieve sustained economic growth, a country needs to overcome the 'threshold' of initial institutional and economic inertia (more on this in section 3). However, contrarily to Myrdal's assertion, simply achieving such rates of growth does not seem to be a sufficient, not to speak of being necessary, condition for successful industrialization. For instance, Indonesia and Malaysia have achieved similar, or higher, rates of employment and output growth than those of some East Asian 'tigers', but Indonesia has not been able to sustain its manufacturing employment growth and Malaysia's industrial dynamism started to wane at levels of per capita income and of MVA significantly short of those of the East Asian 'tigers'. China, in contrast, has been able to reach a high (and still growing) level of employment in manufacturing, despite having a significantly lower growth rate of employment in manufacturing than most of the countries in the sample. This suggests that it is not the high rates of growth in manufacturing employment or output per se but the ability to sustain them that matters.

Interestingly, the countries that have had lower 'peak' employment shares have had weaker manufacturing productivity growth performance afterwards (3.5 per cent or lower with the exception of India) than the richer (Japan and first-tier NICs) countries (3.8 per cent and higher, with the exception of Taiwan). In theory, this can be partially attributed, as in the second Kaldor's law, to the smaller dynamic scale economies and fewer intra-industry linkages.

Particularly notable is the fact that, in the industrialized East Asian countries, manufacturing output has expanded through continued productivity growth, even while manufacturing employment in absolute terms has declined.[6] However, as seen earlier (Table 8.2), in the South and the Southeast Asian economies, manufacturing employment has been growing in absolute terms even after the 'peak' in terms of the employment share (except for India recently), suggesting that their manufacturing employment growth cannot keep up with the growth in workforce. At the same time, their manufacturing sector is still not large enough to drive overall development through its productivity growth.[7] We can notice these different patterns of loss of industrialization dynamism in Figure 8.1.

---

[6] This is also due to shedding sunset industries, which are often more labour-intensive.

[7] It is not to say that sustaining employment growth in manufacturing is desirable under any conditions. If employment in the protected manufacturing sector is expanded without raising its competitiveness, the result may be larger loss of employment if such a sector is exposed to international competition, as it will have little ability to withstand it. This can create higher unemployment in the longer run, which would be difficult to absorb quickly.

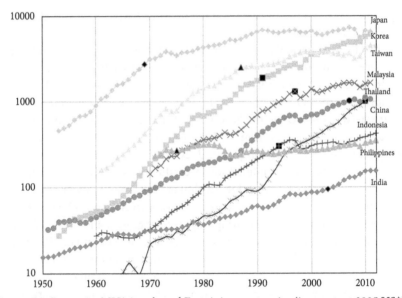

Figure 8.1 Per capita MVA in selected East Asian economies (in constant 2005 US$).

Notes: (a) The **black point** indicates the year in which economy had its manufacturing employment 'peak' as a percentage of population; (b) Graph done in logarithmic scale to illustrate growth rates; (c) Original data is in national currencies at constant 2005 prices—converted to 2005 US$ prices using 'Treasury Reporting Rates of Exchange as of December 31, 2005'.

Source: Authors' calculations from MVA at 2005 national prices data from Timmer et al. (2015), population data from UN DESA Population Division (2017) and exchange rates of national currencies to US$ from US Department of Treasury, Bureau of the Fiscal Service (2005).

Figure 8.1 visually presents some of the previous points. First, it shows that at the heart of the industrialization success of Japan and first-tier NICs was their ability to sustain the rapid expansion of manufacturing output, well beyond their manufacturing employment peak (marked by the black point on the trend line).[8] Second, it shows that, in the case of Southeast Asia (especially Malaysia and Indonesia), the loss of industrial dynamism happened around the time of the employment peak. Beyond it, their industrial growth performance weakens and is increasingly disrupted by contractions.

Most Asian economies in the figure (China and India are the exceptions) experienced a slowdown and even a decline in the growth of MVA following the Asian financial crisis of 1997, despite being at very different levels of MVA per capita.[9] Beyond the 'dip' due to the crisis, the affected countries have experienced a lasting loss of industrial dynamism. The likely cause of this deterioration is the

---

[8] Hong Kong is the exception. It began to rapidly financialize in the 1980s and especially in the 1990s to provide financial services for the gradually liberalizing Chinese economy.

[9] Japan at around US$6,800, Japan and Taiwan at around US$3,800, Malaysia at US$1,300, and Indonesia at US$350 per capita.

change in economic policies and institutions towards the neo-liberal direction, introduced in the aftermath of the 1997 crisis (see Shin and Chang 2005).

One of the main effects of the policy changes after the crisis was on the rate of investment. For both the Southeast and the East Asian regions, gross fixed capital formation (GFCF) as a proportion of GDP fell significantly between 1991 and 1995 and 2001 and 2005 and stayed close to that level in the next decade with the exception of Indonesia (see Chang and Zach 2018: table A2). It fell by the equivalent of about 6 per cent of GDP for Japan, 7 per cent for Korea and Indonesia, almost 8 per cent for Singapore, and over 16 per cent for Malaysia and Thailand. It remained at that level, except in Malaysia, Thailand, and Hong Kong, where it bounced back a little. This decline takes the GFCF/GDP ratio of most of those countries below the world average, around 20 per cent, for the first time since the 1970s. The only major Asian economies with a GFCF/GDP ratio over 30 per cent in that period were Korea, China, and Vietnam.

Interestingly, with this decline, most of those countries have converged to the GFCF/GDP levels of the slower industrializers, like the South Asian economies and the Philippines. This suggests that the inability to sustain the growth in the share of manufacturing in total employment among the Southeast Asian countries after 1997, on the one hand, and the South Asian countries and the Philippines in the earlier period, on the other hand, have similar origins—that is, investments were inadequate to generate manufacturing employment growth faster than the growth of the workforce.

The experiences of China and Vietnam give even more weight to this reasoning. From 2000 to 2010 (and for China in 2010 to 2015 as well), both countries maintained the highest (alongside Korea) rates of GFCF as a proportion of GDP in the region (Vietnam around 30 per cent, China around 40 per cent—see Chang and Zach 2018: table A2), which coincided with them being the only two major economies of the region that experienced growth 'miracles' during the period. In the same period, they significantly improved their MVA per capita level relative to other economies of the region, with China approaching the Malaysian level and Vietnam nearing the Indonesian level.

2.3 Upgrading and Diversification of Industrial Production

Continued upgrading of industrial production is essential for sustaining both industrialization and growth in the standards of living. Industrialization creates demands for a variety of complex machinery and intermediate goods. In an open economy, this can be—and often should be—met by imports, which require foreign exchanges. The rising standards of living lead to an increase in the demand for imported consumer goods and thus for foreign exchanges. The challenge is then to sustain industrialization in the face of rising demands for foreign exchanges (due to increased needs for imports) and of falling abilities to earn them (due to higher wages).

Initially, developing countries earn the necessary foreign exchanges by expanding the exports of existing primary commodities or basic manufactures. However, these will prove insufficient. First, as wages grow, the competitiveness of these goods will deteriorate, as they tend to be more labour-intensive. At the same time, the possibilities for cutting costs become more limited, as these 'basic' goods benefit less from the scale economies than complex ones and have less room for cutting costs through capital investments. Second, the demands for technologically complex goods grow faster than those for primary commodities, structurally constraining their export growths (see Palma 2005).

Thus, the more viable strategy for alleviating the balance of payments (BoP) constraints lies in the diversification of production structure. 'Horizontal' diversification, entailing the expansion of other primary commodities or basic manufacturing goods, increases the economy's foreign exchange earnings, while also 'hedging' the economy against price fluctuations of specific goods. More important, however, is 'vertical' diversification, especially that which involves 'upgrading' towards more technology-intensive industries. It alleviates BoP pressure by making the export basket more 'demand-dynamic', thereby generating more foreign exchanges than it would otherwise. Some studies indicate that the quicker this process occurs, the better the growth outcomes are (e.g., Felipe et al. 2012; also see discussion in Chang and Lin 2009).

In Table 8.4, we can see the change in the leading export items for major Asian economies. We see that the currently industrialized economies have upgraded the most—with high- and medium-technology goods dominating exports. This is especially surprising in the case of Singapore or Korea, which had been exporters of low-tech and resource-based manufactures in 1965. At the same time, no country that has upgraded only moderately has experienced significant industrialization success.

Furthermore, the experiences of China and Vietnam support the idea that countries which upgrade aggressively at relative low-income levels subsequently experience faster rates of economic growth. These countries moved from primary commodity dependence in 1965 to the dominance of mostly high-tech products in 2016. Countries like the Philippines, Malaysia, and Thailand have an even higher concentration of export share in electronic products. However, they, including Malaysia, still significantly depend on primary commodities.

Perhaps unsurprisingly, countries that have not industrialized or grown as rapidly have generally witnessed fewer changes in their exports baskets. Pakistan, for instance, upgraded from plant fibre to garments and from jute to cotton, but is still a largely agro-products exporter. India and Indonesia have largely upgraded from agro-products to mined commodities and natural-resource-based manufactures—into diamonds and jewellery (India) and coal and petroleum (Indonesia)—but have not gone beyond that.

Table 8.4 Technology intensity of top five exports in selected countries in 1965 and 2016 (SITC4 classification)

Country	1965	2016
Japan	Ships and Boats (7932) 7.0% Fabrics, Woven, of Man-made Fabrics (6530) 3.7%	Cars (7810) 15% **Unclassified Transactions (9310) 6.2%**
	Finished Cotton Fabrics (6522) 3.6% Universals, Plates and Sheets, of Iron or Steel (6740) 3.1%	Vehicle Parts and Accessories (7849) 5.4% Machinery for Specialized Industries (7284) 4.0%
	Motorcycles (7851) 2.0%	Electronic Microcircuits (7764) 3.0%
Singapore	Natural Rubber (2320) 34%	Electronic Microcircuits (7764) 24%
	Petroleum Products, Refined (3340) 9.7% Fuel Oils (3344) 5.9%	**Unclassified Transactions (9310) 5.9%** Machinery for Specialized Industries (7284) 2.3%
	Light Oils (3341) 3.4% Gas Oils (3343) 2.9%	Aircraft Parts and Accessories (7929) 2.2% TV and Radio Transmitters (7643) 2.0%
Republic of Korea	Veneers, Plywood, Improved Wood and Other Wood, Worked, Nes (6340) 9.1%	Electronic Microcircuits (7764) 11%
	Universal Plates of Iron or Steel (6741) 7.4% Men's and Boys' Outwear, Textile Fabrics Not Knitted or Crocheted (8420) 5.7% Unbleached Cotton Woven Fabrics (6521) 5.1%	Cars (7810) 8.2% Ships and Boats (7932) 5.5% Vehicle Parts and Accessories (7849) 4.8%
	Miscellaneous Non-Ferrous Ores (2879) 4.8%	Telecom Parts and Accessories (7649) 4.7%
Malaysia	Natural Rubber (2320) 40%	Electronic Microcircuits (7764) 14%
	Unwrought Tin and Alloys (6871) 17% Non-Coniferous Sawlogs (2472) 7.4%	Palm Oil (4242) 5.4% Liquified Petroleum Gases (3413) 4.3%
	Iron Ore and Concentrates (2810) 5.2%	Diods, Transistors and Photocells (7763) 3.8%
	Non-Coniferous Worked Wood (2483) 3.4%	Crude Petroleum (3330) 3.4%
China	Finished Cotton Fabrics (6522) 5.3%	TV and Radio Transmitters (7643) 5.8%
	Soy Beans (2222) 5.0%	Personal Computers (7522) 4.1%
	Milled Rice (0422) 4.7%	Telecom Parts and Accessories (7649) 3.1%
	Miscellaneous Animal Origin Materials (2919) 4.2%	Electronic Microcircuits (7764) 2.7%
	Unbleached Cotton Woven Fabrics (6521) 3.4%	Footwear (8510) 2.3%

Continued

Table 8.4 *Continued*

Country	1965	2016
Thailand*	Milled Rice (0422) 30%	Computer Peripherals (7525) 5.4%
	Natural Rubber (2320) 14% Tin (2876) 7.0%	Cars (7810) 4.7% Trucks and Vans (7821) 4.1%
	Maize (0440) 6.9%	Electronic Microcircuits (7764) 3.4%
	Jute (2640) 6.0%	Vehicle Parts and Accessories (7849) 3.3%
Indonesia	Crude Petroleum (3330) 26% Natural Rubber (2320) 21% Tin (2876) 6.3%	Palm Oil (4242) 10% Coal (3222) 8.6% Crude Petroleum (3330) 3.5%
	Coffee (0711) 6.1%	Footwear (8510) 3.2%
	Fuel Oils (3344) 5.0%	Liquified Petroleum Gases (3413) 3.1%
Philippines	Non-Coniferous Sawlogs (2472) 20%	Electronic Microcircuits (7764) 25%
	Copra (2231) 20%	Computer Peripherals (7525) 8.2%
	Refined Sugars (0612) 14%	Carpentry Wood (6353) 5.2%
	Coconut Oil (4243) 7.7%	Diodes, Transistors and Photocells (7763) 4.3%
	Copper Ores (2871) 6.1%	Electric Wire (7731) 4.1%
India	Tea (0741) 14%	Diamonds (6672) 10%
	Jute Woven Fabrics (6545) 13%	Precious Jewellery (8973) 5.5%
	Iron Ore and Concentrates (2810) 7.4%	Medicaments (5417) 5.2%
	Textile Bags (6581) 5.6%	Cars (7810) 2.8%
	Oilcake (0813) 4.7%	Milled Rice (0422) 2.3%
Vietnam*	Natural Rubber (2320) 42%	TV and Radio Transmitters (7643) 16%
	Coal, Lignite and Peat (3220) 17%	Footwear (8510) 7.6%
	Pig and Cast Iron (6712) 3.9%	Telecom Parts and Accessories (7649) 3.5%
	Green Groundnuts (2221) 3.8%	Personal Computers (7522) 2.7%
	Tea (0741) 3.4%	Electronic Microcircuits (7764) 2.6%
Pakistan	Jute (2640) 35%	Linens (6584) 12%
	Raw Cotton (2631) 12%	Milled Rice (0422) 8.2%

Textile Bags (6581) 10%	Finished Cotton Fabrics (6522) 6.8%
Jute Woven Fabrics (6545) 6.3%	Cotton Yarn (6513) 6.1%
Cotton Yarn (6513) 4.9%	Miscellaneous Textile Articles (6589) 5.2%

Bangladesh	Jute (2640) 53%	Cotton Undergarments (8462) 23%
	Jute Woven Fabrics (6546) 21%	Men's Pants (8423) 17%
	Textile Bags (6581) 12%	Knitted Underwear (8451) 11%
	Crustaceans and Molluscs (0360) 3.0%	Miscellaneous Feminine Outerwear (8439) 7.1%
	Finished Leather (6118)	Men's Shirts (8441) 7.0%

Notes: (a) Products coloured by technology intensiveness. High-tech manufactures, medium-tech manufactures, low-tech manufactures, natural resource-based manufactures, primary commodities. Based on Lall (2000) classification; (b) Countries marked with * use data for 2015—latest available. Bangladesh uses data for 1972 and 2011—first and last entries available; (c) Countries ordered from richest to poorest (2015 per capita GDP UNCTADstat 2017 data).

Source: Authors' construction, Observatory of Economic Complexity (OEC) software, based on Simoes and Hidalgo (2011).

Table 8.5 confirms these observations at a more aggregated level. The table looks at the shares of four main groups of export goods—agricultural goods, both primary and processed (Agr), minerals and oil (M&O), garments, textiles and fabrics (GTF), and hi-tech products like machinery and electronics (M&E).[10]

All the economies in Table 8.5 have seen a very significant decrease in the share of agricultural commodities, both primary and processed (Agr). Excluding Korea (where it was only 20 per cent), these constituted 45–84 per cent of merchandise exports in 1965, but only 2–21 per cent in 2016. This decline was accompanied initially by an increase in exports of garments and textiles (GTF) and, in some countries, mined commodities (M&O). In the case of the four richest countries in the Table, as well as the Philippines and more recently Vietnam, another change was taking place after that initial shift, which was a marked expansion of electronics and machinery (M&E) exports. In these countries, these constituted <1–3 per cent of merchandise exports in 1965 but 39–61 per cent in 2016.

Despite large variations within the trend, we can see that those countries that were growing faster (see Table 8.2 for their respective growth rates) were those that experienced the most dramatic transformation in their export baskets and went through the changes described above most rapidly. This could be seen most clearly in the cases of Korea, Malaysia, China, Thailand, and more recently Vietnam, which all have seen a drastic transition from dominant group Agr to

[10] See note (a) to Table 8.4 for the breakdown of each group. The commodities included in each group are not all goods of a similar nature (for instance, group Agr could also include processed foods and group M&E could also include aircraft). However, we did not include all OEC-SITC2 commodity groups, partly due to the limits of the OEC software, partly because some SITC2 groups encompass a much more diverse range of goods, and partly because some groups had only marginal shares of exports across all selected economies.

Table 8.5 Merchandise export shares of selected commodity groups in selected Asian economies 1965–2016, %

Year	1965				1985				2000				2016			
Commodity group(a)	Agr	M&O	GTF	M&E	Agr	M&O	GTF	M&E	Agr	M&O	GTF	M&E	Agr	M&O	GTF	M&E
Korea	20	12	33	3	4	1	31	28	2	1	10	57	<1	2	3	61
Malaysia	49	11	1	1	23	27	4	19	4	7	3	69	9	11	2	49
China	45	3	23	3	15	21	33	7	3	2	27	45	2	1	17	52
Thailand*	76	3	<1	<1	56	6	16	10	16	4	11	47	13	6	4	50
Indonesia	49	31	2	<1	12	67	3	<1	10	25	15	20	21	27	12	15
Philippines	52	10	4	<1	30	12	14	22	3	2	11	75	6	5	7	61
India	54	13	18	2	30	24	23	7	15	22	29	10	14	21	17	17
Vietnam*	66	20	<1	<1	86	7	2	<1	22	28	34	7	13	4	27	39
Pakistan	68	<1	23	1	39	<1	46	2	13	<1	76	3	20	2	64	3
Bangladesh*	84	<1	15	<1	56	<1	37	<1	12	<1	84	<1	7	<1	89	<1

Notes: (a) Commodity groups based on SITC2 groups as in OEC software: Agr—cereals and vegetable oils, cotton, rice, soy beans and others, fish and seafood; fruit, leather, meat and eggs, misc. agriculture, tropical treecrops and flowers; M&O—oil, coal, mining, precious stones; GTF—garments, textiles and fabrics, M&E—machinery and electronics; (b) Countries marked with * have data for other years included—Bangladesh has 1972 instead of 1965 and 2011 instead of 2016; Thailand and Vietnam have 2015 instead of 2016; (c) The shares are calculated with the exclusion of 'not classified' group. The only exception is 1965 Vietnam data, which includes Coal, Lignite and Peat (SITC4 code 3220) into group B, since it constitutes a very significant portion of exports in that year (17 per cent); (d) Countries are ordered from the richest to the poorest based on their 2015 per capita GDP, as reported in UNCTAD (2017).

Source: Authors' calculation with use of OEC software, based on Simoes and Hidalgo (2011).

M&O, GTF, and then M&E. There are exceptions to this, such as the Philippines, which did not manage a similarly high overall growth rate, or Thailand, which moved directly from agricultural commodities and products to machinery and electronics without much expansion in groups M&O and GTF. However, Table 8.2 shows that none of the countries that did not significantly expand their group M&E exports have managed successful industrialization.

As we have seen in this part of the chapter, the Asian development experience of the past five decades has been defined by remarkable degrees of industrialization and the resulting structural transformation. In the next section, we will examine how the industrial policy approaches adopted by Asian economies during that period have been crucial in that process.

3. Industrial Policy in Asia

3.1 The Purpose of Industrial Policy in the Framework of Circular and Cumulative Causation

To understand the role of industrial policy for industrial development, let us start by considering Myrdal's conceptualization of the development process as that of circular and cumulative causation. It means that a number of positive (or negative) impacts of changing socio-economic conditions reinforce the process in the direction of the initial change. Thus understood, the process of industrial development is underpinned by a number of economic objectives whose achievements contribute to the achievement of others,[11] notably:

- sustaining a high investment rate and maximizing their development impacts
- expansion of manufacturing employment
- expanding the scales of production to reap scale economies
- vertical diversification into higher-technology sectors
- expanding and deepening inter-sectoral linkages
- acquisition of cutting-edge technologies and the development of research and development (R&D) capabilities by domestic producers
- acquisition of organizational, managerial, and technical capabilities by domestic producers
- increasing international market share.

In theory, success in meeting these objectives drives industrialization. In practice, however, the 'virtuous spiral' of cumulative causation rarely happens automatically.

---

[11] As described by Myrdal, industrial development is also strongly related and dependent on institutional and social factors, the discussion of which goes beyond the scope of this chapter. For discussion of these aspects in relation to Asia, see Chapters 5 and 13, this volume.

This is especially true for developing countries that lack potent domestic industrial enterprises. According to Myrdal (1968), this is due to various institutional factors—attitudes, scarcity of certain economic inputs, and political demobilization, which create strong inertia—all of which require a powerful impulse to be overcome, especially through state intervention. State intervention becomes even more necessary if military objectives or ideological aspiration requires acceleration of the pace of structural transformation or if there are counterforces or shocks pushing the economy in the opposite direction. Given all these, Myrdal points out that the core purposes of development planning are: (i) to cause such a 'virtuous spiral' to arise; (ii) to introduce (where missing) and strengthen the forces of cumulative causation that drive it; (iii) to preserve it in the face of bottlenecks, counterforces, or shocks; and (iv) to use newly arising opportunities to propel it further. Correspondingly, the purpose of industrial policy is to guide industrial development in the same manner, using a broad range of policies (for examples, see Chang 2011b).[12]

In the following section, drawing on Myrdal's insights, we will provide overviews of industrial policy in four major Asian economies—in Korea, Malaysia, China, and India—and discuss how and why it has contributed (or not) to industrialization in those countries.[13]

3.2 Selected Case Studies of Industrial Policy in Asian Countries

3.2.1 Republic of Korea

The 'classic' Korean industrial policy started in the 1960s, motivated by revanchism against Japan and by the military threat from its communist neighbours. It was heavily influenced by the industrial planning ideologies of Japan, the USSR, and China, despite the widely advertised allegiance to the 'free world' by its new military government. It was structured by the (indicative) five-year plans of the Economic Planning Board (EPB), with detailed sectoral plans provided by the Ministry of Commerce and Industry (Chang 1994).

The Korean government provided a range of strong incentives to expand into hi-tech sectors at a relatively low level of development—the Heavy and Chemical Industrialization programme was launched in 1973 when the country's per capita income was just over 5 per cent of the US level. First, the government protected

---

[12] The need for co-ordination and for the management of a range of interlinked economic and non-economic processes is one of the reasons why it is difficult, if not outright misleading, to try to define industrial policy in terms of the tools. Such attempts usually yield excessively long lists. We argue that it is better to define it in terms of its goals (that is, industrial development) and in terms of its modus operandi (i.e., selective—and sequential—development of various industrial sectors).

[13] Within the scope of this chapter, we focus on overviewing most standard selective industrial policies. The effect of other policies on industrial development, including macroeconomic and exchange rate policies are explored by Chapter 9 or Chapter 11 in this volume.

'infant' industries from international competition through trade restrictions; quantitative restrictions were prevalent until the 1980s and the average manufacturing tariff was 30–40 per cent until the 1970s (Chang 2005). Second, the government rationed foreign exchanges, giving priority to importers of capital goods and intermediate inputs. Third, subsidies, including export subsidies, were provided conditional on improving the export performance or developing R&D capabilities and retracted whenever the recipient failed to perform. Fourth, foreign direct investment (FDI) was heavily regulated to promote capability acquisition by domestic firms. FDI was banned in many industries and majority ownership was not allowed outside the Export Processing Zones (EPZs), while investors were put under various performance requirements regarding local contents and technology transfer. Fifth, where the private sector was unwilling to invest in sectors deemed strategic, the government set up state-owned enterprises (SOEs)— the most notable example being POSCO (set up in 1968 and privatized in 2001), which is now the fourth largest steel-maker in the world.

In implementing industrial policy, the government promoted the chaebols, the large and highly diversified conglomerates. This policy allowed the concentration of scarce capital and managerial resources while ensuring scale economies and long investment horizons. While promoting fierce competition among the chaebols through innovation, the Korean government also regulated their investments and pricing in order to reduce inefficiencies resulting from 'excessive competition'.[14] It also set up deliberation councils to co-ordinate private investment goals with national targets.

Moderated in the late 1980s and the early 1990s, Korea's 'classic' industrial policy approach was largely dismantled in 1993, when the EPB was abolished and five-year plans terminated. Soon after that, industrial policy was even more diluted by liberalization following the Asian financial crisis of 1997, resulting in the loss of industrial dynamism. By that time, however, Korea had already become a rich industrialized economy.

3.2.2 Malaysia

In its initial phase (1957–1969), Malaysia's industrial policy was aimed at expanding domestic manufacturing employment and alleviating BoP pressures through import-substitution. This was realized by direct and indirect government financing of factory construction in industrial zones. However, there was little to no strategic targeting aimed at things like vertical diversification, technological upgrading, or scale economies in production. There was little pressure for infant industries to 'mature' (Jomo et al. 1997).

---

[14] It was understood to be a situation in which a large number of firms competed in one sector, leading to a waste of resources due to things like unnecessary scrapping of sector-specific capital goods as a result of more frequent bankruptcies, duplication of R&D, and the lack of technology sharing. On the concept of 'excessive competition', see Chang (1994) and Amsden and Singh (1994).

The approach changed in the 1970s to an export-oriented one. While there were attempts to expand comparative-advantage-conforming export industries, like palm oil and petroleum, great efforts were made to enter hi-tech sectors (especially electronics) by attracting multinational companies (MNCs) into free-trade zones. Export-oriented local firms were also given lucrative tax incentives (including deductions on R&D and training), although there was no policy to expand local supply linkages (Jomo et al. 1997). These efforts were combined with the New Economic Policy, aimed at ethnic redistribution. Instead of supporting the most able industrialists (mostly Chinese), the government set up SOEs and subsequently privatized them to Bumiputera owners (the country's majority ethnic group). These enterprises were supported by the industrial licensing system, which handicapped Chinese-owned businesses.

Malaysia's industrial policy took a brief turn towards prioritizing the expansion of domestic productive capabilities with the introduction of the heavy industrialization policy in 1980–1985, which targeted sectors like cement, steel, and automobiles. This effort was mostly abandoned in 1985–1986 due to the poor performance of the targeted industries.

Even after the 1986 liberalization, however, industrial policy continued. The Industrial Development Agency used a variety of tax incentives and investment subsidies to deepen local supplier linkages and technological transfer (Lall 1995). Although less 'heavy-handed' than before 1986, the government continued to support selected sectors, identified in the industrial master plans, launched for 1986–1995, 1995–2006, and 2006–2020, on the bases of growth and technological potentials. Support to these industries was largely provided through 'horizontal' industrial policy measures (e.g., subsidies for R&D, physical investment, worker training), but some trade protection (heavier for more processed products) was also used. Export tariffs on some strategic industrial inputs, such as crude palm oil (which provided targeted support to the oleo-chemical industry reliant on it), were maintained. Investment licensing was continued, favouring capital-intensive investments through rules regarding the minimum investment per worker. Investment incentives were actually extended rather than reduced, after 1986. For example, the pioneer status, which allowed, among other things, exemption from corporate income tax for five (extendable to ten) years for firms entering new industries, was granted to 12–17 per cent of investments in 1983–1985 but to 24–28 per cent of investments in 2001–2003 (Gustafsson 2007). Although yielding limited success in the expansion of domestic productive capabilities, these policies helped the vertical and horizontal diversifications of the Malaysian economy.

3.2.3 China

Initially, China was a Soviet-style administrative-command economy with industrialization efforts geared primarily towards developing the capital goods sector through direct state ownership of enterprises and through state control over the supply, distribution, and pricing of industrial production (Ellman 2014). After the 1978 reform, this evolved towards an activist strategic industrial policy in the context of the market system, private property, and production for profit.

During 1978–2004, China's industrial policy was strongly shaped by two motives—the increased pressure, both international and internal, for economic liberalization, and the need to transform the planned economic system into an internationalized market economy (Heilmann and Shih 2013). By the end of that period, China became one of the most open among the world's major economies— the share of its exports and imports reached 71 per cent of GDP in 2005 (second only to Germany) and its average tariff was reduced to 40.6 per cent in 1992 and 4.9 per cent in 2005 (Dahlman 2009).

However, liberalization was done gradually and selectively. China rejected the 'shock therapy' and used a range of policies to develop domestic productive capabilities while protecting and restructuring domestic industries. One such strategy was the targeted use of FDI in EPZs. The Chinese government attracted FDI into specific sectors with the use of tax incentives, while extracting (formal and informal) concessions from the MNCs regarding local sourcing, joint ventures, technology transfer, and workforce training. The government actively encouraged domestic enterprises—through direct control of SOEs, various subsidies, or direct negotiation with the management—to use EPZs' exposure to actively integrate domestic producers into the international market. For example, enterprises present in EPZs were encouraged to expand their supplier networks to include a larger number of domestic firms into the supply chain of EPZs-based MNCs. They were also integrating into international supply chains, learning organizational capabilities, or upskilling of technical staff. At the same time, the large network of EPZs enabled the country rapidly to expand manufacturing employment and its foreign exchange earnings, which were then used for importing more advanced technologies (machines or technology licences).

Over the course of liberalization, China has continued to promote infant industries. This has been done through a significant degree of state ownership (roughly 30 per cent of Chinese firms in 2013 were state-owned), the use of subsidized credit through state-owned banks, an extensive system of public procurement, various trade barriers for non-EPZ areas, and public investments (Dahlman 2009). It has tried to develop large-scale domestic firms by encouraging and facilitating mergers in an effort to create 'national champions' (Nolan 2001). The most comprehensive support was provided to sectors deemed important for national security, technological advancement, and the secure supply of strategic inputs (especially coal, electricity, telecommunications, and aircraft) (Chang et al. 2013).

Following the success of initial restructuring and the build-up of domestic production capabilities, China's strategy turned towards the development of native R&D capacity, the expansion of domestic linkages, and vertical diversification. These were the main goals of the sectoral industrial policies and national indicative planning programmes, which followed the establishment of the National

Development and Reform Commission in 2003–2004. The number of national industrial policy programmes annually adopted rose from nil in 2003 to 15 in 2011.

Three such programmes deserve special mention. The first, the 2006 Medium- and Long-Term Programme of Science and Technology, provided funding for sixteen megaprojects in hi-tech sectors, such as pharmaceuticals, semiconductors, large commercial aircraft, and military industries (Chen and Naughton 2016). The second programme, Strategic Emerging Industries launched in 2010, aimed to develop twenty industries in seven broad categories, building on the aforementioned megaprojects. These industries accounted for 8 per cent of Chinese GDP by 2015 and 15 per cent by 2020 (Chen and Naughton 2016). Lastly, in 2015, the Made in China 2025 initiative was launched, geared towards upgrading Chinese industries and achieving domestic contents of core components and materials of 40 per cent by 2020, and 70 per cent by 2025. It prioritizes high-tech sectors like aerospace, robotics, IT, energy, and pharmaceuticals.

3.2.4 India

India's industrial policy of the early postcolonial period aimed to achieve economic independence through industrialization (Felipe et al. 2013). Its occupation of industrial 'commanding heights' allowed the Indian government to directly control investment (Singh 2008). Its development vision was implemented through the five-year plans of the Planning Commission, whose primary emphasis was on the development of capital goods industries, to enable indigenous industrialization. These and other key industries were to be state-owned. The private industrial sector was allowed but was to fully conform to the five-year plans through the so-called 'licence raj' system, which controlled all the key aspects of the business (scale and location of investments, minimum and maximum outputs, and imports).

Focused on achieving a high degree of self-reliance, India put little emphasis on competing in international markets and pursued an aggressive import-substitution (IS) policy, supported by high tariffs (the average weighted tariff was 83 per cent in 1990) and comprehensive import controls. FDI was highly restricted, especially following the 1973 Foreign Exchange Regulation Act. Such a degree of protection from international competition, when coupled with price controls, ensured significant margins to industrial enterprises, but there was no East-Asian-style government compulsion to improve performances. Some industrial policy measures during the IS period were successful. For example, the Indian government promoted the generic pharmaceutical industry by 'freeing' product patents through the 1970 Patent Act, setting up the Council of Scientific and Industrial Research labs, and introducing restrictions on MNCs (Chaudhuri 2013).

However, in many cases, industrial policy was constrained by ideological considerations. For example, in the electronics hardware industry, the policy favoured native innovation, even when it would have been much more effective to first acquire more advanced technologies through foreign licensing and then build on them, as did the East Asian countries.[15] As another example, the Indian government restricted the scale of investment of large firms in order to protect small-scale enterprises, which were favoured for ideological reasons, rather than ensuring scale economies of factories set up, as was done in East Asia. Most of these policies were later liberalized. In the 1980s, restrictions on imports of capital goods and on production capacity were relaxed, and targeted FDI became more widely used (Rodrik and Subramanian 2004; Kohli 2006; Nayyar 2006). A more dramatic shift came with the 1991 reform. The investment licensing system and state monopoly were abolished in almost all industries. FDI was allowed in the majority of sectors (at first up to 49 per cent and later up to 100 per cent of ownership). Industrial location policy and the Monopoly and Restrictive Trade Practices Act were abolished (Kohli 2006; Felipe et al. 2013). Trade was gradually liberalized—the average weighted tariff fell from 83 per cent in 1990 to 14.5 per cent in 2005.

More recently, the pendulum has swung back to an extent, with more activist national industrial policy plans. The first major such plan was the 2011 National Manufacturing Policy, which aimed to increase MVA in GDP from 16 per cent to 25 per cent by 2022, with the use of the so-called national investment and manufacturing zones, tax exemptions (e.g., exempting suppliers to Special Economic Zones from indirect taxes), and other incentives (e.g., covering the costs of filing for international patents) (Warwick 2013). Another was the 2014 Make in India initiative, aimed at attracting MNCs to set up production and design facilities through measures like further sectoral de-licensing, the building of industrial corridors, and the facilitation of greater government–business co-operation (especially through the Investor Facilitation Centre and the Invest India initiative).

3.3 Evaluating Industrial Policy Experience in Asia—What Can Be Learnt?

3.3.1 The Choice of Policies

Although the use of industrial policy in the post-Second World War period has enabled the majority of Asian economies to achieve sustained GDP per capita growth, it has yielded dramatically better outcomes in some countries.

It is clear that neo-liberal policies—based on the principles of privatization, liberalization, and stabilization—have commonly brought about a decline in

---

[15] However, some of the investments made in establishing elite engineering institutes and domestic hi-tech hubs (most notably in Bangalore) later created the basis for the success of Indian ITC industries (Balakrishnan 2006).

industrial dynamism. It is also clear that central planning has proven very ineffective in most areas. However, beyond that, there is no policy that has worked—or not worked—everywhere. Infant industry protection worked very well in Taiwan but failed in Pakistan. Export-orientation and FDI-friendly policies have helped Malaysia, but less so the Philippines. Regulation of domestic investment promoted rapid industrialization in Korea but hindered it in India. Moreover, some countries have been able to sustain good growth performance despite significantly changing their policies over time, while others have produced uneven results across time despite a consistent industrial strategy.

The point here is *not* that you can use any policies to succeed, but rather that the same policy tools can be used poorly or even misused. In other words, the difference between success and failure stems not only from *which* policies were used but *for what purpose* and *how* they were used. More specifically, the policy approaches of poorer performers have often neglected or abandoned the objectives crucial to industrial catch-up, whereas successful countries have been willing to use any means at their disposal to pursue them.

Let us consider this in relation to some of the objectives listed at the beginning of section 3. For example, to achieve economies of scale in production, the Chinese government facilitated the mergers of smaller enterprises to create 'national champions', while the Korean state used industrial licensing to encourage the establishment of large-scale factories. In India, in contrast, the same tools were often used to protect small-scale enterprises, with serious negative implications for industrial efficiency and dynamism. As another example, subsidized credits in Korea were rationed in a way that maximized the developmental benefits of the resulting investments. In Malaysia, their rationing was largely guided by ethnic considerations, often restricting the growth of more capable (Chinese-owned) firms. As yet another example, Korea, Taiwan, and India all restricted FDIs and put conditions on them, but the East Asian economies did so to maximize the development of domestic productive capabilities, while India did the same to minimize the involvement of foreign capital.

In short, what distinguishes the less successful performers is less the policy tools used than the neglect of the objectives crucial for achieving industrial catch-up, such as the achievement of scale economies and the development of domestic productive capabilities.

3.3.2 Pragmatism and Adaptability

Common to the success stories of industrialization in East Asia was the degree of pragmatism characterizing their policies. They were willing to adopt any tools or approaches deemed beneficial for industrial catch-up, even when they went against their overall ideological position.

In all the successful industrializers, industrial policy was built neither on blind trust in markets nor on its full substitution by state control. For example, the Korean state severely regulated many markets, but this was done to ensure scale economies (investment licensing) or to prevent 'wasteful competition' (price controls, government-sanctioned recession cartels). While protecting national firms from international market forces through infant industry protection and subsidies, it exposed them to international market forces by pushing them to start exporting early. As another example, despite its initial ideological opposition to capitalism, China liberalized its economy through the dual-track pricing system, which provided (temporary) protection to SOEs from market forces, while allowing them to sell for profit and learn to compete in the market.

We can see the same kind of pragmatism in the choice of concrete policy tools. For example, despite the very aggressive general stance they took against FDI, Korea and Taiwan were flexible enough to actively court MNCs in industries like garments, shoes, stuffed toys, and electronics assembly, in the early days of industrialization, recognizing their abilities to generate the extra foreign exchanges needed for industrial upgrading. Singapore very much relied on FDI, but was selective, rather than 'even-handed', in choosing which firms in which sectors to host. China has relied far more heavily on FDI and imposed far fewer *formal* conditions on MNCs regarding ownership and performance requirements (e.g., local sourcing, export) than Korea or Taiwan have, but has fully exploited its strong bargaining position (coming from large domestic markets, good quality infrastructure, and workers with good skills) to impose many *informal* conditions regarding technology transfer, local sourcing, worker training, and so on.

As another example, the Korean government had a clear preference for domestically owned private sector enterprises, but willingly set up SOEs when necessary (see the case of POSCO referred to earlier), nationalized private sector firms in trouble (although usually privatized them again when they were nursed back to health), and granted 100 per cent foreign ownership to MNCs in the EPZs. The Singapore government may have used free-trade policy and welcomed MNCs, but it heavily uses SOEs (they produce around one-fifth of GDP—one of the highest such ratios outside of the oil economies) and owns 90 per cent of the land (and aggressively exploits the position for industrial policy purposes).

Furthermore, the more successful East Asian economies were willing to quickly and/or significantly adapt their policies to changing internal and external conditions. Korea, despite its huge success in labour-intensive manufacturing industries (textiles, garments, shoes, wigs, and stuffed toys) in the 1960s, started developing heavy and chemical industries in the early 1970s, when the wage costs showed a sign of rising, even though the country was able to remain competitive in most of those industries (except wigs) well into the 1980s. Had it not taken early action to develop a new generation of export industries (e.g., shipbuilding, automobiles, electronics), Korean industrialization may have fizzled out by the 1980s. The most dramatic example of adaptability is China's liberalization. At the turn of the 1990s, the Chinese economy was unable to compete in the international capitalist trading system. However, after rejecting the then prevalent neo-liberal 'shock therapy' in favour of a gradualist approach to industrial policy reform, not only did its economy avoid the traumatic collapse and then the prolonged slump experienced by the USSR and its satellites, but it has become one of the most successful industrializers in recent history.

3.3.3 Enabling Conditions

The question as to why some countries have more effective industrial policy regimes has been discussed broadly in the literature on the so-called developmental state (see Evans 1995; Leftwich 1995; Woo-Cumings 1999, among others). Two broad factors are worth mentioning here.

First, it has been frequently emphasized that the existential threat that the East Asian countries faced from their communist neighbours forced their leaders to prioritize industrial catch-up and enabled them to impose 'harsh' but necessary policies for rapid industrialization, such as suppression of wage demands, repression of consumption, low welfare spending, and restrictions on civil liberties. The logic driving such thinking is perhaps best captured by the quote of Sun Yat-sen that 'the nation without foreign foes and outside dangers will always be ruined' (Wade 1990). In Myrdal's terms, existential threats contributed to the changes in the attitudes of both the (political and economic) elites and the population at large, thereby enabling the institutional changes and policy reforms necessary for economic development.

The importance of existential threat, however, should not be overstated, as there is no inevitable relationship between external threat and successful industrialization. The existential threat posed to each other by Pakistan and India has not led to the emergence of developmental states, while the Korean state itself was not 'developmental' in the 1950s, despite having the same (or an even more serious) existential threat as that of the 1960s. These examples show that human agencies (both of the elites and people) are critical in determining the effect of external threats on industrialization. Moreover, independently of external threats, nationalism—often expressed in the form of revanchism against the Japanese— was a key motive in countries like Korea and (later) China (see Chapter 14, this volume, on the role of nationalism on development in Asia).

Second, the more successful Asian countries have exhibited higher state capacity. Two aspects are important here. One is the technical capacity—namely, the ability of the policymakers to design and implement the context-sensitive and technically demanding policies described above. The other is the political capacity to maintain what Evans (1995) calls the 'embedded autonomy'—namely, the ability of the policymakers to resist the pressure of sectional interests in formulating and implementing industrial policy while being attentive to the needs of different economic actors.[16]

---

[16] Interestingly, the concept of 'embedded autonomy' defines the opposite situation to what was described by Myrdal (1968) as a 'soft state'. He describes it as a situation where the state is not able to enact or enforce its policies against the interests of social groups.

However, it should be noted that high state capacity in East Asia was developed *alongside* success in industrialization, rather than prior to it, as is often believed. A good case in point is Korea, which until the late 1960s was sending its bureaucrats for extra training to the Philippines and Pakistan. It is also not as if China's rapid industrialization since the 1980s was preceded by a vast upgrading of the country's administrative apparatus. It has only been over a period of a couple of decades that these countries have been able to transform their corrupt and incompetent bureaucracies into some of the most efficient state machinery (see Chang 1994 for the Korean and the Taiwanese cases).

4. Conclusion

In the five decades following the publication of Myrdal's *Asian Drama*, developing Asia has witnessed a remarkable structural transformation. Its experience has conformed to the two tenets of early development economics—the belief in industrialization as the key motor force behind economic development and the view that an active industrial policy is instrumental for guiding industrial development.

Each of the Asian growth miracles has been underpinned by comprehensive industrialization. At the same time, while all Asian regions—and almost all Asian economies—have industrialized faster than the world average, there are staggering differences between their performances. The most successful cases, apart from Hong Kong, have been based on activist industrial policy of one kind or another. Even though these countries have seen significant policy liberalization since the 1990s, they still have more active industrial policies than their counterparts elsewhere. Moreover, the fastest-growing major economy since the 1990s— China—has had one of the most comprehensive industrial policies in the region, and indeed in the world.

Although the activist industrial policy has been a common feature among more successful industrializers, what set them apart has been a striking degree of pragmatism in the pursuit of developmental objectives. Their choice of policies, rather than being dictated by dogmas, often strayed from the ideological preferences. Instead, these economies were willing to change policies whenever they were proving to be insufficient or to adapt them to changes in domestic and international conditions. These observations remain just as relevant for the decades ahead. Those sceptical of the continued relevance of industrial policy point to changes in the global production landscape (especially the dominance of 'global value chains' controlled by MNCs from rich countries) and the narrowing of the policy space under the World Trade Organization (WTO) and various bilateral and regional trade and investment agreements (Pack and Saggi 2006; Warwick 2013). Yet the rejection of industrial policy on such bases amounts to interpreting it as another dogmatic policy template.

Even though it is true that a narrower policy space makes some of the old tools of industrial policy (e.g., export subsidies, local content requirements for FDI) unavailable, many of them can still be used. A number of industrial policy measures are not related to trade and are therefore beyond the WTO's jurisdiction (e.g., targeted subsidies for investment or skills development, promotion of strategic M&A), while many of the trade-related measures are still allowed (e.g., tariffs, R&D subsidies, technology transfer requirements for FDI) (for further discussions, see Chang et al. 2016: chapter 5). In these circumstances, the pragmatism in policy design and its adaptability—that have marked the performance of successful Asian policymakers—remain just as important in future years.

The increased importance of global value chains does make it more difficult for developing economies to compete against MNCs in final goods markets. However, global value chains also create opportunities for those countries to specialize in intermediate goods. Rather than making industrial policy obsolete, this creates new roles for it. More policy measures will be needed to help firms develop capabilities in quality control, abilities to co-ordinate R&D with buyer firms, and workers' skills (as intermediate goods tend to be more skill-intensive than final goods), among others. Once again, successful industrial catch-up in the face of these and other challenges will require an ability to skilfully adapt a country's industrial policy.

These considerations are present to a varying degree in the cases of new activist industrial policy initiatives unveiled in countries of the region such as China or India. Although their effectiveness remains to be seen, the upcoming challenges of this century, including the need to face the environmental crisis, require per-haps an unforeseen degree of adaptability in guiding structural change, and policymaking going beyond established dogmas.

References

ADB (Asian Development Bank) (2013). *Asia's Economic Transformation Where to, How, and How Fast? ADB Key Indicators for Asia and the Pacific* 2013. Manila: Asian Development Bank.

Amsden, A., and A. Singh (1994). 'The Optimal Degree of Competition and Dynamic Efficiency in Japan and Korea', *European Economic Review*, 38(3): 941–51.

Balakrishnan, P. (2006). 'Benign Neglect or Strategic Intent? Contested Lineage of Indian Software Industry', *Economic and Political Weekly*, 41(36): 3865–72.

Chang, H.-J. (1994). *The Political Economy of Industrial Policy*. Basingstoke: Macmillan.

Chang, H.-J. (2002). *Kicking Away the Ladder: Development Strategy in Historical Perspective*. London: Anthem.

Chang, H.-J. (2005). *Why Developing Countries Need Tariffs—How WTO NAMA Negotiations Could Deny Developing Countries' Right to a Future*. Geneva: South Centre.

Chang, H.-J. (2006). *The East Asian Development Experience: The Miracle, the Crisis and the Future*. London: Zed Books.

Chang, H.-J. (2007). *Bad Samaritans: The Guilty Secrets of Rich Nations and the Threat to Global Prosperity*. London: Bloomsbury Press.

Chang, H.-J. (2011a). 'Institutions and Economic Development: Theory, Policy, and History', *Journal of Institutional Economics*, 7(4): 473–98.

Chang, H.-J. (2011b). 'Industrial Policy: Can We Go Beyond an Unproductive Confrontation?'. In J. Lin and B. Pleskovic (eds) *Annual World Bank Conference on Development Economics* 2010, *Global: Lessons from East Asia and the Global Financial Crisis*. Washington, DC: World Bank.

Chang, H.-J., and J. Lin (2009). 'Should Industrial Policy in Developing Countries Conform to Comparative Advantage or Defy it? A Debate Between Justin Lin and Ha-Joon Chang', *Development Policy Review*, 27(5): 483–502.

Chang, H.-J., and K. Zach (2018). 'Institutions and Development in Asia', UNU-WIDER, Helsinki, WIDER Working Paper 2018/120.

Chang, H.-J., A. Andreoni, and M.L. Kuan (2013). 'International Industrial Policy Experiences and the Lessons for the UK', Government Office for Science, London, Future of Manufacturing Project: Evidence Paper 4.

Chang, H.-J., J. Hauge, and M. Irfan (2016). *Transformative Industrial Policy for Africa*. Addis Ababa: United Nations Economic Commission for Africa.

Chaudhuri, S. (2013). 'Manufacturing Trade Deficit and Industrial Policy in India', *Economic and Political Weekly*, 48(8): 41–50.

Chen, L., and B. Naughton (2016). 'An Institutionalized Policy-making Mechanism: China's Return to Techno-Industrial Policy', *Research Policy*, 45(10): 2138–52.

Dahlman, C. (2009). 'Growth and Development in China and India: The Role of Industrial and Innovation Policy in Rapid Catch-up'. In M. Cimoli, G. Dosi, and J.E. Stiglitz (eds) *Industrial Policy and Development: The Political Economy of Capabilities Accumulation*. Oxford: Oxford University Press.

Ellman, M. (2014). *Socialist Planning*. Cambridge: Cambridge University Press.

Evans, P. (1995). *Embedded Autonomy: States and Industrial Transformation*. Princeton, NJ: Princeton University Press.

Felipe, J., A. Abdon, and U. Kumar (2012). 'Tracking the Middle-Income Trap: What Is It, Who Is In It, and Why?', Levy Economic Institute, Annandale-on-Hudson, Working Paper 715.

Felipe, J., U. Kumar, and A. Abdon (2013). 'Exports, Capabilities, and Industrial Policy in India', *Journal of Comparative Economics*, 41(3): 939–56.

Gustafsson, F. (2007). 'Malaysian Industrial Policy, 1986–2002'. In J.K. Sundaram(ed.) *Malaysian Industrial Policy*. Singapore: NUS Press.

Heilmann, S., and L. Shih (2013). 'The Rise of Industrial Policy in China, 1978–2012', Harvard-Yenching Institute, Cambridge, MA, Harvard-Yenching Institute Working Paper Series 7.

Jomo, K.S., Y-C. Chen, B.C. Folk, I. ul-Haque, P. Phongaichit, B. Simatupang, and M. Tateishi (1997). *Southeast Asia's Misunderstood Miracle: Industrial Policy and Economic Development in Thailand, Malaysia and Indonesia.* Boulder, CO: Westview Press.

Kaldor, N. (1966). *Causes of Slow Rate of Growth in the United Kingdom.* Cambridge: Cambridge University Press.

Kohli, A. (2006). 'Politics of Economic Growth in India, 1980–2005: Part I and Part II', *Economic and Political Weekly*, 41(13&14): 1251–9, 1361–70.

Lall, S. (1995). 'Malaysia: Industrial Success and the Role of the Government', *Journal of International Development*, 7(5): 759–73.

Lall, S. (2000). 'The Technological Structure and Performance of Developing Country Manufactured Exports, 1985–1998', *Oxford Development Studies*, 28(3): 337–69.

Leftwich, A. (1995). 'Bringing Politics Back In: Towards a Model of the Developmental State', *The Journal of Development Studies*, 31(3): 400–27.

Myrdal, G. (1968). *Asian Drama: An Inquiry into the Poverty of Nations. A Twentieth Century Fund Study, Volumes I, II, and III.* London: Allen Lane.

Nayyar, D. (2006). 'India's Unfinished Journey Transforming Growth into Development', *Modern Asian Studies*, 40(3): 797–832.

Nolan, P. (2001). *China and the Global Economy: National Champions, Industrial Policy, and the Big Business Revolution.* New York: Palgrave.

Pack, H., and K. Saggi (2006). 'Is there a Case for Industrial Policy? A Critical Survey', *The World Bank Research Observer*, 21(2): 267–97.

Palma, J.G. (2005). 'Four Sources of De-industrialization and a New Concept of the Dutch-Disease'. In J. Ocampo (ed.) *Beyond Reforms: Structural Dynamic and Macroeconomic Vulnerability.* Washington, DC: World Bank.

Rodrik, D., and A. Subramanian (2004). 'From "Hindu Growth" to Productivity Surge: The Mystery of the Indian Growth Transition', Centre for Economic Policy Research, London, Discussion Paper 4371.

Shin, J-S., and H.-J. Chang (2005). 'Economic Reform after the Financial Crisis: A Critical Assessment of Institutional Transition in South Korea', *Review of International Political Economy*, 12(3): 409–33.

Simoes, A.J.G., and C.A. Hidalgo (2011). 'The Economic Complexity Observatory: An Analytical Tool for Understanding the Dynamics of Economic Development', Workshops at the Twenty-Fifth AAAI Conference on Artificial Intelligence. Available at: https://atlas.media.mit.edu/en/ (accessed 30 December 2017).

Singh, A. (2008). 'The Past, Present and Future of Industrial Policy in India: Adapting to the Changing Domestic and International Environment', Centre for Business Research, University of Cambridge, Cambridge, Working Paper 376.

Szirmai, A. (2009). 'Industrialization as an Engine of Growth in Developing Countries', UNU-MERIT, Maastricht, Working Paper 10.

Timmer, M.P., G.J. de Vries, and K. de Vries (2015). 'Patterns of Structural Change in Developing Countries'. In M.J. Weiss and M. Tribe (eds) *Routledge Handbook of Industry and Development*. New York: Routledge.

UNCTAD (United Nations Conference on Trade and Development) (2017). *UNCTADstat*. UNCTAD Data Center. Available at: http://unctadstat.unctad.org/wds/ReportFolders/reportFolders.aspx?sCS_ChosenLang=en (accessed 29 December 2017).

UN DESA (United Nations Department of Economic and Social Affairs), Population Division (2017). 'World Population Prospects: The 2017 Revision', DVD Edition, UN DESA Population Division. Available at: https://esa.un.org/unpd/wpp/Download/Standard/Population/ (accessed 29 December 2017).

US Department of Treasury, Bureau of the Fiscal Service (2005). 'Treasury Reporting Rates of Exchange as of December 31, 2005'. Available at: https://www.fiscal.treasury.gov/fsreports/rpt/treasRptRateExch/1205.pdf (accessed 29 December 2017).

Wade, R.H. (1990). *Governing the Market: Economic Theory and the Role of Government in East Asian Industrialization*. Princeton, NJ: Princeton University Press.

Warwick, K. (2013). 'Beyond Industrial Policy: Emerging Issues and New Trends', OECD Publishing, Paris, OECD Science, Technology and Industry Policy Papers 2.

Woo-Cumings, M. (ed.) (1999). *The Developmental State*. Ithaca, NY: Cornell University Press.

World Bank (2017). 'World Development Indicators Database Archives', The World Bank DataBank. Available at: http://databank.worldbank.org/data/reports.aspx?source=wdi-database-archives-%28beta%29 (accessed 28 December 2017).

9

Macroeconomic Perspective on Development

Amit Bhaduri

1. Introduction

As a multidimensional historical process, the development of a country involves economics, politics, society, technology, environment, and culture. Such a process, if forced for long, would create serious distortions, but also becomes sustainable over timethrough strong internal reinforcing mechanisms. Macroeconomic policies have the role of helping this process with supporting government initiatives and institutional set-up, while involvement of the people is at the core. This resonates to some extent with Gunner Myrdal's vision of development in his *Asian Drama* as the merging of many economic, social, and political processes that result in 'cumulative causation' to usher in an overall process of development. Similar, although narrower visions, restricted mostly to the economic aspect, are also to be found in Young (1928), who linked economic progress with 'increasing returns', and Kaldor (1972), who attempts to capture industrialization, especially manufacturing, as a process of 'dynamic increasing returns' characterized by a mechanism of mutually reinforcing strong positive feedbacks. Myrdal's intellectual ventures (1957, 1968/1977) had consistently been wider, integrating many aspects cutting across artificial intellectual boundaries of academic disciplines.

History is essential to this perspective because these processes work on historically inherited specific 'initial conditions'. Consequently, any discussion of usual macroeconomic policy instruments like monetary, fiscal, or exchange rate policies can be misleadingly limiting, unless placed in this wider framework proposed by Myrdal to reckon adequately with the initial conditions and institutional requirements. The objectives of development, as well as the relevant instruments and institutions, are interrelated in an inextricable manner, shaped by the context. Policies and economic performances focusing exclusively on particular aspects like the growth rate of gross domestic product (GDP), rapid industrialization, or international competitiveness might trivialize the problem if they fail to capture adequately the transformative process operating on initial conditions.

From this point of view, the role of macro policy needs to be viewed not merely in terms of economists' traditional preoccupation with efficient allocation of given scarce resources among alternative means and the efficacy of the price mechanism. It must concern itself also with measures needed to augment and transform the resource base for the purpose of development, its utilization through expansion of markets, as well as accompanying income and wealth distribution. The inherited initial conditions set limits but also provide opportunities. Their interplay is the story of successes and failures in development, as would be seen from comparative experiences of various Asian countries.

Reckoning with the variety of factors that come into play in the making of these stories necessarily implies that macroeconomic policies for development are not mere application of a given set of instruments aimed at a given set of targets (Tinbergen 1954). The instruments and their supporting institutions, as well as the targets, are moving over time, with evolving initial conditions throwing up new challenges and opportunities. The perspective on developmental macroeconomic policies presented here attempts to cope with this broader view of development as a dynamic process involving moving targets, instruments, and institutions over time. If the developmental experience of a particular country is captured by time series, experiences of several countries provide a moving cross-section of the grand 'Asian Drama' of development unfolding over time.

Since the capability of a country is always limited in some ways, a major question facing macroeconomic policy for development is the sequence and relative priorities to be assigned to augmenting and transforming resources. The traditional view might leave it to the price mechanism, but that is usually inadequate and, at times, even misleading. To illustrate the point, immediate employment expansion linked to productive asset and infrastructure creation may have priority in the time sequence in situations of vastly underutilized and unemployed manpower, which coexist extensively with precarious livelihoods. The priority would be to deal simultaneously with both resource augmentation and distribution through labour utilization. Human capital development through better education, health, and housing may acquire similar priority in some other situations, while expansion of the market for skilled labour might be an equally pressing need. Other situations may call for access to foreign capital inflow, technology and industrial policy, and strategic integration with the world economy on a priority basis.

Each one of these examples would usually require creating or strengthening supporting institutions as well as different policies like fair price rationing of essential goods for the poor, land reform, agricultural credit or services reform, nature and degree of decentralization, environmental policy linked to decentralization and livelihood, as well as regulatory reforms. They go beyond the reach of standard macro policy instruments relating to monetary, fiscal, or exchange rate policies. These examples also illustrate why actual experiences of development seldom respect the artificial neat boundaries of academic disciplines, and a better appreciation of historical experiences requires us to travel through less chartered territories of macro policies for development.

The strategy we follow is to take up some major themes that have repeatedly arisen in diverse development experiences in Asian countries and comment on their significance from the viewpoint of macroeconomic theory and policy. The discussion in section 2 begins with the question of how to strike a balance between our theoretical understanding and historical description of 'initial conditions' using the diversity of the economies of Asia as background. History enters in an essential way insofar as policies have to be tailored to the stage of development. For instance, utilization of vast surplus labour is often a priority in the early stage of development, which is discussed in section 3 as labour utilization through the strategy of extensive growth followed by some Asian countries. This leads to a macroeconomic discussion in section 4 of the constraints that operate on such labour utilization strategies. Productive utilization of surplus labour also raises the issue of the size and nature of the market that can absorb the output produced. This is discussed in section5 under the issue of domestic versus foreign markets.

The relative importance assigned to them concerns the strategy of export promotion versus import substitution, which in turn is related to issues of technological capability, acquisition of foreign technology, extent of external indebtedness, and international competitiveness. These interrelated issues are the themes of sections 6 and 7. However, usual discussions of these issues overlook decentralization, particularly in large countries, which can add a different policy dimension. The nature of decentralization, which can have a direct bearing on the question of popular involvement in development, is explored in section8, while section 9 discusses the issue of economic and social inequality, which in turn has a direct bearing on decentralization. The concluding observations in section 10 recapture some of the main points. Asian experiences emphasize how some successful experiments with development policies have often meant going against conventional wisdom in development thinking, but invariably paying attention to the specificities of initial conditions and evolving economic context.

2. Initial Conditions

Emphasis on initial conditions has strong deterministic overtones of classical physics. Some decades after the spectacular success of Newtonian mechanics, the great French mathematician Laplace claimed with chilling arrogance that one could completely predict the future and the past on the basis of scientific laws of motion, if only one had knowledge of the initial conditions of all particles. When emperor Napoleon asked how God fitted into this scheme, Laplace is said to have replied that he did not need that particular hypothesis. Replace 'God' by 'uncertainty' and we encounter similar arrogance in a deterministic view of modern macroeconomics. On the assumption of a representative, all-knowing, all-seeing representative rational agent, temporal and inter-temporal optimization techniques are applied to describe the macroeconomy, whose assumed optimal properties naturally minimize the economic role of government intervention and serve an ideological purpose by claiming implicitly that we live in the best of all possible worlds, in which the working of a free market economy cannot be improved upon (Lucas 1983; Sargent 1987). Ironically, this amounts to the same case once made for bureaucratic centralized planning. The distinction between an economy guided by planning from the top and by the market from below is obliterated, merging logical extremes in a display of mathematical virtuosity.

However, the starting point of discussion must be the undeniable fact that historical processes are typically non-repetitive, unlike motions of deterministic classical mechanics, or even that of less deterministic quantum theory at sub-atomic level. The indeterminacy goes deep in economics. Experimental economics at the level of the individual shows not only the limitation of the rationality postulate, but its ambiguity and the pitfalls of viewing economic actions and policies in terms of individual rationality. At the macro level that problem gets hugely magnified as we look for repetitive patterns involving interactions among numerous individuals and groups with diverse interests and power.

With hindsight it might be possible to identify some of the sources of the irregularity of historical processes, but far more difficult to decide how best to deal with them. If macroeconomic policies are viewed as experiments, usually not replicable, a policy may have different outcomes in different situations. Such ambiguity and unpredictability are summed up as 'differences in initial conditions', which arise partly from the inescapable incompleteness of specifying initial conditions. It resonates with the great French mathematician Poincare's (1908) oft-repeated warning: 'we could still only know the initial situation approximately...It may happen that small differences in the initial conditions produce very great ones in the final phenomenon...Prediction becomes impossible' (English translation by Gandolfo 1996: 504).

Given the incompleteness, it usually becomes the historian's prerogative to choose critical elements to characterize the initial condition. At the formal level, the use of a priori (Bayesian), *ex ante* subjective probability in place of statistical frequency distributions is one such attempt; introducing critical nonlinearities may be another. Myrdal's more historical approach laid particular emphasis on analysing the consequences of distortions caused by colonial rule and traditional hierarchical stratification of caste, gender, etc., in India (Myrdal 1977). However, the critical elements would be different when initial conditions differ.

Drawing an analogy from non-linear dynamical systems, one could think of these critical elements as being similar to 'bifurcation points' whose small perturbations tip the balance dramatically. In some cases macro policies can set in motion cumulative changes, due to small changes in some parametervalues, whichaffect the 'structural stability' by altering thequalitative properties of a system. They might give rise to such phenomena as discrete jumps or 'catastrophic change', 'hysteresis', and 'chaotic' dynamics, of which many examples are available, even in simple macroeconomic models (e.g., Day 1983; Bhaduri and Harris 1987). Popularly known as 'the butterfly effect', such sensitivity to initial conditions picturesquely captures how the flap of the wings of a butterfly could create a storm across the ocean in some distant land. In a parallel vein, an insignificant-looking initial advantage of a firm can add up cumulatively to such decisive advantage as to transform the market structure from competition to monopoly (Sraffa 1926) or make an initially inferior technology dominate others under increasing returns (Arthur 1994; David 1995).

The purpose of macro policy analysis would lie in searching for such critical tipping points in relation to initial conditions, so that meaningful policy perturbation can set in motion cumulative causation for escaping from underdevelopment. However, indeterminacy would arise in economic policy precisely because the same policy might not have the same effect of tipping the balance in relation to other initial conditions. Subject to this qualification, some policies in development economics search for greater generalization for breaking the 'vicious cycle of poverty' by tapping unutilized surplus labour (Nurkse 1953). A 'big push' for industrialization' (Rosenstein Rodan 1943; Murphy et al. 1989), advocating simultaneous investment on a range of related industries to create mutual positive feedbacks, and the 'spread effect' on the supply as well as demand side (Myrdal 1977) is another such idea.

Some specific aspects ofinitial conditions may be identified in the Asian context to analyse their possible role as 'critical points' for understanding diversity in development experiences across countries in Asia. They relate to:

(a) Difference in size and natural resource endowment (especially oil).

(b) The initial nature of their political economies—from Chinese and Vietnamese socialism evolving towards one-party market economies, to the strong market orientation of Taiwan, Thailand, Malaysia, and the Philippines, democratic planning trying to combine market and state in India and Sri Lanka and tilting increasingly towards the market, to South Korea's authoritarian model moving towards multiparty democracy, and countries of Central Asia who rather abruptly ceased to be parts of the former economy of the Soviet Union.

(c) Similarities and differences in colonial experience under Britain, Japan, France, Spain, and later the US, which left imprints on the respective colonies as examples of 'hysteresis'.

(d) Culture, identities, and social stratification. India for instance is prolifically full of such divisions—religious, caste, and ethnic. Comparatively, most other countries are more homogeneous, but many also have to deal not merely with distinct minorities but manufactured identities for political purposes. Korea, despite being politically divided, appears more homogeneous in many cultural aspects. While many would argue that considerable similarity exists between India, Pakistan, and Bangladesh in many respects, their differences play a significant role. How the overall situation is shaped, resulting in conflict, cohesion, and co-operation for mutual benefit, must be an integral part in the orientation of macroeconomic policies.

Although the influence of history through initial conditions is crucial, it does not have a decisive influence. Elements of unpredictability, arising from low-probability events like 'black swan' and non-foreseeable sensitivity to initial conditions like 'butterfly effects', defy incorporation in a rigidly predetermined policy framework. A striking example in Asia is the contrasting experiences of oil-rich Gulf States and similarly endowed parts of Central Asia. Their policies towards natural resource extraction and trading shaped by initial conditions of geopolitics differed, leading to unpredictably large macroeconomic differences. They often led to 'hysteresis'in the sense that the effects persisted even when the initial cause was removed.

Since policies towards economic openness and development were conditioned in large parts of Asia by the geopolitics of the Cold War, preferential access, particularly to the North American external market, played a part in making outward-looking industrialization more successful in some countries (e.g., South Korea, Taiwan). Similarly, initial land reform by an authoritarian occupation force (the US) and wider access to basic education as an initial condition created by some colonial powers (especiallyJapan) created unforeseeable preconditions for more balanced industrialization at later stages, when contrasted with the spread of education in some Central Asian countries that were part of the former Soviet Union. Indeed, when asked why India could not carry out a thorough land reform like Japan or South Korea, former Indian Prime Minister Indira Gandhi was said to have retorted that carrying out reform on someone else's land was much easier than on one's own.

Because chance elements that cannot be foreseen, even with best available information about initial conditions, matter in the development process, it should be a humbling lesson against detailed optimality calculation on paper. It is often more desirable to maintain flexibility to respond to unforeseen conditions with policy designed for trade-off between efficiency and flexibility, as suggested in 'bounded rationality' and 'satisfying behavior' (Simon 1979). From this angle we need to consider several important issues usually left out of the development debate, like decentralization, economic social and political mobility, and livelihood opportunities.

3. Labour Utilization and Extensive Growth

The foremost requirement of inclusiveness in development is rapid expansion of employment and livelihood opportunities in situations of huge surplus labour and mass unemployment. Assuring fuller utilization of labour with high employment in the shortest possible time has been achieved most successfully in post-revolutionary situations in China and Vietnam. Using a strategy of 'extensive growth', they showed how underutilized massive 'surplus' labour can be fruitfully absorbed for capital formation in a short time through huge, centralized public projects like building irrigation dams, roads and waterways, infrastructure for production, and delivery through agricultural communes. This helped in taking the first step in development. With various schemes of quantity and price rationing of essential goods, the market mechanism was largely replaced. The link was strong between centralized one-party political systems and institutional support for extensive growth, and this strategy runs the danger of excessive state authoritarianism. Nevertheless, a moderate variation of this model through decentralized programmes could be attempted with smaller projects being decided and implemented by local communities in accordance with their local priorities.

Financial autonomy and respect for traditional local knowledge are necessary prerequisites. India's rural employment guarantee scheme (2005) was a step in that direction, but failed to realize its full potential, partly due to rigid rules set by higher levels of bureaucracy and politicians. The loss of flexibility was visible in many ways: delays in the release of funds for payment of wages; the definition of rural asset creation according to uniform rules set by a bureaucracy distant from the local reality, like 100 days of work per year; payment according to amount of soil moved by manual labour; applying a uniform ratio of human to mechanical power irrespective of soil conditions; and uniform local child care arrangements for female labour. More importantly, perhaps, a lack of arrangements for on-the-spotaccess to public distribution of essential goods reduced the effectiveness of the policy. Generating income without creating locally useful productive assets became normal, as did corruption by following rules on paper without substance. Enormous variation in the performance of the employment guarantee scheme across Indian states pointed not merely to the differences in efficiency and interest taken by bureaucrats and politicians but to the importance of mobilization of public involvement through local activists. At least in India, this showed how greater local involvement of elected representatives at 'Panchyat' and 'Gram Sabha' levels (for which the Indian constitution had made provisions in law) was crucial but largely thwarted by attempts to maintain party control in the competitive multiparty democracy. The broad political economy lesson for macro policy formulation is the need for greater flexibility through greater local autonomy by factoring in more carefully the political compulsions that are typically generated by such schemes.

It is also instructive to note in this context that a 'minimum income support scheme'intended to raise the purchasing power of the poor might strengthen the bureaucratic tendencies further through a'patron–client' relation between the state and poor, leaving even less space for popular initiatives and participation. A decentralized employment guarantee scheme driven by local initiatives on the other hand would have the potential of impacting both income generation and local production, while strengthening a sense of the economic rights of the poor.

4. Macroeconomic Constraints on Labour Use

A critical requirement for any extensive growth strategy is the downward flexibility of the real wage rate. Its purpose is to make 'redistribution of limited wage goods from the already employed to the unemployed' (Kahn 1972), a politically feasible proposition through some version of rationing. The issue of redistribution, if left unattended by macro policy, might get resolved by the market through 'forced saving' imposed on the workers. This is undesirable because it also finances greater consumption out of profit by the rich through 'profit inflation' (Keynes 1930, 1940), or results in a persistent 'inflationary barrier' in the case of downward flexibility of the real wage (Robinson 1956). For financing such programmes, even a direct tax on wages can be more equitable than redistribution through inflation against workers (although its apparently unjust nature makes it politically undesirable), while taxing profit is considered politically unwise in capitalist democracies (Bhaduri 1986). However, this unjust nature of forced saving due to inflation is not a justification for fiscal austerity in financing such programmes. Instead, it calls for rationing of essential consumption goods through the extension of the public distribution system, as was done in post-revolution China and Vietnam or even in immediate post-war Britain.

The basic model of the inflexible real wage rate with unlimited supply of labour in a dual economy was proposed by Lewis (1954). He viewed the shift of labour from traditional agriculture to industry as a voluntary process induced by a higher wage in industry until the 'turning point' is arrived at when all excess labour in agriculture is absorbed by industry (Fei and Ranis 1964). Because of the downward inflexibility of the real wage rate throughout the process, relative price, or the terms of trade, regulates the pace of industrial growth. If it becomes too high, the relative price of agricultural goods rises in relation to industrial goods and reduces industrial profitability. The first order condition for profit maximization requires the marginal product of labour in industry to equal the product wage rate, that is, $MPL_i = w/p_i, = (w/p_c)(p_c/p_i)$, where w is money wage rate and p_c and p_i are price levels of consumption and investment goods respectively. A constant real wage rate in terms of consumption goods (w/p_c) would entail lower product wage in industry (w/p_i) if the terms of trade (p_c/p_i) move in favour of agricultural goods. This would lower profit-maximizing demand for industrial labour and slow down the pace of industrialization. The main lesson is that agricultural surplus becomes the binding constraint when real wage is insufficiently flexible in terms of consumption goods.

In such cases, production technique maximizing investible surplus (or profit) would also maximize long-run economic growth (Dobb 1960; Sen 1960). However, this can be misleading (Kalecki 1993). If limited agricultural surplus is the problem in a predominantly agricultural economy like China, India, Indonesia, or Pakistan in their early stage of industrialization, then the emphasis should be on combining some rationing measures with raising current agricultural output by focusing on decentralized local investments for raising productivity of land rather than that of labour.

In contrast to wage goods, if availability of capital goods is identified as the binding constraint, the macroeconomic policy has to be directed towards choice of industries rather than production techniques. In situations of limited capacity to produce or import capital goods due to foreign exchange constraints, the compulsion to industrialize faces barriers of unavailability of capital goods. China and India, despite differences in their political systems, tried to overcome the constraint by expanding rapidly their capacity to produce capital goods. China's justification for this lay in one of the 'ten great relationships' propounded at that time (1950s) following the Marxian scheme of 'expanded reproduction', which assigns a 'leading role' to capital goods producing Department 1. A similar path was followed by India using a two-sector (later four-sector), non-shiftable, capital goods model (Mahalanobis 1953) closely resembling the Soviet model of industrialization formulated originally by Feldman (Domar 1958).

Nevertheless, a very significant difference arose between China and India. In post-revolutionary China, land reform, agricultural communes, large-scale irrigation, and a transport network created through 'extensive growth' significantly increased the productivity of land and agricultural surplus. Early excesses with the 'Great Leap Forward' for industrialization in China caused acute food shortage and famines that were tackled through liberalization of agricultural communes in the 1980s. In contrast, land reform in post-independence India was moderate, mostly replacing former large revenue-collecting intermediaries for the colonial state by large farmers and moneylenders as Myrdal had perceptively observed (Myrdal 1977). As a result, India faced a chronic balance of payments deficit on account of food imports until the 'Green Revolution' eased the situation in the 1980s. This was followed in the early 1990s with economic liberalization, when India was able to attract sufficient inflow of foreign private capital to cover its continuing current account deficits. China, in contrast, started to have persistent export surplus, with increased openness to trade from around the same time.

5. Domestic versus Foreign Markets

A country's domestic and foreign markets are linked mostly through trade surplus or deficit. An export or import surplus would magnify positively or negatively the size of the domestic market through the foreign trade multiplier. However, when the export surplus is a small fraction of total domestic demand ($Y = C + I + E - M$, in usual notations), which is usually the case with large countries, it provides relatively weak support for expanding the domestic market. It is wiser in such cases to view export promotion as a way of facilitating primarily international payments and earning foreign exchange. The situation is usually reversed for small countries.

However, while this broad direction for openness in trade in relation to the domestic market size might be the guideline for trade policies, national governments' control over them has been weakened not only because of new institutions like the World Trade Organization but also by intra-firm trade by transnational corporations, which accounts for over 60 per cent of foreign trade. As a result, much of the exports generated by corporations become structural, spreading demand as well as employment to various international locations, driven by compulsions of sub-contracting, the international supply chain, and the pull of countries with lower corporate tax rates. This, in turn, has weakened revenue collection by national governments encouraging the ideology of fiscal austerity.

At the same time, to enhance their international competitiveness in a global market, the focus of large corporations shifted from employment generation to raising labour productivity for lowering unit cost, quality control, and on-time delivery through mechanization, automation, and robotization. The main consequence has been a widening gap between output and employment growth. Independent small and even medium-sized firms in developing countries are at a disadvantage insofar as finance, technology, and access to the international supply network are concerned, even when they are better placed to provide more employment. With large corporations as their main players, two of Asia's most populated countries, China and India, succeeded in raising their share in the world economy in manufacturing value-added and export. During their high-growth years (roughly 1993–2013) China grew by nearly three times (approximately 9 per cent) and India two times (approximately 7 per cent) the world average, but regular employment grew by barely more than 1 per cent in China, and slightly less than 1 per cent in India.

The inter-connections of corporate-led jobless growth, rural–urban migration, destitution, an expanding informal sector, and environmental degradation can be illustrated briefly with an arithmetical example (Bhaduri 2018). Suppose ten traditional livelihoods with a low average labour productivity of two are destroyed for land acquisition from traditional agriculture, typically to let corporations have cheap access to natural resources like minerals, rivers and water bodies, village commons, forests, mountains, and coast lines, etc. However, given the limited size of the domestic and foreign markets, corporations with their higher labour productivity, say six times more, that is, twelve, can absorb only two persons. The result is higher output at $12 \times 2 = 24$, but employment is lower at two, with eight unemployed. For corporations to absorb all, displaced labour, the domestic and international market have to be of a much larger size of $12 \times 10 = 120$. And yet, the more corporations try to capture the international market through greater international competitiveness, the greater the pressure for raising labour productivity and the stronger the negative pressure on job creation, leading to a growing informal sector where displaced jobless persons try to make a desperate living by encroaching on natural resources, urban space, and infrastructure. Congestion costs reduce corporate efficiency through shortages of regular water, electricity, and space, lowering corporate competitiveness to complete the vicious circle. This range of problems is increasingly faced by many high-growth Asian countries.

Such Asian experiences of jobless high growth contradict Schumpeterian optimism about 'creative destruction' as well as the Lewisian vision of approaching a 'turning point' at which all surplus labour is absorbed in high productivity industry. With unemployment growing, rural to urban voluntary migration, due to the pull of higher expected industrial wages, is usually not the dominant factor (Harris and Todaro 1970). Instead, the major problem arises from destroyed rural livelihoods, exacerbated by degrading of environment and the taking over of traditional village commons by corporations to produce natural resource-intensive outputs. Adam Smith's observation that the extent of division of labour is limited by the size of the market seems more in conformity with recent Asian experiences when growing pressure on environment and rural livelihood is factored in, rather than with either Schumpeter's or Lewis's versions. The emphasis on the importance of the domestic market particularly in large economies is its main lesson.

6. Import Substitution versus Export Promotion

While the two largest countries of Asia focused on building the domestic base for capital goods production in their early phase of industrialization, some smaller countries successfully followed different paths. The geography of their smaller size had an influence, buttheir initial conditions in other respects might have exerted an even bigger influence.

The spectacular success of export-promoting industrialization in a group of Southeast and East Asian countries such as South Korea, Hong Kong, Taiwan, Singapore, and Malaysia deserves special attention, while Thailand and the Philippines followed a similar path somewhat less successfully. These countries had a distinctly greater orientation towards economic openness from the beginning without concentrating on capital goods industries and import substitution. Although two relatively large countries among them, South Korea and Taiwan, developed quite early some heavy industries with import substitution potential, they maintained their outward orientation, and shifted gradually through quality improvement to outward-looking export promotion policies. While China and

India followed a similar trajectory, their import-substituting heavy industrialization policies lasted longer.

The real contrast is the two little city states of Singapore and Hong Kong. They were poor in land and other natural resources, and depended decisively on international trade in goods and services from the very beginning as an integral part of industrialization, but shared with Korea and Taiwan a massive education drive, and systematically nurtured an industrially skilled labour force. Singapore followed the innovative strategy of using its geographical location by placing itself strategically in the various international supply chains of multinationals, as did Malaysia at a later date. It started with trade in goods but gradually included related services, finally extending to financial services. Hong Kong was more naturally placed as a 'port' for the huge hinterland of China. Both city states have managed to traverse the path of development with considerable skill, which becomes clear when contrasted with the experiences of some other similarly placed small South Asian countries like Sri Lanka, particularly because it is comparable on several social indices like high literacy. In general, small countries that seem to succeed internalize the external market, whereas large countries externalize their internal markets; exports by firms become the beginning of the market expansion path of the former, but are the end destination for the latter (Nayyar 2013).

Developing a domestic capital goods production base in the early phase would be easier the less severe is the foreign exchange constraint. The role of an undervalued currency or exchange rate as a policy instrument tends to be overemphasized due to exclusive focus on the price mechanism. Instead it might be noticed that many East and Southeast Asian countries were placed in a relatively advantageous position regarding foreign exchange availability because of their geopolitical situations, which were absent to varying extents for countries like China, Vietnam, India, and Indonesia, particularly in the early phase. As a result, the compulsion of building a domestic capital base was stronger and lasted longer. This was often exacerbated by the wrong policy of not producing sufficient agricultural surplus, which also needed foreign exchange. In contrast, many Southeast and East Asian countries had a more favourable situation due to their political economy, mostly dictated by geopolitics, which privileged them with preferential trade treatment and access to greater capital inflows. However, this in no way belittles their imaginative macro policies that helped them to exploit these advantages more successfully compared to some others in Asia, such as Pakistan, the Philippines, or Thailand.

An inference about macroeconomic policy might be drawn from these varied experiences. It points to the importance of getting the time sequence right in moving towards economic openness. Successful industrialization of many large and medium-sized countries had an early phase of building infrastructure and a capital goods industry for import substitution, followed by potential for export promotion. The sequence acted as a disciplining device on quality control. Countries that failed were saddled with unwanted 'infant industries', partly discrediting the strategy. However, reversing the sequence would be a mistake of oversimplification. They do not produce the same result, somewhat like 'non-commutivity' (of matrix multiplication) where AB and BA are usually not the same. Unfortunately, the importance of time sequence is often forgotten in many econometric cross-country analyses, leading to oversimplified debates about import substitution versus export promotion.

7. Technological Capability and Capital Account Openness

Prior to financial globalization involving large private capital flows, Asian countries mostly had to depend on aid and grants. With the US dollar as international 'money', countries more closely aligned politically to the United States typically faced fewer problems. Nevertheless, technological capability for industrial success is not a readily purchasable commodity on the international market. Both South Korea and Taiwan developed much of their industrial base simultaneously with domestic technological absorptive capacity and a strong emphasis on education and skill formation. South Korea, like Japan after the Second World War, relied heavily on commercial borrowing instead of direct foreign investment, paying required licence fees while accumulating a very high level of per capita foreign debt. However, it gradually generated a sustained export surplus to pay back and became a member of the OECD with full capital account convertibility, almost like a textbook success story. Singapore and Malaysia also attained comfortable foreign exchange positions with consistent balance of payments surpluses (averaging about 2 per cent of their GDP over two decades), but the latter still maintains some capital account control, which left it relatively unaffected by the late 1990s' (1997) financial crisis in Asia.

State-led industrialization under tariff and non-tariff protection in China and India during the early phase of industrialization moved towards increasing openness in trade under globalization. Both have diversified their exports and increased their share of manufactured goods in world trade, along with six other newly industrialized Asian countries over the last quarter century (Nayyar 2013). However, there are important differences in that China built up huge foreign exchange reserves from the time it gradually opened up its capital account. It attracted foreign investment and increasingly invested abroad. India, too, attracted large foreign capital inflows, but with a high proportion of relatively short maturity portfolio investment to enjoy an apparently comfortable foreign reserve position covering a continued current account deficit. On the trade front, the services sector, especially less-advanced software services rather than manufacturing, has been India's most important export earner since early 2000, and much of its manufactured exports are to other developing countries (Ghose 2016)—whereas, China, like South Korea and Taiwan, is penetrating increasingly into the export market of developed countries. This suggests India's comparatively lower technological capability as a result of its industrial policy in transiting from the import substitution to export promotion phases.

Some of the more successful smaller exporters in Asia had a different industrial policy. Singapore and Hong Kong placed themselves strategically in international supply chains fairly early and became integrated in them. Some others in the ASEAN region received considerable foreign investment related to supply networks first from Japan, then South Korea, and now increasingly from China. Along with trade, they had a high degree of openness in foreign investment and to a lesser extent in finance. Their technological capability was typically influenced by foreign investors' requirements. Occasionally described as the 'flying geese pattern', in which the position vacated by the leading bird is taken over by a follower, the acid test for these countries would be their ability to acquire sufficient independent technological capability. The role of the state also has to change byguiding investment towards channels considered more promising for either attracting foreign investment or directly promoting domestic investment for economic development through a combination of the budgetary, fiscal, and monetary 'carrot and stick' policy that had been typical of Japan, South Korea, and Taiwan. The East and Southeast Asian countries, perhaps best exemplified by South Korea, seemed more successful in this respect. This often verged towards authoritarian 'managed democracy' with restrictions on real wages and long working hours in the early phases, and has emerged only gradually out of this phase (Amsden 1989; Wade 1990; Chakravarty 1993).

Borrowing from private rather than official sources under financial globalization created both unprecedented opportunities for attracting massive inflows coupled with the danger of capital flights. This has become a major challenge for the appropriate fiscal, monetary, and exchange rate policy mix in all countries. Most Asian developing countries have used various degrees of direct control over their capital accounts in addition to these standard policies. Assuming sensitivity of capital flows to interest rate variation, the argument was made that monetary rather than fiscal policy would generally be more effective under flexible exchange rates (Mundell 1968). Fiscal policies based on borrowing heavily from the market were discouraged due to their possible impact in raising the rate of interest, especially in a flexible exchange rate regime, but such fiscal discipline was used very flexibly in the successful cases of East and Southeast Asia. In the cases of accumulated foreign debt with a high fraction of short maturity debt, as in India and Indonesia, expansionary fiscal and monetary policies became more restrictive to comply with the sentiments of international financiers to avoid sudden capital flights. Keynesian policies for fighting unemployment became the most important casualty as austerity was imposed in the name of fiscal discipline.

The ability to service debt depends on several factors, but ultimately on the ability to generate enough export surplus. This requires acquiring technological capabilities through continuous up-gradation and the ability to build complex goods where price competitiveness is not the only factor. Building such a technological niche where product novelty captures increasing market share becomes the goal (Lall 1987). That path was traversed in Asia initially by Japan and later by South Korea and Taiwan, and now probably China. Availability of foreign exchange is not enough to reach this destination, as it requires effective industrial policy. Some oil-rich Middle-Eastern Asian countries with export surplus have so far not been able to acquire similar technological capability, pointing to a gap between their industrial and financial power. Some oil-rich Central Asian countries that were part of the former Soviet Union suffered distortions in industrial development partly due to industrial policy based on regional division. They produced components of heavy and complex industrial products (e.g., large tractors, rockets, space ships, etc.) in a centralized system. After the collapse of the Soviet Union, these industrial sites became largely useless for the newly born sovereign countries, with insufficient reorientation of skills to suit altered demand patterns. The lesson needs to be learnt that availability of external finance is at best a necessary, but not a sufficient, condition for successful industrial policy.

Serviceability of debt becomes critical particularly when countries with limited foreign exchange pursue independent industrial policies. Suppose one unit is borrowed at interest rate i; if invested, it produces a steady flow of b units of output (incremental output–capital ratio). Assuming a constant fraction s of output is saved, $1 > s > 0$ would be the country's ability to repay, and for sb, the repayment becomes viable. Since, by definition, the growth rate of the economy, g equals sb, this implies g has to exceed the interest rate i for servicing debt. This rule provides a useful benchmark against overdependence on foreign borrowing. It may be supplemented by the analogy with a firm whose cash flow may require occasional outside finance, normally manageable as 'hedge finance' from expected profit flows. More frequent dependence on external finance over longer periods becomes 'speculative' but continuous dependence on injections from outside indicates 'Ponzi' finance and financial fragility (Minsky 1985).

However, the problem of debt servicing has been almost reversed in recent years as poorer East Asian countries with high growth and persistent surpluses on current accounts (e.g., South Korea, Singapore, Malaysia, Taiwan, Hong Kong, and now China) have been lending, that is, exporting capital to richer countries (Prasad et al. 2007). In this context, confusion between 'capital' as finance and as physical equipment needs to be avoided. Lucas (1990), for example, puzzled as to why sufficient 'capital' does not flow from relatively capital-abundant-rich countries to relatively capital-poor countries, since the former have lower compared to the latter's higher marginal product of capital. Capital in this context means physical capital, whereas international capital mobility refers to financial capital. It is not only that physical capital does not have that kind of mobility, the very proposition that marginal product of physical capital equals the rate of profit was proved logically unacceptable outside a one-commodity world precisely on account of this confusion between the physical and value of capital (Sraffa 1960; Samuelson 1966).

8. The Role of Decentralization in the State versus Market Debate

Successes and failures in Asian experiences teach us that recognizing the limits of economic and social engineering in formulating industrialization strategy is as important as being flexible in the use of fiscal and monetary policies to suit differ-ent circumstances. Overly rigid macroeconomic policies are faulty in their very design, not merely in implementation. And yet, experience shows that centralized policy formulation in several Asian countries often erred in this respect. At times they have overemphasized rule-bound, bureaucratically top-heavy execution. Such faultily designed policy, even if well implemented by a bureaucracy or a party, soon loses momentum. 'Great Leap Forward' in China in the 1950s might be such an example. Another example from India and elsewhere might be insistence on forcible population control in the 1970s and insistence on large dams causing mas-sive displacement and dispossession. Asia has had its share of such 'authoritarian high modernism' associated with undertaking giant projects due to bureaucratic oversimplification in centralized decision-making (Scott 1998).

The problem is avoidedin the mythical worldof a perfectly competitive market. With numerous atomistic individuals having no price-setting power and working in a complete set of future markets that avoids all hazards of uncertainty, the market economy settles to a Pareto optimal equilibrium (Debreu 1953).Whilethis construction begs most real-life questions this ideologically powerful view of the market economy continues to dominate development discourse with its implied message that government interventiondisturbs optimality, rather 'leaving it to the market' with a minimalist state is optimal.

In reality, however, both the state and the market are open to manipulative abuses of power, and the design of economic policy has to start by escaping the simplistic binary choice between the state and the market. Counter-posing the state and the market in a 'double movement' for balance against excesses by either is desirable (Polanyi 1944) but has the strong possibility of oneoverpowering the other in many political circumstances.Exploration ofalternatives in decentraliza-tion is imperative, particularly in constitutional democracies of large countries. This means bringing communities more directly into decision-making in a wider three-tier federal structure. The counter-argument that there is a large trade-off between efficiency and decentralization is often fictitious. A centralized large dam or a nuclear power project run by a few highly skilled technocrats may appear more efficient, but a larger number of smaller projects for water or unconventional sources of power management that allow greater community participation may turn out to be more efficient in practice due to their greateradaptabilityto local conditions.

The basic logic for decentralization in large countries where the central power isremoteaims atincorporating implementability into the plan, because success often eludes without the involvement ofinterested local communities. The state would still have the role of co-ordinating, resolving disputes, providing assistance to less able communities, and preventing elite capture of local institutions. However, the paradigm of macroeconomic policies for development has the important task of placing the institutions of the state, the market, and the decentralized communities in an effective functioning arrangement. Although the extent to which this is feasible remains an open issue and the jury is still out, not always with a favourable verdict (Crook and Manor 1998; Bardhan and Mukherjee 2006; Brancati 2006), the undeniable importance of the issue in the light of experience requires its integration into the macroeconomic thinking about development.

The problem may be approached from three different angles. The first challenge is creating powerful group incentives for development without leaving it either to the market mechanism or a distant authoritarian bureaucracy. The biggest obstacle is that groups are divided by opposing interests of gender, caste, and religion, which is indeed a replica of society. Typically, such incentives are more likely to be effective when they do not come into sharp conflict with other sectional interests. Perhaps the clearest example of this has been the preservation of forests and the environment by local participants against a few profit-seeking outside contractors. Other examples are the local rather than centralized storage of grains, nurseries suited to local environments, and water conservation. Indeed, during the extensive growth phase of labour utilization, such decentralization may be more effective and less authoritarian. The market solution has often meant the familiar 'free rider' problem and the tragedy of the commons, which would also appear here. Decentralized planning is not merely the intermediate level of planning between the state and market, but a way of exploring how to find the maximum feasible level of achieving direct democracy in developmental projects by raising awareness of the rights and self-regulating capability of citizens against free-riding.

The second challenge lies in dealing with the typical failures of centralized bureaucracy for the delivery of basic needs in areas such as public distribution of food, education, health, housing, child care, and old age insurance. The opposite failure of the market is most glaring in poor countries where poorer sections are excluded through the price mechanism, denying them market access to basic needs. This is the same market logic of 'one dollar one vote'that discourages the production of the most needed goods, such as safe drinking water, basic preventive medicines, and health care, because they are unprofitable. To counter such exclusion in production and consumption, decentralization could be designed to providenovel instruments, like the concept of social rather than private wages paid in terms of improved community services in elementary and preventive local health care, facilities for child and old age care, and better local common schooling. They typically provide labour-intensive employment and greatly help poorer members of the community in particular. One very important characteristic of a social wage that is seldom stressed is that it can achieve a very high degree of incentive compatibility between the provider and the user of these goods and services, and might avoid many of the abuses (e.g., asymmetric information) of either an anonymous bureaucratic or market system. Similarly, community needs are often better served by small and medium local firms, rather than multinational large firms.

Finally, both capitalist multiparty democracies as well as more authoritarian one-party democracies are increasingly showing tendencies of converging insofar as interests of large corporations are concerned. They span diverse areas like globalization of trade, investment and finance, obsessive concern with international competitiveness, and neglect of employment for higher labour productivity through acquisition of latest technology. The rules of the game are increasingly biased in favour of corporations, to the neglect of traditional knowledge and local possibilities. Strengthening communities through greater awareness of their duties and rights and use of community traditional knowledge through participation in the development process can at least partly act as countervailing power,almost a compulsion of our time. This perhaps is the most pressing justification for exploring the role of decentralization in the more conventional state versus market debate.

9. Economic and Social Inequality

The oft-told story of a Latin American military dictator who reported to the American president that his country's economy was doing well, but not its people, sums up the usual consequences of the strategy of 'growth at any cost'. The strategy suits large corporations more than the people because the benefits of growth donot automatically trickle down in the absence of supporting policies. Slow growth in formal employment, livelihood-destroying policies and transferring of common resources to incentivize corporate investment enormously increased corporate wealth, but at the cost of higher inequality. Both China and India witnessed unprecedented growth in their GDPs along with significant increases in inequality of income and wealth during the same period. And yet, several other Asian experiences have shown that reasonably stable income distribution, with social mobility through measures like initial land reform, improved public health, and education, along with labour-intensive infrastructure for generating employment, created preconditions for high growth. An almost exclusive focus on labour productivity and reduction of unit cost, without concern for employment levels, imposes severe restrictions on the home market, pushing economies towards the foreign market.

In this zero-sum game of increasing globalmarket share, even the losers, due to their dependence on large multinational corporations, ignorethe importance of enlarging the home market through greater income equality by raising the level of employment. Instead, social inequality of various kinds based on caste, race, gender, ethnicity, region, and religion tend to increase in situations of shrinking employment and income opportunities. Gender equality suffers greatly, as evidenced in the Indian case, in a disproportionately large fall in the participation rate of women in the work force in times of shrinking employment opportunities. Under pressures of legitimization by the majority or dominant minority, government follows discriminatory policiesencouraging majoritarianism. . Examples are religious conflicts in Sri Lanka (Tamil–Singala), India, Pakistanin contrast to multi-ethnic, multicultural Singapore or Malaysia where similar traditional tensions decreased with greater prosperity. Democratic multiparty politics often has the unfortunate tendency to magnify such tensions, while the one-party totalitarian solution is suppression by force. And yet, rapid employment-generationsocial mobility is seldom considered as part of the solution. 'Structural' anthropology suggests that tensions of different cultures are often subsumed under wider governing principles like the linked kinship system (Levi-Strauss 1963). Increased local employment opportunities under decentralization, which also reduce alienation, and family separation of migrant workers, could be an important component of a similar governing principle.

Several Asian experiences point to the importance of health care, education, land reform, and infrastructure as ways of moving towards more equitable development. And yet, these are necessary but not sufficient conditions for social cohesion or development. For instance, some Central Asian countries of the former Soviet Union, which had attained many of these conditions, have not yet been on a trajectory of sustained development. In particular, their examples show that human capital development through education under the former Soviet regime did not lead to realization of productive potential in the absence of an adequate market on the demand side. Creating better supply conditions including human capital development is like making more powerful boats whichis not useful unless there is enough water in the river. Myrdal's observation sums it up: 'Supply does not create its own demand, while demand does not call forth its own supply' (Myrdal 1977: 227). In more successful cases, the state played a key role in matching demand with supply measures conditioned by its political economy. The mixing of market forces with monetary, fiscal, and exchange rate policies of the state often focused on private investment and directly undertook public investment for economic and social infrastructural development. The idea of 'crowding out' of private investment by public investment and blanket rules of a ceiling on fiscal deficit or public debt found little support.

Based on the experiences of East and Southeast Asian countries, even if industrialization in general is considered to be at the core of the process of development, the importance of manufacturing must be put into proper perspective. The macropolicy framework must not overlook either the need for developmental prerequisites or the unfolding negative implications for employment and the environment of corporate-led emphasis on the growth of manufacturing. Nevertheless, creating the prerequisites of development often runs the danger of a 'managed' democracy with paternalistic overtones. Several economically successful Asian countries have had this experience, from which some are gradually finding their way out, while in the worst cases paternalism persists without the developmental prerequisites. Even greater income equality in face of relatively less-developed political rights generates tension. While multiparty democracies in South Asia might appear better at protecting the political rights of ordinary citizens, their economic rights are diminished greatly by massive poverty and social inequality magnified bysocial divisionfor capturing votes at election times. Thus, the challenge of how best to combine economic with political and social, especially gender, equality-facesdevelopment inAsia.

10. Concluding Observations

Increasing inequality of income and wealth presents serious problems along the trajectory of development. The tensions generated are not only political and social, but also economic.Matching demand with supplymay beaccepted as a general principle but, increased inequality in favour of the richshrinks the size of the domestic market. The rich save more in financial assets and on up-market imported goods which are detrimental to the expansion of the volume as well as thepattern of demand in a poor country.

In relatively large South Asian countries such as India, Bangladesh, and Pakistan, the priority must be to utilize particularly rural labour more effectively as much as possible in rural areas without following the conventional wisdom that industrialization led by corporations with external market orientation would someday solve the problem. Under democratic accountability at regular intervals of elections, the time permitted to any elected government is not compatible with this macroeconomic strategy because labour absorption in high productivity industry is a much slower process. The compulsions for democratic legitimization without moving towards authoritarianism require shifting attention to the domestic market and production of goods needed by ordinary citizens. This is how macroeconomic policies might hope to bring a closer together economic, political, and social equality. However, this requires providing rural areas with better production and earning opportunities, necessitating at least some reforms in land use and ownership rights coupled with land-improving investments for small-scale agriculture.

Whenever necessary, this has to be supplemented by public works providing electricity, infrastructure, and connectivity, but as far as possible on a decentralized basis with smaller, short-yielding, locally operated projects by smaller firms. It would absorb the maximum amount of labour in the shortest possible time.

However, even within the same region of SouthAsia, the policy mix has to be different for small countries with relatively small domestic markets like Sri Lanka, Maldives, orland-locked Nepal. They have to rely more on imports and devise ways of increasing their export earnings through location advantages in international supply chains, tourism, and exploitation of forest and marine resources, accompanied by development of food- andlocalnatural resource-processing industries. When they are able to meet this challenge like some of the smaller Southeast and East Asian countries, they will have a road map pointing to outward-oriented, export-led development.

As a general rule, instead of obsessive concern for catching up with the industrially advanced countries through greater international competitiveness, the focus of industrial policy should be on producing goods compatible with the purchasing power of the ordinary people in the domestic market and its up-gradation through improved technology. Macroeconomic policies for industrialization have to reckon with the problem of producing improved quality goods for the domestic market in poor countries where the vast majority have purchasing power far below the international standard. Otherwise, wrong policies will be promoting inequality by concentrating investible resources on a composition of goods biased in favour of the richer sections, even when they achieve balance between demand and supply. For an alternative macroeconomic policy paradigm, the defining issue for more equitable and inclusive developmentrequiresviewing output growth as the outcome of decentralized high employment growth, rather than employment growth as the outcome of high output growth.

However,emphasiswill vary from case to case, depending on the specificity of the initial conditions and stage of development of a country. In East and Southeast Asian countries that have already achieved greater prosperity and have a greater outward orientation, the consumption pattern of ordinary citizens in many ways would be closer to that of high-income countries, and their path to industrialization and service sector development would be different. Not only catching up, but overtaking, may well become their objective. The main lesson to be learnt from the diversity of experiences of Asian countries is that inclusive development requires compatibility between the level of prosperity of average citizens in a country and the domestic production pattern which must technologically improve over time without undue concern for international image and position. It is not wise in this respect for any country to try to skip the stages of its developmental history by ignoring the majority. This is the essence of strategic, not blind integration with the global economy in terms of openness in trade, investment, and finance, as well as industrial policy and technology acquisition.

In the course of development as a historical process, the meaning and content of the notion of development itself must change. Recalling Wittgenstein, we might say words, utterances, as well as signs acquire their meaning not as abstractions, but through use in an appropriate 'form of live' (Wittgenstein 1958: 8–14). The word 'development' is no exception. Asian countries are a vast laboratory of experiments that attempt to develop in different ways. Some are more successful than others, but all have lessons for us. We are invited to observe this changing and fascinating scene, which was opened to us by Gunner Myrdal half a century ago.

Acknowledgements

I am grateful to Deepak Nayyar, an anonymous referee, and several participants at the authors' workshop in Shanghai, June 2018, for comments on earlier versions of the chapter.

References

Amsden, A. (1989). *Asia's Next Giant: South Korea and Late Industrialization*. New York: Oxford University Press.

Arthur, W.B. (1994). *Increasing Returns and Path Dependence in the Economy*. Ann Arbor, MI: University of Michigan Press.

Bardhan, P.K., and D. Mukherjee (2006). *Decentralization and Local Governance in Developing Countries: A Comparative Perspective*. Cambridge, MA: MIT Press.

Bhaduri, A. (1986). *The Dynamics of Commodity Production*. London: Macmillan.

Bhaduri, A. (2018). 'A Study in Development by Dispossession', *Cambridge Journal of Economics*, 42(1): 19–31.

Bhaduri, A., and D.J. Harris (1987). 'The Complex Dynamics of the Simple Ricardian System', *Quarterly Journal of Economics*, 102(1): 83–94.

Brancati, D. (2006). 'Decentralization: Fuelling the Fire or Dampening the Flames of Ethnic Conflictand Secessionism', *International Organization*, 60(Summer/3): 651–85.

Chakravarty, S. (1993). 'Development Strategies in Asian Countries'. In S. Chakravarty (ed.) *Selected Economic Writings*. Delhi: Oxford University Press.

Crook, R.C., and J. Manor (1998). *Democracy and Decentralization in South Asia and West Africa: Participation, Accountability and Performance*. Cambridge: Cambridge University Press.

David, P.A. (1995). 'Clio and Economics of QWERTY', *American Economic Review, Papers and Proceedings*, 75: 332–7.

Day, R.H. (1983). 'The Emergence of Chaos from Classical Economic Growth', *Quarterly Journal of Economics*, 98(2): 201–3.

Debreu, G. (1953/1972reprint). *The Theory of Value*. New Haven, CT: Yale University Press.

Dobb, M.H. (1960). *An Essay in Economic Growth and Planning*. London: Routledge and Kegan Paul.

Domar, E. (1958). 'A Soviet Model of Growth'. In his *Selected Essays on Economic Growth*. Oxford, Oxford University Press.

Fei, C.H., and G.Ranis (1964). *Development of the Labour Surplus Economy: Theory and Policy*. New Haven, CT: Yale University Press.

Gandolfo, G. (1996). *Economic Dynamics* (3rdedn). Berlin: Springer.

Ghose, A.K. (2016). 'Globalization, Growth and Employment in India', *Indian Journal of Human Development*, 10(2): 127–56.

Harris, J.R., and M.P. Todaro (1970). 'Migration, Unemployment and Development: A Two-Sector Analysis', *American Economic Review*, 60(1): 126–42.

Kaldor, N. (1972). 'The Irrelevance of Equilibrium Economics', *Economic Journal*, 82(328): 1237–55.

Kalecki, M. (1993). *Collected Works of Michal Kalecki. Volume 5: Developing Economies*. Edited by J. Osiatynski. Oxford: Clarendon Press.

Keynes, J.M. (1930). *A Treatise on Money, VolumeII*. London: Macmillan.

Keynes, J.M. (1940). *How to Pay for the War*. London: Macmillan.

Kahn, R.F. (1972). 'The Challenge of Development'. In R.F. Kahn(ed.) *Selected Essays in Employment and Growth*. Cambridge: Cambridge University Press.

Lall, S. (1987). *Learning to Industrialize: The Acquisition of Technological Capability by India*. Basingstoke: Macmillan.

Levi-Strauss, C. (1963). *Structural Anthropology*. Translated from French by C. Jacobson and B.G. Schoepf. New York: Basic Books.

Lewis, W.A. (1954). 'Economic Development with Unlimited Supplies of Labour', *The Manchester School*, 22(2): 131–91.

Lucas, R.E. (1983). *Studies in Business-Cycle Theory*. Cambridge, MA: MIT Press.

Lucas, R.E. (1990). 'Why Doesn't Capital Flow from Rich to Poor Countries?', *The American Economic Review*, 80(2): 92–6.

Mahalanobis, P.C. (1953). 'Some Observations on the Process of Growth of National Income',*Sankhya*, 12(4): 317–2.

Minsky, H.P. (1985). 'The Financial Instability Hypothesis'. In P. Arestis and T. Skouras (eds) *Post Keynesian Economic Theory*. Basingstoke: Wheatsheaf.

Mundell, R. (1968). *International Economics*. London: Macmillan.

Murphy, K.M., A. Shleifer, and R.W. Vishney (1989). 'Industrialization and Big Push', *Journal of Political Economy*, 97(5): 1003–26.

Myrdal, G. (1957). *Economic Theories and Underdeveloped Regions*. London: Duckworth.

Myrdal, G. (1968/1977) (abridged). *Asian Drama: An Inquiry into the Poverty of Nations*. Original in three volumes published in 1968. London: Allen Lane, The Penguin Press. Abridged in S.S. King (ed.) Pelican New Edition (1977).

Nayyar, D. (2013). *Catch Up: Developing Countries in the World Economy*. Oxford: Oxford University Press.

Nurkse, R. (1953). *Problem of Capital Formation in Underdeveloped Countries*. New York: Oxford University Press.

Poincare, H. (1908). *Science etMethode*. Paris: Flammarion.

Polanyi, K. (1944). *The Great Transformation*. New York: Rinehart.

Prasad, E.S., R. Rajan, and A. Subramanian (2007). 'The Paradox of Capital', *Finance and Development (IMF)*, 44(1).

Robinson. J. (1956). *Accumulation of Capital*. London: Macmillan.

Rosenstein Rodan, P. (1943). 'Problem of Industrialization of Eastern and South-Eastern Europe', *Economic Journal*, 59(2): 202–11.

Samuelson, P.A. (1966). 'A Summing Up', *The Quarterly Journal of Economics*, 80(4): 568–83.

Sargent, T.J. (1987). *Dynamic Macroeconomic Theory*. Cambridge, MA: Harvard University Press.

Scott, J.C. (1998). *Seeing Like a State*. New Haven, CT: Yale University Press.

Sen, A.K. (1960). *Choice of Techniques*. Oxford: Blackwell.

Simon, H.A. (1979). 'Rational Decision-Making in Business Organizations', *The American Economic Review*, 69(4): 493–513.

Sraffa, P. (1926). 'The Laws of Returns under Competitive Conditions', *Economic Journal*, 36(4): 535–50.

Sraffa, P. (1960). *Production of Commodities by Means of Commodities*. Cambridge: Cambridge University Press.

Tinbergen, J. (1954). *The Design of Economic Policy*. Amsterdam: North Holland.

Wade, R. (1990). *Governing the Market: Economic Theory and the Role of Government in East Asian Industrialization*. Princeton, NJ: Princeton University Press.

Wittgenstein, L. (1958). *Philosophical Investigations*, 2nd edn. Translatedby G.E.M. Anscombe. Oxford: Basil Blackwell.

Young, A. (1928). 'Increasing Returns and Economic Progress', *Economic Journal*, 38 (Sept 152): 527–42.

10

Poverty and Inequality

Guanghua Wan and Chen Wang

1. Introduction

Poverty reduction featured most prominently among the Millennium Development Goals (MDGs) as well as in the post-2015 development agenda of the Sustainable Development Goals (SDGs). And containing inequality was added to the latter. Against this background, the primary objective of this chapter is to construct and discuss poverty and inequality profiles in Asia[1] for the past 50 years or so. While data on inequality are available from the World Income Inequality Database (WIID) of UNU-WIDER, consistent poverty estimates do not exist for the early years. Thus, household consumption data from the Penn World Table (PWT version 9) have been combined with the inequality observations of WIID to generate poverty profiles for Asia, its sub-regions, and individual economies.[2] The poverty lines are set at US$1.90 and US$3.20 per person per day, adjusted by the 2011 purchasing power parity exchange rates. They correspond to the extreme and moderate poverty lines of the World Bank, respectively.

Our analytical results demonstrate that, contrary to Myrdal (1968) who was rather pessimistic about the future of Asia, Asia has achieved remarkable growth and miracle poverty reduction since the mid-1960s. Beginning with Japan's taking off after the Second World War, followed by the emergence of the four 'tigers' of Korea, Taiwan, Hong Kong, and Singapore in the 1960s and 1970s, Asia's re-rise received a huge boost when China embarked on its reform and opening-up journey in late 1978, reinforced later by the fast growth of the Indian and other Asian economies. Consequently, Asia's share in global gross domestic product (GDP) has been rising rapidly (see Nayyar 2013). The share is expected to rise further (ADB 2011), and could reach more than 76 per cent by 2040 according to Fogel (2007).

The fast growth has helped lift billions of Asians out of poverty. According to the estimates presented in section 2.3, Asia's poverty rate under the US$3.20 poverty line dropped from 73.57 per cent in 1965 to 9.69 per cent in 2014.

---

[1] Unless otherwise specified, Asia or region in this chapter refers to the following economies: China, Hong Kong, Japan, Mongolia, South Korea, and Taiwan from East Asia; Cambodia, Indonesia, Laos, Malaysia, the Philippines, Singapore, Thailand, and Vietnam from Southeast Asia; and Bangladesh, Bhutan, India, Iran, Maldives, Nepal, Pakistan, and Sri Lanka from South Asia.

[2] See https://www.wider.unu.edu/project/wiid-world-income-inequality-database and https://www.rug.nl/ggdc/productivity/pwt/ (accessed 1 July 2018).

The corresponding decrease under the US$1.90 poverty line is from 48.52 per cent in 1965 to 2.58 per cent in 2014. In fact, the MDG on poverty reduction would not have been achieved if Asia were excluded (ADB 2014).

On the other hand, however, the fast growth has been accompanied by rising inequality.[3] For Asia as a whole, the Gini index, an indicator of inequality, increased from 38.43 per cent in 1965 to 42.80 per cent in 2006 before declining in recent years. The recent decline may be attributable to the financial crisis that began in 2007/2008 (see more discussions later in the chapter). In particular, inequality worsened significantly in the most populous countries of Asia: China, India, Indonesia, Bangladesh, and Sri Lanka (see section 2.2).

The rising inequality has far-reaching implications. It can offset the benign effect of growth on poverty (Ravallion and Chen 2004). Furthermore, in highly unequal societies, the elite may hijack the power of the state, adversely affecting the provision of public goods and services that tend to benefit the poor more (Bourguignon and Dessus 2009). Most fundamentally, inequality is expected to undermine future growth through various transmission channels (Wan at al. 2006). In particular, it may raise the likelihood of financial crises and stimulate current account deficits (Rajan 2010; Acemoglu 2011).

Clearly, the interwoven relationship between growth, poverty, and inequality—coined the growth–poverty–inequality triangle by Bourguignon (2004)—is an important and complex subject worth careful examination. While much has been published on Asia's phenomenal growth, Asia's poverty profile is largely absent if one extends the time horizon back to the 1970s or 1960s. Further, existing studies on income inequality are mostly centred on within-country inequality. Even the flagship publication of ADB (2012) and ESCAP (2018) did not take into consideration income gaps between economies. This is regrettable as Asia's welfare depends not only on growth and inequality within individual economies but also on disparities between economies (Sen 1973). In short, to gain a good understanding of the development process in Asia requires a comprehensive and coherent analysis of the growth, inequality, and poverty issues for Asia, its sub-regions, and individual economies.

In addition to the provision of poverty and inequality profiles, this chapter addresses three related issues: what were the impacts of growth and inequality on poverty reduction in Asia? What are the drivers of absolute poverty and inequality? And what is the relationship between growth and inequality? The last two issues will be addressed by estimating various regression models while the first question will be tackled using the framework of poverty decomposition, initially developed by Datt and Ravallion (1992) and modified by Zhang and Wan (2006). This framework can attribute a change in poverty to contributions that are made

---

[3] This chapter only considers inequality of income, which is generally more equally distributed than wealth but more unequally distributed than consumption due to smoothing.

by growth and inequality, respectively (see section 3 for details). It is important to point out that poverty will be estimated using per capita consumption data from the latest PWT. This is recommended by Feenstra et al. (2015) and Anand and Segal (2015) and is also more consistent with the World Bank that uses consumption not income data from household surveys to estimate poverty. However, the level of consumption reported in PWT is usually higher than that from household survey. Also, Asia on average is more developed than Africa. Thus, we focus on results based on the US$3.20 poverty line unless specified otherwise. Our use of the PWT data is supported by Pinkovskiy and Sala-i-Martin (2016).

The rest of the chapter is organized as follows. Section 2 discusses profiles of growth, inequality, and poverty for Asia, its sub-regions, and individual economies. Section 3 focuses on sources of poverty reduction while section 4 is devoted to the study of inequality, with a special emphasis on the costs and drivers of inequality. Finally, section 5 provides a summary and policy recommendations.

2. Growth, Inequality, and Poverty Profiles

According to Sen (1973), the overall well-being of a region such as Asia depends on two variables: regional average income/consumption and regional distribution of income/consumption. The latter can be represented by an indicator of inequality such as the Gini or Theil index. Further, the two variables completely determine the level of poverty for a given poverty line. The aim of this section is to depict the development process of Asia for the period 1965–2014 by constructing and presenting these three interrelated profiles.

2.1 Growth Profile

The importance of growth requires no justification at all. As pointed out by Myrdal (1968), growth is likely to improve almost all other conditions, even attitudes and institutions. In the context of this chapter, growth leads to lower poverty and welfare gains, holding income distribution or inequality constant.

To demonstrate the role of Asia's economic growth in a global picture, Figure 10.1 shows the growth trends of Asia, its sub-regions, and non-Asia countries, where non-Asia countries include both developing and developed countries. As expected, Asia's growth has been phenomenal since the mid- or late 1960s. It outpaced non-Asia countries except during the second energy crisis of the late 1970s and the Asian financial crisis in the late 1990s. This is particularly true in the late 1960s when the four tigers took off and became even more significant when China began its expansion in the late 1970s, with contributions from India and other Asian economies. However, different sub-regions performed quite differently.

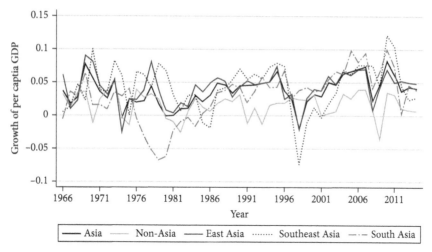

Figure 10.1 Growth of per capita GDP: Asia and sub-regions.

Note: Asia contains countries from East Asia, Southeast Asia, and South Asia; Non-Asia includes all countries except for countries from East Asia, Southeast Asia, and South Asia.

Source: Authors' compilation based on PWT data.

East Asia has been the star performer, and, for most years, Southeast Asia performed well too.

Not surprisingly, heterogeneity in growth performance is even more significant when comparing different individual economies. As figure 2 of Wan and Wang (2018) shows, economies in East Asia not only grew fast but also were relatively stable. The growth fluctuations were more synchronized within Southeast Asia than economies in other sub-regions.

2.2 Inequality Profile

The fast growth in Asia does not necessarily lead to welfare improvement unless the poor gain equally or more than the rich. Societal welfare could even decrease if the growth benefits the rich at the cost of the poor (Sen 1973). In other words, the more the poor benefit, which implies declining inequality, the larger the welfare gains for the society. Unfortunately, growth is often accompanied by rising inequality, as pointed out by Kuznets (1955) and Lewis (1955) and as happened in Asia.

To assess whether Asia's growth was accompanied by worsening distribution, it is necessary to construct an Asia-wide inequality profile, ideally based on household or individual data. In the absence of such data, the methodology derived in appendix B of Wan and Wang (2018) is used to convert the Gini estimates of WIID into Theil estimates (Theil 1967).[4] Adding up these Theil estimates weighted

---

[4] Theil index is another popular indicator of inequality.

by population shares gives rise to the so-called within-economy inequality. Using per capita GDP of individual economies, a Theil estimate representing the so-called between-economy inequality can be obtained. The sum of these two components is the overall inequality (Theil index) for Asia, which can be converted back into the Gini coefficient.

Figure 10.2 depicts Asia's inequality profile which exhibits an inverted-U pattern. The curve at the bottom shows the simple unweighted average of Gini estimates of individual economies. The gap between this curve and the regional Gini reflects two impacts: gaps between economies and the importance of population weights. It is clear that the conventional wisdom of using the unweighted Gini is misleading. More realistic estimates of the regional inequality (the top two curves in Figure 10.2) paint a much more serious picture. Apart from severe underestimation, the unweighted Gini even produces different inequality trends.

An interesting finding from Figure 10.2 is the decreases in inequality during crises, initially noted by Wan (2001). Inequality in Asia grew successively from 1965 until the first oil crisis of 1973. The decline in inequality during this crisis was small and short-lived. Afterwards, regional inequality resumed its climbing trend until the onset of the second oil crisis that began in 1979. This time, the inequality decline lasted several years until the mid-1980s. The decrease in inequality during the 1997 Asian financial crisis was also short-lived. Most importantly, the prolonged and lingering global crisis of 2007/2008 is associated with successive declines of Asia's inequality.

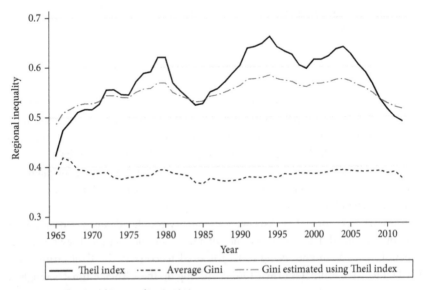

Figure 10.2 Regional inequality in Asia.
Source: Authors' compilation based on PWT and WIID data.

As Lopez-Acevedo and Salinas (2000) demonstrated, the rich usually suffer from severe capital losses during crises, seriously affecting their income. Also, crises cause more income damage to workers of non-tradable sectors such as financial services and to individuals in the top income decile. These can be confirmed by the drop in the income share accruing to top income earners. According to the World Inequality Database, from 2008 to 2009, the share of pre-tax income of the top 1 per cent earners dropped from 12.7 to 11.2 per cent in France, 29.3 to 27.4 per cent in Brazil, 11.4 to 9.7 per cent in Taiwan, 11.3 to 10.4 per cent in Japan, and 15.2 to 13.7 per cent in Singapore. Similarly, from 2008 to 2009 the income share of the top 10 per cent earners dropped from 37.3 to 35.6 per cent in France, 56.2 to 55.0 per cent in Brazil, 36.9 to 33.7 per cent in Taiwan, 43 to 41.3 per cent in Japan, and 43.6 to 39.6 per cent in Singapore. Of course, social protections kick in during crises, helping moderate after-tax income inequality.

Figure 10.3 shows the within- and between-economy components of Asia's inequality. The latter dominated total inequality and yet it has been neglected by the public, the policy, and even research communities. Further, the trend of Asia's inequality is almost completely driven by the between-component. For example, the early ascent of the total inequality was accompanied by the increasing between-component. And the post-1990s decline was accompanied by the decreasing between-component despite the rising within-component.

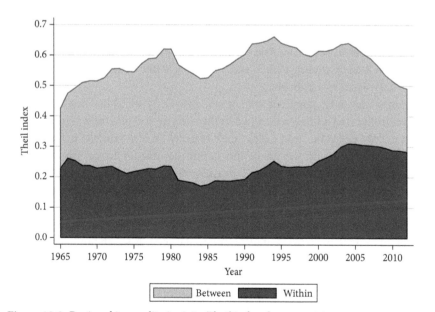

Figure 10.3 Regional inequality in Asia: Theil index decomposition.

Note: Total inequality is the sum of within-country inequality (Theil index (within)) and between-country inequality (Theil index (between)).

Source: Authors' estimation based on PWT and WIID data.

The sub-regional profiles differ from the regional counterpart and from each other. Referring to figure 5 of Wan and Wang (2018), several findings are discernible. First, very much like the regional picture, sub-regions experienced inequality rises and significant declines, with a peak around the height of the second oil crisis. They also experienced an upward trend starting from the mid-1980s. Unlike the inverted-U pattern of the regional profile, East Asia and South Asia exhibit an M pattern. Moreover, the overall inequality is lower in South Asia while East Asia is most unequal. Second, for East Asia, the main contributor of inequality is the between-component while in South and Southeast Asia, the within-component dominates and economies in these two sub-regions are relatively more homogeneous in terms of development level. In fact, the between-component in South and Southeast Asia is relatively stable. Third, East Asia is unique in the sense that the latest declining trend occurred much earlier than in other sub-regions. This is related to the dominance of the between-component in East Asia and is driven by the catching up of China with its two neighbours of Japan and Korea, particularly after 1988 when Japan began to experience the lost decades.

As expected, the inequality profiles at the individual economy level are more diverse, see figure 6 of Wan and Wang (2018). It is interesting to observe that economies within each sub-region share similar inequality trends while trends differ across sub-regions, making one wonder if cultural factors may play a role in driving inequality. In addition to cultural factors that are difficult to quantify, level of development, technical change, unemployment, urbanization, globalization, and ageing are potential drivers of inequality (see section 4 for more details). Note that economies in Southeast Asia experienced more erratic changes in inequality while East Asia (excluding China) and South Asia witnessed more stable distributions with one or two outliers.

Among the most populous economies, inequality in China was low in the pre-reform period and even declined in the early period of reform but rose quite substantially since the mid-1980s until recently. While growth in China was accompanied by rising inequality, this is not the case for Japan, which experienced fairly equal distribution until the early 1980s. Inequality in Japan did grow since then but the level remained low. Inequality in India fluctuated more and stayed at relatively high levels until recently. The trend of inequality in Bangladesh is similar to that in China, while inequality in Indonesia also grew. These countries represent more than 90 per cent of Asia's population. It is worth noting the spatial dimension of inequality in large countries such as China, India, and Indonesia where the rural–urban divide contributes significantly to national inequality (see Shorrocks and Wan 2005). In China, this contribution amounted to more than 50 per cent of total inequality (see Wan 2007; Wang et al. 2014).

Another indicator of income distribution is the labour share in national income. Analytically, a decline in the labour share implies rising inequality as labour income is usually more equally distributed than capital income (Jacobson and

Occhino 2012; Piketty 2014; Luo et al. 2018). Based on PWT data, except Hong Kong, Mongolia, and Singapore, all other economies in Asia experienced decreases in the labour share, with the largest decline observed in India (from 71.75 per cent in 1975 to 49.54 per cent in 2011).

2.3 Poverty Profile

While the impact of growth on inequality is uncertain, its impact on poverty is always benign provided that the distribution does not deteriorate. Since inequality has risen in many parts of Asia (see section 2.2),the poverty profile cannot be determined a priori despite the general growth trends in Asia.

A formidable challenge in constructing the poverty profile lies in the lack of household or individual data. However, under a reasonable assumption, poverty can be estimated using the Gini estimates of WIID and the per capita household final consumption data from PWT (see appendix B of Wan and Wang 2018). Ideally, the Gini estimates should be based on consumption rather than income data. However, if consumption is proportional to income, income and consumption inequalities would be identical. In reality, due to consumption smoothing, its inequality is generally smaller than income inequality. Nevertheless, consumption is highly correlated with income, justifying to a certain extent the mixed use of income Gini estimates from WIID. Note that interpolation and extrapolation were necessary to fill in some of the missing Gini estimates.

Figure 10.4 presents the poverty head count ratios or poverty rate for Asia and its sub-regions under the US$1.90 and US$3.20 poverty lines. It is striking to see that in 1965, 73.57 per cent of Asians lived under the US$3.20 poverty line and half of Asians lived with less than US$1.90 per day. After 50 years of development, Asia has eliminated extreme poverty using the 3 per cent threshold of the World Bank, although Asia is still some way from ending moderate poverty. In 2014, there are still 421.48 million moderately poor in Asia.[5]

Not surprisingly, the poverty profile differs considerably across sub-regions (see figure 9 of Wan and Wang 2018) although they all share a similar declining trend. In terms of poverty rate, in 1965 Southeast Asia was the poorest. By 2014, however, South Asia, which had not managed to end extreme poverty under the 3 per cent threshold of the World Bank, became the poorest. The general declining trends imply the dominating growth impact of poverty reduction. However, the trend became flatter for East Asia since the mid-1980s and for Southeast Asia since the early 1980s. The former may be related to the fast-rising inequality in China and the latter may be explained by growth moderation combined with increases in inequality in Southeast Asia.

---

[5] Asia's total population is 4,349.6 million, according to United Nations (2015).

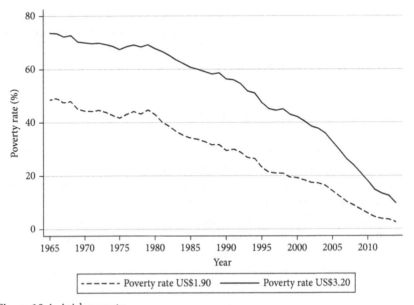

Figure 10.4 Asia's poverty.

Source: Authors' estimation based on PWT and WIID data.

It is useful to note some episodes of poverty increases. For example, South Asia became poorer from the mid-1970s to the early 1980s. This is due to the independence of Bangladesh in 1971 and socio-economic instabilities afterwards. Also, Sri Lanka experienced poverty increases from the early 1970s to the mid-1980s due to a series of wars.

There are large heterogeneities in both the level and fluctuations in the poverty rates across economies (see figure 10 of Wan and Wang 2018). Apart from Japan, all other economies suffered from abject poverty back in 1965. Under the 3 per cent threshold, Taiwan and Hong Kong eliminated extreme poverty in late 1960s, Singapore mid-1970s, followed by South Korea in early 1980s, Malaysia late 1990s, and Thailand and Indonesia in the new millennium. By contrasting the poverty profiles with the corresponding growth profiles, the correlation appears to be quite high, implying that poverty reduction is largely driven by growth. Changes in inequality only played a supplementary role, as discussed further in section 3.

3. Sources of Poverty Reduction

Having provided the poverty, growth, and inequality profiles, this section explores the poverty–growth–inequality triangle, focusing on sources of poverty reduction. This can be achieved by decomposing a poverty change into the growth and inequality components or effects. The methodology to be used here is based on Zhang and Wan (2006) who modified the decomposition framework of Datt and Ravallion (1992). Let ΔP denote a change in poverty P between period 0 and period T:

$$\Delta P = P(Y_T;I_T) - P(Y_0;I_0) \tag{1}$$

where Y denotes average consumption and I denotes distribution or inequality. By definition, the growth component of ΔP is the change in poverty due to a change in Y holding I constant. The inequality or redistribution component is the change in poverty due to a change in the distribution I while holding Y constant. Let $P(Y_i, I_j)$ be the poverty estimate from a hypothetical distribution, $i = 0$ or T, $j = 0$ or T and $i \neq j$. The growth component can be defined as:

$$Growth\ component = P(Y_T,I_0) - P(Y_0;I_0) \tag{2}$$

or, alternatively as

$$Growth\ component = P(Y_T;I_T) - P(Y_0,I_T) \tag{2a}$$

Similarly, the inequality component can be defined as:

$$Inequality\ component = P(Y_0,I_T) - P(Y_0;I_0) \tag{3}$$

or

$$Inequality\ component = P(Y_T,I_T) - P(Y_T;I_0) \tag{3a}$$

Different combinations of the alternative growth and inequality components produce four distinct decompositions of ΔP. If Equations (2) and (3) are used, period 0 is considered as the reference point. By contrast, choosing equations (2a) and (3a) implies the use of period T as the reference point. The results from the two decompositions need not agree, and both are inexact in the sense that the two components do not add up to ΔP. If the combination of Equations (2a) and (3) or (2) and (3a) is used, the decomposition will be exact since:

$$P(Y_T;I_T) - P(Y_0;I_0) = \left[Growth\ component\right] + \left[Inequality\ component\right]$$
$$= [P(Y_T;I_T) - P(Y_0,I_T)] + [P(Y_0,I_T) - P(Y_0;I_0) \tag{4}$$
$$= [P(Y_T,I_0) - P(Y_0;I_0)] + [P(Y_T;I_T) - P(Y_T,I_0)] \tag{5}$$

However, the inequality and growth components are measured against different reference points in Equations (4) and (5), which may produce different results. A solution to the reference point problem is to take the average of Equations (4) and (5) to arrive at:

$$\Delta P = 0.5\left\{\left[P(Y_T;I_T) - P(Y_0,I_T)\right] + \left[P(Y_T,I_0) - P(Y_0;I_0)\right]\right\}$$
$$+ 0.5\left\{\left[P(Y_0,I_T) - P(Y_0;I_0)\right] + \left[P(Y_T;I_T) - P(Y_T,I_0)\right]\right\}$$
$$= \left\{Growth\ component\right\} + \left\{Inequality\ component\right\} \tag{6}$$

Note that the above decomposition of Zhang and Wan (2006) does not have the annoying residual term and is not path-dependent, as in Datt and Ravallion (1992).

The decomposition results for Asia under the US$3.20 poverty line are shown in Figure 10.5, with a positive effect reflecting poverty reduction. Note that the estimated inequality effect is positively correlated with poverty reduction—a rise in inequality implies poverty rise and vice versa. On the contrary, the estimated growth effect is negatively correlated with poverty reduction—growth implies

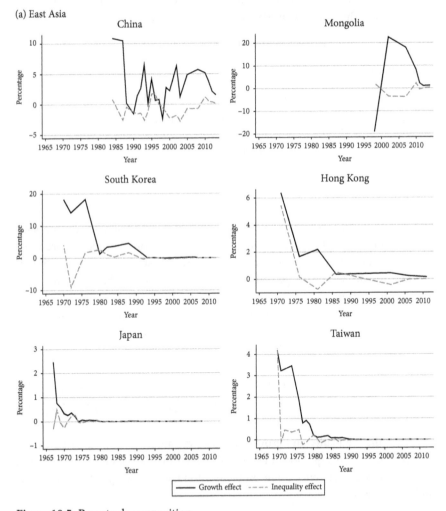

Figure 10.5 Poverty decomposition.
(a) East Asia
(b) Southeast Asia
(c) South Asia
Source: Authors' estimation based on PWT and WIID data.

(b) Southeast Asia

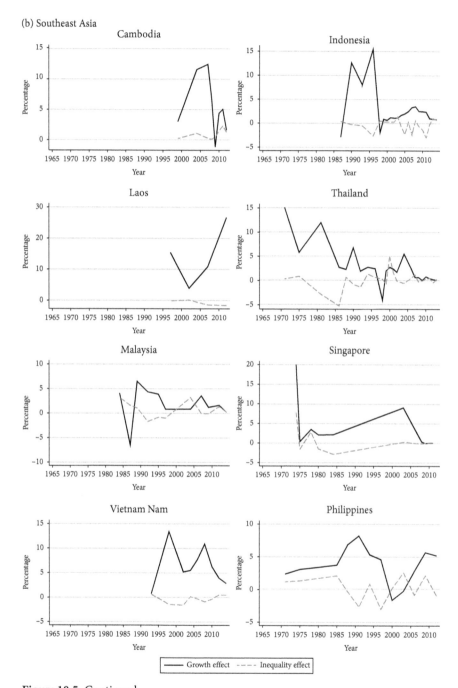

Figure 10.5 Continued

(c) South Asia

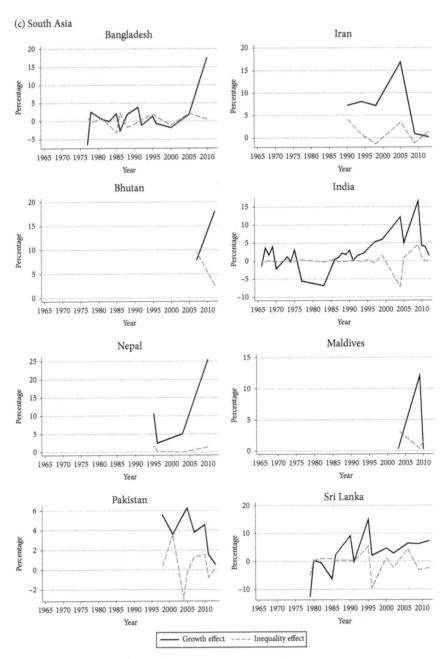

Figure 10.5 Continued

poverty reduction and vice versa. For Asia, the inequality effect is mostly poverty-increasing, echoing the general trend of rising inequality. Meanwhile, the growth effects are negative in most years. Comparing the two effects, the benign growth effect clearly dominates. Therefore, it can be concluded that the impressive achievement in poverty reduction in Asia is largely accounted for by growth. The inequality effect has been detrimental, but it is small in absolute values.

As far as East Asia is concerned, the growth effect for South Korea, Hong Kong, Japan, and Taiwan was large in the early years and began converging to zero since around the early 1990s. In China and Mongolia, the growth effect was also positive although the contributions appeared relatively small. This is not surprising, as China is well known for high savings rate or low consumption rate despite its miracle growth in the last four decades. Inequality improved in Hong Kong and Taiwan in the early 1970s, reinforcing the benign growth impact of growth. In South Korea, the inequality effect also helped reduce poverty in most years, corresponding to the declines in its inequality; see figure 6 of Wan and Wang (2018).

Turning to Southeast Asia, on average the growth effect was larger than that for East Asia although it declined over time. Singapore witnessed the largest growth effect in the mid-1970s, reducing the poverty rate by more than 20 per cent. In Laos and the Philippines, the growth effect has been significant in recent years. Inequality effect in Southeast Asia was similar to that in East Asia, being close to zero.

As far as South Asia is concerned, the pattern of growth effect was opposite to that for most of the other Asian economies where the growth effect decreased over time. For example, in Bangladesh, India, and Nepal, the growth effect increased over time.

Except in East Asia, redistribution effects are close to and fluctuate just above zero, and the growth effects are mostly positive and dominate the total changes in poverty. The growth effect in different sub-regions became small over time in Southeast Asia but expanded in South Asia. Such a difference is attributable to three factors: differences in the growth rate of per capita consumption, the growth impact on poverty, and the base-period level of poverty.

Since the magnitude of the growth effect depends on the growth rate and its impact on poverty, it is useful to divide the growth effect by the growth rate to obtain the growth elasticity of poverty reduction. The results (not presented here due to space consideration) demonstrate the diminishing impact of growth on poverty reduction over time: a same 1 percentage point of growth (in consumption per capita) leads to less and less poverty reduction over time—a typical phenomenon of 'ripping the low-hanging fruits first'. This is why the growth impact is related to the base-period level of poverty.

To further explore fundamental drivers of poverty, Table 10.1 reports regression results using the poverty rate under the US$3.20 poverty line as the

Table 10.1 Drivers of poverty

	m1	m2	m3	m4	m5	m6	m7
	Poverty 3.2	Poverty 3.2	Poverty 3.2	Poverty 3.2	Poverty 3.2	Poverty 3.2	Poverty 3.2
Ln(GDP per capita)	−181.843***	−210.418***	−196.928***	−191.153***	−203.496***	−203.439***	−167.331***
	(17.410)	(20.738)	(25.908)	(29.170)	(30.769)	(31.021)	(31.189)
Ln(GDP per capita)²	10.226*** (1.018)	12.402*** (1.230)	11.630*** (1.652)	11.548*** (1.703)	12.325*** (1.814)	12.021*** (1.815)	10.020*** (1.772)
Total factor productivity (TFP)		−18.952* (10.367)	−36.242** (17.564)	−45.298** (19.845)	−45.832** (19.643)	−29.720 (18.086)	−34.982* (15.680)
Unemployment rate			0.171 (0.368)	0.282 (0.348)	0.329 (0.338)	0.482 (0.332)	0.372 (0.317)
Urbanization				−0.250 (0.227)	−0.264 (0.215)	−0.199 (0.202)	−0.286 (0.195)
Trade					−0.042* (0.024)	−0.037 (0.026)	−0.051* (0.028)
Foreign direct investment (FDI)						−0.231** (0.116)	−0.152 (0.104)
Population share aged >65 years							1.919*** (0.479)
Constant	806.222***	894.919***	851.367***	827.691***	878.279***	885.841***	721.546***
	(76.371)	(89.933)	(103.382)	(116.985)	(124.432)	(125.674)	(129.299)
Country dummy	Y	Y	Y	Y	Y	Y	Y
Year dummy	Y	Y	Y	Y	Y	Y	Y
N	190	145	125	125	125	125	125
Adjusted R²	0.963	0.953	0.943	0.944	0.945	0.947	0.953

Notes: Robust standard errors in parentheses; *P<0.1, **P<0.05, ***P<0.01.

Source: Authors' estimation based on PWT, WDI, and WIID data.

dependent variable. The result shows a U-shaped relationship between GDP per capita (in logarithm) and poverty. Since GDP per capita (in logarithm) ranged from 6.92 to 11.82 in our data, the estimated marginal effect of economic growth is always below zero, confirming that growth is good for the poor in Asia. Technological progress and trade exposure also helped poverty reduction. Also, as expected, ageing is positively related to poverty.

In addition, the unemployment rate is positively correlated with poverty although the coefficient is insignificant. As noted by Gustafsson and Johansson (1999), a weak or non-existent relationship could be attributable to income losses from unemployment, which are masked by unemployment benefits or by increased labour market activity of other family members. Nevertheless, the poor largely live on returns to labour rather than capital. Thus, growth with employment creation reduces poverty far more than jobless growth.

Needless to say, policy matters too. To demonstrate the relevance of policy measures, we take China and India as case studies. In 1986, China set up the Poverty Alleviation Office under the State Council, taking the overall responsibility for poverty alleviation. Early efforts targeted areas inhabited by minorities, remote and border regions, and revolutionary bases. In 2001, the government issued a document entitled 'Outline of Poverty Alleviation and Development for the Rural Area (2001–2010)' and in 2012 it issued the document 'The Twelfth Five-Year Plan for Poverty Alleviation and Development for Whole Villages'. In India, the government proposed strategies, such as 'The National Social Assistance Programme' in 1995, 'Indira Awaas Yojana' in 1996, and the 'Public Distribution System', introduced in 1944, was replaced by the 'Targeted Public Distribution System' in 1997. More recently, India launched the 'Mahatma Gandhi National Rural Employment Guarantee Scheme' in 2005. These policies helped generate jobs for the poor or directly transferred income or consumption to the poor.

4. Drivers and Costs of Inequality

Inequality not only erodes the growth impact, it may directly lower growth itself. In this section, we first model drivers of inequality and then gauge the costs of inequality in terms of lost GDP and poverty that could have been reduced if inequality did not rise.

4.1 Drivers of Inequality

To examine the driving forces of inequality, we run a number of pooled time series cross-section regression analyses. The equations are specified as follows, where *Asia* denotes a dummy variable:

$$Inequality = f(GDP, GDP^2, TFP, Unemployment, Urbanization,$$
$$Trade, FDI, Ageing, GDP \times Asia, GDP^2 \times Asia,$$
$$TFP \times Asia, Unemployment \times Asia, Urbanization \times Asia,$$
$$Trade \times Asia, FDI \times Asia, Ageing \times Asia) \tag{7}$$

Besides GDP, Equation (7) includes a number of socio-economic variables. Technological progress tends to favour capital over labour and skilled labour over unskilled labour—the so-called capital or skill bias. Meanwhile, as an economy becomes more technology and capital intensive, those with capital and skills are paid more. The simultaneous increases in the quantities and prices of capital and skill naturally raise the capital share in the national pie at the cost of the labour share. This leads to worsening distribution because capital income is more unequal than labour income (Piketty 2014) and because the capitalists and the skilled tend to be in the upper segment of the income ladder. To control for technical change, we use total factor productivity (TFP) from PWT.

The linkage between globalization and income distribution has been analysed extensively (Mahler 2004). From the Stolper–Samuelson theorem, exposure to international markets raises demand for skilled labour, causing larger wage gaps (Burgoon 2001). Two measures are included to account for the effect of globalization, namely trade openness (share of import + export over GDP) and net foreign direct investment (FDI) flows as a percentage of GDP. Also, an increase in the elderly dependency ratio implies less employment and fewer taxes (Lam 1997; Gustafsson and Johansson 1999). Meanwhile, the elderly are usually located at the lower part of the income ladder. Thus, ageing could lead to a rise in income inequality (Lindert 1978; Repetto 1978; Razin et al. 2002). Therefore, we control for the percentage of population aged sixty-five years.

Finally, the unemployment rate is added to assess the impact of jobs on inequality. Given the urban–rural gap and different levels of inequality in rural and urban areas, urbanization rate is included. Data for 217 countries and the period 1965 to 2014 are used. Except the Gini coefficient sourced from WIID and TFP from PWT, other variables are from World Development Indicators (WDI).

Table 10.2 presents the estimation results. For Asia, a significant inverted-U shape is found between GDP per capita and the Gini coefficient, confirming the Kuznets hypothesis, although this is not the case when a global sample is used. More significantly, the unemployment rate and population ageing are found to be associated with higher inequality, forcefully demonstrating the importance of jobs in containing inequality.

However, the globalization variables are insignificant, possibly because their impacts changed around 1980 when the current wave of globalization began, but limited data points for the pre-1980 period do not permit separate modelling for the two periods. However, we can simply plot inequality-globalization variables for the two periods (see figure 14 of Wan and Wang 2018). The plots clearly show

Table 10.2 Drivers of inequality

	(1)	(2)	(3)	(4)	(5)	(6)	(7)
Ln(GDP per capita)	−45.418** (12.155)	−34.511** (13.225)	−74.941*** (10.710)	−73.633*** (10.133)	−72.331*** (12.220)	−76.151*** (12.306)	−81.083*** (11.557)
Ln(GDP per capita)^2	2.539** (0.710)	2.097** (0.688)	4.321*** (0.641)	4.268*** (0.614)	4.188*** (0.701)	4.404*** (0.721)	4.558*** (0.669)
TFP		−6.910 (4.346)	−7.594 (3.836)	−8.691* (4.128)	−8.573 (4.270)	−8.865 (4.433)	−7.325 (4.550)
Unemployment rate			0.188** (0.072)	0.199** (0.068)	0.194** (0.069)	0.200* (0.079)	0.178* (0.086)
Urbanization				−0.103 (0.100)	−0.097 (0.121)	−0.074 (0.110)	−0.061 (0.107)
Trade					0.004 (0.012)	0.010 (0.015)	0.007 (0.015)
FDI						−0.002 (0.002)	−0.002 (0.002)
Population share aged >65 years							0.573*** (0.133)
Asia × Ln(GDP per capita)	74.637*** (13.534)	74.770*** (15.722)	119.925*** (7.524)	115.175*** (6.633)	113.592*** (9.711)	116.420*** (9.948)	122.236*** (9.717)
Asia × Ln(GDP per capita)^2	−3.998*** (0.754)	−4.273*** (0.846)	−6.752*** (0.435)	−6.401*** (0.423)	−6.294*** (0.559)	−6.397*** (0.578)	−6.601*** (0.557)
Asia × TFP		14.014*** (3.169)	20.927*** (3.341)	20.063*** (3.613)	19.813*** (3.750)	17.233** (4.874)	16.250** (4.728)
Asia × Unemployment rate			−0.097 (0.109)	−0.029 (0.071)	−0.020 (0.083)	−0.058 (0.114)	−0.054 (0.124)
Asia × Urbanization				−0.014** (0.004)	−0.018 (0.012)	−0.025 (0.014)	−0.024 (0.015)
Asia × Trade					−0.016 (0.088)	−0.040 (0.076)	−0.047 (0.070)
Asia × FDI						0.062 (0.041)	0.071 (0.041)
Asia × Population share aged >65 years							−0.425** (0.130)
Constant	187.117*** (45.555)	132.742* (57.864)	287.351*** (42.268)	289.373*** (33.577)	284.322*** (42.595)	295.917*** (42.919)	316.460*** (40.262)
Country dummy	Y	Y	Y	Y	Y	Y	Y
Year dummy	Y	Y	Y	Y	Y	Y	Y
N	1344	1106	987	982	982	960	960
Adjusted R^2	0.841	0.867	0.898	0.901	0.901	0.900	0.900

Notes: Robust standard errors in parentheses; *$P<0.1$, **$P<0.05$, ***$P<0.01$.

Source: Authors' estimation based on PWT, WDI, and WIID data.

that both trade and FDI are positively correlated with inequality in Asian countries in both periods.

What about the effect of land reform? Land reform broadly means regulation of ownership, operation, leasing, sales, and inheritance of land (Ghatak and Roy 2007). Several countries are known to have undertaken land reform in Asia: China, India, Japan, the Philippines, Sri Lanka, South Korea, Taiwan, and Vietnam (see appendix C of Wan and Wang 2018). To estimate the effect of land reform on inequality, a dummy variable (*land reform* = 1) interacted with the reciprocal of time trend (to ensure that the impacts of land reform possibly decline over time) is added to Equation (7). Here, the country fixed effect must be removed, otherwise the effect of land reform is not estimable. figure 15 of Wan and Wang (2018) indicates that land reform did help reduce inequality. However, this effect was only visible in the first few years after land reform began and it diminishes over time and converges to 0, much as expected.

4.2 Costs of Inequality

Inequality can be detrimental to growth (Wan et al. 2006). First, a higher inequality implies more individuals facing credit constraints under an imperfect capital market. Consequently, they cannot carry out productive investments (Galor and Zeira 1993; Fishman and Simhon 2002). Second, worsening distribution generates a rise in the fertility rate among, and less investment in human capital of, the poor (De La Croix and Doepke 2004). Third, increasing inequality may lead to weaker domestic demand, constraining the economy. This is particularly relevant to Asia, which saves more and consumes less. Fourth, growing disparity increases the pressure for redistribution, deterring investment incentives (Alesina and Rodrik 1994; Persson and Tabellini 1994). Fifth, enlarged gaps mean a more unstable socio-political environment for economic activities (Benhabib and Rustichini 1996). Finally, rising inequality adversely affects crime rate and health (Li et al. 2019; Yao et al. 2019). Empirically, Dabla-Norris et al. (2015) find that a 1 percentage point rise in the income share of the top 20 per cent lowers GDP growth by 0.08 percentage points in the following five years. On the contrary, a 1 percentage point increase in the income share of the bottom 20 per cent is correlated with a 0.38 percentage point rise in economic growth.

To quantify the effect of inequality on economic growth, the following model can be estimated:

$$
\begin{aligned}
GDP\ per\ capita = f\,(& Gini,\ Capital\ stock,\ Human\ capital,\ TFP, \\
& Sector\ ratio,\ Trade,\ Gini \times Asia,\ Capital\ stock \times Asia, \\
& Human\ capital \times Asia,\ TFP \times Asia,\ Sector\ ratio \times Asia, \\
& Trade \times Asia) \qquad (8)
\end{aligned}
$$

where sector ratio is defined as the share of value-added of the manufacturing industry to value-added of the primary industry (see Bourguignon and Morrisson 1998). Other variables are self-explanatory.

Results in Table 10.3 confirm the adverse effect of inequality on GDP per capita. This relationship is rather robust and stable. More specifically, every 1 percentage point increase in the Gini coefficient leads to a decline of GDP per capita, on average, by US$209. Other estimation results are largely consistent with a priori expectations.

As discussed earlier, rising inequality means higher poverty for a given economic pie because transfers from the poor to the rich push more people into poverty. This can be defined as the poverty cost of inequality. This cost can be easily simulated by holding GDP at the level in the base or current year and letting inequality change from the base year level to the latest level. Table 10.4 presents the results, in total, 248.4 million (under US$3.20 poverty line) and 145.09 million (under the US$1.90 poverty line) people who could have been but were not lifted out of poverty due to rising inequality. The cost largely came from China (212.57 million and 114.18 million), followed by India, Indonesia, and Bangladesh.

5. Summary and Conclusions

It is useful to note several limitations of this chapter. First, multidimensional poverty is not considered, largely due to data unavailability. Second, UNU-WIDER is working on the next version of the WIID database, which will provide more and better inequality estimates. One may examine the robustness of our results using the improved database when it becomes available. Finally, the poverty decomposition framework overlooks the dynamic nature of the growth–poverty–inequality triangle. Changes in inequality may affect future growth, indirectly influencing poverty in subsequent years. In particular, it is possible that the higher the initial inequality, the smaller the effect of the same growth on poverty. How to incorporate these dynamics into poverty decomposition represents a topic for future research. Despite these limitations, some important findings and conclusions can be drawn from the analyses and discussions of this chapter, as summarized below.

Asia has experienced rapid growth in the post-Second World War period, where East Asia has been the star performer. Asia's fast growth has contributed to significant poverty reductions in the region. According to our estimates, Asia's poverty rate under the US$3.20 poverty line dropped from 73.57 per cent in 1965 to 9.69 per cent in 2014. The corresponding decrease under the US$1.90 poverty line is from 48.52 per cent in 1965 to 2.58 per cent in 2014, implying eradication of abject poverty at the aggregate regional level under the 3 per cent threshold of the World Bank. At the sub-regional level, in 1965 Southeast Asia was the poorest. By 2014, however, South Asia, which is the only sub-region that had not managed

Table 10.3 The effect of inequality on growth

	(1)	(2)	(3)	(4)	(5)	(6)
Gini coefficient	108.434* (45.961)	25.289 (41.634)	38.611 (33.510)	43.223 (23.206)	43.695 (25.741)	29.962 (22.742)
Capital stock per capita		9.4e+04*** (1.2e+04)	9.3e+04*** (1.3e+04)	1.0e+05*** (9261.137)	5.3e+04*** (1.1e+04)	5.0e+04*** (6765.451)
Human capital index			−1.6e+03 (4081.721)	263.301 (3717.562)	176.738 (3897.517)	−1.3e+03 (3569.102)
TFP				1.2e+04*** (2608.077)	1.1e+04*** (2628.943)	1.2e+04*** (1865.266)
Ratio of manufacturing industry to primary industry					394.522*** (32.538)	346.926*** (34.701)
Trade						43.786*** (6.678)
Asia × Gini coefficient	−211.995** (60.709)	−137.154** (48.045)	−160.447*** (33.972)	−231.866*** (47.420)	−223.370*** (47.829)	−209.261*** (41.207)
Asia × Capital stock per capita		2.8e+04*** (3100.348)	5.3e+04*** (1.8e+04)	4.6e+04** (1.8e+04)	6.5e+04*** (1.2e+04)	6.9e+04*** (1.1e+04)
Asia × Human capital index			−3.2e+03 (3517.043)	−2.9e+03 (2373.827)	−788.000 (2605.179)	229.355 (1470.570)
Asia × TFP				−3.8e+03 (2046.457)	−3.8e+03 (2412.322)	−4.2e+03** (1337.840)
Asia × Ratio of manufacturing industry to primary industry					−367.360*** (37.677)	−317.682*** (39.385)
Asia × Trade						−37.259** (9.935)
Constant	2.0e+04*** (1554.350)	1.5e+04*** (2053.074)	2.1e+04 (1.1e+04)	4199.864 (9355.659)	4345.825 (1.1e+04)	5266.407 (1.0e+04)
Country dummy	Y	Y	Y	Y	Y	Y
Year dummy	Y	Y	Y	Y	Y	Y
N	1343	1309	1224	1105	1027	1018
Adjusted R²	0.979	0.985	0.986	0.988	0.991	0.992

Notes: Robust standard errors in parentheses; *$P<0.1$, **$P<0.05$, ***$P<0.01$.

Source: Authors' estimation based on PWT, WDI, and WIID data.

Table 10.4 The impact of inequality on poverty (in millions)

Economy	Period t_0–t_1	Poverty-reducing impact (US\$3.20)	Poverty-increasing impact (US\$3.20)	Population in poverty due to inequality change	Poverty-reducing impact (US\$1.90)	Poverty-increasing impact (US\$1.90)	Population in poverty due to inequality change	Gini t_0	Gini t_1	Gini t_1 – Gini t_0
Bangladesh	1973–2010	0.00	3.97	3.97	0.00	16.57	16.57	32.44	41.56	9.12
Bhutan	2003–2012	0.10	0.00	-0.10	0.06	0.00	-0.06	46.78	35.95	-10.83
China	1981–2013	0.00	212.57	212.57	0.00	114.18	114.18	31	47.3	16.3
Hong Kong	1966–2011	0.00	0.00	0.00	0.00	0.00	0.00	49	48.7	-0.3
Indonesia	1984–2014	0.00	12.80	12.80	0.00	4.73	4.73	30.98	37.34	6.36
India	1965–2012	0.00	32.22	32.22	0.00	15.94	15.94	31.9	34.1	2.2
Iran	1986–2009	4.33	0.00	-4.33	2.06	0.00	-2.06	47.42	37.35	-10.07
Japan	1985–2008	0.00	0.02	0.02	0.00	0.00	0.00	35.92	36.18	0.26
Cambodia	1994–2012	1.47	0.00	-1.47	1.13	0.00	-1.13	38.5	30.76	-7.74
South Korea	1965–2012	0.58	0.00	-0.58	0.58	0.00	-0.58	37.13	30.7	-6.43
Laos	1992–2012	0.00	0.29	0.29	0.00	0.23	0.23	34.31	37.89	3.58
Sri Lanka	1973–2012	0.00	1.35	1.35	0.00	0.55	0.55	37.67	46.29	8.62
Maldives	2002–2010	0.02	0.00	-0.02	0.01	0.00	-0.01	41.31	37	-4.31
Mongolia	1995–2014	0.01	0.00	-0.01	0.00	0.00	0.00	33.2	32.04	-1.16
Malaysia	1979–2014	1.39	0.00	-1.39	0.59	0.00	-0.59	51	38.23	-12.77
Nepal	1984–2010	0.00	0.58	0.58	0.00	0.99	0.99	30.06	32.84	2.78
Pakistan	1987–2013	3.96	0.00	-3.96	1.10	0.00	-1.10	33.3	30.7	-2.6
Philippines	1965–2012	4.39	0.00	-4.39	2.89	0.00	-2.89	48.78	44.77	-4.01
Singapore	1966–2011	0.04	0.00	-0.04	0.02	0.00	-0.02	49.8	47.3	-2.5
Thailand	1969–2013	1.12	0.00	-1.12	0.68	0.00	-0.68	41.95	37.85	-4.1
Taiwan	1968–2013	0.06	0.00	-0.06	0.02	0.00	-0.02	32.6	30.8	-1.8
Vietnam	1992–2014	0.00	2.06	2.06	0.00	1.06	1.06	35.65	37.59	1.94
Total	—	17.47	265.86	248.40	9.17	154.26	145.09	—	—	—

Source: Authors' estimation based on WIID and WDI data.

to end extreme poverty, became the poorest. Under the 3 per cent criterion, Taiwan and Hong Kong eliminated extreme poverty in the late 1960s, Singapore in the mid-1970s, followed by South Korea in the early 1980s, Malaysia in the late 1990s, and Thailand and Indonesia in the new millennium. However, Asia is still some way away from ending moderate poverty. In 2014, there were still 421.48 million moderately poor (with a poverty rate of 9.69 per cent) in Asia.

On the other hand, however, the fast growth has been accompanied by inequality changes. For Asia as a whole, the Gini index increased from 38.43 per cent in 1965 to 42.80 per cent in 2006 before declining in recent years. At the sub-regional level, South Asia is most equal while East Asia is most unequal. Like the regional picture, the sub-regional inequality all exhibited an inverted-U pattern. Further, Asia's inequality is mainly driven by the between-economy disparities. Inequality profiles of individual economies share common trends with their sub-regional counterparts, notwithstanding significant heterogeneity of inequality trends across economies and sub-regions. In particular, inequality worsened significantly in the most populous countries of Asia, including China, India, Indonesia, and Bangladesh.

Drivers of inequality include level of development, technical change, unemployment, urbanization, globalization, and ageing. In particular, unemployment and ageing are found to be positively associated with higher inequality, forcefully demonstrating the importance of employment in containing inequality. Regarding poverty drivers, it is not surprising to find that growth led to poverty reduction but this benign impact is found to have diminished as economies grow. That is, a same 1 percentage point of growth led to less and less poverty reduction over time— a typical phenomenon of 'ripping the low-hanging fruits first'. Other poverty-reducing factors include technological progress and trade exposure. Ageing and unemployment are also found to be positively correlated with poverty, once again demonstrating the importance of employment in fighting poverty.

Despite its recent declines, rises in inequality had cost Asia dearly. Modelling results in our chapter indicate that every 1 percentage point increase in the Gini coefficient led to a decline of GDP per capita by US$209 on average. The cost of inequality also includes offsetting the benign effect of growth on poverty: a higher initial inequality is associated with smaller impacts on poverty of subsequent growths. In total, 248.4 million (under the US$3.20 poverty line) and 145.09 million (under the US$1.90 poverty line) Asians could have been lifted out of poverty but were not, due to rising inequality in the region. This cost largely came from China (212.57 million and 114.18 million), followed by India, Indonesia, and Bangladesh.

Looking ahead, regardless of the ongoing de-globalization tide and possible clashes between the old and new global powers, growth of India is expected to accelerate and growth of China may re-accelerate (Lin et al. 2016), both providing major impetus for continuous development in Asia and beyond. The expected growth is likely to lead to future declines in inequality, based on our confirming the applicability of the Kuznets curve in Asia. Both the continued growth and predicted improvement in income distribution will lead to further poverty reduction in the region (see appendix B of Wan and Wang (2018) for more details), holding other things constant. According to our baseline projection, the moderate poverty rate could decline to 9.4 per cent in 2015, below 3 per cent in 2028, and 0.6 per cent in 2040. Appendix B of Wan and Wang (2018) also provides alternative inequality and poverty projections, depending on the different growth scenarios that are assumed.

Nevertheless, Asia should not be complaisant with the growth prospect and the declining trend in inequality. As the benign growth impact diminishes, the adverse impact of inequality on poverty will gain more importance. Moreover, inequality could undermine growth and the cost of inequality in terms of lost growth and poverty reduction is quite substantial in Asia.

Apart from confirming the inequality-reducing role of land reform and inequality-rising role of globalization, this chapter concludes that technical change is one of the most important drivers of inequality. Consequently, Asia should remain on high alert as artificial intelligence, big data, and information and communications technology (ICT) continue to advance, displacing manual labour and benefitting the skilled and the capitalists. How to generate jobs and reverse or at least halt the declining labour share in national income is a formidable challenge facing policymakers in Asia and beyond (Piketty 2014). On the other hand, these technology progresses may be used to help fight poverty and lower inequality. For example, 'accurate poverty reduction' recently invented and adopted in China relies on big data and ICT for poverty targeting and monitoring among others, which can be more effective than traditional modality of policy interventions.

Another finding worth reiteration is the role of employment in lowering inequality and poverty. This appeals for more public resources on education and training, upgrading the skills and enhancing the human capital of the disadvantaged. Closely related to this is the challenge of ageing, which directly reduces labour supply and worsens poverty. Postponing the retirement age and strategic retraining of older workers ought to be added urgently to the policy agenda of relevant governments.

It can be said that inequality plays a pivotal role in disentangling the growth–inequality–poverty triangle. While market may be most efficient in discovering prices for resource and output allocations, these allocations need not be optimal for maximizing social welfare. Thus, governments must step in when it comes to solving the distributional issue. However, the conventional wisdom of relying on fiscal tools has been proven to be insufficient. Measures or interventions at the stage of primary distribution must be considered. From this perspective, groundbreaking theories and practice (such as the basic income guarantee) are needed to raise the returns to labour relative to capital and raise the returns to the less skilled relative to the highly skilled.

References

Acemoglu, D. (2011). 'Thoughts on Inequality and the Financial Crisis', AEA meeting, Denver, 7 January. Available at: https://economics.mit.edu/files/6348 (accessed September 2018).

ADB (2011). *Asia 2050: Realizing the Asian Century*. India: Sage Publications.

ADB (2012). *Asian Development Outlook: Confronting Rising Inequality in Asia*. Manila: Asian Development Bank.

ADB (2014). 'Poverty in Asia: A Deeper Look'. In *Key Indicators for Asia and the Pacific*. Manila: Asian Development Bank.

Alesina, A., and D. Rodrik (1994). 'Distributive Politics and Economic Growth', *Quarterly Journal of Economics*, 109(2): 465–90.

Anand, S., and P. Segal (2015). 'The Global Distribution of Income'. In A.B. Atkinson and F. Bourguignon (eds) *Handbook of Income Distribution*. Amsterdam: Elsevier.

Benhabib, J., and A. Rustichini (1996). 'Social Conflict and Growth', *Journal of Economic Growth*, 1(1): 129–46.

Bourguignon, F. (2004). 'The Poverty–Growth–Inequality Triangle', mimeo. Washington, DC: World Bank.

Bourguignon, F., and S. Dessus (2009). 'Equity and Development: Political Economy Considerations'. In S. Levy and M. Walton (eds.) *No Growth Without Equity? Inequality, Interests and Competition in Mexico*. Washington, DC: World Bank.

Bourguignon, F., and C. Morrisson (1998). 'Inequality and Development: The Role of Dualism', *Journal of Development Economics*, 57(2): 233–57.

Burgoon, B. (2001). 'Globalization and Welfare Compensation: Disentangling the Ties that Bind', *International Organization*, 55(3): 509–51.

Dabla-Norris, M.E., M.K. Kochhar, M.N. Suphaphiphat, M.F. Ricka, and E. Tsounta (2015). 'Causes and Consequences of Income Inequality: A Global Perspective', International Monetary Fund, IMF Staff Discussion Note SDN/15/13, June. Available at: https://www.imf.org/external/pubs/ft/sdn/2015/sdn1513.pdf (accessed September 2018).

Datt, G., and M. Ravallion (1992). 'Growth and Redistribution Components of Changes in Poverty Measures: A Decomposition with Applications to Brazil and India in the 1980s', *Journal of Development Economics*, 38(2): 275–95.

De La Croix, D., and M. Doepke (2004). 'Inequality and Growth: Why Differential Fertility Matters', *American Economic Review*, 93(4): 1091–113.

ESCAP (2018). *Inequality in Asia and the Pacific in the Era of the 2030 Agenda for Sustainable Development*. Bangkok: United Nations.

Feenstra, R.C., R. Inklaar, and M.P. Timmer (2015). 'The Next Generation of the Penn World Table', *American Economic Review*, 105(10): 3150–82.

Fishman, A., and A. Simhon (2002). 'The Division of Labor, Inequality and Growth', *Journal of Economic Growth*, 7: 117–36.

Fogel, R.W. (2007). 'Capitalism and Democracy in 2040', *Daedalus*, 136: 87–95.

Galor, O., and J. Zeira (1993). 'Income Distribution and Macroeconomics', *Review of Economic Studies*, 60: 35–52.

Ghatak, M., and S. Roy (2007). 'Land Reform and Agricultural Productivity in India: A Review of the Evidence', *Oxford Review of Economic Policy*, 23(2): 251–69.

Gustafsson, B., and M. Johansson (1999). 'In Search of Smoking Guns: What Makes Income Inequality Vary over Time in Different Countries?', *American Sociological Review*, 64(4): 585–605.

Jacobson, M., and F. Occhino (2012). 'Labor's Declining Share of Income and Rising Inequality', *Economic Commentary*, September: 2012–13.

Kuznets, S. (1955). 'Economic Growth and Income Inequality', *American Economic Review*, 45(1): 1–28.

Lam, D. (1997). 'Demographic Variables and Income Inequality'. In R.R. Mark and O. Stark (eds) *Handbook of Population and Family Economics*. Amsterdam: Elsevier Science.

Lewis, W.A. (1955). *The Theory of Economic Growth*. London: George Allen & Unwin.

Li, J., G.H. Wan, C. Wang, and X. Zhang (2019). 'Which Indicator of Income Distribution Explains Crime Better? Evidence from China', *China Economic Review*, 54: 51–72.

Lin, J.Y., G. Wan, and P.J. Morgan (2016). 'Prospects for a Re-Acceleration of Economic Growth in the PRC', *Journal of Comparative Economics*, 44(4): 842–53.

Lindert, P.H. (1978). *Fertility and Scarcity in America*. Princeton, NJ: Princeton University Press.

Lopez-Acevedo, G., and A. Salinas (2000). 'How Mexico's Financial Crisis Affected Income Distribution', World Bank, Washington, DC, World Bank Policy Research Working Paper 2406. Available at: https://ssrn.com/abstract=630778 (accessed September 2018).

Luo, Z., G. Wan, C. Wang, and X. Zhang (2018). 'Aging and Inequality: The Link and Transmission Mechanisms', *Review of Development Economics*, 22(3): 885–903.

Mahler, V. (2004). 'Economic Globalization, Domestic Politics, and Income Inequality in the Developed Countries: A Cross-National Study', *Comparative Political Studies*, 37(9): 1025–53.

Myrdal, G. (1968). *Asian Drama: An Inquiry into the Poverty of Nations*. New York: Pantheon.

Nayyar, D. (2013). *Catch Up: Developing Countries in the World Economy*. Oxford: Oxford University Press.

Persson, T., and G. Tabellini (1994). 'Is Inequality Harmful for Growth? Theory and Evidence', *American Economic Review*, 84: 600–21.

Piketty, T. (2014). *Capital in the Twenty-First Century*. Cambridge, MA: Belknap.

Pinkovskiy, M., and X. Sala-i-Martin (2016). 'Lights, Camera…Income! Illuminating the National Accounts–Household Surveys Debate', *The Quarterly Journal of Economics*, 131(2): 579–631.

Rajan, R. (2010). 'How Inequality Fueled the Crisis', *Project Syndicate*, 9 July. Available at: https://www.project-syndicate.org/commentary/how-inequality-fueled-the-crisis?barrier=accesspaylog (accessed September 2018).

Ravallion, M., and S. Chen (2004). 'Learning from Success: Understanding China's (Uneven) Progress against Poverty', *Finance and Development*, 41(4): 16–19.

Razin, A., E. Sadka, and P. Swagel (2002). 'The Aging Population and the Size of the Welfare State'. *Journal of Political Economy*, 110(4): 900–18.

Repetto, R. (1978). 'The Interaction of Fertility and the Size Distribution of Income', *Journal of Development Studies*, 14(4): 22–39.

Sen, A. (1973). *On Economic Inequality*. Oxford: Clarendon Press.

Shorrocks, A.F., and G.H. Wan (2005). 'Spatial Decomposition of Inequality', *Journal of Economic Geography*, 5(1): 59–82.

Theil, H. (1967). *Economics and Information Theory*. Amsterdam: North-Holland.

United Nations (2015). *Demographic Yearbook* 2014. Available at: https://unstats.un.org/unsd/demographic-social/products/dyb/index.cshtml (accessed September 2018).

Wan, G., and C. Wang (2018). 'Poverty and Inequality in Asia: 1965–2014', UNU-WIDER, Helsinki, WIDER Working Paper 2018/121. Available at: https://www.wider.unu.edu/publication/poverty-and-inequality-asia (accessed April 2019).

Wan, G.H. (2001). 'Changes in Regional Inequality in Rural China: Decomposing the Gini Index by Income Sources', *Australian Journal of Agricultural and Resource Economics*, 45(3): 361–81.

Wan, G.H. (2007). 'Understanding Regional Poverty and Inequality Trends in China: Methodological and Empirical Issues', *Review of Income and Wealth*, 53(1): 28–34.

Wan, G.H., M. Lu, and Z. Chen (2006). 'The Inequality–Growth Nexus in the Short and Long Run: Empirical Evidence from China', *Journal of Comparative Economics*, 34(4): 654–67.

Wang, C., G.H. Wan, and D. Yang (2014). 'Income Inequality in the People's Republic of China: Trends, Determinants, and Proposed Remedies', *Journal of Economic Surveys*, 28(4): 686–708.

Yao, Y., G.H. Wan and D. Meng (2019). 'Income Distribution and Health: Can Polarization Explain Health Outcomes Better than Inequality?', The European Journal of Health Economics, 20(4), 543–557.

Zhang, Y., and G.H. Wan (2006). 'The Impact of Growth and Inequality on Rural Poverty in China', *Journal of Comparative Economics*, 34(4): 694–712.

11

Education and Health

Sudipto Mundle

1. Introduction

The transformation of Asia's education and health profile over the past fifty years has been breathtaking. Myrdal (1968) had not expected this. Comparing the countries of Asia[1] with the developed countries, Myrdal noted several disadvantages in the initial conditions prevailing in Asia. That led him to believe that development of the social system in Asia, including health and education, would be very challenging.

We now see that his assessment was overly pessimistic. Asia transformed at an unprecedented pace despite the disadvantages of its initial conditions. Ironically, social development has been the most striking in East Asia, a sub-region he unfortunately excluded from his canvas (World Bank 1993; ADB 1997; Sen 1998a). However, Asia's experience has fully validated Myrdal's 'institutional approach' of seeing development as the upward movement of a social system through circular causation of all its constitutive elements. Several key constraints he had identified and the consequences he had anticipated are very much in evidence today.

The central idea of the institutional approach, as Myrdal put it, 'is that history and politics, theories and ideologies, economic structures and levels, social stratification, agriculture and industry, population developments, health and education, and so on, must be studied not in isolation but in their mutual relationship'.[2] Myrdal described this process as development of the social system as distinct from the narrower concept of economic development that primarily focuses on the rise in per capita income.

Three aspects of this approach are particularly important for this chapter. First, initial conditions, that is, elements of the social system, lay down the boundaries of what is possible (Myrdal 1968: chapter 14). Second, education and health—investment in man as Myrdal called it—were central to his conception of

---

[1] Myrdal's study was limited to countries of South Asia and Southeast Asia. He called the whole region South Asia and referred to today's South Asia as either the Indian subcontinent or 'India and Pakistan'. The coverage of this chapter is limited to mainland Asia, excluding West Asia, the Central Asian republics and island economies of the Indo-Pacific region.

[2] Myrdal (1968: preface).

development (Myrdal 1968: vol. III). Third, in the process of cumulative causation the spread of education and healthcare are to be seen not in isolation but in their relationship with all the other elements of the social system (Myrdal 1968: appendix 2).

This chapter traces the spread of education and healthcare in Asia during the past fifty years through a similar methodological lens. After the Second World War, new postcolonial states came to power across much of Asia. Most were 'developmental states' aspiring to lead the transformation of their countries into developed societies at the quickest possible time.[3] Development of education and health services were important components of this agenda. This was partly because of their intrinsic value in improving the quality of life, as was recognized by Myrdal (1968) and much emphasized subsequently by Sen (1998a, 1999). But possibly more importantly it was because political leaders of the time recognized the instrumental value of education and health for promoting growth, the human capital relationship that was originally highlighted in modern economic literature by Schultz (1961) and later incorporated in the endogenous growth theories of the 1990s (Grossman and Helpman 1994; Pack 1994; Romer 1994).[4]

There were differences in the initial conditions under which development programmes were launched in different countries, including differences in levels of income, the nature of the postcolonial states and the specific policies they followed. By the late 1960s there were already large differences in the education and health status of different Asian countries. There were also large differences in the pace of their subsequent development. Social development in South Asia lagged behind social development in Southeast Asia, which lagged behind social development in East Asia, with some important exceptions to this general pattern.

Trends common to most countries are discussed in this chapter, along with the variations across countries. Section 2 presents a comparative analysis of the spread of education across countries along with some country experiences. Section 3 presents a similar comparative analysis of trends in health conditions across countries and some country experiences.[5] Section 4 pulls together the threads of the analysis to draw some conclusions, admittedly tentative, on why the social development outcomes of different countries/sub-regions in Asia have differed

---

[3] Chalmers Johnson (1982) originally formulated the concept of a 'developmental state' in the context of Japan. He contrasted the 'plan rational' state which led state-guided capitalist development to the Western liberal concept of the 'market rational' state that enabled market-led capitalist development. The concept was subsequently applied to South Korea (henceforth Korea) and Taiwan by Amsden (1989) and Wade (1990) among others. A large body of literature has since emerged applying the concept to other countries, the central idea being that of key state actors committed to the goal of rapid development. Accelerated industrialization and industrial policy aimed at achieving global competitiveness in selected industries were core components of their strategies. But, typically, their goal was a wider agenda of comprehensive national development (Wade 2018b).

[4] On the relationship between education, human capital formation, and growth in a specifically Asian context see Tilak (2002).

[5] More detailed country experiences are presented in appendices 1 and 2 of Mundle (2018b). These accounts capture the rich variety of country experiences across the whole region.

widely. Based on these conclusions some speculations are offered about possible trends during the next twenty-five years.

2. The Spread of Education

2.1 The Observed Trends Across Countries

A quantitative picture of the spread of education is presented in Tables 11.1 and 11.2.[6] The spread of primary education is best captured by the net primary enrolment rate (PER), which corrects for enrolment of children older than the normal primary education age cohort. By 1971, most countries in East Asia, the richest sub-region, had already achieved a near universal PER (>95 per cent). China is the only country in the sub-region that experienced some regression. Net primary enrolment in China rose to 94 per cent by 1987 then regressed to 89 per cent (2014).

In South Asia, the poorest sub-region and demographically the largest, PERs in 1971 were among the lowest in Asia, amounting to only 60 per cent, 50 per cent or even less.[7] But the rates have improved significantly in all South Asian countries over the past fifty years. Bangladesh, India and Nepal are approaching near universal PERs now (2014). Sri Lanka is a remarkable positive outlier, having achieved a net PER of over 78 per cent by 1977 and a near universal PER by 1985. Afghanistan and Pakistan are still a long way away from this milestone, but enrolment rates have improved significantly in both countries.

PER trends in the countries of Southeast Asia lie between the trends in East and South Asia, with large variations around this general pattern. A near universal PER had already been achieved by 1971 in Singapore and soon thereafter in the Philippines (1976) and Vietnam (1977). But 1971 PERs were quite low in Lao PDR and Myanmar.[8] Most countries in the sub-region had achieved near universal net PER by 2014. The exception is Indonesia, where the net PER has regressed to 89 per cent after having peaked at 98 per cent in 1985.

The robustness of enrolment trends has been checked against trends in primary completion rates (PCRs)[9] since dropouts can be quite significant in low per capita income countries. In some countries the initial PCR was very low but increased rapidly over the next fifty years. In other countries the PCR was already high in 1971. In China, the PCR in 2014 was lower than in 1987, similar to the

---

[6] The years 1971, 1985, 2000, and 2014 in the Tables are approximate benchmarks. For some countries the data refer to the years nearest to these benchmark years for which they are available. Details are given in the notes to Tables 11.1 and 11.2.

[7] Afghanistan, for instance, had a net PER of only 27% reported in 1974.

[8] No estimate is available for Cambodia until 2000.

[9] The PCR is the ratio of the number of students at the end of the final primary year, net of students repeating the year, to the size of the corresponding age cohort. It does not net out students older than the relevant age cohort. The ratio can therefore exceed 100%.

Table 11.1 Primary education

Country	Population (millions) (1) 2016	Per capita GNI (at current prices in US dollars) (2) 2014	Primary enrolment rate (net) (3) 1971	(4) 1985	(5) 2000	(6) 2014	Primary enrolment rate (net), gender parity index (GPI) (7) 1971	(8) 2014	Primary completion rate (9) 1970	(10) 1985	(11) 2000	(12) 2014	Primary completion rate, gender parity index (GPI) (13) 1971	(14) 2014
East Asia	**1,559.9**	**10,827**	**98.3**	**94.7**	**90.2**	**90.1**	**0.9**	**1.0**	**102.4**	**102.1**	**86.5**	**96.8**	**1.0**	**1.0**
Japan	127.0	39,195	99.3	99.4	97.8	98.3	1.0[e]	1.0[f]	105.1[g]	99.4	102.4	102.1[j]	1.0	1.0[l]
Republic of Korea	51.2	28,099	95.9	98.6	99.0	94.6	1.0	1.0[f]	96.0[g]	105.2	103.6	96.5	1.0	1.0
Mongolia	3.0	3,842	–	94.4[b]	90.0	95.1	1.0[e]	1.0	95.7[g]	98.0[h]	87.0	98.3[j]	–	1.0
China	1,378.7	7,588	–	94.1[b]	89.1[c]	89.1	0.9[e]	1.0[f]	–	102.2[h]	84.4[i]	96.3	–	1.0
Southeast Asia	**638.2**	**4,034**	**79.7**	**95.4**	**93.3**	**93.0**	**0.9**	**1.0**	**56.5**	**87.6**	**92.2**	**100.3**	**0.8**	**1.0**
Singapore	5.6	55,107	–	96.1[b]	95.7	99.9[d]	0.9[e]	1.0	95.1	–	–	98.7	1.0[k]	–
Malaysia	31.2	10,814	86.7	97.2[b]	98.4	99.6	0.9[e]	1.0[f]	80.6[g]	93.9	100.6	101.9	0.9[k]	1.0
Philippines	103.3	3,445	96.8[a]	94.4	89.5[c]	95.7[d]	–	1.0[f]	–	89.2	100.4[i]	101.0	–	1.1[l]
Thailand	68.9	5,633	75.5[a]	–	98.9[c]	90.9	0.9	1.0	37.5[g]	71.4[h]	84.9	93.3	–	0.9[l]
Vietnam	92.7	1,916	97.3[a]	91.1	97.2	98.0[d]	1.0[e]	–	81.5[g]	–	99.0	106.2	–	1.0
Indonesia	261.1	3,484	70.1	97.8	92.0[c]	88.9	0.9	1.0	51.9[g]	94.2	93.8[i]	102.9	–	0.9
Cambodia	15.8	1,032	–	–	92.4	95.1	0.8	1.0	–	46.0[h]	51.1[i]	96.3	–	1.0
Myanmar	52.9	1,272	63.7	–	92.2	96.2	0.9	1.0[f]	35.7[g]	–	76.5	85.1	0.7	1.0[l]
Lao PDR	6.8	1,929	–	64.9[b]	75.6	97.2	0.6	1.0	–	42.1	67.5	100.3	–	1.0
South Asia	**1,765.2**	**1,500**	**59.7**	**74.7**	**78.7**	**89.9**	**0.6**	**1.0**	**35.0**	**58.6**	**69.8**	**93.2**	**0.5**	**1.3**
Sri Lanka	21.2	3,760	78.5[a]	98.3[b]	99.7[c]	97.2	0.9[e]	1.0	63.5	83.7	107.3	98.0	–	1.0

India	1,324.2	1,557	61.4	77.5[b]	79.8	92.3[d]	0.7	1.0[f]	39.7[g]	63.2[h]	71.8	97.5	0.5	1.1
Bangladesh	163.0	1,158	50.8[a]	61.1	91.7[c]	90.5[d]	0.5[e]	1.0[f]	43.3[g]	28.5[h]	64.4[i]	98.5[j]	0.5[k]	1.2[l]
Pakistan	193.2	1,418	–	–	58.9[c]	72.7	0.4	0.9	–	–	64.5[i]	73.7	–	0.8
Nepal	29.0	709	27.1[a]	60.6[b]	72.7	94.1	0.2[e]	1.0	–	46.9[h]	67.2	104.1	–	1.1
Afghanistan	34.7	657	–	28.2[b]	–	85.7	0.2[e]	–	16.8[g]	19.2	29.6[i]	–	0.2[k]	–

Notes: Data are sorted with respect to mean years of schooling in 2014.
Some figures are not for the exact same year mentioned in the Table. Details are given below.

[a] Afghanistan 1974; Bangladesh 1970: Philippines 1976; Sri Lanka 1977; Thailand 1973; Vietnam 1977.

[b] Afghanistan 1993; China 1987; India 1990; Lao PDR 1988; Malaysia 1994; Mongolia 1987; Nepal 1984; Singapore 1990 (from data.gov.sg); Sri Lanka 1986. Earliest available data for Cambodia are for 1997 and the value of NER at primary level was 83.12.

[c] Bangladesh 2005; China 1997; Indonesia 2001; Pakistan 2002; Philippines 2001; Sri Lanka 2001; Thailand 2006; Singapore (from data.gov.sg).

[d] Bangladesh 2010; India 2013; Philippines 2015; Singapore 2016; Vietnam 2013.

[e] Afghanistan 1974; Bangladesh 1970: China 1976; Japan 1975; Malaysia 1970; Mongolia 1975; Nepal 1970; Singapore 1970; Sri Lanka 1970; Thailand 1973; Vietnam 1976. Data collected from Econstat for Cambodia, China, Lao PDR, Malaysia, Mongolia, Pakistan, Singapore, Sri Lanka and Vietnam.

[f] Bangladesh 2010; China 2007; India 2013; Japan 2013; Korea Republic 2013; Malaysia 2006; Myanmar 2010; Philippines 2013. Data collected from Econstat for Cambodia, China and Malaysia. Data for Singapore collected from data.gov.sg.

[g] Afghanistan 1974; Bangladesh 1976; India 1971; Indonesia 1972; Japan 1971; Korea, Rep. 1971; Malaysia 1974; Mongolia 1978; Myanmar 1971; Thailand 1975; Vietnam 1979.

[h] Bangladesh 1981; Cambodia 1994; China 1989; India 1987; Mongolia 1983; Nepal 1988; Thailand 1981.

[i] Afghanistan 1993; Bangladesh 2005; Cambodia 2001; China 2004; Indonesia 2001; Pakistan 2005; Philippines 2001; Sri Lanka 2001.

[j] Bangladesh 2015; Japan 2012; Mongolia 2015; Philippines 2013; Thailand 2015.

[k] Afghanistan 1974; Bangladesh 1976; Malaysia 1974; Singapore 1975 (collected from Econstat).

[l] Bangladesh 2015; Japan 2012; Myanmar 2010; Philippines 2013; Thailand 2015.

Region

East Asia: Japan, Republic of Korea, Mongolia, and China.

Southeast Asia: Singapore, Malaysia, Philippines, Thailand, Vietnam, Indonesia, Cambodia, Myanmar, and Lao PDR.

South Asia: Sri Lanka, India, Bangladesh, Pakistan, Nepal, and Afghanistan.

Regional averages are calculated by applying the population share.

Source: Author, based on data from the World Development Indicators Database.

Table 11.2 Secondary and tertiary education

Country	Secondary school enrolment (gross)				Secondary school enrolment (gross), gender parity index (GPI)		Lower-secondary completion rate				Tertiary school enrolment (gross)				Tertiary School enrolment (gross), gender parity Index (GPI)		Mean years of schooling (primary or higher)			
	(1) 1971	(2) 1985	(3) 2000	(4) 2014	(5) 1971	(6) 2014	(7) 1971	(8) 1985	(9) 2000	(10) 2014	(11) 1971	(12) 1985	(13) 2000	(14) 2014	(15) 1971	(16) 2014	(17) 1971	(18) 1985	(19) 2000	(20) 2014
East Asia	**42.0**	38.7	65.6	95.1	0.7	1.0	82.4	57.6	79.7	98.3	1.8	5.6	13.4	43.2	0.5	1.1	–	4.6	6.7	7.6
Japan	86.5	94.9	101.8	101.7	1.0	1.0	98.5	99.4	103.2[i]	–	17.6	29.0	48.7	63.4	0.4	0.9	–	9.6	10.7	12.5
Republic of Korea	39.7	90.6	98.4	98.5	0.6	1.0	44.4	96.5	98.2	100.1	7.2	31.6	78.4	94.2	0.3	0.8	5.4	9.4	10.7	11.6[s]
Mongolia	64.0	87.5[b]	65.1	91.5[d]	1.0[e]	1.0[f]	52.7[g]	84.6[h]	62.7	106.6[j]	21.0	23.8	30.2	64.3	–	1.4	–	7.7[q]	9.0	10.0[s]
China	38.0	31.4	61.0	94.3	0.7[e]	1.0	–	52.3[h]	76.9[i]	98.2	0.1[k]	2.5	7.7	39.4	0.5[o]	1.2	–	4.0[q]	6.2	7.0[s]
Southeast Asia	**26.3**	39.5	57.7	83.9	0.7	1.0	13.9	40.3	66.3	83.9	5.0	10.4	18.8	32.3	0.6	1.2	3.4	4.2	6.8	7.9
Singapore	–	95.1[b]	98.7	108.1	–	1.0	–	–	–	–	6.5[k]	23.5	45.3[m]	86.6	0.4[o]	1.1	–	3.9[q]	10.5[r]	11.3
Malaysia	35.2	53.7	66.2	77.7	0.7	1.1	–	90.8[h]	87.7	84.7	3.9[k]	5.6	25.7	27.6	0.6[o]	1.5	4.0	4.0[q]	8.6	10.1[s]
Philippines	47.5	67.2	74.7[c]	88.4[d]	–	1.1[f]	–	66.0[h]	67.7[i]	82.2[j]	17.6	27.8	30.3[m]	35.8	1.3	1.3	5.0	6.3	7.7	9.1[s]
Thailand	18.1	30.6	62.8[c]	127.7	0.7	1.0	23.0[g]	–	81.3[i]	84.0[j]	2.9	20.7	34.9	52.5	0.7[o]	1.3	2.8	3.7[q]	7.2[r]	8.3
Vietnam	35.9	34.8[b]	57.8[c]	78.4[d]	1.0[e]	–	11.4[g]	–	68.3	93.8	1.7[k]	1.9[l]	9.4	30.5	0.7[o]	1.0	6.3	6.3[q]	4.0[r]	7.8[s]
Indonesia	18.6	34.3	55.1	82.5	0.6	1.0	12.9	38.8	69.1[i]	91.2[j]	2.9	6.1	14.9	31.1	0.4[o]	1.1	2.3	3.1[q]	7.8	7.8
Cambodia	8.4	27.8[b]	17.2	45.1[d]	0.4	0.9[f]	–	–	17.4[i]	45.1	1.4	0.3	2.5	13.1[n]	0.3[o]	0.8[p]	–	5.2	5.7	5.8[s]
Myanmar	20.1	23.1	36.3	51.3	0.6	1.0	12.9	–	32.6	48.7	1.7	4.8	10.6	13.5[n]	0.6[o]	1.2[p]	1.4	2.7[q]	3.1	4.7
Lao PDR	3.7	21.3	34.2	57.2	0.4	0.9	1.4	22.0[h]	35.3	53.9	0.2	1.5	2.7	17.3	0.2	0.9	–	2.5	3.9	4.6
South Asia	**22.7**	33.5	42.5	69.5	0.4	1.0	20.3	42.0	50.8	79.0	4.2	5.3	8.1	22.2	0.3	1.0	1.3	2.1	4.2	5.3
Sri Lanka	48.3	61.1	76.5[c]	99.7[d]	1.1[e]	1.0[f]	37.6	73.7	89.4[i]	96.2	1.1	3.7	4.8	19.3	0.7	1.3	4.7	5.7[q]	10.5[r]	10.9
India	24.0	37.4[b]	45.1	74.3	0.4	1.0	–	42.4[h]	53.5[i]	85.6	5.0	5.8	9.5	25.5	0.3	1.0	1.3	2.2[q]	4.4	5.4[s]

Bangladesh	20.5[a]	20.1	48.1	63.5[d]	0.3[e]	1.1[f]	–	–	53.2	67.6[j]	2.1[k]	5.0	5.4	13.4	0.1[o]	0.7	1.1	2.1[q]	4.2[r]	5.2
Pakistan	16.7	19.6	22.9[c]	41.6	0.3	0.8	–	–	33.4[i]	50.5	2.3	3.0[l]	2.7[m]	10.4	0.3	1.1	1.6	1.7	2.7[r]	5.2
Nepal	11.1[a]	26.8	36.0	66.9	0.2[e]	1.1	–	31.6[h]	42.7	82.8	1.6[k]	3.4	4.2	15.8	0.3[o]	1.0[p]	0.2	0.6[q]	2.4	3.3[s]
Afghanistan	9.4	13.5	13.0[c]	55.7	0.1	0.6	9.7[g]	13.6	17.0[i]	–	0.9	2.2[l]	1.3[m]	8.7	0.2[o]	0.3	0.7	0.8[q]	2.1	3.1[s]

Notes: Data are sorted with respect to mean years of schooling in 2014.
Some figures are not for the exact same year mentioned in the Table. Details are given below.

[a]   Bangladesh 1973; Nepal 1972; Vietnam 1976.

[b]   Cambodia 1991; India 1986; Mongolia 1986; Singapore 1990 (from data.gov.sg); Vietnam 1990.

[c]   Afghanistan 2001; Pakistan 2003; Philippines 2001; Sri Lanka 1995; Thailand 2001; Vietnam 1998; Singapore (from data.gov.sg).

[d]   Bangladesh 2015; Cambodia 2008; Mongolia 2015; Philippines 2013; Sri Lanka 2013; Singapore (from data.gov.sg); Vietnam (data for 2008 from London 2011).

[e]   Bangladesh 1973; China 1976; Mongolia 1974; Nepal 1972; Sri Lanka 1976; Vietnam 1976.

[f]   Bangladesh 2015; Cambodia 2008; Mongolia 2015; Philippines 2013; Sri Lanka 2013; Singapore (from data.gov.sg).

[g]   Afghanistan 1973; Mongolia 1974; Thailand 1975; Vietnam 1979.

[h]   China 1990; India 1987; Lao PDR 1988; Malaysia 1998; Mongolia 1980; Nepal 1988; Philippines 1990.

[i]   Afghanistan 2005; Cambodia 1997; China 1997; India 2002; Indonesia 2002; Japan 1994; Pakistan 2004; Philippines 2001; Sri Lanka 2001; Thailand 2007.

[j]   Bangladesh 2013; Indonesia 2015; Mongolia 2010; Philippines 2014; Thailand 2015.

[k]   Bangladesh 1970; China 1970; Malaysia 1979; Nepal 1974; Singapore 1970; Vietnam 1976.

[l]   Afghanistan 1986; Pakistan 1986; Vietnam 1986; Singapore (from data.gov.sg).

[m]   Afghanistan 2003; Myanmar 2001; Pakistan 2003; Philippines 2001; Sri Lanka 1994; Singapore (from data.gov.sg).

[n]   Cambodia 2015; Myanmar 2012; Singapore (from data.gov.sg).

[o]   Afghanistan 1979; Bangladesh 1972; Cambodia 1972; China 1974; Indonesia 1972; Malaysia 1979; Myanmar 1972; Nepal 1976; Singapore 1970; Thailand 1976; Vietnam 1976.

[p]   Cambodia 2015; Myanmar 2012; Nepal 2015; Singapore (from data.gov.sg).

[q]   Afghanistan 1979; Bangladesh 1981; China 1982; India 1981; Indonesia 1980; Malaysia 1980; Mongolia 1990; Myanmar 1983; Nepal 1981; Singapore 1980; Sri Lanka 1981; Thailand 1980; Vietnam 1979. Data collected from the Human Development Report (UNHDR) for Cambodia, Japan, Lao PDR, and Mongolia.

[r]   Bangladesh 2001; Pakistan 2005; Singapore 2005; Sri Lanka 2001; Thailand 2004; Vietnam 1989. Data collected from the Human Development Report (UNHDR) for Afghanistan, Cambodia, Japan, Lao PDR, Myanmar, and Nepal.

[s]   Afghanistan 2012; Cambodia 2012; China 2010; India 2011; Republic of Korea 2010; Malaysia 2010; Mongolia 2010; Nepal 2011; Philippines 2013; Vietnam 2009. Data collected from the Human Development Report (UNHDR) for Afghanistan, Bangladesh, Cambodia, Japan, and Lao PDR.

Region

East Asia: Japan, Republic of Korea, Mongolia, and China.
Southeast Asia: Singapore, Malaysia, Philippines, Thailand, Vietnam, Indonesia, Cambodia, Myanmar, and Lao PDR.
South Asia: Sri Lanka, India, Bangladesh, Pakistan, Nepal, and Afghanistan.
Regional averages are calculated by applying the population share.

Source: Author, based on data from the World Development Indicators Database and UNESCO Institute for Statistics (Education Dataset).

regression in PER noted earlier. But it bottomed out in 2004 and is now recovering. This is discussed further below.[10] In Indonesia, another country that experienced regression, the PCR has now gone up to over 100 per cent after having regressed slightly in 2001.

Secondary gross enrolment rates (GERs) were much lower than PERs throughout Asia in 1971 (Table 11.2).[11] But by 2014 East Asia had achieved a near universal secondary GER at 94 per cent. Secondary enrolment had also increased very significantly by 2014 in Southeast Asia and South Asia at 85 per cent and 70 per cent respectively. But there are large variations around these averages. In Southeast Asia it ranges from only 45 per cent in Cambodia to 128 per cent in Thailand. In South Asia it ranges from 42 per cent in Pakistan to 100 per cent in Sri Lanka.

Completion of basic education, six years of primary education plus two years of lower-secondary education, is an important milestone since many countries have mandated eight years of compulsory basic education. Streaming of students between 'academic' education at higher secondary and tertiary levels and technical and vocational education (TVE) also begins at this stage, setting the boundaries of their life chances for the future. East Asia had achieved a near universal lower-secondary completion rate of 98 per cent by 2014. The countries of Southeast Asia and South Asia were not too far behind with 84 per cent and 79 per cent respectively. But again, there are large variations around these averages. It ranges from 45 per cent in Cambodia to 100 per cent in Singapore in Southeast Asia, and from only 17 per cent in Afghanistan to 96 per cent in Sri Lanka in South Asia.

Barring a couple of countries, the general trend of access to primary and secondary education in Asia is one of convergence. The countries of Southeast Asia and South Asia have been catching up with East Asia. The tertiary enrolment rate (TER) picture is different. Starting from negligible levels in 1971, the TER in East Asia went up to 41 per cent by 2014. Southeast Asia and South Asia had somewhat higher TERs initially (Table 11.2) but were then left behind by East Asia. The average TERs in Southeast Asia and South Asia are 32 per cent and 22 per cent respectively.

As usual there are large variations around these sub-regional averages. In East Asia, Korea has achieved a near universal TER. In Southeast Asia, Singapore has a very high TER of 87 per cent. Philippines already had a high TER of 18 per cent in 1971 and this has risen further to 36 per cent. Cambodia and Myanmar on the other hand have TERs of only 13 per cent. In South Asia, India had a TER of

---

[10] See also the China country note in Mundle (2018b: appendix 1).

[11] This is despite the fact that we are comparing gross enrolment rates at the secondary level with net enrolment rates at the primary level, which are by definition lower than gross rates. Unfortunately net enrolment data comparable across countries are not available at the secondary or tertiary levels. Since the numerator in gross enrolment rates does not correct for enrolment of students older than the age cohort used for the denominator, gross enrolment rates can sometimes exceed 100%.

5 per cent in 1971 that has now risen to 26 per cent.[12] At the other end, Pakistan and Afghanistan have TERs of only 10 per cent and 9 per cent respectively.

There was significant gender disparity in PERs and PCRs in the initial period in many countries, especially in South Asia. However, these had been largely eliminated by 2014 (Table 11.1). The picture is very similar for gender disparity in secondary enrolment rates (SERs) and TERs (Table 11.2). The exception is Afghanistan, where there was considerable gender disparity in 1974 in the PER and PCR. Afghanistan being a post-conflict country with patchy information, more recent data on PER or PCR is not available. But estimates available for SER and TER indicate that significant gender disparity still persists.

The quality of education is much harder to assess. The standardized global test Programme for International Students Assessment (PISA) conducted by the OECD enables some limited cross-country comparisons of education quality (OECD 2018). Unfortunately, only six Asian countries participated in the latest 2015 PISA test for mathematics, science, and reading—China, Korea, Indonesia, Singapore, Thailand, and Vietnam. Malaysia did participate but was not rated because it did not meet the required testing standards. India participated in the 2009 test, performed very poorly, being ranked near the bottom, and then pulled out of the tests.

Of the participating Asian countries, Singapore was ranked 1st among seventy-seven countries in mathematics, science and also reading. Korea was another high performer, ranked 7th, 11th, and 7th in mathematics, science, and reading respectively. China was ranked 6th in mathematics, 10th in science, and 27th in reading. But it has been pointed out that it was represented by the provinces of Jiangsu, Guangdong, Beijing, and Shanghai, which are more advanced than most other Chinese provinces and therefore not representative. Vietnam also performed above average, being ranked at 22, 8, and 32 respectively for the three tests. Thailand performed below average with ranks of 55, 56, and 59. Indonesia's performance was near the bottom with ranks of 65, 64, and 66 in mathematics, science, and reading.

We cannot generalize about education quality in Asia from the results of just the six participating Asian countries. However, the non-participation in international quality tests itself indicates that most Asian countries have given priority to the quantity of education supply rather than its quality. This is also confirmed by individual country studies.

2.2 Key Experiences of Selected Countries

The education experiences of a large number of individual countries have been summarized in Mundle (2018b: appendix 1). Here only some of the key experiences

---

[12] On this see the India country note in Mundle (2018b: appendix 1).

of a few selected countries are presented to animate the quantitative picture presented above.

2.2.1 The Best Performers: Korea, Singapore, Vietnam, and Sri Lanka

Korea's education policy priorities gradually shifted from primary to secondary to tertiary education as it developed (Mundle 1998). Another notable feature is its focus on cost efficiency, based on high pupil–teacher ratios, control of teacher salaries, etc. Despite Korea's high public education expenditure, resource constraints and rising costs have led to increasing dependence on private provision and private spending. That has, in turn, led to rising inequality in access to both higher secondary and higher education.

Singapore's special feature in education policy is the public financing and provision of education as a merit good, all the way up to tertiary education, and the emphasis on quality through teacher excellence. It is possibly the only country where teacher salaries are comparable to those of doctors, lawyers, and engineers.

Vietnam and Sri Lanka stand out because of their excellent education performance despite their low levels of per capita income. Education development proceeded in Vietnam only after the war ended in 1975, but it has made remarkable progress since then. Its performance in PISA quality tests is already above average. However, despite its rapid growth, public spending has not kept pace with the spread of education. There is increasing dependence on private spending, leading to increasing disparity in access to education between rich and poor regions, rural and urban areas, and rich and poor households. Sri Lanka's most notable policy feature is the public financing of education as a merit good, all the way up to university.

2.2.2 The Weakest Performers: Afghanistan and Pakistan

Afghanistan's education system collapsed during the 1980s in the wake of the civil war. The worst period was during the Taliban rule of 1996–2001, when misogyny peaked. That is still evident in the gender disparity reported in Tables 11.1 and 11.2. Supported by external donors, the present government is attempting to rebuild the education system, with public provision of free, compulsory education for eight years.

Pakistan is the worst performer in Asia after Afghanistan. The country has been ruled for many years by a military dictatorship, which retains effective power even during periods of civilian rule. Education has evidently been a low priority. It remains to be seen whether this will change under the recently elected civilian government.

2.2.3 The Largest Countries: China, India, and Indonesia

China's education policy since 1977 has been based on the three pillars of decentralization, market orientation, and mass higher education. Decentralization, combined with the 'private responsibility' system in agriculture, led to the collapse of the primary education system and eventually a decline in primary enrolment (Table 11.1). The village government responsible for delivering primary education no longer had the resources to do so after the reforms. Primary education is now recovering after being reassigned to the county government. The combination of decentralization and market orientation, that is, private provision and private spending, has also led to growing disparity between rich and poor provinces, rural and urban areas, and between rich and poor households. Finally, China has ring-fenced an education system for especially meritorious students[13] from 'key' schools to 100 higher education institutions (Project 211) and a few world-class universities (Project 985). This has created another dimension of disparity between elite students and the rest.

India's education policy is striking for its elitist bias, the high priority given to higher education instead of universal primary and secondary education. This situation has improved following the Right to Education Act of 2009, which mandates universal free education for eight years. However, the focus on expanding quantity has led to severe neglect of quality. Annual surveys show that learning outcomes are abysmally low and have declined over time.

Indonesia's education services witnessed a massive expansion during 1975–1987, aimed at providing universal primary education. A wave of decentralization reforms followed since 2000 that empowered the local bureaucracy to deliver primary education. The constitutional amendment of 2002, earmarking 20 per cent of government spending for education, was another remarkable move. It has greatly improved access to education, especially among poor children. However, quality has been a casualty, stemming largely from poor teacher quality and the incapacity of the local bureaucracy. Inequality in access to secondary and tertiary education, accentuated by differences of gender, ethnicity, or location is the other major challenge.

2.3 The Spread of Education: Stylized Facts and Major Challenges

In summary the spread of education in Asia during the past fifty years has been dramatic. It has been mostly led by postcolonial developmental states as part of their strategies of development.[14] Initial conditions varied, as did the motives and capacities of the governments, and so did the pace of education development. However, the similarities in patterns of change are more striking than the differences. The principal goal was to increase the access to education, and universalize access to primary education. Barring Afghanistan and Pakistan, all others have now achieved this goal. The access to secondary education has also seen vast increases throughout the region. Many countries, especially in East Asia, have

---

[13] Though reports suggest that children of rich parents also manage to slip inside the fence.
[14] That includes Thailand, which was never formally colonized but was very much a part of the colonial system.

achieved near universal access to secondary education while a few others have lagged behind. Many countries of the region have also achieved very significant expansion of tertiary education. Moreover, as the leading countries have approached the limits of improvement, the lagging countries have been catching up.[15] There is a tendency towards convergence.

An important aspect of Asia's education development experience is the tension between resource requirements and resource availability. Several countries have significantly raised the education share of government spending, but usually this has not been enough. Most countries, barring Singapore and Sri Lanka, have seen the rapid growth of private spending. This has generated a pattern of nested disparities in the access to education: disparity between more and less prosperous regions, disparity between rural and urban areas within each region, and disparity between rich and poor households within rural and urban areas.[16] Another major challenge is the quality of education. Asian governments have mostly focused on quantitative expansion at the expense of quality. Several countries are now beginning to address the problem of poor quality.

Finally, many Asian governments recognize that the content of education needs to be completely overhauled for the emerging knowledge-based society of the twenty-first century. But for most Asian countries, barring Singapore, Korea, China, and Vietnam, a knowledge-based society remains an aspiration not an operational goal.

3. The Spread of Health Services

3.1 The Observed Trends Across Countries

The improvement in Asia's health profile during the past fifty years has been remarkable. There were differences among individual countries in their initial conditions and the pace of change has varied. But large improvements in health conditions have been registered in *all* countries of the region.

These changes are tracked using a set of demographic indicators (Table 11.3) and a set of nutrition and anthropometric indicators (Table 11.4).[17] Life expectancy is taken as the principal indicator of health conditions. Sen (1998b) has suggested that this is, in fact, the true measure of a country's economic success. Life expectancy

---

[15] There are obviously upper limits to these quantitative indicators. Net enrolment rates (NERs) cannot exceed 100%.

[16] This is evident in the countries discussed in Mundle (2018b: appendix 1). Several studies confirm this also for other Asian countries. See, for instance, Government of Malaysia (2013), Sagarik (2014), Saw and Schneider (2015) and UNESCO (2013).

[17] Comparisons across sub-regions or individual countries need to be interpreted with caution because data are not available for some countries for the indicated benchmark years. In such cases the relevant data for the nearest available year have been used. Details are given in the notes to Tables 11.3 and 11.4.

Table 11.3 Health indicators

Country	Population (millions) (1) 2016	Per capita GNI (at current prices in US dollars) (2) 2014	Life expectancy at birth, total (years) (3) 1970	(4) 1985	(5) 2000	(6) 2015	Gender parity index (GPI) of life expectancy at birth (years) (7) 1970	(8) 1985	(9) 2000	(10) 2015	Infant mortality rate (per 1,000 live births) (11) 1970	(12) 1985	(13) 2000	(14) 2015	Maternal mortality rate (modelled estimate, per 100,000 live births) (15) 1990	(16) 2000	(17) 2014
East Asia	1,559.9	10,827	60.21	69.18	72.84	76.93	1.07	1.05	1.05	1.05	74.13	38.78	27.18	8.42	87.92	52.91	25.72
Japan	127.0	39,195	72.0	77.7	81.1	83.8	1.08	1.08	1.09	1.08	13.4	5.5	3.3	2.0	14	10	6
Korea, Rep.	51.2	28,099	62.0	68.5	75.8	82.2	1.12	1.13	1.10	1.08	48.0	20.7	6.4	3.0	21	16	12
China	1,378.7	7,588	59.1	68.5	72.0	76.1	1.06	1.05	1.05	1.04	80.6	42.4	30.1	9.2	97	58	28
Mongolia	3.0	3,842	55.3	58.4	62.9	69.1	1.09	1.08	1.10	1.13	119[a]	94.6	48.6	16.1	186	161	46
Southeast Asia	638.2	4,034	56.73	63.38	67.68	70.84	1.08	1.07	1.08	1.08	88.72	60.34	35.94	21.67	307.87	189.21	107.19
Singapore	5.6	55,107	68.3	73.9	78.0	82.6	1.10	1.07	1.05	1.06	22	8.8	3.0	2.1	12	18	10
Vietnam	92.7	1,916	59.7	68.9	73.1	75.9	1.19	1.14	1.14	1.13	54.3	42.3	23.6	17.6	139	81	54
Malaysia	31.2	10,814	64.5	69.5	72.8	75.2	1.04	1.05	1.06	1.06	42.2	18.7	8.7	7.0	79	58	41
Thailand	68.9	5,633	59.4	67.9	70.6	75.1	1.09	1.09	1.11	1.11	71.6	38.7	19.6	10.8	40	25	21
Indonesia	261.1	3,484	54.5	61.5	66.2	69.0	1.04	1.04	1.05	1.06	112.7	73.6	41.1	22.9	446	265	133
Philippines	103.3	3,445	60.8	63.8	67.2	69.0	1.06	1.08	1.10	1.10	55.5	49.8	30.0	22.1	152	124	117
Cambodia	15.8	1,032	41.6	50.4	58.4	68.5	1.12	1.09	1.08	1.06	177.4[a]	86.6	79.6	27.5	1,020	484	167
Myanmar	52.9	1,272	51.0	56.9	62.1	66.4	1.10	1.08	1.07	1.07	119.3	89.4	65.6	41.4	453	308	184
Lao PDR	6.8	1,929	46.2	51.0	58.9	66.3	1.06	1.05	1.05	1.05	141.0[a]	123.0	82.5	50.4	905	546	213
South Asia	1,765.2	1,500	48.13	55.99	62.82	68.48	0.98	1.01	1.03	1.04	144.11	103.93	68.45	38.75	558.80	382.17	186.51
Sri Lanka	21.2	3,760	64.3	69.2	71.1	75.0	1.06	1.09	1.11	1.09	54.4	25.2	14.1	8.3	75	57	31
Bangladesh	163.0	1,158	47.5	55.6	65.3	72.2	1.00	1.01	1.01	1.05	149.2	117.9	64.0	29.7	569	399	188
Nepal	29.0	709	40.5	50.1	62.3	69.9	1.01	1.02	1.04	1.05	176.8	119.5	60.3	29.6	901	548	275
India	1,324.2	1,557	47.7	55.8	62.6	68.3	0.98	1.01	1.03	1.05	142.6	100.5	66.6	36.2	556	374	181
Pakistan	193.2	1,418	52.9	58.6	62.8	66.3	1.00	1.02	1.03	1.03	144.2	115.3	88.1	65.7	431	306	184
Afghanistan	34.7	657	36.7	45.6	55.5	63.3	1.04	1.04	1.04	1.04	204.8	141.3	90.8	54.9	1,340	1,100	425

Notes: Data are sorted with respect to life expectancy at birth in 2015.

[a] Mortality rate, infant: figures for some countries are other than 1970. Cambodia 1975; Lao PDR 1978; Mongolia 1978.

Source: Author, based on the World Development Indicators.

Table 11.4 Nutrition indicators

Country	(1) Population (millions) 2016	(2) Per capita GNI (at current prices in US dollars) 2014	Prevalence of undernourishment (percentage of population)				Prevalence of stunting, height for age (percentage of children under five)				Prevalence of stunting, height for age, female percentage of children under five) (11) 2014	Prevalence of wasting, weight for height (percentage of children under five)			
			(3) 1991	(4) 2000	(5) 2014	(6) 2015	(7) 1971	(8) 1985	(9) 2000	(10) 2014		(12) 1971	(13) 1985	(14) 1995	(15) 2014
East Asia	**1,559.9**	**10,827**	**23.24**	**14.76**	**9.07**	**9.17**		**35.77**	**17.28**	**8.99**	**8.51**		**4.50**	**4.99**	**2.25**
Japan	127.0	39,195	–	2.5	2.5[a]	–		8.3[c]		7.1[e]	6.5[f]		1.2[h]	–	2.3[j]
Korea, Rep.	51.2	28,099	5	5	5	5			2.5[d]	2.5[e]	2.7[f]		–	–	0.9[j]
China	1,378.7	7,588	23.9	16.2	9.8	9.3		38.3[c]	17.8	9.4[e]	8.9[f]		4.8[h]	5.0	2.3[j]
Mongolia	3.0	3,842	29.9	38.2	21.5	20.5			29.8	10.8[e]	14.7[f]		–	2.3[i]	1.0[j]
Southeast Asia	**638.2**	**4,034**	**29.62**	**22.61**	**10.06**	**9.74**	**57.7**	**47.9**	**38.0**	**30.2**	**30.1**	**9.8**	**8.5**	**8.4**	**9.7**
Singapore	5.6	55,107	–	–	–	–	10.7[b]		4.4			7.7[g]		3.6	–
Vietnam	92.7	1,916	45.6	28.1	11.8	11		64.1[c]	43.4	23.3[e]	23.2[f]		11.1[h]	13.5[i]	4.4
Malaysia	31.2	10,814	5.1	5	5	5			20.7[d]	17.2[e]	17.2[f]			15.3[i]	–
Thailand	68.9	5,633	34.6	19	7.9	7.4		25.3[c]	18.1[d]	16.3[e]	16.3[f]		6.0[h]	6.7	6.7[j]
Indonesia	261.1	3,484	19.7	17.2	7.6	7.6			42.4	36.4[e]	35.5[f]			5.5	13.5[j]
Philippines	103.3	3,445	26.3	21.3	13.9	13.5	60.2[b]	44.7[c]	38.3[d]	30.3[e]	29.1[i]	9.9[g]	5.7[h]	9.1[i]	7.9[j]
Cambodia	15.8	1,032	32.1	32	15	14.2			49.2	33.5	32.6			13.4[i]	9.2
Myanmar	52.9	1,272	62.6	52.4	14.9	14.2		55.1[c]	40.8	35.1[e]	33.4[f]		12.9[h]	9.4[i]	7.9[j]
Lao PDR	6.8	1,929	42.8	39.2	18.9	18.5			48.2	43.8[e]	42.1[f]			12.3[i]	6.4[j]
South Asia	**1,765.2**	**1,500**	**24.88**	**18.95**	**16.36**	**16.24**	**74.2**	**65.8**	**49.7**	**39.3**	**37.9**	**19.5**	**21.1**	**18.5**	**14.5**
Sri Lanka	21.2	3,760	30.6	29.9	22.9	22	50.4[b]	31.2[c]	18.4	14.7[e]	14.6[f]	15.9[g]	13.3[h]	15.3	21.4[j]
Bangladesh	163.0	1,158	32.8	23.1	16.9	16.4		70.9[c]	50.8	36.4	35.9		17.3[h]	15.7	14.3

Nepal	29.0	709	22.8	22.2	7.7	7.8	75.0[b]	–	57.1[d]	37.4	39.5[f]	15.2[g]	–	7.5	11.3
India	1,324.2	1,557	23.7	17	15.3	15.2	75.1[b]	66.2[c]	51.0[d]	38.7	37.9	20.3[g]	21.3[h]	19.3	15.1
Pakistan	193.2	1,418	25.1	22.4	22	22	70.5[b]	62.5[c]	41.5[d]	45.0[e]	41.7[f]	15.2[g]	24.0[h]	17.2[i]	10.5[j]
Afghanistan	34.7	657	29.5	45.2	26	26.8	–	–	53.2[d]	59.3[e]	–	–	–	18.2[i]	–

Notes: Data are sorted with respect to life expectancy at birth in 2015.

Prevalence of undernourishment, 2014:

[a] Figure for Japan is from https://knoema.com/atlas/Japan/topics/Health/Nutrition/Prevalence-of-undernourishment.

Prevalence of stunting, height for age:

[b] Figures for some countries are other than 1971: India 1977; Nepal 1975; Pakistan 1977; Philippines 1973; Singapore 1974; Sri Lanka 1978.

[c] Figures for some countries are other than 1985: Bangladesh 1986; China 1987; India 1989; Japan 1980; Myanmar 1984; Pakistan 1986; Philippines 1987; Sri Lanka 1987; Thailand 1987; Vietnam 1984.

[d] Figures for some countries are other than 2000: Afghanistan 1997; India 1999; Korea, Rep. 2003; Malaysia 1999; Nepal 2001; Pakistan 2001; Philippines 1998; Thailand 1995.

[e] Figures for some countries are other than 2014: Afghanistan 2004; China 2010; Indonesia 2013; Japan 2010; Korea, Rep. 2010; Lao PDR 2011; Malaysia 2006; Mongolia 2013; Myanmar 2009; Pakistan 2012; Philippines 2013; Sri Lanka 2012; Thailand 2012; Vietnam 2010.

Prevalence of stunting, height for age, female:

[f] Figures for some countries are other than 2014: China 2010; Indonesia 2013; Japan 2010; Korea, Rep. 2010; Lao PDR 2011; Mongolia 2010; Myanmar 2009; Nepal 2011; Pakistan 2012; Philippines 2013; Sri Lanka 2012; Thailand 2012; Vietnam 2010.

Prevalence of wasting, weight for height:

[g] Figures for some countries are other than 1971: India 1977; Nepal 1975; Pakistan 1977; Philippines 1973; Singapore 1974; Sri Lanka 1978.

[h] Figures for some countries are other than 1985: Bangladesh 1986; China 1987; India 1989; Japan 1980; Myanmar 1984; Pakistan 1986; Philippines 1987; Sri Lanka 1987; Thailand 1987; Vietnam 1988.

[i] Figures for some countries are other than 2000: Afghanistan 1997; Cambodia 1996; India 1997; Lao PDR 1994; Malaysia 1999; Mongolia 1992; Myanmar 1994; Pakistan 1994; Philippines 1993; Vietnam 1994.

[j] Figures for some countries are other than 2014: China 2010; Indonesia 2013; Japan 2010; Korea, Rep. 2010; Lao PDR 2011; Mongolia 2013; Myanmar 2009; Pakistan 2012; Philippines 2013; Sri Lanka 2012; Thailand 2012.

Source: Author, based on the World Development Indicators.

data are supplemented by data on infant mortality rates (IMRs) and maternal mortality rates (MMRs). The anthropometric indicators include measures of the incidence of undernutrition, stunting, and wasting.

East Asia has achieved the maximum progress, followed by Southeast Asia, followed by South Asia. Average life expectancy, for instance, has risen to 76 years in East Asia, 71 years in Southeast Asia and 69 years in South Asia (Table 11.3). There are of course large variations around sub-regional averages. Thus, life expectancy ranges from 63 years in Afghanistan to 84 years in Japan. However, there are technical limits to the achievable standards of health.[18] Hence lagging countries are gradually catching up with the leading countries as the latter asymptotically approach these limits. There is no gender bias in life expectancy; it is now higher for women compared to men in *all* countries of the region. However, son preference is exercised by aborting girls before birth in some countries and this is reflected in their distorted sex ratios.[19] Nutrition trends also show large improvements over the period. But disturbingly high levels of undernutrition, stunting, and wasting persist in several countries.

3.2 Key Experiences of Selected Country Experiences

The healthcare experiences of a large number of individual countries have been summarized in Mundle (2018b: appendix 2). Here, only a few key features are highlighted to provide some context to the quantitative picture presented above.

3.2.1 The Best Performers: Singapore, Korea, and Thailand

Singapore's health outcomes are among the best globally and these have been achieved cost effectively. Singapore's health expenditure is less than 4 per cent of GDP as compared to the OECD average of 9 per cent. The public sector dominates the provision of healthcare, accounting for over 70 per cent of hospital admissions, and 75 per cent of beds are subsidized. The most interesting aspect of Singapore's healthcare system is its financing arrangement through Medisave, carved out of the compulsory provident fund system, Medishield for catastrophic care, Eldershield for the elderly and Medifund for poor families. Costs are kept low through co-payments, which minimize moral hazard, and competition among private insurance providers.

Korea's health system is best known for its social insurance (SI) system, which covers virtually the whole population. However, there is a disproportionate concentration of health services in urban areas, with service deficits in rural areas, especially in less-developed provinces. Also, private providers who account for

---

[18] For instance, the IMR or MMR cannot decline below zero. Longevity is also bounded by the present state of medical knowledge even under optimal living conditions.

[19] See Sen (1990).

90 per cent of hospital beds push services, drugs, and diagnostic tests not covered by SI, thereby pushing up the burden of out-of-pocket (OOP) spending. This deters low-income patients from seeking treatment, thereby skewing the incidence of SI benefits in favour of the rich. The rising incidence of chronic non-communicable diseases (NCDs) requiring expensive treatment, a consequence of ageing and increasing incomes, is another challenge testing the viability of the SI system.

Thailand's healthcare system is increasingly seen as a model for other developing countries. Despite its low per capita income, Thailand has a very high standard of health. This has been achieved with remarkably low and declining OOP spending. Thailand has universal health coverage which is entirely SI financed. In the government and corporate sectors, the SI premium is financed through payroll taxes whereas the SI premium for the poor, the informal sector, and others is tax financed. Patients choose their primary care units and SI provides a comprehensive benefit package for a capped capitation fee plus a case-based payment for inpatient and outpatient care. There is almost no co-payment and balance billing is also not allowed. OOP spending is now down to 18 per cent of total health spending.

3.2.2 The Weakest Performers: Afghanistan and Pakistan

Afghanistan is a post-conflict but still violent country where the delivery of essential public services is challenging. The donor-supported government has attempted to deliver an essential package of hospital services (EPHS) in urban areas and a basic package of health services (BPHS) in rural areas delivered through non-government organizations and contract service providers. But the EPHS is mainly limited to Kabul, and the BPHS covers about 60 per cent of the population at best. Service provision is very patchy because of the shortage of health workers and medicines. OOP spending accounts for over 73 per cent of total health expenditure and patients need to travel to Pakistan or India for treatment of any serious ailment.

Pakistan has an elaborate 3-tier structure for public sector health service delivery, from basic rural health units to tertiary care hospitals in the main cities. However the quality of public health services is weak, especially in rural areas. Underfunded, not easily accessible and staffed by unco-operative personnel, healthcare centres also often do not have the required stocks of medicines. Consequently, private service providers now dominate the field, with OOP spending accounting for about 75 per cent of total health expenditure.

3.2.3 The Largest Countries: China, India, and Indonesia

China's health indicators lag behind those of the best performers in Asia but are better than the rest. It has separate 3-tier systems of healthcare provision for urban and rural areas. The urban system has been mostly state funded through the Government Health Insurance System and Labour Health Insurance Scheme for different population segments. Rural communities have had to provide for themselves through the Cooperative Medical System (CMS), with shortfalls being met by the village government. The system worked well until the 1979 reforms, which combined the private responsibility system of agriculture with decentralization, bankrupted the village governments. The CMS, the backbone of the rural healthcare system, collapsed. Hospitals in urban areas also faced financial crisis with soaring drug prices. They started charging for expensive services and drugs, and some doctors started accepting fees informally.

With increasing dependence on OOP spending, disparities between rich and poor provinces, rural and urban areas within provinces, and rich and poor households, soared. In April 2009, the market-oriented reforms were reversed through fresh reforms and the CMS has been revived. The new reform is still work in progress. SI now covers over 92 per cent of the population, but SI coverage excludes many services and drugs. OOP spending accounts for 50 per cent of inpatient care and 60 per cent to 70 per cent of outpatient care.

India's health and nutrition standards have improved markedly over the past fifty years, but lag well behind those of the best performing countries. It has an elaborate 3-tier public sector healthcare system from a base of village-level primary health centres up to federal hospitals that provide secondary and tertiary care. But the system is overloaded, the referral system is broken and patients wait in long queues in overcrowded hospitals to receive treatment from overburdened and uncooperative medical staff. Treatment is supposedly free, but drugs are often out of stock and inpatient beds may not be available for weeks. So even poor patients, when they can afford it, seek private care, which is a flourishing business. Over 80 per cent of total health spending is OOP spending. This has led to rising disparity in access to healthcare and a high incidence of household impoverishment due to expensive catastrophic care. A National Health Mission set up to address the increasing inequity in access to healthcare proved inadequate. Some states started their own SI schemes and the federal government is now initiating a nationwide scheme. Unfortunately these SI schemes are designed for inpatient care when the bulk of OOP spending is for outpatient care.

Indonesia's local health centres, called *pasekamas*, constitute the vital base of its 3-tier public healthcare system. They provide preventive services, primary care, as well as referrals for higher-level care. The *Jamkesmas* SI programme introduced for the poorest 30 per cent of the population, together with pre-existing schemes for the formal sector, provided insurance cover to about 55 per cent of the population. But the middle 45 per cent of informal sector workers and the rest of the population were left out. District officials, significantly empowered by the 2001 decentralization reforms, introduced the *Jamkheda* SI scheme for them. In 2014, the government integrated all three SI schemes into the *Jaminan Kesehatan Nasional* (JKN) scheme, which seeks to achieve universal SI coverage by 2019. Unfortunately, JKN mainly addresses curative care and its coverage excludes many services. Hence, OOP spending still accounts for 60 per cent of total health expenditure. The heavy dependence on private provision and private financing has inevitably led to growing disparity between Java and the other islands, especially the remote outer islands, between the cities and rural areas and between rich and poor families.

3.3 The Development of Healthcare: Challenges and Responses

To summarize, the spread of healthcare during the past fifty years has been remarkable. Postcolonial governments recognized that a collective good like health services could not be left to the market. But the public provision of health services was constrained by the availability of public resources. This compelled most governments to turn to private provision of health services. But that in turn was constrained by the limited capacity of households to meet OOP expenses.

In addition to the tension between the goal of expanding healthcare provision, the limited resources of governments and the budget constraints of households, other important considerations include the contingent nature of demand for healthcare, the asymmetry of information between patients and physicians and the impoverishing impact of catastrophic OOP spending. These necessitated the *ex ante* pooling of risk through health insurance (Arrow 1963; Mundle 1998). Adverse client selection by profit-driven private insurers raised the need for universal SI.

These factors have collectively led to the emergence of a variety of health systems in Asia, ranging from maximum dependence on public funding and public provision as in Singapore and Thailand to maximum dependence on OOP private spending and private provision as in most of the South Asian countries. Some issues arising from the experience of this variety of health systems are summarized below.

The rising burden of NCDs while the burden of communicable diseases (CDs) is yet to be eliminated is a major challenge. Unfortunately, public health measures, such as immunization, that are equitable and cost efficient in dealing with CDs have been neglected, their share of public health expenditure typically being less than 10 per cent. Consequently the benefit incidence of public healthcare spending has been regressive in most countries (O'Donnell et al. 2007).

In most Asian countries this policy bias in favour of expensive curative care has put intolerable pressure on the delivery capacity of public health systems based on a foundation of poorly trained village health workers. It has broken the referral system and overburdened secondary and tertiary hospitals that have ended up providing poor services. Patients have therefore increasingly opted for paid private services when they can afford it. The shift to private health provision, mostly financed by OOP spending, has in turn generated several challenges.

Typically, private providers push over-treatment, expensive diagnostic tests and medication apart from high doctors' fees, leading to huge escalation in treatment costs. The catastrophic impact of high OOP spending has often driven households to impoverishment. Comparisons show that the incidence of catastrophic health episodes has been lower in countries that have tried to contain the share of OOP spending (Doorslaer et al. 2006; Tangcharoensathien et al. 2011).

Rising costs of medical care have forced poorer households to progressively withdraw from seeking medical care as treatment costs have risen. This has resulted in increasing inequality in access to medical care between more and less prosperous regions, rural and urban areas, and rich and poor households. In response to this rising inequality of access, most Asian countries have moved towards SI, with governments often paying the premium. But SI by itself has not prevented private providers from driving up costs. The consequent thinning of SI coverage, co-payments and coverage caps has resulted in continuing heavy reliance on OOP spending. A WHO assessment concluded that a viable SI system requires a separate dedicated safety net programme for vulnerable households and an allocation of 4 per cent to 5 per cent of GDP for health expenditure, of which OOP spending should not exceed 30 per cent to 40 per cent (WHO 2009). In comparison, OOP spending in most Asian countries ranges from 60 per cent to as much as 80 per cent. The high dependence on OOP spending and consequent inequality of access is the principal challenge facing healthcare provision in Asia today.

4. Social Development, Disparity, and the State

Some features stand out clearly in the foregoing account of social development in Asia. The outstanding feature is the remarkable transformation of Asia's education and health profile. Some countries, and regions within countries, have lagged behind. Others have surged ahead. But there were impressive gains in social development in *all* countries compared to their own initial conditions. Second, as the leading countries approach the feasible limits of such development the lagging countries are gradually catching up, a process of convergence is underway.[20] There are, of course, variations in the pace at which the different lagging countries are catching up with the leading countries. Finally, within most countries a pattern of nested disparities has emerged in the access to education and healthcare: disparity between more and less prosperous regions, disparity between rural and urban areas within a region, and disparity between rich and poor households within the urban and rural areas. These disparities have increased with the increasing shift

---

[20] See footnotes 15 and 18.

from public to private provision of education and healthcare in most countries, though there are important exceptions. However, these disparities are likely to decrease over the long term with continuing social development like the variations across countries and for the same reasons.

What accounts for these large variations across countries? Partly, it is differences in initial conditions. This would include differences in colonial legacies[21] or a legacy of conflict in some countries that influenced the course of future development. Equally important are the initial differences in standards of education and health. The close association between initial and current levels of education and health across countries will be evident from Tables 11.1–11.4. Another important factor is the close association between levels of income, hence income growth, and the spread of education and health services. This is also evident from the same tables. As we know from the human capital literature cited earlier, here the causality runs in both directions.

Another critical element that has determined the pace of social development in Asia is the nature of the state. In postcolonial Asia, social development has been led by developmental states.[22] Thus, the spread of education and healthcare was very much a function of the priorities and capacities that reflected the nature of the state. To better understand this relationship, a taxonomy of the different types of states is helpful. The nature of a state is a complex, multifaceted phenomenon not easily amenable to classification in a single taxonomic category. Some characteristics of the state may fit one category and other aspects may better fit another category. Also, the nature of the state can change over time. Nevertheless, framing the discussion within a taxonomy of the different types of Asian states is a helpful analytical device.

To develop such a taxonomy, I start with the binary concepts of extractive versus inclusive institutions and political versus economic institutions that Acemoglu and Robinson (2012) have employed, among other important conceptual innovations, to explain why most nations fail to develop. Simple modifications of the Acemoglu–Robinson (AR) framework give us an alternative taxonomy that can help explain the differing impacts of different types of developmental states on the development of education and health.[23] AR maintained that, except in transitional conditions, extractive or inclusive economic institutions match with the corresponding political institutions.[24] They argued that most nations

---

[21] Breman and Mundle (1991) had initially drawn attention to the very different legacies of European colonialism in South and Southeast Asia and Japanese colonialism in East Asia, and their differentiated impact on agrarian transformation. This idea has now been revived and much extended by Duara (2018) and Wade (2018a).

[22] See the Introduction to this chapter, especially footnote 3.

[23] For an earlier attempt along these lines to explain the long-term growth prospects of twenty-five emerging economies in Asia, Africa, and Latin America see Mundle (2018a).

[24] The similarity of this idea with the somewhat more complex idea of necessary correspondence between relations of production and the superstructure of a society in Marx's theory of historical materialism (Marx 1859) is obvious. However, a failure of such correspondence was one of the drivers

failed to develop because predatory states drained them of resources and enterprise through extractive political and economic institutions. The few developed nations are exceptions where states have maintained inclusive political and economic institutions that *enabled* development. Johnson's conception of the developmental state, which not only enabled but also *led* the process of development, is the antithesis of AR's rather passive 'night watchman' conception of the ideal state.[25]

Let us extend ARs concept of economic institutions to also include social institutions and allow the possibility of stable social systems where exclusive[26] political institutions are combined with inclusive economic and social institutions or, conversely, inclusive political institutions are combined with exclusive economic and social institutions. These simple modifications yield a taxonomy of different types of states, especially developmental states, which is rich enough to capture the observed variations in the nature of states in Asia.

In reading my taxonomy it is important to understand how I have interpreted some key concepts. By *inclusive political institutions* I mean institutions that allow political competition; the existence of a judiciary; a legislature and a free press that are independent, not controlled by the executive; and protection of human rights. A system of political institutions that fails to pass this test would be considered exclusive. Authoritarian regimes ruled by a dictator or a single party would obviously be exclusive. But an apparent multiparty democracy with an elected government where real power is controlled by a deep state that faces no political competition would also be considered exclusive. Similarly, when the same party led by the same individual or family continues to 'win' election after election and rules for decades this, too, would point to the prevalence of exclusive political institutions. However, it must be noted that without the centralized exercise of power, political competition in highly polarized or fractionalized polities can become a hindrance to collective action. The need to accommodate many competing interest groups can fritter away the state's resources and its capacity to deliver collective goods.[27]

The demarcation of exclusive and inclusive socio-economic institutions is more difficult. One clear indicator is whether the pre-existing landed and business elites were protected or removed through land reform and other measures by the new postcolonial states that came to power. Another indicator is the prevalence

---

of change in Marx's theory of history while for AR it is part of a binary classification between nations that develop successfully and those that fail.

[25] This conception of a minimalist, non-interventionist state protecting free market and property rights is similar to those of North and Weingast (2000) and Besley and Persson (2011) among others. For a compelling critique of this paradigm see Bardhan (2013).

[26] I am here replacing AR's term 'extractive' with the term 'exclusive', which I find more appropriate as the opposite of 'inclusive'.

[27] On this see, among others, La Porta et al. (1999), Besley and Persson (2011) and Mundle et al. (2012).

or social acceptance of differentiation based on identity such as caste, religion, ethnicity, or language. A third indicator would be effective state action to provide or finance collective goods, such as universal basic education and universal healthcare, to mitigate the impact of wealth and income inequality. These indicators are only illustrative not exhaustive.

Finally, the concepts of hard and soft states need to be reintroduced with some precision. Myrdal (1968, 1970) introduced the concept of the 'soft' state, a state that has the intention but lacks the capacity or the will to enforce its agenda of state-led development in the face of multiple constraints and competing claims for the resources of the state. By inference, a hard state is one that has the capacity and will to enforce its agenda. Several scholars have since attempted to give some precision to this basic idea in different ways. Evans has introduced the concept of 'embedded autonomy' (Evans 1995; Evans and Heller 2018). Wade (2018a) has distinguished between 'special interest' states and 'common interest' states. Khan (2018) has written about 'enforcement capacity' as a function of 'the political settlement'. Bardhan (2016) has sought to define a measure of state strength in terms of 'commitment ability'. Building on these constructs, especially Bardhan, and the concepts of the developmental state and inclusive versus exclusive political and socio-economic institutions discussed above, I bring back the concept of hard and soft states in presenting the following taxonomy:

1. The **hard developmental state** combines exclusive political institutions with socio-economic institutions that are inclusive. Countries with such states experience rapid social development:[28] China, Malaysia (until the recent election that has ended the United Malays National Organisation (UMNO) party's monopoly of power), Singapore, Thailand, Vietnam, (also Korea and Taiwan in their pre-democratic period).

2. The **soft developmental state** combines inclusive political institutions with exclusive socio-economic institutions. Countries with such states are likely to experience slow social development: Bangladesh, India, Indonesia, Lao PDR, Mongolia, Nepal, and Philippines.

3. The **inclusive developmental state** where political and socio-economic institutions are both inclusive. Countries with such states are likely to experience rapid social development: Japan, Korea, Taiwan, and Sri Lanka.

4. The **predatory state** which is not developmental at all and where political and economic institutions are both exclusive. Countries with such states are likely to lag behind and experience very slow social development: Cambodia, Pakistan, Myanmar (also presumably North Korea, but that country is not analysed here).

---

[28] By social development I mean specifically the spread of education and healthcare.

To understand the differences in the nature of these states it is necessary to recognize the geopolitical conditions under which these different states came into existence. Mundle (2017), Duara (2018) and Wade (2018a) have underlined the importance of the US-led Cold War in Asia in shaping the nature of many of these states.[29]

Wade has shown how the US supported Japan, Korea, and Taiwan, the frontline states in the war against communism, in securing themselves internally through comprehensive land reforms that swept away the landed elite, and in curbing and disciplining the business elite. Externally, the US protected these states through its security cover, large-scale development assistance, and privileged access to the vast US market to enable their rapid industrialization and growth. He has pointed out the subtle difference in the scale of US support to these states and the Philippines, which was also an ally against communism but not a frontline state. There the strong landed elites were protected as US allies in containing the domestic spread of communism. The scale of military, financial and other assistance, or preferential access to US markets, was also not comparable to US assistance to the frontline states.

Duara has argued that this same model of US support on a more moderate scale applies to its allies in Southeast Asia, that is, Thailand, Indonesia, Malaysia, and Singapore.[30] Mundle has pointed out that while the US allies were driven by the fear of communism, the communist states in China and Vietnam were driven by the opposite fear of US domination and the overthrow of communism. On both sides of the Cold War it was the existential threat of that war which legitimized these authoritarian states[31] and also drove them to aggressively pursue strategies of rapid, inclusive growth. Most of these states have been classified as hard developmental states in our taxonomy.

In some cases the replacement of dictatorships by inclusive political institutions led ironically to the emergence of soft states with little ability to transform exclusive economic relations. In the Philippines, the predatory state of the Marcos era was replaced by a soft state with the return of democracy. In Indonesia, Suharto's authoritarian rule, and rent collection by a narrow elite of family and friends, was combined with otherwise inclusive economic policies (Timmer 2018). Political competition following the fall of Suharto led to the emergence of a soft state that lacks the capacity to transform the prevailing exclusive economic institutions.

But the classic example of a soft state is India, the country that led Myrdal to formulate the very concept of the 'soft state'. The Indian state came to power following a remarkable, non-violent independence movement in which Gandhi mobilized all sections of society, including the landed and business elites. The

---

[29] Which became a very hot war with huge casualties in Korea and later Vietnam.

[30] In its early years, the new Singaporean state may also have perceived an existential threat from Malaysia, from which it had broken away.

[31] Duara discusses how nationalism was a powerful legitimizing ideology in this context.

corollary was the continuing dominance of these elites over public policy and the protection of landed and business interests. In addition to elite interests the Indian state has also had to continuously navigate its way through the conflicting interests of a highly fractionalized polity of different castes, religions, regions, and classes.[32] Securing political consensus among all these interests led to what Joshi has described as collective action gridlock (Joshi 2016). Accommodating the many competing interests also exhausted the state's resources in large transfers and subsidies, resulting in persistent fiscal stress and lack of resources for financing collective goods like basic education, healthcare, or infrastructure. India also has an elaborate, multi-layered bureaucracy stretching down to the millions of villages, but this bureaucracy still functions with a colonial mentality of masters ruling over subjects and its incentive system is designed to ensure loyalty to superiors, not delivery of public services.

The classification of states presented above reflects judgements based on the literature cited earlier, the data, the country notes in Mundle (2018b) and my earlier research (Mundle 2017, 2018a). Can these judgements be scrutinized against some objective criteria? The nature of the state is a complex notion not easily measurable by any simple metric. However, public provision or financing of social services is one of many competing demands for the limited resources of the state. Hence, the allocation of public resources for social expenditure is a possible indicator, admittedly crude, of the inclusiveness of the state.

Panel A in Figure 11.1 presents a scatter diagram of the education share of government spending against mean years of schooling, taken as a representative measure of education development. Panel B presents a scatter diagram of the share of healthcare in government spending against life expectancy, taken as a representative measure of health standards in a country. It turns out that most of the countries classified as soft developmental states or predatory states spend less than or close to the median share of public expenditure on education and health services. For the least inclusive countries, clustered in the lower left quadrant of both panels, this has happened even when the achieved standards of education and health are below the regional median. The exceptions that need explanation are Afghanistan and Nepal, and Indonesia in the case of education. Conversely most of the countries classified as inclusive or hard developmental states allocate more than the median share of public expenditure on education and health services. The exception requiring explanation here is Japan in the case of education.

Afghanistan and Nepal are the poorest countries in the region and heavily aid-dependent. The high share of social services in these two countries reflects donor priorities rather than the character of the state. The high allocation for education in Indonesia started with policy reforms in 1975, when Indonesia was a hard

---

[32] On this see, among many others, Bardhan (2010); Kohli (2012); Varshney (2013); Mundle (2017, 2018a).

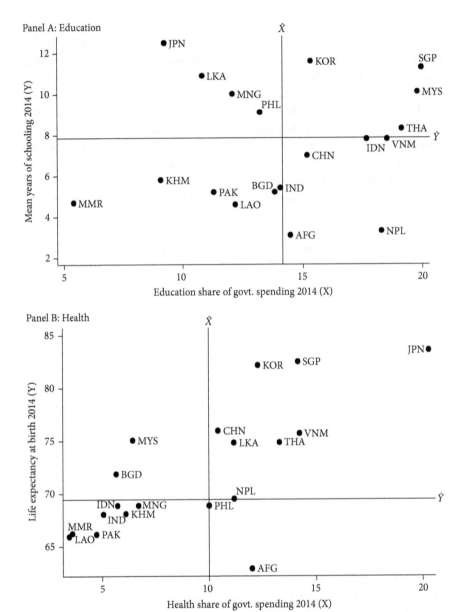

Figure 11.1 Achieved standards and public expenditure shares of education and health in Asian countries.

Note: Country codes: AFG = Afghanistan; BGD = Bangladesh; KHM = Cambodia; CHN = China; IND = India; IDN = Indonesia; JPN = Japan; KOR = Korea, Rep.; LAO = Lao People's Democratic Republic; MYS = Malaysia; MNG = Mongolia; MMR = Myanmar; NPL = Nepal; PAK = Pakistan; PHL = Philippines; SGP = Singapore; LKA = Sri Lanka; THA = Thailand; VNM = Vietnam.

Source: Author, based on World Development Indicators Database and UNESCO Institute for Statistics (education database).

developmental state under Suharto, not the soft state it is today. Japan has already reached the feasible ceiling of schooling per child at over 12 years and it is also a rich country with nearly US$40,000 per capita income. At revenues corresponding to this high level of income the low share of public expenditure allocated to education is evidently adequate to maintain the high education standard Japan has already achieved. With these explanations for the exceptions, it appears that the empirical criteria applied here is consistent with the classification of state character suggested above. It would be interesting to verify the robustness of the classification against other quantitative indicators of state character.

5. A Concluding Remark

The increasing dependence on private provision of education and health services has led to increasing disparity in the access to education and health services in most countries as has been described above. However, the dominant long-term trend is the rapid spread of these services and rising standards of education and health in *all* the countries of the region. Also there is convergence. The leading countries Japan, Singapore, and Korea have already reached or are approaching the best feasible standards of education and health. The lagging countries are gradually catching up. There are, however, large variations among them both in existing standards and in the pace at which they are catching up. An important determinant of these variations, apart from initial conditions and income levels, is the nature of the state in each country. If the classification suggested here is appropriate, it is likely that countries led by the inclusive and hard developmental states—China, Malaysia, Thailand, Sri Lanka, Vietnam—will catch up over the next decade or so. Countries led by soft developmental states will follow. Within this large group, countries with less political fractionalization, stronger commitment ability and greater state capacity will catch up faster than the others.[33] The predatory states are unfortunately likely to catch up last.

Acknowledgements

This chapter is an abridged version of a more detailed UNU-WIDER Working Paper (Mundle 2018b). In writing that paper I benefitted a great deal from discussions with Deepak Nayyar and Pranab Bardhan, and the comments of an anonymous referee. Earlier versions of the paper were also presented at two workshops on Asian Transformation in Hanoi on 9–10 March 2018 and in Shanghai on 29–30 June 2018. The comments of participants at these workshops, especially Amit Bhaduri and Rajiv Malhotra, were very helpful. Excellent research assistance from Satadru Sikdar is also gratefully acknowledged.

---

[33] See Bardhan (2016), Mundle (2017, 2018a), Evans and Heller (2018), and Khan (2018) on these questions.

References

Acemoglu, D., and J.A. Robinson (2012). *Why Nations Fail: The Origins of Power, Prosperity and Poverty.* New York: Crown publishers.

ADB (1997). 'Emerging Asia: Changes and Challenges', mimeo. Manila: Asian Development Bank. September.

Amsden, A. (1989). *Asia's Next Giant: South Korea and Late Industrialization.* New York: Oxford University Press.

Arrow, J.K. (1963). 'Uncertainty and the Welfare Economics of Medical Care', *The American Review,* 53(5): 941–73.

Bardhan, P. (2010). *Awakening Giants-Feet of Clay: Assessing the Economic Rise of China and India.* Princeton, NJ: Princeton University Press.

Bardhan, P. (2013). 'Little, Big: Two Ideas About Fighting Global Poverty', *Boston Review,* 20 May. Available at: http//bostonreview.net/world-book-ideas/pranab-bardhan-little-big, (accessed 16 July 2018).

Bardhan, P. (2016). 'State and Development: The Need for a Reappraisal of the Current Literature', *Journal of Economic Literature,* 54 (3): 862–92.

Besley, T. and T. Persson (2011). *Pillars of Prosperity: The Political Economics of Development Clusters.* Princeton, NJ: Princeton University Press.

Breman, J. and S. Mundle (1991). 'Introduction'. In J. Breman and S. Mundle (eds) *Rural Transformation in Asia.* Delhi: Oxford University Press.

Doorslaer, E.V., O. O'Donnell, R.P. Rannan-Eliya, A. Somanathan, S.R. Adhikari, C.C. Garg, D. Harbianto, A.N. Herrin, M.N. Huq, S. Ibragimova, A. Karan, C.W. Ng, B.R. Pande, R. Racellis, S. Tao, K. Tin, K. Tisayaticorn, L. Trisnantoro, C. Vasavid, and Y. Zhao (2006). 'Effects of Payments for Healthcare on Poverty Estimates in 11 Countries in Asia: An Analysis of Household Survey Data', *The Lancet,* 368: 1357–64.

Duara, P. (2018). 'Nationalism and Development in Asia'. UNU-WIDER, Helsinki, WIDER Working Paper.

Evans, P. (1995). *Embedded Autonomy: States and Industrial Transformation.* Princeton, NJ: Princeton University Press.

Evans, P. and P. Heller (2018). 'The State and Development', UNU-WIDER, Helsinki, WIDER Working Paper.

Government of Malaysia (2013). *Malaysia Education Blue Print* 2013–2025, *(pre School to Post-Secondary Education).* Putrajaya: Ministry of Education, Malaysia.

Grossman, G.M. and E. Helpman (1994). 'Endogenous Innovation in the Theory of Growth', *Journal of Economic Perspective,* 8(1): 23–43.

Johnson, C. (1982). *MITI and the Japanese Miracle: The Growth of Industrial Policy 1925–1975.* Stanford, CA: Stanford University Press.

Joshi, V. (2016). *India's Long Road: The Search for Prosperity.* India: Allen Lane Penguin Books.

Khan, M.H. (2018). 'Institutions and Development in Asia', UNU-WIDER, Helsinki, WIDER Working Paper.

Kohli, A. (2012). *Poverty Amidst Plenty in the New India*. Cambridge: Cambridge University Press.

La Porta, R., F. Lopez-de-Silanes, A. Shliefer, and R. Vishney (1999). 'The Quality of Government', *Journal of Law, Economics and Organisation*, 15(1): 222–79.

Marx, K. (1859). *A Contribution to the Critique of Political Economy*. English translation. Moscow: Progress Publishers.

Mundle, S. (1998). 'Financing Human Development: Some Lessons from Advanced Asian Countries', *World Development*, 26(4): 659–72.

Mundle, S. (2017). 'Employment, Education and the State', *The Indian Journal of Labour Economics*, 60(1): 17–31.

Mundle, S. (2018a). 'Beyond Catch Up: Some Speculations about the Next Twenty-Five Emerging Economies'. In A. Ghosh Dastidar, R. Malhotra, and V. Suneja (eds) *Economic Theory and Policy Amidst Global Discontent: Essays in Honour of Deepak Nayyar*. Oxford: Routledge.

Mundle, S. (2018b). 'Fifty Years of Asian Experience in the Spread of Education and Health', UNU-WIDER, Helsinki, WIDER Working Paper.

Mundle, S., P. Chakraborty, S. Chowdhury, and S. Sikdar (2012). 'The Quality of Governance: How have Indian States Performed?', *Economic and Political Weekly*, 47(49): 41–52.

Myrdal, G. (1968). *Asian Drama: An Inquiry into the Poverty of Nations*. London: Penguin Press, Allen Lane.

Myrdal, G. (1970). 'The "Soft State" and Underdeveloped Countries'. In P. Streeten (ed.) *Unfashionable Economics: Essays in Honour of Lord Balogh*. London: Weidenfeld and Nicholson.

North, D.C. and B.R. Weingast (2000). 'Institutional Analysis and Economic History', *Journal of Economic History*, 60(2): 414–17.

O'Donnell, O., E.V. Doorslaer, R.P. Rannan-Eliya, A. Somanathan, S.R. Adhikari, D. Harbianto, C.C. Garg, P. Hanvoravongchai, M.N. Huq, A. Karan, G.M. Leung, C.W. Ng, B.R. Pande, K. Tin, K. Tisayaticom, L. Trisnantoro, Y. Zhang, and Y. Zhao (2007). 'The Incidence of Public Spending on Healthcare: Comparative Evidence from Asia', *The World Bank Economic Review*, 21(1): 93–123.

OECD (2018). PISA 2015 Results in Focus. Paris: OECD.

Pack, H. (1994). 'Endogenous Growth Theory: Intellectual Appeal and Empirical Shortcomings', *Journal of Economic Perspectives*, 8(1): 55–72.

Romer, P.M. (1994). 'The Origin of Endogenous Growth', *Journal of Economic Perspective*, 8(l): 3–23.

Sagarik, D. (2014). 'Educational Expenditure in Thailand: Development, Trends, and Distribution', *Citizenship, Social and Economics Education*, 13(1): 54–66.

Saw, G.K. and B.L. Schneider (2015). 'Challenges and Opportunities for Estimating Effects with Large-scale Education Datasets', *Contemporary Educational Research Quarterly*, 23(4): 93–119.

Schultz, T.W. (1961). 'Investment in Human Capital', *The American Economic Review*, 51(1): 1–17.

Sen, A. (1990). 'More than 100 Million Women are Missing', *New York Review of Books*, 20 December.

Sen, A. (1998a). 'Human Development and Financial Conservatism', *World Development*, 26(4): 733–42.

Sen, A. (1998b). 'Mortality as an Indicator of Economic Success and Failure', *The Economic Journal*, 108(446): 1–25.

Sen, A. (1999). *Development as Freedom*. New York: Oxford University Press.

Tangcharoensathien, V., W. Patcharanarumol, P. Ir, S.M. Aljunid, A.G. Mukti, K. Akhavong, E. Banzan, D.B. Huong, H. Thabrany, and A. Mills (2011). 'Health Financing Reforms in Southeast Asia: Challenges in Achieving Universal Coverage', *The Lancet*, 377: 863–73.

Tilak, J.B.G. (2002). *Building Human Capital in East Asia: What Others Can Learn*. Washington, DC: International Bank for Reconstruction and Development and the World Bank.

Timmer, P. (2018). 'Pro-Poor Growth in Indonesia: Challenging the Pessimism of Myrdal's *Asian Drama*', UNU-WIDER, Helsinki, WIDER Working Paper.

UNESCO (2013). *Malaysia Education Policy Review*. Paris: UNESCO.

Varshney, A. (2013). *Battles Half Won: India's Improbable Democracy*. New Delhi: Penguin Books.

Wade, R. (1990). *Governing the Market: Economic Theory and the Role of Government in East Asian Industrialization*. Princeton, NJ: Princeton University Press.

Wade, R. (2018a). 'The Developmental State: Dead or Alive?', *Development and Change*, 49(2): 518–46.

Wade, R. (2018b). 'Escaping the Periphery: The East Asian "Mystery" Explained', UNU-WIDER, Helsinki, WIDER Working Paper.

WHO (2009). *Health Financing Strategy for the Asia Pacific Region (2010–2015)*. New York: World Health Organization.

World Bank (1993). *The East Asian Miracle: Economic Growth and Public Policy*. Oxford: Oxford University Press and the World Bank.

12

Unemployment, Employment, and Development

Rolph van der Hoeven

1. Introduction and Overview

This chapter provides a retrospect of, and prospects for, development, labour market, and employment issues in Asia, triggered by Myrdal's *Asian Drama*, published fifty years ago. Following this introduction and overview, section 2 firstly conceptualizes labour markets, employment, underemployment, and unemployment at the time when *Asian Drama* was written. It then traces the evolution of thinking about labour markets and employment in a more or less chronological order up until the adoption of the 2015 United Nations Sustainable Development Goals, before setting out the analytical approach on development and labour markets followed in this chapter.

Section 3 shows how various sub-regional groups and countries in Asia fared from 1965 to 2015 with respect to economic and labour market issues. The first sub-section, compares Asian sub-regions to other developing regions and the second sub-section analyses developments in Asian countries themselves. Asian countries are classified into categories of fast-growing countries with good labour market outcomes, fast-growing countries with weak labour market outcomes, and those that have not grown fast and have weak labour market outcomes.

Section 4 analyses how and why in certain Asian countries policies and institutions have reinforced each other, leading to faster growth and better labour market outcomes—something that Myrdal labelled as 'cumulative causation'. Section 5 discusses six, not entirely independent, factors determining future developments of economies and labour markets in Asia: demographic trends, migration, technology, the future of work, social developments, and income inequalities. Section 6 concludes.

2. The Analytical Framework

2.1 Concepts of Employment and Labour Markets at the Time of *Asian Drama*

Asian Drama (Myrdal 1968) had, at the time of publication, a great influence on thinking on employment and related issues. *Asian Drama* was the only publication with two chapters in the seminal bundle *Third World Employment* (Jolly et al. 1973). Myrdal's understanding of employment issues should, though, be set in the context of his time (decolonization and independence). He is vigorous in rejecting the colonialist or mercantilist approach to economic development and its interpretation of the labour market. However, he is also critical of the 'modern approach', which purports fast growth in the modern industrial sector profiting from a large reserve pool of labour. The modern approach, as depicted by Myrdal, resembles Lewis's theory of unlimited supply of labour, although Myrdal barely makes reference to the writings of Lewis (1954) himself. Myrdal is not fully convinced of the unlimited supply of labour argument. In various passages, especially in part V (Problems of Labour Utilization), he contests the notion of a labour reserve, as substantial parts of the labour force (with different intensity in Asian countries and most pronounced in India) are unable to work in industry because of administrative, caste, and religious practices and a lack of basic skills (because of insufficient education) and stamina (because of ill health and sanitary conditions).

Myrdal questions a mechanistic interpretation of the notion of underemployment and emphasizes issues like duration and productivity of work. He favours the concept of a dual labour market driven by different and separate activities in the so-called formal and informal economies. Under certain conditions, the modern industrial sector can even face a situation of labour shortage, similar to that in developed countries. Myrdal also rejects a strict economic interpretation of the development challenge and prefers an integrated approach combining economic with sociological and political analysis. He emphasizes initial conditions and cumulative causation as explanatory factors for different patterns of development and employment creation.

Myrdal, advancing the work of Mahalanobis (1958), criticizes (in appendix 16) those labour market analyses that studied in-depth unemployment but neglected to take a broader view of employment and development. His analysis gave support to the concept of the informal sector and informal employment. Myrdal, though, did not use the term 'informal sector' himself, a concept firstly observed by the Indian economist Rao (1938) and later also brought to attention by Lewis (1954). It is unclear whether Myrdal built on the ideas of Rao and Lewis or whether he came to similar conclusions.[1]

The notion of the informal sector has not been uncontested, however. For some scholars the informal sector is a temporary phenomenon that would disappear with the transition from agriculture to industrialization. Giving this sector too much attention would only cause a country's development path to deviate. Yet reality was and is different, as Myrdal and several other studies at that time showed. Neglecting the informal sector, and those working in the informal sector, would

---

[1] Hart (1971), after Myrdal had published *Asian Drama*, introduced the term 'informal sector', which was also brought to a larger public by ILO employment reports on Kenya, Sri Lanka, Philippines, and Colombia in the 1970s.

bypass a large, and often the poorest, part of the population. But for some others (de Soto 1989; Maloney 2004), the informal sector is not seen as a problem but as a solution. These authors lament the overbearing role of the central state and local authorities in halting private sector initiative. Supporting and stimulating the informal sector is thus not seen as a way of helping workers in a transition process, but rather as an important way of liberalizing the economy, and so, in the optic of these proponents, of fostering growth through liberalization.

Although the International Labour Organization (ILO) sponsored various analyses and studies on the informal sector, the informal sector remained a contested issue for many years, even in the ILO. Only in 2003 did the ILO develop a comprehensive classification of informal sector activities and employment patterns (ILO 2013). *That classification rejects the existence of an informal sector* per se, *but rather acknowledges the existence of informal activities and an informal economy that are sometimes closely intertwined with the formal economy.* There can be informal employment in the formal sector (Breman 2013).

Myrdal also emphasizes the capability of the labour force as an important factor in development. At various places, he is critical of the labour surplus theory, arguing that, because of restraining factors such as bad health, low literacy, bad living conditions, and cultural inhibitions, a labour reserve army is not fully operational to function properly in all sections of the economy, giving rise to the human capital approach to development. One of Myrdal's closest collaborators Paul Streeten, together with various analysts at the Institute of Development Studies at the University of Sussex and the ILO, expanded the human capital approach to the 'basic needs' approach (or basic human needs) as an objective of development.

Whereas in the human capital approach the quality of employment, measured by education and health, was seen as instrumental for achieving economic growth, the basic needs approach saw the removal of poverty, gainful employment, good education, and health as development objectives in themselves (Hopkins and van der Hoeven 1983). The notion of basic needs was well established in Indian planning (Srinavasan and Bardhan 1974). The basic needs approach, however, was not entirely accepted. According to some developing countries, the basic needs approach focused too much on the poorest developing countries and gave too little attention to international measures to foster national economic growth (van der Hoeven 1988). This fear was fed as *structural adjustment programmes* (SAPs) started to dominate development thinking and financing in the major international financial institutions. Emphasis shifted back to economic growth, to the neglect of employment and basic needs.

2.2 Evolution of Thinking on Labour Markets and Employment

The notion of employment and related issues gained traction again towards the end of the twentieth century, being the main subject of the World Summit for Social

Development in Copenhagen in 1995. The summit called for renewed attention to poverty reduction, employment, and social inclusion. It contained explicit recommendations for incorporating political, legal, economic, and social factors to foster productive employment and to reduce income inequality. Yet these recommendations were not to avail five years later, as full employment was absent in the original formulation of the Millennium Development Goals (MDGs) in 2000—first, because employment was allegedly difficult to measure and second, because concentration on direct poverty alleviation measures led to a relative neglect of policies dealing with employment in general (Amsden 2011). However, political pressure increased on the UN and in 2005 full employment was incorporated into MDG1 as a sub-goal to poverty alleviation but without any indication of necessary structural changes to create more productive employment (see van der Hoeven 2017).

In dealing with the impact of globalization and contributing to the debate on the MDGs, the ILO (1999) and various scholars (e.g., Stiglitz 2002) advanced the notion of productive employment by developing the concept of 'decent work', which emphasizes four elements: employment, social security, workers' rights, and social dialogue. Employment refers to work of all kinds and has both quantitative and qualitative dimensions. In order to *foster coherence of various national policies for decent work* and to measure progress, Ghai (2005) suggested creating a decent work index; that was, however, never accepted as there was no agreement within the ILO on which indicators such an index should contain.

In preparing for the Sustainable Development Goals (SDGs), adopted in 2015 and successor to the MDGs, successful proposals were made to give productive employment more promise in the process of international goal setting (Martins and Lucci 2013; Nayyar 2013a; van der Hoeven 2014). Unlike the MDGs, the SDGs incorporate a labour market perspective by elaborating on the themes of productivity and employment and by adding the perspective of labour rights. The SDGs also advocate a redistributive growth path and policies that promote equality of opportunity and outcome (Luebker 2017). Since the SDGs also intend to foster vast improvements in education and health, as well as participation in decision-making, the concerns expressed by Myrdal about labour market issues have never been accentuated more in international discourse. *However, as Myrdal also argues, what is in the benevolent planner's mind is often not translated into actual policies, as economic, social, cultural, and religious power have a great influence on development in general and also on that in the labour market.*

2.3 Analytical Approach

The next sections analyse how various sub-regional groups and countries in Asia have fared in economic and labour market issues since 1965, first by comparing Asian regions to other developing regions, and second by looking at growth and labour market dynamics in Asian countries themselves. Sets of countries are constructed that have grown fast with good labour market outcomes, those that have grown fast with weak labour market outcomes, and those that have not grown fast and have poorer labour market outcomes.

Various indicators are used that Myrdal proposed in *Asian Drama* to define what good labour market and employment outcomes are. Economic growth is measured by growth in gross domestic product (GDP) per capita, and economic structure by the percentage of workers in agriculture and industry. Poverty rates and the percentage of working poor are indications of socio-economic progress. Indicators of labour market performance are employment-to-population rate, labour force participation rate, unemployment rates, and the percentage of wage and salaried workers, all broken down by gender (something which Myrdal did not apply). Literacy rates and secondary school completion rates are not only indications of the quality of the labour force, contributing to higher productivity, but are also worthwhile goals in themselves. Using such an elaborate set of labour market indicators to get a picture of the employment problem acknowledges that in the relationship between labour markets, employment, and development, the causation runs in both directions, thus considering development, good labour markets, and employment both as a means and an end.

The classification of Asian countries into sets of countries with different growth and labour market regimes provides, in the following sections, a basis for analysing from a macroeconomic perspective how policies and institutions in certain countries have reinforced each other, leading to superior outcomes—something that Myrdal did not quite provide in his analytical framework.

3. The Development Experience

3.1 Asian Regions Compared with other Developing Regions

One can question the conclusion of *Asian Drama* that Asian countries are constrained in their development potential and their ability to create employment. Comparing developments in Asia with other major developing regions suggests that the drama was perhaps developing much more strongly in other regions than in Asia. *Asian Drama* paints a rather pessimistic picture of development in Asia. A few decades after its publication, other publications painted a rather different picture. A World Bank publication in the early 1990s spoke of an East Asian Miracle (World Bank 1993). It singled out five countries and two city-states in East Asia that underwent rapid development in terms of growth and employment. Of the fourteen developing countries to which Nayyar (2013b) attributes the potential to catch up with developed countries, seven are located in Asia.

Over the fifty-year period 1965–2015 one notices a different picture than Myrdal predicted (van der Hoeven 2018: table 1). In comparing developing countries in four regions—East Asia and the Pacific, South Asia, Latin America, and

Sub-Saharan Africa (SSA)—the East Asia and Pacific region, with initially the lowest per capita income of all four regions, shows an average annual GDP per capita growth of 6.2 per cent, which accelerated to 8.1 per cent over the period from 2000 to 2015. Its GDP per capita in 2015 thereby surpassed both that of South Asia and of SSA. Although much lower than in East Asia and the Pacific, average per capita growth over the fifty-year period 1965–2015 in South Asia was 3.1 per cent per annum, which also accelerated to 5.4 per cent in the period from 2000 to 2015. In contrast, annual per capita growth from 1965 to 2015 in the other major developing regions was much slower: 1.4 per cent in Latin America and only 0.2 per cent in SSA. Annual per capita growth in these regions during the 2000 to 2015 period was also much higher; in effect, SSA's growth rate of 2.6 per cent surpassed that of Latin America, which had the lowest rate (2.2 per cent) of that period. These superior growth patterns and the patterns of diversification in Asian economies have been a steady process over the last fifty years as shown by Ocampo et al. (2009: figure 3.1).

Developing country regions also show a great variation in the employment-to-population rate (van der Hoeven 2018: table 1). Concentrating on comparable and reliable figures from 2000, the fastest-growing region (East Asia and the Pacific) shows the highest employment-to-population ratio, and although the ratio declined from 72.1 per cent in 2000 to 67.7 per cent in 2015, it remained the highest of all the developing regions. South Asia was the lowest of all in 2000 with 57.0 per cent, declining to 52.8 per cent in 2015. The difference between the fastest-growing Asian region and the slower-growing Asian region is thus striking. Labour has played a much greater part in the fast-growing Asian Pacific region than in the South Asian region. This can also be seen in the poverty figures, for which comparable data are available from 1980 to 2015. Using the US$3.20 per day poverty line, the percentage of people in poverty in the Asian Pacific region dropped from a staggering 93.5 per cent in 1980 to 17.6 per cent in 2015, while in the South Asian region it dropped from 84.2 per cent to only 52.0 per cent in 2015—a much slower pace of poverty reduction, which is more in line with that in Sub-Saharan Africa and Latin America. The two Asian sub-regions also have lower unemployment rates. In 2000 and 2015, the East Asia and Pacific region and the South Asian region had figures well below 5 per cent, while those of the other two developing regions were, though declining, much higher.

Khan (2012) explains the superior performance of the Asian sub-regions, especially that of East Asia, by continued employment intensive growth, which was stimulated initially by a transformation in agriculture, caused by more egalitarian landholdings, and by a consequent increase in industrial activities, with initial high output employment elasticities stimulated by a strong final demand regime either through exports or through internal consumption. The next sub-section analyses how these and other factors have played out in different categories of Asian countries.

3.2 Diverse Developing Experience in Asian Countries

This sub-section analyses labour market performance and development in South and East Asian countries over the last fifty years and deals with the diversity of Asian experience, covering, unlike Myrdal's study, a substantial number of countries. It traces these countries' various development paths and labour market performance. The analysis examines factors underlying success or failure in labour market performance by constructing a set of Asian countries classified by high or low growth and by good or weak labour market performance that experienced: (a) rapid economic growth with good labour market performance; (b) rapid economic growth with weak labour market performance; or (c) neither rapid economic growth nor good labour market performance, where underemployment persisted in the subsistence sector and grew in the urban informal sector. A fourth theoretical possibility of a country with low growth and good labour market performance can be excluded, based on actual experience over the last decades. Furthermore, because of the great diversity in growth performance in Asia, it is more appropriate, for analytical purposes, to distinguish not two but three different country groupings with various growth performances.

3.2.1 Growth Regimes

Van der Hoeven (2018: tables 2, 4) constructed for thirteen East, South, and Southeast Asian countries, based on growth and labour market outcomes from 1965 to 2015, different country categories:[2]

- 4 fast growers, with an average per capita growth rate of more than 4.5 per cent
- 5 steady growers with an average per capita growth rate of between 4.5 and 3 per cent
- 4 slow growers with a per capita growth rate of less than 3 per cent.

The first group, in descending order of per capita growth, is: China, South Korea, Vietnam (data for 1965 to 1985 missing), and Thailand. However, these countries showed considerable variation in growth performance over the fifty-year period. South Korea had the second highest growth per annum rate of all countries from 1965 to 1975 (8.73 per cent). But, its growth rate was somewhat affected by the financial crisis in 2007, with its annual growth rate being only 2.73 per cent over the period 2006 to 2015, which was more in line with growth in the developed countries in the group to which it belonged in that period.

---

[2] For lack of consistent time series Cambodia, Bhutan, and Myanmar were not retained, while Taiwan also was not retained, as it is not included in the available comparative databases. Furthermore, for reasons explained in Nayyar (2013b), the city economies of Singapore and Hong Kong have not been retained either.

China shows an opposite trend, starting with an annual growth rate of 4.26 per cent in the 1965–1975 period, rising to annual growth rates of over 8 per cent during the 1986–1995, 1996–2005 and 2006–2015 periods. Thailand had steady growth of 4 per cent during the first two periods from 1965 to 1975 and 1976 to 1985, which peaked in the decade from 1986 to 1995 and then fell back, partly as a consequence of the Asian crisis in 1998, to more modest growth rates of 2.5 per cent and 2.75 per cent in the 1996–2005 and the 2006–2015 periods. Vietnam's growth rate (as measured over the ten-year periods from 1986) was continuously steady at around 5 per cent.

The second group, that of steady growers, contains Laos, Malaysia, Sri Lanka, Indonesia, and India. Laos (1965–1985 data missing), though starting at a lower annual growth level of 2.93 per cent in the period 1986–1995, gradually increased annual growth to 6.37 per cent in the period 2006 to 2015. In contrast, Malaysia had strong annual growth during the first three periods (1965–1975, 1976–1985, and 1986–1995), but then tapered off over the last two ten-year periods, dropping to below 4 per cent. Indonesia also grew annually by more than 4 per cent for the first three 10-year periods, but had exceptionally weak performance of only 0.85 per cent annual growth during the period 1996–2005. India and Sri Lanka both showed increasing annual growth levels over the five ten-year periods. India started from a low base of 1.25 per cent and 1.83 per cent growth from 1965 to 1975 and from 1976 to 1985, rising to 5.84 per cent from 2006 to 2015. Sri Lanka started on a somewhat better footing with 2.41 per cent annual growth from 1965 to 1975, gradually nudging up to above 5.49 per cent from 2006 to 2015.

The group of slow growers consists of Pakistan, Nepal, Bangladesh, and the Philippines. Pakistan started with modest annual growth during the first three ten-year periods, falling to low levels of 1.61 per cent and 1.08 per cent during the last two ten-year periods. Bangladesh shows the opposite pattern, starting from strong negative annual growth of −2.30 per cent from 1965 to 1975 and moving to higher growth during the period 2006 to 2015. Nepal shows a similar pattern. The Philippines has a more erratic growth pattern, starting the 1965–1975 period with annual growth of 2.41 per cent, followed by two decades of almost no or negative growth, but only nudging up to 3.64 per cent in 2006–2015. As this description of growth performance over the fifty-year period 1965–2015 shows, development in the countries under consideration was neither uniform nor linear. Some countries did better in the earlier part of the fifty-year period, while others, because of the end of war, internal turbulence, or changes in policies, did better in the more recent decades.

Looking at a more recent period (1986–2015), the picture of economic development changes only slightly. Only three countries are classified differently. In the 1986–2015 period, India belonged to the group of high-growth countries instead of the group of medium-growth countries, Bangladesh to the group of medium-growth countries instead of the group of low-growth countries, and

Table 12.1 Country classifications by economic growth: 1965–2015 and 1986–2015

	High growth	Medium growth	Low growth
1965–2015	China, S. Korea, *Vietnam*, Thailand	Malaysia, Indonesia, *Laos*, India, Sri Lanka	Pakistan, Nepal, Bangladesh, Philippines
1986–2015	China, S. Korea, Vietnam, India	Thailand, Malaysia, Indonesia, Laos, Sri Lanka, Bangladesh	Pakistan, Nepal, Philippines

Note: Countries in italics do not have information for all time periods.
Source: Based on van der Hoeven (2018: table 2).

Thailand to the group of medium-growth countries instead of the group of high-growth countries (Table 12.1).

Thus, out of the thirteen countries, only two made it to a higher-growth league in the later period, while only one degraded. So, the growth dynamism that Asian countries had shown over 1965–2015, at the time when *Asian Drama* was written was reinforced, with a few exceptions, in the period from 1986 to 2015.

3.2.2 Labour Market Regimes

How do the growth regimes in the various countries relate to their labour market regimes? As noted by Myrdal, consistent and comparable information on social development and labour markets is much harder to come by than that on economic development. Thanks to efforts of Asian scholars like Amartya Sen and Mahbub al Haq, consistent and comparable information on social development has gradually become more available since the 1990s. So, in order to appraise how labour markets have performed under different growth regimes in Asian countries, we concentrate the discussion on the 1986–2015 period rather than on the full 1965–2015 period.

Myrdal cautioned against using the Western concept of unemployment to appraise the employment or labour market situation (Myrdal 1968: 998, 1,118, and 2,221), as did Turham (1970). The question is whether such caution is still relevant today. This is indeed the case. Ghose et al. (2008) have convincingly shown that the unemployment rate is not an appropriate measure to distinguish whether a country belongs to a good or weak labour market regime. In countries without any decent form of unemployment benefits, poor and middle-income workers cannot afford to be unemployed, whereas richer workers are often listed as unemployed while they are waiting for more highly paid jobs (Ghose et al. 2008: 79). A country like China, with a rapidly expanding labour market, has consistently higher unemployment figures than India, Nepal, or the Philippines (van der Hoeven 2018: table 4). Thus, the unemployment rate is not a very accurate measure to compare the functioning of labour markets in Asian developing countries. In order to establish whether a country belongs to a good or weak labour market regime, van der Hoeven (2018: tables 2, 4) uses a mixed set of labour market indicators such as working poor, employment in agriculture, employment-to-population ratio, male and female labour force participation rates, percentage wage and salaried workers by sex, literacy rate, and secondary school completion, as indicators of the quality of the labour force itself.

The group of fast growers over the 1986–2015 period (China, Korea, Vietnam, and India) show a mixed pattern in terms of labour market regime.

China, Korea, and Vietnam show:

- fast declining poverty rates (down from 86.8 per cent over the 1986–1995 period to 23.7 per cent over the 2006–2015 period in China and down from 78.3 per cent to 28.1 per cent in Vietnam, while poverty is non-existent in Korea);
- a fast declining percentage of working poor;
- a rapid or steady decline of the percentage of workers in agriculture (down from 17.7 per cent to 6.6 per cent in Korea, from 63.8 per cent to 46.5 per cent in Vietnam, and 58.2 per cent to 35.5 per cent in China);
- high and increasing literacy rates (China 95.1 per cent and Vietnam 93.5 per cent in 2015); and
- a high employment-to-population rate of over or near 70 per cent in 2015.

Furthermore, China and Korea have a high percentage of wage and salaried workers. Yet, the share of wage and salaried workers in Vietnam falls in the same range as that of countries in the group of steady growers and slow growers. However, India's structural and labour market profile resembles more that of countries with a lower growth rate: high levels of poverty, high percentage of workers working in agriculture, lower levels of labour force participation rate, low levels and only gradually increasing levels of wage and salary workers, and low and only slowly increasing literacy rates. The only indicator where India levels with the other countries in the group of high-growth countries is that of secondary school completion rates.

The labour market outcomes of the group of steady growers are rather diverse. In Laos and Bangladesh, the poverty rate has declined by less than in other countries, resulting in a still substantial level of working poor. Sri Lanka, Malaysia, Thailand, and Indonesia have had much faster poverty reduction than Laos and Bangladesh. Literacy rates have declined in Laos and, though growing, remain low in Bangladesh. Only in Malaysia is the share of wage and salaried workers high. The number of individuals who have completed secondary school education varies substantially in this group of steady growers, with the lowest in Bangladesh (17.1 per cent) and highest in Malaysia (56.1 per cent).

The group of slow growers all have still high poverty rates ranging from 37.9 per cent in the Philippines, to 47.3 per cent in Pakistan, and 50.9 per cent in Nepal. Pakistan and the Philippines also have low employment-to-population rates (Pakistan's being the lowest of all countries considered at 47.6 per cent). The rate in Nepal in contrast is the highest in the region. The percentage employed in

Table 12.2 Country classifications by growth and labour market regime: 1986–2015

	High growth	Medium growth	Low growth
Good labour market regime	China, S-Korea, Vietnam,	Malaysia, Indonesia, Thailand	
Weak labour market regime	India	Laos, Sri Lanka, Bangladesh,	Pakistan, Nepal, Philippines

Source: Based on van der Hoeven (2018: tables 2, 3, 4).

agriculture varies considerably in this group, with relatively lower rates in Pakistan and the Philippines (43.9 and 33.0 per cent) and a rather higher rate in Nepal (73.9 per cent). Literacy rates and secondary school completion rates are also very low in this group, except for the Philippines, which has high literacy and secondary school completion rates. The considerations discussed here lead to the following country groupings, which depict various growth and labour market regimes (Table 12.2).

3.2.3 Wages, Productivity, and Wage Shares

How wage developments relate to productivity growth is also important for the characterization of a good labour market regime. If wages lag behind productivity growth, this implies that workers profit less from the growth in the economy, causing in most cases a reduction in final demand, unless the increased profits are invested fully and effectively, leading to rapid future employment creation, in which case lower wages are 'compensated' with higher employment (see also Nayyar 2014). Unfortunately, for most of the countries and time periods considered, there are no complete data sets of wages and productivity, nor of the wage shares in GDP, so analysis of these issues needs to be restricted to a smaller number of countries and also to a shorter time period.

ILO (2016: figure B1) provides information for the 2006–2014 period for Korea, China, India, and Indonesia, countries where the majority of the population considered in this chapter live. Productivity grew fastest in China (80 per cent) and India (60 per cent), but less in Indonesia (about 40 per cent) and Korea (20 per cent). In all countries, real wages grew more slowly than productivity, with the discrepancy being much greater in India than in the other countries, confirming the classification of India as a weak labour market regime.

3.2.4 Female Employment and Labour Force Participation

Another striking point in the classification by growth and labour market regimes is the different position of women in the labour market. The most striking case is that of the group of countries in the fast-growing regime. Countries in this group that also have a good labour market regime all have a much higher female labour

Table 12.3 Female and male unemployment rates: 1996–2015

	Female unemployment rate lower or equal to male unemployment rate	Female unemployment rate larger than the male rate but less than 1.5 times the male rate	Female unemployment rate larger than 1.5 times the male rate
2006–2015	China, S. Korea, Vietnam, Laos, Nepal, Thailand	Malaysia, Indonesia, India, Philippines	Bangladesh, Pakistan, Sri Lanka
1996–2005	China, S. Korea, Laos, Vietnam, Thailand	Bangladesh, Malaysia, Indonesia, India, Philippines, Nepal	Pakistan, Sri Lanka

Source: Based on van der Hoeven (2018: table 4).

force participation rate than the countries with a weak labour market regime (for the 2006–2015 period: China 64.0 per cent and Vietnam 72.9 per cent, compared to India 29.5 per cent). Also, the difference in the percentage of wage and salaried workers is higher on average for the fast-growing countries with a good labour market regime than for those with a weak labour market regime. In general, countries with lower female labour force participation rates belong, whatever their growth regimes, to the group of countries with a weak labour market regime (van der Hoeven 2018: table 4).

As explained earlier, because of country-specific anomalies and a correlation with the state of the economy, we did not consider the unemployment rate as a useful indicator to compare Asian countries over a long time period, but the relation between male and female unemployment rates gives a strong indication of the labour market regime in a particular country. In countries with a high- or medium-growth regime and with a good labour market regime, female unemployment is similar to male unemployment, while in countries with a slow or medium-growth regime female unemployment is higher and sometimes substantially higher (Pakistan, Sri Lanka, Bangladesh) than in other country groupings. Thus, the way women are treated in the labour market has a clear effect on the economic and social status and growth potential of Asian countries (Table 12.3).

4. Policies, Institutions, and Outcomes

Can we distinguish specific policies and institutions for the group of countries with high or medium growth and good labour market outcomes? Common characteristics of the fast-growing countries with good labour market outcomes (Korea, China, and Vietnam) are that these countries did not rely exclusively on the market for allocation of resources and that their macroeconomic policies did not correspond to neoclassical macroeconomic prescriptions. Another important characteristic was their initially low household income inequality. Their low household income inequality was itself the result of more equal factor distribution of income, labelled by Adelman (1979) as redistribution before growth. The most salient examples of equal factor distribution were programmes of land redistribution and early investment in education. This distribution in land and human capital assets resulted in higher factor rewards for workers and peasants when the economic process started to take off, and left fewer factor rewards for capital owners, thus creating spells of virtuous growth.

Amsden (2011) in her assessment of the early developments in East Asia argues that the institutions in these countries constrained, in the development process, the influence of capital ('taming capital'), not through social contracts or labour market agreements, as happened in the equitable high-growth episode in Europe in the aftermath of the Second World War, but through state interventions by enlightened bureaucracy, which either directly (China) or indirectly forced firms to invest, to expand, and to create employment. However, the effect was the same: productivity gains were used to invest, to expand employment, and to increase wages. Taylor (2010) labels such a virtuous growth regime as mildly profit-led, where there is room for wage growth and where profits were reinvested in the economy, which on the one hand added to a demand impulse, but also led, through productivity gains, to an expansion of supply (the so-called Kaldor–Verdoorn mechanism). This virtuous growth pattern of the fast-growing Asian countries was the result of what Khan (2007) calls growth-enhancing governance. Khan contrasts this growth-enhancing governance with market-enhanced governance, a set of policies advocated by the Bretton Woods institutions in the 1980s and 1990s as part of the Washington Consensus.

Two important observations are in order. First, although the fast-growing countries with good labour market regimes started their development process with low-inequality regimes, in some countries household inequality has since risen substantially (for example, in China where income inequality is reaching a Gini ratio of 0.5 or more, UNU-WIDER n.d.). This begs the question of the sustainability of current growth regimes, an issue that we will take up in more detail in the section on future prospects. A second observation is that several countries that did not manifest a high-growth regime, also have, or had at least in the past, a low-inequality regime. Hence, a low-inequality regime is a necessary but certainly not a sufficient condition for a virtuous growth and employment pattern.

Therefore, another common element in the three fast-growing and the three medium-growing countries with good labour market outcomes must be sought in the drivers of growth. All countries in this group made use of external markets to sustain a demand-led growth regime. However, as in the case of their investment regime, external demand was not left to an invisible hand. On the contrary, firms were encouraged to export, with clear export targets. Korean firms were not allocated foreign exchange or further export licences if they had not met earlier agreed export targets and investment (Amsden 2007). All the virtuous growing countries defied the lessons from the 'Washington Consensus', which came to dominate policy advice from the Bretton Woods institutions in the 1980s (van der Hoeven and Taylor 2000).

Government policies to increase agricultural productivity through land redistribution, investment, subsidies, and the provision of 'public goods' for agriculture and for human development have also been a turning point in countries with fast and medium growth and with a good labour market regime. In the case of China, Saith (2016: 85–6) argues:

> Chinese advantage originates not in the market reforms era, but in the socialist period when the countryside was organized in rural collectives. In India, rural institutions were generally obstructive, sticky and posed a constraint to policies of rapid transformation; in China, the institutional profile, far from setting a constraint, was itself converted into a policy instrumental variable, where institutional features were designed and periodically redesigned primarily using the criteria of their functional appropriateness for generating rural accumulation and growth.

The countries with fast and median growth with a good labour market regime, despite different political constellations, manifested a Lewisian development process where labour could move to industry—a process that Myrdal himself had cast doubt upon because of the inability of the rural workforce to be productively engaged in industry. The above makes clear that countries with an explicit growth regime based on strong demand impulses, and managing a fair income distribution regime, showed better performances in the labour market, as employment generation and increasing rewards on the labour factor made a virtuous growth path possible.

The issue of labour intensity in sectors of the economy cannot be left unaddressed. Myrdal himself, in discussing cottage industries (Myrdal 1968: chapter 25), refers to this at various instances and favours development of cottage industries. Designing policies for labour-intensive activities is often heralded together with programmes for poverty alleviation as the magic key to solve the unemployment problem in developing and emerging countries (for an insightful and critical discussion, see Amsden 2011). However, in the countries with virtuous growth patterns, the stimulating cottage industries played a lesser role than in the countries that did not manifest a virtuous growth pattern. The formal industry sector in India is less labour intensive than in the other countries in the group of fast-growing countries (Ghose 2016; Verick 2016). Breman (2013) argues furthermore that maintaining a large informal workforce is a necessary element in India to keep workers' wages low.

Comparing the trajectories of India and China shows the importance of well coordinated industrialization policies for good labour market outcomes. The success of China in industrialization compared to India is well demonstrated by Felipe (2012: 101): whereas the actual share of manufacturing to total output in China is *higher* than its predicted share based on its GDP per capita level (34.5 per cent versus 27.3 per cent), the actual share in India is *lower* than the predicted share (15.85 per cent versus 19.55 per cent, figures for 2000). Female labour force participation, the percentage of wage and salaried workers, employment-to-population rate, and literacy rate are all higher in China than in India.

While India has made efforts to boost industrialization since 2000, its share of manufacturing remains below its potential. Various policies have contributed to this. Nayyar (2018) points to the low level of loans from development banks in India, where the percentage of outstanding loans from development banks to GDP dropped over the period 2000 to 2010 from 7.4 per cent to 0.8 per cent, while the percentage rose in China from 6.2 per cent to 11.2 per cent. Chandrasekhar and Ghosh (2006: 278–9) point to the success of the more dirigisted macroeconomic policies in China:

> There is an overarching conclusion, of wider relevance, that can be drawn from the comparative analysis of the experiences of macroeconomic management in China and India. Discussions on macroeconomic policies counterpose the policies adopted in the dirigiste period, ostensibly characterized by financial repression, with a framework characterized by a reduced role for fiscal policy and for state expenditure and a greater role for the liberalized financial sector in mobilizing and channeling investment. The Chinese experience makes it clear that such either-or dichotomies are not inevitable. India's experience suggests that relent-lessly pursuing the transition to a marketist macroeconomic framework makes it difficult to sustain investment and growth and to translate the benefits of that growth into better outcomes with regard to employment and poverty reduction.

The amalgam of economic and labour market policies in China led to a process of 'cumulative causation' (as Myrdal labelled such processes) that fostered effective transformation and good labour market outcomes, as compared to India.

In order to flesh out why some of the other countries in Asia had high growth and good labour market outcomes and some not, Box 12.1 compares development and labour market patterns in Bangladesh and Vietnam. Because of past wars, these countries shared tremendous development challenges in the 1970s and even later. Bangladesh (created in 1972) and Vietnam (unified in 1975) both emerged from serious armed conflicts costing many lives and destroying large chunks of infrastructure, and needed to transform their economies and society. Box 12.1 concludes that the gradual and interventionist policies in agriculture and manufacturing in Vietnam led to a virtuous growth path and better labour market outcomes than in Bangladesh.

Box 12.1 Transformation policies and labour market outcomes in Vietnam and Bangladesh

---

After unification, Vietnam adopted a very centralized planning economy. Its first five-year plan was somewhat of a failure. Therefore, in 1986 Vietnam adopted a home-grown reform programme, *Doi Moi*, which resulted in the opening up of the economy, but with a strong role for the communist party, with a fair amount of government intervention in agriculture and with vigorous industrial

Continued

Box 12.1 *Continued*

policies (Tarp 2017: chapter 1). Bangladesh also started with a strong socialist-oriented government, but after a period of military rule and later a more democratic regime, free market fundamentals were restored in Bangladesh. Export-processing zones were established from 1983 and Bangladesh became one of the world's largest exporters of garments (Jenkins and Sen 2006).

The interventionist agricultural policy in Vietnam resulted in a system where out of around 2,000 of all rural households 41% were farming purely for the market, 18% were farm labourers, with the remaining households having diversified income sources. In Bangladesh, rural households were dominated by rural households with diversified income (48%) and by households living on farm labour (40%) with only 6% purely engaged in farming (World Bank 2008: 76; Fields 2012). In the 1986–1995 decade the labour market structures were similar in Vietnam and Bangladesh. However, the interventionist industrial policy in Vietnam paid off. While in 1990 the shares of manufacturing in GDP in Vietnam and Bangladesh were more or less the same (12.3% and 13.3% respectively), in 2005, Vietnam's share had greatly surpassed that of Bangladesh (20.6% versus 16.5%) (Szirmai 2012: 406–20).

These different transformation paths in Vietnam and Bangladesh also resulted in better labour market outcomes in Vietnam. In the 1986–1995 period, the shares of agricultural employment and manufacturing employment were the same in both countries (around 64% and 14%). This pattern changed over 2006–2015 to the extent that the share of agricultural employment declined in both countries to around 47%, but the share of manufacturing employment became larger in Vietnam (around 22%) than in Bangladesh (18%). Higher productivity in manufacturing in Vietnam also resulted in drastic changes in poverty profiles. Whereas the percentage of people living below the poverty line in the 1986–1995 period was about the same (78% in Vietnam, 80% in Bangladesh), the rate drastically decreased in the 2006–2015 period in Vietnam to 28%.

Hence, while both countries became export-oriented, the gradual interventionist policies in agriculture and manufacturing in Vietnam led to better economic and labour market outcomes than in Bangladesh.

5. Future Prospects

Myrdal's predictions and the subsequent developments in the majority of Asian countries show that predicting a long-term development trajectory of a country or of a region, and the evolution of the labour market therein, is hazardous. As Myrdal observed, development depends on economic, social, cultural, and religious factors as well as on strengthening institutions for a developmental state. The previous sections showed how a positive mix of these factors lead in some fast-growing countries to a virtuous development path with good labour market outcomes, but also how a negative mix can lead to slower development and weaker outcomes in the labour market.

We see six, not entirely independent, factors determining future development of economies and labour markets in Asia, which all point to the need for a continuation or for a stronger adoption of the demand-led growth which was so successful in some Asian countries.

5.1 Demographic Trends and Challenges

Asian economies have witnessed a substantial lift from demography. Demographic dividends—characterized by falling child dependency, a growing working-age population, and a moderate rise in old-age dependency—have contributed up to 2 per cent to annual GDP growth (ADB 2018). The transition to an older population in the foreseeable future will deprive the region of a main driver of its economic success. While demographic dividends are vanishing in China and Thailand today, Indonesia, Malaysia, and Vietnam are expected to lose their dividends by the 2020s. India and the Philippines should be able to benefit from their youthful populations for a little longer—possibly up until 2030 (Scherpf 2015).

Demographics are not a fate, and countries can develop coping mechanisms that facilitate a sustainable transition towards older societies (ADB 2018). Such mechanisms include immigration and enhanced productivity. In addition, the participation of older people and women in the labour force needs to be encouraged (Scherpf 2015). Across emerging Asia, the retirement age is still fairly low (55 in Malaysia, Indonesia, India, and Thailand, 60 in China and Vietnam, 62 in Singapore, and 65 in the Philippines). Against the background of increasing life expectancy, a rise in the legal retirement age can be a simple yet effective policy response. Eventually, countries need to find meaningful and fair ways to transfer resources from the working population that generate savings to retirees with inadequate income to sustain their consumption. Given the changes in traditional family-based support structures, the development of comprehensive public transfer schemes has to be a key policy priority (Scherpf 2015). Asia's financial systems still lag substantially behind the region's dynamic real economy, and many Asian countries have labour markets that discourage employers from hiring older workers (Park et al. 2015).

5.2 Migration

Demographic developments also affect international migration. But migration is even more affected by economic and political factors. ESCAP (2016: 51) observes a great divergence between countries in the Asian region and classifies the region into three groupings: those with a GDP per capita below US$10,000 (PPP in 2012 US$), those with a GDP per capita between US$10,000 and US$20,000, and those with a GDP per capita greater than US$20,000. In countries in the last group, which contains, for example, South Korea and Malaysia, in-migration is greater than out-migration; in the middle-income group (containing, for example, China and Thailand), in- and out-migration are more or less equal; and in the lowest income category (containing all the other countries we analysed in section 3) out-migration still predominates. For these countries, remittances (from countries in as well as outside the Asian region) still remain a considerable part of GDP. For Bangladesh, Nepal, Pakistan, Philippines, Sri Lanka, and Vietnam, remittances still contributed over 5 per cent to GDP in 2016 (ADB 2018: 56). However, as other countries in the region that have grown quickly have shown, out-migration and remittances can change quickly.

The UN estimates that, based on population and economic projections, China, South Korea, Thailand, Malaysia, and Sri Lanka will need immigrants to maintain dependency rates and economic growth, while countries in South Asia as well as Indonesia and Laos can 'afford' out-migration (*The Economist* 2017). Furthermore, technological development also changes the characteristics of migration. The World Bank (2009: 158) observes that skilled out-migration from East Asia and the Pacific and from South Asia is already over 60 per cent, the highest for all regions in the world. Binding labour shortages in the Asian region over the next 25 years can only be avoided, if Asian countries improve their collaboration for an orderly migration regime.

5.3 Technology, Industrialization, and Labour Replacement

Technological development and industrialization have played a major role in the fast-growing Asian countries with a virtuous growth path and superior labour market outcomes (Lin 2012). For the fast-growing countries that have reached a certain level of industrialization and with good labour market performances (like China), the question is whether further industrialization should be pursued or whether more attention should be given to developing various activities in the high-end service sector, as manufacturing costs are rapidly rising (McKinsey 2017a). In the transition to more service-oriented activities, artificial technologies can dramatically boost productivity. McKinsey (2017b) argues that this increased productivity could be a crucial capability for China to sustain its future economic growth as the country's working-age population declines. It estimates that automating workplaces with artificial intelligence could add 0.8 to 1.4 percentage points to GDP growth annually, depending on the speed of adoption. However, realizing this potential in China also depends on automating workplaces across China's traditional industries and not just among the technology giants. If China manages to combine this with its continued demand-based economic growth, it will become a strong growth pole for the whole Southeast and East Asian region. Countries in Asia at the lower end of development would still gain from industrialization. A recent World Bank report (Hallward-Driemeier and Nayyar 2017: 6) concludes:

> With reform priorities becoming more urgent, one key lesson is that new technologies and changing globalization patterns increase the complementarities between economy wide and targeted approaches. Yet it may be more feasible, at least in the immediate future, to meet the requirements to be competitive by targeting locations and sectors rather than attempting to reform and provide public investments throughout the whole economy and that given the growing uncertainty about the pace of technological change, horizontal policies that develop transferable skills would reduce risks in the future.

5.4 Future of Work

A related issue to technological development is the future of work in Asian countries. The discussion on the future of work is often couched in terms of how automatization is affecting the high-end and profitable manufacturing industries in Asia and how robots are penetrating the industrial production processes. Yet this seems mainly to apply to China and South Korea. UNCTAD (2017) observes that robotization has been primarily employed in the automotive, electrical, and electronics industries, but that in many labour-intensive industries, such as garment making, widespread automatization is not yet suitable and that in countries with large numbers of low-skilled workers entering the labour force (as in the set of Asian countries with low growth and weak labour market regimes considered in this chapter) automatization may still drive up production costs. Governments in these countries therefore need to apply judicious policies for encouraging new technologies but not rely on the effects of these solely, or massively subsidize these technologies. The experience of China of 'walking on two legs' when it developed its industrial base while maintaining agricultural output and employment, could also be applied by combining more traditional labour-intensive manufacturing and high technological activities.

5.5 Social Development, Education, and Health

A strong improvement in literacy and secondary education is a common characteristic of Asian countries with high or medium growth rates and good labour market outcomes. This conclusion has at least two important pointers for the future development of Asian countries. First, in countries that lag behind in achieving full literacy and secondary education, growth and productive employment will remain constrained. Attaining full literacy and investment in education as part of an overall growth strategy is warranted in these countries. Second, countries that have progressed well in these areas need to be cognizant of the fast changes in the labour market caused by the technological development discussed above. This requires changes in school curricula and in developing systems of continuous learning and upgrading of skills. Failing in this will lead to a slowdown of growth, deteriorating labour market conditions, and increasing wage and income inequality.

5.6 Income and Wealth Inequalities

Income inequality, in most of the Asian countries analysed, went up or remained stable over the period considered. Most notable is the increase in India and China where the Gini ratio increased from the 0.26 to 0.35 range in the 1966–1970 period to the 0.45 to 0.55 range in the 2011–2015 period, while in other countries the Gini ratio went up one range or stayed in the same range (UNU-WIDER n.d.).

Income inequality has increased for various reasons, but a strong contributing factor is the declining wage share, indicating that capital owners capture productivity gains to a larger degree than workers. This, combined with increases in wealth inequality, is leading to an increase in the income share of the top one per cent of the population. McKinsey (2017b) argues that the fast-growing artificial intelligence in China and in other fast-growing Asian countries will raise the premium placed on digital skills, while reducing demand for medium- and low-skilled workers, potentially exacerbating income inequality. It is difficult to predict whether this trend of rising inequality will continue, but there are clear signs that a continuing rise in inequality is socially and economically untenable. Few countries in the region have explicit policies to reduce income and wealth inequality. With growing inequality, the economic growth of the past is not sustainable (van der Hoeven 2011; Nayyar 2013b), and high inequality and faltering growth will lead to social unrest and to deteriorating labour market outcomes, undoing for some countries the gains achieved in this area (Nayyar 2017).

Domestic policies to face these challenges in Asian countries can be reinforced or compromised by international developments. If, as UNCTAD's *Trade and Development Report* (2017) strongly advocates, a global social contract on global growth and employment creation could be achieved (van der Hoeven 2012), then economic and social developments in Asia would certainly progress faster than they would without such a global social contract. But whether such a global social contract will emerge is not at all a given in the current international political constellation.

6. Conclusions

This chapter reviewed how economic development and labour markets have interacted in Asian countries since the publication of Myrdal's *Asian Drama* in 1968. It found that Myrdal was correct in rejecting the Western approach to, and the definition of, employment by emphasizing the role of 'informal' employment, but that he underestimated the effects of the Lewisian development process. A classification of Asian countries by growth regimes and labour market regimes showed that in fast-growing countries with a good labour market regime, initial conditions played a certain role, but less than Myrdal had predicted. Myrdal's concept of cumulative causation explains development in Asian countries better: all fast-growing countries with a good labour market regime have pursued a developmental state and applied a host of interventionist policies in agriculture, industry, and macroeconomics, as well as in social policies and in the treatment of women in the labour market. Successful countries are also characterized by initial low-income inequality and targeted redistribution of factors of production. For some countries, though, growing inequality, together with other development challenges (demographics, migration, technology, the future of work, and social policies) may, if not attended to, become a problem in the future. Furthermore, domestic policies to face these challenges may be reinforced or compromised by international developments that are difficult to predict.

Acknowledgements

I would like to thank Deepak Nayyar, Guanghua Wan, an anonymous referee, as well as participants at seminars in Hanoi (Central Institute for Economic Management, March 2018) and in Shanghai (Institute of World Economy, Fudan University, June 2018) for useful comments and suggestions.

References

ADB (2018). *Labor Migration in Asia, Increasing the Development Impact of Migration through Finance and Technology*. Manila: Asian Development Bank.

Adelman, I. (1979). 'Redistribution before Growth'. In *Institute of Social Studies, Development of Societies, the Next Twenty-five Years*. The Hague: Martinus Nijhoff.

Amsden, A.H. (2007). *Escape from Empire, the Developing World's Journey through Heaven and Hell*. Boston, MA: MIT Press.

Amsden, A.H. (2011). 'Say's Law, Poverty Persistence, and Employment Neglect'. In R. van der Hoeven (ed.) *Employment, Inequality and Globalization: A Continuous Concern*. London: Routledge.

Breman, J. (2013). *At Work in the Informal Economy of India: A Perspective from the Bottom Up*. Delhi: Oxford University Press.

Chandrasekhar, C., and J. Ghosh (2006). 'Macroeconomic Policy, Inequality and Poverty Reduction in China'. In G.A Cornia (ed.) *Pro-poor Macroeconomics, Potential and Limitations*. Houndmills: Palgrave.

ESCAP (2016). *Asia-Pacific Migration Report 2015, Migrants' Contributions to Development*. Bangkok: Economic and Social Commission for Asia and the Pacific.

Felipe, J. (2012). *Inclusive Growth, Full Employment, and Structural Change: Implications and Policies for Developing Asia*. London and Manila: Anthem Press and Asian Development Bank.

Fields, G. (2012). *Working Hard, Working Poor: A Global Journey*. Oxford: Oxford University Press.

Ghai, D. (2005). 'Decent Work: Universality and Diversity', International Institute of Labour Studies, ILO, Geneva, Discussion Paper 159.

Ghose, A.K. (2016). *Indian Employment Report 2016 Challenge and the Imperative of Manufacturing-led Growth*. New Delhi: Oxford University Press.

Ghose, A.K., N. Majid, and C. Ernst (2008). *The Global Employment Challenge*. Geneva: ILO.

Hallward-Driemeier, M., and G. Nayyar (2017). *Trouble in the Making? The Future of Manufacturing-Led Development*. Washington, DC: World Bank.

Hart, K. (1971). 'Informal Income Opportunities and Urban Unemployment Opportunities in Ghana', Paper delivered at Conference on Urban Employment in Africa, IDS, University of Sussex, 12–16 September.

Hopkins, M., and R. van der Hoeven (1983). *Basic Needs in Development Planning*. Aldershot: Gower.

ILO (International Labour Organization) (1999). *Decent Work, Report of the Director General, to the International Labour Conference 1999*. Geneva: International Labour Organization.

ILO (2013). *Measuring Informality: A Statistical Manual on the Informal Sector and Informal Employment*. Geneva: International Labour Organization.

ILO (2016). *Wages in Asia and the Pacific and the Arab States*. Bangkok: ILO Regional Office for Asia and the Pacific.

Jenkins, R., and K. Sen (2006). 'International Trade and Manufacturing Employment in the South: Four Country Case Studies', *Oxford Development Studies*, 34(3): 299–322.

Jolly, R., E. de Kadt, H. Singer, and F. Wilson (1973). *Third World Employment, Problems and Strategy*. Harmondsworth: Penguin Education.

Khan, A.R. (2012). 'Employment in Sub-Saharan Africa: Lessons to be Learnt from the East Asian Experience'. In A. Noman, K. Botchwey, H. Stein, and J.E. Stiglitz (eds) *Good Growth and Governance in Africa, Rethinking Development Strategies*. New York: Oxford University Press.

Khan, M.H. (2007). 'Governance, Economic Growth and Development since the 1960s', United Nations, New York, UNDESA Working Paper 54.

Lewis, W.A. (1954). 'Economic Development with Unlimited Supplies of Labour', *Manchester School*, 22: 133–91.

Lin J. (2012). *The Quest for Prosperity: How Developing Economies Can Take Off*. Princeton, NJ: Princeton University Press.

Luebker, M. (2017). 'Poverty, Employment and Inequality in the SDGs: Heterodox Discourse, Orthodox Policies?'. In P.A.G. van Bergeijk and R. van der Hoeven (eds) *Sustainable Development Goals and Income Inequality*. Cheltenham: Edward Elgar.

Mahalanobis, P.C. (1958). 'Science and National Planning', *Sankya, The Indian Journal of Statistics*, 20(1&2): 77–8.

Maloney, W.S. (2004). 'Informality Revisited', *World Development*, 32(7): 1159–78.

Martins, P., and P. Lucci (2013). 'Recasting MDG 8: Global Policies for Inclusive Growth', Overseas Development Institute, London, Working Paper.

McKinsey Global Institute (2017a). *Artificial Intelligence: Implications for China*. London and Shanghai: McKinsey.

McKinsey Global Institute (2017b). *Jobs Lost, Jobs Gained: Workforce Transitions in a Time of Automation*. San Francisco, CA, London and Shanghai: McKinsey.

Myrdal, G. (1968). *Asian Drama: An Inquiry into the Poverty of Nations*. New York: Pantheon.

Nayyar, D. (2013a). 'The Millennium Development Goals Beyond 2015: Old Frameworks and New Constructs', *Journal of Human Development and Capabilities*, 14(3): 371–92.

Nayyar, D. (2013b). *Catch Up, Developing Countries in the World Economy*. Oxford: Oxford University Press.

Nayyar, D. (2014). 'Why Employment Matters: Reviving Growth and Reducing Inequality', *International Labour Review*, 153(3): 351–64.

Nayyar, D. (2017). 'Can Catch up Reduce Inequality?'. In P.A.G. van Bergeijk and R. van der Hoeven (eds) *Sustainable Development Goals and Income Inequality*. Cheltenham: Edward Elgar.

Nayyar, D. (2018). 'Financing Reindustrialization: Bring Back Development Banks?', MINT, New Delhi, Friday 11 May.

Ocampo, J.A., C. Rada, and L. Taylor (2009). *Growth and Policy in Developing Countries: A Structuralist Approach*. New York: Columbia University Press.

Park, D., S.-H. Lee, and A. Mason (2015). *Aging, Economic Growth, and Old-Age Security in Asia*. Cheltenham and Manila: Edward Elgar and Asian Development Bank.

Rao, V.K.R.V. (1938). 'The Problem of Unemployment in India', *Indian Journal of Economics*, 18(4): 627–34.

Saith, A. (2016). 'Transforming Peasantries in India and China: Comparative Investigations of Institutional Dimensions', *Indian Journal of Labour Economics*, 59: 85–124.

Scherpf, A. (2015). 'Asian Demographic Trends: A Threat to Growth', *Global Risks Insight*, 22 February, p. 1ff.

de Soto, H. (1989). *The Other Path: The Invisible Revolution in the Third World*. New York: Harper and Row.

Srinavasan, T.N., and P.-K. Bardhan (1974). 'Perspectives of Development: 1961–76: Implication of Planning for a Minimum Level of Living in Poverty and Income Distribution in India'. In P.K. Bardham and T.N. Srinavasan (eds) *Poverty and Income Distribution in India*. Calcutta: Statistical Publishing Society.

Stiglitz, J. (2002). 'Employment, Social Justice and Societal Wellbeing', *International Labour Review*, 141(1–2): 9–29.

Szirmai, A. (2012). 'Industrialization as an Engine of Growth in Developing Countries, 1950–2005', *Structural Change and Economic Dynamics*, 23(4): 406–20.

Tarp, F. (ed.) (2017). *Growth, Structural Transformation, and Rural Change in Viet Nam*. Oxford: Oxford University Press.

Taylor, L. (2010). *Maynard's Revenge: The Collapse of Free Market Macroeconomics*. Cambridge, MA: Harvard University Press.

The Economist (2017). 'Asia's looming Labour Shortage', 11 February.

Turham, D. (1970). *The Employment Problem in Less Developed Countries*. Paris: OECD.

UNCTAD (2017). *Trade and Development Report 2017*. Geneva: UNCTAD.

UNU-WIDER (n.d.) 'WIID—World Income Inequality Database'. Available at: https://www.wider.unu.edu/project/wiid-world-income-inequality-database (accessed October–December 2017 and May–June 2018).

van der Hoeven, R. (1988). *Planning for Basic Needs: A Soft Option or a Solid Policy, A Basic Needs Simulation Model Applied to Kenya*. Aldershot: Gower.

van der Hoeven, R. (ed.) (2011). *Employment, Inequality and Globalization: A Continuous Concern*. London: Routledge.

van der Hoeven, R. (2012). *Emerging Voices: A Global Social Contract to Follow the Millennium Development Goals*. Washington, DC: Council on Foreign Relations.

van der Hoeven, R. (2014). 'Full Employment Target: What Lessons for a Post-2015 Development Agenda?', *Journal of Human Development and Capabilities: A Multi-Disciplinary Journal for People-Centered Development*, 15(2–3): 10–21.

van der Hoeven, R. (2017). 'Can the SDGs Stem Rising Inequality in the World?'. In P.A.G. van Bergeijk and R. van der Hoeven (eds) *Sustainable Development Goals and Income Inequality*. Cheltenham: Edward Elgar.

van der Hoeven, R. (2018). 'Employment and Development in Asia', UNU-WIDER, Helsinki, WIDER Working Paper 2018/107.

van der Hoeven, R., and L. Taylor (2000). 'Introduction: Structural Adjustment, Labour Markets and Employment: Some Considerations for Sensible People', Special Section on Structural Adjustment and the Labour Market, *Journal of Development Studies*, 36(4): 20–32.

Verick, S.S. (2016). 'Manufacturing and Jobs: Is India Different?', *The Indian Journal of Labour Economics*, 59(1): 57–84.

World Bank (1993). *The East Asian Miracle*. Washington, DC: World Bank.

World Bank (2008). *World Development Report*. Washington, DC: World Bank.

World Bank (2009). *World Development Report*. Washington, DC: World Bank.

13

Institutions and Development

Mushtaq H. Khan

1. Introduction

Gunnar Myrdal's *Asian Drama* (1968) was arguably the first systematic analysis of the role of institutions in Asia's development. Myrdal described his magisterial work as an 'institutional approach' that aimed to explain why conventional economic analysis was providing inappropriate policy advice. Economic policies that worked in advanced countries were failing in Asia, Myrdal argued, because of Asian behavioural norms.[1] Conventional economics assumed that people would respond flexibly and rationally to market incentives, but social, institutional, and political factors made Asians respond in different ways.

Like Myrdal, later institutional economists such as North (1990) or Acemoglu and Robinson (2012) began to explain the poor performance of some developing countries by comparing their market-supporting institutions and informal norms with advanced countries. But like Myrdal, they ignored the Asian countries that performed remarkably well with unorthodox institutions, and they did not ask why similar unorthodox institutions failed to work in other Asian countries. The new institutional analysis failed to explain these variations because, first, it focused only on an analysis of *institutions*, both formal and informal, ignoring how characteristics of organizations and the distribution of *power* between them affected the operation of institutions and the persistence or otherwise of particular behavioural patterns. Second, they also downplayed the critical role of institutions in responding to market failures. Later developmental state theorists did focus on institutions that addressed market failures, in particular, industrial policy institutions. But they, too, ignored the role of power in explaining the effectiveness of *these* institutions. The 'political settlements framework' looks at the interdependence of institutions and organizations, and how the distribution of power across organizations affects the effectiveness of institutions and the persistence of particular types of informal behaviour. This framework can explain the diversity of Asian experiences better and can help to formulate more effective policy.

---

[1] Myrdal's work takes in India, Pakistan, Ceylon, Burma, Malaya, Thailand, Indonesia, and the Philippines, with occasional references to South Viet Nam, Cambodia, and Laos. However, his in-depth analysis is largely based on India and to a lesser extent Pakistan, with references to other countries supporting the main lines of argument.

One of Myrdal's most influential observations was that states in South Asia were 'soft' and could not enforce social discipline. Political leaders tolerated social indiscipline and inefficiency on the grounds that this was part of 'democratic planning' while engaging in corruption themselves. Myrdal argued that this regressive collective behaviour was the product of attitudes, cultures, and institutions. He was describing something important, but it was an incomplete observation. The soft states were only 'soft' in some areas. They were very hard in others, for instance in repressing communists or secessionists. The weak implementation of *some* institutions and policies is more likely to have been due to the interests of powerful organizations in specific countries and sectors rather than a general feature of their cultures and attitudes. The 'political settlement' describes the distribution of power across different types of organizations. The distribution of organizational power can vary greatly across countries and sectors, and over time, and can help to explain significant differences in institutional outcomes and behavioural patterns.

The relationship between institutions and political settlements can be explored through the lens of industrial policy institutions, which played an important role in many Asian countries. Success with industrialization depended not just on the country's initial conditions, but also on the implementation of transformative industrial policy institutions. Successful industrial policy in Taiwan and South Korea in the 1950s and 1960s involved the allocation of resources to new firms and sectors as conditional policy rents. The aim was to accelerate technology adoption and learning-by-doing to raise productivity and achieve competitiveness in new sectors. The critical condition for success, as developmental state theorists later pointed out, was that industrial policy agencies could effectively discipline the recipients of policy rents. This capability allowed mistakes to be corrected and ensured that productivity growth was rapid. In China in the 1980s, the industrial policy was different but the enforcement of conditions ensuring productivity growth was again effective, achieving dramatic outcomes.

At the other end of the spectrum were countries in South Asia in the 1960s where the beneficiaries of industrial policy rents were much more difficult to discipline. Powerfully connected business houses, and groups linked to them, captured policy rents and could not be disciplined. Not surprisingly, these countries achieved less significant industrial outcomes. Southeast Asian countries were somewhere in between and achieved moderate success. However, the 1980s saw the beginning of a different type of industrialization in South Asia, led by sectors like automobiles and pharmaceuticals in India and garments and textiles in Bangladesh. Institutions and policies successfully supported capability development in these sectors because policy rents were now delivered in ways that could not be unproductively captured, even in these political settlements.

Developmental state institutions worked in North East Asia and China not because these countries already had market-supporting behavioural norms, nor because they were less corrupt or otherwise better at following market rules. If the appropriate rights, norms, and behaviour already existed, social transformations would not be required (Khan 2004, 2007). Transformational policies are required precisely because pre-existing rights and institutions have to change and new capabilities developed. They inevitably disrupt pre-existing rights and require the creation of many rents as important market failures are targeted. Transformational institutions are successful when they are effective in changing rights and behaviour to achieve more productive societies. For this to happen the enforcement of these institutions has to be aligned with the interests of the powerful.

This chapter is structured as follows. Section 2 outlines Myrdal's contribution to institutional analysis and how modern institutional analysis has built on his analysis. Section 3 sets out an alternative institutional analysis based on political settlements, and the implications for the analysis of the effectiveness of institutions. Section 4 draws on the experiences of Asian countries to explore how developmental policies and institutions worked across political settlements and how appropriately designed transformative institutions can work even in apparently adverse political settlements. Section 5 concludes by discussing incremental versus radical strategies for reforming governance and institutions. While Myrdal advocated radical change, he recognized, with some pessimism, that the incremental approach was the one that most countries would adopt. However, a deeper evaluation of the experiences of the last fifty years suggests that the incremental approach can have less pessimistic prospects than Myrdal thought, particularly if it takes into account the interdependencies between organizational power and institutions.

2. Myrdal and Institutional Analysis

Myrdal posed a question that continues to motivate institutional analysis: why do people not respond to incentives in the same way everywhere (Myrdal 1968: 16–24)? Myrdal rightly criticized economists who assume that responses to economic incentives will be the same everywhere. This was not the case, he argued, because behavioural norms may prevent individuals from responding rationally to economic incentives. He called these patterns of behaviour 'institutions', and in India, Myrdal's main case study, the regressive institutions he identified included the caste system, the taboo on cow slaughter, dysfunctional pre-capitalist structures of land rights, and the management of firms based on caste, family, and ethnic allegiances. What Myrdal describes as institutions include what we would today call formal institutions like property rights or laws against cow slaughter, as well as informal institutions like caste, that are either self-enforced or enforced by informal extra-legal processes (North 1990).

Myrdal's argument was that formal and informal institutions reinforce each other and are therefore difficult to change. Their persistence can prevent the emergence of the behavioural patterns necessary for a modern market economy, including efficiency, diligence, flexibility, enterprise, and even honesty. He concluded that regressive behavioural regularities needed to change, but this was only likely if *compulsion* was used to change these attitudes. But the 'soft' South Asian states were unable or unwilling to impose any social discipline on citizens (Myrdal 1968: 60–3). His response was to propose a big push to change institutions and attitudes because '[i]t is often not more difficult, but easier, to cause a big change rapidly than a small change gradually' (Myrdal 1968: 115). But he did not make clear where he thought such a push would come from.

Figure 13.1 summarizes the links in Myrdal's analysis. The parallels with the later institutional economics of North and his followers are obvious. The argument begins with formal institutions and informal behavioural norms. In Asia these were often regressive, with roots going back to pre-colonial and colonial periods, which Myrdal loosely describes as 'feudal'. These pre-existing institutions include dysfunctional property rights over land, hierarchical caste systems, or other social attitudes that were inimical to the effective operation of a capitalist market economy. Individuals and firms could not respond flexibly to price signals or market opportunities in such a context. To deal with the economic underperformance that followed, states found it necessary to operate a raft of discretionary top-down controls like licensing economic activities, providing subsidies, protecting markets, and so on. The result was the resolution of some problems but the creation of new inefficiencies, since these interventions too could not be properly policed or enforced. We would today describe this as rent creation and corruption. Anticipating subsequent debates over rents, rent-seeking, and governance, Myrdal

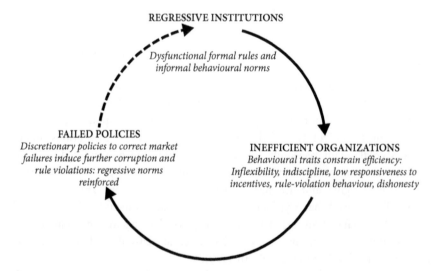

REGRESSIVE INSTITUTIONS

*Dysfunctional formal rules and
informal behavioural norms*

FAILED POLICIES
*Discretionary policies to correct market
failures induce further corruption and
rule violations: regressive norms
reinforced*

INEFFICIENT ORGANIZATIONS
*Behavioural traits constrain efficiency:
Inflexibility, indiscipline, low responsiveness to
incentives, rule-violation behaviour, dishonesty*

Figure 13.1 Myrdal's institutional analysis.
Source: Author's illustration based on Myrdal (1968: 901–35).

argued that these interventions created 'extraordinarily high profits' (rents) for privileged companies in the private sector (Myrdal 1968: 926). Given the low social discipline, the interventions induced further rule violations and regressive behaviour, completing the loop in Figure 13.1 (Myrdal 1968: 901–35).

Myrdal's analysis anticipated modern institutional analysis whose logical structure is quite similar. It also anticipated the literature on how corrections to market failures can lead to government failures (Bhagwati 1982, 1983; Krueger 1990). Myrdal sometimes argues that regressive institutions persisted because powerful interests benefitted from them, but at other times he argues that they reflected the values and cultures of these societies. In the early part of his work, it appears that regressive institutions are protected by powerful interests. But later Myrdal argues that gradual changes were possible in Europe because reforms were aligned with the values of Western civilization, while in South Asia, regressive social behaviour, stratification, and attitudes were sanctioned by old cultures and popular religion, and so gradual reform was more likely to be overturned (Myrdal 1968: 2114–15).

The distinction between the two positions is important for Myrdal's justification of radical change. If regressive behaviour is embedded in rigid mental models of large numbers of people, there may be no alternative to radical cultural revolutions to break down these ways of thinking. But if the resistance comes from the powerful, attempts at big changes are likely to be violently resisted and incremental reform strategies may in any case work better. For instance, the resistance of different elites may be better dealt with using sequential reforms, or by working in alignment with the interests of some of the powerful to achieve greater productivity and welfare gradually.

The interests of the powerful and the evolution of cultures can clearly interact. Powerful groups can be expected to invest in cultures that support their interests, but these can also become widely shared and provide affirmation and identity to many other groups. A wide range of groups can then use cultural and identity symbols in their own mobilizations. It may therefore appear that culture has an independent existence because it does not mechanically reflect the interests of particular groups. Nevertheless, culture persists because a variety of groups invest in its reproduction and it is therefore important to assess the dominant direction of causality over time. Myrdal's earlier argument that regressive institutions and attitudes are protected by configurations of interests is more in line with my own thinking and with the evidence discussed in section 4. If on the other hand, cultures and norms persist entirely independently because of mental models, we are in a thicker soup. Much later, Douglass North came to a similar impasse when he was trying to explain the persistence of dysfunctional institutions. North resisted explanations based on the distribution of power, and so he had to fall back on mental models to explain institutional stagnation by a process of exclusion (North 1995). The problem is that this can easily descend into a genetic explanation because we then have to explain why some population groups fail to update or reject their dysfunctional mental models in the light of evidence. Fortunately, North abandoned this line of argument before it drove him in that direction.

This is not to say that values, cultures, or religions never have independent effects on the evolution of institutions and organizations. Cultures and norms can influence how different groups across society identify themselves and the narratives they use to mobilize their supporters in conflicts with other groups. As a result, the evolution of organizational power and institutions can be affected by culture and history. Myrdal's warnings about the regressive role of culture and religion can hardly be ignored in the context of the backward slide towards populism and identity politics in large parts of contemporary South Asia and beyond. Even so, the question remains as to whether progress requires substantial social upheavals to destroy these ideological frames or whether incremental strategies can change evolutionary institutional paths. If institutions and policies can be designed to be effective in particular power configurations, and if they support the development of new productive capabilities, the distribution of power can gradually change and allow new groups to invest in the propagation of new cultures and attitudes. We will return to these questions.

The questions Myrdal raised became the subject of a vast outpouring of research in institutional economics and political economy. Liberal rent-seeking analyses drew on the work of Krueger (1974) and Posner (1975) to argue that liberalization was required to reverse discretionary policy interventions of the type that Myrdal had described. This, it was argued, would reduce rent-seeking and corruption and make economies more efficient. The work of North and his associates (North 1981, 1990; North et al. 2007; North et al. 2009; North et al. 2013) and later of Acemoglu and Robinson (2012) identified the formal and informal institutions that supported efficiency (essentially institutions that made market transactions more efficient) and the 'extractive' or redistributive ones that destroyed value. The role of political power found a place in mainstream institutional analysis in the work of Acemoglu and Robinson (2000, 2012).

But the emerging analysis suffered from many of the limitations of Myrdal's original work. The emerging work on rents and rent-seeking ignored the rents created by welfare-enhancing state interventions. If we recognize the possibility of value-enhancing rents, rent-seeking and corruption can be associated with very different development outcomes (Khan 2000a, 2000b, 2006). Similarly, the mainstream work on property rights and formal institutions ignored the fact that capitalist development requires the destruction of many pre-existing rights and institutions. Developing societies are unlikely to have well-enforced formal institutions when their pre-existing rights are going through huge disruptions. Using the institutions and governance structures of advanced countries as the benchmark for developing countries is therefore deeply problematic not only in Myrdal, but also in later authors like Acemoglu and Robinson (Acemoglu et al. 2001; Khan 2012).

Acemoglu and Robinson's (2000, 2012) analysis of power, and their argument that inclusive political institutions empower market-supporting groups, is also based on an inappropriate generalization. Advanced countries are advanced because they have many productive organizations that can benefit from market institutions. Market-restricting monopolies benefit small groups but hurt the majority. Inclusive political institutions in such a context can plausibly empower the productive majority to resist monopolists. The problem of power is more complex in developing countries where the majority may not necessarily support market institutions because they do not yet have the productive capabilities to benefit from them. Instead, large groups can be mobilized with populist or iden-tity politics to demand value-reducing rents or to block the productive restruc-turing of property rights. In *these* contexts, inclusive political institutions do not necessarily empower market-supporting groups. This is not an argument against inclusive politics, because restricting rent-seeking opportunities in these contexts may sometimes trigger violence and more regressive results. The challenge is to devise incremental institutional changes that can nudge developing societies towards better evolutionary paths.

3. Political Settlements and Institutional Evolution

Given these limitations, it is not surprising that Myrdal and the new institutional economists who followed could not provide convincing explanations for *differ-ences* in performance across developing countries. The high-growth countries in Asia did not have the cultures and values of Western capitalist societies, they did not have well-enforced formal institutions during their transitions, and they did not have very inclusive political institutions. And yet they achieved dramatic capitalist transitions. Moreover, from the 1980s, there were significant growth accelerations in South Asia as well, without the massive disruptions in cultures and attitudes that Myrdal thought would be required.

The 'political settlements' framework addresses this challenge and provides a different analysis of institutions. It builds on three analytical propositions. First, the effectiveness of any institution depends on the responses of the organizations affected by that institution. The horizontal activity of organizations in punishing or isolating rule-violators is at least as important in ensuring adherence as the occasional vertical enforcement by the state. Second, as any institution implies different costs and benefits across organizations, some organizations may support the institution while others resist it. The overall adherence to, or enforcement of, an institution will therefore depend on *the distribution of power across different types of organizations* (the political settlement). Finally, apart from market-supporting institutions (like property rights) a range of other institutions is required to address market failures and maintain political stability. During periods of crisis or rapid transformations, institutions are also involved in organizing changes in rights and creating new capabilities. The operation of 'transformative' institutions can be decisive, particularly in these contexts. The political settlements framework uses these propositions to provide an alternative analysis of institutional performance and policy (Khan 2010, 2018).

The role of organizations in enforcing institutions was highlighted in the work of Greif (2006). He used a game-theoretic approach to describe how institutions can endogenously emerge in repeated prisoner's dilemma games. Institutions for Greif were simply the equilibrium behaviour of organizations. The formal specification of an institution was therefore less important than the actual behaviour of organizations in adhering to particular rules and enforcing them on each other. An implication of this approach, though Greif did not put it like that, is that if equilibrium behaviour diverged from the description of a formal rule, it would appear that the formal rule was being distorted or modified by the behaviour of organizations. His models did not consider the distribution of power across organizations, but in games with multiple equilibria with different distributions of benefits, powerful organizations can be expected to hold out in distributive conflicts until the equilibrium behaviour of other organizations adjusts to support the institution desired by the more powerful (Knight 1992). This takes us to our second proposition. The behavioural regularities that emerge will depend not just on particular punishment strategies, but also on the relative holding power of the organizations involved.

Marxist historians of capitalist transitions in Europe have also identified the importance of distributions of power for understanding the emergence and effectiveness of institutions (Brenner 1976, 1985; Wood 2002). The puzzle they addressed was that the first transition to capitalism was in England rather than in more commercialized or more culturally sophisticated parts of Europe. The Italian city states, the Baltic states, or the Netherlands were more commercialized centres of long-distance trade. The Renaissance was centred in continental Europe. England's advantage could not have been its more advanced culture or its market institutions. Rather, these theorists argued, the first capitalist transformation in England was the outcome of a fortuitous balance of power between peasants, lords, and monarchs that allowed lords to enclose the commons, yet prevented them from reducing the peasantry to serfdom as in Eastern Europe and Russia. The Enclosures gradually privatized common village lands over several centuries, but allowed richer peasants to become capitalist tenant farmers by leasing land from enclosing landlords. This created a landless proletariat and capitalist farmers, but also new inequalities which, far from being aligned with 'Western values', were strongly resisted by the Church (Tawney 1938). Nevertheless, the emergent agrarian capitalism drove innovation and productivity growth. Intense competition between capitalist farmers who had to raise productivity to pay rising rents to landlords led both to the development of technology and the imposition of discipline on workers who adhered to new rules because being landless they had no exit options.

The configuration of power was therefore critical for the English transformation, rather than a hard state or specific cultures and values, though cultural and other factors may have played some role. Similar institutions did not emerge in much of Europe till military competition with Britain persuaded Bismarck, Napoleon, and other state leaders to organize political coalitions to push through institutional transformations from above that achieved capitalist transitions. Similar state-led transitions began in Asia with the Meiji revolution in Japan in the nineteenth century, which foreshadowed transitions in Taiwan and South Korea in the twentieth. In each case, the transition was driven by different types of state and non-state organizations but, in all cases, a specific distribution of organizational power enabled outcomes that led to the emergence of new institutions and more dynamic societies. These institutional changes were mostly gradual rather than revolutionary breaks with pre-existing cultures and norms, though the latter changed over time as production systems and power configurations changed.

In every case, there was resistance from losers, but the losers were typically not the small groups of privileged monopolists, as in Acemoglu and Robinson's analysis. The resistance to the Enclosures in Britain came from peasants. Far from inclusive institutions assisting the majority, the dispossessed peasants could not block these changes because parliament was *not* inclusive enough. Representation was restricted to property owners. Nor did parliament play a role in ensuring that peasants were rapidly or fairly compensated. They were not compensated at all. Parliament therefore played no direct role in the institutional transformation. The transition was successful because landlords could expropriate common lands without much peasant resistance, but they could not expropriate the peasant's own land because peasants had sufficient collective power at the village level. This fine balance of power ensured a capitalist transformation of agriculture that eventually led to an improvement in welfare across classes. The configuration of organizational power and political institutions mattered, but in more complex ways than Acemoglu and Robinson suggest.

Finally, a large heterodox literature has discussed the role of institutions in addressing market failures and transforming rights and capabilities during social transformations. The diversity of outcomes can be examined through the lens of rents and the management of rents (Stiglitz 1996; Khan 2000a, 2000b, 2004). Rents can be defined in a number of ways, but they usually refer to incremental incomes associated with specific institutions. Some institutional changes, like the creation of artificial monopolies, create rents that are socially damaging. But welfare-enhancing interventions that create or reallocate property rights or address market failures also create incremental incomes somewhere. What types of rents are created and how they are allocated and managed can serve as a useful lens for assessing the rent-creating institutions. Dynamic societies have institutions that allow growth-enhancing transformations of rights and the creation and management of rents that drive learning, innovation, and political stability. Less dynamic societies mismanage rents, allowing some groups to capture assets and rents without delivering results, or they create rents that are directly unproductive, like monopoly rents or conflict-inducing redistributive rents.

Since all institutional changes create new incomes, they inevitably create rents. Not surprisingly, the emergence of institutions is usually driven by rent-seeking and they create incentives for further rent-seeking. Outcomes depend on the institutions regulating rent-seeking and the distribution of power across relevant organizations. Rent-seeking can result in the creation of socially useful institutions, distortions in the implementation of useful institutions, or the creation of damaging institutions (Khan 2000b). Rent-seeking is just as ubiquitous in advanced countries but the adherence to a rule of law means that rent-seeking processes here are generally rule-following and part of 'normal' politics. However, legality does not ensure good social outcomes, and the converse is also true. Both legal rent-seeking (like lobbying) and illegal variants (like bribing and patron–client politics) can be associated with socially damaging, less damaging, or beneficial institutional outcomes.

In developing countries, powerful organizations typically do not support a rule of law. This is because even organizations that are not predatory are often not productive enough to survive against more productive competitors elsewhere without informal rents. And because they are few in number, they can also transact with each other using informal contract enforcement, without a rule of law. Adherence to a rule of law by the powerful is therefore unlikely in these contexts and rent-seeking, too, is likely to be illegal or extra-legal, often taking the form of corruption. Politics is therefore likely to have a rule-violating character. Low tax revenues also mean that promises to spend the budget in rule-following ways are unlikely to attract powerful organizations to support particular parties. These characteristics of developing-country rent-seeking can explain why patronage and political corruption are typically part of their 'normal' politics (Khan 2005).

Given the nature of rent-seeking in these countries, it is not surprising that developing countries, including successful ones, typically suffer from high levels of corruption. South Korea in the 1960s or China in the 1980s had significant levels of corruption and yet achieved rapid development. Myrdal's analysis of corruption and later mainstream analysis does not address this challenge. The variations in the outcomes of corruption become explicable once we recognize that the real differences between countries are in the types of rents created by organizations and how they are managed by other organizations. Where the conditions of allocating and withdrawing rents support productivity growth, desirable results can be achieved despite rent-seeking. Corruption declines over time in these countries as productive capabilities develop and the growth in the number of productive organizations creates growing organizational support for formalization and rule-following behaviour (Khan 2005, 2006).

The management of industrial and technology policies allows us to examine the significance of the distribution of power for the management of rents. Developing-country firms typically have low initial capabilities. Myrdal recognized the critical importance of learning-by-doing, a process later analysed by Amsden (1989) and others. Developing countries do not have to invent new technologies; they can just learn how to use existing ones (Myrdal 1968: 691–6). However, market failures may prevent investments in learning-by-doing, a problem Myrdal did not adequately recognize. Amsden (1989) argued that learning needed to be supported by targeting conditional rents to emerging business, but the latter also had to be disciplined, and rents sometimes withdrawn to ensure that these were not wasted.

Evans (1995) later contributed the concept of 'embedded autonomy' to explain why intervention by strong East Asian states achieved productivity growth rather than rent extraction. These states had the power to extract resources from business, but they used their power to raise productivity instead. Evans argued that this happened because government agencies were embedded in dense business–government networks that allowed the knowledge and interests of the business sector to be incorporated into policy.

While developmental state theorists provided a deeper analysis of institutions and rents and went beyond the focus on market institutions, their analysis was still largely a purely institutional one. They ignored the configurations of power that enabled some institutions to work in specific contexts but not others. The rent-granting and rent-withdrawal institutions that Amsden and others identified in East Asia existed in similar forms in South Asia where they achieved far less impressive results. South Asian states had sufficient autonomy to destroy or constrain many good businesses, but they did not discipline the bad ones. Similarly, dense networks between business and government in South Asia and sometimes in Southeast Asia resulted in crony capitalism rather than efficiency-enhancing information sharing. The differences between these cases cannot be understood by looking at institutional structure alone, we need to understand how specific configurations of organizational power made similar institutions operate differently.

Figure 13.2 summarizes our distinction between a 'pure institutional analysis', which focuses on the incentives created by formal and informal institutions that *may* result in particular outcomes, and the political settlements extension, which looks in addition at how the specific distribution of power across organizations affects the *actual* adherence to and enforcement of these institutions. Note that the introduction of particular institutions and policies on the left-hand side is not entirely predetermined by existing power structures. Otherwise, societies would be completely trapped by the interests of those who are already powerful. There is always some policy space for the introduction of new institutions and policies

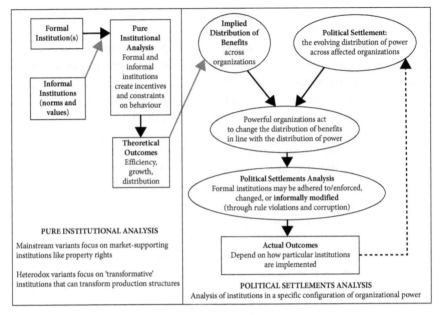

Figure 13.2 Political settlements and institutional outcomes.

Source: Author's illustration based on Khan (2010, 2018).

that innovative political leaderships or organizations can exploit, but their implementation and final effects do depend on the reaction of a broader range of organizations.

The distribution of power across organizations is the 'political settlement' at the top right-hand corner of Figure 13.2. This describes the holding power of organizations affected by a particular institution. The country and sector-specific configurations of organizational power can only be inferred from a reading of history, which is why institutional analysis cannot be generalized from particular cases or derived from first principles. Holding power is not just based on the economic power of organizations but also on their organizational power to hold out in conflicts while inflicting costs on others. Ignoring the power and interests of organizations is one reason why pure institutional analysis remains deficient, both the mainstream variants focusing on market institutions and heterodox variants looking at transformative institutions. Every institution or policy has distributive implications, and organizations can be expected to support or resist their implementation. If institutions create rents or seek to manage rents in ways that are against the interests of powerful organizations, the latter will resist by trying to change the institution or to informally modify its implementation using corruption or informal violations. Fully effective adherence is a boundary case. Note that informal modifications here have little to do with norms and everything to do with the alignment or otherwise of the distribution of rents and the distribution of power. Actual economic outcomes depend on how particular institutions or policies are implemented, not just their theoretical effects. Figure 13.2 also shows that the political settlement is itself affected by economic outcomes which change the distribution of power over time. It is this evolutionary dynamic that a historical analysis of institutions must attempt to capture.

Depending on how the outcomes of particular policies and institutions affect the development of organizations, the relative power of organizations will evolve in particular ways. Radical change from this perspective is only necessary if the existing political settlement allows no incremental improvements in outcomes. The radical change in question would involve political mobilizations and the creation of new organizations that sought to *directly* change the political settlement at the top right-hand corner of Figure 13.2. The danger is that mobilizations on this scale can just as well trigger counter-mobilizations of even more regressive coalitions, while incrementalism may actually result in more sustainable progressive changes in the political settlement over time.

4. Comparative Institutional Experiences

The analytical links described in Figure 13.2 can help to make sense of comparisons between North East Asian and South Asian experiences in the 1960s, the period that Myrdal looked at. They can also help us to understand institutional evolution since that time. South Korea began its industrial take-off shortly after Park Chung Hee took power in a military coup in 1961. By then South Korea had already carried out substantial land reforms as the Japanese occupation had forcefully dispossessed the most powerful elements of the Korean *yangban* landed elite and converted much of their land to Japanese ownership. With the departure of the Japanese, land reform based on the redistribution of Japanese land and the compulsory purchase of land from the remaining landlords was relatively easy to achieve. These reforms led to a significant equalization of landholdings and a dramatic reduction in the number of tenants as they became smallholders. However, it did not create a class of yeoman tenants on the English pattern who could drive an agrarian capitalist revolution from below. The global conditions were not right for smallholding agriculture to make much of an impact on South Korea's economic progress. At best, the land reform created political stability in the countryside in the face of the communist threat from the North, expanded the domestic market somewhat, and perhaps created a greater demand for education in the countryside (Kohli 1994; Putzel 2000).

The real impetus to South Korean modernization came with its industrial push in the 1960s. A critical feature of the new institutional structure was the provision of significant rents to the *chaebol* (the large family-owned conglomerates of South Korea), to enable them to engage in learning-by-doing to improve their organizational and technical capabilities (Amsden 1989; Khan 2000b). The institutions supporting their learning also compelled the *chaebol* to rapidly acquire international competitiveness by withdrawing support if they failed to perform. The credibility of the withdrawal threat created compulsions for rapid productivity growth and ensured that infants did not require permanent support. Myrdal's fear that unproductive rent capture would compound the problems that any interventions tried to solve did not materialize in South Korea.

Why did South Korea not fall into this trap? Pakistan provides a good comparison with South Korea because it attempted a similar mix of import substitution and export promotion, and provided rents to large holding companies using similar instruments (Khan 1999). Indeed, in the early years, South Korean planners came to Pakistan to learn about planning strategies. While there were many differences between the two countries, the decisive difference was that large Pakistani companies were connected to powerful and dense networks within the bureaucracy, army, and political parties, and could use their help to successfully retain rents even when their failure to become competitive had become obvious.

The organization of patronage networks in Pakistan was fragmented, but each network was powerful enough to resist disciplining by others or by state agencies. In the late 1960s, the media openly reported how 'twenty-two families' had captured public resources, but the military regime was unable to impose discipline on its inefficient clients. There was much corruption in this process, as Myrdal recognized, but it was more than just a problem of corruption. The value-reducing rent capture by powerful networks hurt the legitimacy of the ostensibly powerful military government. It tried unsuccessfully to rein in its clients, including revealing their names and the money they owed, but it failed. The regime was eventually brought down in 1971 as a result of popular mobilizations against cronyistic elites. The failure was deeper than knowledge, values, or interests. The top leadership had strong incentives to limit rent capture by uncompetitive business groups but they failed to overcome their resistance. The nature of the failure suggests that a different policy design, perhaps supporting smaller, less-connected capitalists, or rewarding investors after they had achieved some results rather than giving all the rents upfront, may have worked better in this political settlement. Indeed, we find that other strategies of supporting learning worked much better in a number of sectors in South Asia in the 1980s.

We know as a result of later revelations by the *chaebol* that the allocation of industrial policy rents in South Korea in the 1960s involved much corruption. But, here, corruption did not featherbed inefficiency. The *chaebol* receiving support knew they had an opportunity to become competitive, but they also knew that the option of capturing the rents while remaining uncompetitive was not feasible. This was because the state agencies monitoring them were more powerful than the networks that individual businesses could mobilize. The agencies figured out that their formal *and* informal payoffs would be higher if they reallocated rents to *chaebol* that could grow and generate additional profits rather than inefficient ones that could not. Corruption still happened, but here it was of a profit-sharing type. The *chaebol* needed the support of the state, and they were willing to treat the political leadership as informal business partners who could claim a share of profits as 'dividends'. The logic was simple, and both sides soon worked out that profit-sharing corruption was not only *not* contrary to productivity growth, given the distribution of power, it created incentives and compulsions to achieve productivity growth. The rent allocation rules could not be distorted because critical agencies had the interest and the power to prevent it (Khan 1998, 2000b).

Where did this capacity come from? It is hard to argue that contemporary South Korea had a culture with attitudes of rationality and discipline that were significantly superior to South Asia. True, it had a more developed industrial history as a result of Japanese colonialism, but this cannot explain why inefficient firms were not allowed to capture rents. The capacity to withdraw rents and discipline the *chaebol* is more plausibly explained by a specific political settlement. The historical roots of this can be traced back at least to the impact of Japanese colonialism. The latter was brutal, but it did not create a fragmented and competitive set of political organizations in its colonies, as the divide-and-rule strategies of British colonialism created in South Asia and elsewhere. The post-war South Korean political settlement was marked by an absence of powerful *competitive* networks within the state and bureaucracy, so individual *chaebol* could not collude and share rents with parts of the network to prevent themselves being disciplined by other parts.

When the South Korean state began its industrialization drive, its leaders did not have pre-conceived ideas about how to make rent allocation achieve dynamic results. Rather, trial and error revealed that making support to a *chaebol* conditional on the achievement of export targets resulted in rapid productivity growth because the rule could be enforced. The *chaebol* put in lots of effort to raise productivity, knowing that the alternative would be disastrous for them. Once the enforceability of these rules became known, the system evolved in a particular direction, with more ambitious learning strategies emerging. In contexts where state support could be combined with rules that compelled companies to achieve productivity growth, similar types of corrupt but 'efficient' profit sharing emerged in a number of Asian countries, including China in the 1980s.

Trial and error revealed a very different political settlement to South Asian state leaders. Leaders in Pakistan and India were soon aware that industrial policy rents were being unproductively captured and though this was not in their interest they failed to discipline their clients. While individual bureaucrats and politicians benefitted, the higher-level leaderships lost out in terms of overall revenue and legitimacy. Individual businesses constructed alliances with powerful political and bureaucratic networks that undermined any possibility of disciplining them. The failure to govern rents was ultimately not due to flawed mental models but rather a configuration of power that made it impossible to impose discipline on these firms.

In India, Myrdal argued that productivity growth was not even an explicit goal of import protection, the latter was justified simply by the need to conserve foreign exchange (Myrdal 1968: 1158). This is not true. Using protection as a rent allocation instrument to develop domestic productive capabilities was a demand of the nationalist movement, and it was supported by emerging Indian capital in the Bombay Plan of 1944. Moreover, the failings of the industrial licensing system were of great concern to the Indian state (Chakravarty 1987). However, when state leaders discovered that efficiency could not be achieved, they would occasionally justify their policies by saying this was not even their intention.

We know from the report of the Industrial Licensing Policy Inquiry Committee (Dutt 1969) that Indian policymakers were painfully aware that businesses they supported were not meeting their licence conditions and instead using their licences to behave like monopolies. The Dutt Committee recommended sanctions on business houses that failed to comply with licence conditions, but this was not implemented. As in Pakistan, the problem was clearly neither ignorance nor the interests of state leaders. Rather, the peak agencies that wanted to achieve productivity growth were weak relative to the powerful networks below them who saw greater benefit in capturing rents without delivering results and using the rents to sustain their power through patronage networks. The distribution of power was the real source of this prisoner's dilemma outcome, while the ability of political leaderships in developmental states to discipline free riders allowed the pie to increase for everybody. Institutions and institutional outcomes reflected the political settlement rather than values or norms.

We turn now to Myrdal's analysis of the soft state. It is true that planning agencies in South Asia could not discipline businesses protected by political entrepreneurs from the intermediate and upper classes and their clientelist networks. But other state agencies *were* able to discipline subaltern classes or regional separatist movements. In these conflicts, states in India and Pakistan were ready to use overwhelming force to 'discipline' segments of their societies. The enforcement problem was therefore limited to specific sectors and institutions rather than being a general malaise of social indiscipline. The *specific instruments* that were used, particularly for promoting industrial development, had governance and disciplining requirements for *specific organizations* that could not be adequately enforced. The implication is that other institutions and instruments allocating rents to a different set of organizations may have achieved better development results.

This insight can help to explain the significant growth accelerations in a few sectors in India and Bangladesh in the 1980s with relatively minor institutional and policy innovations. The previous industrial policy had achieved *output* growth in many sectors, but *productivity* growth was low because of poor disciplining. As a result, competitiveness was typically not achieved in most sectors (Acharya et al. 2003: table 2.2; Virmani 2004: table 1; Bosworth et al. 2007: table 3). The growing economic openness from the 1980s helped imports of capital and machinery, which supported productivity growth. But the achievement of competitiveness also required policies that assisted learning and capability development. What is interesting is that relatively minor institutional and policy innovations created the compulsions for productivity growth that were previously missing.

The new policy and institutional innovations in a few sectors were successful because rents were delivered to organizations that did not have the power to protect them unconditionally. Conditions could be credibly enforced that would hurt the firms if they failed to deliver results. An important feature in several of these take-offs was that investors were induced to *first* invest their own resources in learning, with policy promising sufficient *ex post* rents to give a high return on their risky investments if they succeeded.

I have discussed these examples at greater length elsewhere; they included automobiles and pharmaceuticals in India and garments and textiles in Bangladesh, sectors that drove growth accelerations in these countries from the 1980s onwards (Khan 2011, 2013a, 2013c). The cases are different, but we can summarize the Bangladeshi garments and Indian automobiles cases to illustrate their common features. In these two cases *ex post* rewards were created for a foreign partner to transfer capabilities to domestic firms. In a third sector, Indian pharmaceuticals, the story was slightly different. Here *ex post* rents were created for domestic firms if they succeeded in developing manufacturing capabilities by backward engineering based on the application of the Indian Patent Act of 1970. But all these sectors were similar in rewarding successful capability development *ex post* as a way of encouraging prior private investments and being successful in the implementation of these rules.

In the Bangladesh garments sector, the critical instrument was an agreement in 1979 between a Bangladeshi company, Desh, and a South Korean company, Daewoo, backed by the Bangladeshi state. The context was the Multi-Fibre Arrangement of 1974, which created potential *ex post* rents for least-developed countries like Bangladesh if they could achieve sufficient quality and competitiveness to sell garments in the quota-protected US market. The protection created quota rents in the US market, and the agreement was to pass on the potential quota rents to Daewoo as its reward for transferring export capability to Desh (Khan 2013b). The rule essentially transferred a percentage of future sales revenue to Daewoo, and this was sufficiently rewarding for it to invest in capability transfer. What made the rule easy to enforce was that unless Desh acquired the capability to export, no one would make any money. No *ex ante* rents were allocated to powerful businesses in Bangladesh, so there was no possibility of capturing these rents. The rule for transferring quota rents to Daewoo was also credible because the Bangladeshi state could prevent a relatively small firm from violating a contract that the President saw as vital for the country.

This combination of credible *ex post* rents for Daewoo and compulsions for investors to recover their investments resulted in dramatic capability development. Desh became a competitive firm within months of sending an army of supervisors to South Korea to learn factory and supply chain organization. As the organizational design that it adapted was appropriate to Bangladeshi conditions and could be easily imitated, thousands of Bangladeshi entrepreneurs entered the garments industry. The explosive growth of the sector created millions of jobs and within two decades Bangladesh had become the second biggest garment producer after China, though still far below China in absolute terms.

In the Indian automobile industry, the government signed a joint venture agreement in 1982 between Suzuki, a Japanese company, and Maruti, a public sector Indian company, allowing Suzuki to sell in the highly protected Indian market if it could produce an Indian car with sixty per cent domestic content within five years. Given that Indian tier one and two producers already had basic technical capabilities, the incentive of capturing significant tariff rents *ex post* was sufficient for Suzuki to invest in developing the capabilities of its Indian suppliers. Here, too, the mechanisms of rent allocation were credible to the parties, as was the enforceability of the conditions.

Rents could not be captured by Indian components producers because no *ex ante* rents were transferred to them. A failure to achieve international standards with Suzuki's help would simply be a lost opportunity for future profits. Suzuki knew that the strong opposition to its operations from domestic automobile and machine tools producers meant that a failure to achieve the domestic content conditions would result in exclusion from the Indian market. There was no question of the capacity of the Indian state to enforce this condition. As Suzuki was investing first, it had strong compulsions to succeed as that was the only way to capture the *ex post* tariff rents. Once again capability development was rapid and successful, and similar deals with other foreign companies followed. By the 1990s, India's auto components industry had become globally competitive. By the turn of the century, the sequential upgrading of auto components producers enabled India to produce its own branded cars. It became one of the few global car producers that could produce globally competitive national brands.

In both these cases incremental institutional and policy changes turned out to be enforceable from the perspective of specific developmental goals, given the distribution of power across the organizations involved, including relevant governance agencies. This is potentially a promising escape from the bind of weak enforcement, because it exploits the observation that in most states, enforcement failure does not extend to all dimensions. Economic development would be more rapid, and strategies of inclusion more effective, if these opportunities were more thoroughly exploited. The importance of the appropriate design of policies and institutions across different political settlements is insufficiently understood, which is why Bangladesh and India have not been able to replicate their own successes in many other sectors.

Looking at South Korean or Taiwanese industrial policy as paradigmatic has been very damaging for follower countries. These North East Asian states inherited political settlements from Japanese colonial times that were characterized by the absence of powerful factional political organizations. These states had the capacity to enforce conditions on firms receiving rents because the latter could not construct coalitions with powerful factions to protect their rents for a price. As politicians and bureaucrats discovered their enforcement capacity, sequential improvements in policy design followed. These countries did not have the cultural norms of the West, but the gradual productive transformation of their societies through the development of capabilities and competitiveness created a very similar impetus for investments in education, health, and culture. This took them in the direction of modern societies, including a transition from learning to innovation societies. With the transition to innovation increasing in pace over the last two decades, the dominance of institutions supporting catching up has been gradually superseded by institutions supporting innovation. While the achievements of these 'developmental states' have been truly impressive, the institutions and policies that they used to achieve development are not replicable in other states, even in Asia, where the political settlements are substantially different.

South Asia inherited a very different political settlement. Both democratic and authoritarian governments in India, Pakistan, and Bangladesh discovered their enforcement capabilities were limited when they faced powerful political and bureaucratic factions organized by the 'intermediate classes'. Myrdal described a moment in the history of these countries when they were using policy instruments that were seriously distorted in their implementation. Subsequent developments in the 1980s and beyond show that substantial growth could be achieved with policies and institutions allocating rents in other ways, even though these have not been developed to their full extent. Nevertheless, the long-run pace of development in South Asia is likely to be slower and more uneven than in North East Asia. South Asian states do not have the political and institutional capacity to support development across a broad range of sectors and regions all at once, as these strategies typically require disciplining a broad range of policy rents. Moreover, the poor results of bureaucratic management and the involvement of politicians and bureaucrats in value-reducing variants of corruption have had negative effects on morale. The very best graduates no longer find a career in the civil service sufficiently rewarding in most parts of South Asia, and this has had negative cumulative effects on bureaucratic capacity.

Southeast Asia has been somewhere in between in terms of the complexity of their internal power structures, and therefore in the constraints on enforcement set by their political settlements. Over the longer term their success has been somewhere in between South and North East Asia. From the perspective of the political settlements framework, it is not surprising that we find a great diversity of economic strategies and institutions that have worked and failed across these countries (Khan 2000b, 2007). Southeast Asian countries, too, have come a long way in the half-century since Myrdal wrote his *Asian Drama*, and some now face new challenges of progressing from learning to innovation societies while dealing with emerging challenges of populist politics.

5. Incremental versus Radical Reform and Prospects for the Future

On one critical question, the jury is still out. Myrdal posited that incremental changes were not only more painful than radical or revolutionary changes in the long run; incremental strategies were also more likely to fail. The case against incrementalism that Myrdal posited still affects many variants of modern institutional analysis. Acemoglu and Robinson are arguably in the same tradition in ruling out the sustainability of growth without a big shift towards inclusive political and economic institutions. For Myrdal, incrementalism was an excuse for unproductive elites to keep tolerating indiscipline and regressive practices (1968: 1909–10). However, neither Myrdal nor Acemoglu and Robinson have a convincing explanation of where the big changes will come from. Even if leaderships emerged in these countries with very different beliefs and a willingness to unleash discipline on society, or even if the critical junctures that Acemoglu and Robinson identify as the prelude for big changes came around (Acemoglu and Robinson 2012: 110–23), there is no guarantee that the radical reform strategies that may follow would be sustained over time.

If we are right in arguing that the distribution of power in society is relevant for institutional outcomes, attempts by political movements to enforce radical changes on the powerful could unleash substantial counter-mobilizations, violence, and very high 'transition costs' (Khan 1995, 2012). Nor is it clear that incremental strategies are more likely to fail if they can be appropriately constructed. What is clear is that many of the formal institutional and policy strategies that Myrdal looked at did indeed fail in India because their requirements of enforcement and adherence were unrealistic. But a leadership that was developmental could have followed an incremental strategy that took into account issues of enforcement to identify institutions and policies that were more likely to be effective for achieving development in that social context.

The elephant in the room for making these comparisons is China, a country that Myrdal did not include in his original study and one that Acemoglu and Robinson write off as unlikely to succeed given its 'non-inclusive' institutions (Acemoglu and Robinson 2012: 428–46). In fact, China is not only the most dramatic developmental transformation in human history, it also went through massive upheavals and revolutionary changes in the organization of its society. These radical changes could have contributed to its success in two quite different ways: the upheavals could have destroyed pre-existing regressive cultures and attitudes in Myrdal's sense, or they could have helped to create a disciplined organization, the Communist Party, with a new power structure that was effectively a new political settlement. The distinction is important. The cultures and attitudes that the communist revolution tried to root out were precisely the individualistic profit-seeking attitudes and property rights that were revived after 1979 during the growth transformation. One could argue that the upheaval helped to reboot pre-existing norms, to make them more appropriate for modern capitalism, but surely a less costly route could have been tried. Tens of millions of lives were lost or disrupted in the Great Leap Forward and the Cultural Revolution and yet many aspects of pre-revolutionary culture survived.

A more compelling case for the potentially positive effects of revolutionary disruption is that it may have enabled the construction of a relatively disciplined and inclusive political organization, the Communist Party, with the political power to allocate resources and discipline their use on a scale not possible in other developing countries. The Communist Party gradually came to include within it almost all of the politically active Chinese population, and it developed formal mechanisms for reaching compromises and enforcing agreements on collective rent allocation decisions. Decades of conflict and organizational activity were necessary to create this political structure but once it had emerged, the enforcement of collective decisions about resource and rent allocation was much more effective relative to other developing countries. The political settlement that the Chinese Communist Party represents may not be a permanently sustainable one, nor may it be the most appropriate one for enforcing the new types of rights and contracts that will be required as China moves from a learning to an innovation society. But it was very effective in organizing the post-1979 economic miracle based on adopting and adapting existing technologies and attracting significant foreign investments.

While the end results of the revolution were clearly positive, regardless of how we explain it, the policy implications are not clear. If the construction of a disciplined and inclusive political organization is the element that explains China's subsequent institutional success, this is by no means assured as an outcome of an upheaval. Upheavals can destroy pre-existing institutions and organizations without necessarily leading to the emergence of a disciplined and inclusive organization. Massive upheavals are more likely to create unmitigated chaos for long periods. The answer to Myrdal's social discipline and soft state problem may be to look much more seriously for incremental answers that take us in the direction of more organized and disciplined societies. I find very promising the examples of successful sectoral development in Myrdal's 'soft states' in the 1980s and beyond. These provide rich but all-too-rare examples of strategies that may work to accelerate the social transformation of countries in progressive and inclusive directions. If incremental strategies can be sustained across sectors and regions (and that is admittedly a big if), these strategies could gradually result in the multiplication of successful sectors and organizations, which may eventually want a better formal enforcement of social rules in general.

The growth and empowerment of powerful productive organizations that will eventually *demand* the enforcement of rules in their own interest is the only sure way of eventually creating an effective demand for a transition to a rule-following society. As against this, regressive interests and organizations in these societies can also be expected to mount their own rent-seeking and influencing activities. We can expect them to try and distort institutions in ways that can be described as social indiscipline, corruption, regressive social norms, and impunity. The pace of, and prospects for, development are likely to depend on the contest between these contending forces.

Acknowledgements

I am very grateful to Deepak Nayyar, two anonymous referees, and workshop participants for very useful comments on an earlier draft.

References

Acemoglu, D., and J.A. Robinson (2000). 'Political Losers as a Barrier to Economic Development', *American Economic Review Papers and Proceedings*, 90(2): 126–30.

Acemoglu, D., and J.A. Robinson (2012). *Why Nations Fail: The Origins of Power, Prosperity and Poverty*. London: Profile Books.

Acemoglu, D., S. Johnson, and J.A. Robinson (2001). 'The Colonial Origins of Comparative Development: An Empirical Investigation', *American Economic Review*, 91(5): 1369–401.

Acharya, S., I. Judge Ahluwalia, K.L. Krishna, and I. Patnaik (2003). 'India: Economic Growth 1950-2000', Global Research Project on Growth, Indian Council for Research on International Economic Relations, New Delhi.

Amsden, A. (1989). *Asia's Next Giant: South Korea and Late Industrialization*. Oxford: Oxford University Press.

Bhagwati, J.N. (1982). 'Directly Unproductive, Profit-seeking (DUP) Activities', *Journal of Political Economy*, 90(5): 988–1002.

Bhagwati, J.N. (1983). 'DUP Activities and Rent Seeking', *Kyklos*, 36(4): 634–7.

Bosworth, B., S.M. Collins, and A. Virmani (2007). 'Sources of Growth in the Indian Economy', National Bureau of Economic Research, Cambridge, MA, NBER Working Paper Series 12901. Available at: http://www.nber.org/papers/w12901 (accessed 1 August 2018).

Brenner, R. (1976). 'Agrarian Class Structure and Economic Development in Pre-Industrial Europe', *Past and Present*, 70: 30–75.

Brenner, R. (1985). 'The Agrarian Roots of European Capitalism'. In T.H. Aston and C.H.E. Philpin (eds) *The Brenner Debate: Agrarian Class Structure and Economic Development in Pre-Industrial Europe*. Cambridge: Cambridge University Press.

Chakravarty, S. (1987). *Development Planning: The Indian Experience*. Oxford: Oxford University Press.

Dutt, S. (1969). 'Report of the Industrial Licensing Policy Inquiry Committee', Department of Industrial Development, Government of India, New Delhi.

Evans, P.B. (1995). *Embedded Autonomy: States and Industrial Transformation*. Princeton, NJ: Princeton University Press.

Greif, A. (2006). *Institutions and the Path to the Modern Economy*. Cambridge: Cambridge University Press.

Khan, M.H. (1995). 'State Failure in Weak States: A Critique of New Institutionalist Explanations'. In J. Harriss, J. Hunter, and C.M. Lewis (eds) *The New Institutional Economics and Third World Development*. London: Routledge.

Khan, M.H. (1998). 'Patron–Client Networks and the Economic Effects of Corruption in Asia', *European Journal of Development Research*, 10(1): 15–39.

Khan, M.H. (1999). 'The Political Economy of Industrial Policy in Pakistan 1947–1971', SOAS University of London, London, Department of Economics Working Paper. Available at: http://eprints.soas.ac.uk/9867/ (accessed 1 August 2018).

Khan, M.H. (2000a). 'Rents, Efficiency and Growth'. In M.H. Khan and K.S. Jomo (eds) *Rents, Rent-Seeking and Economic Development: Theory and Evidence in Asia*. Cambridge: Cambridge University Press.

Khan, M.H. (2000b). 'Rent-seeking as Process'. In M.H. Khan and K.S. Jomo (eds), *Rents, Rent-Seeking and Economic Development: Theory and Evidence in Asia*. Cambridge: Cambridge University Press.

Khan, M.H. (2004). 'State Failure in Developing Countries and Strategies of Institutional Reform'. In B. Tungodden, N. Stern, and I. Kolstad (eds) *Toward Pro-poor Policies: Aid Institutions and Globalization*. Proceedings of Annual World Bank Conference on Development Economics. Oxford: Oxford University Press and World Bank. Available at: http://eprints.soas.ac.uk/3683 (accessed 1 August 2018).

Khan, M.H. (2005). 'Markets, States and Democracy: Patron–Client Networks and the Case for Democracy in Developing Countries', *Democratization*, 12(5): 705–25.

Khan, M.H. (2006). 'Determinants of Corruption in Developing Countries: The Limits of Conventional Economic Analysis'. In S. Rose-Ackerman (ed.) *International Handbook on the Economics of Corruption*. Cheltenham: Edward Elgar.

Khan, M.H. (2007). 'Governance, Economic Growth and Development since the 1960s'. In J.A. Ocampo, K.S. Jomo, and R. Vos (eds) *Growth Divergences: Explaining Differences in Economic Performance*. Hyderabad, London, and Penang: Orient Longman, Zed Books and Third World Network. Available at: http://www.un.org/esa/desa/papers/2007/wp54_2007.pdf (accessed 1 August 2018).

Khan, M.H. (2010). *Political Settlements and the Governance of Growth-Enhancing Institutions*. SOAS, University of London, London, Research Paper Series on

Governance for Growth. Available at: http://eprints.soas.ac.uk/9968 (accessed 1 August 2018).

Khan, M.H. (2011). *India's Evolving Political Settlement and the Challenges of Sustaining Development*. London: SOAS, University of London. Available at: http://eprints.soas.ac.uk/12844/ (accessed 1 August 2018).

Khan, M.H. (2012). 'Governance and Growth: History, Ideology and Methods of Proof'. In A. Noman, K. Botchwey, H. Stein, and J. Stiglitz (eds) *Good Growth and Governance for Africa: Rethinking Development Strategies*. Oxford: Oxford University Press.

Khan, M.H. (2013a). 'Technology Policies and Learning with Imperfect Governance'. In J. Stiglitz and J.Y. Lin (eds) *The Industrial Policy Revolution 1. The Role of Government Beyond Ideology*. London: Palgrave. Available at: http://eprints.soas.ac.uk/id/eprint/17296 (accessed 1 August 2018).

Khan, M.H. (2013b). 'The Political Settlement, Growth and Technical Progress in Bangladesh', Danish Institute for International Studies, Copenhagen, DIIS Working Paper 2013: 01. Available at: http://www.diis.dk/graphics/Publications/WP2013/WP2013-01.Bangladesh%20-%20Mushtaq-H-Khan.pdf (accessed 1 August 2018).

Khan, M.H. (2013c). 'Political Settlements and the Design of Technology Policy'. In J. Stiglitz, J.Y. Lin, and E. Patel (eds) *The Industrial Policy Revolution 2. Africa in the Twenty-First Century*. London: Palgrave. Available at: http://eprints.soas.ac.uk/id/eprint/17297 (accessed 1 August 2018).

Khan, M.H. (2018). 'Political Settlements and the Analysis of Institutions', *African Affairs*, 117(469): 636–55. Available at: https://doi.org/10.1093/afraf/adx044 (accessed 1 April 2019).

Knight, J. (1992). *Institutions and Social Conflict*. Cambridge: Cambridge University Press.

Kohli, A. (1994). 'Where Do High Growth Political Economies Come From? The Japanese Lineage of Korea's "Developmental State"', *World Development*, 22(9): 1269–93.

Krueger, A.O. (1974). 'The Political Economy of the Rent-Seeking Society', *American Economic Review*, 64(3): 291–303.

Krueger, A.O. (1990). 'Government Failures in Development', *Journal of Economic Perspectives*, 4(3): 9–23.

Myrdal, G. (1968). *Asian Drama: An Inquiry into the Poverty of Nations. A Twentieth Century Fund Study, Volumes I, II, and III*. New York: Pantheon.

North, D.C. (1981). *Structure and Change in Economic History*. New York: W.W. Norton.

North, D.C. (1990). *Institutions, Institutional Change and Economic Performance*. Cambridge: Cambridge University Press.

North, D.C. (1995). 'The New Institutional Economics and Development'. In J. Harriss, J. Hunter, and C. Lewis (eds) *The New Institutional Economics and Third World Development*. London: Routledge.

North, D.C., J.J. Wallis, S.B. Webb, and B.R. Weingast (2007). 'Limited Access Orders in the Developing World: A New Approach to the Problem of Development', World Bank, Washington, DC, World Bank Policy Research Paper 4359.

North, D.C., J.J. Wallis, S.B. Webb, and B.R. Weingast (eds) (2013). *In the Shadow of Violence: Politics, Economics and the Problems of Development*. Cambridge: Cambridge University Press.

North, D.C., J.J. Wallis, and B.R. Weingast (2009). *Violence and Social Orders: A Conceptual Framework for Interpreting Recorded Human History*. Cambridge: Cambridge University Press.

Posner, R.A. (1975). 'The Social Costs of Monopoly and Regulation', *Journal of Political Economy*, 83(4): 807–27.

Putzel, J. (2000). 'Land Reforms in Asia: Lessons from the Past for the 21st Century', LSE Development Studies Institute, London, LSE DESTIN Working Paper Series 00–04.

Stiglitz, J.E. (1996). *Whither Socialism?* Cambridge, MA: MIT Press.

Tawney, R.H. (1938). *Religion and the Rise of Capitalism*. Harmondsworth: Penguin.

Virmani, A. (2004). 'Sources of India's Economic Growth: Trends in Total Factor Productivity', Indian Council for Research on International Economic Relations, New Delhi, Working Paper 131.

Wood, E.M. (2002). *The Origins of Capitalism: A Longer View*. London: Verso.

14

Nationalism and Development

Prasenjit Duara

1. Introduction

Gunnar Myrdal is justly remembered for his expanded vision of development that accounted for institutions. However, he tended to see nationalism in Asia, fuelled by ignorant and superstitious religiosity, as a principal block to development. In contrast, he viewed European nationalism favourably in relation to development, declaring that 'in Europe, nationalism despite its association with romanticism, remained secular and rational at its core' (Myrdal 1968: 2112). I aim to show that there is a more complex dialectical relationship between nationalism and economic development than Myrdal imagined, not only in post-Second World War Asia, but also globally.

Nationalism reveals a common underlying structure of a self–other relationship, which may be expressed variously in different countries and at different times. The nation-state's goal has been to strengthen the nation. Economic development is an important dimension and means of achieving this goal, but equally the demand for the integration of the nation frequently based upon the exclusivism of the self–other binary has periodically raised its head. Meanwhile, popular or alternative views of the nation have also occasionally reshaped development policies and goals. While many Asian nations have successfully used nationalism to achieve high levels of growth and development, this same nationalism has also generated forms of exclusivism and competitiveness that may not easily permit addressing contemporary global problems such as environmental crises.

The analysis in this chapter develops a chronological framework that attends to regional distinctiveness. It begins by assessing the legacy of European nationalism in Asia as the twinned ideology of development and exclusion. This legacy entailed national homogenization—often proceeding from a religious base overlain by racial, ethnic, and linguistic expressions of 'othering'—that contributed to national integration and global economic competitiveness. The global spread of this model eventuated in the two World Wars of the twentieth century. In its aftermath, the UN model of national development, which promoted an inclusive, civic nationalism, tended to prevail in many parts of the world for the next few decades.

Next, the chapter considers the role of historical factors in shaping the development outcomes of the post-war period, particularly probing the different legacies of state capacities between Japanese and European imperialism in Asia. While the cruelties of Japanese colonialism have led to its denunciation, the institutions and programmes they established were far better suited to modern development in the Japanese colonies than those of the Europeans. During the Cold War, many of the ex-Japanese colonies and puppet states in the Asian Pacific littoral came under the US security umbrella. The high rates of growth in Korea and Taiwan were achieved by a combination of adapting Japanese colonial institutions and the top-down model of nationalism with the security and economic opportunities afforded by the United States. By the late 1970s, a counterforce of grass-roots nationalism forced through more participatory modes of political and economic governance.

Turning to the populous nation-states of China and India, the chapter explores their distance from US hegemony and experiments with more socialistic forms of development. These alternative forms were enabled by the powerful nationalist movements, and particularly revolutionary nationalism in China, premised upon a more equitable contract with the population than the older imperialist order. In both countries, by the last decades of the century, the pattern of national development and the ideals of redistributive justice began to change as a result of economic and political failures and the rise of new classes demanding change and even expressing separatist sentiments.

In Southeast Asia, the relationship is examined for the 1970s to 1990s period, when a Japan-centred regional economy emerged. Developments in the 1990s culminated in the Asian financial crisis of 1997–1998, leading in turn to political crises in several countries. The region came out from this downturn with new ideas for cementing interdependence within it. The Association of Southeast Asian Nations (ASEAN) has emerged as a significant economic region and even while nationalist competition within it continues, it represents a major force integrating the national economies. Finally, the nationalism–development relationship is explored for the twenty-first century, in which time there appears to be an emergent co-relation between neo-liberal globalization and exclusivist nationalism.

2. The Legacy of European Nationalism

Since the publication of *Asian Drama*, the study of nationalism may well have emerged as one of the most extensive areas of inquiry across the interpretive social sciences and humanities. The rose-tinted view of European nationalism prevalent during Myrdal's time has been stripped to reveal nationalism's twin faces: a developmental approach towards citizens of the majority group coupled with the practical denial of rights to minorities and a periodically hostile, competitive, and warring approach to nations outside its claimed territories. Minorities frequently serve as the hinge group between the outside and inside of the nation, or as the 'internal other' of this nationalism. This dualism of nationalism—the mother of all identity politics—is built upon a self–other distinction and emerges as the deep structure of nationalism that has been apparent over the last 300 years.

Nationalism in Europe was closely linked to imperialism, thus expressing this dualism well into the twentieth century. As Eric Hobsbawm (1990: 102) pointed out, imperial expansion was justified by a nationalism, one that was more racist than rational. Arendt (1948: 152–3) observed that imperialists appeared as the best nationalists because they claimed to stand above the reality of national divisiveness and represent the glory of the nation. Whether in Europe, America, Asia, or Africa, nationalism has periodically expressed itself in both inclusive ways and in more hateful, warlike ways.

Moreover, contrary to Myrdal's narrative of Europe, religion has turned out to be an extremely significant factor in the history of nationalism. The self–other form in which the communal self is represented by the state, whether in reality or aspirationally, arose out of the wars of religion in the sixteenth and seventeenth centuries. The confessional communities of Reformation Europe—Calvinist, Lutheran, Anglican, Catholic—were the historical antecedents of nation-states, where church, state, and subjects became rolled into one as the 'chosen community' antagonistic towards non-believers, whether in the vicinity or beyond the continent. The sovereign nation emerged in the late eighteenth and nineteenth centuries, only after the confessional polity and the accompanying disciplinary revolution enabled the successful formations to become competitive in global capitalism. The states created a relatively homogenized political formation with a common language, national culture, and education system equipped to function in an industrial society and gain competitive control of global resources. While the national community retained the self–other identity form of confessional communities, I have argued that the nation-state translated the holy compact into what has been called the 'congruence of state and culture' defining the nation.[1]

Religion remained an important force until well into the twentieth century, but its role was transformed. More than working as an obstacle to development, confessional religion often became the basis of national exclusivism, even when it was not always so recognized. Carl Schmitt, the German philosopher who joined the Nazis, recognized this clearly:

> All significant concepts of modern theory of the state are secularized theological concepts not only because of their historical development—in which they were transferred to the theory of the state, whereby for example, the omnipotent God became the omnipotent lawgiver—but also because of their systematic structure, the recognition of which is necessary for a sociological consideration of these concepts.   (Schmitt 1985)

---

[1] For the congruence of state and culture see Gellner (1983). For 'confessional nationalism', see Duara (2015).

Schmitt's notion of the 'confrontation of friend and enemy' in the modern nation-state is ultimately at a metaphysical level—one between faiths. Note that Schmitt's religious model for the modern state came not from Christian universalism but from the confessional faiths of the seventeenth and eighteenth centuries.

Myrdal did not quite grasp the three-way relationship between development, nationalism, and religion that European history itself had demonstrated. Religion as 'superstition' has not played a significant role as an obstacle to economic development in Asia, even in the medium term. Rather, religion, which in many parts of Asia—East, Southeast, and South Asia—had not been exclusivist, came to be seen by elites as creating the basis of national homogenization and cohesiveness. State Shinto in Meiji Japan, Hindutva in India, and Islamism in many Muslim-majority countries often represented nationalist elite efforts to suppress local religious orientations and practices and transfer their devotions to what I call 'confessional nationalism'. As in the earlier history of Europe, these sentiments were often expressed more as political loyalties and passions rather than as religious practices. The relevant point here is that religious ideas and sentiments work in a different way in relation to nationalism and development. They typically operate as the basis of exclusivist nationalism, but this can be used for national exclusivism as much as for economic expansion. While religions in the modern world can by no means be so reduced, it has also become an instrument of nationalism.

Writing before Myrdal, Polanyi noted a basic relationship between the inclusive/exclusive polarity and the fluctuations of the global economy. The alternation between capitalist expansion and a closing off of the national economy based on 'the principle of social protection aiming at the conservation of man and nature as well as productive organizations, relying on the varying support of those most immediately affected by the deleterious action of the market' was central to the modern history of nation-states (Polanyi 1957: 132). To be sure, the closing off was not always protective of all and nationalist exclusivity is not always related to economic protectiveness. The two are more complexly related. But there does appear to be a broad relationship that makes clear that nationalism—in its different forms—will recur with fluctuations in global capitalism into the foreseeable future.

Scholars of nationalism often present a difference between two types of nationalism: an ethnic nationalism (built on race, religion, language, etc.) versus a 'civic nationalism' in which citizenship rights are equally granted to all citizens, regardless of race, ethnicity, language, religion, or culture. In the European context, German nationalism is often condemned as ethnic/racist, whereas Anglo-French nationalism is seen to be civic and inclusive. This is likely the model that Myrdal had in mind when conducting the comparison between Europe and South Asia. Moreover, it may have represented the dominant model during the first few decades after the Second World War, when the UN effectively embedded this model in its vision of the family of nations. The notion of development was also sanctioned by the UN's mandate to eradicate poverty and promote higher standards of living and well-being across all nations (United Nations n.d.). Yet in the decades since the 1980s, a narrower ethnic-cultural, if not racist, vision of the nation, aided by global capitalist volatility, has reasserted itself, which can be seen in the American support for Donald Trump today. This represents, of course, only the most recent expression of the deeply embedded self–other form of the nation.

3. Post-war Asian Nationalisms

Most international studies of economic development typically take the nation-*state* as the stable basis of their analysis. When comparing the economic achievements or failures of nations, analysts refer to the state's aggregate indices and policies towards, say, capital formation, foreign debt, currency controls, or balance of trade (Bergeron 2004). While indispensable, these analyses can miss how changes in socio-political forces transform development strategies and vice versa. National development may be more accurately seen as a moving target—or the site of struggle—responding to both global forces and to nationalism as an imaginary constituted as much by identity factors as the changing configuration of interests and power. Given that the *raison d'être* of economic development is the nation, economic strategy and policy is as much about social and political imperatives of the nation-state as it is about development.

I attend to the historical and institutional factors that shape what we might call the 'national imaginary' or 'nation-scapes'. How do histories, institutions, and expectations shape the configuration of the national interests and its power struc-ture at different moments? How might the national imaginary affect the profile of resource allocation, redistribution, stratification, and, not least, the environment? The imaginary can be integrative or contentious, leading even to separatist forces. It has periodically restructured the goals and strategy of the nation-state with regard to development. To take the most evident expressions of how imaginaries have reshaped society and the world, consider the difference between Maoist and contemporary China or, for that matter, between Nehru's and contemporary India. While the broad goals of national development may remain, the frontiers of community inclusion, the class configuration, and possibilities of nationalism have changed dramatically.

Nationalism, and economic nationalism in particular, has informed most Asian nation-states since the Second World War. While patrimonial tendencies—the tendency of leaders to treat national resources as their patrimony—have periodically been parasitic on economic strategy, by and large the pursuit of national advantage has been the primary thrust of Asian nation-states. Import-substitution industrialization or export-oriented strategies have sometimes been sequential, but they often have been subtly combined, especially in East Asian nations, from the 1960s. Economic nationalism in the era of post-Cold War globalization continues to prevail, although with considerably different approaches as Asian nations have come to accept global integration and seek to make their domestic firms more competitive in the global market.

The UN-sanctioned civic model of nationalism and stabilization of economic flows under the Bretton Woods regime of monetary exchange produced a breathing space for many emergent nation-states in the post-war period to cultivate their national models of development and progress. Between 1950 and 1980, the role of developing economies in the world economy and trade shrank greatly compared with the past century and a half, and also with their later growing involvement after 1980. As late as 1970, their share in world trade was under 20 per cent, but had risen to more than 40 per cent by 2010, and included trade in services (Nayyar 2013: 97). Moreover, as most of these erstwhile colonies had been multi-ethnic, nationalist leaders developed policies principally of civic nationalism to accommodate minorities.

Indeed, decolonizing nations were created with the commitment to create a new and more just world order. A series of anti-imperialist and non-alignment conferences led by Jawaharlal Nehru, Sukarno of Indonesia, and, later, Zhou Enlai, most notably during the Asian–African Conference of Bandung in 1955, reiterated this commitment. They developed the principles of Panchasheela—a doctrine of non-interference in each other's internal affairs—a kind of Westphalian doctrine for postcolonial nations. To be sure, territorial conflicts between these newly created states, as well as other geopolitical pressures of the Cold War, led to the dissipation of the movement by the early 1960s. Nonetheless, the strong anti-imperialist and anti-capitalist sentiments upon which many of these nationalist movements were cultivated continued to have an enduring influence in the larger nations of Asia.

4. Colonial Legacies in Asia

The region of Asia that concerns us can be divided into two parts, those in South and Southeast Asia that fell under European, chiefly British but also Dutch and French empires, and those that came under Japanese control. Those that were colonized or controlled by Japan before the Second World War had an entirely different experience of development and nationalism than those in the old European empires. Although Japanese colonialism is abhorred by many Korean and Chinese because of historical crimes, the memories of which have been kept alive, Japanese investment in the development of its colonies in Korea, Taiwan, and the puppet state of Manchukuo (which was more populous than Japan) was far greater than in the British and French colonies of Asia. For example, 50 per cent of Korean and Taiwan school children were receiving elementary education by 1940, compared to 2 per cent in Vietnam at the time, while literacy in India at the time of independence was 12 per cent (Nayaka and Nurullah 1974; Cumings 1999).[2]

Generally speaking, East Asia should be historically distinguished from much of the rest of the continent because of the strong influence of German models of statist nationalism associated with early nineteenth-century theorists like Friedrich List. The main conduit of this model was of course Japan itself, but the fascist *dirigiste* influence on the Kuomintang (KMT) in the 1930s was also significant. Here it is crucial to note that the impact of statism and mobilization on the Chinese Communist Party derived, of course, from Soviet communism, but strong mobilizational apparatuses were developed all over East Asia during the inter-war period. The Japanese puppet state of Manchukuo developed a Leninist-like mobilizational apparatus called the Concordia Society, as well as other controlled mass organizations capable of bringing vaccination, electricity, and heavy-handed surveillance to the most remote villages of Manchuria in a way that was unknown and unseen in European colonies (Duara 2003).

The question of how and why Japanese imperialism turned out to be so different is a larger question that cannot be addressed in depth here, but it has a bearing on our analysis. Japan was a latecomer to the new industrial and imperialist powers at the turn of the twentieth century, including the Germans, Russians, Italians, and Americans, who sought to challenge the global supremacy of Britain and France. These powers discovered nationalism to be a powerful means to mobilize resources, integrate the lower classes, and discipline the population for competition, often with the promise of imperial glory and rewards. For instance, calls to maximize production, rein in consumption, and ban strikes during the First World War were associated to national loyalty in Europe (Arendt 1948 [1973]; Giddens 1987: 234–9; Hobsbawm 1990: 132).

Japan, operating outside the Eurasian theatre of this war, was one of the war's great beneficiaries, seizing German territories and expanding its footprint in East Asia. At the same time, it also noted the necessity of total preparedness for future wars. Upon observing insufficient civilian support for the war among Europeans, it was the first to develop administered mass organizations. A second feature of nationalism among latecomer imperial powers was the recognition, especially among the Japanese, of the necessity to extend some of the *formal* features of nationalism to their colonies and puppets—the idea of the 'regional bloc' or the 'yen bloc' in the case of Japan. This strategy may be seen in the German New Order, the US Monroe Doctrine, the Soviet Union and later the Soviet bloc, the Sterling Zone, and others.

---

[2] Cumings maintains that 70 per cent of children were getting primary education in Taiwan and Korea, whereas Kohli cites the figure for Korea at 50 per cent (Kohli 2004: 39).

In part because of its own humiliation as an inferior Asiatic race, as well as the rise of nationalism in the colonies at the end of the First World War, Japan also sought to match the idea of the regional bloc with the paradoxically anti-(Western) imperialist ideology of pan-Asianism. Encouraged partly by Woodrow Wilson's doctrine of national self-determination and the Soviet revolution, the aftermath of the First World War saw the momentum of popular nationalism in East Asia rise to its greatest heights with the 1 May 1919 movement in Korea and the 4 May 1919 movement in China. Responding to this nationalism, Japanese empire builders actively re-conceptualized their imperial strategy with ideas of regional co-operation under their dominance. This train of ideas and policies eventuated in the Greater East Asian Co-Prosperity Sphere of the Pacific War. The Japanese often kept or set up the national form of the occupied states and claimed to modernize and develop them. However, ideology and policies should not be seen simply as a cloak for imperialist nationalism. Rather, the conditions of war and internal conflicts exacerbated the tension in the Japanese imperialist structures between a commitment to develop the colonies and puppet states and a confessionalist Shinto nationalist tendency to impose their domination.

The impact of Japanese nationalist imperialism left its most important legacy, of course, upon its earlier colonies and puppet states of Korea, Taiwan, and Manchukuo, the last of which was perhaps the most developed state in Asia outside Japan. This legacy included a relatively autonomous and interventionist bureaucratic state drawing on native Confucian statecraft and Prussian–German statism (*Staatswissenschaften*), involving state direction of the economy, total surveillance, a disciplined workforce, high levels of mass education, involvement in the regional political economy, and, not least, an ideology of national essence.

According to Korean economist Sub Park, the yearly mean growth rate of gross domestic production in Korea was 3 per cent between 1915 and 1940, while Indian growth between 1900 and 1946 was under 1 per cent annually (Park 2003: 5). The accumulated per capita British investment in India and Japanese investment in Korea were US$8 and US$38, respectively, in 1938 (Park 2003). By 1936, heavy industry accounted for 28 per cent of total industrial production in Korea, with half a million workers, a number that tripled by 1945 (Cumings 1999: 76).

Taiwan is justly famous among the export-driven industrializing economies of its time. The success of its export expansion was dependent on low-cost labour and the import of production goods at close to world prices. Both were made possible by active government intervention (Chou 1985). Note, however, that after the 'takeoff' of the 1960s, the ratio of imports and exports to gross domestic product (GDP) was 38 per cent in 1975; in fact, colonial Taiwan had already achieved this figure in 1937.[3]

---

[3] It was 39 per cent, with imports at 16 per cent and exports at 23 per cent (Cumings 1999: 78–9).

Sanctioning, if not sanctifying, the Meiji Japanese model of development and expansion was the nationalist ideology of *kokutai*. By the end of the nineteenth century, the Meiji state had developed and disseminated the idea of a unique Yamato race with a common ancestry and divine origins in Amaterasu, organized by a nationwide system of Shinto shrines reaching into every community and school (Hardacre 1989: 32–3, 43–55). Even apart from colonial dominance, the spread of Japanese (and Germanic) ideas into the rest of East Asia led to efforts to mimic these ideals from the early twentieth century. Chinese nationalists sought to derive the nation from the ancestry of the mythic Yellow Emperor (also pursued by the KMT and revived in today's People's Republic of China (PRC)), and Korean nationalists sought to raise the mythic Tangun to the same status (Schmid 2002).

In contrast to the Japanese colonial developmental state, which reinforced the top-down confessionalist model, the European colonial legacy in South and Southeast Asia reflected a weak capacity for penetration and development. However, and particularly in the British Empire, its legacy was reflected in the creation of the representative political institutions discussed below. East Asian nationalism was channelled through corporatist social surveillance structures such as the (updated) Chinese imperial system of *baojia*, in which an ascending hierarchical agglomeration of decimal family units was responsible for all members under them. The massively expanded role of the *baojia* system in colonial Taiwan was as much responsible for the development of the communities as was their surveillance. So, too, in Manchukuo, where together with the police they also attended to vaccination, hygiene, and marketing, as well as political surveillance projects. Little wonder that post-war South Korea was taken over by authoritarian and military leaders with deep connections to the Japanese colonial establishment. Park Chung-hee, who came to power in a military coup to rule as president (1963–1979) during the takeoff years, was a career officer in the Manchukuo Imperial Army and a great admirer of Meiji Japan and the Bushido cult (Eckert 2016: 1–2). The Chinese Communist Party's Leninist cell units embedded within communities were also like confessional units in which people converted and were reborn into a communist faith (*fanshen*) with the goal of purifying the nation (and, more remotely, the world).

5. The Cold War Framework

The ascendance of US power over the former Japanese-occupied territories of maritime East and Southeast Asia during the Cold War, including Japan itself, South Korea, Taiwan, and to a lesser extent Singapore, Malaysia, Thailand, Indonesia, the Philippines, and other countries, played a significant role in the rise of the Asian tigers. Several of these countries—especially Japan and the colonies—were devastated by war but they possessed high levels of education, strong traditions of state activism, and a disciplined workforce. Significantly, the post-war British colonial state in Hong Kong and Malaya also became much more active in building infrastructure, public education, housing, and health services. The United States evolved a pattern of relationships with these militarily, and often economically, dependent allies. Development aid, military protection, and favourable access to American markets were exchanged for firm anti-communist, frequently dictatorial, authoritarian, and monarchical regimes loyal to American interests. As Japan re-built its economy and the US dollar weakened in the 1970s, Japan came to play an important intermediary role in the regional economy of East and Southeast Asia.

Atul Kohli has argued that Asian economies performed better than those in Latin America through the post-Second World War period because they pursued *national* capitalist models of development rather than the more foreign-dependent capitalist models of the latter. The economically successful states in Asia created conditions to support profitability for private domestic investors by various means, including exercising considerable autonomy from foreign capital and power, fostering high domestic saving rates, limiting foreign debt, and channel-ling foreign investment to manufacture for exports (Kohli 2009). We will explore here how these national structures and strategies emerged and developed—quite differently and with different consequences—in Asia.

In the two big countries, China and India, the powerful nationalist and national-ist-socialist movements allowed them to limit foreign economic involvement and experiment with different modes of development until the 1990s. But what was the process whereby national models came to dominate in countries like South Korea and Taiwan, where the United States exercised considerable power com-parable to that in Latin America? Were not nationalist ideals, aspirations, and ambitions in these countries, including South Korea, Taiwan, the Philippines, Thailand, Malaysia, Singapore, and Indonesia, as well as Pakistan, subordinated to regimes that supported the interests of the United States during the Cold War?

Perhaps the most critical factor in this problematic is the nature of US–Cold War concerns in Asia. East and Southeast Asia did not see much of a 'cold' war; rather, there were many bloody hot wars, only most notably in Korea and Vietnam. Communist insurgencies and counter-insurgencies spread across the region well into the 1970s until after the United States–China rapprochement. The security concerns of the United States, which encountered several communist powers on this eastern front, created important conditions for the relative autonomy of the littoral nation-states in its Asian bloc. Between 1946 and 1975, economic and military aid to South Korea and Taiwan was US$69 billion and US$42 billion, respectively. US-sponsored land reforms defused tensions and created stronger domestic markets. It also used aid to steer these countries away from import-substitution policies to the export strategy based on US domestic and military demand in Asia. To be sure, the United States spent even greater amounts—US$115 billion between 1954 and 1975—in South Vietnam, so it is clear that other factors were at work in the success of South Korea and Taiwan (Gray 2014: 42). The colonial legacy of strong institutions, educated populace, and strategically minded state leadership arguably made the difference in these two countries.

US Cold War allies in Asia emerged as highly authoritarian, if not dictatorial, states backed by the US military and its security imperatives. Where possible, monarchies were supported in East and Southeast Asia (and, especially, in the Middle East). Even when they were constitutional monarchies, they represented the symbolic centre of anti-communist nationalism. While the US–Thai military alliance hunted the communists, the cult of the Thai monarch, King Bhumibol, became closely identified with agricultural development and compassion without significant rural reforms (Baker and Phongpaichit 2005).

In South Korea and Taiwan, the national interests of this leadership were generated less by *national movements* than by the historical factors and the corporatist structure of the colonial society they inherited. Both Park Chung-hee and Chiang Kai-shek were deeply nationalist, but their power during the post-war period was not based on an autonomous national movement. To the contrary, they sought to create and mobilize a national movement to support their political and economic strategies. To secure power during his lifetime, Park Chung-hee promulgated the Yushin (Restoration, as in Meiji Restoration) Constitution granting him lifetime presidency.

The New Community Movement (*Saemaul Undong*, 1971–1979) and the militarization of modern society served as the apparatuses for Park's anti-communist national mobilization. The New Community Movement was launched as a rural development project but turned into a movement of 'spiritual discipline' affecting all aspects of life. It emphasized egalitarianism and produced 'enthusiastic warriors of industrialization'. It worked through core cells and did not expend many funds; it also neglected the growing numbers of urban workers. In some ways, this top-down mobilization, which began to be seen as oppressive after the first few enthusiastic years, ironically fostered the subsequent *minjung* movement that was directed sharply against military rule (Han 2004).

The role of nationalism in Korean development may be assessed, interestingly, through the optic of popular views of Park Chung-hee that have poured out in the political climate of the late 1990s. The divisive consequences of this history can still be seen in the recent political career of his daughter, the recently ousted President Park Geun-hye, and *chaebols* closely associated with the family. Conservative forces regard him as among the greatest national heroes for the radical modernization and strengthening of the nation while reviving national culture and identity, and leading an austere and corruption-free life. They justify his service to, admiration of, and re-opening of ties with Japan and deny his role in hunting down Korean independence fighters in Manchukuo. The 'progressive' critique, including those of the unifiers with the North and other leftists and liberals, depicts him as a dyed-in-the-wool would-be Japanese fascist, a brutal dictator, and a corrupt leader who fostered the business and political cabal that would rule South Korea (a phenomenon that analysts of the Korean miracle dub the state's 'embedded autonomy') (Moon 2009: 7–9).

The role of nationalism in Taiwan under the KMT government of Chiang Kai-shek, which underwent an economic miracle similar to that of South Korea in the 1960s and 1970s, resembled the Korean pattern in important respects, but was distinctive in others. The KMT imposed martial law in China soon after its arrival, and the February 1947 massacre took perhaps 30,000 Taiwanese lives. It set up a brutal dictatorship that was most draconian during the White Terror (*baise kongbu*) of the first two decades. This institutional terrorization was accompanied by the effort of the mainland ruling emigrants, who represented about 15 per cent of the population, to nationalize or Sinicize the local population who, they claimed, had become slavish under 50 years of Japanese rule (Harrison 2006: 103–8).

Chiang revived the nationalist–fascist–Confucian–Christian ideological concoction called the New Life Movement. This was essentially a highly surveilled code of conduct and behaviour. In the mainland it had included items such as accounting for the proportion of foreign product in one's clothing and consumption, as well as punishments—sometimes draconian—for keeping long hair or wearing short skirts. In Taiwan it was imposed through schools, media, family, and military. Additionally, Taiwanese were instructed and expected to speak only in Mandarin (a foreign language to most of them, who spoke the regional languages of South China). Chiang declared that the New Life Movement was meant to 'thoroughly militarize the life of the people of the entire nation. It is to make them nourish courage and alertness, a capacity to endure hardship, and especially a habit and instinct for unified behavior. It is to make them willing to sacrifice for the nation at all times' (cited by Harrison 2006: 102). In both Taiwan and South Korea, the communist 'other' without and within the nation also enabled the repression and disciplining of the population in their strategy of development.

By the time these states achieved their development goals in the 1970s, especially at the end of the Vietnam War and after the Sino–US rapprochement, there was a slackening of political control. Efforts were made in Taiwan to reconcile the native population with the regime. Over the next few decades, the Taiwanese opposition developed into a full-fledged anti-KMT and 'Taiwan independence' movement which now rules the island state through the Democratic Progressive Party (DPP).

The waning of Cold War pressures led more generally to popular movements reflecting disaffection with repression and inequality among the Cold War Asian allies of the United States. The South Korean student movements protesting the Gwangju massacre of 1980 led to the *minjung* movement of the later 1980s. The protests against Marcos emerged almost simultaneously in the Philippines; foment in Taiwan resulted in the electoral defeat of the KMT in 1996; subsequently in 1998, the Suharto regime was toppled in Indonesia. Opposition continues to fester in Thailand, although here the long political continuity of the monarchy has tended to diffuse the opposition. All of these movements expressed themselves as national movements embodying the will of the ordinary people and seeking genuine or grass-roots democracy. In Taiwan, it is also expressed as a guarded separatism, whereas in South Korea there is a deep underlying stratum of desire to seek reunification with the North.

6. Nationalism in China and India

If the developmental capacities of postcolonial societies were shaped considerably by their colonial legacies, China remains an outlier with respect to colonialism. To be sure, the foreign settlements in the treaty ports of China and the impact of Japanese state-building activities in Manchuria, Tianjin, and later in several Japanese-occupied regions did have an impact, but a powerful Chinese nationalism was neither enabled nor hampered by existing colonial structures. The Japanese occupation and the course of the Pacific War provided the opportunity for the Chinese Communist Party (CCP) to emerge as revolutionary nationalists. Chinese communism was premised on the idea that Leninism was the most powerful way to establish a strong, equitable, and wealthy *nation*; this was also the case in Vietnam. Ho Chi-Minh stated: 'I loved and admired Lenin because he was a great patriot who liberated his compatriots' (Ho Chi-Minh 2004: 30). China's break with other communist nations such as the Soviet Union and Vietnam was shaped as much by issues of national territory, honour, and interests as by any ideological factor. The most empowering factor enabling the CCP to follow its own agenda was the revolutionary nationalism that it had awakened, particularly in rural China, and that it managed to secure and contain through land redistribution and the mobilization and control apparatuses of the CCP.

India, under the Indian National Congress, shared with China the command over a vast national movement that also enabled it to develop its own pathways. However, mass mobilization in the Indian context was relatively superficial and did not penetrate deeply enough to alter the lives of the masses. Nor was the state structure in British India or the first decades of independent India capable of mobilization and development. Critical to the differences between East and South Asia is the elimination of traditional landed-class control in the East. In Japan, the Meiji Restoration was effectively a revolution that eliminated historical control of the landed classes by means of state-led mobilization. In South Korea and Taiwan, it was the legacy of Japanese colonial mobilization, together with the US Occupation, which supervised major land reform. In older European colonies, large landed classes and interests retained local control well into the twentieth century.

Regardless of the depth or strength of national mobilization, the enormous national movements in China and India reinforced their conviction to remain non-aligned, or at least not subordinate themselves to the emerging superpowers. To some extent this was also true of Indonesia under Sukarno. This nationalism predisposed these states to hold oppositional stances towards free-market ideologies, albeit with different degrees of hostility in the different societies. It is notable that even the Republic of China in Taiwan advocated strong state controls until the 1960s, when it came more directly under the influence of the United States as its protective superpower. Despite the weakness of the non-aligned movement, its most important outcome may have been that the two largest players in Asia—China and India—managed to maintain their non-aligned status, especially after China pulled away from the Soviet bloc from the late 1950s.

The nationalist and nationalist–socialist movements in the two societies allowed them to experiment with different modes of development until the 1990s. In China, both the CCP and KMT, as observed earlier, were deeply influenced by Germanic ideas of state science (whether via Japan, the Soviet Union, or directly). In addition, during the revolution, the CCP developed a formidable Leninist organizational structure with arguably the widest and deepest penetration of any political structure in the world. Contrary to Marx's dismal view of the peasants as a 'sack of potatoes', Mao turned the theory on its head and led a powerful peasant revolution. During the revolution, and particularly during the anti-Japanese war of resistance, it was by no means a merely top-down structure, but actively mobilized the hearts and minds of very large segments of the population through rituals of deep identity conversion embodied in the community stagings of re-birth and 'speak bitterness' campaigns.

In a brilliant analysis, Apter and Saich (1994) discuss how, through a process they call 'exegetical bonding', during the revolution Mao fashioned a nested hierarchy of three narratives, disseminated through pedagogical and political practices, which validated the role of the communists and Mao himself. The master narrative is a tale of loss of the nation to imperialists following the Opium Wars and loss of livelihood, particularly of peasants. The second narrative represents the struggle for Sun Yat-sen's inheritance between Mao and Chiang. The third is about inner-party struggles, of renegades and adventurists overcome by Mao. To the extent that there is any Marxism in these narratives, it is about forging the correct or *true* path to gain national liberation and social justice (Apter and Saich 1994: 14–15).

To be sure, the CCP closely supervised these ritual events and did not allow them to stray too far from the script. Moreover, as the CCP settled into power after 1949, and especially during and after the Great Leap Forward disaster of 1958–1959, these rituals of self-formation came to be seen as routinized and 'ritualized'—in the modern sense—and even more as acts of propaganda and surveillance. Disenchantment came to a head during the Cultural Revolution of

1966–1976. After the death of Mao and the arrest of the Gang of Four, these campaigns moderated considerably, but they have not entirely disappeared.

A second dimension of Chinese communist nationalism refers to the broader revolutionary strategy of the party. In the Second United Front between the CCP and KMT, a very weak coalition forged during the anti-Japanese resistance between 1937 and 1945, Mao crafted an enormously influential text called *On New Democracy*. The task ahead of the CCP was national resistance and, to that end, only traitors and collaborators with the Japanese army were targeted for elimination. Rich peasants and even patriotic landlords were spared, as were national capitalists. Over the next 30 years, to simplify drastically, policy alternated between radicalism and a more moderate approach towards people who would be regarded as 'class enemies' during periods of radicalism, such as during the land revolution (1946–1949), the Great Leap Forward, and the Cultural Revolution. But even during these last two major campaigns, the nation's greatness was foremost in the minds of the leaders. The Great Leap Forward urged the people to overtake Britain and France's iron and steel production within fifteen years. During the Cultural Revolution, class enemies, domestic and foreign, were often merged because China was the only true revolutionary power in the world, barring Enver Hoxha's Albania. The enemies of the revolution were automatically the enemies of China.

As is well known, China's development during the Maoist period was creditable compared to other developing countries, particularly in basic education and healthcare. GDP also grew 6 per cent between 1953 and 1978 (Zhang and Kanbur 2005: 192; Hirst 2015). It is interesting to note that Deng Xiaoping did not think that the reforms he unleashed in 1979 would end socialism. He felt that capitalist society could not eliminate the fundamental problems of extraction of super-profits, exploitation, and plundering. Deng was responding to the social and economic problems of revolutionary nationalism that stressed non-material incentives to increase production in rural and urban society. In the process, however, the national imaginary began to change from a civic union of nationalities (*minzu tuanjie*) to an extraterritorial conception of the Han nation, particularly to engage overseas Chinese investments during the 1980s and 1990s. Meanwhile, the rapid growth of the Chinese economy in the coastal regions—significantly fuelled by these investments—over the hinterland, contributed to dissatisfaction and separatist nationalisms in ethnic regions of Tibet, Xinjiang, and Mongolia.

It is not clear how prepared Deng was to drive a Faustian bargain with neoliberal capitalism for the sake of uplifting the nation (Xiaoping 1984: 175). As capitalism—led by the state—advanced in leaps and bounds in China and the socialist-nation ideals were increasingly eroded, an ideological and moral vacuum has emerged in which the party-state has installed a raw nationalism. Indeed, it would appear that Xi Jinping has now thrown overboard Deng's dictum, '*tao guang yang hui*' (to hide one's advantage and improve on the disadvantage), and gone on to assert China's 'rightful place' among the world's nations.

If the legacy of Japanese colonialism was a developmental state (and continued political hatred by many ex-colonials), the legacy of British imperialism in South and Southeast Asia was represented by Britain-inspired political institutions and the weak developmental capacity of the state. Civil society in India fostered a nationalism that has probably had the longest history of any modern nationalism in Asia. Dadabhai Naoroji, the second president of the Indian National Congress in 1886, was also the author of the Drain Theory, which documented the drain of wealth perpetrated by the British in India and the negative economic impact of British policies. The Indian National Congress was centrally concerned with economic issues, agitating for reduced taxes and greater state expenditure; it launched the Swadeshi movement in 1905—simultaneously with the Chinese economic boycott of American goods—urging Indians to buy Indian-made cloth over British cloth. Under Gandhi, the idea of economic boycott grew into a vast non-co-operation movement that eventually fuelled Indian independence.

The history of Indian colonialism and a 'negotiated' nationalism ensured that despite the impoverished condition of the nation, democracy would remain the only viable means of sustaining the fledgling nation. Economically, Indian nationalism was a fertile ground for developing ideas and plans for independent India. Between Gandhian ideas of restoring the traditional village economy with its utopian ideals of self-governance, and Stalinist notions of total state control of the economy and society, were many hybrid ideas championed by Gandhian socialists of various stripes, including Ram Manohar Lohia and Jawaharlal Nehru himself.

Nehru's ideas were implemented during the first decades of the Republic through the Five-Year Plans of the Planning Commission, which he chaired. Other South Asian countries also developed national plans that stressed self-sufficiency, national markets, growth, and reduction of poverty and inequality. To be sure, these plans were not anti-market, but rather pro-national market (Ludden 2005). The Nehruvian model of a mixed economy and a secular, democratic (bottom-up) political system remained a powerful imaginary of the nation that also became deeply entrenched as different interests and path dependencies became fixed into it.

As a democracy, the political leaders of India cannot simply be focused on growth and development, but have to respond more directly to a multitude of constituencies, redistribution, welfare, and territorial tensions with neighbouring countries. Moreover, India inherited a weak state structure compared to East Asian states. A study of the colonial state's effort to prepare for the Japanese invasion in 1942 revealed how utterly incapable it was of expanding its fighting forces, raising finances, controlling prices, or rationing food (Kamtekar 2002: 187–221). This administrative structure was inherited by the Republic of India without major structural change.

Given the weak administrative capacity and its greater penetration by social interests compared to other East Asian states, national policies in India had to evolve through negotiation and consensus building. It stabilized its territorial unity through the creation of linguistic states and military build-up in Kashmir and the northeast. There have been several turning points in Indian economic policy that have a relationship to the nature of nationalism in India. During the late 1940s and 1950s, the policies of import-substitution and national planning that prevailed represented perhaps a midway path—the outcome of a political stalemate—between socialist influence and big business interests in the Indian National Congress (Mukherji 2009: 84). While the socialists split, creating their own Socialist Party in 1948, Nehru steadily increased the proportion of government investment in relation to private investment, although the latter continued to have a legitimate role in the economy.

During the Indira Gandhi years, Indian non-alignment was compromised as the nation-state was forced to ask for US food aid and financial assistance. In return, India had to liberalize its trade policy and devalue its currency. In 1969, policy veered in the other direction as the government nationalized a massive quantum of private sector assets, including the banking sector. Foreign multinationals also saw their power and autonomy reduced and departed the country during the 1970s. Such a confused zigzag of economic policy reflected weak economic development, popular unrest, and, not least, inner-party conflict, which culminated in the populist policies of the Emergency Period (1975–1977) (Kaviraj 1986). This variety of populism not only decimated the inner organization of the old Congress party—which may have been imploding anyway—but the highly undemocratic measures and failures also *catalysed* changes in the national imaginary.

By the late 1970s, the growing middle classes were coming into their own and their rise was accompanied by an explosion of the media and civil society. Urban protest and anger against government corruption and mis-governance—also expressed in Bombay cinema of the time—in addition to weak economic development, laid the foundations of a changing national imaginary that was in favour of alternative models of development. At the same time there was, in some regions and communities, a tearing at the national consensus as regional and communal movements began to assert themselves. Counter-national movements appeared during the 1980s in the Punjab, Assam, and Kashmir, the last of which has yet to be resolved (Rajagopal 2011; Roy 2015).

Finally, the liberalization measures of 1991 sealed the transformation of the Nehruvian national self-image, although hard reforms would still take a long time, given the nature of Indian national politics. Indeed, it took the dire threat of a fiscal crisis—in addition to the political tragedy of the death of the prime minister—for national leaders and policymakers to accept this change (Mukherji 2009: 90). More than ten years before, Deng Xiaoping and the reformists in the party had effected similar systemic changes with positive economic consequences and equally powerful consequences for its imaginary of a socialist nation.

7. The Asian Financial Crisis and the Question of National Autonomy

Just as in China and India, popular dissatisfaction with existing strategies of development and changing ideas of redistributive justice during the postcolonial decades in Southeast Asia forced changes in the policies and strategies of the regimes. Indeed, it led to regime change in Korea, Taiwan, the Philippines, and Indonesia. In Southeast Asia, domestically driven tensions and opposition combined with geopolitical changes particularly after the United States–China rapprochement, the end of the Vietnam War, and the winding down of the Cold War in the mid-1970s. From this period, several of these nations, including Malaysia, Thailand, and Indonesia—came to be integrated in the regional economy centred in Japan, together with the earlier generation of the newly industrialized countries of Korea, Taiwan, Hong Kong, and Singapore. Japan was not only a source of inspiration: Japanese investment created production systems in the region during the 1980s, and the availability of cheap credit in Japan since then also fuelled speculative investments.

While some of these nation-states, particularly Indonesia and the Philippines, had relatively weak state capacities and poor governance structures, they sought to follow the Japanese path of development. This, as we have seen, was a form of East Asian neo-mercantilism involving close, co-operative relationships between the state and business on the one hand, and the planned nature of economic development on the other. The weak version of the East Asian model in Southeast Asia, while successful in some areas, however, tended to exacerbate the undemocratic characteristics of the regimes, which sometimes led them to unleash ethnic nationalism.

The 'race riots' of 1969 in Malaysia between Malays (*bumiputera*) and the large Chinese (and Indian) minority represents the most evident change in economic development policies resulting from competing nationalisms. In the major countries of Southeast Asia, the overseas Chinese community were typically entrepreneurial and often wealthy, but represented what Fred Riggs called 'pariah entrepreneurs' (quoted in Baker and Phongpaichit 2005: 153) due to their low status in the ideology of national purity, and were the frequent object of rent-seeking bureaucrats and military. (Part of the community was also identified with communism, which did not help their situation.) After the 1969 riots, the Malay state sought to redistribute economic power to the Malay population by increasing its control of key economic sectors, nationalizing many foreign enterprises and targeting 30 per cent *bumiputera* ownership of economic enterprises and employment (Chapter 20, this volume).

In Indonesia, the slaughter of communists organized by Suharto and the military in 1965 overlapped considerably with a massacre of the Chinese community (alleged to be communist), and the ethnic violence reappeared in 1998 when the Suharto regime fell. The situation remains uneasy with the rise of Islamism. The Thai monarchy, however, was the most agile in transitioning to a post-Cold War regime. Soon after the military suppressed the student and rural unrest in the mid-1970s, the Thai royalty was the first to host Deng Xiaoping in his post-1978 tour of Southeast Asia. The principally Chinese Thai merchant classes were appeased and the leftists were isolated (Wongsurawat n.d.).

The years after the end of the global Cold War brought the Washington Consensus to the region. The United States and the International Monetary Fund (IMF) persuaded these erstwhile Cold War partners through their membership in APEC (the Asia-Pacific Economic Cooperation) to privatize, deregulate, and liberalize their trade regimes and capital markets. The loosening of national controls led to a wave of private capital inflows into Indonesia, South Korea, Malaysia, Thailand, and the Philippines; the total value increased from US$48 billion to US$93 billion between 1994 and 1996. In 1997, the figure declined precipitously to *minus* US$12 billion (*Financial Times*, 16 February 1998: 21, cited by Beeson 1998: 357–74; see also Higgott 1998).

What came to be called the Asian financial crisis of 1997–1998 was triggered by currency devaluation in China and Japan, which made these other Asian economies uncompetitive at both ends of the value chain. The Chinese devaluation of the yuan in relation to the US dollar in 1994 led to a 50 per cent decline in its value on top of the introduction of a 17 per cent VAT rebate for exports (Higgott 1998: 335). The depreciation of the Japanese yen to the US dollar in 1995 (by 40 per cent) and the weakening of Japanese consumer markets caused the steep and unsustainable appreciation of these Asian currencies, which were all pegged to the dollar (Corsettia et al. 1999: 355). Although the crisis began in Thailand, it quickly spread to neighbouring countries, revealing the close relationships between these economies. Riots broke out in several countries, including South Korea and Thailand. Certain weaker economies such as Suharto's military technocratic regime, which could not manage the volatility, collapsed.

One may legitimately inquire, despite the comparatively developed national autonomy in Asia compared to Latin America, whether this autonomy was sufficient. While some Southeast Asian countries may have expressed poor governance, it was ultimately the dependence on the United States–Japan-centred regional economy and the pressures they faced for liberalization that underlay the crisis. Paul Krugman observed in 1998:

> Why hasn't China been nearly as badly hit as its neighbors? Because it has been able to cut, not raise, interest rates in this crisis, despite maintaining a fixed exchange rate; and the reason it is able to do that is that it has an inconvertible currency, a.k.a. exchange controls. Those controls are often evaded, and they are the source of lots of corruption, but they still give China a degree of policy leeway that the rest of Asia desperately wishes it had.
>
> (Krugman 1998, quoted by Corsettia et al. 1999: 364)

The political consequences of the crisis in the context of regional development is worth noting. The US allies in the region had formed into ASEAN in 1967, initially as a security organization. Subsequently, as these economies 'took off', their economic relationships with each other grew greatly and increasingly, as noted, under a Japan-centred regional economy. While economic and cultural nationalism continued to shape these countries, by the 1990s they had developed sufficient confidence to announce a distinctive identity—although it was more ideology than identity—of 'Asian values', particularly in those societies influenced by Confucian values. This ideological bubble, however, burst soon after the financial crisis. Nonetheless, as the crisis revealed, these economies had become highly interdependent.

The economic integration of East, South, and Southeast Asia, which had increased steadily under imperialist-dominated trade, declined precipitously at the end of the Second World War (Petri 2005: 11–14). Intraregional trade began to pick up in the 1980s, but it was the shock of the common crisis that seems to have awakened the states to the reality of regional networks and focused their attention on co-operation. Ten years on from the crisis, what the Asian Development Bank (ADB) calls 'integrating Asia', including ASEAN, China, Japan, South Korea, India, Hong Kong, and Taiwan, conducted over 50 per cent of its trade with itself in comparison to trade with the outside world, compared with only 33 per cent in the 1980s. In 2016, the Asian interregional trade share of world trade rose to 57.3 per cent. Six major indicators of interdependence tracked for the sixteen Asian economies have increased markedly in the ten years since the financial crisis (ADB 2008: 70, 97–8; see also ADB 2017). Financial integration has been weaker, but several of these countries have entered into bilateral swap agreements since the Asian financial crisis. The ADB reported in 2017 that twenty years after the financial crisis, wide-ranging reforms and safety net systems against the impact of externals had been developed, 'as seen by Asia's relative resilience to and rapid recovery from the 2008/09 global financial crisis' (ADB 2017: 8).

In the twenty-first century, ASEAN has sought to create a framework to enmesh the major powers in regional affairs through commercial diplomacy (e.g., free-trade agreements), thereby avoiding dependence on a single great power. In recent years, the admirable balance it had achieved has tended to be overcome by the increasing dependence on Chinese economic development and fear of political intervention.

8. Nationalism and Development in the Twenty-first Century

The end of the Cold War and the onset of the neo-liberal era of the Washington Consensus has created a different scenario for Asian nations. The impact of global capitalism was felt most severely during the Asian financial crisis by the frontline nations of East and Southeast Asia. While, as we have seen, these nations have succeeded in creating some protections and escaped the global financial crisis of 2008–2009 less damaged than others, the economic, political, and cultural impacts of globalization have generated a changed pattern of both state and popular nationalism.

Many of the economically powerful Asian nations, including Japan, South Korea, China, Vietnam, Malaysia, Thailand, Indonesia, and India have accepted the premise of international economic integration and their businesses have gained considerably from this integration. This has changed the nature of state economic nationalism, but they have by no means rejected it. Instead of blatant moves like expelling multinationals or raising protective tariffs, these states have taken on new roles in supporting national and domestic firms to compete successfully in the global economy. In this context, state intervention has tended to favour private domestic corporations, often at the expense of public investment and services (D'Costa 2012: 14, 28).

Saskia Sassen has written about restructuring of the contemporary state as a consequence of globalization: 'The encounter of a global actor—firm or market—with one or another instantiation of the national state can be thought of as a new frontier zone. It is not merely a dividing line between the national economy and the global economy. It is a zone of politico-economic interactions that produce new institutional forms and alter some old ones' (Sassen 1999: 151). The Chinese state expresses this changed structure aptly since the 1990s. The special economic zones and decentralized formats governing regional and international relationships can be found, most famously, in the Hong Kong–South China relationship, the Yellow Sea zone, and the Taiwan–Fujian–Shanghai interactions.[4] Provincial government economic activism plays a particularly important role, for instance, in southwest Yunnan–Southeast Asia ties, and more recently in the Belt Road Initiative.

While this has led to high growth rates in the GDP of Asian economies, especially for China and India, the population has also been exposed to the volatility of global capitalism. Partially in response to these changes, the role of popular nationalism in Asia, as elsewhere, has changed. Over the previous fifty years, the nation-state's project to mobilize its citizens for development, sacrifice, and repression had, with notable exceptions, led to its shaping the identities of the people through the educational and other apparatuses, state and non-state. In the current era, this nationalism has tended to become a reactive—and often reactionary—movement in a populist version of Polanyi's defensive or protective phase.

In the absence of an alternative vision to socialism, the PRC state has emphasized the raw goals of restoring national power and glory and reached back to its imperial history. The decades of state-led nationalism, first directed against US imperialism

---

[4] See, for example, Hook (2001); see also Chen (2000).

and subsequently against Japanese war crimes, led in the twenty-first century to mass nationalism that often slipped out of state control. Internet nationalism is of course the latest phase of a series of events over the last twenty years, including demonstrations against the Belgrade bombings and the numerous protests regarding territorial conflicts with Japanese and other neighbouring countries. Similarly, popular nationalisms have forced the hand of the Vietnamese government, generated conflicts between Thailand and Cambodia, between Indonesia, Malaysia, and Singapore, among many others. Islamic nationalism in Indonesia and to a lesser extent in Malaysia, regional Muslim uprisings in Southern Thailand and the Philippines, and Buddhist nationalism in Myanmar have also stoked violence in the ASEAN region just as it has begun to gain some traction as an economic formation (Vu 2013).

In India, the rise of the Bharatiya Janata Party (BJP) has seen both state activism in the global and national economic sphere as well as the intensification of Hindutva communalism. A recent expression of the relationship between the two reported in the *New York Times* is revealing. In the 2017 elections in Gujarat, the *New York Times* reported that many supporters of Prime Minister Narendra Modi, who had been a long-time chief minister of Gujarat with a strong following among the business community in particular, were poorly affected by recent economic measures, such as the demonetization of the economy:

> Kailash Dhoot, a textile exporter, said that Mr. Modi's recent policies had wounded his business but that Mr. Modi's party was still his first choice.
>
> When asked why, Mr. Dhoot was quick, and curt, with an answer. 'Hindutva,' he said. And he closed his mouth firmly, signaling the discussion was over.
>
> (Gettleman and Kumar 2018)

The legacy of confessional nationalism has produced loyalty, if not identity, with the state, which was mobilized for economic advancement and political integration. The particular example cited from the *New York Times* above reveals that the two need not be completely aligned, but can also function as supplementary or substitutive. In other words, the state in India deploys both goals—exclusivist integration and economic development—to substitute one for the other when needed. While this relationship certainly pre-existed contemporary polities, the scapegoating function is very relevant to contemporary states, democratic and non-democratic, in both the developing and developed world.

9. Conclusion

Since the Second World War, nationalism in Asia has revealed many visages—revolutionary, top-down, anti-communist, participatory, civic, ethnic, religious, and more. The immediate post-war decades saw a largely inclusive civic model across much of the globe, permitting the new nation-states to develop their domestic capabilities and resources without strong ethnocentric biases (but not excluding anti-communism). The prevalence of the post-war inclusive model had much to do with the geopolitical circumstances of the victory of the Allied Forces in the Second World War, but it was also enabled by strong anti-imperialist national movements across much of the colonial and semi-colonial world. As movements, these were fertile and rich sources of ideas and practices, including co-operatives and rural re-constructionist practices across Asia. They were also movements for the reduction of inequalities, inequities, and social justice. Nationalism as a grass-roots movement is important because it urges us to view the costs of efficient modernization on people and the environment. In East Asia, the reckoning—in the places where it has come, like South Korea and Taiwan—is being made after a certain level of development has been attained. In the more democratic countries, the processes are merged and development is slow, but we also have to contend with the thought that without grass-roots national movements, development may not happen.

Each dominant mode has also transmuted over time, reflecting changes in domestic and international forces. In turn, changes in the political and national imaginaries have affected economic policies and distributive outcomes, and vice versa. We saw decisive transformations in the Cold War littoral where non-inclusive rapid growth was replaced by greater participation and more redistributive models. In China and India, the inadequacies of development strategies also led to political upheavals, which led the state to economic policies that were more capital-friendly. In Southeast Asia, the reliance on US military power and Japanese investments broke down during the Asian financial crisis, leading to changes in leadership, and more importantly, the emergence of a regionally integrated, transnational economy. ASEAN became a significant player able not only to absorb global economic shocks, but also to enmesh global powers within a framework of its own making, at least until the recent activities of the PRC.

More recently, the dialectic between national political movements and economic development has taken a more sinister turn, baring the self–other binary that underlies the nation-form. The ascendance of neo-liberal capitalism globally has been accompanied by the rise of chauvinistic, populist nationalism. The connection between nationalism and development appears to have come full cycle from over a century ago, although, of course, there are important differences. Nationalism is at work today to protect against real or perceived predation as well as to integrate the nation for competitive advantage.

The challenges ahead, particularly with the environmental crisis, will require nations to cultivate new ways of addressing problems of poverty and inequality in combination with sustainable development. While economic globalization has made the world more interdependent than ever, nationalism makes it very difficult to translate interdependence into co-operation. Relatedly, among the impediments to planetary sustainability are contemporary models and conceptions of *prosperity* among competitive nation-states, which tend to perceive development and sustainability as a zero-sum game.[5] The forces of civil society and transnational agencies and institutions committed to sustainable development will be needed to shift the will of nation-states to respond to this crisis.

Acknowledgements

I would like to thank Aditya Balasubramaniam, Kanchana Ruwanpura, Srirupa Roy, and Viren Murthy for their help. Asian Transformations workshop participants Robert Wade and Deepak Nayyar gave especially constructive comments.

References

Apter, D.E., and T. Saich (1994). *Revolutionary Discourse in Mao's Republic.* Cambridge, MA: Harvard University Press.

Arendt, H. (1948 [1973]). *The Origins of Totalitarianism.* New York: Harcourt Brace.

Asian Development Bank (2008). *Emerging Asian Regionalism.* Manila: ADB.

Asian Development Bank (2017). 'The Era of Financial Interconnectedness', ADB, Manila, Asian Economic Integration Report 2017.

Baker, C., and P. Phongpaichit (2005). *A History of Thailand.* Cambridge: Cambridge University Press.

Beeson, M. (1998). 'Indonesia, the East Asian Crisis and the Commodification of the Nation-State', *New Political Economy*, 3(3): 357–74.

Bergeron, S. (2004). *Fragments of Development.* Ann Arbor, MI: University of Michigan Press.

Chen, X. (2000). 'Both Glue and Lubricant: Transnational Ethnic Social Capital as a Source of Asia-Pacific Subregionalism', *Policy Sciences*, 33: 269–87.

Chou, T.-C. (1985). 'The Pattern and Strategy of Industrialization in Taiwan', *The Developing Economies*, 23: 138–57.

Corsettia, G., P. Pesentib, and N. Roubini (1999). 'What Caused the Asian Currency and Financial Crisis?', *Japan and the World Economy*, 11: 305–73.

Cumings, B. (1999). 'Colonial Formations and Deformations'. In: *Parallax Visions: Making Sense of American–East Asian Relations at the End of the Century.* Durham, NC: Duke University Press.

D'Costa, A.P. (2012). 'Capitalism and Economic Nationalism', *Oxford Scholarship Online.* DOI: 10.1093/acprof:oso/9780199646210.003.0001.

---

[5] See the important work of Jackson (2009).

Duara, P. (2003). *Sovereignty and Authenticity*. Lanham, MD: Rowman and Littlefield.

Duara, P. (2015). *The Crisis of Global Modernity*. Cambridge: Cambridge University Press.

Eckert, C. (2016). *Park Chung-hee and Modern Korea*. Cambridge, MA: Harvard University Press.

Gellner, E. (1983). *Nations and Nationalisms*. Ithaca, NY: Cornell University Press.

Gettleman, J., and H. Kumar (2018). 'India's Economic Woes are Piercing Modi's Aura of Invulnerability', *New York Times*, 6 January. Available at: www.nytimes.com/2018/01/06/world/asia/india-modi-economy.html (accessed 23 August 2018).

Giddens, A. (1987). *The Nation-State and Violence*. Berkeley, CA: University of California Press.

Gray, K. (2014). 'US Aid and Uneven Development in East Asia', *Annals of the American Academy of Political and Social Sciences*, 656: 41–58.

Han, S.-M. (2004). 'The New Community Movement', *Pacific Affairs*, 77(1): 69–93.

Hardacre, H. (1989). *Shinto and the State, 1868–1988*. Princeton, NJ: Princeton University Press.

Harrison, M. (2006). *Legitimacy, Meaning and Knowledge in the Making of Taiwanese Identity*. Basingstoke: Palgrave Macmillan.

Higgott, R. (1998). 'The Asian Economic Crisis', *New Political Economy*, 3(3): 333–56.

Hirst, T. (2015). 'A Brief History of China's Economic Growth', *World Economic Forum*, 30 July. Available at: www.weforum.org/agenda/2015/07/brief-history-of-china-economic-growth (accessed 23 August 2018).

Ho Chi-Minh (2004). 'The Path That Led Me To Leninism'. In P. Duara (ed.) *Decolonization*. London: Routledge.

Hobsbawm, E. (1990). *Nations and Nationalism since 1780*. Cambridge: Cambridge University Press.

Hook, G. (2001). 'Region-Building and Integration in Post-Cold War East Asia', Asian Studies Frontier Research Project, Working Paper 9.

Jackson, T. (2009). *Prosperity Without Growth*. London: Sustainable Development Commission.

Kamtekar, I. (2002). 'A Different War Dance', *Past & Present*, 176: 187–221.

Kaviraj, S. (1986). 'Indira Gandhi and Indian Politics', *Economic and Political Weekly*, 21(38–9): 1697–708.

Kohli, A. (2004). *State Directed Development*. Cambridge: Cambridge University Press.

Kohli, A. (2009). 'Nationalist Versus Dependent Capitalist Development', *Studies in Comparative International Development*, 44: 386–410.

Krugman, P. (1998). 'Saving Asia', *Fortune Investor*, 7 September.

Ludden, D. (2005). 'Development Regimes in South Asia', *Economic and Political Weekly*, 40(37): 4042–51.

Moon, S. (2009). 'The Cultural Politics of Remembering Park Chung-hee', *Asia-Pacific Journal*, 7(19): 1–33.

Mukherji, R. (2009). 'The State, Economic Growth, and Development in India', *India Review*, 8(1): 81–106.

Myrdal, G. (1968). *Asian Drama: An Inquiry into the Poverty of Nations. A Twentieth Century Fund Study, Volumes I, II, and III*. New York: Pantheon.

Nayaka, P., and J.S. Nurullah (1974). *A Students' History of Education in India (1800–1973)* (6th edn). Mumbai: Macmillan.

Nayyar, D. (2013). *Catch Up*. Oxford: Oxford University Press.

Park, S. (2003). 'Exploitation and Development in Colony', *Korean Journal of Political Economy*, 1(1): 5.

Petri, P.A. (2005). 'Is East Asia Becoming More Interdependent?', Paper prepared for session on European and Asian Integration, American Economic Association, Boston, 8 January.

Polanyi, K. (1957). *The Great Transformation*. Boston, MA: Beacon Press.

Rajagopal, A. (2011). 'The Emergency as Prehistory of the New Indian Middle Class', *Modern Asian Studies*, 45(5): 1003–49.

Roy, S. (2015). 'Angry Citizens', *Identities*, 23(3): 362–77.

Sassen, S. (1999). 'Servicing the Global Economy'. In P. Dicken, P.F. Kelly, L. Kong, and K. Olds (eds) *Globalization and the Asia-Pacific*. London: Routledge.

Schmid, A. (2002). *Korea Between Empires, 1895–1919*. New York: Columbia University Press.

Schmitt, C. (1985 [2005]). *Political Theology* (2nd edn). Trans. George Schwab. Chicago, IL: University of Chicago Press.

United Nations (n.d.) 'About Economic and Social Development'. Available at: www.un.org/esa/about_esa.html (accessed 23 August 2018).

Vu, T. (2013). 'Southeast Asia's New Nationalism', *TRaNS*, 1(2): 259–79.

Wongsurawat, W. (n.d.). 'The Crown and the Communists', unpublished paper.

Xiaoping, D. (1984). 'Uphold the Four Cardinal Principles'. In: *Selected Works (1975–82)*. Beijing: Beijing Foreign Languages Press.

Zhang, X., and R. Kanbur (2005). 'Spatial Inequality in Education and Health Care in China', *China Economic Review*, 16: 189–204.

PART III

COUNTRY AND SUB-REGION STUDIES

COUNTRY STUDIES

15

China

Justin Lin Yifu

1. Introduction

Myrdal did not cover China in his monumental book, *Asian Drama*. When he published the book in 1968, China was approaching the twenty-year anniversary of the victory of the socialist revolution, led by Mao Zedong, in 1949. Its publication also came ten years after the launch of the failed ultra-leftist Great Leap Forward;[1] and ten years before the beginning of Reform and Opening Up, launched by Deng Xiaoping,[2] in 1978. In 1968, China was in the middle of the chaotic Cultural Revolution, which was launched by Mao Zedong himself in 1966 and did not end until his death in 1976.[3]

Unlike other Asian countries studied in *Asian Drama*, China had a strong rather than a soft state. China had also carried out, since 1953, a big push for its industrialization drive, recommended by Myrdal in *Asian Drama* to Asian countries for changing their miserable underdeveloped status. China, starting in the

---

[1] The Great Leap Forward aimed for China to overtake the United Kingdom in ten years and to catch up with the United States in fifteen years. It set ambitious industrialization targets, for example, doubling the steel output from 5.35 million ton in 1957 to 10.7 million ton in 1958. The program boosted industrial output like a balloon but soon failed, as shown in Figure 15.1a. However, the efforts to industrialize China persisted. The Great Leap Forward also made parallel dramatic changes in the rural area, for example, the adoption of People's Commune as the basic farming system. After the socialist revolution, the Chinese government first confiscated landlords' land and distributed the land to poor farmers in 1949–1952 and consolidated the private farms into agricultural collectivizes step by step afterwards. The first attempt was the Mutual Aid team of 3 to 5 households in 1953, then progressed to the Primary Agricultural Cooperative of 20 to 30 households in 1954–1955, to Advanced Agricultural Cooperatives of around 200 households in 1956–1957, and peaked at the People's Commune of an average farm size of 5,000 households. After the failure of the People's Commune, the farm system changed to the Production Team system of 20 to 30 households in 1962. The system remained until the introduction of individual-based farming, the Household Responsibility System, in 1978, when the Reform and Opening Up began.
[2] Deng Xiaoping, born in 1904, was one of the first generation revolutionary leaders. He became general secretary of the Chinese Communist Party in 1956, purged in 1966 at the beginning of Cultural Revolution, restored in 1973 by Chairman Mao, purged again in 1976 by the leftist Gang of Four, Chairman Mao's heirs, when Mao died. He returned to power again in 1978 after the Gang of Four was overthrown.
[3] Mao's ostensible reason for the Cultural Revolution was to prevent China from falling back onto the capitalist road. However, one of the true reasons behind his motivation was to regain his political dominance in China after stepping aside from the first line of policymaking in 1962, due to the setback of the Great Leap Forward and People's Commune in 1958–1961, which led to the Great Famine with in excess of 30 million deaths and 33 million postponed births (i.e., the decision to have a pregnancy) (Lin 1991).

first Five-Year Plan in 1953, adopted a state-led planned economic system to pursue a heavy industry-oriented development strategy for the purpose of quickly building up a comprehensive system of modern capital-intensive industries. With the big push of the Stalinist planning model as well as Chinese bureaucrats' mobilization and implementation capability, China was quickly transformed from an agrarian economy in 1952 to an economy dominated by industry, as shown in Figure 15.1a, with the capability to test nuclear bombs in 1964 and launch a satellite in 1970.

Nevertheless, when *Asian Drama* was published, China was still trapped economically in a dire situation worse than most other countries analysed in the book. Measured in current US dollars, China's per capita GDP in 1968 was US$91.5, compared to US$98.8 in India, US$65 in Indonesia, US$323.4 in Malaysia, US$146.9 in Pakistan, US$224.6 in Philippines, and US$150.2 in Sri Lanka.[4]

Real change in China did not occur for another ten years until the Reform and Opening Up began in 1978. In that year, 70.5 per cent of the labour force was employed in the primary sector and 82 per cent of China's population was living in rural areas, as shown in Figures 16.1b and 16.1c. Moreover, 84 per cent of its population was living below the international poverty line of US$1.25 a day. China's per capita GDP was US$156, about 25 per cent below India's US$204 and less than one third of the average of US$490 in Sub-Saharan African countries. Like other poor countries, China was also an inward-looking economy with trade consisting of merely 9.7 per cent to its GDP. Myrdal did not have the opportunity to spend another ten years doing the research on China and publish a sequel to *Asian Drama* in 1978. If he had done, he, like many economists at that time, would most likely have painted a pessimistic outlook for China, similar to his outlook for other Asian countries in his 1968 book, even though China had implemented many of his proposed programmes, such as big-push industrialization and land reform, for three decades.

From the above humble starting point, Deng Xiaoping and other veterans initiated at the end of 1978 the Reform and Opening Up programmes to transit the Chinese economic system from a planning economy to a market economy. Deng and his associates were purged during the Cultural Revolution and did not return to power until the death of Mao and the downfall of Mao's hand-picked ultra-left successors, the Gang of Four, in 1976.

China is celebrating the fortieth anniversary of Reform and Opening Up this year. In the past forty years, predictions of the coming collapse of the Chinese economy surged repeatedly in the world's news media and international forums. However, to the surprise of almost every China observer and economist around the world, China achieved a sustained growth miracle. Instead of collapse,

---

[4] The data for per capita GDP used in this chapter are all taken from the World Bank's World Development Indicators (https://datacatalog.worldbank.org/dataset/world-development-indicators).

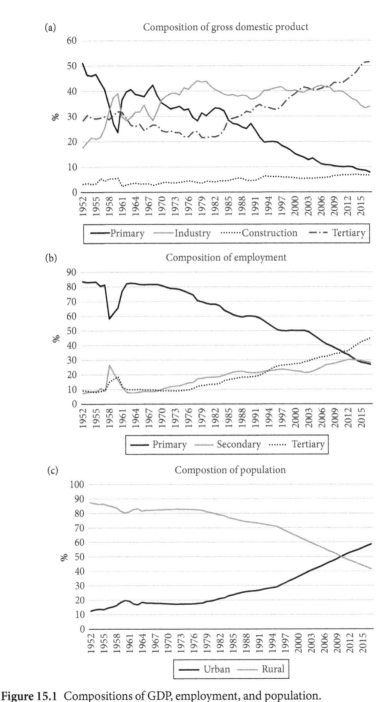

Figure 15.1 Compositions of GDP, employment, and population.

Source: Author's illustration based on data from National Statistical Bureau, *Compilation of New China Statistical Data, 1949–2013*; National Statistical Bureau, *China Statistical Abstract* 2018.

stagnation, and frequent crises—as in many transition economies in East Europe, the former Soviet Union, Africa, and Latin America at the same period of time—the average annual growth rate of GDP reached 9.5 per cent in the period 1978–2017. This performance was far exceeding the expectation of Deng Xiaoping himself. When he initiated Reform and Opening Up, the target was to quadruple the Chinese economy in twenty years. The GDP growth rate required for that was 7.2 per cent per year for twenty years. I was a graduate student at Peking University at that time. None of my classmates, including myself, and my professors, including those visiting professors from the West, thought the above growth target was possible to achieve.

In addition, China's trade growth was also unprecedented. The average annual growth rate of trade volume, measured in US dollars, reached 14.8 per cent in 1978–2017. With such an extraordinary growth performance, China overtook Japan to be the second largest economy measured by market exchange rate in the world in 2009, overtook Germany to be the world's largest exporter in 2010, overtook the US to be the world's largest trading country in 2013, and in 2014, China's GDP, measured by purchasing power parity, exceeded the US to become the world's largest economy. China's per capita GDP reached US$8,640 and trade consisted of 31.1 per cent of GDP in 2017. During this period of time about 800 million people were lifted above the international poverty line of US$1.25 a day, contributing to more than 70 per cent of poverty reduction in the world. Moreover, not only was China the only emerging market economy to avoid a systemic financial and economic crisis in the past forty years, it also helped the Asian economies to quickly pull out of the 1997/1998 financial crisis by not devaluing Chinese currency and maintaining dynamic growth and helped the world economy avoid a downward spiral in the 2008 global crisis by using fiscal stimulus to achieve quick recovery, and contributing more than 30 per cent of global growth annually.

In this chapter, I discuss six related questions: why was China's growth performance poor before 1987? Why was it possible for China to achieve such an outstanding performance after the transition in 1978? Why was China able to avoid collapse and stagnation as was occurring in other transition economies? What were the prices China paid for its success? What are the prospects for China's growth in the coming decades? What lessons can we draw from China's development experiences in view of the *Asian Drama*?

2. Why was China Trapped in Poverty before 1978?

Rapid, sustained increase in per capita income is a modern phenomenon. Studies by economic historians, such as Angus Maddison (2001), show that average annual per capita income growth in the West was only 0.05 per cent before the eighteenth century, jumping to about 1 per cent in the nineteenth century, and reaching about 2 per cent in the twentieth century. That means that per capita income in Europe took 1,400 years to double before the eighteenth century, about seventy years in the nineteenth century, and thirty-five years thereafter. Before the coming of modern times in 1700 AD, the gap of per capita GDP in China and India, compared with that of West European countries, was only about 50 per cent and due to their enormous population size, China and India together contributed about 50 per cent of global GDP (Lin and Rosenblatt 2012).

A continuous stream of technological innovation is the basis for continuous improvement of productivity and income and thus sustained growth in any economy. The dramatic surge in growth in modern times is a result of a paradigm shift in technological innovation. Before the industrial revolution in the latter half of the eighteenth century, technological innovations were generated mostly by the experiences of craftsmen and farmers in their daily production. After the industrial revolution, experience-based innovation was increasingly replaced by experimentation and, later, by science-based experiments conducted in scientific laboratories (Lin 1995; Landes 1998). This paradigm shift accelerated the rate of technological innovation, marking the coming of modern economic growth and contributing to the dramatic acceleration of income growth in the nineteenth and twentieth centuries (Kuznets 1966).

The industrial revolution not only accelerated the rate of technological innovation, but also transformed industrial, economic, and social structures, as the historical materialism articulated by Karl Marx and Friedrich Engels (1848) in *Manifesto of the Communist Party*. Before the eighteenth century, every economy was agrarian; 85 per cent or more of the labour force worked in agriculture, mostly in self-sufficient production for the family. The acceleration of growth was accompanied by the movement of labour from agriculture to manufacturing and services. The manufacturing sector gradually moved from very labour-intensive industries at the beginning to more capital-intensive heavy and high-tech industries. Finally, the service sector came to dominate the economy. Accompanying the change in industrial structure was an increase in the scale of production, required capital and skill, market scope, and risks. In order to exploit the potential unleashed by new technology and industry and to reduce transaction costs and share risks, it requires innovations as well as improvements in an economy's hard infrastructure, such as power, road networks, and port facilities, and its soft infrastructure, including rules and values, the legal framework, financial institutions, and the education system (Lewis 1954; Kuznets 1966; North 1981; Lin 2011, 2012b).

A developing country like China, which started its modernization drive in 1949 after the victory of the socialist revolution, potentially has latecomer advantages in its pursuit of technological innovation and structural transformation. In advanced, high-income countries, technological innovation and industrial upgrading require costly and risky investments in research and development, because their technologies and industries are located at the global frontier. Moreover, the institutional innovation required for realizing the potential of new technology and industry often proceeds in a costly trial-and-error, path-dependent, evolutionary process (Fei and Ranis 1997). By contrast, a latecomer country in the catching-up process can borrow technology, industry, and institutions from the advanced countries at low risk and costs. So, if a developing country knows how and introduces necessary conditions to tap the latecomer advantage in technology, industry, and social and economic institutions, it can grow at an annual rate several times that of high-income countries for decades before closing its income gap with those advanced countries (Lin 2009; Vu 2013).[5]

In pre-modern times, China was the largest economy and among the most advanced, powerful countries in the world (Maddison 2007). Mao Zedong, Zhou Enlai, and many other Chinese social and political elites joined the socialist revolution for the purpose of realizing the dream of China's rejuvenation. The lack of industrialization—especially the lack of large-scale, capital-intensive, technologically advanced, heavy industries that were the foundation for high labour productivity, and thus high income, and the basis for the production of military machineries, and thus military strength—was perceived as the root cause of China's backwardness. It was natural and seemingly intuitive for the social and political elites in China to prioritize the development of large, heavy, advanced industries when they started the process of nation building after the success of the socialist revolution. In the nineteenth century, the political leaders of France, Germany, the United States, and other Western countries pursued effectively the same strategy, motivated by the contrast between Britain's rising industrial power and the backwardness of their own industry (Gerschenkron 1962; Chang 2003).

Starting in 1953, China adopted a series of ambitious Five-Year Plans to accelerate the building of modern advanced industries, with the goal of overtaking Britain in ten years and catching up to the United States in fifteen years. Because those advanced industries were not only protected by patents, but their access to knowhow was also prohibited by advanced countries due to their national security consideration, China needed to 'reinvent the wheel' when it wanted to build up those advanced industries. Such a strategy effectively gave up the latecomer's advantage in technology innovation and industrial upgrading.

---

[5] The concept of latecomer advantages is related but has a subtle difference to the advantages of backwardness made popular by Gerschenkron (1962). The latecomer advantages refer to a country at a lower development stage that can learn from the existing technology, industry, and institution of a country at a higher development stage to reduce the cost and risk of innovation in its development process. The advantage of backwardness refers to a country at a lower development stage that has a lower opportunity cost than an advanced country in adopting the newest technology, as the former can adopt directly the newest technology when it first enters a new industry while the latter is already in the advanced industry and will have to replace the equipment that embodied the old technology with new equipment using the newest technology as and when the newest technology becomes available (Lin 2016).

Moreover, China was a lower-income agrarian economy at that time. In 1953, 83.1 per cent of its labour force was employed in the primary sector, and its per capita income (measured in purchasing power parity terms) was only 4.8 per cent of that of the US (Maddison 2001). Given China's employment structure and income level, the country did not possess a comparative advantage in the modern advanced industries of high-income countries, whether latent or overt, and Chinese firms in those industries were not viable in an open, competitive market.

To achieve its strategic goal, the Chinese government needed to protect the priority industries by giving firms in those sectors a monopoly in product markets and subsidizing them through various price distortions, including suppressed interest rates, an overvalued exchange rate, and lower prices for other inputs, including wages for labour. The price distortions created shortages and the government was obliged to use administrative measures to mobilize and allocate resources directly to the non-viable firms in priority industries (Lin 2009; Lin and Li 2009).

These interventions, as shown in Figure 15.1c, enabled China to quickly transform the production structure from an agrarian economy to an industrialized economy with the ability to test nuclear bombs in the 1960s and launch satellites in the 1970s. However, the modern capital-intensive industries generated only a few employment opportunities, resulting in little change in China's employment and population structure from its agrarian past before the end of the 1970s, as shown in Figures 16.1b and 1c. The costs of such a development strategy were not only the voluntary giving up of the latecomer's advantage but also the inefficiency arising from the misallocation of resources, the distorted incentives, and the repression of labour-intensive sectors in which China held a comparative advantage. As a result, economic efficiency was low and growth before 1978 was driven mainly by an increase in inputs. Despite a very respectable average annual GDP growth rate of 6.1 per cent in the period 1952 to 1978 and the establishment of large modern industries, China's household consumption grew by only 2.3 per cent a year, in sharp contrast to the 7.9 per cent average growth after 1978.

3. Why could China have an Extraordinary Performance after the Transition in 1978?

As discussed in the previous section, a sustained growth relies on continuous technology innovation in the existing industries and constant upgrading to new, higher value-added industries. A developing country has the latecomer advantage in technological innovation and industrial upgrading and can potentially grow faster than advanced countries. In the post-Second World War period, thirteen of the world's 200+ economies found the way to tap into the potential and achieved average annual growth of at least 7 per cent for twenty-five years or more. After the economic transition started in 1978, China became one of the thirteen.

The Commission on Growth and Development, headed by Nobel Laureate Michael Spence, finds that these thirteen economies have five common features: openness, macroeconomic stability, high rates of saving and investment, a market system, and committed, credible, and capable government (Commission on Growth and Development 2008: 22). Spence suggests that the above five features are the ingredients for a recipe but that they alone are not a recipe for successful development (Spence 2016). In fact, there is a recipe for success. The recipe is to follow a country's comparative advantages to develop its industries and to upgrade its industries according to the changes in comparative advantages in the country's development process (Lin 2009, 2013).

Lin and Monga (2012) show that the first three features are the result of following the economy's comparative advantages in developing industries at each stage of its development and the last two features are the institutional preconditions for the economy to follow its comparative advantages in developing industries. If a country develops its industries according to its comparative advantages, it will produce whatever the country can produce at low cost and export the goods. Otherwise, the country will import from other countries. The country will be an open economy with trade consisting of a larger share of its GDP than a country adopting a comparative advantage-defying import-substitution strategy. The country will be competitive in domestic and international markets with fewer homegrown crises and better ability to mitigate external shocks due to the government's sound fiscal position than a country adopting an inefficient comparative advantage-defying development strategy. Therefore, a country will have a good record of macro stability. The return to investment will be high in industries that are consistent with a country's comparative advantages, resulting in a high saving and high investment in the country. For the entrepreneurs to make investments according to a country's comparative advantages spontaneously, requires a price system that can reflect the relative scarcities of each production factor. Such a price system will exist only in a competitive market, which is the fourth feature among the five features of the thirteen successful economies. The economic development is a process of structural changes, which will require a committed, proactive, capable state to help overcome the inevitable externality and co-ordination issues for a dynamic transformation.

After the transition from a planning economy to a market economy, initiated by Deng Xiaoping at the end of 1978, China switched its development strategy. The government liberalized the entry of private enterprises, joint ventures, and foreign direct investment to labour-intensive industries, in which China had comparative advantages but were repressed before the transition. With liberalization of entry into the new sectors, in addition to providing incentives for investment, the Chinese government recognized the need to help private firms overcome all kinds of inherent hurdles in the transition process: The overall business environment was poor,[6] the nationwide infrastructure in China was bad,[7] and the nation's investment environment was inhospitable.[8] The Chinese government mobilized its limited resources and capability to build up special economic zones and industrial parks (Zeng 2010, 2011). Within the zones and parks, the infrastructure and business environment were made very attractive. The labour costs were low because of the large amount of surplus labour in rural areas when China started the transition. But China lacked the knowledge about how to turn that surplus labour to its advantage by producing labour-intensive goods of acceptable quality for the international market. And international buyers were not confident that Chinese firms would be able to deliver the goods in a timely manner. To overcome those difficulties, the Chinese governments at all levels and in all regions proactively approached prospective foreign investors, especially those manufacturers in developing Asia that were about to upgrade their operations in the value chain and relocate their labour-intensive processing to other low-wage economies because of rising wages in their own economies. China provided tax holidays to incentivize foreign manufacturers to make investments in the special economic zones and industrial parks (Graham and Wada 2001; Wei and Liu 2001).

In addition, when the transition started in 1978, the official exchange rate was overvalued. To facilitate the trade, the government adopted initially a dual-track exchange rate system, allowing the market-determined exchange rate to operate parallel with the overvalued official exchange rate, and the dual-track system converged to a managed floating system in 1994 (2012a). The government also used innovatively the countercyclical fiscal policies in the 1997/1998 East Asian financial crisis and 2008 global financial crisis to improve infrastructure, especially the inter-regional infrastructure, such as highways and high-speed railroads, which contributed to the rapid integration of domestic markets and linkage to the global markets.[9]

---

[6] In 2013, after more than three decades of market-oriented reform, China still ranked 91 in the World Bank's Doing Business survey (http://www.doingbusiness.org/rankings).

[7] I still remember vividly the experience of my travel by car from Guangzhou, the capital city of Guangdong province, to Shenzhen, the newly established special economic zone, for the first time in 1984. The car had to cross rivers by ferry three times and it took me more than twelve hours to travel the distance of 300 km. The infrastructure at that time in China was worse than any of the African countries to where I travelled extensively as the Chief Economist of the World Bank in 2008–2012.

[8] In the World Bank's *Investing Across Borders* 2010, China's investment environment was ranked the worst among the eighty-seven economies covered in the study. See http://iab.worldbank.org/~/media/FPDKM/IAB/Documents/IAB-report.pdf.

[9] In 1997, China only had 4800 km of highway, compared to 86,000 km in the US, although the territory size in both countries is about the same. The length of highway in China expanded to 25,100 km in 2003 after the investments supported by countercyclical fiscal expansion in the East Asian financial crisis, and to over 136,000 km now after the investments supported by the fiscal expansion in the 2008 global financial crisis. Moreover, China had more than 22,000 km of high-speed rail by 2016, contributing to more than 65 per cent of the high-speed rails in the world (NBS 2018).

With the pragmatic transition approach, accession to WTO in 2001, the favourable exchange rate policy, and infrastructure improvement, China developed labour-intensive light manufacturing and quickly became the world's factory, thereby tapping into the potential of latecomer advantage in the process of industrial upgrading. While in 1978 primary and processed primary goods accounted for more than 75 per cent of China's exports, by now the share of manufactured goods had increased to more than 95 per cent. Moreover, China's manufactured exports upgraded from simple toys, textiles, and other cheap products in the 1980s and 1990s to high-value and technologically sophisticated machinery and information and communication technology products in the 2000s. The exploitation of the latecomer's advantage has allowed China to emerge as the world's workshop and to achieve extraordinary economic growth by reducing the costs of innovation, industrial upgrading, and social and economic transformation.

4. Why did other Transition Economies not Perform Equally Well?

After the Second World War, all other socialist countries and most developing countries, including those studied in *Asian Drama*, adopted a development strategy similar to that of China. The strategy was influenced by the elites' intuitive perception of modernization in the developing countries, the Soviet Union's experience of rapid industrialization before the Second World War and the prevailing structuralist development thinking at that time (Lin 2012b, 2012c). Most developing countries shed colonial or pseudo-colonial shackles and gained political independence after the Second World War. They started in earnest the modernization drives under the leadership of their revolutionary national fathers, in a manner similar to China before transition in the late 1970s. Compared with developed countries, these newly independent developing countries had extremely low per capita income, high birth and death rates, low average educational attainment, and very little infrastructure—and were heavily specialized in the production and export of primary commodities while importing most manufactured goods before their modernization drive. The development of modern, advanced industries to control the commanding heights was perceived as the only way to achieve rapid economic take-off, become an advanced country, and avoid exploitation by Western industrial powers (Prebisch 1950).

It became a fad after the 1950s for developing countries in both the socialist and non-socialist camps to adopt a capital-intensive, large-scale, heavy industry-oriented development strategy (Lal and Mynt 1996). But the capital-intensive modern industries on their priority lists could not develop spontaneously by market in their countries, retrospectively, due to those industries' defiance of comparative advantages and the resulting lack of viability for firms in those priority industries in the open, competitive market (Lin 2009, 2011). Nevertheless, the perception at that time was the inherent structural rigidities in the economy causing the market failures for developing modern industries.[10] The structuralist thinking at that time thus advised a developing country to adopt an import-substitution strategy to develop the modern capital-intensive industries by direct state intervention to overcome market failures with institutional arrangements similar to what were adopted in China's planning system, including market monopoly, price distortions, and direct allocation of financial and other inputs.[11] This strategy made it possible to establish some modern industries and achieve investment-led growth for one or two decades in the 1950s to the 1970s. Nevertheless, the distortions led to pervasive soft budget constraints, rent-seeking, and misallocation of resources. Economic efficiency was unavoidably low. Stagnation and frequent social and economic crises began to beset most socialist and non-socialist developing countries by the 1970s and 1980s. Structuralism was replaced by neo-liberalism after the 1970s (Lin 2012b, 2012c). As encapsulated in the neo-liberal Washington Consensus, liberalization from excessive state intervention became a fad in the 1980s and 1990s.

From the perspective of new structural economics, which advocates the use of the neoclassical approach to study the determinants and impacts of structure and structural change in the process of economic development, the industrial structure in an economy at a given time is endogenous to the comparative advantages determined by the economy's endowment structure at that time. The state's interventions and distortions before the transition were second-best institutional arrangements endogenous to the needs of providing protections and subsidies to non-viable firms in the priority sectors. But the Washington Consensus reforms, advocated by the academic and policy communities in the 1980s, did not realize the root causes and endogeneity of those interventions. As a result, policymakers and academics recommended that socialist and other developing countries adopt a big bang approach to eliminate immediately all distortions and interventions by implementing simultaneously programmes of privatization, marketization, liberalization, and fiscal stabilization with the aim of quickly establishing a well-functioning market to achieve efficient, first-best outcomes.

But if those distortions were eliminated immediately, many non-viable firms in the priority sectors would collapse, causing a contraction of GDP, a surge in

---

[10] From the new structural economics perspective, the reason why those capital-intensive industries could not develop spontaneously in a low-income agrarian country was not because of market failures due to structural rigidity but the lack of comparative advantages and non-viability of firms in those capital-intensive industries in an open, competitive market (Lin 2011).

[11] There are different explanations for the pervasive distortions in developing countries. Grossman and Helpman (1996), Engerman and Sokoloff (1997: 260–304), and Acemoglu et al. (2005) propose that these distortions were caused by the capture of government by powerful vested interests. Lin (2009, 2003) and Lin and Li (2009) propose that the distortions were a result of conflicts between the comparative advantages of the economies and the priority industries that political elites, influenced by the dominant social thinking of the time, targeted for the modernization of their nations.

unemployment, and acute social disorders. Moreover, some of those advanced industries were the backbones to national defence. To avoid the dreadful social consequence and/or for the needs of national defence, many governments continued to subsidize the non-viable firms in those advanced, capital-intensive, large-scale industries through other, disguised, less efficient subsidies and protections even after the privatization (Lin and Tan 1999). Transition and developing countries thus had even poorer growth performance and stability in the 1980s and 1990s than in the 1960s and 1970s (Easterly 2001, Lin 2014).

During the transition process, China adopted a pragmatic, gradual, dual-track approach. The government first improved incentives and productivity by allowing farmers in agricultural collectives to adopt the family farm-based household responsibility system. The farmers became residual claimants and were allowed to sell at the market freely after delivering the obligatory quota to the state at fixed prices (Lin 1992). At the same time, the government introduced a profit retention system to the state-owned enterprises, giving workers the right to a partial share of productivity improvements. The government also liberalized the entry of private enterprises, joint ventures, and foreign direct investment in labour-intensive sectors, in which China had comparative advantages but that were repressed before the transition. In addition, as discussed in the previous section, the government also proactively facilitated the growth of the new industries by setting up enclaves such as special economic zones and export processing zones to overcome the bottleneck of hard and soft infrastructure in their growth.

This transition strategy allowed China to maintain stability by avoiding the collapse of old priority industries and to achieve dynamic growth by simultaneously turning its comparative advantages into competitive advantages. The quick accumulation of capital and upgrading of comparative advantages also allowed China to tap into the potential of latecomer's advantages in the industrial upgrading process. In addition, dynamic growth in the newly liberalized sectors created the conditions for reforming the old priority sectors. The quick accumulation of capital gradually turned those capital-intensive industries from China's comparative disadvantages to comparative advantages. Firms in those sectors became viable in the open, competitive market, and as a result, protections and subsidies became unnecessary for their survival. The government could eliminate the remaining protections and subsidies as they became redundant. Through this gradual, dual-track approach, China achieved 'reform without losers' (Naughton 1995; Lau et al. 2000; Lin et al. 2003; Lin 2012a) and moved gradually but steadily to a well-functioning market economy.

The similar gradual, dual-track approach also worked in a few other socialist economies—such as Vietnam, Cambodia, and Laos in Asia, and in Poland, Slovenia in East Europe and Belarus and Uzbekistan in the Former Soviet Union. In these small groups of transition countries, they all avoided mass privatization of their large-scale state-owned enterprises and instead of encountering economic collapse, they maintained stability and growth in the transition process (Lin 2014).

5. What Price did China Pay for its Success?

Although the economic performance during the transition in the last four decades was extraordinary, China paid a very high price for its success. In addition
to environmental degradation and food safety issues, which draw much public
complaint and are the results of rapid industrialization and a lack of appropriate
regulations, the main issue during the transition is widespread corruption and
the worsening of income disparities. Before 1978, China had a rather disciplined
and clean bureaucratic system and an equalitarian society. According to the
Corruption Perception Index published by Transparency International, China
ranked number 79 among all the 176 countries or territories in 2016; and based
on the estimates of the National Bureau of Statistics and various scholars' research,
China's GINI coefficient exceeded 0.45, higher than the international warning
level, after 2000 (Li and Sicular 2014). These problems were related to China's
pragmatic, dual-track transition strategy.

As already mentioned, the Chinese government adopted a pragmatic, dual-
track approach in the transition. The government, one the one-hand, provides
transitory protection and subsidies to the non-viable state-owned enterprises in the
old, capital-intensive sectors so as to maintain stability, and on the other hand,
liberalizes and facilitates the entry to the new, labour-intensive sectors which are
consistent with China's comparative advantages so as to achieve dynamic growth.
One of the most important costs for the old capital-intensive sectors was the cost
of capital. Before the transition in 1978, the government used fiscal appropriation
to pay for investments and cover working capital; the SOEs did not have to bear
any cost for capital. After the transition, the fiscal appropriation was replaced
by bank loans. The Chinese government set up four large state banks and a stock
market to meet the capital needs of large enterprises. To subsidize the SOEs, the
interest rates and capital costs were artificially repressed.

When the transition started, almost all firms in China were state-owned. With
the dual-track transition, private-owned firms grew dynamically and some of
them became large enough to get access to bank loans or list in the equity market.
As interest rates and capital costs are artificially repressed, whoever could borrow
from the banks or list in the stock market are therefore subsidized. These subsidies
were paid for by the low returns to savings in the banks or in the stock market
made by individual households, farms and micro, small and medium-sized firms
in industries and services. Those people providing the funds are poorer than the
owners of the large firms they financed. The subsidization of the operation of rich
people's firms by poorer people was one reason for increasing income disparities.
Moreover, access to bank loans and the equity market generates rents for the recipients, leading to the bribery and corruption of the officials who control the access.

Similarly, before 1979 natural resources mining was operated free of concession fees by large-scale state-owned enterprises (SOEs) and their outputs were
provided to other state-owned enterprises at very low prices. After 1983, the

government allowed private firms to enter the mining sectors and liberalized controls over output prices in 1993. Concession fees and output taxes are kept low as a measure to compensate for state-owned mining enterprises' social policy burden of employing redundant workers and covering the pension of retired workers (Lin et al. 1998; Lin and Tan 1999). For new private mining companies, they do not have those social policy burdens. Acquiring a concession promises them overnight enrichment and becomes a source of income inequality and corruption. In addition, banking and other large-scale service industries, such as power and telecommunications, are operated by state-owned monopoly enterprises. These monopoly rents were also sources of inequality and corruption.

It is noteworthy that in general the marginal propensity to consume decreases with income. Therefore, if wealth is disproportionately concentrated in the higher income group, the nation's consumption-to-GDP ratio will be lower and the savings ratio will be higher. The concentration of wealth in the large firms has a similar effect. A consequence of the widening of income disparities is relatively high household savings and extraordinarily high corporate savings in China as shown in Figure 15.2 (Lin 2013).

For coping with the corruption issue, the Chinese government under President Xi Jinping, after taking office in 2013, launched a wide-ranging, persistent anti-graft campaign. However, the root of widespread corruption is found in the rents arising from the distortions embodied in the dual-track transition for the purpose of protecting and subsidizing large-scale SOEs in capital-intensive industries defying China's comparative advantage. In the 1980s and 1990s, China was a poor country and capital was scarce. After four decades of rapid economic growth,

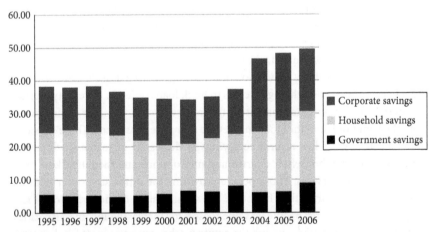

Figure 15.2 China's corporate, household, and government savings as percentage of GDP.

Source: Author's illustration based on data from National Statistical Bureau, *China Statistical Yearbook* (1998–2009).

capital becomes relatively abundant and comparative advantages in China evolve accordingly. Many capital-intensive industries turn from defying China's comparative advantages to becoming consistent with China's comparative advantages. As a result firms in those industries become viable and should be competitive and profitable in domestic and global markets as long as they have good management. The nature of subsidies and protections to the recipient firms changes from a necessity for survival to a pure rent. It is imperative and the time to eliminate all remaining distortions and protections so as to complete the transition to a well-functioning market economy and to uproot the cause for corruption and income disparity. Indeed, this is exactly the intention of the comprehensive reform agenda adopted in 2013 by the third plenary session of the 18th party congress of the Communist Party of China. The government sets up a national committee for deepening reform, headed by President Xi Jinping himself, for the purpose of completing the transition to a well-functioning market economy. Hundreds of reforms have been introduced. The implementations take time. However, the direction of the transition is clear and the government's determination for moving China in that direction is strong.

6. Can China Maintain Dynamic Growth and become a High-Income Country in the Years Ahead?

The question that arises is, if China removes all remaining distortions and completes this transition to a well-functioning market economy, how long can it maintain dynamic economic growth and realize its dream of becoming a high-income country? This question is hotly debated in China and closely followed globally. The reason for the question is that China's annual growth rate dropped continuously from 10.6 per cent in 2010 to 6.7 per cent in 2016. A growth of 6.7 per cent was the lowest that China has ever reached since 1990 and it was the first time that China experienced six concessive years of deceleration after the transition started in 1978.

To answer the question as to whether, after more than thirty years of extraordinary growth, China can maintain dynamic economic growth in the coming years, one needs to answer two further related questions. The first, how large is China's growth potential? And the second, what were the reasons for the persistent deceleration of China's growth after 2010?

Pritchett and Summers (2014) project that China's growth rate will decrease to a range of 2.3 per cent to 5.5 per cent in the next twenty years. Eichengreen et al. (2012) suggest that, based on international experiences of rapid-growing catch-up economies after reaching US$17,000, measured in purchasing power parity and the 2005 constant dollar, a level of which China will reach soon, China's growth rate will slow down to around 6 per cent. From the analysis of this chapter, the potential for rapid economic growth depends on the size of the latecomer advantage that China still enjoys. To measure the size of the remaining latecomer advantage, in my view, one should compare China's per capita GDP with the per capita GDP in advanced countries, such as the US. This is because per capita GDP is a proxy for a country's average labour productivity and average labour productivity is a measure of the average level of technology and valued-added of industries in a country.

According to the data for 2008, which was the last published by Maddison,[12] the per capita GDP in China, measured at purchasing power parity, in 2008 was 21 per cent of the United States' figure in the same year. This proportion was similar to that for Japan in 1951, Singapore in 1967, Taiwan China in 1975, and South Korea in 1977. All stood at 21 per cent of the US figure in their relevant years.

In the twenty years from 1951 to 1971, Japan grew at an average annual rate of 9.2 per cent. From 1967 to 1987, Singapore grew at 8.6 per cent. From 1975 to 1995, Taiwan China grew at 8.3 per cent. From 1977 to 1997, South Korea grew at 7.6 per cent. These four East Asian economies were among the thirteen economies referred to in section 2 as having tapped into the growth potential from the latecomer advantage and as having enjoyed high growth rates of 7 per cent or more continuously for twenty-five or more years. Just as these economies were able to utilize the technology gap and exploit the latecomer advantage to grow for twenty years at 7.6 per cent to 9.2 per cent per year, so too potentially China can grow for twenty years at 8 per cent per year from 2008. Ten years have passed since 2008. Another ten years of potential growth at 8 per cent per year remain.

If China has the potential to grow at 8 per cent, why has the growth rate declined persistently down to below 8 per cent since 2010 and reached 6.7 per cent in 2016? The potential growth rate reflects the possibilities for technological innovation and industrial upgrading judged from supply side. The realization of this potential growth rate depends as well on demand-side conditions. From a demand-side point of view, growth has three components: net exports, investment, and consumption. High-income countries have not yet recovered from the global financial crisis of 2008: in these countries per capita GDP is stagnant, there is a large debt overhang, which they need to reduce, and consumption has increased very slowly. The stagnation of the US, western European countries and Japan has depressed international trade with a major impact on Chinese exports as China is a major global supplier of consumption goods. From 1979 to 2015, China's annual average export growth was about 16 per cent. It was −2.8 per cent in 2015 and −7.7 per cent in 2016. The poor export performance was one of the reasons for a deceleration in China's growth.[13]

---

[12] The Maddison-Project (http://www.ggdc.net/maddison/maddison-project/home.htm, 2013 version).

[13] China's growth bounced back to 6.9 per cent in 2017. The main reason was the export growth recovered from −7.7 per cent in 2016 to 7.9 per cent in 2017.

The second reason was that China, like most countries, adopted countercyclical fiscal expansion to support investment and growth after the 2008 global crisis. These projects were completed but the global economy has not fully recovered from the aftermath of the crisis. As such, incentives for private investment remain low. Without a new round of stimulus programmes, investment growth rates will drop.

The above two factors affect all countries: growth has decelerated not just in China but also, and often more sharply, in other BRIC countries and many other countries. Fortunately, China maintains a high employment rate, and its household income has continued to grow rapidly at about 8 per cent per year, with consumption growing at a similar rate. This is the reason why China was able to maintain a growth rate higher than other BRIC and emerging market economies.

Looking forward, high-income countries are very likely to have a secular stagnation (Summers 2014), similar to that of Japan after 1991 due to the lack of structural reforms. These economies are likely to grow at less than their normal growth rate of 3 per cent to 3.5 per cent per year. The external demand is likely to remain sluggish.

How much China can turn the 8 per cent growth potential to actual growth in the coming years depends largely on domestic demand, including investment and consumption. There is a popular view that China needs to switch its unstainable investment-led growth model to a consumption-led growth model. This is not the right prescription for China or any country. Consumption is a desirable goal of development but its growth can be sustainable only with an increasing household income. The latter requires continuous improvement of labour productivity through technological innovation and industrial upgrading, both of which rely on investment. In fact, as shown in Figure 15.3, due to rapid income growth resulting in high consumption growth, consumption has been the major source

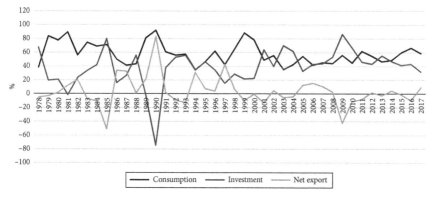

Figure 15.3 Components of GDP growth.

Source: Author's illustration based on data from National Statistical Bureau, *China Statistical Abstract 2018*.

394 ASIAN TRANSFORMATIONS

of growth in China since the transition started in 1978. Except for a few years with investment surges as a result of events such as the entry to WTO in 2001 and the countercyclical fiscal stimulus in 2009, consumption contributed more to China's growth than investment did.

The key for assessing how much China's growth potential can be realized in the coming years depends on whether China has good investment opportunities in the face of the existence of excess capacity in many industries as a result of lingering global crisis, and whether China has sufficient resources to support the investment. Although there is excess capacity in many industries, such as steel and cement due to slack demands, as an upper-middle-income country China has very considerable room for investment in upgrading the industries to higher value-added industries, urbanization and intra-urban infrastructure, and environmentally friendly green technologies. Such investments will increase efficiency and environmental sustainability while taking the latecomer advantages. China also has plenty of resources for investments. Its fiscal position is very sound. In 2015 national, provincial, and local governments' combined debt was less than 60 per cent of GDP, among the lowest in the world. Private savings are around 50 per cent of GDP, one of the highest in the world. China also has more than US$3 trillion of foreign exchange reserves. With good investment opportunities and abundant funding, China will maintain a reasonable rate of investment growth, create jobs, and increase household income and consumption. With these conditions and depending on reforms to eliminate remaining distortions from the dual-track transition, there is no reason why China cannot reach its annual growth target of 6.5 per cent or more before 2020 and 6 per cent in the following decade. If China does reach these targets, it is very likely that around 2025, Chinese per capita GDP will reach the threshold of US$12,700, making China a high-income country (Lin et al. 2016).

7. Final Remarks

There are three additional questions to answer before I conclude the chapter:

1) Why did China start the Reform and Opening Up programme in 1978 to transit from the planning economy to a market economy?

2) Why did China not follow the popular, seemingly more logical, neo-liberal shock therapy of privatization, marketization, and stabilization encapsulated in the Washington Consensus and instead adopt a gradual, dual-track transition, which was regarded as the worst possible transition strategy, although retrospectively this approach is the best?

3) What lessons can we draw from China's experiences in the past half-century for other developing countries?

For the first question, I think it is because when Deng Xiaoping came back to power by purging Mao's hand-picked successors, the Gang of Four, in a palace revolt, he needed to justify his actions in order to gain the support of the people and consolidate his power. After almost thirty years of socialist revolution, Chinese people still lived in poverty. The need to shift from the ultra-left policy to improve people's living was good justification for his action to purge the Gang of Four (Lin 2012a).

Then why did Deng adopt a gradual, piecemeal transition approach? There is no theory at that time to support this approach. On the contrary, a gradual, piecemeal transition approach was considered the worst possible transition strategy as the prevailing theory at that time suggested that such an approach would make the economy worse than a planning economy (Murphy et al. 1992). The accepted wisdom in the 1980s/1990s was that the correct way to transit from a planning economy to a well-functioning market economy was to implement the Washington Consensus of privatization, marketization, and stabilization simultaneously in shock therapy (Summers 1994). In the Marshall Lectures (Lin 2009), I argue: First, pragmatism has been a virtue in Confucianism, probably sharpened by the need for survival in a land with high population pressure and frequent natural disasters. Second, Deng himself was one of the first-generation political leaders who started the socialist revolution and introduced a planned economy to China. In an authoritarian regime the power of a leader is not delineated by his/her formal, official position but based mainly on the personal trust and prestige that a leader receives from his people.[14] If a leader is to renounce policies that he or she pursued in the past, he may lose his/her prestige in people's minds.[15] Therefore, it was rational for Deng to adopt a tinkering strategy to reform and open up the system instead of a comprehensive overhaul or a complete replacement of the system. Vietnam and Lao also adopted a gradual, dual-track reform approach. In both countries, like in China, the first-generation revolutionaries, who had brought socialism and planned economies to their countries, initiated the transition. In Eastern European and former Soviet Union countries, their leaders were all second or even third or fourth generation leadership when they adopted the shock therapy to transit from the planning system. They were not accountable for the

[14] In his final years, Deng's only formal title was an honorary chairman of China's Bridge Society. He was, however, the *de facto* supreme leader until his death. Similarly, Mao Zedong was regarded as the ultimate leader by members of the Chinese Community Party for more than ten years before he was elected chairman in the party congress in 1945 due to his extraordinary wisdom and strategy in the revolution against the Nationalist Party and the fight against Japanese invasion.

[15] As argued in the previous note, in China a leader's prestige is accumulated through the merits of their contributions to the people and the nation during their career, and people's trust in their wisdom to provide good guidance for the nation's future. If a political leader openly admits that they made a mistake in a major policy in the past, their prestige and authority will be hurt. This was the main reason Chairman Mao stepped aside from the central stage of power in 1962 after admitting his mistakes in the Great Leap Forward and the motivation for him to launch the Cultural Revolution to regain power.

introduction of the planning system and could replace the old system with a new one in a wholesale way.

Finally, what can we learn from China's experience? When China started the transition in 1978, pessimism about China's future prevailed and, even up to recent years, the coming collapse of Chinese economy was a repeated theme in the economic profession. Myrdal did not review China's situation in his *Asian Drama*, if he did he would have most likely been pessimistic. In fact, post-Second World War, the economic profession's view about East Asia's future was gloomy. The irony is that China, East Asian economies, and Mauritius were all considered basket cases by the economic professions but beat the odds to be the most successful newly industrialized economies. Moreover, the developing countries, which followed the right development approach based on the prevailing theories advocated by the economic profession, all performed poorly. The dominant development thinking was structuralism when development economics became a sub-discipline of modern economics post-Second World War. The import-substitution strategy, which advocated structuralism, was adopted widely in Latin America, Africa, and South Asia in the 1950s to 1960s. Their economies performed poorly. Their income gap with advanced countries widened instead of narrowed. After the 1970s, neo-liberalism replaced structuralism as the dominant thinking in the economic profession. The transition approach based on neo-liberalism was the Washington Consensus, which advocated the use of shock therapy to establish a well-functioning market economy by the simultaneous implementation of marketization, privatization, and stabilization. East Europe and the former Soviet Union, as well as many developing countries in the 1980s to 1990s, followed this approach, resulting in 'lost decades' with a lower average growth rate and a higher frequency of crises than before the transition. On the contrary, the few economies that performed well in development, for example the East Asian economies' export-oriented strategy in the 1950s/1960s, and the successful transition economies like China's gradual, piecemeal dual-track approach, were considered the wrong approaches by the mainstream economic professions.

Why was the economic profession's perception of developing countries, in general, pessimistic? Why did the developing countries, in general, fail by following the guidance from mainstream ideas to formulate their development and transition policies, and the few successful economies' development and transition policies, in general, considered wrong? The reasons are likely because the economic professions always use high-income countries as their reference to see what the developing countries do not have and cannot do well. Developing countries do not have advanced industries and their market institutions do not perform well, compared to advanced countries. Based on the above observations, the mainstream theories in their policy recommendations advise developing countries to own what the advanced countries have and to do what the advanced countries are doing. The intentions are good but the results are disappointing.

Using the high-income countries, especially an ideal high-income country, as a reference, a developing country must be inefficient, beset with traditional, low-productivity industries, and backward or distorted institutions. However, these seemingly inefficient industries and institutions are either endogenous to its stage of development, for example, the traditional agriculture and the related agrarian institutions, or the legacy of previous policy interventions, for example, the inefficient SOEs and related government interventions. Without understanding the roots of the endogeneity in industries and institutions and the appropriate theories to guide the change of endogenous phenomena, economists often become pessimistic about developing countries. Myrdal's outlook about Asian countries is an example. The repeated prediction, for the past forty years, by economic professions about the coming collapse of the Chinese economy is another example. Pessimism arises because structural backwardness and distortions not only cause the market to be inefficient and the government to be ineffective, especially compared to the ideal case, but are also rigid and hard to eliminate.

The mainstream theories fail to guide successful development and transition because, in general, those theories neglect the endogeneity of the backwardness and distortions present in the developing and transition countries. To have successful development and transition in developing countries, it is essential for the economic professions to change the reference from the developed countries to the developing countries themselves. From the experiences of China and East Asian economies in the last half-century, a successful development in a country should start with what a country has and what the country can do well. What a country has, refers to the country's endowments, such as an abundant supply of labour force, at a given time and what the country can do well is the comparative advantage based on its endowments. The state's development and transition policy is to mobilize the limited resources under the state's command, proactively and pragmatically for the purpose of removing bottlenecks in the hard and soft infrastructure, in order to facilitate the country's comparative advantages so that they become the country's competitive advantages in the domestic and international market. This is exactly what the new structural economics, which I advocate as the third edition of development economics, intends to achieve (Lin 2011, 2012b, 2012c; Lin and Monga 2017). If the state in a developing country can play such a facilitation role in its catch-up and or transition process, the country can be competitive and grow dynamically even though it is beset with a backward or distorted structure and turn from a low-income country to an industrialized high-income country within one or two generations. As Keynes (1935) said, 'it is ideas, not vested interests, which are dangerous for good or evil'. The Chinese experiences in the past half-century suggest, as long as the ideas for development and transition are right, every developing country can be optimistic about its future.

References

Acemoglu, D., S. Johnson, and J.A. Robinson (2005). 'Institutions as the Fundamental Cause of Long-Run Growth'. In P. Aghion and S.N. Durlauf (eds) *Handbook of Economic Growth*. Amsterdam: Elsevier.

Chang, H. (2003). *Kicking Away the Ladder*. London: Anthem Press.

Commission on Growth and Development (2008). *The Growth Report: Strategies for Sustained Growth and Inclusive Development*. Washington, DC: World Bank.

Easterly, W. (2001). *The Elusive Quest for Growth*. Cambridge, MA: MIT Press.

Eichengreen, B., D. Park, and K. Shin (2012). 'When Fast-growing Economies Slow Down', *Asian Economic Paper*, 11(1): 42–87.

Engerman, S.L., and K.L. Sokoloff (1997). 'Factor Endowments, Institutions, and Differential Paths of Growth among New World Economies'. In S. Haber (ed.) *How Latin America Fell Behind*. Stanford, CA: Stanford University Press.

Fei, J., and G. Ranis (1997). *Growth and Development from an Evolutionary Perspective*. Malden, MA: Blackwell.

Gerschenkron, A. (1962). *Economic Backwardness in Historical Perspective: A Book of Essays*. Cambridge, MA: Belknap Press of Harvard University Press.

Graham, E.M., and E. Wada (2001). 'Foreign Direct Investment in China: Effects on Growth and Economic Performance', Institute for International Economics Working Paper No. 01–03.

Grossman, G.M., and E. Helpman (1996). 'Electoral Competition and Special Interest Politics', *Review of Economic Studies*, 63(2): 265–86.

Keynes, J.M. (1935). *The General Theory of Employment, Interest and Money*. New York: Harcourt, Brace and World.

Kuznets, S. (1966). *Modern Economic Growth: Rate, Structure and Spread*. New Haven, CT: Yale University Press.

Lal, D., and H. Mynt (1996). *The Political Economy of Poverty, Equity, and Growth: A Comparative Study*. Oxford: Clarendon Press.

Landes, D. (1998). *The Wealth and Poverty of Nations*. New York and London: Norton.

Lau, L.J., Y. Qian, and G. Roland (2000). 'Reform without Losers', *Journal of Political Economy* 108(1): 120–43.

Lewis, W.A. (1954). 'Economic Development with Unlimited Supply of Labour', *Manchester School of Economic and Social Studies*, 22(2): 139–91.

Li, S., and T. Sicular (2014). 'The Distribution of Household Income in China', *China Quarterly*, 217: 1–41.

Lin, J.Y. (1991). 'Collectivization and China's Agricultural Crisis in 1959–1961', *Journal of Political Economy*, 98: 1228–52.

Lin, J.Y. (1992). 'Rural Reforms and Agricultural Growth in China', *American Economic Review*, 82(1): 34–51.

Lin, J.Y. (1995). 'The Needham Puzzle', *Economic Development and Cultural Change*, 43(2): 269–92.

Lin, J.Y. (2003). 'Development Strategy, Viability and Economic Convergence', *Economic Development and Cultural Change*, 53(2): 277–308.

Lin, J.Y. (2009). *Economic Development and Transition*. Cambridge: Cambridge University Press.

Lin, J.Y. (2011). 'New Structural Economics: A Framework for Rethinking Development', *World Bank Research Observer*, 26(2): 93–221.

Lin, J.Y. (2012a). *Demystifying the Chinese Economy*. Cambridge: Cambridge University Press.

Lin, J.Y. (2012b). *The Quest for Prosperity*. Princeton, NJ: Princeton University Press.

Lin, J.Y. (2012c). *New Structural Economics: A Framework for Rethinking Development and Policy*. Washington, DC: World Bank.

Lin, J.Y. (2013). 'Demystifying the Chinese Economy', *The Australian Economic Review*, 46(3): 259–68.

Lin, J.Y. (2014). 'The Washington Consensus Revisited', *Journal of Economic Policy Reform*, 18(2): 96–113.

Lin, J.Y. (2016). 'The Latecomer Advantages and Disadvantages'. In M. Andersson and T. Axelsson (eds) *Diverse Development Paths and Structural Transformation in Escape from Poverty*. Cambridge: Cambridge University Press.

Lin, J.Y., and F. Li (2009). 'Development Strategy, Viability, and Economic Distortions in Developing Countries', World Bank, Washington, DC, Policy Research Working Paper 4906.

Lin, J.Y., and C. Monga (2012). 'The Growth Report and New Structural Economics'. In J.Y. Lin (ed.) *New Structural Economics*. Washington, DC: World Bank.

Lin, J.Y., and C. Monga (2017). *Beating the Odds*. Princeton, NJ: Princeton University Press.

Lin, J.Y., and D. Rosenblatt (2012). 'Shifting Patterns of Economic Growth and Rethinking Development', *Journal of Economic Policy Reform*, 15(3): 171–94.

Lin, J.Y., and G. Tan (1999). 'Policy Burdens, Accountability, and Soft Budget Constraints', *American Economic Review*, 89(2): 426–31.

Lin, J.Y., F. Cai, and Z. Li (1998). 'Competition, Policy Burdens, and State-owned Enterprise Reform', *American Economic Review: Papers and Proceedings*, 88(2): 422–7.

Lin, J.Y., F. Cai, and Z. Li (2003). *The China Miracle*. Hong Kong: Chinese University Press.

Lin, J.Y., G. Wan, and P. Morgan (2016). 'Prospects for a Re-acceleration of Economic Growth in the PRC', *Journal of Comparative Economics*, 44(4): 842–53.

Maddison, A. (2001). *The World Economy: A Millennial Perspective*. Paris: OECD Development Centre.

Maddison, A. (2007). *Chinese Economic Performance in the Long Run—Second Edition, Revised and Updated: 960–2030 ad*. Paris: OECD Development Centre.

Marx, K., and F. Engles (1848). Manifesto of the Communist Party. Available at: https://www.marxists.org/archive/marx/works/1848/communist-manifesto/.

Murphy, K., A. Schleifer, and R.W. Vishny (1992). 'The Tradition to a Market Economy', *Quarterly Journal of Economics*, 107: 889–906.

Naughton, B. (1995). *Growing Out of the Plan*. New York: Cambridge University Press.

NBS (National Bureau of Statistics) (2018). *China Statistical Abstract* 2018. Beijing: China Statistics Press.

North, D. (1981). *Structure and Change in Economic History*. New York: W.W. Norton.

Prebisch, R. (1950). *The Economic Development of Latin America and Its Principal Problems*. New York: United Nations. Reprinted in 1962 in *Economic Bulletin for Latin America*, 7(1): 1–22.

Pritchett, L., and L.H. Summers (2014). 'Asiaphoria Meets Regression to the Mean', National Bureau of Economic Research, NBER Working Paper No. 20573.

Spence, M. (2016). 'In Search of Growth Strategies', Project Syndicate, 28 January. Available at: https://www.project-syndicate.org/commentary/global-economy-growth-strategies-by-michael-spence-2016-01?barrier=accesspaylog.

Summers, L. (1994). 'Comment'. In O.J. Blanchard, K.A. Froot, and J. Sachs (eds) *The Transition in Eastern Europe*. Chicago, IL: Chicago University Press.

Summers, L. (2014). 'Reflections on the "New Secular Stagnation Hypothesis"'. In C. Teulings and R. Baldwin (eds) *Secular Stagnation*. London: CEPR Press.

Vu, K.M. (2013). *The Dynamics of Economic Growth*. Cheltenham: Edward Elgar.

Wei, Y., and X. Liu (2001). *Foreign Direct Investment: Determinants and Impact*. Northampton: Edward Elgar.

Zeng, D. (2010). *Building Engines for Growth and Competitiveness in China*. Washington, DC: World Bank.

Zeng, D. (2011). 'How Do Special Economic Zones and Industrial Clusters Drive China's Rapid Development?', World Bank, Washington, DC, Policy Research Working Paper 5583.

16
India

Kaushik Basu

1. Myrdal and India

My first encounter with Gunnar Myrdal's *Asian Drama* was a year after its publication. I joined Delhi University's St. Stephen's College as an undergraduate in 1969. One of our professors, Kalyanjit Roy Choudhury, a voracious reader, told us with excitement about this mammoth publication. Soon the book became a fashion statement for students on our campus. To be seen crossing the college yard with one of the volumes of the book raised one's stature. To be seen talking about it raised it even more. It was a case of good competition, which helped enhance the level of erudition of my generation of students.

The publication of this three-volume magnum opus, focused on South Asia, predominantly India, and more tangentially on several Southeast Asian nations, marked a turning point for all those engaged in the study of economic history, political economy, and development. Treating the region as focus, Myrdal ranged over economics, history, and politics. What Myrdal was attempting, admittedly in an inchoate way, was an early precursor of both new institutional economics and behavioural economics, by insisting that to understand the performance of economies, we have to view economics as a discipline embedded in sociology, psychology, and politics.

Because Myrdal was charting such a new course, *Asian Drama* was both pioneering and flawed, as we now know with the hindsight of contemporary research. We can see these twin traits in his analysis of India's economy. In looking at India's sluggish growth and the vast numbers living in extreme poverty, Myrdal often allowed his pessimism to show through. As he wrote,

> If in a country like India the government were really determined to change the prevailing attitudes and institutions, and had the courage to take the necessary steps and accept the consequences, then these would include the effective abolition of caste, prescribed by the constitution, [...] land reform and tenancy legislation, [...] the eradication of corruption at all levels [...] and so on.
>
> (Myrdal 1968: 368)[1]

---

[1] All page references to *Asian Drama* are to the widely used 1972 version edited by Seth King and published by Allen Lane.

402 ASIAN TRANSFORMATIONS

One senses in this a pessimism that stems from frustration with a newly independent nation he wishes would succeed. The remark, however, suggests an inadequate understanding of the complexity of interaction between economics and politics and the troublesome idea of the endogeneity of institutions. His questioning 'If [...] the government were really determined' and suggestion that the 'abolition of caste' and 'eradication of corruption' are matters of choice by the government reveals a rather simplistic view of government as an exogenous institution.

It is not clear that governments have within their wherewithal the ability to control many of the social ills like discrimination and corruption. The persistence of these ills is not necessarily evidence of political leaders condoning them, even though it often is. We have to use more sophisticated analysis to separate out the cases where the corruption is being condoned or even encouraged, and where it is being haplessly suffered because its mitigation is beyond the leader's reach or any individual's reach for that matter. Many of our worst social ills are *collective* traps.

While Myrdal deserves credit for venturing out to some of these, rather treacherous, multidisciplinary terrains so early, the social sciences at that time did not have the tools and theoretical constructs to do justice to such interdisciplinary trespassing. As a consequence, we can now share the concern that Myrdal had for the theatre of Asia and at the same time bring some of the more contemporary, multidisciplinary social science methods to bear on the project. That is what I attempt to do in this chapter.

India is today a changed country from what it was half a century ago. It still has huge challenges but the country has long since broken with the 'Hindu rate of growth', and its population below the poverty line has fallen steadily since the late 1960s, and sharply over the last decade. One way of celebrating *Asian Drama* is to take stock of what India has done since the time of its publication in 1968 and peer into the future and at the challenges that lie ahead, and that is what I propose to do in this chapter.

2. Politics First

From the vantage point of hindsight, it seems quite remarkable that India did what no other newly independent developing country did. It invested in politics first—establishing democracy, free speech, independent media, and equal rights for all citizens. At one level all progressive leaders around the world tried this. Following the end of the Second World War, as nations broke from the yoke of imperialism and became independent, we had not just Jawaharlal Nehru in India, but Sukarno in Indonesia, Jinnah in Pakistan, Nkrumah in Ghana, Nyerere in Tanzania, and several other leaders trying to put their nation on an even keel politically, and build political institutions to promote inclusive economic development. But in most cases it did not last. Coups, chaotic responses, and the lust for power caused democracy to collapse in one nation after another, bringing in military rule and conflict. A map of democracy around the world in 1985 would show a bleak landscape in virtually all developing and emerging nations. India was the exception.

While a large part of the credit for this does go to the early political leaders— Mahatma Gandhi, Nehru, and Ambedkar, and to progressive writers and intellectuals like Rabindranath Tagore, Periyar E.V. Ramaswamy, and Sarojini Naidu—as in all matters of history, luck also plays a role. And India had it in ample measure. In any case, the upshot was that in terms of political design and structure, with regular elections, a progressive constitution, secularism, free media, and an empowered supreme court, India resembled an advanced nation, and in this respect had very few peers in the developing world.[2]

India's downside turned out to be its economy. With growth sluggish, large swathes of population living in poverty, and widespread illiteracy, the country trudged along for decades, while several other nations, like South Korea, Taiwan, Singapore, and Hong Kong, starting from roughly the same level of economic prosperity in the 1950s, took off in spectacular ways. Some would argue that this sluggishness was in part *caused* by India's democracy and progressive politics, and that, if there were a dictator, he or she would have pulled the economy out of the vicious circle. I shall comment on this later. But whether or not this causal explanation from politics to economics has any merit, two facts do stand out: early India's remarkable political achievements and the persistent economic stagnation for at least three decades after its independence.

Two caveats to the above claim ought to be made. First, the description should not convey the impression of nothing happening during these first decades. Despite the overall growth remaining subdued at around 3.5 per cent per annum, much was happening beneath that. Taking a page out of the Soviet model, India tried to institute five-year planning, with an effort to set up heavy industries, large-scale steel production, and building dams to generate electricity on a large scale. Second, somewhere in the mid-1960s, India had a successful 'green revolution' and broke out of the trap of low agricultural productivity and frequent famines. Though this was most visible in Punjab, Haryana, and western Uttar Pradesh, its benefits were felt across the nation.

The second caveat is that the slow growth of the early years should not be taken as an indicator of the nation's independence not having an impact on the economy. Independence was good for India. Sivasubramonian's (2000) comprehensive statistical study shows that annual growth, from being negligible during the first fifty years of the twentieth century, moved up to somewhere between 3 and 3.5 per cent in the decades immediately after the country's independence in 1947.

---

[2] For discussion, see Sen (2004, 2005) and Basu (2009). For one of the most authoritative studies of the interface between politics and economics in India, see Bardhan (1998).

Nayyar (2006) identifies 1951 and 1980 as the two turning points in India's growth in the twentieth century. I will have occasion to dispute his second turning point but that will come later.

There would be a short interruption in democracy in 1975, when the Prime Minister, Indira Gandhi, declared an emergency and took dictatorial control over the nation. For those who believe dictatorship helps economic growth, the emergency seemed like a godsend because, in 1975/76, India's GDP growth rate hit 9 per cent, an unimaginable figure at that time (and, it is also believed, the trains ran on time). However, if these hardliners studied the growth trend thereafter, they would be deflated. Growth declined and, by 1979/80, it had plummeted to –5.2 per cent, the worst year in India's history from 1947 to now.[3] In fact, after that year, India has not had a single year of negative GDP growth, though it grazed past it in the early 1990s.

Luckily, the emergency lasted just under two years and, unlike most dictatorships, it was brought to an end by an election, called by Indira Gandhi herself, in 1977, when she was roundly defeated. It remains a mystery why she behaved so differently from other dictators—namely, calling an election and then not rigging it. One theory, to which I subscribe, is that she was troubled by the fact of having destroyed her father's legacy of establishing a vibrant democracy in India and wanted the legitimacy of an election and was prepared to lose.[4] The other hypothesis is hubris, namely, that she was confident that, though the opposition and much of the media cried foul, she would win and then she would consolidate her power. In any case, fortunately for all supporters of democracy, she was defeated.

When Indira Gandhi returned to power in the 1980s, India's policies began to change. I would argue that, unlike her father, Jawaharlal Nehru, she did not have an innate economic ideology. While she had strong political convictions, on matters of economics, she had few deep convictions. When it came to economic policy, her career can be broken into two parts—the first when she was her father's daughter, driven largely by Nehru's ideology, and the second when she was her sons' mother, steered largely by her sons' convictions.

In her early years as leader, Indira Gandhi was largely her father's daughter and she did what Nehru would have done. Nehru's own ideology was broadly Fabian socialist, with an instinctive internationalism. As he wrote to Amiya Chakravarty in a letter dated 29 November 1935, 'I have far more in common with English and other non-Indian socialists than I have with non-socialists in India'. And later, when he was prime minister, he had joked with the US Ambassador to India, John Kenneth Galbraith, that, to understand India, Galbraith ought to realize that

---

[3] As this topic has been so much in the news since the demonetization of 8 November 2016, I should point out that the only other time demonetization was tried in independent India was in 1978, when Morarji Desai was prime minister. This was before the year when growth plummeted in a way not seen since India's independence.

[4] This is the view taken by Pranab Mukherjee, who was close to Indira Gandhi and would later become president of India. (I know this from my personal conversation with Mr Mukherjee).

Nehru was 'the last Englishman to be ruling over India'. His socialist instinct—the belief that there should be vastly greater equality of income and wealth—was genuine. Commenting on what differentiates Western and Indian political thinking, Myrdal had written, 'Another fact is South Asia's commitment to egalitarianism, which is an integral part of their ideology of planning' (Myrdal 1968: 120). Despite this, Nehru balked at the centralization of power that he saw in China and the Soviet Union.

Questions remain about whether these two instincts are compatible. In the end, the form of socialism India followed is best described as state capitalism. A few large public sector firms and banks were established; there were lots of private firms and enterprises, with some polarization between the very large and very small (with a missing middle); the state tried to command and direct from the top; and, finally, all this was wrapped up in a profuse rhetoric of socialism. It is interesting to note that Myrdal (1968) himself had toiled to make sense of India's 'socialism' and observed how this involved a certain amount of 'verbal jugglery'. The evidence for this comes from the fact of enormous income and wealth inequality that prevails in India (see, for instance, Bardhan 2007). Some observers of India's political economy have argued that, despite this rhetoric, in practice, India drifted to 'neo-liberalism' (Kohli 2012).

This is an important observation. India never practised socialism in the sense of having a centralized ownership of the means of production in the hands of the state, though using the term socialism had become mandatory in all government documents and declarations pertaining to the economy, well into the 1990s. What India meant by the term socialism (and pursued that, too, without much success) was a kind of welfare state, in which there would be support for the poor in terms of healthcare, education, and basic food. But even this was more often present in writings emerging from the government than in actual action. In terms of the government owning the means of production, India was nowhere near a social-ist state: India had roughly 14 per cent of GDP coming from state-owned enter-prises, whereas for China this was 40 per cent. These data are not easy to compute and there is indeed a big margin for error (see Basu 2009) but the large difference is significant.

In her early years, Indira Gandhi pursued a policy similar to that of Nehru, the nationalization of banks in 1969 being the most aggressive move along those lines. By the time she returned to power in the 1980s, three years after her electoral defeat in 1977, her strategy had shifted, this time under the influence of, primarily, her younger son, Sanjay Gandhi, and later under the influence of Rajiv Gandhi, which would have large implications for India's economic trajectory, the story of the next section.

Indira Gandhi also had deep influences on India's politics and the nature of the state. Even leaving aside the emergency, she had centralized power, often in her own hands, much more than Nehru. As Kothari (1977) argued, this in turn tended to take away power and initiative from the grass-roots level, and resulted in a centralization of power that Nehru had resisted. According to Kothari (though there is scope to contest his view), this had a negative effect on economic growth.

Similar issues arise in evaluating India's democracy. Thanks to the adoption of the principle of 'one person, one vote', independent India established representative government right from the start, but questions remain about how 'responsive' India's 'representative' state is. In a compelling essay, Mehta (2012) examines these questions. Echoing Myrdal's view that distant histories can have deep influences on the nature of contemporary politics and institutions, Mehta points to the social inequalities that go far back into Indian history, having legacy effects on the nature of democracy.

One of the most major historical sources of social inequality in India is its caste system. While in itself caste is a deplorable inheritance and, at least in speech, most founding political leaders of India spoke out against it, it has been argued by some that the castes have played a role in nurturing India's democracy by providing focal points of coalition and political mobilization for disadvantaged groups (see Varshney 2013). What complicates the story is that many of these caste identities are local and regional, which has thwarted mobilization across the nation—an outcome that has both its plusses and minuses.

It must also be recorded that the nature of India's politics has changed much since the mid-1970s. The domination of a few big parties and in particular the Congress has diminished vastly. Regional parties have sprung up all over the nation and India has seen the rise of coalition politics also on the national stage, as parties have had to reach out to others to make sure they have the majority necessary to form a government. This has put a new set of brakes and challenges on policy experimentation, and, at the same time, brought a certain agility to politics, as all parties that matter have had to master the art of accommodation and compromise.

One major shift in the trajectory of India's political economy is the arrival of 'coalition politics' in the late eighties. Though there was a short period of coalition governance immediately after the emergency, the paradigmatic shift to coalition politics began in 1989. This did create new strains. As Nayyar (1998) argued, there was an 'absence of consensus' rarely seen earlier. But this also created a kind of stability whereby the nation learned not to destabilize economic policy every time there was a shift in power at the nation's helm. Indeed, despite all these caveats, despite the two-year retreat from 1975 to 1977 caused by the emergency, and despite its complicated and many-splendoured manifestation, democratic stability is a remarkable achievement for India. While research and activism must persist in analysing and correcting the weaknesses of India's democracy, it needs to be appreciated that this, like good infrastructure, is an institutional and political investment for stable economic policy that modern India has inherited and it would be folly to damage it just when the nation has reached a stage to take advantage of and build on it to power its economy, promote development, and even step up the GDP growth rate.

While this is not the central concern of this chapter, the political story that I have laid out in this section is of considerable relevance. There is a small but undeniable build-up of opinion in India that is questioning the value of India's early commitment to cultural and political openness, secularism, and commitment to freedom of speech, for the media and also for individuals—from university cam-puses to the street-corner coffee house. It is regrettable that there are now forces that would like to reverse this. I believe that democracy, cultural openness, and secular-ism are traits that make for a better society and also more growth, at least of a sustainable kind. Whether or not India's early investment in this kind of politics was the right choice at that time (I believe it was but am aware that this is not beyond contestation), to squander this social and political capital just as the economy is taking off would be a mistake of enormous proportions, akin to making early invest-ment in large ports, roadways, and railways, and then deciding not to use them.

3. India's Economic Trajectory Since Independence

In a project commemorating Myrdal's *Asian Drama* there should be no need to remind the reader that economic growth does not occur solely because of good economics, but is due to many other factors that lie beyond economics (see Chapters 3 and 13, this volume). Growth is the outcome of various factors, from the nature of institutions, the prevalent social norms, and the positioning of the nation in the global polity, to the nature of economic policy. Some of the drivers of growth are beyond the control of any individual or organization. But there are also drivers that can be controlled by citizens and government. The purpose of economic analysis is to identify these.

What marks India's economic history since the nation's independence is the relative lack of drama, compared to other Asian countries. Barring the growth spike in 1975, mentioned above, India chugged along at a steady rate, of around 3.5 per cent per annum, for the first three decades. Given that population was initially growing at over 2 per cent per annum, this meant a growth of barely 1 per cent for per capita income. Table 16.1 summarizes the essential numbers. Annual GDP growth rate, averaged over decades, shows India growing at 3.91 per cent, 3.68 per cent, and 3.09 per cent over the 1950s, 1960s, and 1970s, respectively. In decadal terms, the big break was in the 1980s, when the growth breached the 5 per cent mark for the first time.

I believe this initial sluggishness was, in part, a consequence of the nature of Indian politics. Democracy with a vibrant media and regular elections makes governments wary of policy experiments, because the politicians are likely to be out of office if the policies backfire. So what Park Chung Hi could do in South

Table 16.1 India's growth and investment rates

Year	Annual GDP growth rate	Investment rate	Savings rate
1951–61	3.91	11.82	–
1961–71	3.68	14.71	9.03
1971–81	3.09	17.86	12.96
1981–91	5.38	21.04	17.32
1991–2001	5.71	24.14	24.27
2001–11	7.68	32.44	31.42
2011–18	6.61	35.78	31.17

Source: Economic Survey 2017–2018, Government of India, 2018.

Korea, or Mao Zedong could in China, or Lee Kuan Yew in Singapore was not feasible for leaders in India's democratic setting.[5]

All this is well reflected in the anecdotes of history and comparative statistics. In the 1950s, South Korea and India were almost equally poor and, in fact, most advanced nations treated South Korea as the basket case that would need support and aid to prevent major suffering but there was not much hope of a growth surge, whereas India was treated as ready to take off. However, Park Chung Hi took commanding control of the economy, took some daring policy decisions, some of which backfired massively and had to be retracted (see Krueger 1998). However, and maybe because of this policy agility, the economy stumbled a few times but also grew at a remarkable clip. South Koreans are now a little more than seventeen times as rich as Indians, in per capita income terms, which shows what a combination of good policies and institutions can do.

Turning to China, in contrast to India, we find it, all the way up to 1976, experiencing fluctuations in growth that would have been unimaginable, and also intolerable, in India. The broad picture of India's growth, captured in Table 16.1 reflects this relative tranquillity, which is in sharp contrast to China. In 1961, following the Great Leap Forward and the famine it unleashed—arguably the biggest famine in world history—China had a negative growth of 27 per cent. That is, more than a quarter of its GDP disappeared.

The Cultural Revolution would again result in a drop in growth much greater than India ever saw. On the other hand, China had several years of double digit growth during the 1960s and 1970s. Until the arrival of Deng Xiaoping, the most notable feature of China's economy was not how high or how low growth was, but the fluctuations in growth. This would change in the early 1980s, when China would move to a sustained high-growth path over a thirty-year period. When the Latin American crisis of 1982 happened, caused by the huge international debt build-up, it

[5] Lest this misleads the reader, I should add that just as China, Singapore, and South Korea are examples of authoritarian control and high-growth coinciding, there are many more examples of nations with totalitarian control at the helm and low growth and devastated economies.

had a negligible effect on China, which was by then on a fairly steady 10 per cent per annum growth path. China's growth is gradually slowing down now, currently just below 7 per cent per annum, but that is probably a reflection of the economy's maturity. It is beginning to look like a proper upper-middle-income nation.

For India, in contrast to China—barring relatively small dips in 1957–1958 and 1965–1966, and a very occasional 8 per cent growth and one year of 9 per cent growth (in 1975–1976)—the trajectory remained quite uneventful for the first three decades after Independence. Growth picked up through the 1980s as a changed Indira Gandhi tried to free up markets and ease controls, which were beginning to smother the country's growth. But by the end of the 1980s, more than anything else, it was fiscal laxity that helped India grow faster and also set the stage for the big crisis of 1990–1991, when the first Gulf War precipitated a massive slowdown and a balance of payments crisis for India.

This is where there is scope for some debate on whether the growth pick-up that India saw in the early 1980s can be described as a turning point, as Nayyar (2006) called it. Rodrik and Subramaniam (2004b) take a similar view, pointing to an 'attitudinal shift' in the government in the 1980s. At one level, this is a semantic controversy. It is indeed true that while in a pure comparison of numbers in terms of decadal growth, as captured in Table 16.1, where the broad direction of India's growth is upward, there is indeed a sharp rise in growth between the 1970s and 1980s.

There were some important policy drivers behind the growth pick-up, including Indira Gandhi's small steps towards liberalization, but there was, at least from the mid-1980s, also some short-termism, in terms of fiscal fuelling, which contributed to the growth but also to the economic crisis of 1990–1991. The proximate cause of the crisis was the first Gulf War, which put a sudden stop to the inflow of foreign exchange to India. At that time, the main inflow of foreign exchange was from remittances sent by Indian workers in the Gulf countries. The Iraqi invasion of Kuwait and the subsequent crisis put a virtual halt to this. One reason why this spun into an even bigger crisis than need have been the case was the growing fiscal burden of the previous years.

The crisis of the 1990s enabled India to do what China had been able to do in the 1960s and 1970s, and South Korea in the 1970s—experiment with policy shifts and reforms, and the rewards were visible. The economic reforms of 1991–1993 in India have been analysed extensively (see Nayyar 1996; Ahluwalia 2002; Mohan 2002). They caused many changes, most notably in India's international sector, best captured by India's foreign exchange reserves, which increased exponentially after 1993. There was also the removal of India's notorious licensing system, which drew attention to the larger subject of the costs of doing business, which in India were (and still are) very high. I shall return to this later.

In India, since foreign exchange reserves used to be so low, it had become standard wisdom that people and corporations should not be allowed to take foreign exchange out of the country. What this wisdom missed out on was the fact that if you do not allow people to take their foreign currency out of the country, they will not bring their foreign currency into the country in the first place. Hence, it is likely that one reason India had so little foreign reserve is that there were such severe restrictions on taking foreign money out of the country. This was changed during the reforms of 1991–1993 and the results were visible within three or four years.

Of course, at the time of such a policy shift there is a risk of crisis, because once the restrictions to take foreign exchange out are lifted, the first instinct of people will be to take their foreign reserves out and this can cause a sudden balance of payments crisis. India reached out to the IMF for support at the time of the reforms, to ensure that there would be a backup in the event of a sudden currency haemorrhage. Once that immediate risk of crisis was overcome, the benefits were visible. The country's foreign exchange reserves began to rise exponentially from the mid-1990s and the level that used to hold steady roughly at US$5 billion now stands at over US$400 billion.

The nation's growth rate also picked up from 1994, and hovered between annual rates of 6–8 per cent, with a small drop in and after 1997, almost certainly caused by the East Asian crisis. The growth rate picked up once again in 2003 and from 2005 it was at a level of over 9 per cent for three consecutive years, for the first time drawing comparisons with China's.

Such major shifts have many precursors and I would be remiss not to mention some less dramatic but important changes that began in the late 1960s and played an important role in preparing the ground for India's later high growth. I do believe that the early political investments of Nehru that I have already referred to played an important role in the long-run strength of the Indian economy. Turning to economic policy, the most important story was that of savings and investment. On these dimensions India today resembles East Asian economies, with savings and investment rates somewhere between 30 and 40 per cent. But this was not always the case.

What arguably gave a boost to savings and investment was the controversial move to nationalize all banks in 1969. This may have had other negative effects but one consequence of this was a sharp rise in the number of bank branches in relatively remote rural areas (a consequence of a directive from the government to the banks). This made it easier for people to save money, and through the 1970s there was an unprecedented rise in India's savings rate (Basu and Maertens 2008). A comprehensive study by Athukorala and Sen (2004) confirmed that the 'spread of banking facilities' played a positive role in India in promoting savings. What India saw subsequently was a most unusual growth pattern for a developing country. It was not the manufacturing sector that led India's growth but the services sector (Murthy 2005; Nayyar 2012; Basu 2015). Over the next fifteen years India topped the chart of nations in terms of service sector growth and this was primarily because of the information technology sector, in which the country excelled, but there is more to the story.

The growth story of India's services sector is an outlier. It has been argued that the services sector growth tends to occur in two waves, one which takes an economy from the low- to middle-income category, and a second one which occurs in middle-income economies, giving them a further boost (Eichengreen and Gupta 2009). The first consists of various informal sectors growing rapidly, whereas the second gets its boost from more sophisticated sectors, such as information technology and finance, triggering the overall service sector growth. It is this second-stage services sector growth that happened in India, rather early and with a vigour rarely seen anywhere else. As Nayyar's (2012) estimation shows, between 1980 and 2009 India's service sector growth was so large that it picked up 85 per cent of the decline in share of agriculture. That the share of agriculture will decline in the process of development is normal. What this statistic shows is both the remarkably good performance of India's service sector and the remarkably poor performance of India's manufacturing sector.

The factors that drove India's success in the service sector are several and make for interesting economic analysis. First, there was an early policy shift that was rooted in politics but had an unintended, beneficial effect. This had to do with the computing sector. Following a spat with IBM in 1977, India asked the company to leave the country. This caused big disruptions to the computing sector in India, but it also became an inadvertent application of the infant industry argument, whereby India was forced to make its own innovations and advances in this sector (Murthy 2005). This prepared the initial ground and then, when the economic reform of 1991–1993 happened, India's information technology sector was ready for take-off. As has been emphasized by Murthy (2004), the reforms were critically important because they cut down government bureaucracy and enabled speed in a sector that depends on that.

I have argued in Basu (2015) that two of India's big stumbling blocks, a cumbersome bureaucracy and poor infrastructure, explain a significant part of both its success in the services sector and stagnation in the manufacturing sector. The manufacturing sector, which needs to transport its products over roads and use the nation's ports to ship goods out for global sales, and has to negotiate the bureaucracy to pay taxes and get permits, was naturally stunted. The services sector, and in particular IT products, on the other hand, was initially largely tax exempted and so did not have to interact much with the bureaucracy. Further, its outputs did not, for the most part, have to be carted across roads or negotiate ports since they could be digitally sent to the user. Hence, this sector could bypass the nation's two big stumbling blocks.

Another interesting connection, which fits so well with the kinds of concern that Gunnar Myrdal had, is between democracy and service sector growth. Eichengreen and Gupta (2009) argue that the second wave of service sector growth has a connection with democracy, with more vibrant democracies having an advantage. They create an ethos of openness and connectivity that are crucial to this sector. One obvious factor is Internet connectivity. Many nations with severe top-down state control place restrictions on digital connectivity to thwart dissent and the amassing of popular opinion. Fortunately, India had the advantage of a democratic system, and it is arguable that this played a significant role in the success of its service sector.

This pattern of growth, coupled with India's over-production of engineers through from the 1960s to the 1980s, had a political fallout. As Silicon Valley took off in the USA and there was a growing need of expertise there, India became the main partner of the USA in this segment of the economy. This caused a warming of relations between the USA and India, which had hit rock bottom at the time of Bangladesh's independence in 1971 when Indira Gandhi refused to toe Nixon's line. This political development has been of great help to both the United States and India, with FDI flowing in both directions between the two countries and greater geopolitical co-operation between them. With Indians getting more than 50 per cent of the H1B visas, which is the category meant for professionals, that the USA issues, these links have continued to grow.

All these drivers had fallen into place by the early years of this millennium and, by 2003, India seemed to have moved another step up the growth ladder. In 2003–2004, India's GDP grew by 8 per cent and then from 2005 to 2008 it grew at over 9 per cent for three consecutive years. It is likely that India has moved up to a higher growth path, even though there have been some trying years subsequently. Immediately after 2008, the great global recession had its effect on India. After 2010, some major corruption scandals rocked the entire economy and in 2016 an ill-conceived demonetization put the brakes on the economy. It is, however, arguable that India is now on a higher growth path overall, despite these occasional interruptions.

To complete the picture of how India has developed overall, it is important to look at other indicators of progress—literacy, poverty, inequality, and health. The story here has been less encouraging. For a nation committed to equality and socialism, India did surprisingly poorly on these important indicators. Literacy is a striking example. In higher education, India did remarkably well for a developing economy (though it has, of late, been losing rank).[6] We could see this from the large presence of Indians in international gatherings of science, engineering, and other areas of higher learning and research. Yet, in terms of basic literacy, it trailed behind much poorer nations. In 1961, India's adult literacy was 28 per cent and life expectancy at birth was 28 years. These improved slowly till 1991 when the figures were, respectively, 52 per cent and 58 years. Thereafter there was some pick-up and latest available numbers (for 2011) are literacy 74 per cent and life expectancy 67 years.

---

[6] See Agarwal (2009); Patra et al. (2017).

Given that it is easier to make progress on a low base, the performance was very disappointing up to 1991. It is also worth noting that there is a great deal of variance across the country, with two states—Kerala and Mizoram—having over 90 per cent adult literacy, whereas in several states it is barely above 60 per cent. These figures hide large gender differences in most parts of India. There is only one state where female literacy is over 90 per cent. This is Kerala. At the other end, there are states with abysmally low female literacy, such as Rajasthan (52.7 per cent) and Bihar (53.3 per cent).

The above numbers are symptomatic of other social indicators, like poverty, health, and malnutrition. India's poverty rates, using the simple headcount ratio, have also been declining. In 1977 there were 60 per cent and 87 per cent of the population living on less than US$1.90 and US$3.20 dollars a day, respectively. There was a sharp fall after 2009, but with over 20 per cent of the population living on less than US$1.90 and 60 per cent living on US$3.20, there is still a great distance to go.

Finally, a comment on inequality. The numbers here are dismaying and reveal what was discussed earlier in this chapter, namely, that socialism in India was mainly a rhetorical exercise. The measurement of inequality is, of course, a vexing problem, the classic work being that of Sen (1977).[7] The Gini coefficient of income or consumption inequality is high but there are other measures, based on wealth and the tracking of the difference between the super-rich and the median person, which shows very high and worsening inequality (Bardhan 2007; Mishra 2012), which is likely to have negative spillovers in the long-run, and maybe not that long. The numbers on poverty quoted above, in a nation that now has several individuals listed among the world's wealthiest individuals, tell us that India does have work to do in reversing some of these inequality trends.

4. Contemporary Challenges

While India's growth picked up in the last few decades, and especially since 2005, as just discussed, India still faces formidable challenges—of deep-seated poverty, endemic corruption, growing inequality, and other anxieties of early growth. How should the nation deal with these hurdles? How should India turn the march of technology that is happening around the world, and creating turmoil in so many places, to its advantage? How should it attend to the disquiet of the disenfranchised class, a necessary concomitant of high inequality? The aim in this section is not to be even-handed but to comment on four special areas, where India has work to do and on which I have comments on offer.

---

[7] For an excellent short summary of the numbers and also the challenge of measurement in the context of India, see Mishra (2012).

4.1 Bureaucratic Costs

In India, the cost of transactions with the bureaucracy is too high. This curbs enterprise and handicaps small businesses, which cannot afford to operate large legal departments to deal with government sanctions and permits. India's disadvantage in this is caught well by the World Bank's Doing Business indicator. Among the 190 countries studied by the World Bank, India currently has a rank of 100 in terms of the 'ease of doing business', where rank 1 indicates an economy with the least bureaucratic inefficiency.

A snapshot of how India performs in comparison with a group of Asian economies in terms of select indicators is dismaying. Consider, for instance, the number of days it takes to get the basic permits to start a small enterprise. In Singapore it is 3 days, in South Korea 4, in Bangladesh 20, and in India 30. An enterprise pondering whether to start a new business venture will surely consider how difficult it would be to close and exit, should the business fail. For this reason, one of the ten indicators that make up the overall ease of doing business is the time it takes to resolve insolvency and close down a firm. The data on this are quite remarkable. Resolving insolvency in Singapore takes 9 months, in Malaysia 1 year, in South Korea 1.5 years, and in India 4 years and 3 months. The story is similar for the time required to enforce a contract and the time needed to obtain export clearance and customs clearance for imports. In the light of all this, it is not hard to understand why India's manufacturing sector has failed to take off.

In moving on I should make three warnings. First, in reality there are thousands of dimensions to measuring a business environment. The aim must not be to target the World Bank's indicators and work specifically on them. Yet there is a tendency in contemporary India to do just that, because the Doing Business ranking has suddenly become a visible and much talked about indicator. That can move a nation up the World Bank's chart and yet miss the substantive improvements the indicators are supposed to approximate. Second, it is important to remember that ease of doing business is not the same as overall welfare. It would be foolhardy to concentrate on ease of doing business to the exclusion of other measures of a nation's welfare. One important dimension of human life is how difficult or easy it is for ordinary people to interact with the government. How easy is it to get a driving licence, to pay one's electricity bills, or to file an income tax return? Doing Business measures the ease of business groups' interaction with the state, but there is also a need for a measure that captures ordinary people's ease of interaction with the state. Such a 'living life' index would capture an important dimension of economic life alongside what is measured by the Doing Business index.

Finally, the need to eliminate unnecessary hurdles must not be equated with a call for doing away with regulation. No modern economy can run well or enhance the well-being of its overall population if it is left entirely to the dictates of profit making. We need regulation to direct the economy, and we certainly need laws and controls to curb environmental damage. We cannot allow enterprises to choke our rivers and lakes with plastic and chemicals on grounds of free-market efficiency. But what has happened in India is a stacking-up of old and new rules, many of which serve no purpose other than to slow down decision-making and fuel corruption as people are forced to cajole and bribe those in authority to get the necessary permissions.

4.2 Corruption Control

The above topic naturally leads us to the problem of endemic corruption, which was a major concern of Myrdal. However, his emphasis was on the determination of leaders as a potential remedy. While this may be of some importance, it may not address the crux of the problem. At the same time, it would not be right to treat corruption as inevitable, as some take it to be. Corruption can be curbed and vastly diminished. But to do this needs analysis and careful reasoning, as much as determination and grit on the part of leaders. The world has had leaders who were deeply troubled by corruption and determined to end it in their nation, and were themselves incorruptible, and yet failed. To understand this, we need to dissect the problem carefully.

First, many observers make the mistake, looking at the corruption all around them, of treating corruption as an inherent part of society. There are some passages in Kautilya's *Arthashasthra* that have nurtured this belief. Consider this: 'Just as it is impossible not to taste honey or the poison on the tip of the tongue, so it is impossible for a Government servant not to eat up at least a part of the King's revenue.' This beautiful imagery, characteristic of Kautilya, expresses a rather pessimistic view, and nurtures a sense of helplessness in the face of corruption.

Fortunately, there is enough evidence now that corruption can be controlled. There are developed countries in the world that had a high level of corruption in the early nineteenth century. In Myrdal's own country, Sweden, there was the ubiquitous institution of the '*sportler*', which was something between a tip and a bribe, given to a bureaucrat to get some 'job' done. It is gone now. Today, the Scandinavian and Nordic nations are among the least corrupt countries in the world. There are examples of economies where corruption has gone down over an even shorter period—a couple of decades. Singapore and Hong Kong are good examples. According to Transparency International's data, Singapore has less corruption than the UK and USA; Hong Kong less than the USA.[8]

Much of the challenge of corruption control arises from unrealistic assumptions about the behaviour of the agents of the state. Once we recognize that they are

---

[8] See https://www.transparency.org/news/feature/corruption_perceptions_index_2017#table.

human, with their own motivations and aims, we can attempt to draft appropriate laws. This is essentially a problem of mechanism design. I shall stay away from such micro issues here; I have discussed these at some length elsewhere, in the context of controlling bribery (Basu 2015, 2018). I want instead to address here one widespread challenge that arises in countries where corruption is endemic, such as Brazil, India, and China. To put the problem in perspective, it may be pointed out that these three countries have ranks of 96 (Brazil), 81 (India), and 77 (China) in terms of the perceived level of corruption among the 180 countries analysed by Transparency International, the least corrupt country (which happens to be New Zealand) having a rank of 1 and the most corrupt (Somalia) a rank of 180.

The problem I am referring to occurs when a leader has a surfeit of options when it comes to deciding where to start cleaning up corruption. Consider a nation where corruption is endemic. This can be because there is a natural self-reinforcing element to corruption: If lots of people are corrupt, it seems fine for you to be corrupt. And this logic can lead to a corruption trap (World Bank 2015). There is also the problem of nations with a complex history of law-making, such as India,[9] where there has been such a build-up of layers of law and custom that it is now virtually impossible to avoid violating the law. Debroy's (2000) estimate is that, between central government and the (29) state governments, India has over 30,000 laws, a disproportionate number gathering dust. Therein lies the problem.

Consider a leader in some such nation who is genuinely keen to put an end to corruption. With corruption everywhere, the leader faces a choice of where to start. She can pick anybody and find him guilty of some violation of the law. Now, every political leader knows that if she wishes to survive politically it is best to arrest not friends but those in the opposition. But once she begins to go after her enemies it becomes clear that the anti-corruption policy itself is a handy instrument to silence the opposition and to go after a press that is critical of her policies. In other words, what begins as an anti-corruption policy becomes an instrument of disciplining the opposition and the media. This is the danger that is faced by Xi Jinping, by Narendra Modi, by Michel Temer. It is an important reason why corruption persists and why the persistence of corruption is not necessarily a sign of the leader not being serious about removing corruption but simply a manifestation of a political-economic trap in which nations tend to get caught. And India is no exception.

One way for a leader, serious about crime control, to handle this is to set up some broad parameters and hand over corruption control to an autonomous authority, with the explicit commitment that, once this authority begins to function, it would have full autonomy, in the way a nation's supreme court is supposed

---

[9] For an elegant commentary on this history, see Roy and Swamy (2016).

to have. In Asia, Indonesia is the only country that has had some experience of this kind of institution, though even it has run into problems recently.

4.3 Norms and Institutions

Turing to broader issues, the challenge of mitigating corruption entails thinking of the state as an endogenous institution consisting of individuals with their own objectives and motivations, as assumed in the literature on new institutional economics, of which Myrdal's work was clearly a precursor (see Evans 1995; Stiglitz 2017; Basu 2018). Such a perspective opens up new ways of thinking about the law and how to control corruption.[10] I want to discuss one that relates to social norms and, more generally, sociology.[11]

In controlling corruption, the design of incentives with which economists have been concerned matters, but the social and political setting is as important. This is often missed by neoclassical economists, who treat social and cultural variables as exogenous and redundant for the economy. In reality, we can try to eliminate or modify cultural traits that have harmful consequences on the economy and encourage the ones that aid efficiency and progress. And even though it is true that, at this stage, we do not fully understand *what causes* norms to change, the recognition that they do change and can potentially respond to policy is important and can help set up a useful research agenda. Second, even when our norms and culture are fixed, knowing how they intertwine with economic variables enables us to think of new policy interventions and assess more accurately the costs and benefits of interventions.

As illustration, consider the problem of teacher absenteeism in government-run schools. A multi-country study in which researchers made surprise visits to government-run primary schools shows that in terms of teacher truancy, India is second only to Uganda (Kremer et al. 2004)—and by a short head. At any time, 25 per cent of teachers are found missing from government-run schools in India. What should be done? In answering this, economists have typically looked to *economic* variables. This can indeed be useful. Analysts have rightly stressed the role of incentives and sanctions—both carrots and sticks—in creating greater work discipline among the teachers. However, I believe that much of the problem is rooted in culture and social norms. Economists assume that, once we cite culture, we are planning to do a disappearing act in a welter of words and vague generalities. That is not true. There is now an increasing body of knowledge that is beginning to give shape and structure to these topics. For one, we know that our behaviour is affected by echo chamber effects within groups and by notions of

---

[10] See Basu (2011), Abbink et al. (2014), Berlin et al. (2017), and Mishra (2017).

[11] For an innovative scheme of corruption control, which does not involve the government but entails self-enforcing contracts among private sector firms and corporations, see Dixit (2015).

social stigma. It is otherwise hard to explain why, though teachers are paid the same salary and subjected to the same rules of economic incentives and punishments across the nation, teacher truancy in Jharkhand is about three times as high as that in Maharashtra, as the Kremer et al. (2004) study shows. Our behaviour is often guided not by monetary considerations but by notions of dignity, stigma, and self-respect.

In reality, unlike in the neoclassical model, people, including those indulging in corruption, are aware of the moral dimensions of corruption. However, when corruption is widespread, it may seem a more tolerable form of behaviour. It can then be like an equilibrium-selection norm. As is pointed out in World Bank (2015: 60), through much of history and in many contemporary societies, corruption is 'a shared belief that using public office to benefit oneself and one's family and friends is widespread, expected and tolerated. In other words, corruption can be a social norm.'

An interesting study by Abbink et al. (2014) checks this out by artificially *creating* the social norm in a laboratory setting, and measuring people's behavioural response.[12] The study found that the probability of offering a bribe doubles when the subject is paired with a more corrupt partner rather than a more honest partner. The social setting influences individual behaviour. The moral quality of leadership in society can make a difference. And there is now a large body of literature which outlines social and institutional interventions that can be as powerful as economic incentives in changing some of these adverse behaviour patterns in society.

4.4   Technology and Labour

Turning finally to the challenge of technology and labour, for India this is as yet a problem in its early stages, but it may come to be the dominant problem in the medium to long term. Worldwide and in high- and upper-middle-income countries the problem is acute. Thanks to the rise of two kinds of technology—the 'labour-saving' kind, which is leading to machines and robots replacing labour, and the 'labour-linking' kind, which is allowing workers in low-wage nations to do some of the work for rich economies without having to leave their shores—there is a clear trend of wage shares falling and inequality rising.

The problem is affecting India (Kotwal 2017). Since the reforms to India's economy during 1991–1993, growth has been higher but job creation has lagged behind growth quite significantly (Ghose 2016; Nayyar 2017). During the real-high-growth period for India, 2005–2008, for instance, when GDP

---

[12] See also Bicchieri and Xiao (2009) and Banerjee (2016).

was growing at roughly 9.5 per cent per annum, annual job creation was barely 2 per cent. I believe that this will become an inevitable problem once India becomes a high-income or even an upper-middle-income economy, since it is a global problem. However, there is no reason why India should not be able to take advantage of labour-linking technologies and create more jobs for now. However, to continue to be competitive in this dimension, India will have to build skills and continue to improve and modernize its education system. As Ghose's (2016) recent study shows, not only is India's labour force very poorly educated, the distribution of education is also abysmal. This will cause a large problem because the demand for unskilled work is bound to go down. Mechanical work will soon not need labour because machines will out-compete labour, but when it comes to creative work and research, human skills will continue to be critical, at least in the foreseeable future. This is what takes us back to what was stressed above—the importance of education, especially the development of creative skills.

To absorb labour, it is also important to grow and nurture both the agricultural and manufacturing sectors. India's services sector, the engine of India's good performance, is virtually on autopilot now. Attention needs to be directed to the other sectors, which also happen to be more labour-intensive. For this, work is needed in two areas that have already been mentioned: namely, creating better infrastructure and cutting down bureaucracy.[13] There will be a challenge later when wages rise and India becomes part of the global story. My belief is that India will need radical reforms such as some form of profit sharing across the population. But that is not a problem special to India, and so it is of no direct concern in this chapter.

5. The Next Twenty-five Years

Peering into the distant future is not easy for any discipline. In the case of economics, its intertwining with politics and sociology makes forecasting even more hazardous. With that caveat in mind, here is some speculation about what the next twenty-five years may hold in store for India.

It has been a remarkable half-century since when Myrdal's seminal work drew global attention to this newly-independent nation. All the portents are that India will continue to grow rapidly and will take on the mantle of a growth leader in the world.[14] At this moment, this sounds overly optimistic since, politically and socially, India is going through a bleak patch. The reason for my optimism is that

---

[13] There have been some, more specific, exciting new ideas, such as the development of coastal economic zones, that have been discussed in recent times (see Singh 2018).

[14] See discussion in Basu (2015). See also Rodrik and Subramaniam (2004a).

I expect this to pass. A run of 9 per cent annual growth, which began in 2005 but has slackened off since then, maintained over a twenty-year period is not a pipe dream. If the country can get back onto such a growth path five years from now, it will be a transformed nation by 2043. But there are risks and one would be remiss not to point to them.

First, agriculture as a share of value-added in GDP has, over the last fifty years, become quite small but it is still a vital sector that employs around half of the nation's labour force. Even a small decline in its production can cause food inflation, large welfare losses among the poor, and even political instability. Therefore, agriculture as a sector will continue to need nurture.

Second, as pointed out above, while technology will eventually create a global challenge that will affect India, for some time still to come India can take advantage of its cheap labour and boost its manufacturing sector. But to nurture this sector, more investment is needed in infrastructure, the reduction of bureaucratic costs, and also good macroeconomic policy, because a wrong exchange rate policy, or another move like demonetization, can blight the nation's prospects.

Third, we have the challenge of inequality. As Ghatak (2017) documents, India has a growing inequality problem, and unless it invests in health and education and also taxes to curtail dynastic intergenerational transfers more effectively, it may have growth but at the cost of true development. This will be a problem for India for some time to come. While the growth story has been exemplary, various indicators show that growth has not been distributed well across society (see Subramanian 2016). This shows up clearly if we compare two countries that have had similar growth, Vietnam and India. In terms of child malnutrition, for example, India has performed markedly less well than Vietnam (Ray 2008), showing that the spoils of growth may not have been shared well; and, further, as Vietnam's experience shows this is not inevitable.

India has all these challenges but with its early investment in the political institutions of democracy, secularism, and openness, as well as in good universities and institutes of higher learning, India has the potential to be in the frontline of the world economy within the next quarter-century.

Acknowledgements

Early drafts of this chapter was presented at UNU-WIDER conferences in Hanoi on 9–10 March 2018, and in Shanghai on 29–30 June 2018. It has benefitted greatly from discussions with Tony Addison, Alaka Basu, Amit Bhaduri, Prasenjit Duara, Guanghua, Rolph van der Hoeven, Sudipto Mundle, Siddiq Osmani, Daniel Poon, Frances Stewart and Finn Tarp. I am grateful to Deepak Nayyar and an anonymous referee for detailed comments. I thank Aviv Caspi, Gowtham Muthukkumaran, Xinyue Pei and Haokun Sun for research assistance.

References

Abbink, K., U. Dasgupta, L. Gangadharan, and T. Jain (2014). 'Letting the Briber Go Free: An Experiment on Mitigating Harassment Bribes', *Journal of Public Economics*, 111: 17–28.

Agarwal, P. (2009). *Indian Higher Education: Envisioning the Future*. New Delhi: Sage.

Ahluwalia, M.S. (2002). 'Economic Reforms in India since 1991: Has Gradualism Worked?', *Journal of Economic Perspectives*, 16(3): 67–88.

Athukorala, P., and K. Sen (2004). 'The Determinants of Private Savings in India', *World Development*, 32(3): 491–503.

Banerjee, A.V. (2016). 'Policies for a Better-fed world', *Review of World Economics*, 152(1): 3–17.

Bardhan, P. (1998). *Political Economy of Development in India*. Oxford: Oxford University Press.

Bardhan, P. (2007). 'Poverty and Inequality in China and India: Elusive Link with Globalization', *Economic and Political Weekly*, 42(38): 3849–52.

Basu, K. (2009). 'China and India: Idiosyncratic Paths to High Growth', *Economic and Political Weekly*, 44(38): 43–56.

Basu, K. (2011). 'Why for a Class of Bribes the Act of Giving a Bribe should be Treated as Legal', Ministry of Finance, Government of India, Working Paper. Available at: www.kaushikbasu.org/Act_Giving_Bribe_Legal.pdf (accessed 8 September 2018).

Basu, K. (2015). *An Economist in the Real World: The Art of Policymaking in India*. Cambridge, MA: MIT Press.

Basu, K. (2018). *The Republic of Beliefs: A New Approach to Law and Economics*. Princeton, NJ: Princeton University Press.

Basu, K., and A. Maertens (2008). 'The Pattern and Causes of Economic Growth in India', *Oxford Review of Economic Policy*, 23(2): 143–67.

Berlin, M., B. Qin, and G. Spagnolo (2017). 'Leniency, Asymmetric Punishment and Corruption: Evidence from China', mimeo, Stockholm School of Economics.

Bicchieri, C., and E. Xiao (2009). Do the Right Thing: But Only If Others Do So', *Journal of Behavioral Decision Making*, 22(2): 191–208.

Debroy, B. (2000). *In the Dock*. New Delhi: Konark.

Dixit, A. (2015). 'How Business Community Institutions can Help Fight Corruption', *World Bank Economic Review, Papers and Proceedings*, 29(sup. 1): S25–S47.

Eichengreen, B., and P. Gupta (2009). 'The Two Waves of Service Sector Growth', NBER Working Paper 14968.

Evans, P. (1995). *Embedded Autonomy: States and Industrial Transformation*. Princeton, NJ: Princeton University Press.

Ghatak, M. (2017). 'India Needs to Create Greater Economic Opportunities for All', *Economic Times*, 9 October.

Ghose, A. (2016). *India Employment Report* 2016: *Challenges and the Imperative of Manufacturing-led Growth*. Delhi: Oxford University Press; Institute for Human Development.

Kohli, A. (2012). 'State and Redistributive Development in India'. In R. Nagaraj (ed.) *Economic Growth, Inequality and Social Development in India: Is Inclusive Growth Possible?* Basingstoke: Palgrave Macmillan.

Kothari, R. (1977). *Democratic Polity and Social Change in India*. Mumbai: Allied Publishers.

Kotwal, A. (2017). 'The Challenge of Job Creation'. *Ideas for India*, 15 December. Available at: http://www.ideasforindia.in/topics/macroeconomics/the-challenge-of-job-creation.html.

Kremer, M., K. Muralidharan, N. Chaudhury, J. Hammer, and H. Rogers (2004). 'Teacher Absence in India: A Snapshot', *Journal of European Economic Association*, 3(2–3): 658–67.

Krueger, A. (1998). 'Contrasts in Transition to Market-Oriented Economies: India and Korea'. In Y. Hayami and M. Aoki (eds) *The Institutional Foundations of East Asian Economic Development*. London: Macmillan.

Mehta, P.B. (2012). 'State and Democracy in India', *Polish Sociological Review*, 178(2): 203–25.

Mishra, A. (2012). 'Inequality'. In K. Basu and A. Maertens (eds) *New Oxford Companion to Economics in India*. Delhi: Oxford University Press.

Mishra, A. (2017). 'The Many Faces of Corruption'. In A. Mishra and T. Ray (eds) *Markets, Governance and Institutions, in the Process of Economic Development*. Oxford: Oxford University Press.

Mohan, R. (2002). 'A Decade after 1991: New Challenges Facing the Indian Economy', *Reserve Bank of India Bulletin*, 56: 771–88.

Murthy, N. (2004). 'The Impact of Economic Reforms on Industry in India: A Case Study of the Software Industry'. In K. Basu (ed.) *India's Emerging Economy: Performance and Prospects in the 1990s and Beyond*. Cambridge, MA: MIT Press.

Murthy, N. (2005). 'Making India a Significant IT Player in this Millennium'. In R. Thapar (ed.) *India: Another Millennium*. New Delhi: Penguin Books.

Myrdal, G. (1968). *Asian Drama: An Inquiry into the Poverty of Nations. A Twentieth Century Fund Study, Volumes I, II, and III*. New York: Pantheon, (all page references are to the 1972 edition by Allen Lane, edited by Seth King).

Nayyar, D. (1996). *Economic Liberalization in India: Analytics, Experience and Lessons*. Kolkata: Orient Longmans.

Nayyar, D. (1998). 'Economic Development and Political Democracy: Interaction of Economics and Politics in Democratic India', *Economic and Political Weekly*, 33(49/ December): 3121–31.

Nayyar, D. (2006). 'India's Unfinished Journey: Transforming Growth into Development', *Modern Asian Studies*, 40(3): 797–832.

Nayyar, D. (2017). '25 Years of Economic Liberalization', *Economic and Political Weekly*, 52(2): 41–8.

Nayyar, G. (2012). *The Service Sector in India's Development*. Cambridge: Cambridge University Press.

Patra, S., T. Ray, and A.R. Chaudhuri (2017). 'Impact of Education Loans on Higher Education: The Indian Experience', mimeo. New Delhi: Indian Statistical Institute.

Ray, R. (2008). 'Diversity in Calorie Sources and Undernourishment during Rapid Economic Growth', *Economic and Political Weekly*, 43(23, February).

Rodrik, D., and A. Subramanian (2004a). 'Why India Can Grow at 7 Per Cent a Year and More: Projections and Reflections', *Economic and Political Weekly*, 51–7.

Rodrik, D., and A. Subramanian (2004b). 'From "Hindu Growth" to Productivity Surge: The Mystery of the Indian Growth Transition', National Bureau of Economic Research, NBER Working Paper 10376.

Roy, T., and A. Swamy (2016). *Law and the Economy in Colonial India*. Chicago, IL: University of Chicago Press.

Sen, A. (with J. Foster) (1977). *On Economic Inequality: An Expanded Edition*. Oxford: Oxford University Press.

Sen, A. (2004). 'Democracy and Secularism in India'. In K. Basu (ed.) *India's Emerging Economy: Performance and Prospects in the* 1990s *and Beyond*. Cambridge, MA: MIT Press.

Sen, A. (2005). *The Argumentative Indian: Writings on India's History, Culture and Identity*. New York; London: Farrar, Straus and Giroux; Picador.

Singh, N. (2018). 'Job Growth in India: Development Means Creating Good Jobs', *Financial Express*, 21 March.

Sivasubramonian, S. (2000). *The National Income of India during the Twentieth Century*. Delhi: Oxford University Press.

Stiglitz, J. (2017). 'Markets, States and Institutions'. In A. Mishra, A. Ray, and T. Ray (eds) *Markets, Governance and Institutions, in the Process of Economic Development*. Oxford: Oxford University Press.

Subramanian, S. (2016). 'The Quintile Income Statistic, Money-Metric Poverty, and Disequalising Growth in India: 1983 to 2011–12', *Economic and Political Weekly, Economy*, 51(5): 73–9.

Varshney, A. (2013). *Battles Half Won: India's Improbable Democracy*. New Delhi: Penguin.

World Bank (2015). *World Development Report* 2015: *Mind, Society and Behavior*. Washington, DC: World Bank.

17

Indonesia

C. Peter Timmer

1. Introduction

Two powerful, vicious circles drove Gunnar Myrdal's pessimism about the development prospects of South and Southeast Asia. The first was the pervasive poor governance that he termed the 'soft state', usually controlled by corrupt, rent-seeking elites who were uninterested in economic policies that might bring widespread gains in welfare. The second was the debilitating nutritional status of most of the rural population, too poor and unproductive to even put enough food on the tables for their families, thus reducing their productivity even further. These downward spirals, visible in many countries in the early-to-mid-1960s when Myrdal was researching and framing *Asian Drama*, were especially 'dramatic' in Indonesia. No one at the time seemed to doubt his judgement that the country was the showcase example for development pessimism. This chapter tries to explain why that pessimism turned out to be unfounded.

When the First Five-Year Plan of the Suharto government (REPELITA I) (1969–1974) was drafted, the economic team was aware of Myrdal's pessimism about development prospects in South Asia broadly, and his especially harsh judgement about the prospects for Indonesia. The Plan anticipated growth in per capita incomes of about 3 per cent per year, and this was widely viewed as optimistic. But the subsequent half-century proved that far more was possible. Per capita economic growth of nearly 5 per cent per year was sustained over more than three decades, pulling tens of millions of Indonesians above the nutrition-based poverty line. The trauma of the Asian financial crisis in 1998 hit Indonesia hard, both economically and politically. But it recovered from this as well, in the context of a surprisingly smooth transition from military dictatorship to widespread participatory democracy. Much of the story of the democratic era is necessarily about politics and governance, and this chapter focuses on these and the accompanying economic trade-offs.

Three themes run through this chapter, interconnected yet discrete enough to merit their own headings: (1) the story of economic growth and its accompanying structural transformation of what was a largely rural economy in 1968; (2) the record on poverty alleviation that was mostly a result of that economic growth, but which was enhanced by a *conscious policy* of connecting poor households to the growing economy; and (3) the political transformation that began well before the 1998 fall of the Suharto regime, and which continues to this day.

The main message from this is succinct but powerful—Indonesia's poor have been very closely connected to economic growth in the country, benefitting differentially when the economy was growing rapidly, and suffering disproportionately when the economy is not growing, or suffers a major crisis, as in 1998. Of all the countries discussed by Myrdal, Indonesia's record from the late 1960s to the mid-1990s was one of the most 'pro-poor', and from the late 1990s to the mid-2000s one of the most traumatic. But once again the country recovered from chaos to build a successful economy with a rising middle class and aspirations of regional leadership.

The chapter closes with a review of the economic record of the various democratically elected presidents since 1999, and a prognosis of likely progress for the next quarter-century. Indonesia will celebrate the centenary of its independence in 2045.

2. Understanding Indonesia's Pathway out of Poverty

Myrdal was fully aware of the historical significance of the structural transformation in Western societies as the route out of poverty for agrarian populations, although he apparently did not think the process was relevant to the Asian societies he was observing in the mid-1960s.[1] The structural transformation of poor, agrarian economies into rich, industrial- and service-based economies located largely in urban areas is arguably the only sustainable pathway out of poverty. Surplus labour from agricultural households migrates to more productive off-farm employment, generating a process of economic growth. Productivity growth in the agricultural sector is also needed as a way to feed workers in the cities and keep labour productivity in agriculture from falling too far behind labour productivity in urban areas. A large gap in incomes between the two sectors creates severe political tensions, and we will see these play out in Indonesia after 1998.

2.1 The Dynamics of Structural Transformation

Two variables drive the structural transformation story: the share of agriculture in gross domestic product (GDP) (AgGDPshr) and the equivalent share of the agricultural labour force in total employment (AgEMPshr). The difference

---

[1] The term 'structural transformation' does not appear in the 35-page index to the three-volume set of *Asian Drama* (Myrdal 1968).

between these two shares measures the gap in labour productivity between the agricultural and non-agricultural sectors (AgGAPshr). AgEMPshr is nearly always larger than AgGDPshr, and thus labour productivity in agriculture is lower than in non-agriculture (Timmer and Akkus 2008); Timmer 2015; see Table 17.1.

Figure 17.1 shows these three basic variables for Indonesia during 1880 to 2016. The common pattern of structural transformation is readily apparent—both sectoral employment and contribution to GDP decline smoothly after the economic chaos of the Great Depression and the Second World War. The gap between these two variables also tends to decline (absolutely; by definition it tends to be negative), but remains negative. Even most advanced countries did not reach parity between rural and urban incomes until late in their development. The United States, for example, reached parity around about 1980 (Gardner 2002).

Labour productivity in agriculture has two components: the physical yield of commodities on the land at the disposal of the farm household, and the value of that output in home consumption or in the market. Agricultural labour

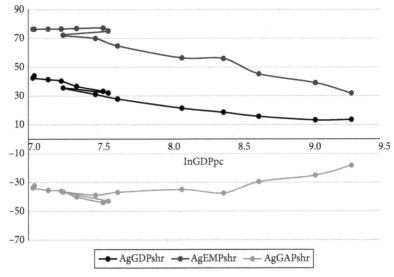

Figure 17.1 Long-run patterns of structural transformation in Indonesia, 1880–2016.

Note: The data used in this figure for measuring structural transformation include four variables, of which the first three are:

(1) AgEMPshr: percentage share of agricultural employment in total employment;
(2) AgGDPshr: percentage share of agricultural GDP in total GDP; and
(3) AgGAPshr: percentage share of agricultural employment in total state employment minus the percentage share of agricultural GDP in total GDP (AgGDPshr–AgEMPshr).

Values for the third variable are typically negative because the share of the labour force working in agriculture is nearly always larger than the contribution of those workers to GDP. This definition makes Figure 17.1 easy to interpret.

The fourth variable is the logarithm of per capita GDP for each decade (lnGDPpc) (see Table 17.4 for source and details). The decadal data used in Figure 17.1 are presented in Table 17.1.

Source: Author's illustration based on updated data from Timmer (2017) and Bolt et al. (2018).

Table 17.1 Decadal data used in Figure 17.1

	1880	1890	1900	1910	1920	1930	1940	
AgGDPshr	44.1	42.5	41.4	40.4	36.7	33.1	32	
AgEMPshr	76.3	76.3	76.4	76.5	76.8	77.1	75	
AgGAPshr	−32.2	−33.8	−35.5	−36.1	−40.1	−44.0	−43	
GDPpc	1,147	1,134	1,267	1,392	1,551	1,876	1,944	
lnGDPpc	7.045	7.034	7.144	7.238	7.347	7.537	7.573	
	1950	1960	1970	1980	1990	2000	2010	2016
AgGDPshr	35.5	31.0	27.8	21.4	18.5	15.7	13.9	13.5
AgEMPshr	72.2	69.9	64.7	56.4	55.9	45.3	39.1	31.8
AgGAPshr	−36.7	−38.9	−36.9	−35.0	−37.4	−29.6	−25.2	−18.3
GDPpc	1,410	1,776	2,074	3,283	4,414	5,664	8,425	10,911
lnGDPpc	7.251	7.482	7.637	8.097	8.393	8.642	9.039	9.298

Source: Author's illustration based on updated data from Timmer (2017) and Bolt et al. (2018).

productivity, and farm incomes, can be raised by policies affecting output prices, as well as by investments that raise physical yields of crops and livestock. Of course, markets also affect agricultural commodity prices and significantly influence the cost of policy choices to alter them. For tradable commodities it is much easier for policy to affect the domestic market price than the farm yield. High rice prices help close the gap between rapidly rising urban incomes and lagging rural incomes. They also encourage domestic rice self-sufficiency, which has been the politically articulated approach to poverty reduction and food security in Indonesia since the mid-1970s.

2.2 Initial Conditions: Where does the Path Begin?

Booth (2016) makes a powerful argument that the initial conditions for much of modern Indonesia's economic development were laid down by Dutch colonial policies in the nineteenth and early twentieth centuries. Certainly Myrdal, when writing *Asian Drama*, was acutely aware of the differential impact of British, French, and Dutch colonial legacies on the development paths of their former colonies, and the Dutch come out rather badly in his assessment. But does that matter fifty years on? Are the relevant 'initial conditions' the reality that Myrdal was observing in the mid-1960s, which was quite grim, or does the story need to start much earlier?

As Booth emphasizes, there is no neat answer to this question. The title of her book indicates that her preference is to start with the colonial legacy.[2] A short

---

[2] The full title is *Economic Change in Modern Indonesia: Colonial and Post-Colonial Comparisons*.

chapter does not have that luxury, but Figure 17.1 does provide useful historical perspective. Indonesia suffered greatly from the Depression and Second World War—the level of per capita GDP was still depressed (by 10 per cent) in 1950 compared with 1920. Compounding the problem, Indonesia missed much of the growth spurt experienced in other parts of Asia between 1950 and 1970—per capita GDP was only 15 per cent higher in Indonesia after those two decades (and almost all of that growth came between 1967 and 1970, after the fall of Sukarno), whereas Japan had per capita GDP that was more than 400 per cent higher.

The basic starting point for this chapter is the mid-1960s, when Myrdal was writing and when much of the development profession was forming its first impressions of Indonesia. Based on his review of the Dutch colonial and Sukarno era economic record, he is unrelenting in his pessimism for Indonesia's future economic prospects:[3]

> It was in their refusal to permit any significant advance toward responsible gov-
> ernment that the Dutch, together with the French, stood out in comparison with
> the British as the guardians of a reactionary imperialism...Holland's stubborn
> refusal to accede to the moderate demands of indigenous nationalists, as well as
> its practice of reserving even the less elevated positions in the colonial adminis-
> tration to Dutch and Eurasian residents, drove the forces of nationalism into
> conspiratorial channels and militant agitation.   (p. 164)

> Without collective cabinet responsibility for major policy directives, govern-
> ment proved grossly ineffective and unstable. There were six cabinets between
> 1945 and 1948, seven between 1949 and 1957...Corruption, graft and fraud on
> a colossal scale were conspicuous features of public life.   (p. 367)

> Furthermore, it has been suggested that Indonesian 'national income per head
> in the middle of the fifties was below the 1939 level,...probably below the 1929
> level and may even be below the level of 1919', [citing Benjamin Higgins] and
> the evidence shows a sharp decline since 1957. As things look at the beginning
> of 1966, there seems to be little prospect of rapid economic growth in Indonesia.
> (p. 489)

The next 50 years played out quite differently.

3. The Evolution of the Indonesian Economy

Indonesia is the original home of the dual economy. Boeke's experience during the Dutch colonial administration of Java led him to identify two types of economic agents—'rational' and 'traditional'—with almost entirely separate spheres of economic activity (Boeke 1946). Lewis (1954) built his Nobel Prize-winning

---

[3] The quotes are from volume I of *Asian Drama* (Myrdal 1968).

model of the dual economy with unlimited supplies of labour on the behaviour of such agents. Indonesia's history has modern lessons.

3.1 The Historical Setting for Indonesia's Growth Experience

Indonesia is an archipelago nation. The soils are mostly volcanic on Java, and they support intensive rice cultivation. The laterite soils on the Outer Islands are most productive in tree crops and natural rainforest. Indonesia's agriculture is dominated by wet- and dry-season rice cultivation and a variety of tree crops for export. There has been long-term experience with international trade, and Muslim traders established Islam peacefully by the sixteenth century.[4]

Under Dutch colonial rule, which started in the fifteenth century and ended with independence in 1945, the trade and tax regime favoured Dutch extraction of income, except for a brief period at the beginning of the twentieth century when Dutch public opinion supported a more developmental approach known as 'ethical policy'. However, this policy collapsed with world prices for export commodities in the 1920s, and Indonesia experienced especially poor economic management during the Great Depression. The Dutch forced the Netherlands East Indies to stay on the Gold Standard well after their regional competitors devalued. The colonial authorities did build a significant network of irrigation canals, roads, ports and shipping facilities, and railroads. There was, however, very little investment in the education of the local population. Only 3.5 per cent of the population was attending school in 1939, compared with 13.3 per cent in 1995. The historical record suggests there was severe poverty in the mid-nineteenth century, which fell gradually until the 1920s. Poverty increased rapidly from the Great Depression until the end of the Second World War.

The Sukarno government took control after declaring independence in 1945, and put 'politics in command' after 1958. It neglected agriculture and adopted an 'inward looking' development policy; the result was economic and political chaos by the mid-1960s. Incomes fell and the hyper-inflation in 1965–1966 had an impact on everyone. The post-war recovery had helped reduce poverty, but the poverty rate increased rapidly as inflation soared and the economy collapsed. Probably 70 per cent of the population was 'absolutely poor' by 1966. Average food energy intake was about 1,600 kilocalories per day. Hunger was widespread.

3.2 Pro-poor Growth in Historical Perspective

Thanks to the painstaking historical research of Pierre van der Eng (1993a, 1993b, 2000, 2002), it is possible to construct a long-run indicator of how the poor

---

[4] Much of this early history is drawn from Timmer (1975).

have fared since 1880 (see Table 17.2). Van der Eng's time series data for 1880 to 1990 can be divided into five main epochs: Dutch colonial exploitation of the Indonesian economy (1880–1905); the 'ethical policy' era when efforts were made to improve living standards of native Indonesians (1905–1925); the tumultuous period during the Great Depression, Pacific War, and fight for independence (1925–1950); the Sukarno era (1950–1965), whose 'guided economy' after 1958 created the economic turmoil that was observed by Myrdal; and President Suharto's 'New Order' regime in the 1965–1990 period, which is the main focus of this chapter. The original van der Eng data end in 1990 and the results reported here depend on that dataset.

Three sets of calculations for each epoch are shown in Table 17.2. The first column shows the trend growth rate of incomes per capita (YPC), as estimated from a semi-logarithmic time trend for the respective time period. These growth rates vary widely. There was a sharp deterioration over the quarter-century of economic chaos from 1925 to 1950, which contrasts equally sharply with strong growth in both the 'ethical policy' era under the Dutch and, strikingly, in the Suharto era. Over the entire time period for which van der Eng reports, per capita incomes rose 0.89 per cent per year.

The second column in Table 17.2 shows the similarly estimated time trend for intake of food energy, as measured from food balance sheet data on kilocalories (KCAL) consumed per capita per day, on average for each year for 1880–1990. During two epochs this trend was negative, which indicates a decline in nutritional status on average for the whole society and the strong likelihood of significant increases in hunger among the poor. During such episodes, poverty was rising. A sharply positive trend in food energy intake, however, as during the 'ethical policy' era and the early Suharto era, suggests that income growth was reaching the poor and improving their access to food. Over the entire time period, the trend in food energy intake was just 0.2 per cent per year.

The relationship between the variables underlying these two trends is also reported in Table 17.2. The third column reports the average income elasticity of demand for food energy (KCAL), which is estimated from the annual data for each epoch. Importantly, the pattern of coefficients is similar for the income elasticities and the rate of change in food energy intake. The logic connecting the two is straightforward. Engel's law suggests that the income elasticity of demand for food (of which energy is an important component for the poor) is a declining function of income level. When income growth includes the poor, their higher income elasticities for food energy raise the income elasticity observed on average. It is thus possible to infer what is happening to the poor during long-run periods of economic growth (or decline) by analysing these changes in food energy intake (Timmer 1996).

This approach works, of course, only for those societies in which the poor wish to increase their food energy intake when their incomes increase—that is, when they are still on the rising part of the Engel curve. This is the case for Indonesia.

Table 17.2 Long-run patterns of pro-poor growth in Indonesia[a]

Time period	Growth rates (%)		Income elasticity for KCAL	Index of pro-poor growth (IPPG)[b]
	YPC	KCAL		
Dutch colonial exploitation, 1880–1905	0.33	−0.34	0.051 0.165	0.05
'Ethical policy' under the Dutch, 1905–1925	1.63	1.39	0.878 2.805	4.57
Depression, the Pacific War, and the fight for independence, 1925–1950	−2.42	0.78	0.333 1.064	−2.57
The Sukarno era, including the 'guided economy' period, 1950–1965	1.46	0.68	0.509 1.626	2.37
The 'New Order' regime of Suharto, 1965–1990	3.45	2.10	0.595 1.901	6.56
The long-run averages, 1880–1990	0.89	0.22	0.313 1.00	0.89

Notes: (a) Details of the regressions are shown in Timmer (2004b), which also provides a full explanation of the analytical relationship between the overall incidence of poverty and the average income elasticity of demand for food energy. (b) The IPPG is calculated as the product of the growth rate in per capita income times the 'standardized' income elasticity of demand for food energy (KCAL), where the base income elasticity is the value for the entire time period from 1880 to 1990 (0.313). Growth rates are calculated as least squares time trends of logarithmic values of incomes per capita (YPC) and average daily per capita food energy intake per capita (KCAL). The 'top' value for the income elasticity of demand for food energy for each epoch is estimated as a constant elasticity value from a double logarithmic function. The 'bottom' value re-scales this estimated value, with the 1880–1990 average of 0.313 equal to 1.000. As an example, the IPPG value of 6.56 for the Suharto era from 1965 to 1990 results from the OLS-estimated rate of growth in per capita income of 3.45 per cent, times the 'standardized' income elasticity of 1.901. This standardized value is computed by scaling up the OLS-estimated income elasticity for the period of 0.595 from the historical base income elasticity of 0.313. Thus 0.595/0.313 = 1.901, and 3.45 × 1.901 = 6.56.

Source: Based on Timmer (2004b).

Even in 2002, at least the bottom half of the income distribution had significantly positive Engel elasticities for food energy. This half of the population subsisted on less than US$2 per day (World Bank 2003a, 2003b).

Finally, Table 17.2 carries this inference process to its logical conclusion, by constructing a crude 'index of pro-poor growth'. The scale is somewhat arbitrary, but it is based on an analytical relationship between the overall incidence of poverty and the observed, average income elasticity of demand (see the derivation and proof in Timmer 2004b). The income elasticity of food energy for the entire period from 1880 to 1990, estimated to be 0.313, is used as the long-run base, scaled to 1. It is multiplied by the long-run growth rate in per capita incomes, 0.89 per cent per year, to generate the long-run average Index of Pro-Poor Growth (IPPG) of 0.89. The income elasticity for each separate epoch is then scaled relative to the long-run average, and multiplied by the growth rate in per capita incomes to generate the IPPG for each epoch. Note that *the IPPG incorporates both the growth and the distributional dimensions of pro-poor growth*, and this index is thus a country-specific version of equation 1 in 'Concept paper on operationalizing pro-poor growth' (World Bank 2004).

As shown in Table 17.2, the IPPG has varied dramatically over time, from −2.53 during the 1925–1950 epoch, to 4.57 during the 'ethical policy' era of 1905–1925. The index is surprisingly high during the Sukarno era, when economic policy is widely regarded to have been a disaster. But a combination of a modest recovery from the quarter-century of depression and wars, with average per capita incomes rising 1.5 per cent per year, and a large average income elasticity for food energy, suggest that what growth there was did actually reach the poor.

The strongest pro-poor growth has been from 1965 to 1990. The data analysed in Table 17.2 only carry the story to 1990, well before the Asian financial crisis in 1997/98. The quarter-century from 1965 to 1990 has an IPPG of 6.56, which is more than seven times the long-run average and nearly half again as large as during the next best epoch, from 1905 to 1925. Clearly, something quite outside earlier historical experience was going on during the first two and a half decades of the Suharto era. What made this era so pro-poor?

3.3 The 'New Order' Government of Suharto: Why was Growth so 'Pro-poor'?

In the early years of the Suharto government, pre-OPEC (1966–1973), there was a need to establish stability and consolidate political power. There was an important role for the food logistics agency (Bulog) in stabilizing rice prices, and for donor assistance, especially the provision of food aid. Major investments were made to stimulate agriculture: irrigation rehabilitation, the introduction of high-yielding rice varieties from the International Rice Research Institute (IRRI), fertilizer imports and distribution, and the BIMAS programme of extension and farm credits. Because median farm size was less than 1 ha, rice intensification had widespread benefits, although larger farmers (those who cultivate about 1 ha of land) benefitted the most in the early years (Afiff and Timmer 1971).

Macroeconomic stability was achieved through a balanced budget and donor-provided foreign borrowing, with all proceeds going to the Development Budget (World Bank 1968; Hill 1996). Poverty fell rapidly as the economy stabilized and grew 5–6 per cent per year in per capita terms, and as food production and over-all food supplies rose sharply. Still, absolute poverty was thought to be about 60 per cent in 1970. The first official poverty estimates, based on the 1976 National Socio-Economic Survey (SUSENAS), indicate a national poverty rate of about 40 per cent (see Table 17.3).

Even for an oil exporter, coping with high oil prices (1973–1983) is not the luxury it might seem. There was rapid expansion of the economy as the role of

Table 17.3 Measures of inequality and poverty in Indonesia, 1932–2016

Year	Gini coefficient[a]			Share of the population below the poverty line[b]		
	Rural	Urban	Total	(50 per cent of median)		BPS poverty line
				Indonesia	People (million)	
1932	0.52	0.57	0.56	26.3	16.4	–
1939	0.58	0.53	0.60	–	–	–
						–
1942	0.60	0.53	0.60	27.6	20.0	–
						–
1953	0.51	0.49	0.55	25.4	21.1	–
1959	0.46	0.47	0.51	23.9	22.3	–
						–
1975	0.16	0.31	0.28	9.4	12.2	–
1976	–	–	–	–	–	40.1
1980	0.13	0.27	0.24	5.4	8.0	28.6
1985	0.19	0.20	0.24	5.4	8.9	–
1987	–	–	–	–	–	17.4
1990	0.15	0.20	0.24	6.2	11.1	15.1
1993	0.16	0.27	0.31	10.2	19.1	13.7
1999	0.17	0.23	0.32	11.7	23.9	–
2005	0.16	0.19	0.34	13.3	29.8	16.0
2008	0.12	0.22	0.37	15.4	36.2	15.2
2012	–	–	0.42	–	–	12.0[c]
2014	–	–	0.42	–	–	11.0[c]
2016	–	–	0.38	–	–	10.5[c]

Source: Author's illustration based on: (a) van Leeuwen and Foldvari (2016: 386, table 5); (b) van Leeuwen and Foldvari (2016: 391, table 6); (c) World Bank (2017: 30–1).

the state expanded, but much of this expansion was in inefficient public-sector investments. Accompanying the real appreciation of the rupiah was declining profitability of tradable goods production, especially in agriculture (Warr 1984). During the mid-1970s there was a growing sense of income inequalities and severe poverty in rural areas, although the regional and commodity dimensions of the poverty masked its economic roots.

Table 17.3 shows estimates of income distribution and the share of the population below the poverty line, using data that are from a variety of sources, including from official Indonesian government statistical sources. These historical data provide comparisons of poverty and inequality from several methodological approaches and update the key data to 2016. Further historical data are illustrated at the sectoral level in Figure 17.1, which charts the structural transformation of the economy from 1880–2016.

Income distribution deteriorated sharply between 1976 and 1978, confirming the growing anxieties. The technocrats took a highly original strategic approach to what was then diagnosed as 'Dutch disease', with a devaluation in November 1978 that came as a big surprise to financial markets. After this, tradable goods production rapidly recovered, especially in agriculture. Poverty rates after 1978 fell, driven by a significant recovery in the share of income garnered by the bottom 40 per cent of the distribution (Papanek 2004).[5]

By the early 1980s the oil boom was over. It became necessary to restructure the economy for a world of low commodity prices, which is the basic story from 1983 to 1993. Agriculture continued to grow, and rice prices were stable (this stability amounted to protection against the low prices in world markets). The government pursued aggressive exchange rate protection via further devaluations in 1983 and 1986 (Thorbecke 1995; Hill 1996). Massive investments in rural infrastructure from earlier oil revenues began to pay off in higher production and lower transactions costs for marketed goods (and improved labour mobility). Industrial output surged in the latter part of the period, led by labour-intensive manufactured exports.

The manufacturing sector contributed 29.2 per cent of the growth in GDP between 1987 and 1992, a radical increase from the 10 per cent contributed during the recovery from 1967 to 1973 (Hill 1996, 2000). Large-scale and sustained economic deregulation led to better incentives for exports, and these were matched by incentives for foreign direct investment (FDI). Manufactured exports responded even faster than policymakers had hoped, and contributed almost *half* of all exports by 1992, up dramatically from the 3 per cent in 1980. The fortuitous 'push' in FDI from Japan and the 'pull' from the attractive climate in Indonesia thus allowed manufactured exports to play a significant role in employment generation by the end of the 1980s.

There was also a boom in the non-tradable economy. National income accounts, however, are not kept according to this distinction, hence the data are more impressionistic.[6] Nonetheless, just as the export economy was booming in the late 1980s and early 1990s, and overall GDP was growing by nearly 7 per cent per year, roughly half of that growth was made up of non-tradable goods and services. According to the Mellor model of poverty reduction (Mellor 2000, 2017), production of non-tradable goods and services, especially in rural areas, provides the economic link between higher incomes from both agriculture and

---

[5] A sharp debate, totally confidential, took place in mid-1978 between advisors concerned about 'Dutch disease' and its impact on rural incomes and poverty, who argued for a significant devaluation of the rupiah, and the trade and industry advisors, who argued for a revaluation because of foreign exchange surpluses (Timmer 1994). The devaluation in November 1978 set the exchange rate at Rp 625 per US$, instead of revaluing to what the market expected, Rp 380 per US$.

[6] It is hard to define the components of the non-tradables sector—although some items are obvious, such as local services, construction, and low-quality local manufactured goods with a limited market appeal beyond the immediate vicinity. Even modern industrial goods produced at high cost behind tariff barriers are non-tradable. Obviously, poor transportation facilities lead to high marketing costs, meaning that many potentially tradable goods are non-tradable. Lower transactions costs and lower tariff barriers are among the surest ways to improve competition and market efficiency.

manufacturing wages, and serves to pull people out of underemployment in rural areas—and out of poverty.

The Mellor model stresses the role of producing *rural non-tradables* that are locally consumed—processed foods, construction, trade, and small-scale manufactures—as the 'ladder' for underemployed workers in agriculture to begin the climb to modern jobs at higher wages. *In most poor, rural economies this non-tradable sector is demand-constrained.* That is, expanding it, and the number of jobs it creates, does not depend on better access to capital or to management skills, but on greater purchasing power among local consumers. Thus Mellor emphasizes rising profitability of agriculture—through higher productivity, not higher prices. Higher prices for agricultural output, especially food, do not contribute much to added demand for non-tradable goods and services because the higher food prices choke off demand for non-food items, except from farmers with significant surpluses to sell. The growing wages of workers in a rapidly expanding manufacturing export sector also contribute to higher demand for the output from the non-tradables sector.

This Mellor model is a three-sector version of the standard Lewis model of the dual economy. In Mellor's version there are two 'commercial' sectors—industry and modern agriculture. The latter has come to use modern technology and is market-driven, a departure from the traditional rural economy envisioned by Lewis (1954). Relatively separate from the commercial sectors is the 'non-tradable' sector, which is informal and mostly rural. The two commercial sectors are the 'engines of growth' because of their potential for rapid productivity gains. Connecting them to the 'non-tradable' sector, however, is the key to a high 'elasticity of connection' between overall economic growth and rapid poverty reduction. This is the sector in which most of the poor make a living (Timmer 1997, 2002). *Unless demand from rising incomes in the commercial sectors spills over to this non-tradables sector, the poor tend to be left out of the growth process.*

The combined boom in agriculture, manufacturing, and non-tradables means the period from the late 1970s to the mid-1990s is one of the most 'pro-poor growth' episodes in modern economic history. This result is a surprise to many. The extensive economic restructuring that took place in the 1980s was expected to create widespread unemployment and lead to lower wages for unskilled labour. Instead, agricultural growth continued, labour-intensive exports surged, and poverty continued to decline throughout the period of restructuring (Ravallion and Huppi 1991).[7]

Figure 17.1 provides an illuminating view of the structural dimensions of this growth. AgGDPshr declines steadily as the economy is growing fairly rapidly—about 3.6 per cent per year per capita between 1970 and 2010. But AgEMPshr declines only slowly in the early stages of growth, from 1970 to 1990, and then

[7] It should be noted that the rice sector in particular was protected from the worst pressures of low prices in world markets, and the substantial devaluations in 1983 and 1986 provided enhanced profitability for the rest of the tradable sector, with spillover effects on incomes in the non-tradable sector.

declines quite rapidly as the rural economy is integrated into the dynamic urban economy via better roads, communications, and an educated rural labour force in search of economic opportunities. The rapidly narrowing AgGAPshr after 1990 reflects the falling poverty rates shown in Table 17.3.

Corruption and increasing distortions in resource allocation during 1993–1998 followed the interests of the Suharto family, especially the children (and grand-children!). These interests distorted trade policy and public-sector investments, and had visible effects on competitiveness, which were partly masked by the inflow of FDI (Cole and Slade 1996). As the economy boomed, deregulation lost steam, first in the Bulog commodities, then more broadly. The performance of the overall economy started to suffer, although poverty levels in 1996, the last SUSENAS report before the crisis, dropped to their lowest levels ever. Absolute poverty, measured in a comparable fashion to the poverty statistics reported first in 1976, fell below 12 per cent.

The three decades of superb economic results were over. The Asian financial crisis hit in late 1997. Investors started to lose confidence in the ability of the Suharto government to cope, especially after the new cabinet was named in April 1998, packed with Suharto cronies and relatives. The crisis caused a massive depreciation of the rupiah, eventually leading to chaos in the domestic rice market (Schydlowsky 2000). Spiralling rice prices late in 1998 led to huge increases in poverty, which is estimated to have reached over 30 per cent of the population by late 1998, early 1999. This was a dismal period for economic growth and poverty reduction.

3.4 The 'Democratic Era' (1999–)

After Suharto's surprise resignation in late 1998, Indonesia successfully elected a democratic legislature in 1999, which in turn selected a new president, Abdurrahman Wahid, a popular Islamic scholar and cleric who headed Nahdlatul Ulama (NU), the country's largest Islamic organization. Wahid attempted to reform the military's role in government and was ultimately impeached by parliament for that effort and accompanying corruption scandals. He was replaced by his vice-president, Megawati, the daughter of Sukarno. She served for three years, but was defeated in the election by her former co-ordinating minister for politics and security, Susilo Bambang Yudhoyono.

Representative democracy brought forth a new political economy of economic policy. Populist voices ostensibly spoke on behalf of the poor. With two decades of experience, it remains to be determined whether Indonesia's pro-poor growth experience under a highly centralized and politically dominant regime put down sustainable, even irreversible, roots, or whether the very foundations of the strategy will come undone under political challenge.

It is already clear that the transition from the autocratic rule of Suharto, an era of economic policy designed and administered by an insulated group of skilled technocrats, to a politically responsive system has been difficult for both economic growth and its connection to the poor. There are few public institutions in place to protect economic policy from polemicists.

As part of a broad effort to help Indonesian development, after the fall of Suharto the World Bank led an effort to help the country cope with corruption in the national government. The main vehicle was to promote decentralization of political power (World Bank 2001). Domestic reform groups supported this agenda and responsibility for most local services devolved to *kabupaten* ('county') levels in 2002 in a 'big bang' political decentralization. Not surprisingly, this transfer was made without adequate funding, policy guidelines, or training of local officials (Alm et al. 2001).

Inevitably, perhaps, corruption at the local level has become rampant. Local 'trade' policies are being used to enforce commodity taxes and trade barriers, especially for rice. Partly because of the resulting 'compartmentalism' in the economy, and the higher transactions costs for most economic activities caused by these activities, donor interest and activity have focused on improved local governance. The stakes are high. Ongoing research by the Social Monitoring and Evaluation Research Unit (SMERU) indicates that measures of the 'quality' of local governance were closely associated with the rate of poverty reduction between 1999–2002 (Sumarto et al. 2004).

The country is clearly paying the price for decades of forgone institution building, especially in the arenas of property rights and rule of law. The new democratic governments have found it difficult to make rapid progress in these arenas, although more has been accomplished than many observers credit (MacIntyre 2003; Ramage 2004). The government of Susilo Bambang Yudhoyono (known universally as SBY) (2004–2014) and the current government of Joko Widodo (again, universally known as Jokowi) (2014–) have made significant strides in strengthening transparency in government and addressing corruption.

Their records on economic growth and poverty reduction are respectable but not outstanding relative to regional and historical performance. The data on per capita GDP in Table 17.4 show Indonesia's record of economic growth per capita by political era since 1880. Per capita GDP in constant 2011 US dollars fell by 4.38 per cent per year from 1996 to 1999 during the Asian financial crisis, and then recovered by 3.31 per cent per year from 1999 to 2005. Still, from its peak in 1996, before the crisis, until the previous peak in per capita incomes was restored in 2005, incomes per capita grew just 0.6 per cent per year. It took a long time for democratic governments to figure out how to manage the economy.

By 2005, however, the new SBY government was able to restore investor confidence, both foreign and domestic, and the economy started growing rapidly again. Between 2005 and 2016, per capita GDP grew by 4.59 per cent per year,

Table 17.4 Economic growth in Indonesia, 1880–2016

Year	RGDPNApc (2011 US dollars)	Average annual increase/ decrease (%/year)	Notes on historical era
1880	1,147	0.36	Dutch colonial exploitation
1905	1,255	1.37	Dutch 'ethical policy'
1925	1,648	−0.62	Depression, war, fight for independence
1950	1,410	1.14	Sukarno era
1966	1,690	4.47	Suharto era
1996	6,269	−4.38	Asian financial crisis
1999	5,481	3.31	Fall of Suharto; recovery to previous peak
2005	6,663	4.59	Democracy in command
2016	10,911		

Note: The average annual rate of economic growth from 1996, the peak year before the crisis, and its full recovery nine years later, in 2005, is just 0.6 per cent per year. Maddison Data Project note: 'In addition to the *CGDPpc* series, we provide a measure of growth of GDP per capita that relies on a single cross-country price comparison, for 2011. This series is also expressed in 2011 US dollars (and *CGDPpc* = *RGDPNApc* in 2011), but its defining feature is that it tracks the growth rate of GDP per capita as given in country National Accounts (or their historical reconstructions). Following PWT [Penn World Tables], we refer to this measure of real GDP per capita as *RGDPNApc*. This series is primarily useful for comparing growth rates of GDP per capita over time.'

Source: Author's calculation based on data from the Maddison Data Project (Bolt et al. 2018).

slightly faster than during the thirty years of the Suharto regime (see Table 17.4). But the return to rapid economic growth was not mirrored by changes in poverty. Between 2010 and 2016, the poverty rate only declined from 13.3 per cent to 10.9 per cent. Most other welfare indicators track these statistics on the poverty rate. This is respectable progress, but leaves Indonesia lagging other countries in its region and income category. Economic growth is no longer 'pro-poor'.

4. Political Economy and Governance

The standard story to explain the political economy of the Suharto regime's emphasis on agriculture (and pro-poor growth) relies on conflict between traditional political forces—communist-inspired peasants and workers faced opposition from an authoritarian military (Simpson 2008). Buying off the peasants was cheaper than repression. Rural development was seen as the least-cost approach to political stability. Large-scale ethnic (Chinese) businesses bought protection from Suharto and his military allies and received lucrative import and operating licences in return. When these highly protected businesses, and their closely associated banks, collapsed in the Asian financial crisis the entire regime unravelled. The vacuum of political institutions, deliberately created by Suharto to remove any challenge to his authority, exposed the country to years of political chaos and weak leadership. This standard story suggested there was only modest hope that the presidential election in September 2004, when Megawati ran against SBY, would return the country to strong leadership and rapid, pro-poor growth.

As with most stories based on conventional wisdom, there are substantial elements of truth in this one. But it misses what distinguishes the Suharto regime from otherwise similar military dictatorships around the world: its focus on *development* and the effort to improve the welfare of the poor by connecting the rural economy to rapid economic growth. Fear of radical peasants wielding scythes simply does not explain this passion, or the massive budgetary resources devoted to it. Oil revenues helped, but the basic strategy was already laid down before the OPEC price shock. A more nuanced story is needed, one that includes the complexities of the structure of political power and the role of leadership. The remainder of this chapter attempts to provide some of that nuance by tracing the political economy of poverty through a governance lens to the problems caused by the massive decentralization that was the first priority of the new democratic government.

4.1 The Political Economy of Pro-poor Growth

Political scientists speculate on the nature of the political coalition assembled by Suharto to maintain and strengthen his hold on power. This coalition was held together by the distribution of economic resources, often in the form of lucrative access to such easily marketable commodities as oil or timber. Import licences for rice, wheat, sugar, and soybeans were equally lucrative. Bulog controlled these closely in the interests of the Suharto regime. Whether the pro-poor policies, and results, of the regime were tied to keeping these interest groups satisfied, even at the expense of faster economic growth in the short run, is the subject of active debate, especially because Bulog, despite being 'privatized' in 2003, established close ties with the husband of President Megawati and successfully lobbied for renewal of Bulog's monopoly control over trade in most agricultural commodities. The ability of Bulog to stall the deregulation process in the early 1990s is seen by some observers (including this one) as an early signal that the entire growth process was running off the rails into corrupt and distortionary cronyism. From this perspective, the collapse of the formal sector during the Asian financial crisis was not such a surprise, as it had become increasingly dominated by these interests (Cole and Slade 1998; Stern 2003, 2004).

The most debated political economy aspect of the New Order government was the near-schizophrenia between macro and sectoral policies. What is so puzzling is why macroeconomic policy was left largely in the hands of very talented, but highly apolitical, technocrats. Persuasive arguments are made that they provided access to the donor community, which has been a strong, almost lavish, supporter of Indonesia since the late 1960s (Simpson 2008). But another argument is simply that the technocrats delivered the economic growth the country desperately needed. In a comparison of the political economy of growth in the Philippines and Indonesia, Thorbecke (1995) came to the following conclusion:

> ...the most fundamental difference between the development environments in the two countries relates to the macroeconomic policy management and the role of the technocrats. In Indonesia, the latter followed a consistent, far-sighted, credible, and enlightened macroeconomic policy that was outward-oriented and provided a framework within which both economic growth and poverty alleviation could occur...the key policy instrument that the technocrats relied on was an appropriate exchange rate. Even at the height of the oil boom, when Indonesia was swimming in petro-dollars and was generating large balance-of-payments surpluses, and when the natural inclination would have been to let the rupiah appreciate, instead the technocrats devalued the currency to protect the traditional tradable sectors...and recycled large parts of these windfall profits back into agriculture. This policy contributed substantially to the phenomenal poverty alleviation process in the rural areas that characterized Indonesia in the seventies and eighties.   (Thorbecke 1995: 34–5)

The technocrats had no political base of their own. They depended entirely on their patron, Suharto, to implement their plans and policies. The president was an active participant in every major macroeconomic decision, especially changes in the exchange rate. Widjojo Nitisastro, the acknowledged dean of the technocrats, receives high praise for his ability to manage the economic team and to consolidate their advice when he explained pressing economic issues to the president. His close colleague, Radius Prawiro, makes the following observation:

> ...the economic team were intelligent and dynamic men with no shortage of self-esteem. It was Widjojo, however, who quickly became the unofficial yet acknowledged head of the group. Widjojo was an expert in both demographics and economics. He was a brilliant strategist and a person of vision with a long-term focus. He was an excellent listener and without resorting to domination... Widjojo was able to guide a team comprising many of Indonesia's most capable and influential economists...He kept meetings moving without imposing rigid procedures or formality. Widjojo was a natural leader. Throughout his career, he deliberately kept a low profile and yet if there is anyone who deserves the title of 'architect' of Indonesia's economic development, it is Widjojo.   (Prawiro 1998: 83)

Despite the control of the economic team over macroeconomic policy, with the president's equally clear support and blessing, Suharto used trade policy to protect special interests in his circle and even beyond, sometimes with no more apparent rationale than a nationalist interest to develop a modern industrial capacity. The role of good economic governance and political commitment to poverty reduction is a key lesson here, but the paradox is why the autocratic Suharto regime provided both ingredients for so long, and why the new democratic governments have not.

Part of Suharto's commitment to the rural economy seems to have come from the highly visible politics, and power, of food security. The drive for higher agricultural productivity—a key ingredient in pro-poor growth in the circumstances Indonesia faced during this period—was fuelled in part by the desire for households, and the country, to have more reliable supplies of rice than were available from world markets. When the world rice market quite literally disappeared for several months during the world food crisis in 1973, Indonesia's dependence on imported rice to stabilize domestic prices highlighted its vulnerability to external markets beyond its control—the opposite of food security in the minds of most Indonesians—and showed how important it was to increase rice production (Timmer 2000). A ratcheting up of policy attention to agriculture and budget support for rural infrastructure followed the traumatic loss of control of rice prices in 1972–1973.

From this perspective, the political economy of pro-poor growth since the tumultuous events surrounding the Asian financial crisis seems quite perverse, especially policies with respect to the rice economy which are intended to generate that growth. There is, however, a rationale that explains the new political economy. Behind the Suharto regime's commitment to pro-poor growth were two important constituencies: one that backed economic growth itself; and the other that expressed concern for the poor. The growth coalition was made up of the modernizing elements of the military, the business elite not already comfortably protected by anti-growth protectionist measures, and most of the rural sector, which was near starvation in the mid-1960s.

The voices for the poor included many of this same coalition, but for somewhat different reasons. The military was concerned about rural unrest. It did not have the coercive resources to suppress it by force alone. The Jakarta political elite, led by Suharto, increasingly staked its credibility on political stability. Both the urban and rural poor could pose a threat to that, as the 1974 Malari riots demonstrated.[8] Increasingly, the donor community stressed the importance of poverty reduction. The World Bank made a major commitment in the late-1980s to the analytical work that surfaced in its 1990 report on poverty (World Bank 1990).

The fortuitous intersection of the growth and poverty coalitions thus offered the Suharto regime a political opportunity to do well by doing good. In the context of powerful opportunities to stimulate rapid growth in rural areas through high-payoff investments in rehabilitating irrigation systems and rural infrastructure

---

[8] A major grievance of the student rioters was the loss of control over rice prices in the previous year, and the continuing high prices.

and the importation of new rice technologies, a cumulative process started that built both rapid growth and poverty reduction into the basic dynamics of the Indonesian economy. *But the process started in the agricultural sector.*

This cumulative process appeared to have ended in the early 1980s, as prices for agricultural commodities collapsed in world markets, oil prices declined, and the whole growth process seemed threatened. Fortuitously, again, but under the determined guidance of the technocrats, and with the full support of the president, the economy was restructured to make it more open to foreign trade and investment, just as Japan and Korea came looking for opportunities to invest in labour-intensive manufacturing facilities. Only with the economic and political collapse in 1998 did this source of pro-poor growth disappear (and with it the patron of the technocrats). In its place, a new populist-driven strategy of poverty alleviation has emerged.

The political appeal of the new democratic strategy for dealing with poverty—direct fiscal and food transfers to the poor—is obvious. In principle, these transfers have an immediate and visible impact on the recipients, and the political 'pitch' for the programmes makes it sound as though the government is actively committed to poverty reduction. Although democracy has probably *increased* the size and influence of the political coalition concerned about poverty, it has greatly *undermined* the coalition supporting economic growth as the main mechanism for dealing with it.

In the political rhetoric since 2003, poverty reduction is no longer linked to economic growth. Instead, the agency distributing subsidized rice to the poor, Bulog, has built an 'anti-poverty' political coalition similar to the one that long supported food stamps in the US Congress. Support in the USA came from conservative rural legislators eager to have additional markets for the food that is produced in surplus by their farm constituents and from urban liberals who have in their constituency many poor people who use food stamps as a major source of income.[9]

Similarly, Bulog is the agency that procures rice domestically with budget support from parliament, and distributes this rice to the poor at low prices that are, again, subsidized by the budget. Bulog has mobilized political support from two constituencies concerned with poverty: first, for its rice procurement programme, on the grounds that it helps rice farmers; and second, for its implementation of the 'special market operations' (OPK) programme that delivers subsidized rice to the poor. As Mink (2004) of the World Bank observed, no parliamentarians have been willing to take on both dimensions of the rice programme simultaneously. As a result, the huge budget subsidies that accrue to Bulog to run these programmes, and the corruption that accompanies them, go unchallenged.[10]

---

[9] Political polarization in the USA now threatens this long-standing coalition between rural farm interests and interests determined to help the urban poor.

[10] The most complete historical analysis of the Indonesian experience with direct food deliveries to the poor (originally OPK, but then called RASTRA, and now about to disappear in favour of cash transfers for most recipients) is offered by Timmer et al. (2018).

Rebuilding the economic growth coalition in support of the poor is proving difficult. It depends on the underlying conditions of economic governance—political stability, rule of law, control of corruption, and so on—that moved in the wrong direction for several years after democratic governments were elected. Probably the best that can be done in the short run is to minimize policy damage to the interests *of the poor* while trying to improve the effectiveness of the programmes transferring resources directly *to the poor*.[11]

4.2 Trends in Governance at the National Level

A focus on the quality of governance at the national level is an essential component of any effort to understand, in political economy terms, the historical and emerging patterns of support for pro-poor growth. The poor themselves seldom have a voice in the strategies that influence the growth process, and they rely on government officials to act on their behalf. In addition to its 'voice' on behalf of the poor, governance is now seen as a major factor in the growth process itself. First, such dimensions as government effectiveness and regulatory quality influence growth directly. Second, dimensions such as rule of law and control of corruption influence growth indirectly and in the longer run.

Understanding the quantitative significance of this influence is difficult because the components of governance are hard to measure. Still, measures of voice and accountability improved between 1996 and 2002, and this improvement signalled the switch to reasonably representative democratic government. There have been steep declines, however, in political stability, regulatory quality, and control of corruption (Kaufmann et al. 2003). This deterioration has immediate ramifications for the pace of economic growth, as it affects investment in a direct manner. FDI was negative between 1998 and 2004. A concern is that such poor governance affects the extent to which economic growth actually reaches the poor. That is, governance itself might be a decisive factor influencing *both* dimensions of pro-poor growth performance.[12] There is accumulating evidence of this connection at the regional level. Indonesia conducted a massive decentralization of many governmental functions in 2001. Research has attempted to judge the quality of local governance and its impact on poverty reduction between 1999 and 2002.

---

[11] Early in 2018, the Jokowi government announced significant changes in how the 'rice for the poor' programme would be administered. Most urban poor now receive pre-paid debit cards that can be used to buy essentials in local markets. Direct deliveries are still used in many areas of the Outer Islands where food markets are not well developed.

[12] The analytical effort to measure the components of governance at the national level was sponsored by the World Bank but never officially adopted. Its directors objected to the often-critical characterization of their own countries.

4.3 The Role of Governance at the Regional Level

The experiment with decentralization of government services to the *kabupaten* level presents challenges and opportunities. The challenges are obvious enough, and have stimulated important efforts by the government of Indonesia and its major donors to provide legal guidelines and financial incentives to make the new structure work. The opportunities are equally obvious. Design and implementation of many basic services in health, education, and business regulation are now closer to the people and far more transparent. Whether they become more responsive is the key challenge to democracy.

One opportunity for researchers that stems from the decentralization is the introduction of a great deal of variance into local government activities, which had been precluded by the strong centralization of power during the Suharto regime. With variance comes an opportunity to analyse what works and what does not. Obviously, it is too early to see many systematic effects, but researchers at SMERU have examined initial data to determine if rough measures of the quality of local governance matter for poverty reduction (Sumarto et al. 2004). Perhaps the most interesting result comes from a survey of eighty-seven cities and *kabupatens* for which a research team was able to construct an index of bureaucratic culture at this level. There were four levels: 'disruptive, less conducive, conducive, and very conducive' in fostering the local business environment. None of the districts had a disruptive climate, and twelve were 'less conducive', sixty-one were 'conducive', and fourteen were 'very conducive' (Sumarto et al. 2004: 28).

Using *kabupaten*-level reports from the SUSENAS reports for 1999 and 2002, the researchers then compared the mean level of poverty reduction for each of these categories of local bureaucratic culture. The overall mean level of poverty reduction for all eighty-seven cities and districts was 7.8 per cent between the two years, but it was only 3.4 per cent in the 'less conducive' environments, 7.0 per cent in the 'conducive' environments, and 15.1 per cent in the 'very conducive' environments. Local 'good governance', at least as measured by this index of bureaucratic culture with respect to business climate, is associated with an immediate impact on poverty reduction.

5. Looking Forward to 2045: Optimism or Pessimism?

Much of this chapter has been spent looking backward, trying to understand the historical, and positive, reversal in the fortunes of Indonesia's poor after 1967, and the challenges the poor have faced in the transition from the authoritarian Suharto regime to real democracy. The issue here is to look forward: can the poor place their hope in economic growth guided by democratic governments, or will they need to seek redress through other venues?

First, a brief restatement of the results of the economic and political history of the past fifty years is in order. The declining role of agriculture in the economy and employment is the clearest lesson, especially because Indonesia has used investments in the rural economy and policies to increase financial incentives for the sector as a way to connect poor households to rapid economic growth. A significantly reduced agricultural sector, in relative terms vis-à-vis labour force and GDP contributions, removes a number of policy instruments to help the rural poor (see Figure 17.1 for a graphical depiction of the declining share of agriculture in both employment and GDP).

These historical lessons are interesting, but the most important reason for spending the time and energy to understand the, often paradoxical, record is to offer useful insights into the future. In particular, how do democratic governments move forward on an agenda of pro-poor growth?

Press reports out of Indonesia were not encouraging after the Asian financial crisis in 1997/8 and Suharto's decision to resign in mid-1998. The country had been through a historic drought. Only imports of six million metric tonnes of rice in 1997/8—20 per cent of consumption—kept per capita supplies at their trend level. The Asian financial crisis swept Indonesia in its fullest fury. The dominant political regime, which had spent thirty years building a support structure to ensure its continued survival, collapsed. When that structure collapsed, it seemed that there was nothing. But in fact the Suharto government had left a legacy of political involvement on the part of the entire population. Every five years, elections were held for members of parliament, who subsequently elected the president. No serious doubts existed about the ultimate outcome of these elections, but they were taken very seriously by the government. Jakarta routinely voted against the government, as did Aceh in Northern Sumatra. High-level officials in the government were tasked to ask 'why?' What was the government doing wrong? The end result was a population that was used to voting, and counting on their votes being heard. When Suharto stepped down in mid-1998, general elections were called to elect a new parliament. It was empowered to name a new president.

The question remains: how does a society cope with three such massive shocks in the span of just a year? If 1966, in the famous words of President Sukarno, was 'the year of living dangerously', what was 1998? The quiet answer, in retrospect, is 'the year of transformation to a freer and fairer society'. This is not the stuff of headlines. The headline grabbers are the Bali and Marriott bombings, judicial ineptitude and outright corruption, human rights abuses by the military, and continuing games played by Jakarta's political elite (McBeth 2003). Little noticed is the steady progress that is being made. If occasional jabs at foreign companies by local courts still roil investors, the clear competence of the new constitutional court is unreported. The petty (and not so petty) corruption of newly empowered local governments makes news and is troublesome. But the open competition to create good business environments at the local level will probably have more long-term impact (Ramage 2004).

Amid the gloom and doom, the historical resilience and successes of Indonesian society need to be appreciated. From a long-run perspective, the Indonesian experience with pro-poor growth provides genuine hope that desperately poor societies can escape from the worst manifestations of poverty in a generation, provided appropriate policies are followed. Much of East and Southeast Asia provide evidence for the reality of this hope. This is a direct challenge to Myrdal's pessimism. This is also a critically important message for the Indonesia of the future, unsure as it is over what path to follow under democratic governments. In its broadest outlines, that path is clear. The three-tiered strategy of growth-oriented macroeconomic policy, linked to product and factor markets through progressively lower transactions costs, which in turn are linked to poor households whose capabilities are being increased by public investments in human capital, is a general model accessible to all countries, including the future Indonesia (Timmer 2004a).

Investments in infrastructure and human capital are at the heart of the public-sector dimensions of this model, and the Jokowi government clearly recognizes this (*The Economist* 2018). The pace of investments in infrastructure to lower transactions costs and in human capital to improve the capabilities of the poor depends on the country's ability to generate public revenues and incentives for private participation (World Bank 2017). A fairer and more effective form of public taxation is essential if the new government is to make these investments. The design of these pro-poor mechanisms of public finance is urgent, because foreign resources, from donors and foreign consumers of petroleum, are becoming less available, although FDI could increase substantially with the right policies in place. There is no escaping the hard fact that these resources dictate not only the pace of economic growth but also the extent to which that growth reaches the poor. With the right pro-poor growth model in place, continued foreign assistance and private investment could have a very high payoff in both dimensions.

Indonesia's success from 1967 to 1997 did not just happen as the accident of market forces. It was planned, nurtured, and largely financed by a government intent on rapidly reducing poverty. Although Myrdal was pessimistic in the late 1960s that such a 'developmental state' could emerge in Indonesia, he likely would have agreed that the authoritarian Suharto government did what was necessary for economic success and rapid poverty reduction. Democratic governments with similar commitment can do the same in the future.

Acknowledgements

I would like to thank Deepak Nayyar for extremely helpful guidance as we went through several iterations of this chapter. I also acknowledge comments from other authors in this project, although I was not able to cope with all of them. Mistakes and opinions remain my own.

References

Afiff, S., and C.P. Timmer (1971). 'Rice Policy in Indonesia', *Food Research Institute Studies in Agricultural Economics, Trade, and Development*, 10(2): 131–59.

Alm, J., R.H. Aten, and R. Bahl (2001). 'Can Indonesia Decentralize Successfully?', *Bulletin of Indonesian Economic Studies*, 37(1): 83–102.

Boeke, J.H. (1946). *The Evolution of the Netherlands Indies Economy*. New York: Institute of Pacific Relations.

Bolt, J., R. Inklaar, H. de Jong, and J.L. van Zanden (2018). 'Rebasing "Maddison": New Income Comparisons and the Shape of Long-Run Economic Development', University of Groningen, Groningen, GGDC Research Memorandum 174.

Booth, A. (2016). *Economic Change in Modern Indonesia*. Cambridge: Cambridge University Press.

Cole, D.C., and B.F. Slade (1996). *Building a Modern Financial System*. Melbourne: Cambridge University Press.

Cole, D.C., and B.F. Slade (1998). 'Why has Indonesia's Financial Crisis been so Bad?', *Bulletin of Indonesian Economic Studies*, 34(2): 61–6.

Gardner, B.L. (2002). *American Agriculture in the Twentieth Century*. Cambridge, MA: Harvard University Press.

Hill, H. (1996). *The Indonesian Economy since 1966*. Cambridge: Cambridge University Press.

Hill, H. (2000). *The Indonesian Economy since 1966* (2nd edn). Cambridge: Cambridge University Press.

Kaufmann, D., A. Kraay, and M. Mastruzzi (2003). 'Governance Matters III: Governance Indicators for 1996–2002', World Bank, Washington, DC, Working Paper.

Lewis, W.A. (1954). 'Economic Development with Unlimited Supplies of Labor', *The Manchester School*, 22: 3–42.

MacIntyre, A. (2003). *Indonesia as a Poorly Performing State?* Canberra: Australian National University.

McBeth, J. (2003). 'Leadership: The Betrayal of Indonesia', *Far Eastern Economic Review*. Cover story, 26 June.

Mellor, J.W. (2000). 'Agricultural Growth, Rural Employment, and Poverty Reduction', Paper for World Bank Rural Week 2000, March.

Mellor, J.W. (2017). *Agricultural Development and Economic Transformation*. Basingstoke: Palgrave Macmillan.

Mink, S. (2004). 'Comments on Presentation by Jorge Garcia-Garcia on the Costs and Benefits of Bulog's Commodity Interventions from 1993 to 1998', World Bank, Washington, DC.

Myrdal, G. (1968). *Asian Drama: An Inquiry into the Poverty of Countries*. New Delhi: Kalyani Publishers.

Papanek, G. (2004). 'The Poor During Economic Decline, Rapid Growth and Crisis'. Paper for USAID Project on Pro-Poor Growth conducted by DAI and BIDE.

Prawiro, R. (1998). *Indonesia's Struggle for Economic Development*. Kuala Lumpur: Oxford University Press.

Ramage, D. (2004). 'The Political Dynamics of Indonesia's Elections', Presentation, Asia Society and US Indonesian Association (USINDO), 29 April.

Ravallion, M., and M. Huppi (1991). 'Measuring Changes in Poverty', *World Bank Economic Review*, 5(1): 57–82.

Schydlowsky, D.M. (2000). *Misperceived Corporate Exchange Risk and Hyperinflation in Indonesia 1998–99*. Washington, DC: American University and Boston Institute of Developing Economies.

Simpson, B.R. (2008). *Economists with Guns*. Stanford, CA: Stanford University Press.

Stern, J.J. (2003). 'The Rise and Fall of the Indonesian Economy', Harvard University, Cambridge, MA, CID Working Paper 100.

Stern, J.J. (2004). 'The Impact of the Crisis: Decline and Recovery'. Harvard University, Cambridge, MA, CID Working Paper 103.

Sumarto, S., A. Suryhadi, and A. Arifianto (2004). 'Governance and Poverty Reduction', SMERU Research Institute, Jakarta, Working Paper.

The Economist (2018). 'The Hard-Hat President', 5 May, p. 39.

Thorbecke, E. (1995). 'The Political Economy of Development: Indonesia and the Philippines', Frank H. Golay Memorial Lecture, Southeast Asia Program, Cornell University, Ithaca, NY.

Timmer, C.P. (1975). 'The Political Economy of Rice in Asia', *Food Research Institute Studies*, 14(3): 197–231.

Timmer, C.P. (1994). 'Dutch Disease and Agriculture in Indonesia', Harvard Institute for International Development, Cambridge, MA, HIID Development Discussion Paper 490.

Timmer, C.P. (1996). 'Economic Growth and Poverty Alleviation in Indonesia'. In R.A. Goldberg (ed.) *Research in Domestic and International Agribusiness Management, Volume 12*. Greenwich, CT: JAI Press.

Timmer, C.P. (1997). 'How Well do the Poor Connect to the Growth Process?', Harvard Institute for International Development, Cambridge, MA, CAER II Discussion Paper.

Timmer, C.P. (2000). 'The Macro Dimensions of Food Security', *Food Policy*, 25: 283–95.

Timmer, C.P. (2002). 'Agriculture and Economic Growth'. In B. Gardner and G. Rausser (eds) *The Handbook of Agricultural Economics, Volume II*. Amsterdam: North-Holland.

Timmer, C.P. (2004a). 'The Road to Pro-Poor Growth', *Bulletin of Indonesian Economic Studies*, 40(2): 173–203.

Timmer, C.P. (2004b). 'Indonesia Country Study', World Bank Project on Operationalizing Pro-Poor Growth, World Bank, Washington, DC.

Timmer, C.P. (2015). 'Managing Structural Transformation', 18th Annual WIDER Lecture. WIDER, Helsinki.

Timmer, C.P. (2017). 'The Structural Transformation in Japan, Indonesia and Malaysia from 1880 to 2010'. Available at: http://www.ehm.my/publications/articles/the-structural-transformation-in-japan-indonesia-and-malaysia-from-1880-to-2010-part-1-data-and-trends.

Timmer, C.P., and S. Akkus (2008). 'The Structural Transformation as a Pathway out of Poverty', Center for Global Development, Washington, DC, Working Paper 150.

Timmer, C.P., H. Hastuti, and S. Sumarto (2018). 'Evolution and Implementation of the Rastra Program in Indonesia'. In H. Alderman, U. Gentilini, and R. Yemtsov (eds) *The 1.5 Billion People Question*. Washington, DC: World Bank.

van Leeuwen, B., and P. Foldvari (2016). 'The Development of Inequality and Poverty in Indonesia, 1932–2008', *Bulletin of Indonesian Economic Studies*, 52(3): 379–402.

van der Eng, P. (1993a). *Agricultural Growth in Indonesia since 1880*. Groningen: Rijksuniversiteit Groningen.

van der Eng, P. (1993b). 'Food Consumption and the Standard of Living in Indonesia, 1880–1990', Australian National University, Canberra, Economics Division Working Papers Southeast Asia 93/1.

van der Eng, P. (2000). 'Food for Thought', *Journal of Interdisciplinary History*, 30(4): 591–616.

van der Eng, P. (2002). 'Indonesia's Growth Performance in the Twentieth Century'. In A. Maddison, D.S. Prasada Rao, and W.F. Shepherd (eds) *The Asian Economies in the Twentieth Century*. Aldershot: Edward Elgar.

Warr, P.G. (1984). 'Exchange Rate Protection in Indonesia', *Bulletin of Indonesian Economic Studies*, 20(2): 53–89.

World Bank (1968). *Economic Development in Indonesia*. Jakarta: World Bank.

World Bank (1990). *Indonesia: Strategy for a Sustained Reduction in Poverty*. Washington, DC: World Bank.

World Bank (2001). *Indonesia: Poverty Reduction in Indonesia*. Washington, DC: World Bank.

World Bank (2003a). *Indonesia: Beyond Macro-Economic Stability*. Washington, DC: World Bank.

World Bank (2003b). *Indonesia: Country Assistance Strategy, FY 2004–2007*. Jakarta: World Bank.

World Bank (2004). 'Concept Paper on Operationalizing Pro-Poor Growth', mimeo, World Bank, Washington, DC.

World Bank (2017). *Indonesia Economic Quarterly. October*. Washington, DC and Jakarta: World Bank.

18

Vietnam

Finn Tarp

1. Introduction

When Gunnar Myrdal's *Asian Drama: An Inquiry into the Poverty of Nations* was published in 1968, Vietnam was in the middle of a devastating war. The United States (US) had escalated her military involvement drastically during the previous years as *Asian Drama* was written, and whatever data were available for socio-economic analysis were extremely poor. Importantly, *Asian Drama* contains a series of pointed observations on the nature and wide-ranging consequences of French colonial domination from the early 1860s to 1954 and the associated severe exploitation of the country. Moreover, US action in Vietnam is character-ized as 'awkward', '...in the name of democracy the Vietnamese should be pre-vented from following their own will' (Myrdal 1968: 399).

Accordingly, while little could be done in the mid-1960s to forecast future political and socio-economic developments in Vietnam in any meaningful way, it does in retrospect strike the reader's eye that Myrdal observed: 'The Vietnamese were by far the most numerous and most cultured of the Indo-Chinese people and it was from them, with their age-long tradition of opposition to Chinese invaders, that early resistance to French rule emerged' (1968: 170). Determination, unity, and willingness to experiment and recognize failure within the country's leadership came to play a critical role in Vietnam's subsequent economic history and development process. *Asian Drama* also highlights that:

> The French intransigently discouraged even moderate nationalists, and then wreaked terrible vengeance on the innocent and guilty alike when violent agitation and conspiratorial activity became the customary mode of political expression...The predictable consequences of this stern policy of repression was to leave the underground Communist Party in the forefront of the Vietnamese struggle for independence.   (Myrdal 1968: 171)

Struggle was certainly to continue as the Vietnamese went on to resist the world's largest military power; and the Vietnamese Dragon initially took a very costly path to post-war reconstruction and development after peace from 1976 where much went wrong. At the same time, few would now dispute that Vietnam did eventually rise from the ashes in a most respectable manner. Gross domestic product (GDP) per capita rose from US$231 in 1985 to US$2,171 in 2016.

This chapter aims to provide an up-to-date country study, which sets out an analytical narrative of the Vietnamese development experience over the past five decades. The story begins with historical background in section 2, and then moves on to the war period until 1975, the subsequent decade guided by the Second and Third Five-Year Plans (1976–1980 and 1981–1985), and a summary of initial conditions in place in 1986. Moving on from history, section 3 outlines the process of economic growth, structural transformation, and rural change from 1986 onwards; while sections 4 and 5 discuss, respectively, the phased transition from planning to markets, and key themes associated with economic openness. Section 6 reviews what was achieved in human development; and section 7 concludes, relating back to *Asian Drama* and reflecting on future prospects and challenges for this dynamic Southeast Asian economy with an unusual history.

The overall narrative is linked together by an effort to identify turning points in economic strategies, policies, and performance, situated in the wider context of polity and society, with focus on the role of history, policymaking, state interventions, and socio-economic performance. The essential insight—or development lesson—is that gradualism and prudence in managing the process of economic change in a centralized yet responsive political system—whether speed or sequence—combined with embedded history are at the foundation of Vietnam's success.

2. History

2.1 Pre-reunification

Myrdal notes that the social structure of the Vietnamese society traditionally based on land ownership remained essentially unchanged under French rule. Overall, some 82 per cent of the economically active population derived their livelihood from traditional, exceedingly low-productivity, village-based subsistence agriculture in the mid-1950s, and only 8 per cent of the population was urban in 1950 (see Myrdal 1968: 427, 467, 494). The level of human development was extraordinarily low, landlessness extreme, and the Vietnamese were generally excluded from more modern sectors of the economy. Colonial rule also brought French-style institutions to support an exploitative production system. While the French imported cheap raw materials from Vietnam they exported tariff-protected industrial products the other way. It is no surprise that 'from this type of colonial domination the emergence of a substantial Westernized upper class was hardly to be expected' (Myrdal 1968: 170).

During the Second World War, where Vietnam was occupied by the Japanese, the Viet Minh was founded by Ho Chi Minh in 1941 as a nationalist independence movement. It quickly established itself as the only organized movement opposing the Japanese, and after the end of the Second World War it started 'a radical land reform by distributing land to the tenants in the part of the country they had gotten control of in their fight against the French' (Myrdal 1968: 1316). As Viet Minh was trying to respond to the underlying land conflicts, negotiations with the French failed, and a decade-long war known as the First Indochina (or French) War (1945–1954) followed. It ended with French defeat at Dien Bien Phu and the Geneva conference in 1954 that divided the country into North and South Vietnam.

In the North, Viet Minh took over the civil administration in early October 1954 and Ho Chi Minh became President of North Vietnam, established as a socialist state led by the Vietnam Workers' Party that changed its name to the Communist Party of Vietnam (CPV) at the Fourth Party Congress in 1976, and with Hanoi as capital. In the non-communist South, Ngo Dinh Diem assumed control based in Saigon. Yet, Viet Minh cadres remained active and fought the Diem government with support from the North. Myrdal notes that '...many tenants who had obtained land free under the Viet Minh, lost it again or had to pay rent and even back rent or compensation', and he goes on to point out that 'this contributed to the rebellion against the Saigon government that started in 1956 and it is one of the powerful undertones to the present conflict' (1968: 1316). The conflict just referred to was the Second Indochina War (1954–1975), also known as the American War or the Vietnam War. It forms a crucial part of world history in the twentieth century and ended with US defeat and withdrawal. Viet Cong captured Saigon on 30 April 1975, and after national elections on 2 July 1976, reunification of North and South Vietnam took place. The Socialist Republic of Vietnam was formed under the leadership of the CPV, and the CPV remains firmly in control and, since 1988, is the only legal political party in Vietnam.

The 1954–1975 war brought gigantic destruction on top of French colonial exploitation, and the human and economic costs of the conflict went very deep. Production and the vast majority of the labour force had been squarely focused on the wartime effort; and human casualties and injuries were immense (see Rummel 1998; Obermeyer et al. 2008). Out-migration of more than 1 million people, who fled after reunification, and the imprisonment of large numbers of former associates of the government of South Vietnam in re-education camps, formed a ruthless part of the initial post-war state of affairs. The professional and entrepreneurial classes in the South were decimated and private ownership was abolished.

2.2 Post-reunification, 1976–1985

The task of unifying a fractured economy and people in what was in 1975 one of the poorest countries in the world can only be characterized as daunting. The prevailing ideology at the time led to the adoption of a heavily centralized, socialist-inspired command-type approach to economic policy and management for the whole of Vietnam, with very ambitious goals. While the command-type model was already established in the North and had indeed worked well under wartime conditions, it marked a radical as well as risky change in economic organization in the South; especially when recalling earlier land conflicts. The way forward, including an emphasis on restoring infrastructure, building heavy industry, and promoting state ownership and entrepreneurship, was to be mapped out in five-year development plans; and in spite of the difficulties faced, ambitions were high and self-confidence pronounced. Building a unified socialist economy in Vietnam was to be achieved in a mere two decades! And the Fourth National Congress was united in the vision adopted. Notably, while the Second Five-Year Plan for 1976–1980 aimed at unifying the shattered (although markedly different) economies of the North and South in one socialist system, no role was permitted for market prices, private trade, and individual entrepreneurship. The plan also set ambitious goals for economic development including a 13 to 14 per cent aggregate annual growth rate. It was soon to become evident that the model was not working.

There was real GDP growth in Vietnam in the early 1970s, after which growth first spiked from a very low level as peace set in and then went on to drop badly in the later years of the Second Plan. While agricultural crop production, then dominated by village collectives, did not collapse outright from its already very low wartime level, production was extremely volatile from one year to the next. Severe food shortages were quickly experienced as a consequence, and in light of pent-up needs. Food-rationing was reintroduced, and Vietnam had to rely on large amounts of food aid support from the World Food Programme and on financial and material support from the former Soviet Union and the Eastern European countries (see *ReliefWeb* 2000).

In sum, the Vietnamese economy was plagued by serious structural constraints and policy failures at the end of the Second Five-Year Plan. Aggregate growth turned negative and agricultural crop production did not recover from wartime lows. In any case, individual land ownership was abolished in 1980 in the whole country in line with the policies of the socialist transformation that had been promoted in North Vietnam after the adoption of the 1959 Constitution. This course of action was taken even if the collectivized production sector was clearly inefficient. In addition, unemployment was high, and there were material and technological shortfalls alongside the serious deficits in food and consumer goods supply.

Far from dynamic economic progress and transformation from an extremely low wartime base in a context of high expectations, central planning was yielding stagnation, and the role of the state continued to be paramount. Heavy state-led industrialization was prioritized in government budget allocations and in international collaboration (with foreign assistance flowing in from socialist partners including China, the Soviet Union, and Eastern Europe as discussed in section 5). Some industrial growth did take place but at a very high cost, and the industrial sector was in any case too small to have any impact on overall economic performance and living standards in the short term where food supply was the overriding concern.[1] The Vietnamese intervention in Cambodia in late 1978 added international isolation and even a Chinese attack along the northern border in early 1979 to the challenges faced.

Cognisant of the failures of the Second Five-Year Plan, the CPV adopted a somewhat more gradual planning approach during the next five-year period (1981–1985). The government presented plans for one year at a time, and policy nuances were introduced in response to policy experimentation at the local level referred to as 'fence breaking' by Rama (2008).[2] Industrial policy started stressing development of small-scale industry to provide goods for domestic markets and export and to support heavy industry. Some room was also allowed for free enterprise activity; in agriculture policy started encouraging the 'family economy' in which family units instead of collectives were responsible for farming. In parallel, it was the stated aim to improve crop production by intensive cultivation, crop specialization, and employing advanced technologies.

As experimentation, learning, and policy dialogue was going on both inside the CPV and in the public more widely during the first half of the 1980s, shortfalls had become endemic, and the country continued to experience high poverty and unemployment rates. In addition to unemployment, underemployment was high; inflation exploded, and the current account was in persistent deficit. The wide-ranging nature of the crisis was manifest, and conditions were ripe for initiating a response in the form of a comprehensive reform programme.

3. Economic Growth, Structural Transformation, and Rural Change from 1986

The Sixth National Congress of the CPV in December 1986 adopted the *Doi Moi* 'renovation' programme that had been in the making. *Doi Moi* was a far-reaching and comprehensive set of policy moves, and in its adoption the CPV recognized that serious policy shortcomings and mistakes had been made and that they were responsible for Vietnam's economic disappointments. A five-point action plan was issued, and Vo Van Kiet (later to become prime minister during the 1990s) delivered the Economic Report to the Congress. He highlighted that the production of grain and food products would be the main objective of the Fourth Five-Year Plan; that material incentives and end-product contracts would play a

---

[1] See McKay and Tarp (2015) for a more recent account of how this concern has influenced policy-making in Vietnam for decades.

[2] Rama (2008: 15–16) highlights that 'Fence breaking experiments in agriculture mainly involved allocating land to farmers and directly contracting with them at prices above those set by the plan', and that these experiments involved fairly high-level local leaders, who had in common that they were seen as ' "bullet proof", given their track records during the wars'. See also Thanh (2011).

prominent role; and that the export of agricultural products would be emphasized as would FDI (see Thayer 1987: 15–16). All in all, a set of quite remarkable policy initiatives, designed to promote the establishment of a socialist-oriented market economy, not so dissimilar to what was happening in other socialist economies at the time. The party leadership had, in the formulation of Rama (2008: 18), first tolerated, then embraced, and finally scaled up 'fence breaking'. A multitude of practical measures and steps was subsequently taken in the rural sector including prominently the liberalization of the price of rice, the phasing out of agricultural co-operatives, and the redistribution of agricultural land to peasants (while keeping in place restrictions on the use of the land for rice production) (see Markussen et al. 2011). Concerted programmes for development of agricultural technology and inputs were also initiated. Of particular note, the land reform initiative was implemented in a remarkably egalitarian manner that came to serve Vietnam well in the coming decades (see Ravallion and van de Walle 2008).[3]

Economic growth reacted quickly to the *Doi Moi* reforms and has remained high, and also relatively stable, ever since. Very significant progress in the level of real GDP per capita was achieved over the years. Inflation got under control, and savings and investment increased considerably.[4] While investment was driven initially by state investment, domestic credit to the private sector was expanded fast as well. Moreover, even if private consumption as a share of GDP soon started falling to a level around 60 per cent, absolute increases in household consumption were impressive. Agricultural output also responded soon after *Doi Moi*. Crop production expanded quickly, and growth has remained positive. Importantly, the politically sensitive food deficit started declining quite significantly, alongside the substantial drop in undernourishment of the Vietnamese population. A major reason behind this progress lies in the phenomenal progress in rice production. In a short span of years, Vietnam turned herself into a major producer and exporter of rice and other agricultural products, from having depended heavily on significant amounts of food imports.

Looking at sector shares of value-added and total employment (see Tarp 2018), it becomes immediately clear that Vietnam is a case of successful structural transformation. Workers have over the past three decades gradually migrated to urban areas and have been employed there. In contrast to the strict traditional Lewis (1954) dual-sector model, agriculture was by no means ignored in *Doi Moi*. In fact, agriculture was very much at the core and was actively supported by state co-ordinated support measures. Consequently, and importantly for the process of

---

[3] More recently, attention has shifted to the efficiency costs associated with operating the large number of plots that individual households were allocated, and consolidation of fragmented plots is presently a priority on the policy agenda. See Khai et al. (2013) for background on farmers' access to land and land transactions.

[4] For a study on rural household savings, social capital, and network effects, see Newman et al. (2014); on formal and informal credit, see Barslund and Tarp (2008).

structural transformation, agriculture has grown substantially in absolute terms.[5] In sum, the general economic transformation story that emerges from Vietnam includes a combination of labour moving out of agriculture to be absorbed in expanding higher value-added industry and services sectors. This implies that structural change contributed to aggregate growth over and above the impact from high levels of investment and technical change.[6] At the same time, significant changes took place in rural organization and life (see Tarp 2017).[7]

The CPV National Congresses have, from 1991 onwards, maintained a strong focus on the continued shift towards a more market-oriented rural economy and an enhanced role of the private sector, while at the same time stressing state control and co-ordination as fundamental characteristics of the Vietnamese economy and society. Goals and strategies continue to be articulated in five-year plans, which play an important role in resource allocation. As regards macroeconomic and rural sector policies, they have in general been focused on very ambitious investment and infrastructure development programmes (across the whole economy), and countercyclical measures have on many occasions been taken. Vietnam managed the 1997 East Asian financial crisis and 2007–2008 financial crisis and its aftermaths much better than other countries. This was achieved through a combination of substantial fiscal stimulus and keeping in place controls of capital movements.[8] In spite of the occasional instability, macroeconomic management has over the years been solid. Growth versus inflation aims has been balanced while responding to severe external shocks (in particular the global financial crises) and generally holding to the objectives of growth and poverty reduction.

4. From Planning to Markets: Increasing SOE Autonomy and Fostering Entrepreneurship

State-owned enterprises (SOEs) were central to the pre-*Doi Moi* reconstruction and industrialization drives in North Vietnam, and from 1975, in the whole of

---

[5] The Vietnamese structural transformation process may therefore be said to be better captured by the Ranis and Fei (1961) two-sector model formulation than Lewis's (1954) original formulation.

[6] McCaig and Pavcnik (2013) conclude that structural change accounted for a third of the growth in aggregate labour productivity. Abbott et al. (2017) argue that a significant part of growth originated from technological change that benefitted agriculture as well. For the importance of industry switching firms for productivity change, see Newman et al. (2013); for industry agglomeration, see Howard et al. (2016).

[7] For detailed panel data studies on the development of the rural sector in Vietnam since 2002, see also UNU-WIDER (2018). A recent book is Tarp (2017) on structural transformation, and two recent papers are Markussen et al. (2017) on happiness, and Newman et al. (2015a) on property rights; but there are many more studies such as Markussen and Tarp (2014) on political connections and investment in land. Also, detailed bi-annual research reports are available from 2006 on the characteristics of the Vietnamese rural economy (see Ayala-cantu et al. 2017).

[8] See Abbott and Tarp (2012) and Thurlow et al. (2011) for detailed studies.

Vietnam. Heavy industry was prioritized in government budget allocations within the planned economy framework; market prices had no role to play; private trade was not recognized; and the role of the SOEs was restricted to implementing plans and achieving production targets decided on and passed down from central levels. No company law existed, and all industrial and service firms were in principle to be brought under state ownership and management. This created obvious disruptions in the South, where drastic nationalization efforts were taken after reunification;[9] but in spite of the fact that none of the industry targets set for the 1976–1980 Five-Year Plan were met,[10] state ownership was pushed forward, and in 1986 SOEs accounted for 40 per cent of GDP (Frank 2013: 2). SOEs were given more flexibility in decision-making and planning in the 1981–1985 plan and from 1986 *Doi Moi* included a series of further important steps to gradually give the SOEs autonomy. Detailed targets were reduced to broader socio-economic guidelines; price controls for consumer goods were abolished; and industrial production was to focus on food, consumer goods, and exports. At the same time government subsidies were significantly reduced. This forced SOEs to become more self-reliant. It also brought out in the open their lack of efficiency and that many were loss-making entities. From the early 1990s this led to the liquidation of many SOEs across the economy. The total number of SOEs fell drastically (see Ngu 2002: 7; Thanh 2011: 5). In contrast, the number of private small and medium-sized enterprises (SMEs) started growing.[11]

The somewhat tentative changes during the 1990s were to accelerate drastically after the Enterprise Law was enacted in 1999 (National Assembly 1999). It made it easier for private enterprises to enter and operate. Nguyen et al. (2016, 2014) document the industry sector changes in detail, including both the continued drop in SOE numbers and that the number of private sector firms (including both industrial and service sector firms) shot up to over 200,000 by 2006. Other telling data is that the number of micro firms with fewer than ten employees increased their employment share from 22.4 per cent in 2002 to 44.7 per cent a decade later. Manufacturing accounted for more than 80 per cent of industrial activity, and annual industrial sector growth was generally around 15 per cent with far lower growth rates in SOEs in the first decade of the 2000s. Service sector developments were quite similar, and in 2005 over half of Vietnam's enterprises were in services, with the highest percentage being in wholesale and retail commerce. The vast majority of very small and small enterprises were in services, with wholesale and retail trade having three-quarters of the enterprises with fewer than five

[9] Ngu (2002) reports that by early 1978 a total of 1,500 private enterprises in the South, with 70 per cent of privately employed workers, had been converted into 650 SOEs.
[10] For example, Ngu (2002: 4) notes target achievement rates of 32 per cent, 21 per cent, and 24 per cent for cement, steel, and chemical fertilizers, respectively.
[11] Further comments on the foreign-invested companies, which were allowed entry after the 1987 Law on Foreign Investment, and which form a critically important part of the changed enterprise landscape in Vietnam, are made in section 5.

employees (see UNDP 2005: 10). An impressive part of the services sector development has been the very rapid expansion of the tourism sub-sector, which in 2015 accounted for 13.9 per cent of GDP, more than 11 per cent of total employment, and 5.6 per cent of exports (*Voice of Vietnam Online* 2016).

Over the past decade, the above developments have been intensified through a vast number of further legal and economic policy steps. One highlight is the 2005 Enterprise Law that unified the legal foundation for all enterprise types (i.e., SOEs, FDIs, and private firms) to create a level playing field for their operations. The shift away from a completely state-dominated economy to one where the private sector and foreign invested firms tower was very distinct.[12] Moreover, the developments over the last couple of years where available statistics are less systematic, confirm that these trends continue (see *Nhân Dân* 2018). For example, the government has announced further ambitious SOE divestment and restructuring plans for the period until 2020; meanwhile, the number of private SMEs continued to grow with around 100,000 new firms in 2016 (see *Vietnam Briefing* 2017).[13] In conclusion, and looking ahead, it merits stressing that while labour value-added in agriculture and services has generally been on an upward trend, this is not the case for industry. Although the rapid expansion and greater absorption of labour in industry is clearly welcome,[14] this point has attracted considerable attention in the domestic policy debate in Vietnam, and we shall revert to this topic in section 7.

5. Openness: Aid, Trade, and FDI

Turning to the role of foreign aid in the Vietnam development experience, it merits recalling that North Vietnam received significant financial and technical support from the USSR and China before reunification, and that from 1954 onwards South Vietnam became heavily dependent on foreign aid from the US, in particular. After reunification, foreign aid continued to flow in, though amounts are not known in detail. Cima (1987: 150–1) estimates that the Soviet Union, China, and Eastern Europe provided foreign assistance during the Second

---

[12] Eckardt et al. (2018) stress that foreign companies include major global players such as Samsung, Intel, and LG, and that they are primarily active in export-oriented, labour-intensive manufacturing.

[13] For detailed panel data studies on the development of the SME non-state manufacturing sector in Vietnam since 2005, see UNU-WIDER (2018). The two most recent papers are Calza et al. (2019) on drivers of productivity in SMEs and Sharma and Tarp (2018) on managerial personality; but there are many more studies of interest, such as Hansen et al. (2009) on whether government support matters, Rand and Tarp (2011) on gender as well as corruption issues in Vietnamese SMEs, and Howard et al. (2016) on industry agglomeration. Detailed bi-annual research reports are also available on the characteristics of the Vietnamese business environment (see Brandt et al. 2016).

[14] Eckardt et al. (2018) note that manufacturing added an estimated 1.5 million new manufacturing jobs in Vietnam between 2014 and 2016 alone.

Five-Year Plan from 1976–1980 worth US$3–4 billion, whereas Western aid amounted to roughly US$1–1.5 billion.[15] Cima paints the following picture:

> In the late 1970s, Vietnam relied heavily on economic assistance from both Western and Soviet-bloc donors to finance major development projects. [However, following Vietnam's membership of the Council for Mutual Economic Assistance (Comecon) and the associated] closer ties with the Soviet Union, its incursion into Cambodia in December 1978, and its border fighting with China in early 1979, aid from China and from Western countries and multilateral organizations dropped … Aid from China, reportedly close to US$300 million in 1977 and 1978, dropped to zero in 1979 … Following Vietnam's occupation of Cambodia, only Sweden continued to provide any significant amount of economic help. Some multilateral assistance, such as that for development of the Mekong River, was made available by the United Nations Economic and Social Commission for Asia and the Pacific, however. Western and multilateral assistance, therefore, did not stop entirely, although the yearly average of about US$100 million through 1986 provided only a fraction of the country's hard-currency needs.   (1987: 176)

Vietnam was clearly in a vulnerable situation and becoming very dependent on the USSR. Moreover, frictions were frequent. Cima states:

> … in the early 1980s, announcement of the Third Five-Year Plan was delayed until the Fifth National Party Congress of March 1982 while Vietnam waited for the Soviet Union to confirm its aid commitments; and that Vietnam in the mid-1980s suffered first reduction, and then elimination of Soviet price subsidies for purchases of Soviet oil.   (1987: 166)

This provides a telling insight into the massive difficulties in macroeconomic management in those early years after reunification, though remittances from overseas Vietnamese played a moderating role at the household level.

One of the institutional decisions of the Sixth National Congress in 1986 was to establish a Commission for Economic Relations with Foreign Countries, and Vietnam clearly aimed at stimulating foreign aid inflows as part of the *Doi Moi* renovation effort. The response came forth once Vietnam had withdrawn from Cambodia in the late 1980s and the world had witnessed the downfall of the former USSR.[16] Aid flows doubled and rose more than five-fold during the decade from 1993 and Japan quickly established itself as the leading donor, with the

---

[15] To compare: the total Vietnamese government budget amounted to US$2.5 billion in 1976 while investments amounting to US$7.5 billion were planned for the 1981–1985 Five-Year Plan (Cima 1987: 150). This suggests that an amount equivalent to two-thirds of the investment programme came from abroad.

[16] Hansen and Tarp (2004) provide an overview of aid flows and management from 1993 on which this paragraph draws.

World Bank and the Asian Development Bank in important second and third place. Countries in the European Union added important amounts that have nevertheless all but disappeared in most recent years as Vietnam has achieved lower-middle-income status. Specifically, Vietnam's dependence on foreign aid has been falling quite steadily since the turn of the millennium where aid accounted for some 5 per cent of GDP to now 1.5 to 2 per cent.[17] Importantly, Trinh (2014) concludes that foreign aid had a significantly positive role in promoting economic growth in Vietnam from 1993 to 2012; a result that is in line with the positive assessment results from the general literature over the past decade (e.g., see Arndt et al. 2016). So the drop in the aid/GDP ratio is both a result of aid phasing out from some donors (the nominator) and of substantial GDP growth (the denominator).

In parallel with the domestic reforms in agriculture, industry, and services, Vietnam began in 1986 an extraordinary process of opening up its economy to regional and global economic forces; and as discussed by Tarp et al. (2003), both the quantity and composition of international trade have changed dramatically. A first, and critical, monetary policy step was the unification of the various official exchange rates in 1989, where the dong was devalued significantly to approach the market parallel rate. By 1992, the parallel premium had fallen to less than 1 per cent (see Dodsworth et al. 1996: box 1), and significant measures had been taken to change the mono-bank system into a commercial banking system (see Kovsted et al. 2005). Subsequently, Vietnam joined the Association of Southeast Asian Nations (ASEAN) in 1995 as relations with the US normalized, and is also a member of the Asia-Pacific Economic Cooperation (APEC). The key economic and trade programme for ASEAN is the ASEAN Free Trade Area (AFTA), and AFTA's core instrument is the Common Effective Preferential Tariff. By joining ASEAN, Vietnam therefore undertook early on international commitments in trade policy, which have had a profound impact as set out in what follows.[18] Other subsequent significant initiatives included the US–Vietnam Bilateral Trade Agreement in 2000 and Vietnam's accession to the WTO in 2007 as WTO member number 150.

Abbott et al. (2009) and Abbott and Tarp (2012) review the host of institutional and policy changes involved; and it stands out that rather than being a standard

---

[17] Raghuram Rajan, during his term as Chief Economist of the IMF, presented an early version of Arvind Subramanian and his own much cited paper on what the cross-country evidence really has to say about aid's impact on growth (Rajan and Subramanian 2008). The Vietnam context could hardly have been more at odds with the thesis presented and the empirical evidence has since been refuted (see Arndt et al. 2010).

[18] Focus in what follows is on major overall trends. For analytical papers on the impact of globalization crises, lessons from trade agreements, technology transfers, productivity spillovers, enterprise behaviour, and income growth related to international trade and foreign investment, see, for example, Tarp et al. (2002), Abbott et al. (2009), Abbott and Tarp (2012), and Newman et al. (2015b, 2017, 2018); and on firm-level technology and competitiveness, see Central Institute for Economic Management et al. (2015).

case of export-led growth, Vietnam saw more limited declines in investment than in export and import around the 1997–1998 and 2008–2009 global crises. There is, therefore, much to suggest that solid investment and macroeconomic management and trade policy, combined with an impressive record on sticking to the programme of building up the necessary institutional framework to benefit from continued international integration, including a strong and focused co-ordinating role by the state, had a lot to do with the success achieved.[19] Moreover, Vietnam has stayed on track since accession to the WTO, and presently has sixteen bilateral and multilateral free trade agreements; in 2018 Vietnam became one of the eleven signatories of the Comprehensive and Progressive Agreement for Trans-Pacific Partnership (TPP), the successor of the TPP after the US withdrew (see Eckardt et al. 2018). A particularly significant element of the opening-up process has been the effective promotion of development zones. They have included industrial zones, economic zones, export-processing zones, and high-tech zones, and firms that have been willing to invest have benefitted from preferential governmental policies, modern infrastructure, and access to utility services (for details, see Ernst & Young 2013). UNIDO (2015: 88) reports that in 2015 there were 313 economic zones in Vietnam; and that 40 per cent of Vietnam's total exports originate from the economic zones.

A first and quite impressive impact of the changes in international monetary and trade policy is the consistent increase in the openness of the Vietnamese economy as measured by the foreign trade (export plus import) share of GDP. It increased from a mere 20 per cent in 1986 to more than an impressive 180 per cent in 2016. While the trade balance during a significant part of the 1986–2016 period was in deficit, it has since 2011 been in surplus, suggesting that the long-term growth strategy has indeed paid off. Vietnam's main exports are rice, coffee, textiles, and machinery. Textiles and machinery, in particular, have become more important export commodities in the 2010s. Oil discoveries were made in the early 1980s in offshore fields, and crude oil exports peaked in 2004. However, since then the production has decreased, and Vietnam is currently a net importer of oil products (World Energy Council 2018). While impressive success in the production and export of agricultural export goods was experienced early on after 1986, declines have been experienced in value terms in more recent years. However, this fall has been more than compensated by manufacturing exports. Main imports are, as could be expected, machinery, chemicals, metals, and oil products, and manufacturing success from 2007–2008 onwards is clearly visible

---

[19] It is striking that many in the international community, including in particular the International Monetary Fund (IMF), argued for a strategy that emphasized stability over growth and faster SOE reform (see IMF 2010), and did not seem to grasp what it actually took to steer the reform process safely and successfully through difficult times. The World Bank was much more receptive, and, as Rama (2008) explains, built up its concessional lending programme to the point where the lending to Vietnam from the International Development Association was second only to that of India.

from the trade balance by goods categories. Despite the global economic crisis, Vietnam maintained focus on investment and expansion and certainly managed to reap the economic benefits in global manufacturing markets after WTO membership became a reality.

Finally, *Doi Moi*, including domestic reforms, trade opening, and accession to the WTO increased the credibility of Vietnam among international investors, and foreign direct investment (FDI) increased very significantly from 1989 onwards and has been high ever since. From 2005, the IMF balance-of-payments statistics also registers outflows of Vietnamese investments abroad. Doanh (2002) analyses the difference between registered and implemented capital, and adds that the decline in the case of Vietnam should also be related to domestic investment climate factors.[20] In any case, the total registered FDI capital has reached a very significant level, reported to amount in 2017 to a record high of almost US$36 billion. Among the nineteen industries and sectors that attracted FDI capital in 2017, the manufacturing–processing industry remained on top with almost 45 per cent (see *Viet Nam News* 2017). Accordingly, the relative size of FDI to investment by the state and non-state sectors has changed drastically over the years, underlining that FDI is a key source of investment funding in addition to the derived agglomeration, technology transfer, and productivity impacts that FDI is associated with. Moreover, the gradually shifting balance between state and non-state investment is fully in line with the discussion about the move from planning to markets in section 4.

6. Human Development

While Vietnam's growth record is impressive, many observers would argue that it is surpassed by achievements in terms of human development. The poverty rate was 58 per cent in 1993, and though poverty has not been eliminated it has fallen significantly: in 2016, it was less than 6 per cent for Vietnam as a whole, with the rural rate being 7.5 per cent and the urban rate being 2.0 per cent. Remaining poverty is particularly associated with poverty among the ethnic minorities in North and Central Vietnam that account for about 10 per cent of the population.[21] Inequality measured by the Gini coefficient for consumption rose moderately from 33.4 per cent in 1993 to 39.3 per cent in 2010. It then fell to 35.6 per cent after which it has risen again to 37.6 per cent. While it does appear that inequality has risen, this is an encouraging performance, and arguably reflects that the

[20] Hansen et al. (2003) provide regional context and further data on the distribution of the FDI received.

[21] Glewwe et al. (2004) provide 628 pages of excellent background and analysis on poverty in Vietnam during the 1990s based on the 1993 and 1998 rounds of the Vietnam Household Living Standard Survey (VHLSS). See Tarp (2017) for more recent panel data analysis and further information on the ethnic minorities, and the World Bank (2012) overview with the telling title *Well Begun, Not Yet Done*.

majority of Vietnamese have had their share of growth benefits.[22] However, it should be highlighted that the Gini measures relative inequality and, therefore, hides changes in absolute differences in income and consumption.

McKay and Tarp (2017: 213) document that in the Vietnam Access to Resources Household Survey (VARHS) rural panel, overall living conditions have in general improved according to three measures of welfare: (i) food consumption, (ii) household income, and (iii) household ownership of assets. However, there are exceptions such as the province of Lao Cai, and the data also document that even in provinces where average living conditions improved, the situation deteriorated for a sizeable minority of households. Migration of some household members seems to have a positive impact on the remaining household members; yet belonging to a non-Kinh[23] minority is significantly associated with smaller increases in food consumption and income. In sum, what has been achieved in Vietnam in terms of growth and poverty reduction is impressive, but important challenges remain.

Turning to other dimensions of human development, life expectancy at birth was more than seventy-six years in 2016 and infant mortality 17.3 per 1,000 births. Access to basic services (electricity, drinking water, sanitation) has expanded rapidly, reflecting substantial public investment in these social goods. Though child malnutrition has continued to fall, stunting nevertheless is around a relatively high 25 per cent and the share of underweight children below five years of age is 14 per cent, indicating that more remains to be done. Finally, tertiary school enrolment is now at almost 30 per cent, reflecting the progress achieved since the mid-1990s where only 2–3 per cent entered tertiary education.

7. Conclusions and Reflections

This study took as its starting point what Myrdal (1968) had to say about Vietnam in the context of the *Asian Drama*. It was clear that little detailed information and data were available at the time in the middle of the war. However, Myrdal was right in pointing to the decisive nature of the Vietnamese people, and subsequent developments have demonstrated that amply. Vietnam emerged victorious in the war and the CPV went on to take a dogged and, in retrospect, very costly position on economic policy and management from 1976. At the same time, when the approach taken did not produce the hoped-for results, the CPV pursued *Doi Moi*

---

[22] Jensen and Tarp (2005) analysed spatial inequality following trade liberalization in a Computable General Equilibrium model relying on data on all of the 5,999 households surveyed in the VHLSS and a 2000 Social Accounting Matrix (SAM) for Vietnam. They concluded that the government should be proactive in combining trade liberalization measures with a pro-poor fiscal response to avoid increasing poverty and inequality. This is exactly what the government has done. See Thurlow et al. (2011) for an illustration.

[23] The majority of the Vietnamese population are of Kinh background.

in an equally persistent manner; and it has certainly paid off. Vietnam has come a long way indeed since the *Doi Moi* reform process was initiated in 1986, and the past more than three decades have witnessed one of the best performances in the world in terms of both economic growth and poverty reduction. People's living standards have improved significantly, and the country's socio-economic achievements are impressive from a human development perspective. Wide-ranging institutional reform has been introduced, including a greater reliance on market forces in the allocation of resources and the determination of prices. The shift from an economy completely dominated by the state and co-operative sectors to one where the private sector and foreign investment play key and dynamic roles should also be highlighted. Significant strides have been made to further the transition from a centrally planned to a market economy, without giving up strategic leadership and influence by the state.

In sum, the key line of argument in this chapter was that gradualism and prudence in managing the process of economic change in a centralized yet responsive political system, combined with embedded history, have shaped socio-economic outcomes in a significant way. The chapter was structured to first set out the historical context and background, moving on to outlining the structural reforms undertaken and explaining how they have played themselves out and impacted on socio-economic and human development in the Vietnamese historical and political setting. This setting has throughout been characterized by a strong focus on egalitarianism, and this has clearly influenced both the nature and content of policy formulation. As was clear, much went wrong in the early years after 1975, but the willingness to learn from mistakes and ability to absorb lessons from experimentation paved the way for an important course correction from 1986 onwards. The importance of history was highlighted already by Myrdal, and the political system as it has evolved has so far kept in place the necessary checks and balances on individual power.[24]

Vietnam, over many years, depended heavily on the USSR and the Comecon members, and only after a reluctant start in the 1980s did the international community start engaging more broadly. Large-scale investment programmes were pursued during the 1990s, and the international community assumed responsibility for supporting a wide variety of social and economic reform initiatives. Importantly, the determination of Vietnam to maintain 'ownership' of the reform process has been evident and absolutely fundamental to the success achieved (see Hansen and Tarp 2004). The reforms were truly generated by Vietnam herself in an impressive manner where search for workable and mutually

[24] Vietnam has no principal ruler and is officially led by the President, the Prime Minister, the Party Secretary General, and the Chair of the National Assembly. Whether the CPV decision of nominating Nguyen Phu Trong to simultaneously assume the posts of Party Secretary General and State President following the untimely passing of Vietnam's President Tran Dai Quang on 21 September 2018, will change existing practice in any fundamental way is unclear.

agreed solutions with a minimum of losers was central, at a time when so many other countries were giving in to heavy-handed pressure from the Bretton Woods institutions and others (Tarp 1993). In contrast, in Vietnam the international community had to adopt patient dialogue, bargaining, and technical advice to find effective ways of securing the attention of the Vietnamese authorities and people. Much can be learnt from this experience for international relations and for foreign aid more generally at a conflict-prone moment in world history.

In the midst of the success achieved it is equally important not to lose track of the fact that Vietnam remains a lower-middle-income country according to the World Bank classification, with GDP per capita considerably lower than in some other Southeast Asian countries. How the country can rapidly and sustainably continue to transform itself and its economy to a wealthier and modern high-income society is a critical policy challenge. While future success cannot be taken for granted, it would fortunately seem as if there is a lot of awareness about this in Vietnam. Caution is justified for many reasons.

First, Vietnam has, as documented in detail by Hoai et al. (2019) in their SAM-based analysis, stressed that it is time for the country to make focused efforts targeted at transforming the economic growth model towards a more sustainable one which does not rely to such a large extent on expanding capital and labour inputs.[25] Technological upgrading has so far played a relatively modest role in Vietnam's success, though by no means has it been completely absent. Nonetheless, the advantages of low labour costs have started to run out of steam and more technological upgrading will be required across the board. This has already been touched upon in section 4 in relation to industry sector performance, where it was noted that labour value-added in industry has not been on a consistent upward trend. This reflects that much of the employment created is in quite basic functions that do not add greatly to the value-added per worker. While the trend may have turned from 2010 onwards, efforts need to be scaled up in combination with continued export engagement. External demand extension can, in addition to generating foreign exchange, also help strengthen internal economic integration and technological upgrading further (e.g., see Newman et al. 2015b, 2017), and productivity dynamism will no doubt be needed to sustain growth in the future. So, it is time to pursue a proactive policy approach to avoid being caught in what is sometimes referred to as a 'middle-income trap'. Vietnam can, in many ways, be said to have by now harvested the relatively easy 'low-hanging fruits',[26] achieved by a strong focus on an expansionist (domestic and foreign) investment-driven model of growth coupled with recovery from a very repressed level. Furthermore,

[25] The SAM dataset is available in Hoai et al. (2016).
[26] As shown by Arndt et al. (2012) in their comparative path analysis of Vietnam and Mozambique, a specific dimension of this is that Vietnam has benefitted greatly from inherent economic multiplier-effects due to a more tightly linked-up economy than Mozambique, as demonstrated in their respective SAMs. Vietnam has, so to speak, got more 'bang for the buck' in terms of poverty reduction for the exact same policies.

what stands out is that this process has been guided by a strong co-ordinating state. Nonetheless, it is time to look ahead—development policy challenges never go away; they simply change in nature, because of past failures and/or successes. One specific future dimension of this will surely be how Vietnam will handle (or not) issues associated with the increasing digitalization of the global economy and the availability of labour-saving technology.

Second, significant differences in the level of sector labour value-added continue to prevail. This reflects that Vietnam has by no means arrived at the 'modernization' point where labour is optimally allocated across sectors. Moreover, existing differences contribute to visible disparities in income and living standards in spite of the efforts of the government to redistribute towards poorer groups of people. In spite of recent progress, the ethnic minorities are far from included on an equal basis and gender equity also leaves much to be desired. In addition to gender- and group-based policy initiatives, this implies that productivity in agriculture will have to increase a lot more. This will have to involve both further investment and technology-driven productivity increases in agriculture and relocation of workers to other non-farming-based activities. While much can be achieved in improving processing of agricultural products, significant shifts of people towards dynamic urban centres will also have to be factored in. How to manage the inherent equity issues in such a process and ensuring no one is, in UN-SDG terminology, 'left behind', will no doubt remain a challenge. The same goes for the need for forward-looking urban and spatial planning, which leads us to the next point, climate change.

Third, Vietnam is typically expected to be susceptible to climate change for a number of reasons. They include the following: (i) much of Vietnam's population depends on agriculture; (ii) the position of Vietnam at the end of the Red and Mekong Rivers exposes the country to inland flooding; and (iii) the long, low-lying coastline is vulnerable to cyclones. The combination of rising sea levels and cyclones is likely to be particularly challenging: it could lead to displacement of large numbers of rural people and undermine valuable transport, energy, and urban infrastructure and impact on longer-term development. At the same time, Arndt et al. (2015) conclude that the negative impacts on agriculture are modest until 2050. Instead, larger costs are caused by rising sea levels and cyclone strikes that undermine urban infrastructure and capital. The insight is that costs are more limited for agriculture, which is a shrinking sector in relative terms in relation to both people and output, while present spatial patterns of urban areas are highly vulnerable, especially in scenarios that go beyond 2050. The implication is that there is a window of opportunity to act, at least with standard rates of depreciation of the existing capital stock. However, the window is quickly narrowing and spatial planning shifting focus towards higher-lying areas of the country is going to be an essential requirement to adapt effectively to climate change.

Fourth, Rama (2008) pointed out a decade ago that the task of managing the Vietnamese economy and society has become a much more complex set-up as a result of the changes associated with Vietnam's transformation following *Doi Moi*. This includes obviously the radically increased openness of the domestic economy to the world economy, which makes it increasingly important to be able to adapt policies and courses of action to changing circumstances outside Vietnam's control. It also means that the number of domestic stakeholders with conflicting interests has become much larger; and this inherently makes the consensus-seeking (growth-focused) approach adopted in the past harder to maintain and pursue successfully. Furthermore, the legitimacy of the existing state and party apparatus depends critically on what will happen to the by now widespread corruption.[27] It is therefore clear that 'new feedback mechanisms from society to state' (Rama 2008: 48) will be needed in the coming years. One development of note in this regard is the increasing role of the National Assembly,[28] but there are many other issues looming here. Overall, none of these challenges referred to here have become less important over the past ten years; and Vietnam continues to be ranked relatively low in indices such as the Worldwide Governance Indicators and the Transparency International corruptions perceptions index (see World Bank 2018c), trying to capture voice, accountability, and control of corruption.

Finally, while caution is required for the above reasons, there is also a lot of reason for optimism as regards the future of development in Vietnam. The Vietnamese people are not prone to rest on their laurels (see Rama 2008; Eckardt et al. 2018), as history has taught us over and over again. The economy is increasingly being focused on forward-looking manufacturing, information technology, high-tech industries, and agriculture, and Vietnam will for years to come be able to harvest a demographic dividend with a relatively young and growing labour force. Eckardt et al. (2018) note that half the Vietnamese population is below 35 years of age and stress that Vietnam has invested heavily in education. They also argue that 'Vietnam's efforts to promote access to primary education and to ensure its quality through minimum quality standards have paid off' and note Vietnam's ranking as 8 in the latest 2015 OECD Programme for International Student Assessment (see OECD 2018).

---

[27] See Rand and Tarp (2012, 2016) for one dimension hereof.
[28] This includes the series of leadership changes introduced at the Tenth CPV Congress in 2006 (see Koh 2008), including that the Eighth Five-Year Plan had to be approved by the National Assembly before being implemented. Moreover, '... if the use of laws and rules to regulate government and state affairs was a dominant theme of political reform in the past two decades, the trend was now seen in the running of party affairs... Another outcome is allowing different opinions on alternatives to be articulated, while retaining the power to accept or reject them within the Central Committee and the Political Bureau. It would be reasonable to say that these changes constitute political reforms designed to democratize the Party through raising the status of the Central Committee, especially in respecting the collective's decision on personnel decisions, and in reducing the roles of powerful individuals in making such decisions' (Koh 2008: 671–2).

Whether one agrees with the exact ranking or not,[29] this does bode well for the future when taking account of what will be required to do well in the global economic environment where global technological and IT advance will be a determining factor for economic and social progress. At the same time, Vietnam will as a *sine qua non* have to continue the process of institutional reform across the board to turn this potential into reality in the coming decades. This is so in general for the economy as a whole and in particular for the higher education and vocational training systems. Vietnam continues to lack workers with the necessary technical and soft skills, illustrated by the fact that, despite the improvement of language proficiency of Vietnamese students over the years, a major breakthrough is yet to materialize. If this does not change it will soon emerge as a key bottleneck for continued economic development and become a major stumbling block in the context of global technological and IT advance.

Acknowledgements

The author is grateful for excellent research assistance from Risto Rönkkö, who constructed a comprehensive set of background tables and figures, available in a detailed WIDER Working Paper (Tarp 2018). This chapter is a summary thereof. The author also appreciates advice, comments, and constructive criticism from Vu Xuan Nguyet Hong, Thi Thu Hoai Dang, and Tony Addison, and from Deepak Nayyar, who invited the contribution of this study to the UNU-WIDER project on Asian Transformations, and provided most helpful critique and suggestions on how to sharpen the key messages. All the usual caveats apply.

References

Abbott, P., and F. Tarp (2012). 'Globalization Crises, Trade and Development in Vietnam', *Journal of International Commerce, Economics and Policy*, 3(1): 1–23.

Abbott, P., J. Bentzen, and F. Tarp (2009). 'Trade and Development: Lessons from Vietnam's Past Trade Agreements', *World Development*, 37(2): 341–53.

Abbott, P., F. Tarp, and C. Wu (2017). 'Structural Transformation, Biased Technological Change, and Employment in Vietnam', *European Journal of Development Research*, 29(1): 54–72.

Arndt, C., A.F. Garcia, F. Tarp, and J. Thurlow (2012). 'Poverty Reduction and Economic Structure', *Review of Income and Wealth*, 58(4): 742–63.

Arndt, C., S. Jones, and F. Tarp (2010). 'Aid, Growth, and Development,' *Journal of Globalization and Development*, 1(2): article 5.

Arndt, C., S. Jones, and F. Tarp (2016). 'What is the Aggregate Economic Rate of Return to Foreign Aid?', *World Bank Economic Review*, 30(3): 446–74.

---

[29] For a critical view, see Jerrim (2017).

Arndt, C., F. Tarp, and J. Thurlow (2015). 'The Economic Costs of Climate Change', *Sustainability*, 7(4): 4131–45.

Ayala-cantu, L., T. Beni, T. Markussen, G. Narciso, C. Newman, A. Singh, S. Singhal, F. Tarp, and H. Zille (2017). 'Characteristics of the Vietnamese Rural Economy', UNU-WIDER report, UNU-WIDER, Helsinki. Available at: https://www.wider.unu.edu/publication/characteristics-vietnamese-rural-economy-0 (accessed September 2018).

Barslund, M., and F. Tarp (2008). 'Formal and Informal Rural Credit in Four Provinces of Vietnam', *Journal of Development Studies*, 44(4): 485–503.

Brandt, K., J. Rand, S. Sharma, F. Tarp, and N. Trifković (2016). 'Characteristics of the Vietnamese Business Environment', UNU-WIDER report, UNU-WIDER, Helsinki. Available at: https://www.wider.unu.edu/publication/characteristics-vietnamese-business-environment (accessed September 2018).

Calza, E., M. Goedhuys, and N. Trifković (2019). 'Drivers of Productivity in Vietnamese SMEs', *Economics of Innovation and New Technology*, 28(1): 23–44. Available at: https://www.tandfonline.com/doi/full/10.1080/10438599.2018.1423765 (accessed 10 April 2019).

Central Institute for Economic Management (CIEM), General Statistics Office (GSO), and Development Economics Research Group (DERG), University of Copenhagen (2015). 'Firm-Level Technology and Competitiveness in Vietnam', a report. Available at: http://web.econ.ku.dk/ftarp/Publications/Docs/Sacnned%20Pubs/Tech%20report%202009–2013%20April%202015.pdf (accessed 14 July 2018).

Cima, R.J. (ed.) (1987). *Vietnam: A Country Study*. Washington, DC: Federal Research Division, Library of Congress. Available at: https://cdn.loc.gov/master/frd/frdcstdy/vi/vietnamcountryst00cima_0/vietnamcountryst00cima_0.pdf (accessed 15 July 2018).

Doanh, L.D. (2002). 'Foreign Direct Investment in Vietnam', Paper presented at the International Monetary Fund Conference on Foreign Direct Investment, Hanoi, 16–17 August. Available at: https://www.imf.org/external/pubs/ft/seminar/2002/fdi/eng/pdf/doanh.pdf (accessed 15 July 2018).

Dodsworth, J.R., A. Chopra, C.D. Pham, and H. Shishido (1996). 'Macroeconomic Experiences of the Transition Economies in Indochina', IMF, Washington, DC, Working Paper 96/112.

Eckardt, S., D. Mishra, and Viet Tuan Dinh (2018). 'Vietnam's Manufacturing Miracle', Brookings blog post. Available at: https://www.brookings.edu/blog/future-development/2018/04/17/vietnams-manufacturing-miracle-lessons-for-developing-countries/ (accessed 15 July 2018).

Ernst & Young (2013). *Doing Business in Vietnam*. Hanoi: Ernst & Young Vietnam. Available at: https://www.ey.com/Publication/vwLUAssets/Doing_Business_in_Vietnam/%24FILE/Doing_Business_in_Vietnam_16000319.pdf (accessed 14 July 2018).

Frank, S. (2013). 'State-Owned Enterprises and Economic Reform in Vietnam', Paper submitted to the Faculty of the Naval War College in partial satisfaction of the requirements of the Department of Joint Military Operations. Available at: http://www.dtic.mil/dtic/tr/fulltext/u2/a594023.pdf (accessed 13 July 2018).

Glewwe, P., N. Agrawal, and D. Dollar (eds) (2004). *Economic Growth, Poverty, and Household Welfare in Vietnam*. Washington, DC: World Bank.

Hansen, H., and F. Tarp (2004). 'Feasibility Study Concerning Possible Future Danish Budget Support and Support to Complementary Activities in Vietnam', a report to Danida, Copenhagen and Hanoi. Available at: http://web.econ.ku.dk/ftarp/miscellaneous/Docs/VNBudgetSupportRep.pdf (accessed 14 July 2018).

Hansen, H., J. Rand, and F. Tarp (2003). 'Are FDI Inflows Complements or Substitutes Across Borders?', MPRA Paper 72834. Available at: https://mpra.ub.uni-muenchen.de/72834/1/MPRA_paper_72834.pdf (accessed 15 July 2018).

Hansen, H., J. Rand, and F. Tarp (2009). 'Enterprise Growth and Survival in Vietnam', *Journal of Development Studies*, 45(7): 1048–69.

Hoai, D.T.T., D. van Seventer, and F. Tarp (2019). 'Growth and Structural Transformation in Vietnam during the 2000s'. In C. Monga and J. Lin (eds) *Handbook of Structural Transformation* (pp. 513–30). Oxford: Oxford University Press. Also available as WIDER Working Paper 2016/108. Available at: https://www.wider.unu.edu/sites/default/files/wp2016-108.pdf (accessed 16 July 2018).

Hoai, D.T.T., D. van Seventer, F. Tarp, Ho Cong Hoa, and Tran Trung Hieu (2016). *A 2012 Social Accounting Matrix (SAM) for Vietnam*. Hanoi: Finance Publishing House.

Howard, E., C. Newman, and F. Tarp (2016). 'Measuring Industry Coagglomeration and Identifying the Driving Forces', *Journal of Economic Geography*, 16(5): 1055–78.

IMF (2010). 'Vietnam. Staff Report for the 2010 Article IV Consultation', IMF Country Report 10/281. Washington, DC: IMF. Available at: https://www.imf.org/external/pubs/ft/scr/2010/cr10281.pdf (accessed September 2018).

Jensen, H.T., and F. Tarp (2005). 'Trade Liberalization and Spatial Inequality', *Review of Development Economics*, 9(1): 69–86.

Jerrim, J. (2017). 'Why Does Vietnam do so well in PISA?', *FFT Education Datalab*, 19 July. Available at: https://ffteducationdatalab.org.uk/2017/07/why-does-vietnam-do-so-well-in-pisa-an-example-of-why-naive-interpretation-of-international-rankings-is-such-a-bad-idea/ (accessed September 2018).

Khai, L.D., T. Markussen, S. McCoy, and F. Tarp (2013). 'Access to Land: Market and Non-Market Land Transactions in Rural Vietnam'. In S. Holden, K. Otsuka, and K. Deininger (eds) *Land Tenure Reforms in Asia and Africa: Assessing Impacts on Poverty and Natural Resource Management* (pp. 162–86). Houndmills: Palgrave Macmillan.

Koh, D. (2008). 'Leadership Changes at the 10th Congress of the Vietnamese Communist Party', *Asian Survey*, 48: 650–72.

Kovsted, J., J. Rand, and F. Tarp (2005). *From Monobank to Commercial Banking: Financial Sector Reforms in Vietnam*. Copenhagen: NIAS Press.

Lewis, W.A. (1954). 'Economic Development with Unlimited Supplies of Labor', *The Manchester School*, 22: 139–91.

Markussen, T., and F. Tarp (2014). 'Political Connections and Land-related Investment in Rural Vietnam', *Journal of Development Economics*, 110: 291–302.

Markussen, T., M. Fibæk, F. Tarp, and Nguyen Do Anh Tuan (2017). 'The Happy Farmer', *Journal of Happiness Studies*, 19(6): 1613–36. Available at: https://link.springer.com/article/10.1007/s10902-017-9858-x?wt_mc=Internal.Event.1.SEM.ArticleAuthorOnlineFirst (accessed 24 July 2018).

Markussen, T., K. van den Broeck, and F. Tarp (2011). 'The Forgotten Property Rights', *World Development*, 39(5): 839–50.

McCaig, B., and N. Pavcnik (2013). 'Moving out of Agriculture', National Bureau of Economic Research, Cambridge, MA, NBER Working Paper 19616.

McKay, A., and F. Tarp (2015). 'Distributional Impacts of the 2008 Global Food Price Spike in Vietnam'. In D. Sahn (ed.) *New Directions in the Fight Against Hunger and Malnutrition: The Role of Food, Agriculture, and Targeted Policies* (pp. 373–92). Oxford: Oxford University Press.

McKay, A., and F. Tarp (2017). 'Welfare Dynamics: 2006–14'. In F. Tarp (ed.) *Growth, Structural Transformation, and Rural Change in Vietnam: A Rising Dragon on the Move* (pp. 205–21). Oxford: Oxford University Press.

Myrdal, G. (1968). *Asian Drama: An Inquiry into the Poverty of Nations, Volumes I, II, and III*. Allen Lane: The Penguin Press.

National Assembly (1999). 'Law on Enterprises', Ministry of Planning and Investment, Vietnam. Available at: http://www.vietnamlaws.com/freelaws/Lw13na12Jun99Enterprises[XIV1033].pdf (accessed on 14 July 2018).

Newman, C., J. Rand, T. Talbot, and F. Tarp (2015b). 'Technology Transfers, Foreign Investment and Productivity Spillovers', *European Economic Review*, 76: 168–87.

Newman, C., J. Rand, and F. Tarp (2013). 'Industry Switching in Developing Countries', *World Bank Economic Review*, 27(2): 357–88.

Newman, C., J. Rand, F. Tarp, and T.T.A. Nguyen (2017). 'Exporting and Productivity', *Journal of African Economies*, 26(1): 67–92.

Newman, C., J. Rand, F. Tarp, and N. Trifković (2018). 'The Transmission of Socially Responsible Behaviour through International Trade', *European Economic Review*, 101: 250–67.

Newman, C., K. van den Broeck, and F. Tarp (2014). 'Social Capital, Network Effects, and Savings in Rural Vietnam', *Review of Income and Wealth*, 60(1): 79–99.

Newman, C., K. van den Broeck, and F. Tarp (2015a). 'Property Rights and Productivity', *Land Economics*, 91(1): 91–105.

Ngu, V.Q. (2002). 'The State-Owned Enterprise Reform in Vietnam', Visiting Researchers Series 4, Institute of Southeast Asian Studies. Available at: http://citeseerx.ist.psu.edu/viewdoc/download?doi=10.1.1.201.2122&rep=rep1&type=pdf (accessed 13 July 2018).

Nguyen, T.T.A., M.D. Luu, and D.C. Trinh (2014). 'The Evolution of Vietnamese Industry', WIDER Working Paper 2014/76. Available at: https://www.wider.unu.edu/publication/evolution-vietnamese-industry (accessed 14 July 2018).

Nguyen, T.T.A., M.D. Luu, and D.C. Trinh (2016). 'The Evolution of Vietnamese Industry'. In C. Newman, J. Page, J. Rand, A. Shimeles, M. Söderbom, and F. Tarp (eds) *Manufacturing Transformation: Comparative Studies of Industrial Development in Africa and Emerging Asia* (pp. 235–56). Oxford: Oxford University Press.

Nhân Dân (2018). 'Vietnam Sees Decline in State-Owned Enterprises'. Available at: http://en.nhandan.com.vn/business/economy/item/5785902-vietnam-sees-decline-in-number-of-state-owned-enterprises.html (accessed September 2018).

Obermeyer, Z., C.J.L. Murray, and E. Gakidou (2008). 'Fifty Years of Violent War Deaths from Vietnam to Bosnia', *British Medical Journal*, 336(7659): 1482–6.

OECD (2018). 'Vietnam—Programme for International Student Assessment (PISA)'. Available at: http://www.oecd.org/pisa/aboutpisa/vietnam-pisa.htm (accessed September 2018).

Rajan, R.G., and A. Subramanian (2008). 'Aid and Growth' *The Review of Economics and Statistics*, 90(4): 643–65.

Rama, M. (2008). 'Making Difficult Choices: Vietnam in Transition', Commission on Growth and Development, World Bank, Washington, DC, Working Paper 40. Available at: http://documents.worldbank.org/curated/en/270911468327590018/pdf/577390NWP0E0an10gcwp040bilingualweb.pdf (accessed 24 July 2018).

Rand, J., and F. Tarp (2011). 'Does Gender Influence Fringe Benefits Provision?', *Feminist Economics*, 17(1): 59–87.

Rand, J., and F. Tarp (2012). 'Firm-Level Corruption in Vietnam', *Economic Development and Cultural Change, University of Chicago Press*, 60(3): 571–95.

Rand, J. and F. Tarp (2016). 'Bribes and Taxes'. In T. Gong and I. Scott (eds.) *Routledge Handbook on Corruption in Asia* (pp. 129–43). London and New York: Routledge.

Ranis, G., and J.C.H. Fei (1961). 'A Theory of Economic Development', *The American Economic Review*, 51(4): 533–65.

Ravallion, M., and D. van de Walle (2008). *Land in Transition: Reform and Poverty in Rural Vietnam*. Washington, DC: World Bank.

ReliefWeb (2000). 'Economic Success in Vietnam Allows WFP to Close Doors', Report from World Food Programme, 18 December. Available at: https://reliefweb.int/report/viet-nam/economic-success-vietnam-allows-wfp-close-doors (accessed September 2018).

Rummel, R.J. (1998). *Statistics of Democide: Genocide and Mass Murder Since 1900*. Münster: LIT.

Sharma, S., and F. Tarp (2018). 'Does Managerial Personality Matter?', *Journal of Economic Behavior & Organization*, 150: 432–45.

Tarp, F. (1993). *Stabilization and Structural Adjustment*. London and New York: Routledge.

Tarp, F. (ed.) (2017). *Growth, Structural Transformation, and Rural Change in Vietnam*. Oxford: Oxford University Press.

Tarp, F. (2018). 'Vietnam: The Dragon that Rose from the Ashes', WIDER Working Paper 2018/126. Available at: https://www.wider.unu.edu/publication/viet-nam-1.

Tarp, F., D. Roland-Holst, and J. Rand (2002). 'Trade and Income Growth in Vietnam', *Economic Systems Research*, 14(2): 157–84.

Tarp, F., D. Roland-Holst, and J. Rand (2003). 'Economic Structure and Development in an Emergent Asian Economy', *Journal of Asian Economics*, 13(6): 847–71.

Thanh, V.T. (2011). 'Vietnam Economy', Central Institute of Economic Management (CIEM) submission to APEC. Available at: http://mddb.apec.org/Documents/2011/SOM/WKSP/11_som_wksp_006.pdf (accessed 13 July 2018).

Thayer, C. (1987). 'Vietnam's Sixth Party Congress', *Contemporary Southeast Asia*, 9(1): 12–22.

Thurlow, J., F. Tarp, S. McCoy, N.M. Hai, C. Breisinger, and C. Arndt (2011). 'The Impact of the Global Commodity and Financial Crises on Poverty in Vietnam', *Journal of Globalization and Development*, 2(1): article 6.

Trinh, T. (2014). 'Foreign Aid and Economic Growth', Master's thesis. Aalto University School of Business, Helsinki. Available at: https://aaltodoc.aalto.fi/bitstream/handle/123456789/15276/hse_ethesis_13848.pdf?sequence=1&isAllowed=y (accessed 15 July 2018).

UNDP (2005). 'Services Sector Development', UNDP, Hanoi. Available at: https://www.undp.org/content/dam/vietnam/docs/Publications/22090_4447_ssde.pdf (accessed 14 July 2018).

UNIDO (2015). 'Economic Zones in the ASEAN', UNIDO Country Office, Hanoi. Available at: https://www.unido.org/sites/default/files/2015–08/UCO_Viet_Nam_Study_FINAL_0.pdf (accessed 14 July 2018).

UNU-WIDER (2018). 'Structural Transformation and Inclusive Growth in Vietnam', UNU-WIDER, Helsinki, UNU-WIDER Project. Available at: https://www.wider.unu.edu/project/structural-transformation-and-inclusive-growth-viet-nam (accessed September 2018).

Viêt Nam News (2017). 'FDI in VN Rose 44% to Hit New Record in 2017'. Available at: https://vietnamnews.vn/economy/420011/fdi-in-vn-rose-44-to-hit-new-record-in-2017.html (accessed September 2018).

Vietnam Briefing (2017). 'Facilitating SME Growth in Vietnam'. Available at: http://www.vietnam-briefing.com/news/facilitating-sme-growth-vietnam.html/ (accessed 14 July 2018). September 2018).

Voice of Vietnam Online (2016). 'Vietnam Enjoys Growing Tourism Contribution to GDP'. Available at: http://english.vov.vn/travel/vietnam-enjoys-growing-tourism-contribution-to-gdp-319524.vov (accessed 14 July 2018).

World Bank (2012). 'Well Begun, Not Yet Done', Report of World Bank, Hanoi. Available at: http://documents.worldbank.org/curated/en/563561468329654096/pdf/749100REVISED00al000Eng000160802013.pdf (accessed 16 July 2018).

World Bank (2018c). 'Worldwide Governance Indicators'. Available at: http://info.worldbank.org/governance/WGI/#home (accessed September 2018).

World Energy Council (2018). 'Oil in Vietnam', WEC oil data. Available at: https://www.worldenergy.org/data/resources/country/vietnam/oil/ (accessed 28 May 2018).

SUB-REGION STUDIES

19

East Asia

Robert H. Wade

1. The fast growth of the developing countries, which used a lot of import protection and other forms of dirigisme 'had a lot of *mystery* for me [and for all of us] who advocate hands-off markets'

(Easterly 2002, emphasis added).

2. '[A] nation that opens its economy and keeps government's role to a minimum invariably experiences more rapid economic growth and rising incomes'

(Louis Uchitelle (2002), reporting on the consensus among business executives and government leaders at the World Economic Forum meeting in 2002).

3. 'The most important thing in life is to have a goal, and the determination to achieve it'

(in English and Chinese, on plaque in entrance to Industrial Development Bureau, Taipei; reported in Weiss and Thurbon 2004).

1. Introduction

When historians look back on the second half of the twentieth century they will likely see the economic renaissance of East Asia as one of the seminal events. Starting with Japan in the 1950s, it rolled on to Taiwan, South Korea, Hong Kong, and Singapore in the 1960s and 1970s; later (but less so) to Southeast Asia; and into China in the 1990s. It represents the first major challenge to the global hierarchy of military, economic, and cultural power created by the British Empire and its European counterparts in the eighteenth and nineteenth centuries, and led by the United States since the Second World War. It has begun to restore the region to the forefront of world development, which it earlier occupied for more than a thousand years before being eclipsed in the new Western-centric world order (Arrighi 2007).

Our focus is on the world order of Northeast Asia, created by Japan in the late nineteenth and early twentieth centuries and then integrated into the emerging American empire after the Second World War. Myrdal's (1968) *Asian Drama* said little about Northeast Asia, focused as it was on South Asia and secondarily on Southeast Asia.

2. Exceptional Economic Performance in Northeast Asia

Today the Northeast Asian countries remain among a small set of non-Western economies to have escaped the typical structural constraints on developing countries. But instead of 'developing countries' or 'emerging economies' we should speak of 'peripheries' in the core–periphery structure of the world economy. The core emits impulses; the periphery receives impulses and supplies the core with inputs that sustain the core's technological, economic, financial, and military dominance—including supplies of skilled people (Fischer 2015).

The Northeast Asian countries remain among a still smaller set of non-Western countries which have developed *mostly indigenously-owned firms* across a broad range of major global industries, able to act as first-tier suppliers to (Western or Japanese) multinational companies (MNCs) and even compete head-to-head with them. The range includes chemicals, petrochemicals, electronics, steel, shipbuilding, cars, and car parts, and more recently, biotech, advanced semi-conductors, artificial intelligence, nanotechnology, and space exploration. This achievement reflects their development of an *indigenous capacity for technological innovation-on-the-world-frontier.* Yet they are located some 9,000 kilometres across the Pacific from the world's biggest and most innovative market, while next-door Mexico has languished.

Just how exceptional is the economic performance of Northeast Asia is clear from the answer to the question: how many non-Western countries have reached the general level of prosperity of Western Europe and North America in the past two centuries? Fewer than ten. The small number of catch-ups makes the point that the main long-term growth pattern in the world economy has been: 'divergence, big time' (Pritchett 1997). A World Bank (2013) study confirms this conclusion. It identified 101 countries in 1960 as 'middle-income' and found that, of those, only thirteen reached 'high income' almost five decades later, by 2008.

Table 19.1 (panel A) shows, for 1970 and 2010, the average income of several East Asian countries as a percentage of US average income, plus Indonesia, India, and Brazil. Taiwan and Korea, together with China, stand out for the magnitude of their catch-up. Most of the rest of the world looks more like Indonesia, India, and Brazil.

Taiwan held the world record for the number of years of continuous 6 per cent or more growth until 2010, at 32 years (1962 to 1994). Korea came second, at 29 years (1962 to 1991). China broke Taiwan's record in 2010; by then it had grown continuously at more than 6 per cent for 33 years, if its growth statistics can be trusted (Pritchett and Summers 2014).

Investment rates underpinning these growth performances are shown in Table 19.1 (panel B). By way of comparison, the UK figure for 1990 was 19 per cent and the US figure was 17 per cent.

We have to keep in mind that most of the non-Western countries that 'made it' into developed country status have small populations (future China aside).

Table 19.1 Comparison of income and investment in Asian countries

Panel A: Country average income as % of US real average income, 1970 and 2010

	Japan	Taiwan	S. Korea	Malaysia	Indonesia	China	India	Brazil
1970	50	20	10	15	5	5	5	15
2010	70	80	70	45	20	25	10	30

Panel B: Gross capital formation/GDP, selected entities, %

	1970	1990	2012	1980–2014
China	33	36	47	40
East Asia & Pacific minus China	23	32	30	28
LICs & MICs minus East Asia	22	22	25	23

Note: Panel A: Penn World tables 9.0, based on 2011 purchasing power parity (PPP) numbers, rounded to nearest ventile. Panel B: LICs = low-income countries, MICs = middle-income countries.

Source: Panel A: Author's update from Cherif and Hasanov (2015). Panel B: World Development Indicators, 22 December 2015.

The *rarity* of income and production catch-up on the scale of Northeast Asia, and the relatively small 'demographic mass' involved, suggests that the world economy contains a segmentation analogous to a 'glass ceiling' or 'middle-income trap'. The idea is at odds with mainstream or neoclassical development theory, which presumes the world economy is an open-ended system with no overall structure of a core–periphery kind, analogous to a marathon race in which the position of each runner is a function of internal fitness.

The next section discusses the causes proposed by analysts writing in the mainstream tradition, often called neo-liberalism. Their interpretation—emphasizing market liberalization in Northeast Asia—has been the most influential in the more general debate about economic development, including in the World Bank. I suggest that its influence stems less from the power of confirming evidence than the power of sheer simplicity (Occam's Razor) plus fit with a pro-Western-capital ideological story.

3. Northeast Asia's Rise in the Neo-liberal Paradigm

By the 1980s, when Northeast Asia's rise began to attract sustained attention from Western policy analysts, most economists and the Western-controlled multilateral development organizations (including the World Bank, the IMF, and the OECD and its Development Centre) viewed their subject through the lens of neo-liberalism—the newly resurgent economic faith in the West, including in development economics.

Neo-liberal philosophy says that 'the market' is the best institution for both economic growth and liberty. Even where unambiguous 'market failures' are identified, they are generally best left untreated, because the societal costs of correcting them through 'state intervention' are likely to be higher than the societal gains. The optimum degree of openness to the international economy is close to maximum openness, because global integration raises competitive pressure on all domestic producers and thereby makes national economies more flexible and channels resources to their most efficient uses. The idea that governments should curb competition in the interests of helping some firms and industries reap economies of scale, and curb global integration in the interests of national social cohesion and national employment, has little value in this way of seeing (Wade 1992a, 2017a, 2017b).

The World Bank's (1993) book, *The East Asian Miracle*, is a relatively sophisticated case in point. It examined the causes of success in eight 'high-performing Asian economies': Japan, the three first-generation newly industrialized economies of South Korea, Taiwan, and Singapore, and three second-generation Southeast Asian economies of Thailand, Malaysia, and Indonesia, plus Hong Kong. The book argues that the states made important contributions to the fast growth of these countries by ensuring 'the fundamentals': low inflation and competitive exchange rates; human capital; effective and secure financial systems; low price distortions; easy access to foreign technology; and low bias against agriculture.

In other words, the states implemented effective 'horizontal' policies, applied across all sectors. But 'strategic' interventions—sector-specific policies to promote specific industries or even specific firms—'generally did not work' (World Bank 1993: 354; Wade 1996). The take-away message: 'openness to international trade, based on largely neutral incentives, was *the* critical factor in East Asia's rapid growth' (World Bank 1993: 292, emphasis added).

This argument makes Northeast Asia powerfully confirm the neo-liberal answer to Adam Smith's question: how does market capitalism generate human welfare? The answer is market liberalization—and in a global context, global integration, or moving towards 'the world as one economic country', having no more restrictions on economic flows or ownership claims across borders than US states have across theirs. It is an argument not just for free trade but also for free capital movement; conversely, it downplays the value of both national sovereignty and democracy. In short, the World Bank concluded that, contrary to William Easterly in epigraph one, East Asia's rise was no mystery. The main causes are identified in epigraph two, the pro-Western-capital argument from the World Economic Forum.

4. The Rise of the Developmental State

We can give a more interesting answer by asking: what conditions enabled Myrdalian cumulative causation between rising state capacity, rising internal peacefulness, and rising incomes. Put the other way, what conditions enabled Japan, Taiwan, and Korea to avoid the common fate of the periphery—the 'weak state', with a well-entrenched ruling group fighting internal enemies, supplying narrowly focused public goods to favour its own supporters, and loosely enforcing the rule of law? What conditions enabled them to begin with the 'special-interest state' (a well-entrenched ruling group able to maintain internal stability, tending to favour its own supporters in order to fortify its grip on power but also focusing over time on long-term national goals), and then transition towards the 'common-interest state' providing broadly based public goods, thereby helping to raise incomes and reduce discontent (Besley and Persson 2011).

We need to keep in mind the point made by Francis Fukuyama: 'Holding on to a certain structure of political power is often a life-and-death issue for leaders of poor countries' (Fukuyama 2004: 49). This holding on to power often results in low state capacity and low commitment to national development goals, even to the point of the rulers creating antagonistic relations between government ministries in case rival groups benefit from the new economic opportunities created by a national development project and use their new wealth to try to replace the incumbents, perhaps by investing in violence (Kohli 2004).

It turns out that the answer to how Northeast Asia sustained the cumulative causation between rising state capacity, rising incomes, and rising internal peacefulness is closely related to the geopolitics of Northeast Asia and the US, and the resulting structure of the regional economy. The rise of Northeast Asia is far from a story of a small group of marathon runners forging ahead in an open race.

4.1 The 'Luck' of Location, Endowments, and Timing

The historian Bruce Cumings reminds us: 'If there has been an economic miracle in East Asia, it has not occurred just since 1960; it would be profoundly ahistorical to think that it did' (Cumings 1984: 3). In a longer treatment we would begin with causes of East Asia's economic pre-eminence up to the seventeenth century. Cutting short this *longue duree*, I begin in the late nineteenth century and the three 'orders' in East Asia at that time (Woo 2016). The first was the world of state-capitalist Northeast Asia, created by Japan with its late nineteenth century colonization of Korea and Taiwan, followed in the 1930s and first half of the 1940s by colonization of Manchuria and down the east coast of China. The Japanese colonial government treated Korea and Taiwan as offshore farms, mines, and industries, closely integrated to the core. It replicated similar economic and political institutions and policies as earlier in Japan—nationalistic, insular, militaristic, state-permeated, focused on raising productivity in agriculture, mining, and early manufacturing, and committed to providing mass elementary school education. By 1940, somewhere between 50 to 70 per cent of Korean and Taiwan children were in elementary school. All three countries were more homogeneous in terms of ethnicity and religion than most other countries.

The second world order, created by Western colonialists, comprised Hong Kong and Southeast Asia. The colonialists transformed the economy (entrepôt Hong Kong apart) into commodity production for Western markets, mainly in the form of plantations, empowering big landlords. But outside the extractive sectors, colonial governance was more passive, more accepting of incumbent landed elites than in Japan's empire. By 1940 only about 2 per cent of children were in elementary school in the French colony of Vietnam. Also, the host societies were ethnically and religiously much more diverse than in Northeast Asia. The third world order was China, which later, in the post-Second World War decades, came to be seen as an enemy of the new US-shaped order in capitalist Northeast Asia.

Our interest is the Japanese–centred world of Northeast Asia, starting with Japan's forced opening in the mid-nineteenth century. For some 250 years before the mid-nineteenth century Japanese rulers isolated the country. In 1853, Commodore Perry of the US navy sailed into Edo (now Tokyo) harbour with a fleet of warships and demanded that Japan open up to American commerce. His visit sent shockwaves through the country's leaders, who feared that America might colonize Japan as it strove for dominance across the Pacific. News had already reached Japan of European states gobbling up chunks of China through what later came to be known as the Unequal Treaties, from 1839 to 1849, by which European states imposed European laws on foreigners in China and set tariffs on goods imported through the treaty ports. Would Japan be next? The Japanese government responded with wholesale reforms to create a centralized state and national identity as the basis for a strong military. The guiding spirit was expressed by a Japanese leader in the wake of Perry's visit: 'If we take the initiative, we can dominate; if we do not, we will be dominated.'

The Meiji restoration of 1868 launched a frenzy of industrialization and militarization lasting several decades, guided by the developmental mindset that emerged from the brutal collective choice of 'sink or swim'. The government undertook a Big Push in state capacity, including fiscal, legal, and public goods. It sent teams of officials around the Western world to investigate ways to organize a modern society, such as a tax system, a post office, a railroad, an army, a state constitution, a parliament, a judiciary, and the like, and then implemented the best models at home.

Japan militarized so fast and effectively that in 1894–1895 its navy defeated China's and a decade later defeated Russia's. The latter sent a shockwave through Western governments, as the first time in the modern era that an Asian state had defeated a European state (as Russia was then considered). Japan went on to become the first non-Western country to catch up with the West in broad measures of production structure, military strength, and mass living conditions. At the same time a powerful group of chauvinist ideologues began to advocate for a new pan-Asian order led by Japan, to fend off Western empires. This group paved the way for Japan to take Korea and Taiwan as colonies in the late nineteenth and early twentieth centuries, and later, large swathes of China.[1]

Following Japan's defeat in the Second World War, Korea reverted to the unified kingdom it had been for a thousand years before it became a Japanese colony— now with a president rather than a king or emperor. Taiwan reverted to a neglected province of the Chinese polity, as before it became a Japanese colony in 1895.

After the war, Japan continued to be ruled by the developmental mindset institutionalized during the Meiji restoration and fortified in the 1930s in the build-up to war. A similar mindset began to be institutionalized in national elites of independent Korea and Taiwan, building on the developmental legacy of Japanese colonialism. Having emerged in Japan in response to the external threat of the US, it re-emerged in Japan and was created anew in Korea and Taiwan in response to another external threat, from close-by communist states of China, North Korea, and Russia. More broadly, the developmental mindset emerged from the combination of:

- a lack of natural resources, above all, land and energy, which allowed the countries to escape 'the natural resource curse' (overvalued exchange rate hindering manufactured exports, and government based on control of natural resource enclaves, ignoring the rest of the population), and on the other hand, abundance of people, with a high ratio of working age people to young-and-old dependents, and a long history of mass literacy and elementary education, which made them outliers for countries at their income levels;[2]

- huge post-war challenges to reconstruct (as distinct from create *de novo*) physical and organizational infrastructure;

---

[1] Following its victory in the Sino–Japan war of 1894–1895, Japan formally annexed Taiwan into the Japanese Empire in 1895, as the first (formal) step in implementing the Southern Expansion Doctrine. The annexation lasted until Japan's Second World War defeat in 1945. Japan began creeping colonial rule in Korea in the 1870s and made Korea a 'Protectorate' in 1905 and a full-fledged colony in 1910. Japanese rule broke the pre-colonial Yangban's (landed elite's) hold on the state. Senior positions in the state were filled with Japanese bureaucrats, who applied economic development lessons from the Meiji Restoration (1868–1912) to Korea. They encouraged Korea-based Japanese business groups, similar to the zaibatsu at home, with state-financed credit, cheap electricity, and other benefits. It is widely believed in Korea that Japanese colonialism heavily damaged the economy's growth potential. We should qualify this belief with the fact that factories left behind at the end of the war fairly quickly regained pre-war levels of production, thanks to the know-how in the heads of Koreans who had worked as middle managers in Japanese-owned companies. Also, the pre-war experience of Japanese zaibatsu made it easier for President Park Chung Hee and his government to nurture Korean equivalents, the chaebol, in a similar relationship to the state. Other favourable long-term causes include ethnic homogeneity, cultural propensity to take organizational goals as one's own personal goals up and down the hierarchy, and more. On organizational incentives in Korean and Indian bureaucracy, see Wade (1982a, 1982b, 1985, 1992b).

[2] Irma Adelman and Cynthia Morris compiled 1961 data for seventy-four developing countries. Taiwan was 44th in per capita income, 12th by 'socio-political' development, and 4th by 'development potential' (Wade 1990b/2004: 109). The median age in Japan in 1970 was 28.8 years; Hong Kong 21.7; Singapore 19.7; South Korea 19.0. The UK median age was 34.2 years, same as Germany's.

- the imperative of building up industry to escape low value-added activities and grow the exports needed to pay for industrialization and military imports; and

- a perception of immanent and existential threat from nearby communist countries, which necessitated a strong military, US protection, and high-speed industrialization, while at the same time allowing mass consumption and living conditions to improve by enough to limit domestic unrest—which enemy neighbours could exploit.

Early post-war Taiwan, with a population of six million, received a turbulent influx of between one and two million in 1949 as the Nationalist (Kuomintang) army and government lost the long-running civil war with the Red Army and Chinese Communist Party, and its leaders, officials, military, and sympathizers fled to Taiwan, 150 kilometres from the mainland. The incomers, under Chiang Kai-shek, claimed to still constitute the rightful ruling regime of China; so they planned merely to regroup in Taiwan for later resumption of the civil war on the mainland. The native Taiwanese, most of whose ancestors had come from the mainland two and more centuries before and had experienced fifty years of total separation from the mainland under Japanese rule, saw the incomers as foreign, and vice versa. With little need for support from the local elite, the Nationalists implemented a disciplined one-party state on Taiwan, applying lessons from their disintegration on the mainland, and discriminating economically and politically in favour of themselves. They constantly invoked the threat of communist invasion or subversion to justify authoritarian rule. The threat was real. For example, the Red Army bombarded Nationalist-held small islands close to the mainland in 1954 and 1958. In short, Taiwan at this time was a 'special-interest' state, but the well-entrenched (and semi-foreign) ruling group was disciplined to provide broader (rather than narrower) public goods both by the external threat and by the US government.

The Korean War of 1950 to 1953 pitted communist North Korea backed by China and the Soviet Union against South Korea backed by the US and a coalition of allies. The numbers 'killed and missing' were: South Koreans—210,000 from the military and one million civilians; North Koreans—406,000 from the military and 600,000 civilians; Chinese—600,000 from the military; and American theatre deaths—37,000. The war ended with an armistice but no peace treaty, the peninsula divided into North and South. The two sides are technically still 'at war'. From the end of the war till today the North Korean regime has undertaken sustained provocation and terror in the South. At the time of my fieldwork in South Korea in 1979, every metre of beach on the country's long coastline was raked at sunset and inspected at dawn in the hunt for footprints of North Korean sea-coming saboteurs.

As in Taiwan, South Korea's rulers—following the military coup led by Park Chung-hee in 1961—implemented a tightly disciplined military dictatorship, using the external threat as its justification. Park had been educated in a Japanese military academy and served in the Japanese army in Manchuria, when he studied the history of the Meiji Restoration and the role of the state in Japan's industrialization. He was chief architect and driving force of Korea's developmental state from 1961 until his assassination in 1979—his core belief was 'we can do anything if we try', as though all problems could be overcome by sheer willpower. Soon after taking power, he arrested leading businessmen and threatened them with jail (for 'corruption') unless they left for the US and returned with export orders; he expropriated houses of senior military (clustered in one part of Seoul), on grounds that their salaries could not possibly have afforded such houses, and handed the area to the diplomatic colony; and he closed down the golf course in the heart of Seoul, built as a facility for American troops and the Korean elite. Both governments sustained intense surveillance over their populations. In Seoul, some rubbish collectors and street sweepers were equipped with unobtrusive communications devices, which marked them out—it was said—as surveillance agents as they went about their work, especially in the poorer districts.

Korea and Taiwan transitioned to a democratic regime as late as the second half of the 1980s, well after they had passed through the demographic transition. Even Japan was almost a one-party state; the Liberal-Democratic party was the majority party in nearly every government from 1955 to the present. The dominant political philosophies of these countries emphasized 'order' and 'nationalism' more than 'liberty' and 'free enterprise', in contrast to neo-liberal philosophy, despite Western media presenting them as lovers of liberty and free enterprise and the American way of life, the better to justify aid against communists.

4.2 The US Role in Northeast and Southeast Asia

Before the Second World War the US had little presence in Northeast Asia. It entered in force as part of its hegemony strategy. In East Asia and in Western Europe it saw severe and persisting communist state enemies. So 'containment of communism' became the top US foreign policy priority in both East Asia and Western Europe (Lee 2017). After several decades of close ties to Chiang and the Nationalists, including the Second World War alliance, the US after 1949 plunged into Cold War with communist China and then into hot war in Korea. The US saw communist China and North Korea—with communist Russia close by—as a severe threat to its emerging 'Pacific sphere of influence'. But despite powerful voices in Washington wanting the US to help Chiang re-start the civil war on the mainland, Secretary of State Dean Acheson prevailed in his call for 'strategic restraint' and a less aggressive policy of building 'a great crescent' of containment around China.

The US poured in assistance to its three Northeast Asian allies—troops, economic advisors, political advisors, teachers, Christian missionaries, accompanied by large financial transfers. Drawing on New Dealers' experience of trying to foster pro-development governments in Latin America before the war, US advisors helped construct centralized, top-level agencies to plan the use of very scarce capital and helped construct an effective civil service, police, judiciary, and education system. During the American Occupation of Japan (1945–1952) the Japanese government instituted 'the most restrictive foreign-trade and foreign exchange control system ever devised by a major free nation', with American blessing (Hollerman 1979). The country's renaissance was much helped by the Korean War, 1950–1953, because it made Japan the main source of American procurements. The prime minister at the time, Shiguru Yoshida, later declared, the war was a 'gift of the gods'.

The US government gave strong backing for expropriative land redistribution in all three countries. The land reforms helped establish political order and support for industrialization by curbing the landed classes and strengthening peasant support for the state—making the rural population a less fertile site for communist subversion. They created a small farmer agrarian structure receptive to intense state efforts to raise agricultural productivity as a condition for fast industrialization (Dore 1965; Wade 1982a). The US government made clear that assistance would not be sustained indefinitely. It gave assistance in the spirit of raising the capacity of the state to finance and man its own bureaucracy and military, so that US resources and personnel could be scaled back without danger to Cold War containment. The periods of intense US involvement in helping to create the developmental state and ward off military attack were: Japan 1948–1964; Taiwan 1950–1965; and South Korea 1945–1965.

Note that the ending of intense US involvement came as the US and allies geared up military efforts on behalf of South Vietnam, fearing that 'communism' might triumph in Indochina after semi-failing in Korea. Korea sent 320,000 troops to fight alongside South Vietnamese and American troops and received in return tens of billions of dollars in grants, loans, tech transfer, and preferential markets from the Johnson and Nixon governments.

In short, thanks to the threat of communist state expansion in a region the US sought to make its sphere of influence (having been attacked from the Western Pacific at Pearl Harbour), the US transferred huge resources to the East Asian three. It raised their foreign exchange reserves (allowing them to run sustained current account deficits), boosted their investment ratios to unusually high levels, and helped to *discipline the use of investable funds* by strengthening the commitment of national elites to transform the production structure towards manufacturing and away from agriculture and commodities, and create appropriate planning and implementation organizations. Also, it gave the aid and loans *in a form that did not dilute national ownership of the industrial sector*, in contrast to Latin America's reliance on US firms to establish subsidiaries. And it gave Northeast Asian countries privileged access to its giant high-income market for manufactured goods.

In the case of Taiwan, the US financial transfers averaged about US$600 million a year from 1951 to 1965 (2016 dollars), the biggest US aid transfers per capita in the world through that period. The US civilian and military aid officials were particularly attentive to ensuring the appropriate use of the resources they transferred to the Nationalist government, well aware of the history of wanton corruption during the Nationalist Party's decades of misrule on the Chinese mainland before retreating to Taiwan in 1949. US resources went directly to firms in the fertilizer, shipping, cement, aluminium, paper, glass, sugar, chemical, synthetic fibre, and pharmaceutical industries. US officials helped draw up regulations for property rights, investment, export-processing zones, and the like. They consistently opposed the many senior people in the Nationalist government committed to establishing new enterprises as *public* rather than private enterprises. They put their weight behind those wanting *strong state leadership of a largely private sector economy*.

In 1959, the director of the US aid mission to Taiwan proposed an eight-point economic reform programme, which included unification of the exchange rate, liberalization of controls on foreign exchange, and privatization of state-owned enterprises. Based on this proposal, the government launched its Nineteen-Point Program of Reform in early 1960, which amounted to a cautious, controlled sequence of promoting exports, opening the economy, replacing some imports in line with an industrial strategy, privatizing a few state-owned enterprises (leaving the commanding heights—the upstream input supplying firms—in public ownership, contrary to American wishes), plus creating or strengthening several agencies to pilot the programme. The US offered a large loan conditional on fulfilling certain goals of the programme.

Lee (2017) sums up: 'By the end of the official aid program in 1965, Taiwan had acquired a developmental state, in which the instruments of state guidance remained but the basis of development was private industry'. The US sponsored similar reforms in Japan and South Korea.

Compare US strategy in its former colony, the Philippines, where the US saw no existential threat.[3] In response to a communist-led insurgency in parts of the countryside, the government and the US relied on a counter-insurgency strategy— and did not try land reform, which would have upset the existing landlord– government complex. The US did not provide anything close to its Northeast Asia level of assistance for the Philippines' own attempt at indigenous industrialization, or encourage effective state planning. It remained relaxed as aid resources fed into existing landlord-dominated patronage networks, as it was not relaxed further north.

---

[3] The Philippines was under Spanish rule for centuries before the US took it as a colony in 1898. US rule lasted till 1941. The US colonial administration was much less dense than the Japanese administration in Korea and Taiwan, and ruled through landed elites.

The US supported the Filipino government's emphasis on intensification of agricultural goods and raw materials, not industrial goods (Lee 2017; Rock 2017). Why? The US saw the Philippines as a periphery of the regional economy focused on threatened Northeast Asia. The top American priority was to industrialize Japan, Taiwan, and South Korea, so as to give them the ability to stand up to their enemies and provide frontline defence of the US. Filipino commodities exported to these countries would provide cheap inputs for people and industry, and help their industrialization while also removing their temptation to import commodities from nearby communists. So the Philippines 'suffered' from not having a communist enemy able to threaten the survival of its pro-American state. Neither its own elite nor the US government pushed for a 'production transformation' coalition. The Philippines remains a periphery in the wider East Asian economy to this day.

Three broader points about the geopolitics and timing should be made. First, in the US and Japanese vision, Japan was to be tied to the US by economic, political, and ideological means, and was itself to be the restored core of the Northeast Asian regional economy. Taiwan and South Korea were to be lower-cost semi-peripheries (though this terminology was not used). All three were to receive easy access to the US market, and favoured for public procurement, on account of their security importance to the US. Encouraged by their governments' commitment to the vitality of these economies, US and Japanese firms took their first steps of importing cheap-labour manufactures from domestic producers or from their own operations there (not from next-door Mexico, in the case of US firms).

Second, timing mattered. The Big Push development efforts in Northeast Asia coincided with the US leading a big multilateral trade and investment liberalization project through the General Agreement on Tariffs and Trade (GATT), which placed more pressure on developed countries to open their markets than on developing countries to open theirs. Northeast Asian firms, and branches of Western multinational corporations, were the 'first movers' to take advantage of the new export opportunities, using Western demand to compensate for relatively low domestic demand out of low incomes and small populations. In particular, they rode the wave of post-war mass consumption of oil-automobile-mass production products of the fourth great technological revolution, and then, from the 1970s, the wave of emerging demand for the information and telecommunication products of the fifth revolution. With their head start, they were well established and moving up value chains and down cost curves by the time producers in other developing countries came into the game.

The regional economy developed a pattern of integration famously known as the 'flying geese' model. As Japan grew fast by the late 1950s some firms began to offshore to Taiwan or Korea (or switched supply to local producers, often in joint ventures); as costs rose in Taiwan and Korea, the process repeated to cheaper sites in Southeast Asia and Indochina—and over the 1990s, China. But an often-overlooked qualification to the flying geese model is that whole industries generally did not move; the high value-added parts remained at home and the lower value-added activities were offshored. Rather, Northeast Asia saw an early development of what would later be called 'global value chains' and should more accurately be called 'regional value chains'. But contrary to today's orthodoxy about GVCs, which suggests that integration into GVC is a better alternative to building a domestic integrated supplier base, these governments promoted both at the same time.

Here is an example of the flying geese mechanism. In the 1970s, Japanese electronics firms like Cassio, Canon, and Sharp began to offshore the assembly of low-end calculators to Taiwan firms in the role of 'original equipment manufacturers'. The production equipment and key components (such as liquid crystal displays) came from Japan, and the calculators were branded as Japanese. One of the main Taiwanese companies was Jinbao Electronics. In 1990, after extensive consultation with Sharp, Jinbao decided to open its own factory in Thailand and sell calculators (and related items) mainly to Sharp. The key components and production equipment in Thailand came from Japan; the procurement and administration came from Taipei; the management in Thailand was Taiwanese; and Thailand provided the lower skilled labour force and the land. All the production was exported. The production appeared in international trade statistics as Thai; the investment in Thailand appeared in international investment statistics as Taiwanese; Japanese firms got most of the profit; and the customers thought the product was Japanese (Bernard and Ravenhill 1995).

The third contextual point is that high levels of US support enabled the East Asian three to run sustained *external payments deficits* during their stage of fast industrialization and urbanization—financed by US assistance. Even as they used substantial and strategic levels of *protection* to foster import replacement, they sucked in huge volumes of imports *in selected sectors*. In contrast, most developing countries, lacking large-scale external assistance, could not sustain the external payments deficits that would have been necessary for fast industrialization and urbanization—unless financed by loans from the multilateral development banks, which have carried mostly neo-liberal conditionalities since the 1980s, unlike US conditions in its assistance to the East Asian three.

I now turn to the role of the state and the arrangement of power in Northeast Asia, comparing it to the model of the neo-liberal regulatory state.

5. Characteristics of the Northeast Asian Developmental State

'Developmental state' was coined by Chalmers Johnson (1982) in his study of Japan's rise, *MITI and the Japanese Miracle*.[4] He used the phrase to refer to a 'plan-rational state', in contrast to a 'market-rational state', two broad types of capitalism. The market-rational state concentrates on 'horizontal' policies to improve productivity across the economy, including market regulation, transport

---

[4] For succinct accounts of the history of the idea see Woo-Cumings (1999) and Haggard (2018).

infrastructure, education, as typified by the US (he said, wrongly (Wade 2017b)). The plan-rational state carries out these same horizontal policies but also uses more 'vertical' (sectorally selective) policies to steer the production structure towards state-set goals (mostly by influencing market allocations, in contrast to communist states which relied on plan-allocation more than market-allocation). Johnson took Japan as his case study of the developmental state in action, focusing briefly on the decades after the country's forced opening in the mid-nineteenth century and then at length on the post-war fast-growth decades.[5]

Since Johnson's book on Japan, a sizeable literature has applied the idea of the developmental state to other cases as a way to understand relative long-run economic performance. This literature emphasizes: (1) the 'developmental mindset' of key state actors—the normative and cognitive models with which they conceive and implement the idea of a state-led national development project, in contrast to the basic idea of neo-liberal economics that states are inherently inefficient and predatory as compared to markets; (2) the remaking of power relations so as to secure the dominance of state actors with a developmental mindset; and (3) institutions, strategies, and policies supporting the developmental mindset (Haggard 1990; Wade 1990; Ravenhill 1993; Weiss 1998; Amsden 2001; Thurbon 2016; Haggard 2018; Khan 2018; Wade 2018).

5.1 The Developmental Mindset

The developmental mindset (a super-social-norm of appropriate actions), as it emerged in the threatening environment of Northeast Asia, included elite agreement on the following:

- high and sustained economic growth rates so as to catch up with developed countries 'quickly' (within a few decades);

- high rates of investment to gross domestic product (GDP) so as to achieve rapid movement of the production structure into more productive sectors;

- the state to co-ordinate the catch-up strategy and promote some sectors and functions ahead of others, whether through public enterprises or through steering private actors into sectors they would otherwise not enter;

- the state to curb the growth of consumption by the urban labour force and farmers, so as to free up more resources for investment;

---

[5] Myrdal's idea of the 'hard state', in contrast to the 'soft state', is an obvious precursor. Myrdal defined 'soft state' to mean the societal 'indiscipline' prevalent in South Asia and by extension much of the developing world, as compared to the states which had emerged in Western Europe. 'Indiscipline' referred to, in his words, 'deficiencies in legislation,...law observance and enforcement, widespread disobedience by public officials and, often, their collusion with powerful persons and groups...whose conduct they should regulate' (Myrdal 1970: 208).

- the state to promote exports intensively, so that the high investment could be profitable despite restrained growth of consumption at home, but at the same time, state industrial policy must target feasible replacement of imports and concentrate foreign exchange on imports of capital goods, intermediate goods, and raw materials (not consumer goods) by means of a managed trade policy, not free trade and not 'neutral incentives' between export promotion and import substitution;

- the state to invest heavily in education (people being the primary endowment, not natural resources), especially engineering, including sending students to the West for university education and putting them under obligation to return; and

- the state to boost the take-up of Western technology, including by establishing public research and development (R&D) centres able to 'domesticate' technologies purchased or imitated from abroad or brought in by branches of Japanese or Western companies, and by industrial extension services to push 'learning in production', especially in small and medium-sized enterprises.

Underpinning this elite consensus was recognition that investment resources were very scarce and had to be carefully husbanded. The elite had no commitment to the idea that 'free markets' or unstrategic integration into the world economy would produce a catch-up production structure over time, nor did American advisors push this agenda, in contrast to their later counterparts in other parts of the world and the World Bank.

The content of the production structure to be aimed at was influenced by popular metaphors of economic development, like descending a river or flying in a V-shaped formation of geese. Officials in South Korea and Taiwan saw their economies descending the same stretch of river, or flying in the same V-formation, as Japan some ten to twenty years before. They could look to Japan's past production structure for a *tangible* guide to what they should be investing in (qualified, of course, by knowledge of current developments in technology and markets, especially in Japan and the USA). The neo-liberal model deliberately has no such compass.

Northeast Asian officials recognized, more implicitly than explicitly, that *a unit of GDP from some sectors gives a larger boost to longer-run growth than a unit from other sectors*. Sectors which are more closely linked to others with higher value-added potential (in manufacturing) have a higher impact on growth than less connected ones. They recognized, second, that in the early stages in most sectors, few domestic firms have the ability to compete internationally without subsidies or protection, or if they do, it is as subordinate producers in low value-added portions of global or regional value chains, exposed to pressure from the lead firms (mostly Western or Japanese) 'to run faster to stay in the same place'. In sectors with high potential to boost longer-run growth, they saw that the question was not *whether* to give state support in order to help reap economies of scale and provide 'externalities' to other firms and sectors (beneficial but unpaid for spillovers), but *how*.

Officials recognized, third, that import replacement in sectors vital to industrial transformation required high levels of imports of raw materials, capital equipment, and technology; and therefore fast growth of export earnings. Business people learnt that export performance was one of the main criteria by which government responded to them across the board. If their export performance was good, government would help when they faced unexpected injury in whatever context. In all three countries, the government created an export 'culture', in the sense that exporting became a 'focal point' for decisions in wider government–business relations.

5.2 State Capacity and Bureaucracy–Business Institutions

Neo-liberal economics has a 'good governance' model, which emphasizes checks and balances between the various government ministries concerned with economic policy; so at central government level, authority should be horizontally decentralized, without a strong co-ordinating centre. And it emphasizes arms-length relations between government agencies and business, to avoid the ever-present danger of business capturing government, given the propensity for government officials to behave 'opportunistically'.

The developmental state model emphasizes the likely need to remake power relations so as to make them support the developmental mindset and the institutions and interventions through which the state tries to accelerate production transformation. In Northeast Asia the land reforms were crucial in removing a potential blockage to industrial development in the form of a landlord–state alliance (as in the Philippines). Also, all three governments in the post-war decades were able to wield a big stick over business. Taiwan and Korea were a mix of one-party states and military dictatorships until the late 1980s.

In the developmental state model the state gains high 'capacity' in economic governance not only from its fiscal and legal capacity but also from its institutional arrangements of 'embedded autonomy', to use Peter Evans' apparently oxymoronic phrase (Evans 1995). The state and its officials have a close working relationship with capitalists, plus the capacity to discipline capitalists and capital. They have the autonomy needed to formulate and implement a strategic vision for the economy's future growth and to discipline the owners and managers of capital in line with that vision (not be captured by specific groups of capitalists to work in their own interest at cost to the larger project). They also maintain close enough relationships with these owners and managers of capital to get information feedback and corporate buy-in to the national project. In Taiwan, when there were more than five firms in an industry the government required them to form an industry association (hence, a Taiwan Feather Exporters' Association). The firms elected the officials—but the government or Kuomintang (KMT) party appointed the secretary.

The 'embedded' part of embedded autonomy did not include much input from labour unions, especially in South Korea and Taiwan before the late 1980s. Labour repression, political marginalization of the working class, was part of the model, to keep down labour costs, prevent consumption demand from eating into the cycle of investment–profits–reinvestment, and keep the state–business vision of future transformation on track (Kohli 2004). Also, non-governmental organizations were tightly constrained.

Comparing public infrastructure bureaucracies in Korea and India, my research found that the Korean agency gave multiple incentives, individual and collective, for staff to act in line with the agency's objectives, while the Indian counterpart had virtually none—its incentives inclined the operational staff to threaten poor service so that clients would pay them under the table to receive normal service (Wade 1982b, 1985). The bureaucracies of Taiwan and Korea were certainly not 'squeaky clean'; corruption was well institutionalized in certain parts of the state, with the exception of the pilot agencies, the central bank, and a few others. But corruption functioned more as a tax or profit-sharing mechanism than as a price. Bidders on civil works contracts knew the conventions about how much had to be kicked back to officials, who, since the kick-back was much the same between different bids, were more inclined to allocate according to 'merit'. In India, by contrast, bidders would offer different amounts of kick-back, and officials allocated more in line with who offered the most.

5.3 The Policy Level

Chalmers Johnson summarized the array of instruments for influencing industry in Japan's post-war decades through the 1960s:

> control over all foreign exchange and imports of technology, which gave them [MITI officials, and US aid officials] the power to choose industries for development; the ability to dispense preferential financing, tax breaks, and protection from foreign competition, which gave them the power to lower the costs of the chosen industries; and the authority to order the creation of cartels and bank-based industrial conglomerates... which gave them the power to supervise competition.   (Johnson 1982: 199)

Johnson argues that bureaucratic dirigisme or administrative guidance played a central role in industrial structure policies into the 1970s and was even significant in Japan's move into more-technology-intensive industries later on.

The underlying rationale (which mainstream economics has long neglected) was to reduce the uncertainty facing investors at home—using trade protection to restrict competition from foreign producers; concessional finance for selected sectors; national procurement in favour of domestic firms; restricting competition among domestic firms, such as by government licensing of entry to particular industries; and also by taking the lead in the domestication of new technologies developed elsewhere.

Japan's methods for shaping the industrial structure provided models for the governments of Taiwan and South Korea. They deployed a wide range of instruments, including directed credit, fiscal investment incentives (such as tax rebates on production of products currently on the country's technology frontier), trade protection (combined with a tariff-rebate system so that producers could get tariff-free import of inputs which went into their exports while they paid the tariffs on what they sold on the domestic market), and hard bargaining with multinationals intending to make foreign direct investments within the national territory (such as local content requirements on a proposed ethylene plant or chip plant) (Wade 1990b/2004, 1991). Richard Luedde-Neurath (1988) documents the elaborate, and often covert, trade and investment controls used by the Korean government at the same time as it boasted to the world of its waves of market liberalization (see also Wade 1993, for Korea and Taiwan).

In contrast to many other governments which used broadly similar instruments from time to time, the developmental states in Northeast Asia normally imposed *performance conditions* of one kind or another to accompany state assistance (Wade 1990b/2004; Amsden 2001). The conditions might relate to closing the price and quality gap between imports and domestic substitutes within a fixed time, or to pushing out the technological frontiers of domestic production (for example, tax incentives for the first few producers to make electrical transformers above a certain capacity).

All three governments managed their exchange rates to ensure that trade protection did not yield overvalued exchange rates. So the combination of exchange rate management and performance conditions meant that trade protection did not insulate producers from international competitive pressure. It *buffered* producers from international competitive pressure until such time as the producers succeeded in (almost) matching the price and quality of competing imports, or failed to do so (Wade 1990b/2004, 1993). Howard Pack is right to criticize the common use of 'a generalized, blunderbuss industrial policy where you say, "Let's protect an entire industry"', but wrong to imply that it is the only way to give trade protection (Pack 2012).

Whereas mainstream economics tends to see learning as happening in R&D entities and deployed fairly automatically in firms' production, all three governments worked actively to accelerate learning in production by combining public R&D with industrial extension services, parallel to agricultural extension services, to accelerate industrial upgrading at the firm level (as distinct from relying on 'learning by doing'). Korea and Taiwan instituted technology development programmes as US aid came to an end in the mid-1960s. For example, the Korean government established the Science and Technology Agency as a department of the Prime Minister's Office in 1967. Its central location in the state gave it power, and it had freedom to hire top-level staff *outside of civil service rules*. Separately, the government established a network of government research institutes (GRIs), such as the Korea Institute for Science and Technology and the Korean Advanced Institute of Science, both in the late 1960s. They had strong links direct to President Park and the top levels of the military; and received ample assistance from the US. The GRIs took 'localizing foreign knowledge' as a core objective, meaning above all, getting this knowledge into the heads of locals, in the spirit of the Korean motto, 'We never learn anything twice'.

Taiwan created the Industrial Development Bureau within the Ministry of Economic Affairs, to operate as an industrial extension service (with a staff of about 150 by the early 1980s, mostly engineers). For decade after decade its engineers, divided into sectoral teams, travelled the length and breadth of the country (their job contracts required them to be out of the office so many days per month), visiting factories, giving advice, listening to problems, and feeding back into policy discussions. See epigraph three.

The government began to institutionalize a 'Science and Technology' complex of organizations at about the same time as Korea. The two countries watched each other closely and sent teams to learn from each other (a Korean team spent weeks inside Taiwan's Ministry of Economic Affairs, making a detailed copy of the country's duty drawback system in the early 1980s). Both countries sent large numbers of students to study science and engineering in the US, with inducements to return. The Taiwan government established a special office dedicated to organizing the diaspora: contacting Taiwanese working in US firms in sectors of high priority in Taiwan (for example, IBM), offering them expenses-paid trips back to Taiwan for conferences and networking, and facilitating full-time repatriation to Taiwan. Taiwan also established a Science and Technology Advisory Group (STAG), comprised of the minister of science and technology, plus between seven and ten *foreign* experts and a local secretariat. The group met for several days at a time, twice a year, to review investment proposals and to draw in knowledge about global technology developments. The Industrial Technology Research Institute (ITRI) by the early 1980s had a staff of some 10,000, divided into sub-institutes such as the Electronics Research and Service Organization (ERSO), with a staff of around 700. ITRI had a secretive military twin with a staff roughly twice as big.

These policies helped sectors and firms produce more, upgrade quality, and diversify into other product and capability domains—helped some more than others. Managing the inevitable tensions between the favoured and not-favoured was essential to their effectiveness. Beyond instruments for managing specific conflicts (for example, over excess capacity in industries like shipbuilding or cars), the authoritarian state managed conflicts through its domination in state–capital relations, and its assistance to capital in dominating capital–labour relations.

6. Singapore and Hong Kong

Singapore was a British colony from 1830 to 1963 (with a brutal Japanese interregnum from 1942 to 1945). It became a sovereign state as recently as 1965. Its development story is similar to that of the Northeast Asian three in that it had no significant natural resources beyond people, and location on one of the world's main East–West communication routes. Starting in the 1950s, it underwent a fast production transformation and integration into the world economy, led by manufacturing. And it experienced a super-fast rise in the world income hierarchy, from about 15 per cent of US average income in 1965 to nearly 70 per cent by the mid-1990s. Like the Northeast Asian cases (minus Hong Kong), it had a developmental state of strongly authoritarian character. (Regular parliamentary elections were held from 1959, but virtually all seats were won by the People's Action Party.) The state 'intervened' in labour markets to keep wage levels well below productivity levels. It engineered forced savings through government-controlled vehicles. It owned the land and ensured that a high and rising portion of the population lived in publicly owned housing, rented out on long leases: by the mid-1970s, half of the population lived in this accommodation (owned by the Housing and Development Board), today, 95 per cent. The state covered all Singapore citizens with a public health system, which today combines a very low percentage of GDP spent on health care and exceptionally high health indicators. Both housing and health tended to make people feel obliged to the state.

But the story also differs from that of the other three. Singapore had no significant agriculture population. It relied heavily on foreign firms establishing mostly wholly owned operations—together with state-owned enterprises. Missing in action was a local capitalist class, for the governing party sought to avoid the possibility of state capture by local capitalists. Also, the authoritarian regime has remained resilient throughout, from the late 1950s until today. Pressure from the population for political liberalization has been conspicuously lacking, in contrast to Taiwan and South Korea through the 1980s (Barth 2017). The state has avoided demands for democratization by: overseeing a high growth economy; being responsive to demands for social protection; ruling loosely enough that Singaporeans are often able to sidestep some state constraints in everyday life; and maintaining a highly meritocratic and squeaky clean civil service—keeping public sector senior salaries closely in line with private sector equivalents, and inverting the normal rule of law, 'innocent till proven guilty', to make civil servants subject to 'guilty [of corruption] till proven innocent'.

As for Hong Kong, mainstream economists like to cite its economic success to affirm that any non-neoclassical explanation of Northeast Asia's success is doomed, because, according to John Williamson, Hong Kong practised 'the most laissez-fare development strategy of any economy in history' (Williamson 1999), and the causes of the others' success must be similar to those of Hong Kong. The second part of Williamson's argument is impure nonsense (impure in that it contains a grain of truth).

Hong Kong was a British colony 1842–1997. Britain took it as 'spoils of war' when the British military defeated the Chinese military and forced the economic opening of China in the First Opium War. Like Singapore, it developed as a service centre for a vast hinterland. The economy flourished on the back of entrepôt trade, as a base for British–India exports of opium into China and for coastal China trade, and for the vast emigration from the mainland to the rest of the world. By 1900, tiny Hong Kong handled 40 per cent of giant China's exports and 42 per cent of its imports (Haggard 1990: 116). In the late 1940s it 'imported' an entrepreneurial light-industrial class already formed on the mainland under Nationalist (KMT) auspices when Shanghai textile capitalists with their modern machinery fled from the prospect of communist victory in the civil war.

For the entire period to 1997 (the brutal Japanese interregnum from 1941 to 1945 aside), it was governed largely by British businesses and senior civil servants in an emphatically non-democratic regime but with an independent judiciary. Virtually all the land belonged to the British Crown, which auctioned long-term leases—and kept taxes low on the proceeds; taxes were also low because the social security system was minimal. Functions which, in the other cases were carried out by state agencies, were performed in Hong Kong by well-institutionalized commercial and banking enterprises drawing personnel and organizational culture from Britain. But the Hong Kong state did intervene to provide a range of public goods for industry: it initiated the Federation of Hong Kong Industries in the 1950s, and established a Trade Development Council in 1967 to promote exports, a Productivity Council and Centre in 1967 to provide training and consultancy, and an Export Credit Insurance Company in 1966 for risks not commercially insurable.

Stephan Haggard summarizes similarities and differences with the others: 'although Hong Kong's *economic policy* may constitute an anomaly [close to laissez faire], its *political structure* shows surprising parallels to the East Asian pattern: a highly insulated state; limited representation [especially of "labour"]; and a concentrated and internally cohesive economic decision-making structure' (Haggard 1990: 115).

7. Conclusion

Northeast Asia undoubtedly benefitted from capitalism (private profit-driven production), and from access to the world market. To this extent the mainstream is correct. But several qualifications have to be made.

First, the ethnic and religious homogeneity of Japan, Taiwan, and South Korea, and the long history of dense populations and institutionalized political order, helped to generate dense, hierarchical social networks through which the natural human tendency to free-ride on the collectivity could be checked and collective interests fostered. This basic cultural pattern of individualism checked by powerful group norms was reinforced by intense state permeation of the society, driven and disciplined by external threats: Japan under the threat of US colonization in the nineteenth century; Korea and Taiwan colonized by Japan as it created an empire to ward off American and European empires; and all three under communist state threat after the Second World War.

Second, they came into the post-war decades with high ratios of working-age people to dependents, as seen by much lower median ages in 1970 than in Europe at that time.

Third, the post-war threat perception of national and US elites kept national elites relatively unified and not at each other's throats—and kept the inevitable tensions between favoured and not-favoured sectors and firms, and favoured and non-favoured regions, within limits. On the spectrum of 'weak state/special-interest state/common-interest state' these were special-interest states moving towards—with a lot of American help in the first decades—common-interest states.

Fourth, for the first several decades the Northeast economies relied not so much on 'the world market' as on 'empire preference' to the US market—and to US technologies, US capital, US military and civilian aid, and US public procurement—thanks to their role in the US's geopolitical strategy to contain communism and show the world that 'capitalism' was superior to 'communism'.

Fifth, steered by a developmental mindset, the developmental state was organized differently than the model neo-liberal state. The latter has no strong centre of co-ordination (because markets played by private capitalists, not states, are the resource co-ordinating institution), and has arms-length relations between the various ministries and between ministries and business. The developmental state has one or a few powerful centres of co-ordination and market leadership, a limited role for the legislature in matters of economic, financial, and security policy, and well-developed mechanisms of consultation and co-ordination with private capitalists, in the spirit of 'embedded autonomy'.

Sixth, these governments operated on the premise that increments of GDP from some sectors brought higher potential future growth than from others, and made intensive use of steerage policies and institutions frowned upon in the neoliberal playbook—such as managed trade, sectoral industrial policy (not 'picking winners' but 'making winners'), targeted concessional credit, and capital controls. These instruments were intended to buffer (not insulate) producers in selected sectors from international competitive pressure and volatility—so profit-raising protection and subsidies came with performance conditions, which were enforced. The whole complex would have scored poorly by Washington Consensus criteria. For example, Taiwan's financial system was and remains the despair of visiting Western economists. That said, there is no knockout evidence on the effects of these 'government interventions'. The causality is too difficult to disentangle 'rigorously'.

Finally, as the governments encouraged firms to integrate into global value chains while simultaneously encouraging the growth of backwards and forwards linkages (filling up the input-output table), they undertook to develop domestic technological capacity, with public laboratories, high enrolments in university and vocational science and engineering faculties, and organized efforts to attract back overseas graduate students (seen as 'brain bank' rather than 'brain drain'). Singapore, as noted, did rely more than the others on incoming Western multinationals—which were left in no doubt as to who called the shots.

These points help to understand how Northeast Asian countries overcame two logics of power which keep most of the periphery as a periphery, and which intertwine like a double-helix to produce the result we know as the glass ceiling or the middle-income or middle-capability trap: first, the centrifugal pressures emanating from the Western core (including several mechanisms of net resource transfer from periphery to core); second, the drive to hold on to a certain structure of political power on the part of leaders of poor countries, even at cost to national development, in case rival groups use the wealth created by access to new opportunities to oust the incumbents.

The full-fledged East Asian developmental states were self-limiting, in the sense that the package of (1) elite consensus around the national development project, (2) bureaucracy of industrial planning, (3) array of industrial steerage instruments, and (4) repression of labour, came out of shared elite conviction of the imperative of high rates of investment to upgrade the production structure quickly, raise mass living conditions, inhibit domestic revolt, and support a strong military, coupled with knowledge that many domestic firms could not compete 'on a level playing field' with firms in developed countries.

Some analysts say that, as of today, the Northeast Asian developmental state has eroded to the point that 'the developmental state is dead' (Pirie 2017). It is true that as the economies achieved 'high income' they moved in a neo-liberal direction, both for structural reasons and also to bolster their alliances with the West. Structurally, they faced the problem common to developed countries: they became less able to generate enough profitable investment opportunities to absorb domestic savings (especially given the various policies in place to restrain consumption). Far from a severe shortage of capital, they began to experience an abundance. At the same time, the general level of productivity became high enough for most firms not to need subsidies or protection to compete domestically or abroad. The state has withdrawn from the capital–labour relation (withdrawn from negotiations about wages and working conditions), and relied on the 'discipline of the market'—the threat of unemployment and the threat of bankruptcy—to keep labour under capital's control. The state has also substantially withdrawn from the allocation of credit, as seen in the now 'independent' central banks and in the large majority of lending having no link to the creation of new productive capacity. So, in both Taiwan and Korea the capital–labour relation and the allocation of capital have been marketized; the state is mostly out.

These neo-liberal trends have been all the easier because during their history as developmental states the state resisted moves in a social democratic direction to build up social protections. Today, public welfare is still underdeveloped and legal obstacles block collective action among the working class. Public social spending as a share of GDP remains far below the OECD average, and the share of the labour force in independent trade unions also falls far short of the OECD average. The governments have allowed the share of wages in national income to keep falling. Income inequality has steadily risen since the 1980s. The growth model relies on rising household debt plus foreign demand—exports—to close the demand gap, and both are sources of vulnerability. Both countries have become highly exposed to an economic crisis in China, or Chinese arm-twisting.

At the same time, the Northeast Asian states (and Singapore) are still characterized by a developmental mindset driving the state to keep pushing for production transformation. The developmental state has not so much 'declined' or 'disappeared' in East Asia in favour of the neo-liberal state, as Iain Pirie (2017) claims; it has 'evolved' in response to changing parameters. In Christopher Dent's words: 'while the policy tools and means may have changed, developmental states still preside over various adaptive-cum-transformative economic projects that increasingly involve a partnering with transnationalized capital' (Dent 2007: 227).

Much of the state's market leadership takes the form of overarching 'societal missions' driven by a varying mix of economic and national security objectives. Over the past several decades, all the Northeast Asian (capitalist) cases have experienced a dizzying number of organizational restructurings in the pursuit of national innovation objectives. Standing back, one can see, first, a fairly steady movement from state-led efforts to domesticate foreign innovations and deploy them in the domestic economy (lowering risks for adopters), to managing uncertainties of innovating on the global techno-economic frontier. Second, one can see a zig-zagging path over time, often coinciding with changes of government: from fairly centralized, top-down control (using methods of formulating, legitimating, and implementing innovation policies drawn from the principles of the old developmental state), to more decentralized, 'peripheral islands' of innovation agencies (drawing on the approach of states like the US and UK), and back to more central control, drawing on an updated version of the developmental mindset (Karo 2018). In short, we should talk not of the death of the developmental state in Northeast Asia and the rise of the neo-liberal or the post-developmental state, but of the transformation of the developmental state from 1.0 to 2.0.

Beyond Northeast Asia, the North Atlantic financial crisis of 2007 to 2012 and ensuing long recession has somewhat weakened credence in the neo-liberal development consensus, reawakening interest in 'respectable' circles in industrial policy and the developmental state. The evidence is clear that economic development that is fast enough to bring mass living conditions close to developed countries is really difficult – because of intersecting logics of the 'special interest' state and the centrifugal forces from the Western core. Catch-up requires, above all, that a powerful coalition within a country embraces a 'developmental mindset' and sustains an institutional process for eliciting information from the private sector about investment opportunities and obstacles, nudging private firms to upgrade and diversify, sponsoring investment initiatives in promising directions that the private sector would not otherwise undertake, pushing education in engineering and science, and managing the inevitable conflicts. But the developmental state is not 'all or nothing'. It can be institutionalized at the subnational regional level and at sector level. Even where bureaucracy-in-general is a swamp, equivalents to Taiwan's Industrial Development Bureau and its Science and Technology Advisory Group (described earlier) can be established to accelerate production upgrading, provided they have top-level political support. But the first step is to accept that the Washington Consensus policy agenda is useful enough as a recipe for improving the performance of a thoroughly crony capitalism, but not for powering upwards through the centrifugal dynamics of the middle-income trap.

References

Amsden, A. (2001). *The Rise of 'The Rest'*. Oxford: Oxford University Press.

Arrighi, G. (2007). 'States, Markets, and Capitalism, East and West', *Positions*, 15(2): 251–84.

Barth, J. (2017). 'The PAP-State: Housing, Health, and Resilient Authoritarianism', DPhil thesis, University of Oxford.

Bernard, M., and J. Ravenhill (1995). 'Beyond Product Cycles and Flying Geese', *World Politics*, 47(2): 171–209.

Besley, T., and T. Persson (2011). *Pillars of Prosperity*. Princeton, NJ: Princeton University Press.

Cherif, R., and F. Hasanov (2015). 'The Leap of the Tiger', IMF Washington, DC, IMF Working Paper WP/15/131.

Cumings, B. (1984). 'The Origins and Development of the Northeast Asian Political Economy', *International Organization*, 38: 1–40.

Dent, C. (2007). 'The State and Transnational Capital in Adaptive Partnership'. In H. Wai-Chung Yeung (ed.) *Handbook of Research on Asian Businesses*. Cheltenham: Edward Elgar.

Dore, R. (1965). 'Land Reform and Japan's Economic Development', *Developing Economies*, 3(4): 487–96.

Easterly, W. (2002). 'The Failure of Economic Development', *Challenge*, 45(1): 88–103.

Evans, P. (1995). *Embedded Autonomy*. Princeton, NJ: Princeton University Press.

Fischer, A. (2015). 'The End of Peripheries?', *Development and Change*, 46(4): 700–32.

Fukuyama, F. (2004). *State-building, Governance and World Order in the Twenty-First Century.* London: Profile Books.

Haggard, S. (1990). *Pathways from the Periphery.* Ithaca, NY: Cornell University Press.

Haggard, S. (2018). *Developmental States.* Cambridge: Cambridge University Press.

Hollerman, L. (1979). 'International Economic Controls in Occupied Japan', *Journal of Asian Studies*, 38(August): 719.

Johnson, C. (1982). *MITI and the Japanese Miracle.* Stanford, CA: Stanford University Press.

Karo, E. (2018). 'Mission-oriented Innovation and Bureaucracies in East Asia', *Industrial and Corporate Change*, 27(October): 867–81.

Kattel, R., and M. Mazzucato (2018). 'Mission-oriented Innovation Policy and Dynamic Capabilities in the Public Sector', *Industrial and Corporate Change*, 27: 5.

Khan, M. (2018). 'Institutions and Development in Asia', UNU-WIDER, Helsinki, WIDER Working Paper.

Kohli, A. (2004). *State-directed Development.* Princeton, NJ: Princeton University Press.

Lee, J. (2017). 'US Grand Strategy and the Origins of the Developmental State', mimeo, Princeton University, Princeton, NJ, Department of Political Science.

Luedde-Neurath, R. (1988). 'State Intervention and Export-oriented Development in South Korea'. In G. White (ed.) *Developmental States in East Asia.* London: Macmillan.

Myrdal, G. (1968). *Asian Drama: An Inquiry into the Poverty of Nations. A Twentieth Century Fund Study, Volumes I, II, and III.* London: Allen Lane.

Myrdal, G. (1970). 'The "Soft State" in Undeveloped Countries'. In P. Streeten (ed.) *Unfashionable Economics: Essays in Honour of Lord Balogh.* London: Weidenfeld and Nicolson.

Pack, H. (2012). 'Does it Make Sense to have an Industrial Policy?', Knowledge@Wharton [online], 11 April. Available at: http://knowledge.wharton.upenn.edu/article/does-it-make-sense-to-have-an-industrial-policy-ask-howard-pack/ (accessed 27 August 2018).

Pirie, I. (2017). 'Korea and Taiwan', *Journal of Contemporary Asia*, 28(1): 133–58.

Pritchett, L. (1997). 'Divergence, Bigtime', *Journal of Economic Perspectives*, 111(3): 3–17.

Pritchett, L., and L.H. Summers (2014). 'Asiaphoria Meets Regression to the Mean', National Bureau of Economic Research, Cambridge, MA, NBER Working Paper 20537.

Ravenhill, J. (1993). 'State and Market: Review of Robert Wade, Governing the Market', *Asian Studies Review*, 16(3): 111–20.

Rock, M. (2017). *Dictators, Democrats, and Development in Southeast Asia.* Oxford: Oxford University Press.

Thurbon, E. (2016). *Developmental Mindset: The Revival of Financial Activism in South Korea.* Ithaca, NY: Cornell University Press.

Uchitelle, L. (2002). 'Challenging the Dogmas of Free Trade', *New York Times*, 9 February. Available at: www.nytimes.com/2002/02/09/arts/challenging-the-dogmas-of-free-trade.html (accessed 27 August 2018).

Wade, R. (1982a). *Irrigation and Agricultural Politics in South Korea*. Boulder, CO: Westview Press.

Wade, R. (1982b). 'Employment, Water Control, and Water Supply Institutions: South India and South Korea', IDS, Sussex University, Brighton, DP182.

Wade, R. (1985). 'The Market for Public Office', *World Development*, 13(4): 467–97.

Wade, R. (1990a). 'Industrial Policy in East Asia'. In G. Gereffi and D.L. Wyman (eds) *Manufacturing Miracles*. Princeton, NJ: Princeton University Press.

Wade, R. (1990b/2004). *Governing the Market*. Princeton, NJ: Princeton University Press.

Wade, R. (1991). 'How to Protect Exports from Protection', *World Economy*, 14(3): 299–309.

Wade, R. (1992a). 'East Asian Economic Success', *World Politics*, 44(2): 270–320.

Wade, R. (1992b). 'How to Make "Street Level" Bureaucracies Work Better', *IDS Bulletin*, 23(4): 51–4.

Wade, R. (1993). 'Managing Trade', *Comparative Politics*, 25(2): 147–67.

Wade, R. (1996). 'Japan, the World Bank, and the Art of Paradigm Maintenance', *New Left Review*, 217: 3–36.

Wade, R. (2017a). 'Is Trump Wrong about Trade?'. In E. Fullbrook and J. Morgan (eds) *Trumponomics: Causes and Consequences*. London: College Publications.

Wade, R. (2017b). 'The American Paradox', *Cambridge Journal of Economics*, 41(3): 859–80.

Wade, R. (2018). 'The Developmental State: Dead or Alive?', *Development and Change*, 49(2): 518–46.

Weiss, L. (1998). *The Myth of the Powerless State*. Ithaca, NY: Cornell University Press.

Weiss L., and E. Thurbon (2004). 'Where There's a Will There's a Way', *Issues and Studies*, 40(1): 61–72.

Williamson, J. (1999). 'Economic Reform: Content, Progress, Prospects', Presentation at the 50th Anniversary Celebration of the University of Baroda, 23 November, Peterson Institute for International Economics, Washington, DC.

Woo, M. (2016). 'Industrial Diversification in Korea'. In R. Cherif, F. Hasanov, and M. Zhu (eds) *Breaking the Oil Spell: The Gulf Falcons' Path to Diversification*. Washington, DC: International Monetary Fund.

Woo-Cumings, M. (ed.) (1999). *The Developmental State*. Ithaca, NY: Cornell University Press.

World Bank (1993). *The East Asian Miracle*. Washington, DC: World Bank.

World Bank (2013). *China 2030: Building a Modern, Harmonious, and Creative Society*. Washington, DC: World Bank.

World Bank (2015). *World Development Indicators 2015*. Washington, DC: World Bank.

20

Southeast Asia

Manuel F. Montes

1. Introduction

This chapter examines the development experiences of Six Southeast Asian countries, Malaysia, the Philippines, Thailand, Cambodia, Lao People's Democratic Republic (hereinafter 'Lao PDR'), and Myanmar—here collectively called 'the Six'—fifty years after Gunnar Myrdal's (1968) *Asian Drama*. A companion piece, (Montes 2018), which is longer but with the same structure, presents more elaboration on the data and analyses.

In *Asian Drama*, Myrdal took an unambiguously pessimistic view of Asian prospects for development on the basis of (1) obstacles to raising agricultural productivity and (2) the low perceived level of capability of governments to intervene effectively in favour of industrial development, the latter being a handicap that included extensive corruption at all levels of government. For the most part, the record of the Six defied Myrdal's prognosis, raising agricultural productivity faster than population growth and displaying sufficient state capability to direct change towards a respectable level of industrial development.

The Six comprise a diverse grouping of countries in terms of natural endowments, historical precedents, and polities. Five, all except Thailand, are former colonies. Three—Cambodia, Thailand, and Malaysia—are constitutional monarchies. Three—Malaysia, the Philippines, and Thailand—are long-running market economies. Two—Myanmar and Lao PDR—are formally socialist economies; at the other end of the scale, free enterprise is deemed as the foundation of the Philippines' democratic way of life (Myrdal 1968: 387). Three states—Cambodia, Malaysia (until May 2018), and Myanmar (until 2016)—have been de facto one-party states.

In terms of standard categories, there are two distinct groups within the Six. There are the three middle-income economies—Malaysia, the Philippines, and Thailand—and three least-developed countries (LDCs)—Cambodia, Lao PDR, and Myanmar—sometimes also referred to as the Socialist Three. The Socialist Three spent part of the post-*Asian Drama* period overcoming economic isolation and embargo, but managed to develop and expand the international dimensions of their economies.

A memorable contribution of Myrdal's *Asian Drama* is the idea of the 'soft state', introduced in the 'value premises chosen' section at the start of *Asian Drama*.

He categorized Asian countries as having 'all "soft states"' (Myrdal 1968: 66). For Myrdal, a soft state comprises two faces of a coin: (1) policies, whether or not they are actually decided, are poorly enforced and (2) authorities 'are reluctant to place obligations on people'.

Subsequently, a discussion arose on the indispensable role of a 'strong state' or a 'developmental state', based on an interpretation of the record of successful East Asian economies (Wade 1990). According to this view, as 'strong states', East Asian states engineered state-led development. This view was an antidote to the rapid rise of the view—propagated by Bretton Woods staff and Official Development Assistance (ODA) agencies in the wake of the developing country debt crises of the 1980s—that an interventionist state is the main obstacle to development. According to this view, if a society is saddled with a soft state susceptible to elite capture, it might as well let domestic and international market forces discipline both the state and the private sector.

The Six threaded the space between these two exhortations, with the exception of two countries. The Philippines has been dismantling state intervention since 1984 and Myanmar has long relied on a planned economy with direct state control over the enterprise sector, despite efforts at reform since 1988. In between, the other Four, despite not being 'strong states', exhibit relatively better performance despite widespread state interventions, governance weaknesses, and gradualist reform paths. These contrasts could suggest that one does not have to choose between corner solutions to obtain some measure of structural change.

Table 20.1 presents the broad contours of overall growth among the Six. For the three LDCs (Cambodia, Lao PDR, and Myanmar), per capita growth rates are distinctly lower in the conflict-ridden 1970–1990 period; per capita growth rates more than doubled in the 1990–2015 period. Starting from below the average in 1970, by 2015 these three had caught up and exceeded the average per capita income of LDCs. Among the three market economies, Malaysia and Thailand achieved high growth in the first half of the post-*Asian Drama* period, until 1990, subsiding in the second half, while the Philippines shows an upturn from low levels in the first period. On per capita income comparisons, Malaysia and Thailand are clearly strong performers. Malaysia's per capita income is practically double that of average developing country per capita income; Thailand's per capita income is 20 per cent higher than average developing country per capita income. The Philippines has lost ground in per capita income comparisons among developing countries.

A discussion of the factors behind this overall pattern will be grouped around four issues:

(1) raising agriculture output and transitioning from agricultural dependence;

(2) industrial development, the state, and the private sector;

(3) openness, trade, and foreign investments; and

(4) employment, inequality, and social development.

Table 20.1 Economic growth indicators, %

	Per capita GDP growth[a]		GDP growth rate[a]		Per cent of 'group'[b] per capita income	
	1970–1990	1990–2015	1970–1990	1990–2015	1970	2015
Cambodia	−2.3	5.0	−1.0	7.4	78.0	119.0
Lao PDR	2.5	5.0	4.8	6.9	31.5	220.9
Myanmar	0.5	8.0	2.7	9.1	72.4	122.1
Malaysia	4.9	3.5	7.7	5.7	162.6	198.0
Philippines	1.0	2.2	3.8	4.2	94.1	59.1
Thailand	5.0	3.4	7.3	4.2	90.9	119.4
Developing countries	2.2	3.6	4.5	5.2		

Notes:

[a] Growth rates are compounded growth rates calculated from end-points based on real values.

[b] Per capita incomes are based on current prices at current exchange rates; for Cambodia, Lao PDR, and Myanmar, the 'group' denominator is LDC per capita income; for Malaysia, the Philippines, and Thailand, the 'group' denominator is developing country per capita income.

Source: Author, based on data from UNCTADStat (http://unctadstat.unctad.org/EN), Data Center, folder Economic trends/National accounts/Gross domestic product/Gross domestic product: total and per capita, current and constant (2010 prices), annual and/Gross domestic product: total and per capita, growth rates, annual.

2. Raising Agriculture Output and Transitioning from Agricultural Dependence

Variations in the record among the Six uphold the view that strong progress in agriculture is an essential element of structural change. There were two vital dimensions in this record: (1) institutional reform and (2) output increases mainly but not solely enabled by the dissemination of 'high-yielding varieties' (HYVs) of rice.

The record suggests that markets and private incentives, while having a necessary role, are insufficient for the purpose of agricultural development and diversification. While the introduction of HYV in rice was fortuitous to the agricultural challenge, successful cases among the Six point to the larger role of institutional changes traceable to state policies and interventions.

2.1 Institutional Reforms

For the Six, these reforms concerned issues of tenancy and collectivization and the role of foreign, indigenous, and state-owned enterprises. Except for Thailand, which was never colonized, plantations for export on one hand and farming for local consumption on the other were the two main production modes in agriculture. As independent states, the Six faced the problem of sustaining commodity export earnings while responding to the inequities in access to land in the rural areas bequeathed by colonial trade.

2.1.1 The Socialist Three

In the Cambodia Lao PDR, agrarian reform—meaning a deliberate withdrawal from collectivized farming, during the 1980s after the failure of initial attempts to secure food security through collective farms—constituted the crucial event in institutional reform in Lao PDR and Cambodia (van Arkadie 1995).

In 1986, Lao PDR began encouraging a return to family farms, de-emphasizing collectives that had generated resistance, 'leading many to retreat into subsistence' (van Arkadie 1995: 31). With state ownership of land, Cambodian non-plantation agriculture in principle was organized in co-operatives, but, in practice, the rules did not displace family farming. By 1989, private property ownership had replaced collective production.

In Myanmar, where all land is the property of the state, formal agrarian reform efforts began after 2010. About one-third of the country's rural residents, are landless labourers. In early 2018, the government enacted two new laws to provide a legal framework that offers a path to widening land ownership: the Farmland Law and the Vacant, Fallow, and Virgin Land Management Law (Hiebert and Nguyen 2018).

2.1.2 The Market Economy Three

In the three market economies of Malaysia, the Philippines, and Thailand, arguments of equity, tinged with the possibility of raising agricultural productivity by unleashing individual initiative, underpinned various state efforts to expand farmer families' access to agricultural assets.

In Malaysia, a postcolonial disposition promoted indigenizing commodity processing and the resettling of landless rural households in rubber and palm oil estates in the 1960s. Under the Bumiputera programme, private, foreign-owned plantations were nationalized so that by the early 1980s, the state had gained control of the whole plantation sector (Lim 1985).

In the Philippines, tenancy-based production—and a matching social structure ('pre-capitalist' (see Chapter 13, this volume) or 'feudal' (Myrdal 1968)) from the Spanish colonial period—held sway in all major crops. The Philippines have attempted a major 'land reform' programme in every decade with indifferent results despite high ambitions (Borras 2007; also Chapter 5, this volume).

Thailand's previous political history, including reforms in 1874 and, again, in the 1930s, afforded a much less skewed distribution in access to land.

Owners and financiers have to take greater responsibility in introducing new technology where tenancy is dominant. Large landowners control not only production but also local labour markets. The next section explores how these kinds of differences in institutional resources shaped the speed and the impact of efforts to raise agricultural productivity.

2.2 The Green Revolution

The propagation of HYV rice, the first of which was introduced in 1966, two years before Myrdal's volume, played a significant part in raising agricultural production and attaining food security in the Six. HYV technology was input-intensive in terms of water, fertilizer, and pesticide, and induced its own pressures on institutions and on state provisioning. Rural institutions and the capabilities of the state, in turn, affected how increases in agricultural output were shared among members of society.

2.2.1 Raising Agricultural Production and Yields

There is a vast body of literature on the positive impact of the Green Revolution on the economies of Southeast Asia, and it suffices to touch on the highlights. The spread of the Green Revolution and HYVs proceeded at a strong pace in the 1970s. By 1976/77, HYVs accounted for 7 per cent of crop area planted in Myanmar, 37.4 per cent in west Malaysia, 68.1 per cent in the Philippines, and 11.3 per cent in Thailand (Darlymple 1979: 708).

For rice, the most telling impact of HYVs was to allow two rice crops per year in irrigated areas. The increase in output was significant enough to turn the terms of trade against agriculture, greatly benefitting consumers, especially those in the lower-income strata who spend more on food.

For the whole of Southeast Asia between 1961 and 2010, the record shows that total agricultural production grew by 3.44 per cent per year, substantially faster than the population (Timmer 2015: 99), a record that includes not just the Green Revolution in rice, but diversification in production and consumption as incomes rose.

Cambodia achieved rice self-sufficiency in 1995. Production targets for rice incorporate a surplus for export (Chhair and Ung 2016). Inadequate infrastructure to transport agricultural produce hampers further investment in productivity and crop diversification. Lao PDR achieved rice self-sufficiency in 1999. However, with 70 per cent of the population living in rural areas, agricultural productivity per worker remains low (World Bank 2014: 26). These two cases argue for sustained state investment in agriculture at low-income levels.

2.2.2 Impact on Society

The impact of the Green Revolution on farmers themselves depended on whether the 'technology enabled their costs of production to decline more than prices declined' (Evenson 2004: 548). Farmers who could use the technology were positively affected; those farmers without access to the technology were negatively affected since they sold their produce at lower market prices.

In the literature, pre-existing inequality is seen as the main determinant of the distribution of gains from the Green Revolution (Ruttan 1977: 20; see also Wong 1987, for Malaysia).

On the consumer side, in the context of Myrdal's warning of a reinforcing interaction between low agricultural productivity and low labour productivity, Timmer (2015: 91) finds that, compared with the rest of the world, Southeast Asia as a whole made substantial progress in reducing food insecurity in the two decades since 1990, with the region transforming a 'large negative gap of 12.3 per cent to a very large positive gap of 15.7 points'. The underlying process Timmer implicates is the rise in the productivity of agricultural labour, which, in the standard narrative, is a precondition for the transition from agriculture to industry.

2.3 Transitioning Out of Agricultural Dependence

Led by Malaysia and Thailand, the Six have managed creditable transitions in shifting the weight of economic activity from agriculture to industry and services at rates that exceeded those achieved a generation earlier by Northeast Asian 'tiger economies' (Coxhead 2015: 4). All of the Six have reduced the sectoral contribution of agriculture to gross domestic product (GDP); all, except Myanmar, see the proportion of GDP in services rise, with the Philippines showing the greatest increase; see Montes (2018: table 2).

The extractive industries represent a high proportion of GDP in Cambodia, Lao PDR, and Myanmar; for these countries, the bulk of the difference between the proportion of GDP in industry and the proportion in manufacturing is associated with the extractive industries. These countries have the advantage of relatively low population densities and thus much room to rely on this sector. Figure 20.1 depicts the steep shift of value-added proportions from agriculture to manufacturing, particularly most recently in Myanmar and Cambodia, with a more moderate but steady long-run reallocation for Malaysia and Thailand. Between 1993 and 2007, the share of manufacturing in Cambodia increased from 12 to 25 per cent. In most countries, the growth rate of manufacturing subsided after the Asian financial crisis.

In the case of the Philippines, the long-term trend has been a declining share of agriculture with no perceptible increase in manufacturing as a proportion of value-added; services, especially in recent years, have absorbed labour from agriculture. A portion of the Philippines' increase in services contribution comes from its capturing second position to India in the international business process outsourcing sector.

3. Industrial Development, the State, and the Private Sector

There is a policy controversy over whether the state had any positive role in the Six's industrial development. One side of the debate holds that successful Southeast

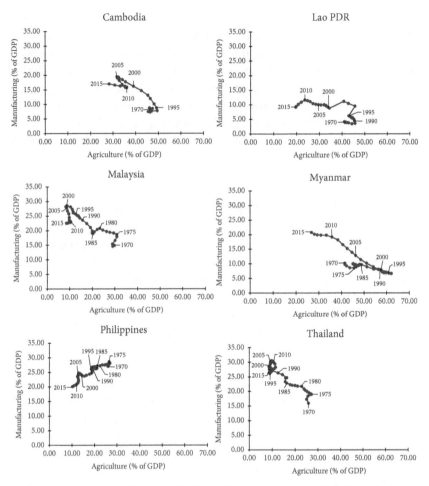

Figure 20.1 Structural change in Southeast Asia: percentage of GDP in agriculture and manufacturing.

Note: Three-year moving averages, except for end-points.

Source: Author, based on data from UNCTAD, http://unctadstat.unctad.org/wds/ReportFolders/reportFolders.aspx in folder Economic trends/National accounts/Gross domestic product: GDP by type of expenditure, VA by kind of activity, total and shares, annual, 1970–2016.

Asian states did *not* intervene significantly and that the unsuccessful ones intervened too much; the other side holds that evidence of extensive intervention on the part of successful economies cannot be ignored. Even for those recognizing that, indeed, extensive state interventions occurred, one side of the argument takes the view that state policies did not have significant impact on industrial upgrading in the successful cases and that external trade, foreign investment, and macroeconomic stability—the latter a distinctly Southeast Asian advantage in the 1980s but not in the 1990s—were the decisive important factors. A related view holds that, by being export-oriented, market conditions were simulated (Bhagwati 1988), thereby enforcing market conforming behaviour on both the state and the enterprise sector. The opposite view is that state policies defied market signals and played an indispensable role in structural change.

The evidence presented here is that successful economies among the Six did intervene and distorted market signals—both as industrial policy and as state-led investment. This contradicts the view detailed in the 'East Asian miracle' study by the World Bank (1993), that the successful economies relied mainly on macroeconomic stability to drive structural change. Except for the Philippines, industrial policy regimes in the countries in all economies have persisted, albeit still evolving, since 1968. State-led investment played a significant role in the early stages. Instead of being dismantled, industrial policies expanded to benefit export sectors beginning in the 1980s. The rest of this section develops this narrative in three sub-parts: (1) a review of the actually existing policies among the Six; (2) the role of state-led investments; and (3) the role of the state and the large domestic private sector. Much of the discussion in this section will be on the three middle-income countries. The three LDCs can be seen as following the path of the successful three middle-income countries, with state-led investments in early stages and state-enabled efforts to penetrate export sectors in extractives and light manufacturing.

3.1 Actually Existing Industrial Policies in Southeast Asia

In 1968, import-substituting policies were unchallenged among the three Southeast Asian market economies (Malaysia, the Philippines, and Thailand), while state dominance over the economy in the three LDCs (Cambodia, Lao PDR, and Myanmar) was inescapable in their conflict-ridden and embargo-restricted contexts.

A system of sectorally targeted exchange controls, cascading tariffs, multiple exchange rates, tax incentives, and subsidies lay at the heart of industrial policy for Southeast Asian countries. There were preferential exchange rates, import controls on competing final goods or intermediate inputs, tariff exemptions on imported equipment, tax holidays, restrictions on entry of new capacity in the industry, preferential interest rates, and access to credit (Montes 1993: 12–13).

3.1.1 Developing while Import-Substituting

After the racial riots of 1969, as part of its Bumiputera programme, Malaysia state protectionist intervention became widespread. However, these programmes sought also to strengthen competitiveness in key export industries, including palm oil. State intervention paved the way for the extensive relocation of US semiconductor companies to Malaysia, exploiting the country's supply of low-cost, semi-skilled female labour (Montes 1993: 15). The net effect of these interventions involved an economy whose degree of price distortion did not differ significantly from that in the Philippines or Korea in 1975 (Salleh et al. 1992: 20).

Thailand has maintained significant import protection for selected industries. Among the most highly favoured sectors were textiles, automobiles, and pharmaceuticals. Industrial promotion benefitted capital-intensive manufactures in defiance of the country's static comparative advantage as a resource-rich, labour-abundant economy (Montes 1993: 17).

3.1.2 Contrasting Approaches to External Liberalization

The 1980s saw a decided shift towards external liberalization among the Six. However, there were contrasts in degree and strategy among these countries. For the Socialist Three, privatization and exchange rate consolidation were critical elements of outward reorientation. For Thailand, this meant the redeployment of import-substituting policies in support of export promotion. For the Philippines, outward reorientation involved import liberalization. In 1981, Thai industrial policy shifted to incorporating export promotion. Even with these reforms, Christensen et al. (1992) report the Thai effective protection rate for manufacturing to be 52 per cent, still higher than Korea (28 per cent), Malaysia (23 per cent), and the Philippines (23 per cent).

The Philippines chose a different path towards an internationally competitive industrial sector, embarking on an ambitious trade and import liberalization programme, starting in 1984 during a balance-of-payments crisis. The new trajectory aimed at eliminating the disincentives imposed by protection (Hill 2015), in a series of structural adjustment programmes under the aegis of the Bretton Woods institutions. The programmes, in line with other such programmes in other debt-distressed countries, did not afford additional financing specifically for industrial adjustment. State financing is analytically incompatible with a liberalization-based effort, which is predicated on a private discovery of international competitiveness.

Lao PDR introduced the New Economic Mechanism in 1986, to begin the transition from a centrally planned to a market-oriented economy. In a 'step by step' gradual manner, price controls were removed, the exchange rate system was unified, and the government's monopoly on trade ended, with the number of state enterprises reduced and the establishment of private firms. With the achievement of peace in 1992, the reintroduction of private ventures in Cambodia began. With the support of international financial institutions, Cambodia and Lao PDR expanded their infrastructure and utilities. Lao PDR benefitted from multilateral programmes to develop the Mekong region and the market for hydropower to Thailand. Cambodia became a big player in contract production in textiles and clothing. Myanmar's industrial sector was under state control throughout this period but in 1988 the registration of private ventures was opened. Table 20.2 indicates that Cambodia, Lao PDR, and Myanmar doubled the contribution of manufacturing to GDP between 1985 and 2015, after stagnating for the previous twenty-five years.

3.2 State-led Investments and State-owned Enterprises

Among the Six, rapid transitions to industry and manufacturing were enabled by high national investment rates. Except for Myanmar, a socialist state, private investment rates played a key role. However, what distinguishes the successful economies is the sizeable role of government investment. Before the Asian financial crisis in 1997, national investment rates exceeded 20 per cent of GDP in Malaysia and Thailand, with government investment at over 8 per cent (see Montes 2018: table 3); the exception was the Philippines, where government investment never exceeded 3 per cent. An acceleration of investment rates after 1997 is evident in Cambodia and Lao PDR. With various levels of effectiveness and through bouts of nationalization and privatization, all of the Six deployed state-owned enterprises (Myanmar exclusively until 1988) and none permanently collectivized agriculture. All of the Six engaged in a fluctuating degree of national economic planning.

Among the Six, the variation in the record of state enterprises mirrors the same range of success and disappointment in the developing world—with Myanmar's experience of stasis uniformly across sectors at one end (Booth 2003; Tin 2006), and successful cases such as palm oil processing in Malaysia at the other (Teoh 2002). What deserves mention is how the private sector in successful cases such as Malaysia achieved productivity increases and industrial development while exploiting state-provided economic subsidies and protection.

3.3 The Role of the State and the Private Sector

In Southeast Asian development, it is not realistic to discuss the role of the state without addressing the nature of 'the' indigenous private sector. Large business conglomerates dominate the economic landscape in Malaysia, the Philippines, and Thailand. Linked politically, including through state and military control, large enterprises play a leading role in basic sectors, such as in food and trade, in Cambodia, Lao PDR, and Myanmar. How this configuration in most of the Six except for Myanmar and the Philippines has not proven an obstacle to respectable, if not vigorous, rates of economic growth in Southeast Asia is a key question.

Unlike Northeast Asian states, which obliged favoured enterprises to reinvest 'policy rents' (Akyüz and Gore 1996; Chapter 13, this volume), Southeast Asian states were 'too soft' to impose accountability on favoured elites for their economic actions. Southeast Asian growth based on delivering economic advantages to political 'cronies' has been called 'ersatz capitalism' (Yoshihara 1988; Jomo 2003a).

3.3.1 Relational Contracting

Among the successful economies of the Six, the nurturing of a rentier incentive structure through industrial policies can be seen as a dimension of their soft state status. In the Six, conglomerates, led by well-connected businessmen, many with foreign business partners, operated in the leading and most profitable sectors of the economy, which for the most part were located in the region's growing external sector.

The domination of economic policy by a state-connected clique provided an infrastructure for co-ordination. Accountability on the part of privileged businesses consisted of political support for the regime and continued commercial success, including the timely servicing of subsidized financing. Myrdal (1968: 957) was profoundly sceptical of such a configuration. This configuration shares many features of medieval guilds in Europe (Montes 2018), where it played a role in regulation, contract enforcement, and co-ordination. In game-theoretic terms, in a repeated game, members enforced commercial accountability among themselves (Greif et al. 1994). The term 'relational contracting' is a shorthand for this kind of governance approach. The clique-based configuration has periodically spawned spectacular corruption episodes, such as the scandals associated with the Port Klang Free Zone (Juego 2015) and the 1MDB holding company in Malaysia.

3.3.2 Business Dominance by a Minority of a Minority

The dominant role of business minorities is also a common phenomenon among the Six. Business conglomerates are owned by a minority within a minority, with prominent businessmen sharing their ethnicity with many other residents who are not wealthy at all. The pervasiveness of Chinese minority groups highlighted by Myrdal (1968: 691) in business endures to this day in Southeast Asia. In Malaysia, while constituting 30 per cent of the population (as estimated in 2001 by *The Economist* 2001: 5), Chinese-descended businessmen account for 69 per cent of market capitalization in large conglomerates; in the Philippines, Chinese constitute 2 per cent of the population and control 50–60 per cent of the market capitalization; in Thailand, the comparable numbers are 14 per cent of the population and 81 per cent of the market capitalization.

In Thailand, Thai export promotion was built on top of the conglomerates from the import-substitution era, with the specific red line that foreign participation in domestic markets is effectively at the 'consent' of indigenous business (Rock 2001). Thai legislation, National Development Plans, and Board of Investments rulings from the 1970s to the present have 'reserved' the most lucrative domestic market for Thai business companies (Montes and Cruz 2017). Thai business conglomerates have enjoyed stable access to state-provided commercial advantages. In contrast, in the Philippines, Montes and Cruz (2017) suggest that outcomes of political contests have caused significant reallocations of state-provided privileges. Spending for political contests, including in the maintenance of a coterie, is counted as consumption in the national accounts. Such consumption expenditures represent forgone investment spending by business conglomerates (Montes 1995).

In contrast to Thailand, where large conglomerates dominated policy design, in non-socialist Malaysia the business sector faced a coherent state which 'sought to guide industrial change through a detailed sector-by-sector strategy laid out in the Industrial Market Plan 1986–95' (Felker 2001: 135).

Myanmar, whose commodity-exporting potential is enormous, is in the early stages of creating an indigenous business class. In Cambodia and Myanmar, the rapid rise of the garment export industry relies primarily on investment and loans from 'Greater China' (a term that includes the People's Republic of China, Taiwan, China, and the Special Administrative Region) to local businessmen, many of minority descent.

'Family-style' management of domestic conglomerates was diagnosed—erroneously[1]—as the 'Asian' governance explanation behind the Asian financial crisis. Nevertheless, it bears asking whether this structure can mobilize capital and operations of sufficient scale to continue to play a prominent role among those economies of the Six seeking to escape the middle-income trap. The contrast is with China, where large state-sponsored corporations are becoming global players. In contrast to those in the Republic of Korea (Amsden 2008), these family-based conglomerates are not known for technological prowess and innovation.

4. Openness, Trade, and Foreign Investments

Most of the Six are renowned as successful globalizers. While it is undisputed that international trade and foreign investment played an indispensable role in the Six's growth and economic diversification, scepticism remains about the manner in which these economies integrated internationally. One side[2] of the debate holds that openness in the customary sense of low tariffs, minimum application of quantitative restrictions, and unrestricted foreign investment were decisive in Asian, including Southeast Asian, development. The alternative view[3] is that successful economies integrated themselves internationally without dismantling their industrial policies or abruptly exposing their domestic enterprises to foreign competition. The record reviewed here argues for the second view. It is also necessary to differentiate between the role of external developments (sometimes called 'luck') and the domestic policies involved in the hosting of foreign investment. Domestic hosting policies in Southeast Asia made it possible to benefit from foreign investment, while retaining industrial policies.

---

[1] See Montes (2017) for the contrasts between the set of analyses that took the view that the 1997–1998 crisis was principally due to domestic governance failures versus those that recognized the role of external factors.

[2] See, for example, Krueger (1992), a piece which gained attention in transition economies when it was published.

[3] See, for example, Amsden (2008) or Wade (1990).

4.1 Performance and Diversification in External Trade

It is proper to start by outlining the role of trade in the Six's overall economic performance. External sources of growth played an important part in the sub-region's development (Phung et al. 2015: 76–7). For example, of Malaysia's 3.8 per cent annual growth in output per worker in the 1980s and 1990s, 1.75 percentage points is from world economic growth, the rest coming from domestic investment, resource endowments, and openness.

The rapid increase in exports as a proportion of GDP in the sub-region would be the envy of other parts of the world. Between 1985 and 2005, Lao PDR increased goods exports as a proportion of GDP from 2.3 to 20.2 per cent; for Malaysia from 41.8 per cent in 1965 to 99.7 per cent in 2005. In the 1990s, Malaysia export volume was growing at 14.2 per cent, the Philippines at 15.1 per cent, and Thailand at 11.2 per cent. Even accepting the susceptibility of the numbers to commodity price cycles, at the end of the period in 2015, the trade outcomes among the Six fell into two groups: (1) the hyper-traders of Cambodia, Malaysia, and Thailand, whose goods exports-to-GDP ratios are near or exceed 50 per cent; and (2) the slower traders of Lao PDR, Myanmar, and the Philippines, with goods exports-to-GDP ratios at or below 20 per cent (see Montes (2018: table 4).

Each of the Six began their transition to more outward-looking policies in the 1980s. Except for the Philippines, it would be inaccurate to propose that the Six began practising openness in the mid-1980s through the path of import liberalization. The persistence in the 1980s and beyond of—costly and inefficient—industrial policies belies this view. In Nayyar's (2013: 118) telling, Malaysia and Thailand 'were non-conformists without being liberalizers' whose economies performed well.

In the 1980s, the Six followed varied transition paths out of import-substitution industrialization. The Socialist Three ended state monopolies in key areas such as external trading, undertook a controlled opening to foreign investment, and relaxed price controls, with Myanmar moving more slowly than the other two. Among the three market economies, Malaysia and Thailand retained industrial policies and refined these tools to apply them to export promotion. The salubrious outcomes for both investors and host countries of these projects established the international reputation and the standards of foreign investor hosting of Southeast Asia. As a sharp contrast, the Philippines, beginning in 1984, embarked on a classic import liberalization programme. Myanmar maintained the dominant position of state enterprises even after embarking on gradual liberalization in 1988.

In Southeast Asia in the 1980s and to the present, the spectacular growth in exports has been strongly driven by foreign investment inflows. In the 1980s, foreign investors produced components in host countries which were exported to home countries for assembly in the final product; eventually, final product assembly moved into the region. Low-cost, pliant labour was the main host-country input;

the operation required no important industrial input from the host country. The investment-driven trade expansion enabled the diversification of the host country's export structure; components for electronic and electrical goods were the key sector. Southeast Asian trade still relies more heavily on component production than East Asian trade (Athukorala and Kohpaiboon 2015: 147, table 7.3).

Cambodia, Myanmar, and Lao PDR are the 'late-traders' among the Six. Like Bangladesh, Cambodia seized the opportunity of the termination in 1985 of the World Trade Organization's Agreement on Textiles and Clothing (the 'ATC', more popularly known as the 'multi-fibre arrangement') to build a garment exports industry, collaborating with the international network of clothing jobbers. Natural gas represents the most dynamic element of the export sectors in Myanmar and Lao PDR. These exports do not absorb much labour, being capital-intensive and highly dependent on foreign investment, but provide foreign exchange.

4.2 Policies towards Foreign Investment

There are possibly two ways to interpret the origin of Southeast Asia's reputation as a platform for foreign investor activities. A widespread view is that 'market-friendly'[4] government policies by host countries led to the region's attractiveness to foreign investment and its success in globalization. The alternative view—for example, Jomo (2003b)—is that external events and decisions had greater impacts than domestic policy in explaining the large-scale inflows into the region.

In the mid-1980s, domestic policy on the part of Southeast Asian states cannot be considered the main driver of the enormous inflow of foreign direct investment (FDI). The unexpected advantage from FDI initially flowed from Japanese companies seeking low-cost labour following the abrupt realignment of the world's major currencies in the mid-1980s from the Plaza–Louvre agreements. In that decade, because of perceived instability on the part of investors, these flows did not land in Hong Kong,[5] the least regulated economy in the region. FDI landed in economies populated by highly protected domestic enterprises—both state-controlled and private. Success in exploiting FDI, instead, depended on state policies to provide these investments with a reliable location to profitably operate production activities for export. Earlier, Nayyar (1978: 77) found that, in location decisions of such export activities, political stability and labour docility are the most decisive factors.

---

[4] There is no standard definition of 'market-friendly' policies, of course. The usage of the phrase here is as a shorthand for economic liberalization and deregulation; see, for example, World Bank (2002).

[5] Athukorala and Kohpaiboon (2015: 141) point to China's Cultural Revolution occurring at that time. Apropos, almost a decade earlier, Nayyar (1978: 68) quotes as typical a statement from a multinational executive that 'We wanted a site where we could have the US Navy between us and Mainland China'.

The key element of the domestic 'hosting' strategy was the expansion of special economic zones for foreign investors, a tool from the 1960s intended originally to facilitate non-traditional exports while preserving the industrial protection of domestic enterprises. Standard economic analysis deemed this strategy extremely costly in terms of domestic resource costs (Warr 1989). Whether in special zones or not, a contrary view is that countries do not need a liberalized economy to productively host FDI, but instead require affordable utilities and infrastructure and facilities for reducing variable costs (Montes 1997a: 178).

In non-special zones, Malaysia and Thailand eventually removed restrictions on 100 per cent-owned foreign ownership, but with sectoral- and market-restricted conditions. By 1992–1993, net FDI into Malaysia as a proportion of the gross fixed capital formation reached 7.3 per cent (Rasiah 2001: 95).

In Thailand, since the 1959 inception of import-substitution, domestic sectoral groups operating in large conglomerates had been capitalizing on a triad of (1) government promotional/protectionist provisions; (2) financing from large indig-enously-owned commercial banks operated meticulously along commercial lines; and (3) technology sourced from foreign, mainly Japanese, companies (see Rock 2001: 268–70). After the yen revaluation, the entry of foreign investment basically followed the private channels established during import-substitution.

The transitions to outward orientation in Lao PDR and Cambodia began about a decade later in the 1990s and in Myanmar in 2016, after the lifting of the trade embargo by advanced economies.

In the international garment industry, the supply-side aspects of foreign investment-driven trade remain a powerful force among the second-tier Southeast Asian countries, benefitting Cambodia and Myanmar. In an arrangement originally necessitated by the quota dispersion for developed country markets during the era of the ATC, the international garments trade became dependent on subcon-tractors organized by the main supplier companies. The rise of garment subcon-tracting companies facilitated rapid employment absorption of rural labour. In Cambodia, 91 per cent of industrial establishments in 2011 were micro-firms employing fewer than five workers (Chhair and Ung 2016), mainly in the gar-ment business. In Myanmar, the garment sector grew rapidly even in the midst of the international embargo in the 2000s (Myint et al. 2015).

4.3 Balance-of-Payments Financing and the Asian Financial Crisis of 1997–1998

Fragile balance-of-payments conditions and periodic commodity price slumps, including the almost simultaneous payments crisis episodes in the mid-1980s, are part of the Six's growth record. Montes (2018: table 5) summarizes the patterns in accumulated current account deficits in five of the economies through the period leading up to the Asian financial crisis of 1997. These ten-year deficits are not higher than an annual rate of 3 per cent of GDP, but leave the economies vulnerable to commodity slumps. After the 1997 Asian financial crisis, the middle-income countries' current accounts switched to surpluses. However, the region's most harrowing balance-of-payments episode did not originate with a commodity price slump. The Asian financial crisis of 1997–1998 came from a sudden reversal of flows in the capital account, sparked by the Thai baht devaluation on 2 July 1997. Abetted by World Bank staff in the 1990s, Malaysia, the Philippines, and Thailand succumbed to the siren call of capital account deregulation starting in the late 1980s. Authorities were forced to intervene against currency appreciation triggered by the unprecedented portfolio inflows to defend their built-up export competitiveness, a policy that further fed short-term capital inflows (Montes 1997b). The domestic impact was a financial sector laden with long-maturity receivables in property development funded by volatile, short-term, hard currency liabilities; thus, the seeding of a financial crisis with foreign characteristics.

The flight of portfolio funds out of the region only ended in the last quarter of 1998 in conjunction with a series of financial crises elsewhere (Montes 2017: 131). These events signalled to portfolio investors that the sub-region was not such a bad bet, within a choice set rife with bad portfolio bets.

Rapid economic recovery in Thailand ensued in 1999, after a fall in output of 10.2 per cent through 1997 and 1998. Malaysia, which had responded to the crisis with effectual capital account controls,[6] lost 0.6 per cent in the same period.

5. Employment, Inequality, and Social Development

In chapter 9 of *Asian Drama*, Myrdal highlighted the deep economic and ethnic divides in business and political participation specific to each country and their roles in national politics and social stability. What role did economic growth and structural transformation play in bridging the social divides inherited from the colonial era in the Six? How did economic growth and structural change affect poverty, inequality, and social development?

The record among the Six is a mix of spectacular reductions in poverty incidence during periods of rapid employment growth and little progress, if not a worsening, in equity. This mix can be attributed to three trends: (1) income gains by the richest strata outstripping income gains obtained by workers moving from rural sectors to industrial activities; (2) state investment in social development, including in education, being inadequate to increase the access of the general population to skills premia introduced by structural change and international integration; and (3) the indifference, if not hostility, of the development model to

---

[6] See Khor (2005) for a description of these capital controls and their impacts.

more widespread political participation and to the strengthening of citizens' rights and labour protections. These three trends are incorporated in the discussion, grouped into the following three topics: (1) employment absorption and poverty reduction; (2) social and political (in)equity; and (3) state investments in social development.

5.1 Employment Absorption and Poverty Reduction

Southeast Asia has an exceptional record in employment absorption and employment redeployment out of agriculture. Much of the redeployed labour was absorbed in enterprises whose markets were overseas, including the Philippines where the labour redeployment was directly overseas. At the national level the poverty impact of the labour redeployment has been spectacular in specific periods among the Six. In Malaysia, the incidence of rural poverty fell from 27.3 per cent in 1985 to 18.6 per cent by 1993 (Government of Malaysia 1996). The performance of Cambodia, Lao PDR, and Myanmar as they moved rural labour into labour-intensive manufacturing for export follow the Malaysian pattern; see Montes (2018: table 6).

In terms of poverty reduction, Thailand's performance—reflecting the greater progress achieved in the rural sector—outshines that of the Philippines, with poverty incidence that is little over half that of the Philippines' 21 per cent, a level in the same vicinity as that of Cambodia, Lao PDR, and Myanmar; see Montes (2018: table 6). Malaysia's poverty incidence was around 5 per cent in 2005 and has shrunk to practically zero by 2015.

With the foreign investment influx after the yen revaluation, Malaysia's proportion of employment[7] in agriculture fell from 30.4 per cent in 1985 to 20.0 per cent by 1995, matching an increase in the proportion of employment in industry from 23.8 to 32.3 per cent in the same period. The proportion of Thai employment in agriculture fell from 66.6 per cent in 1980 to 52.0 per cent in 1995, in step with an increase in industry's proportion from 12.1 to 20.0 per cent by 1995. The Malaysia and Thai precedent became a model for mobilizing unskilled workers, particularly young female workers, from rural areas into industry. Cambodia built its export garment sector more than a decade later using this model. At present, garment workers, recruited principally through personal networks, constitute 80 per cent of the industrial labour force. Remittances to rural areas amplified[8] the poverty impact of the new labour opportunities.

The most dynamic element in the redeployment process involved women's work in light manufacturing. The pattern of redeployment mirrors the FDI-driven export trends in the previous section (Table 20.2). For Malaysia, the Philippines,

---

[7] All data cited in this paragraph are from the World Bank database.
[8] See Chhair and Ung (2016: 228) in the case of Cambodia.

Table 20.2 Ratio of female-to-male labour force participation rate: national estimates, %

	1970	1975	1980	1985	1990	1995	2000	2005	2010	2015
Cambodia						98.7	94.3	89.4	93.5	
Lao PDR						97.2	99.0	99.3	96.0	
Myanmar				49.5	41.5	46.1	50.6	55.2	59.8	64.3
Malaysia			49.4	53.6	56.0	53.0	58.2	57.4	60.5	67.1
Philippines	43.6	51.9	30.2	59.7	58.1	59.7	60.2	62.3	64.0	64.8
Thailand	83.6	62.8	87.2	87.1	87.0	79.4	80.5	81.3	79.6	78.4

Source: Author, based on the World Bank's World Development Indicators.

and Thailand, female labour force participation rates peaked around 1990 with the influx of foreign investment. Studies in the garment and textiles sectors have revealed that as firms expanded their operations and increased mechanization, female workers were being let go in favour of male operators.

Into the 1990s, the mobilization of women's labour into export industries gave foreign companies access to Lewis's (1954) fabled unlimited supply of unskilled labour, initially in Malaysia and Thailand, then in the other four. Women gained employment in subcontracting companies producing for multinational corporations and in related informal work. Women's employment was 'characterized by long hours, job insecurity and unhealthy working conditions, as well as low pay' (Çağatay and Ertürk 2004: 20), but nevertheless coveted by women facing harsher forms of work otherwise. Feminist research from the late 1990s indicated that, instead of competitive pressures driving a decline of discrimination against women and minorities as predicted in mainstream economics, the low cost of non-unionized, and therefore docile, women's labour often played the same role as an undervalued exchange rate in preserving international competitiveness in East Asia.[9]

5.2 Social and Political (In)equity

The lagging progress in social and political equity in the Six can be traced to the economic model and the efforts of postcolonial elites in these countries to maintain their political dominance. The performance of the three market-oriented economies of Malaysia, the Philippines, and Thailand is quite weak in terms of improving social and political equity (You 1999). Chongvilaivan (2014) suggests that rising inequality in Southeast Asia has been driven primarily by the extent to which incomes of the rich have outstripped income growth of the poor despite significant reductions in the poverty headcount ratio. These are reflected in the relatively

[9] See, for example, Berik et al. (2004).

stagnant trends at high levels of inequality in the Gini coefficient. These patterns are consistent with an economic model in which the key driver is the movement of rural labour to low-skill, export-oriented jobs. Low labour costs were the original source of attraction for the relocation of production facilities to the sub-region, 'militating against rapid wage growth in these countries' (Jomo 2003b: 203).

In Malaysia, intra-elite conflicts have not expanded popular political participation within the state and across the society (Weiss 2006; Juego 2015). Single-party control in Cambodia, Lao PDR, Malaysia, and Myanmar over long periods has kept intra-elite competition out of the public eye. The Philippines is distinguished in relying on periodic elections, enabling sweeping shifts in power over economic policy but only within the elite. In Thailand, periods of military control restrained intra-elite conflict; in the 2000s, a rural-based movement led by Prime Minister Thaksin Shinawatra threatened to broaden political participation.

5.3 State Investments in Social Development

Among the Six, a profile of exceptional growth and structural change is not matched by a strong record of investments in the social sector and social protection. The mobilization of rural workers, especially women, into the industrial labour force had a strong impact on poverty reduction in its heyday; but this was not accompanied by a ratcheting up in capabilities in the labour force because of shortfalls in the expansion of education, health, and other social programmes. In this section, we shall review the extent of these programmes and illustrate how these now represent a binding constraint for development, even for successful countries among the Six.

Social programmes and protections in the Six cannot be considered generous. Many of the customary programmes are still to be introduced or with coverage only for urban populations or the employed, and their long-term sustainability is weak (Chongvilaivan 2014). Among the Six, Thailand, followed by the Philippines, has made the most progress in terms of the existence of statutory social provisions at the national level. Lao PDR leads the three LDCs in introducing statutory protections (see Montes 2018: table 8). As in other developing countries, the existence of statutory national protections among the Six can fall far short of the extent of actual funding or its transfer component, the quality of provision, and equality of access by gender, social class, and urban/rural location (ILO 2015; Mundle 2018). For development purposes, the most critical investments are in health and education.

5.3.1 Health: Limited Progress towards Universal Coverage

There is progress in health provision among the Six, but increasing coverage and keeping out-of-pocket costs low is difficult among the three LDCs because of the undeveloped health infrastructure. Malaysia and Thailand have achieved universal coverage for essential health problems, while the Philippines had just crossed 80 per cent coverage in 2015 (ILO 2015). Health coverage in Cambodia and Lao PDR are in the range of 25 per cent of the population. Various strategies have been tried to increase coverage. Out-of-pocket expenditures as a proportion of total health expenditures tend to be high among the LDCs (Montes 2018).

5.3.2 Education: A Prospective Binding Constraint

Inadequate investment in education has implications for the long-term sustainability of the export-oriented model. The quality of education in the region is low and the expansion of access is often at the cost of quality (Phan and Coxhead 2015). Trends in inequality in access to education among the Six have stayed at stagnant levels in most countries experiencing rapid economic growth.

In Thailand, school completion rates are not distinguished. Skills shortages have become quite noticeable. Further expansion of the Thai automobile sector is now hampered by the lack of engineers (Orihashi 2010: 228) Thailand must also contend with a shortage of supporting industries, inadequate organizational capacity, and poor capabilities of small- and medium-scale enterprises.

The extractive industries represent a high proportion of GDP in Cambodia, Lao PDR, and Myanmar. With low levels of education and social services, extractive industry earnings could be channelled to investments in human development; however, very few developing countries, including the other three members of the Six, which in earlier decades had important mining sectors, have managed this potential well.

6. Southeast Asian Development Narratives

Why is the development record in the Six stronger than most other developing countries? What did Myrdal miss in 1968? One could group the flaws in Myrdal's (1968) otherwise deeply grounded and wide-ranging social analysis into three types: (1) unexpected events that would have been difficult to predict; (2) mistaken inferences drawn from observations at the time; and (3) blind spots arising from the underlying analytical framework. The most important unexpected event would be Japan's seizure of the United States' private sector's global dominance in leading global manufacturing areas, which triggered a drastic fall in the value of the dollar. The resulting yen revaluation required many industries in Japan to seek to relocate their labour-intensive activities to Thailand and Malaysia.

Another unforeseen event would be the experimentation and institutional reforms by Southeast Asian states in the agricultural sector, including a retreat from the socialist experiment of collectivized farming, and the significant allocation of state investments in agriculture. HYV also played a strong role in boosting national agricultural productivity, though the technology favoured large land-holders. State successes through institutional reforms and investment, which mitigated existing inequalities in rural areas, affected agricultural performance via their impact on unleashing private incentives.

In the case of the mistaken inferences from observation, an important example could be made about the undervaluing of a possible positive role of the elite in development processes, perhaps from an overemphasis on obstacles from corruption and poor governance. Against social democratic benchmarks, Myrdal (1968) pinpointed cultural impediments and the dominance of an unprogressive elite as villains in the Asian drama. Gradual reform could have fallen afoul of Myrdal's warning that such a pace of change could be self-defeating. Among the Six, the exertions of postcolonial elites to protect their supremacy have shaped economic policies and reforms. This has meant that except for Malaysia, with its explicit programme to raise the social position of Malays, and the Philippines with its efforts at radical economic liberalization, changes have been gradual in order not to jeopardize elite economic interests.

In terms of blind spots arising from Myrdal's (1968) underlying social democratic framework, it cannot be denied that the rent-driven industrial policies were occasions for corruption and extended inefficiency. However, there were sufficient opportunities for socially productive private wealth creation in the interface between state intervention and the external economy during and after import-substitution. Contrary to Myrdal's expectations, elites in the region, even those without a socialist mindset, have been relatively successful in nation-building efforts, including through evolving, though socially costly, industrial development interventions.

Especially within ethnic networks, capitalist motivations appear to have been sufficiently strong to mobilize adequate reinvestments of state-provided rent surpluses without the need for heavy state supervision to substitute for market discipline. In the Six, the pursuit of development and export success relied heavily on existing technology and foreign investment, thus making the government burden lighter; the difference is that most governments dared to sustain sectoral industrial policy.

The ability of the societies in the Six to productively and profitably participate in international production networks was facilitated by the practices of relational contracting, reminiscent of the mercantilist period, which Myrdal considered unsuitable. Shortfalls in social development and technological upgrading are the consequences of the chosen, elite-protecting, development path. These shortfalls, in line with Myrdal's earlier insights, could impose a ceiling on an otherwise relatively successful development record. A second blind spot from an underlying social democratic framework could be the undervaluing in the Six of the commercial and innovative drives of the small farmers, who responded well to economic incentives and to access to higher-yielding farm technologies. In rural

Cambodia, Lao PDR, and Myanmar, the spread of modern farming techniques, with state assistance, was rapid, even though the process could have worsened the existing economic and political imbalances against small farmers.

Myrdal's analytical framework did not imagine the resilience and adaptability of the rentier economy in poor countries operating within a global capitalist economy. A lot of international trade and investment does not take place in an 'arm's length' manner, but relies heavily on international business networks and their engagement with local businessmen. Myrdal also did not foresee how workers' overseas remittances and business process outsourcing could extend the life of a rentier economy in the Philippines, even though he predicted in 1968 either a thoroughgoing democratization based on agrarian reform or a communist regime in the Philippines (Myrdal 1968: 390). Myrdal expressed scepticism of the diffuse form of socialism in Myanmar (then Burma); in actual operation, this regime, which relied heavily on state-owned enterprises, survived economic isolation with an extended operation of a command-and-control system but lagged in growth and industrial development.

In the other four, the record suggests that domestic rentiers can engage in capital accumulation while interacting with global capitalist processes. The Six's experience suggests that a globally friendly postcolonial elite could play a positive role in coherently taking advantage of opportunities in the global economy to raise economic growth rates. But it is not a guarantee of long-term development, especially because sustaining growth will require upgraded domestic technological capabilities which, in turn, requires building internationally capable indigenous enterprises and workers.

To an extent not foreseen by Myrdal, the development achievements of the Six have been predicated on a benign influence of the external economy—both in short-term events and long-term evolution.

In the short term, the three LDCs' dependence on commodity exports signals continuing vulnerability to global economic cycles; with state facilitation, these economies have been increasing their participation in global production networks. In the case of the three middle-income countries, the short-term external vulnerability derives from their open capital accounts susceptible to highly volatile private capital flows. The prospects are poor regarding concerted private capital re-regulation or global institutional reforms to constrain global economic cycles, commodity price cycles, and private capital flow volatility. In the long term, climate change represents the first external binding constraint (Montes 2018).

The inadequate level of social development and provisioning constitutes the most binding internal constraint in the context of the Six's reliance on international trade. Capturing greater value-added from participation in international value chains requires an increasingly capable labour force and private sector.

Extending the model of exporting goods does not augur well for further development. While there is still some room for climbing up the value chain among the three LDCs, for the middle-income countries the threat is stagnation in the middle-income category. Growth among the Six is not distinguished by significant upgrading of human or technological capabilities. Southeast Asia does not have large international companies that participate actively in international technological advances. The social structure—including a narrow private-sector base—and internal politics among the Six also do not portend an ample change in attention to investment in social development or a ratcheting-up of technological capabilities. Within the constraints imposed by global rules in international institutions, such as the WTO, these countries, seen by many other countries as successful globalizers, must find a way to overcome the limits of their domestic social structures to continue to advance their development ambitions. It will not be easy.

Acknowledgements

I am extremely grateful for the comments and suggestions of Deepak Nayyar, an anonymous referee, and participants in the March 2018 workshop in Hanoi where the first draft of this chapter was presented. I am grateful for Justin Chan's excellent research assistance. I am solely responsible for all errors, opinions, and analyses.

References

Akyüz, Y., and C. Gore (1996). 'The Investment–Profits Nexus in East Asian Industrialization', *World Development*, 24(3): 461–70.

Amsden, A.H. (2008). 'Nationality of Firm Ownership in Developing Countries: Who Should "Crowd Out" Whom in Imperfect Markets', Initiative for Policy Dialogue, New York, Initiative for Policy Dialogue Working Paper 174.

Athukorala, P., and A. Kohpaiboon (2015). 'Global Production Sharing, Trade Patterns, and Industrialization in Southeast Asia'. In I. Coxhead (ed.) *Routledge Handbook of Southeast Asian Economics*. London: Routledge.

Bautista, R.M., and D.A. DeRosa (1996). 'Agriculture and the New Industrial Revolution in Asia', International Food Policy Research Institute, Washington, DC, TMD Discussion Paper 13.

Berik, G., Y.M. Rodgers, and J.E. Zveglich (2004). 'International Trade and Wage Discrimination: Evidence from East Asia', *Review of Development Economics*, 8: 237–54.

Bhagwati, J. (1988). 'Export-Promoting Strategy: Issues and Evidence', *World Bank Research Observer*, 3(1): 7–57.

Booth, A. (2003). 'The Burma Development Disaster in Comparative Historical Perspective', *South East Asia Research*, 11: 141–71.

Borras, S.M. (2007). ' "Free Market", Export-Led Development Strategy and its Impact on Rural Livelihoods, Poverty and Inequality: The Philippine Experience Seen from a Southeast Asian Perspective', *Review of International Political Economy*, 14(1): 143–75.

Çağatay, N., and K. Ertürk (2004). 'Gender and Globalization: A Macroeconomic Perspective', Policy Integration Department, World Commission on the Social Dimension of Globalization, ILO, Geneva, Working Paper 19.

Chhair, S., and L. Ung (2016). 'Cambodia's Path to Industrial Development: Comparative Studies of Industrial Development in Africa and Emerging Asia'. In C. Newman, J. Page, J. Rand, A. Shimeles, M Söderbom, and F. Tarp (eds) *Manufacturing Transformation: Comparative Studies of Industrial Development in Africa and Emerging Asia*. Oxford: Oxford University Press for UNU-WIDER.

Chongvilaivan, A. (2014). 'Inequality in Southeast Asia'. In R. Kanbur, C. Rhee, and J. Zhuang (eds) *Inequality in Asia and the Pacific*. London: Routledge.

Christensen, S.R., D. Dollar, A. Siamwalla, and P. Vichyanod (1992). 'Institutional and Political Bases of Growth Inducing Strategies in Thailand', Paper prepared for World Bank Workshop on the Role of Government and East Asian Success, East-West Center, 19–21 November.

Coxhead, I. (2015). 'Introduction: Southeast Asia's Long Transition'. In I. Coxhead (ed.) *Routledge Handbook of Southeast Asian Economics*. London: Routledge.

Dalrymple, D.G. (1979). 'The Adoption of High-Yielding Grain Varieties in Developing Nations', *Agricultural History*, 53(4): 704–26.

Economist (2001). 'Asian Business Survey', 7 April.

Evenson, R.E. (2004). 'Food and Population: D. Gale Johnson and the Green Revolution', *Economic Development and Cultural Change*, 52(3): 543–70.

Felker, G. (2001). 'The Politics of Industrial Investment Policy Reform in Malaysia and Thailand'. In K. Jomo (ed.) *Southeast Asia's Industrialization Industrial Policy, Capabilities and Sustainability*. London: Palgrave.

Government of Malaysia (1996). *Seventh Malaysia Plan 1996–2000*. Kuala Lumpur: Government Press.

Greif, A., P. Milgrom, and B. Weingast (1994). 'Coordination, Commitment and Enforcement: The Case of the Merchant Guild', *Journal of Political Economy*, 102: 745–76.

Hill, H. (2015). 'The Political Economy of Policy Reform: Insights from Southeast Asia'. In I. Coxhead (ed.) *Routledge Handbook of Southeast Asian Economics*. London: Routledge.

ILO (2015). *The State of Social Protection in ASEAN at the Dawn of Integration*. Bangkok: ILO Regional Office for Asia and the Pacific.

Jomo, K.S. (ed.) (2001). *Southeast Asia's Industrialization: Industrial Policy, Capabilities, and Sustainability*. New York: Palgrave.

Jomo, K.S. (2003a). 'Growth with Equity in East Asia?' In K.S. Jomo (ed.) *Southeast Asian Paper Tigers? From Miracle to Debacle and Beyond*. Oxford: RoutledgeCurzon.

Jomo, K.S. (ed.) (2003b). *Southeast Asian Paper Tigers? From Miracle to Debacle and Beyond.* Oxford: RoutledgeCurzon.

Juego, B. (2015). 'Elite Capture and Elite Conflicts in South Asian Neoliberalization Processes'. In IDEAS, CLACSO, and CODESRIA, *Inequality, Democracy and Development Under Neoliberalism and Beyond.* New Delhi: IDEAS.

Khor, M. (2005). *The Malaysian Experience in Financial-Economic Crisis Management: An Alternative to the IMF-Style Approach.* Penang: Third World Network.

Krueger, A.O. (1992). *Economic Policy Reform in Developing Countries: The Kuznets Memorial Lectures of the Economic Growth Center, Yale University.* London: Blackwell.

Lewis, W.A. (1954). 'Development with Unlimited Supplies of Labour', *The Manchester School*, 22(2): 139–91.

Lim, M.H. (1985). 'Contradictions in the Development of Malay Capital: State, Accumulation and Legitimation', *Journal of Contemporary Asia*, 15(1): 37–63.

Montes, M.F. (1993). 'Understanding Development Strategy in Southeast Asia', Paper presented the Conference on Development Strategies in East and Southeast Asia by the Development Research Center, State Council of the People's Republic of China, Guangzhou, 8–11 October.

Montes, M.F. (1995). 'The Private Sector as the Engine of Philippine Growth: Can Heaven Wait?' *Journal of Far East Business*, 1(3): 132–47.

Montes, M.F. (1997a). 'Direct Foreign Investment and Technology Transfer in ASEAN', *ASEAN Economic Bulletin*, 14(2): 176–89.

Montes, M.F. (1997b). 'Private Deficits and Public Responsibilities: Philippine Responses to Capital Inflows'. In *Papers and Proceedings of the International Symposium on Macroeconomic Interdependence in the Asia-Pacific Region.* Tokyo: Economic Research Institute, Economic Planning Agency, Government of Japan.

Montes, M.F. (1998). *The Currency Crisis in Southeast Asia: Updated Edition.* Singapore: Institute of Southeast Asian Studies.

Montes, M.F. (2017). 'Indonesia's 1997–1998 Economic Crisis: A Teachable Case Wasted'. In J.P. Bohoslavsky and K. Raffer (eds) *Sovereign Debt Crises: What Have We Learned?* Cambridge: Cambridge University Press.

Montes, M.F. (2018). 'Six Development Paths in Southeast Asia: Three plus Three', UNU-WIDER, Helsinki, WIDER Working Paper 2018-94, August.

Montes, M.F., and J.P. Cruz (2017). 'Foreign Investment and Philippine Development: A Comparative Approach', Manuscript for the 'Bugkos: Putting Equitable Development at the Center of the Asian Century' Program.

Mundle, S. (2018). 'Fifty Years of Asian Experience in the Spread of Education and Healthcare', UNU-WIDER, Helsinki, WIDER Working Paper, forthcoming.

Murray, H., and P. Nguyen (2018). 'Land Reform: A Critical Test for Myanmar's Government', Center for Strategic and International Studies, Washington, DC. Available at: www.csis.org/analysis/land-reform-critical-test-myanmar%E2%80 %99s-government (accessed 20 April 2018).

Myint, M.M., R. Rasiah, and K. Singaravelloo (2015). 'Globalization of Industrialization and its Impact on Clothing Workers in Myanmar', *Journal of the Asia Pacific Economy*, 20(1): 100–10.

Myrdal, G. (1968). *Asian Drama: An Inquiry into the Poverty of Nations, Volumes I, II, and III*. New York: Pantheon.

Nayyar, D. (1978). 'Transnational Corporations and Manufactured Exports from Poor Countries', *The Economic Journal*, 88(349): 59–84.

Nayyar, D. (2013). *Catch Up: Developing Countries in the World Economy*. Oxford: Oxford University Press.

Orihashi, S. (2010). 'Manufacturing and Management Systems of Japanese Manufacturers in Southeast Asia: The Case of the Automobile Industry in Thailand'. In P. Intarakumner and Y. Lecler (eds) *Sustainability of Thailand's Competitiveness: The Policy Challenges*. Singapore: Institute of Southeast Asian Studies.

Phan, D., and I. Coxhead (2015). 'Education in Southeast Asia: Investments, Achievements, and Returns'. In I. Coxhead (ed.) *Routledge Handbook of Southeast Asian Economics*. London: Routledge.

Phung, T.T.T., I. Coxhead, and L. Chang (2015). 'Lucky Countries? Internal and External Sources of Southeast Asian Growth since 1970'. In I. Coxhead (ed.) *Routledge Handbook of Southeast Asian Economics*. London: Routledge.

Rasiah, R. (2001). 'Southeast Asia Ersatz Miracle: The Dubious Sustainability of its Growth and Industrialization'. In K.S. Jomo (ed.) *Southeast Asia's Industrialization: Industrial Policy, Capabilities, and Sustainability*. New York: Palgrave.

Rock, M.T. (2001). 'Selective Industrial Policy and Manufacturing Export Success in Thailand'. In K.S. Jomo (ed.) *Southeast Asia's Industrialization: Industrial Policy, Capabilities, and Sustainability*. New York: Palgrave.

Ruttan, V.W. (1977). 'The Green Revolution: Seven Generalizations', *International Development Review*, 19(4): 16–23.

Salleh, I., Y.K. Leng, and S. Meyanathan (1992). 'Growth, Equity, and Structural Transformation in Malaysia: Role of the Public Sector', Paper for the World Bank Workshop on the Role of Government and East Asian Success, East–West Center, 19–21 November.

Teoh, C.H. (2002). 'The Palm Oil Industry in Malaysia: From Seed to Frying Pan', WWF Switzerland, Zurich. Available at: http://assets.panda.org/downloads/oilpalmchainpartaandb_esri.pdf (accessed 28 November 2017).

Timmer, C.P. (2015). 'Agricultural Development and Food Security'. In I. Coxhead (ed.) *Routledge Handbook of Southeast Asian Economics*. London: Routledge.

Tin, M.M.T. (2006). *State Dominance in Myanmar: The Political Economy of Industrialization*. Singapore: Institute of Southeast Asian Studies.

van Arkadie, B. (1995). 'Economic Reform and Policy Issues in Vietnam, Laos, and Cambodia'. In M.F. Montes, R.A. Reyes, and S. Tambunlertchai (eds) *Macroeconomic Management in Southeast Asia's Transitional Economies*. Kuala Lumpur: Asia and Pacific Development Centre.

Wade, R. (1990). *Governing the Market: Economic Theory and the Role of Government in East Asian Industrialization*. Princeton, NJ: Princeton University Press.

Warr, P.G. (1989). 'Export Processing Zones: The Economics of Enclave Manufacturing', World Bank, Washington, DC. Available at: http://documents.worldbank.org/curated/en/893611468773056389/pdf/multi-page.pdf (accessed 28 November 2017).

Warr, Peter (2004). 'Globalization, Growth, and Poverty Reduction in Thailand', *ASEAN Economic Bulletin*, 21(1): 1–18.

Weiss, M.L. (2006). *Protest and Possibilities: Civil Society and Coalitions for Political Change in Malaysia*. Stanford, CA: Stanford University Press.

Wong, D. (1987). *Peasants in the Making: Malaysia's Green Revolution*. Singapore: Institute for Southeast Asian Studies.

World Bank (1993). *The East Asian Miracle: Economic Growth and Public Policy*. New York: Oxford University Press.

World Bank (2002). *Globalization, Growth and Poverty*. London: World Bank and Oxford University Press.

World Bank (2014). 'Lao Development Report 2014: Expanding Productive Employment for Broad-Based Growth', World Bank Group, Washington, DC.

World Bank (2017). *World Development Indicators*. Available at: https://data.worldbank.org/products/wdi (accessed 8 December 2017).

Yoshihara, K. (1988). *The Rise of Ersatz Capitalism in Southeast Asia*. Singapore: Oxford University Press.

You, Jon-Il (1999). 'Income Distribution and Growth in East Asia'. In Y. Akyüz (ed.) *East Asian Development: New Perspectives*. London: Frank Cass Publishers.

21
South Asia

S.R. Osmani

1. Introduction

This chapter tells the story of the South Asian economy (excluding India) in the last fifty years. Soon after independence from British rule around the middle of the last century, the region seemed to have a better prospect than many other parts of the Third World. In the event, however, South Asia crawled while the neighbouring East and Southeast Asia galloped away. In fact, in the 1970s, soon after Gunnar Myrdal finished writing his *Asian Drama*, South Asia (including India) plunged into a crisis, that made future prospects look even worse than Myrdal had anticipated. Nonetheless, after traversing a chequered path, a large part of the region seems finally able to look forward to a much brighter future than seemed possible at the time the *Asian Drama* was being written. This chapter describes and explains this story in terms of economic strategies and political economy of the region—focusing on Bangladesh, Pakistan, Sri Lanka, Nepal, and Bhutan.

It ought to be recognized at the outset that although South Asia has failed to keep pace with East and Southeast Asia, in absolute terms the region has made great strides in the last fifty years—in both economic and social spheres. South Asia was among the most populous parts of the world in the 1960s and excessive population pressure was widely deemed to be a serious obstacle to the region's socio-economic progress. After fifty years, the population has more than trebled, and yet the spectre of population explosion is no longer as haunting as it used to be. This is because the region has succeeded in bringing down the rate of population growth considerably. From an average of over 2.5 per cent per annum, population growth has come down to about 1.5 per cent, the only exception being Pakistan, where population growth has slowed only marginally. The slowdown in population growth was brought about by an unusually early demographic transition that is still ongoing in most of the region.

Slowing population growth and respectable economic growth have together ensured that, despite more than a trebling of the population, the region has experienced an improvement in living standards that did not seem possible fifty years ago. Per capita income has almost trebled, life expectancy at birth has gone up from less than fifty years (except in Sri Lanka) to nearly seventy years, and enrolment at the primary level has become near universal.[1]

This chapter tells the story of how this progress was achieved and what challenges lie ahead. Section 2 sets out the background to the story by looking at the initial conditions that Myrdal would have observed in the 1960s. Section 3 provides an overview of the economic growth and structural transformation of the region over the fifty years since the writing of *Asian Drama*. Sections 4 and 5 then attempt an analytical narrative of the major forces—including policies and exogenous factors—that underlie the growth process. Next, the record of performance in the spheres of poverty reduction and human development is discussed in section 6. Finally, section 7 offers some brief observations on the prospects of the region in the coming decades.

2. Historical Context and Initial Conditions

As the countries of the region embarked on the path of economic development around the middle of the twentieth century, they naturally shared some common initial conditions, stemming from a common historical legacy, most notably nearly two hundred years of British colonial rule.[2] Nonetheless, there were some important differences among the countries—stemming from cultural, geographical, and to some extent historical differences—that had a significant bearing on their subsequent trajectories of development.

Nepal and Bhutan, the two landlocked countries of the region, were geographically very different from the rest. A rugged mountainous topography posed a serious hindrance to the development of agriculture and infrastructure, in particular. The same topography, however, also endowed them with a rich potential of hydropower, which they were to harness to great advantage in the years to come. In contrast, Bangladesh was a plain riverine land, whose soil fertility was regularly replenished by the rich alluvial deposits that came with the annual flooding of several mighty rivers and their numerous tributaries. Geography made the pursuit of traditional rice-based agriculture especially convenient, but it also made the development of physical infrastructure especially difficult and made the country susceptible to excessive flooding and devastating tidal surges. Pakistan had a combination of rugged mountains and plain land. The latter was made fertile by the rich network of modern irrigation developed under the Indus Valley Development Project, initiated during British rule. Sri Lanka, as an island economy, was geographically at the opposite pole of landlocked Nepal and Bhutan.

---

[1] For more on the quantitative indicators of socio-economic progress, see Osmani (2018: table A1).

[2] Although Nepal and Bhutan were never colonized by India, they were not altogether immune from the economic and political consequences of British colonialism.

Like Pakistan, it too had a fair mix of rugged mountains and plain land, but the land was naturally fertile, blessed as it was with generous rainfall from a double annual monsoon. Unlike agriculture in the rest of the region, however, Sri Lanka's agriculture was not singularly oriented towards the production of subsistence crops (rice and wheat). Sri Lanka was unique in the region in having a predominance of plantation agriculture (mainly tea, followed by rubber and coconut), as a direct legacy of British colonial policy.

There were significant differences in the political sphere as well. Nepal and Bhutan were ancient kingdoms, ruled by powerful dynasties, which did not allow democratic freedom of any sort. The cost of unfreedom in the two countries was very different, however, owing to deep-seated religious and cultural differences. Nepal was a deeply caste-divided Hindu society, where the lower castes faced severe discrimination in all spheres of life—in some ways, more severe than even the worst cases of caste discrimination in India. Bhutan, in contrast, was a much more peaceful homogeneous Buddhist society, where the general populace was largely content with meagre living in material terms, and the elite faced little resistance in maintaining its grip on both political and economic levers. While both these kingdoms were internally powerful, they were externally vulnerable, because of their small size and landlocked nature; and they responded to this vulnerability by forging very close political and economic ties with India.

Pakistan and Bangladesh, which were parts of the same country when Myrdal was writing, had a very different political and cultural disposition. There were stirrings of democracy following independence from colonial rule in 1947, but they soon dissipated as the country came to be ruled by military dictatorship within a decade of independence; and by the time Myrdal began to study this region in the 1960s, autocracy had become firmly entrenched. However, the underlying discontent at the loss of democratic freedom never disappeared at the grassroots level, especially in Bangladesh (East Pakistan, as it was then called), for which military dictatorship was tantamount to forceful subjugation of their people by the military junta of (West) Pakistan. Over time, the undercurrent of discontent was to culminate in the break-up of Pakistan and the emergence of Bangladesh as an independent nation in 1971. But the legacy of prolonged military rule had already done lasting damage to the polity in both countries, especially in Pakistan, as military rule was repeatedly reimposed under various pretexts. Bangladesh has succeeded somewhat better in removing the shackles of autocracy in recent years, practising parliamentary democracy since 1990, albeit in a deeply flawed fashion; but Pakistan continues to be haunted by the recurrence of military rule every time the prospect of democracy appears on the horizon.

Among all the countries under review, Sri Lanka was the most advanced in terms of success in forging democratic institutions. The practice of limited self-rule that the British had initiated in the 1930s had already instilled a culture of democratic practice even before the British left, and, by the time Myrdal was writing, democracy had taken a firm hold in Sri Lanka. There was trouble ahead, though, as the eruption of violent conflict between the majority Buddhist Sinhalese community and the minority Hindu Tamils threatened to destroy the fabric of the society.

Apart from a more democratic polity, the initial conditions of Sri Lanka differed from those of the rest of the countries in several other important respects. Most significantly, Sri Lanka was well ahead of the rest (including India) in terms of per capita income. This advantage was owed almost entirely to its plantation economy, which had enabled Sri Lanka to gain handsomely from successive commodity booms both before and after political independence. Sri Lanka was also way ahead in terms of human development—its achievements in health and education were well above the levels obtaining in other countries with similar per capita income.

Despite many differences in the initial conditions noted above, the majority of the countries shared one common initial condition that was fundamental to their subsequent transformation. This commonality lay in the choice of development strategy. Inspired by the example of India, they adopted the then popular strategy of economic planning in which the state was expected to play a predominant role in guiding the process of economic development.

There were a couple of significant exceptions, however. While Sri Lanka did follow in the footsteps of India by adopting a state-led development strategy, it continued at the same time to sustain—and indeed strengthen—its unique welfare state policies, which were inherited from the terminal years of colonial times. The other exception was Bhutan, which had no development strategy in the conventional sense. This was consistent with the de-emphasis on material prosperity that had become ingrained in Bhutanese culture, which received rather colourful expression in the royal proclamation that Bhutan would pursue the goal of gross national happiness (GNH) as distinct from the pursuit of gross national product (GNP) that is embodied in conventional development strategies.

Some quantitative indices of the initial conditions are presented below:[3]

(a) In terms of per capita income, the region was poorer than most developing regions in the world but not in comparison with the rest of Asia. Within the region, Sri Lanka was by far the most prosperous country and Nepal the poorest.

(b) There was a negligible manufacturing base in Nepal and Bangladesh, with GDP shares of 3.3 per cent and 5.4 per cent respectively. Pakistan and Sri Lanka were relatively advanced in this regard but they, too, were well below the East Asian and Latin American standards.

(c) Bangladesh and Pakistan were the most populous countries of the region, accounting for some 85 per cent of the total population of the region. Bhutan was by far the tiniest, with a population of about 200,000.

---

[3] For more details, see Osmani (2018: table A2).

(d) With more than 400 people per square kilometre, Bangladesh had an exceptionally high population density. For comparison, South Asia as a whole (including India) had a density of 128, East Asia 59 and the other developing regions only around 10–12.

(e) With a life expectancy of fifty-nine years and 94 per cent enrolment at the primary level, Sri Lanka was way ahead of the rest of the region as well as most other developing regions in terms of health and education. Within the region itself, Bhutan and Nepal lagged the furthest behind, with Pakistan and Bangladesh occupying a position somewhere in between.

3. Growth and Structural Transformation

Growth performance has been slightly uneven across the region (Table 21.1, Panel A). Bangladesh, Nepal, and Sri Lanka experienced a growth acceleration between the two halves of the fifty-year period from 1965 to 2015. The acceleration was the sharpest in Bangladesh, where the growth rate doubled from 2.7 per cent per annum in the first half to 5.4 per cent in the second. In comparison, the acceleration in Nepal and Sri Lanka was marginal. Bhutan and Pakistan, in contrast, experienced a deceleration of growth. Between the two, Bhutan's case is somewhat special because its initial growth rate (10.1 per cent in the 1980s) was a bit artificial, built as it was on a low base. The only genuine deceleration is observed in Pakistan, where the growth rate went down from 5.8 per cent in the first half of the period to 4.1 per cent in the second.[4]

All the countries in the region have gone through significant structural changes over time, as one would expect to happen in conjunction with economic growth. The share of agriculture in national income has declined sharply in all the countries and the share of industry increased. However, industry is a broad category that includes hydropower (e.g., in Bhutan and Nepal) and plantation (in Sri Lanka) as well as construction and manufacturing. Considering the narrower category of manufacturing alone, the extent of transformation in the sense of economic modernization has been relatively modest. This is true especially of Nepal and Bhutan, where the share of manufacturing remains well below 10 per cent in recent years. Even in the other three countries, the share is currently less than 20 per cent, whereas, for comparison, the share of manufacturing in the GDP of the East Asia and Pacific region during the same period was close to 30 per cent.

The growth and structural transformation of the last fifty years have been underpinned by a considerable increase in the rate of capital formation and trade orientation (Osmani 2018: table A2). Pakistan is a notable exception with

---

[4] The pattern of change in the growth of per capita income is very similar to that of the overall growth rate. However, differential success in reining in population growth did make a difference, especially in sharpening the contrast between Bangladesh and Pakistan.

Table 21.1 Growth performance of South Asia: 1966–2015

Panel A	Growth of GDP: 1966–2015 (% per annum)					
	Per capita GDP owth		GDP growth		Population growth	
	1966–1990	1991–2015	1966–1990	1991–2015	1966–1990	1991–2015
Bangladesh	0.1	3.6	2.7	5.4	2.6	1.7
Bhutan	7.1	5.0	10.1	6.6	3.0	1.6
Nepal	1.1	2.7	3.3	4.4	2.2	1.8
Pakistan	2.7	1.8	5.8	4.1	3.1	2.3
Sri Lanka	2.8	4.5	4.6	5.4	1.8	0.9
India	*2.1*	*4.9*	*4.4*	*6.6*	*2.3*	*1.7*

Panel B	Growth reversal in the 1970s and subsequent transition (growth of GDP; % per annum)		
	1966–1970	1971–1980	1981–2015
Bangladesh	3.4	1.0	5.0
Bhutan	n.a.	n.a.	7.6
Nepal	2.6	2.1	4.5
Pakistan	7.1	4.7	4.7
Sri Lanka	5.8	4.4	5.1
India	*4.6*	*3.1*	*6.3*

Notes: (1) The initial figures for Bhutan relate to the decade 1981–1990, since national income data are not available for Bhutan prior to 1980.

(2) In this, and the next table, we include Indian data, purely for a quick comparison, but without any comments in the text, because the Indian experience is not in the purview of this chapter.

Source: Compiled by the author from the World Bank's World Development Indicators database.

regard to the rate of investment, which has actually declined over the period—from 16.2 per cent at the beginning of the period to 14.9 per cent towards the end, which goes a long way towards explaining why Pakistan has been unique in the region in facing a growth deceleration between the two halves of the period. As for trade orientation, Sri Lanka was by far the most trade-oriented country at the beginning of the period, thanks mainly to its reliance on the plantation sector. Over the years, Sri Lanka has increased its trade ratio slightly—from 46.7 per cent in the beginning to 51.1 per cent at the end. By the end of the period, Bhutan had turned into the most open economy of the region, with a trade ratio of over 100 per cent, which is a consequence of the country's overwhelming dependence on India for all its hydropower exports as well as most of its consumer goods imports.

There has also been a significant change in the region's dependence on foreign aid: all the countries are now much less dependent on foreign aid than they used to be. In this sense, the region has become much more self-reliant. The most significant change in this regard has taken place in Sri Lanka and Bangladesh. During the last three decades, the flow of foreign aid has gone down in Sri Lanka from 8.4 per cent of GDP to less than 1 per cent, and in Bangladesh it has fallen from almost 6 per cent to 1.3 per cent. The flow of foreign aid to Nepal and Bhutan—originating mostly from India, on which both countries continue to be highly dependent—remains high in absolute terms, but even there it has fallen somewhat as a percentage of GDP.

A final noteworthy feature of the structural change in the region is its heavy reliance on workers' remittances. In all the countries except Bhutan, the flow of remittances is high and has increased sharply over the years. The magnitude of increase has been the most spectacular in Nepal, where remittances amounted to 27.5 per cent of GDP during 2011 to 2015, making it an exceptionally remittance-dependent country by international standards, not just by the standards of the region.

The main features of growth and structural transformation of the region may be summarized as follows. First, all the countries except Pakistan have experienced a substantial growth acceleration in the period since around 1990. Second, the growth acceleration has been underpinned by a rapid increase in the rates of savings and investment on the one hand and increasing trade openness on the other. Third, the rise in investment rates is especially remarkable in view of the fact that the region's dependence on foreign aid has fallen drastically. Higher rates of investment have been sustained partly by internal resource mobilization, and largely by a sharp rise in the flow of workers' remittances. Fourth, the structural transformation that has accompanied growth acceleration has been characterized by a sharp decline in the share of agriculture in national output, but without a correspondingly sharp increase in the share of manufacturing; it is services that have led the way. Finally, Pakistan, with stagnant investment rate and sluggish growth, has been an exception to the general pattern prevailing in the region.

The preceding summary makes it clear that the growth acceleration that has occurred since 1990 (except in Pakistan) is what one would expect from the basic tenets of development theory. Rise in investment rates and in the degree of trade openness are widely recognized to be among the major factors (though by no means the only ones) that propel economic growth, both on their own and through their interaction with each other. Both these factors have improved significantly in the second half of the period under consideration (except in Pakistan), making the growth acceleration possible. At the same time, the comparison of these factors with those of East Asia helps explain why the region is lagging behind. Most of the countries of the region have failed to reach the levels that East Asia has achieved—in terms of both investment rates (43 per cent in 2011–2015) and trade openness (56 per cent during 2011–2015).[5]

---

[5] East Asia here refers to the region classified by the World Bank as 'East Asia and Pacific (excluding high-income countries)' and the data are taken from the World Development Indicators database.

4. Growth Reversal of the 1970s

Before attempting to unravel the forces behind the patterns of growth and struc-tural transformation in South Asia, it is necessary to note that, soon after Myrdal wrote *Asian Drama* in the mid-1960s, growth prospects actually dimmed in South Asia (including India) before they began to improve. For most of the 1970s, the region faced a reversal of the growth momentum that had been generated in the preceding decades. For this reason, this decade has been described as the 'dis-mal decade' of South Asia (Osmani 2009).[6]

The rate of growth declined in the 1970s from the rates achieved in 1966–1970 in all countries for which data are available (Osmani 2018: table A1, panel B).[7] It was only in the 1980s, and in some cases in the 1990s, that signs of transition to a higher growth path began to emerge. The setback that happened in the 1970s, and the struggles the countries had to go through to recover from this setback, explain in some measure why South Asia has lagged behind East and Southeast Asia in the last fifty years in spite of starting from roughly comparable positions. In order to understand the overall growth performance of the region, it is therefore neces-sary to understand why the reversal happened in the first instance and how the countries attempted to climb out of it in the subsequent decades.

In explaining the growth reversal of the 1970s in South Asia (including India), it is common to attribute a central role to the alleged inefficiencies of a restrictive trade and industrial policy regime—in particular, of the import substitution strat-egy of development that was pursued throughout the region in the 1950s and 1960s.[8] It is, of course, acknowledged that South Asia was not unique in pursuing the import substitution strategy and that East Asia was also pursuing a similar strategy around the same time and still achieved much bigger success in subse-quent decades. The argument is rather that South Asia persisted with this strategy for far too long and implemented it much more rigidly than East Asia, and as a consequence suffered much more from the inefficiencies induced by the strategy. While this argument may have some validity in explaining a part of South Asia's growth shortfall relative to East Asia over the long term, it is a mistake to single out the cumulative effect of import substitution as the primary reason for the growth debacle of the 1970s. A number of conjunctural factors combined with a

---

[6] The 1970s was of course a bad time for the global economy generally, owing mainly to the oil price shock and the policy responses to it. But the situation was especially bad for South Asia for reasons that were specific to the region, which is what justifies describing the 1970s as the dismal dec-ade for South Asia, much more so than for any other developing region. For more on this, see Osmani (2009).

[7] The precise period during which the growth reversal happened varied between countries, and the record of growth during those periods is a lot worse than the average for the entire decade of the 1970s shown in the table. For details of these variations, see Osmani (2009).

[8] The exception was Bhutan, which did not pursue any kind of industrialization strategy to speak of until the 1980s.

range of policy failures to cause that debacle, and the policy failures that occurred went far beyond mere persistence with import substitution.[9]

The overwhelming importance of conjunctural factors is obvious in Bangladesh, which emerged as an independent nation in December 1971 after a prolonged war of liberation. The problem of physical devastation caused by the war was compounded by the disappearance of almost the entire entrepreneurial class, which came predominantly from West Pakistan. In the process, a large number of modern industries became ownerless, leaving the government with the choice of either nationalizing them or auctioning them off to private entrepreneurs. In the event, the first option was chosen, partly because of the absence of a strong indigenous entrepreneurial class, and partly in deference to the socialist ideal of the leadership of the newly independent country. At the same time, unrelenting balance of payments crises forced the government to adopt various restrictive measures including high tariffs, quantitative restrictions on imports, and import licensing, resulting in high and variable incentives for import substitution. It is thus fair to say that the restrictive trade and industrial policies of this decade were more a consequence than a cause of the economic meltdown, which was due primarily to exogenous factors.

In Pakistan, too, the poor performance of the economy in the dismal decade must be attributed mainly to factors other than the trade regime. To begin with, half of the country's export market suddenly disappeared with the cessation of East Pakistan as independent Bangladesh in December 1971. At the same time, agricultural output was severely disrupted by a series of floods and pest attacks. The effects of these shocks were compounded by the radical programme of economic reform adopted by Prime Minister Zulfiqar Ali Bhutto. He came to power in December 1971 with an avowedly socialist agenda of land reform and nationalization of industries. In the event, the implementation of land reform fell far short of its aim, but the disruption caused by government rhetoric and the piecemeal nature of its implementation created enough uncertainty to dampen the growth of investment in agriculture. The nationalization programme proved to be especially damaging. It had a severely dampening effect on private investment—the driving force behind Pakistan's growth in the preceding decades (Burki 1980). By 1974/75, total investment in large-scale manufacturing had dwindled to just one-third of the level of 1969/70. The precipitous decline of manufacturing in the dismal decade was but the inevitable consequence of this slump in investment. It is thus reasonable to argue that the slump of the 1970s owed much more to the joint squeeze delivered by exogenous shocks and Bhutto's anti-private enterprise policies than to the inefficiencies of import-substituting industrialization in the preceding decades.

---

[9] For an elaborate development of this argument for the whole of the South Asia region, including India, see Osmani (2009).

In the case of Sri Lanka, two different aspects of the policy regime have generally been blamed for the growth debacle of the 1970s. One of them is the common theme of excessive reliance on import-substituting industrialization. The other is unique to Sri Lanka—viz. its policy of maintaining persistently high levels of welfare expenditure until the 1980s. Several commentators have argued that whatever contributions these welfare expenditures might have made towards human development in Sri Lanka, they entailed a trade-off with economic growth, and that the crisis of the 1970s was but an inevitable consequence of this anti-growth bias of the welfarist regime.

Neither of these lines of argument stands up to careful empirical scrutiny.[10] As in the case of Pakistan, policy mistakes did aggravate the crisis, but the real problem did not lie either in the pursuit of import substitution or in the commitment to the welfare state. The problem lay in the creation of an overbearing state—in particular, in excessive reliance on the public sector as the principal vehicle for driving growth. The Ten-Year Plan for 1959–1968, which launched Sri Lanka on the path to industrialization, was deeply influenced by the Nehru–Mahalanobis strategy prevailing in India at the time, but Sri Lanka went far ahead of India in its reliance on the public sector. In the event, the Ten-Year Plan never became fully operational, and prior to 1970 the scope of the public sector remained smaller than was originally envisaged. However, soon after the left-wing collation, led by Srimavo Bandaranaike, came to power in 1970, the overbearing state spread its tentacles to all aspects of the economy—industry, agriculture, trade, and key service sectors. Thus, the economy that evolved in the 1970s was characterized by complete dominance of the state, which induced widespread rigidities and inefficiency.[11]

It is thus evident that the genesis of the 'dismal decade' in South Asia was a complex phenomenon going far beyond trade strategy. In all the countries, a series of supply shocks played a major role in precipitating the crisis. Erroneous policies were certainly responsible for aggravating the crisis, but the real culpability lay not so much with the policy of import substitution as with the excess of state intervention engulfing every sphere of the economy.

5. Attempted Transition to a Higher Growth Path

The dismal decade of South Asia came to an end towards the end of the 1970s. The first country to try to break out of the shackles was Sri Lanka, around 1977–1978, followed by Pakistan and then Bangladesh and Nepal. The transition was marked by a decisive shift in policy regime in each of the countries. The new regimes had many common features across the countries, although the vigour

---

[10] For a detailed rebuttal of both these lines of argument, see Osmani (1994).

[11] For evidence and further elaboration of these arguments see, among others, Athukorala and Jayasuriya (1994), Athukorala and Rajapathirana (2000), and Osmani (2009).

and consistency with which they were implemented varied from country to country. On the whole, the new regimes entailed a significant softening of the administrative grip on the economy, allowing a freer play of market forces both within the domestic sphere and in the conduct of external economic relations.[12]

5.1 The Reform Process

In Sri Lanka, the reform process started in 1977 when the right-wing United National Party (UNP), led by J.R. Jayawardene, returned to power with massive popular support. With the help of Bretton Woods institutions, the new government embarked upon an ambitious reform programme. The list of reform included the replacement of quantitative restrictions by tariffs on most import items, across-the-board reduction in tariff rates, hefty devaluation of the currency against the dollar, removal of exchange control for current account transactions, withdrawal of state monopoly over import trade and distribution of essential commodities, elimination of price controls, rationalization of state-owned enterprises, and special incentives to exporters of manufactures. A radical change also occurred in social welfare policy with the abolition of direct consumer subsidies. The rice ration system was replaced by a system of food stamps targeted at low-income groups.

In Pakistan, on his assumption of power in 1977, General Ziaul Haq initiated reforms with the avowed aims of reversing the statist strategy of the previous regime and restoring business confidence within the private sector. To this end, steps were taken to denationalize a few of the industries, to soften the grip of the investment licensing system and to encourage the private sector to enter the areas not reserved for the public sector.

In Bangladesh, a major thrust towards liberalization came with the launching of the New Industrial Policy (NIP) in 1982, which initiated a process of denationalization and stimulation of private enterprise. By 1985, only about 40 per cent of industrial assets remained in the public sector as compared with 90 per cent in the early 1970s. Nepal moved much more slowly than the others in the early 1980s, relying mainly on a depreciation of the currency aimed at boosting exports.

These early reforms had very little impact on the real economy, however. There was indeed an economic upturn at that time, but in all cases it was engineered by an unprecedented expansion of demand that brought about higher growth through fuller utilization of the excess capacity that had emerged in the 1970s.

In Sri Lanka, the expansion of domestic demand came from two main sources. First, the government embarked upon an investment programme of unprecedented magnitude with two major components—one involving large-scale irrigation

---

[12] The following discussion leaves out Bhutan, whose story has some unique features. That story is told briefly in a separate sub-section at the end of this section.

and land development under the Mahaweli Development Project and the other involving an ambitious housing programme. Second, the investment effort was supported by an exceptionally generous flow of foreign assistance from Western donors who were keen to ensure the success of Sri Lanka's pioneering effort at economic liberalization. In the process, the budget deficit soared from about 8 per cent of GDP during 1970–1977 to 19 per cent during 1978–1983.

In Pakistan and Nepal, too, the initial boost to domestic demand came from expansionary fiscal policy. The fiscal deficit increased from an average of 5.3 per cent of GDP in the 1970s to 7.1 per cent in the 1980s in Pakistan,[13] and from 3.1 per cent to 6.7 per cent in Nepal.[14] Bangladesh was slightly different in the sense that credit policy was the principal vehicle for demand expansion. In order to ensure the success of the privatization programme that stemmed from the NIP launched in 1982, the potential buyers of state-owned enterprises were lured with cheap credit from the nationalized banking system, resulting in a credit boom.

It is arguable that some degree of demand expansion made sense in the 1980s for all these countries as it helped exploit the slack that had been generated by the crisis of the 1970s. The problem, however, was that, in all cases, the expansion of demand was carried to the extreme, thereby storing up macroeconomic imbalances for the future, which led invariably to growth retardation, principally through fiscal squeeze and partly through appreciation of the real exchange rate that resulted from higher inflation.

Deep-rooted structural problems eventually began to outweigh the stimulus of demand expansion, resulting in the slowdown of growth. The emerging crisis prompted a series of structural adjustment programmes starting from the second half of the 1980s, which apart from trying to stabilize demand also aimed at implementing far-reaching market-oriented reforms in both domestic and external sectors.

5.2 Post-reform Growth Trajectories

While the nature of reforms was very similar in all the countries, the results were very different, mainly because of the different ways in which the political economy of the countries evolved in the subsequent period. The biggest problems were faced by Pakistan and Nepal; Sri Lanka somehow muddled through, and

---

[13] Three other factors also contributed: depreciation of currency, a surge in workers' remittances, and a large inflow of Western aid, which poured in mainly to help Pakistan train and arm the Afghan mujahideen who were fighting against the Soviet invasion of Afghanistan. Average annual foreign aid committed to Pakistan increased from US$1.45 billion during 1970–1978 to as much as US$2.29 billion during 1983–1988 (Ahmad and Laporte 1989).

[14] At the same time, money supply also increased rapidly, the supply of broad money rising from 16.2 per cent of GDP to 27.2 per cent. For more on the reforms in Nepal, see Osmani and Bajracharya (2008).

Bangladesh was the only country that was able to enjoy sustained benefits from the reforms.

In Pakistan, the decade of the 1990s was marked by an intense power struggle among the major political parties on the one hand, and the military–bureaucratic nexus on the other, which resulted in the dismissal of four elected governments, culminating in yet another military coup in 1999. The fallout of this turmoil was a severe deterioration in economic performance—so much so that during the five-year period 1997–2002, GDP growth plummeted to an average of barely 3 per cent, which was even lower than had been achieved in the 'dismal decade'. There was a brief turnaround after 2002–2003, but this too did not last long as it was stimulated by unsustainable fiscal expansion rather than long-overdue structural reforms (Hasan 2008). The history of growth in Pakistan is thus one of a series of booms and busts. Political uncertainty has played a huge part in causing these economic cycles, which in turn has had a deleterious long-term effect on the economy by causing a secular stagnation of investment. Since 1980, Pakistan's investment ratio has been the lowest in the region; not surprisingly, its growth performance has also been the weakest.

In Nepal, too, the potential benefits of reforms were swamped by the fallout from political turmoil. For a while, the reforms instituted in the early 1990s did seem to yield some tangible results, but the growth rate slumped after 2000. This slump was caused by the political turmoil emanating especially from a severe Maoist insurgency and a protracted power struggle between politicians and the Royalty. Despite the economic progress made in the previous period, Nepal's development was fragile and fraught with deficiencies. Most importantly, not all regions or groups were able to participate equally in growth and human develop-ment. In particular, the Western and Far Western regions, *Dalits* (the lowest caste or 'untouchables') and indigenous peoples lagged behind badly. Growing inequal-ity sowed the seeds of a Maoist insurgency, which started in 1996, and intensified after 2001, leading to a serious deterioration in security and disruption in devel-opment and governance in large parts of Nepal. Furthermore, an increasingly competitive global environment, brought about by the phasing out of the quota that was guaranteed under the Multi-Fibre Arrangement (MFA), resulted in a steady loss in the market share of Nepali exports. When the conflicts finally ended in 2007, and a new political compact was reached around a new interim Constitution, it was hoped that the economy would finally turn a corner. However, a large peace dividend that many had hoped for failed to materialize, and the economy sput-tered along at an average growth rate of 4.7 per cent during this period.[15]

Sri Lanka's post-reform growth trajectory also went through ups and downs, but on the average, the economy kept growing at the moderate rate of around

---

[15] The opportunities and challenges emerging in the post-conflict era are insightfully analysed in Pant et al. (2017) and World Bank (2017).

5 per cent during 1985 to 2005. Several structural bottlenecks were responsible for Sri Lanka's failure to move on to an even higher growth path after the initial recovery. Some of these bottlenecks were legacies of the profligate macroeconomic policy the country pursued after 1977.[16] These included slow growth of public investment, high rates of inflation leading to the appreciation of the real exchange rate and negative real interest rate. By the mid-2000s, a widespread disenchantment had set in among Sri Lankans with the unfulfilled promises of the liberalized policy regime. A decisive shift in policy orientation came when the coalition government of the United People's Freedom Alliance (UPFA) came to power in 2004, and it became intensified when Mahinda Rajapakse, the candidate of the left-leaning Sri Lanka Freedom Party (SLFP), won the Presidential elections of November 2005.

The new government's development ideology and policy directions marked a deliberate attempt to move away from many of the fundamental tenets of the preceding regime.[17] The government placed special emphasis on social development, distributive policies, extensive government intervention and 'domestic' economic activities of the rural populations. In the process of pursuing this agenda, the government reverted to the inward-looking protectionist development policy of the past. Restrictive trade policies created a strong anti-export bias, which was reflected in a dramatic decline in the trade-to-GDP ratio—from 89 per cent in 2000 to 48 per cent in 2016. Overall growth performance did not, however, suffer in the short run. In addition to policy actions that boosted domestic demand, the end of the decades-long civil war in the North in 2009 provided a significant boost to the economy. The ensuing peace dividend, in combination with the domestic-demand-oriented policy, has enabled the country to maintain a steady enough growth over a prolonged period. There is, however, no sign of the growth acceleration that many expected the peace dividend to yield.

In Bangladesh, the eventual transition to a higher growth path coincided with its democratic transition at the outset of the 1990s. Improved performance of both agriculture and manufacturing contributed to the acceleration of growth. A combination of policy interventions and favourable external conditions helped to bring about this transformation.[18]

In agriculture, a major boost came from the liberalization of markets for agricultural inputs, especially elimination of non-tariff barriers to the importation of cheap irrigation equipment with effect from 1988. Growth in manufacturing was led by the export-oriented garments sector, which benefitted from a combination of policy reform and conjunctural factors. On the policy front, trade

---

[16] Kelegama (2008) provides a perceptive analysis of the legacies left by the fiscal profligacy of the 1980s.

[17] See World Bank (2016b) for detailed discussion of this policy shift and its implications.

[18] For a fuller analysis of the growth acceleration in Bangladesh since the 1990s, see Osmani et al. (2006).

liberalization played a key role. Between the late 1980s and early 1990s, Bangladesh embarked upon one of the most remarkable episodes of trade liberalization in the contemporary world, slashing tariff rates much faster than most other developing countries in Asia and elsewhere (Mahmud 2004). Reduced protection, coupled with a variety of direct incentives offered to the export-oriented firms, resulted in a substantial reduction in anti-export bias within the existing incentive structure. To a significant extent, export growth was also helped by external factors such as the MFA, which ensured easy access of Bangladeshi garments to Western markets. A couple of other factors also helped—namely, stronger mobilization of domestic resources and increased flow of workers' remittances. All these have enabled Bangladesh to maintain a steady acceleration in GDP growth since around 1990. From an average of 3.8 per cent in the 1980s, the growth rate has accelerated steadily, reaching an average of 6.3 per cent during 2010 to 2015. Such a sustained acceleration in growth over a quarter of a century makes Bangladesh an exceptional performer in the region—in sharp contrast to Pakistan, Sri Lanka, and Nepal, all of which have struggled to sustain growth, let alone to accelerate it, during the same period.

Bangladesh's relative success can be attributed to a couple of distinctive features of its development process. First, continuity in the practice of democratic politics—which sets Bangladesh apart from Pakistan, Sri Lanka, and Nepal—has clearly helped by providing a relatively stable socio-political environment. Second, more than in any other country of the region, the NGO community of Bangladesh has played a very strong role in softening some of the constraints to growth and development. For example, they have softened the credit constraint faced by poor entrepreneurs by providing affordable microcredit, strengthened the female labour force through various programmes of women's empowerment, and helped improve the level of human capital at the grassroots level through innovative initiatives for providing informal education and healthcare to the poor.[19]

5.3 The Story of Bhutan

The story of Bhutan is rather different from that of the other countries in the region; it does not fit the pattern described so far, if only because modernization of the Bhutanese economy is a much more recent phenomenon. Ever since the mid-1980s, the economic growth of Bhutan has been inextricably and almost exclusively linked to the development of hydropower. Apart from earning valuable exports revenue, hydropower has also contributed to GDP growth indirectly by boosting the construction sector through both backward and forward linkages

---

[19] In the process, the NGO community has also made a significant contribution towards poverty reduction and human development, as discussed in section 6 below.

and by facilitating the growth of power-intensive industries. The combined contribution of the energy sector itself, and of energy-related activities such as construction and power-intensive industries, has enabled Bhutan to sustain a remarkably high growth rate of around 8 per cent over a period of three decades, despite slow growth in agriculture.

Hydropower also makes an overwhelming contribution to the public exchequer, through both tax and non-tax revenue. Most of the government revenue earned from the sale of hydropower has been used to maintain high levels of social expenditure and to fund infrastructural development. At the same time, most of the earnings from electricity exports have been used to import consumer goods, including essential foodstuffs, from India. Without these imports, the social expenditure as well as construction and other activities spurred by hydropower development would have faced serious problems due to the wage goods constraint. The softening of the wage goods constraint has been one of the principal pathways through which hydropower has contributed to sustaining the growth process in Bhutan.[20]

Yet another distinctive feature of Bhutan is that for the past three and a half decades, the development strategy of Bhutan has been underpinned by an overarching philosophy of human well-being that goes under the rubric of the GNH approach to development. By deliberately juxtaposing itself against the traditional pre-occupation with GNP, this philosophy explicitly rejects the purely materialistic approach to development and calls for a holistic approach to development embracing material, environmental, cultural, and spiritual goals. For operational purposes, the GNH approach has been defined in terms of four pillars, viz. (1) equitable development, ensuring equity between individuals as well as regions, (2) environmental sustainability, (3) cultural and spiritual upliftment and (4) good governance. Although there exists some uncertainty as to how exactly to translate these principles into actual policymaking, the government of Bhutan continues to make serious attempts to ensure that its development strategy conforms to these principles as closely as possible.[21] The choices made by the government in pursuit of these goals invariably entailed trade-offs with the demands for material progress. So far, the government has managed the trade-offs without much sacrifice of material welfare, but they remain a concern for the future.[22]

6. Poverty Reduction and Human Development

The economic transformation of South Asia is reflected not only in rising per capita income but also in sharply falling poverty rates and all-round human

[20] For further development of these arguments, see Osmani et al. (2005, 2008).

[21] For an attempt to operationalize the concept of GNH in terms of practical policymaking, see, among others, RGOB (1999).

[22] Some of the policy choices are analysed in ADB (2013) and World Bank (2014).

development. As measured by the international poverty line, the extent of poverty was in the range of 44 to 62 per cent in the early 1990s—except in Sri Lanka, where it was less than 10 per cent. Since then, it has fallen drastically every-where—to 15 per cent in Nepal, 13 per cent in Bangladesh, 6 per cent in Pakistan and only about 2 per cent in Bhutan and Sri Lanka.[23]

Long-term economic growth, and the accompanying structural transformation in occupational patterns, has played a major role in achieving this remarkable reduction of poverty across the region by opening up opportunities for gainful employment for increasing numbers of people.[24] But other country-specific factors have also contributed. In Bangladesh, a major contribution has come from the microfinance revolution, which has reached nearly two-thirds of the rural population. By providing affordable credit to poor self-employed people, microfinance has enabled a significant number of them to climb out of poverty by seizing the opportunities opened up by the growth process.[25] In Sri Lanka, the egalitarian policies pursued by the government since the middle of the 2000s has helped render the growth process distinctly pro-poor. In Nepal and Pakistan, the huge amount of remittances sent by overseas migrant workers has been a major driver of poverty reduction. In Bhutan, the egalitarian philosophy underlying the GNH approach has helped translate the riches of hydropower into higher living standards for the general population.

Impressive gains have been made in other dimensions of human development as well. Sri Lanka is well known for its stellar achievements in various dimensions of human development from the earliest stage of its development. In the 1960s and 1970s, when most developing countries were almost obsessively preoccupied with growth, Sri Lanka set up an elaborate welfare state, quite atypical of countries at comparable levels of income. As a consequence, the health and educational outcomes of the people of Sri Lanka surged ahead of the levels achieved not just in South Asia but in most other developing countries, and even some developed countries of the world. In the process, Sri Lanka became a role model for the human development paradigm.[26] Since the early 1990s, other countries in the

---

[23] See figure 1 in Osmani (2018). The international poverty line has been used for the sake of comparability across countries. Estimates of poverty based on national poverty lines tend to be some-what higher, but long-term trends are roughly similar.

[24] For a detailed analysis of the processes of poverty reduction in the region, see, among others, Osmani et al. (2006), World Bank (2013), Osmani (2017), Sen and Ali (2017) and on Bangladesh; ADB (2014) and NSB (2014) on Bhutan; Uematsu et al. (2016) and World Bank (2016a) on Nepal; López-Cálix et al. (2014) on Pakistan; and Gunatilaka et al. (2009) and World Bank (2015b; 2016b) on Sri Lanka.

[25] A recent carefully conducted econometric exercise has estimated that, in the absence of microfinance rural poverty, would have been 46 per cent in 2010 instead of 33 per cent, the actual poverty rate. In other words, microfinance has helped make rural poverty 28.5 per cent lower than it would otherwise have been (Mahmud and Osmani 2016: chapter 7).

[26] Some commentators have argued that the contribution of welfare expenditures to human development in Sri Lanka has been vastly exaggerated and that the country's unusually high level of human development owes more to favourable initial conditions than to policy—a view that has been hotly contested by others, and now stands discredited. For a comprehensive review of this debate, see Osmani (1994).

region have also made impressive progress, though not quite achieving the levels of human development obtaining in Sri Lanka.

South Asia (including India) has historically been notorious for having an exceptionally high prevalence of malnutrition, even compared with regions such as Sub-Saharan Africa, which have been economically more backward in most respects than South Asia. In the mid-1990s, UNICEF coined the term 'Asian Enigma' to refer to this perverse scenario. Much has changed in the two decades since then. While the level of malnutrition still remains unacceptably high in all South Asian countries (with the exception of Sri Lanka), the speed of improvement has been quite remarkable (Osmani 2018, figure 2). The sharpest decline has occurred in Bangladesh, where the prevalence of stunting has come down from around 69 per cent in 1995 to just 36 per cent in 2014. Nepal has also achieved a very rapid speed of improvement, followed closely by Bhutan. Sri Lanka, which had less than half the stunting rate of the other countries to begin with, has been able to reduce it further—to just 15 per cent by 2014. Pakistan is the sole exception to this pattern of sustained improvement. Some improvement did occur until the early 2000s, but there seems to have been a reversal since then. Poor progress in human development in Pakistan is underlined by low public spending on social sectors, which has actually declined as a share of GDP in recent years.

At the opposite end in the spectrum of progress in human development lies Bangladesh. Among the low- and lower-middle-income countries in the world, Bangladesh's performance in health and education makes it a significant outlier— with a much better performance than might be predicted on the basis of per capita income alone. What is more, Bangladesh has been able to achieve these results with a much lower public expenditure on health and education (as a percentage of GDP) than countries with comparable performance. This unique feature of Bangladesh's achievement reflects to a large extent the sterling role that its NGO community has played in promoting social development, much more than in any other part of South Asia (Asadullah et al. 2014).

One aspect of the NGO movement in Bangladesh that is especially salient in this context is its singular focus on women's empowerment. Since its very inception, the microfinance movement, led by the *Grameen* Bank, has targeted women as the main beneficiaries. BRAC (Bangladesh Rural Advancement Committee), the largest development NGO in the world, has also kept women at the centre of its wide-ranging activities, involving microcredit, health, education, and entrepreneurship development. Most other NGOs have similarly engaged in women-focused activities. The Government of Bangladesh has also made a major contribution in this regard by giving special incentive to girls' education through stipends—first at primary and subsequently at secondary level. All these have enabled Bangladesh to achieve gender parity in school much sooner than the rest of the countries (other than Sri Lanka);[27] and the advancement in girls' education, coupled with the general empowerment of women, has in turn helped the country achieve exceptional performance in the fields of health and nutrition despite low public spending in these areas.

While the region as a whole can be proud of the overall progress in human development that has taken place in the last two to three decades, a number of concerns are beginning to appear on the horizon. As these economies move on to the next stage of development and brace themselves to face the challenges of global competition on the one hand and rapid technological change on the other, they will need to improve the skill-base of their population. While some improvement has indeed occurred, it has been from a very low base, and the current level of human capital among the countries' labour forces is still very low by international standards. One indication of this is the low ratio of young people with access to tertiary education, which has been in the range of 10 to 18 per cent in recent years.

Another, related, concern is rising inequality in various dimensions. Income inequality, as measured by the Gini coefficient, is generally on an upward trend in most of the countries (Osmani 2018, figure 4). The upward-rising first half of Kuznets' celebrated inverted U-shaped relation between growth and inequality is evident for all countries except Sri Lanka, where the second, downward-sloping, part has begun to emerge in recent years—thanks to the egalitarian policies pursued by the present regime.

There are signs of growing inequality also in educational and health outcomes. It was noted earlier that the current level of human capital is generally low across the region. What makes the situation more worrisome is that, for the countries for which information on the distribution of human capital is available, it is the children from richer families who are acquiring an increasing share of whatever human capital is being formed. For instance, the difference in access to tertiary education between the richest and the poorest quintiles of the population has widened considerably since the early 1990s in Bangladesh, Nepal, and Pakistan (Osmani 2018, table A3.) Similarly, the difference between the richest and the poorest quintiles in the prevalence of child malnutrition has also widened during the same period (Osmani 2018, table A4). If unchecked, this trend of increasing inequality in human capital is likely to perpetuate income inequality through the intergenerational transmission mechanism—as children from poorer families accumulate less human capital and earn less income than children from richer families, they would transmit the inequality to the next generation. In the

---

[27] Pakistan is the only country in the region (including India) that has yet to achieve gender parity in schooling; in fact, its gender parity index still hovers around just 50 per cent.

process, not only would inequality be perpetuated, but persistent inequality may also weaken the foundations of long-term growth.[28]

There is a good deal of commonality in the experience across the region, especially in the trends since the 1990s—as seen in the significant reduction in poverty and the sharp improvement in various dimensions of human development in most of the countries, accompanied, however, by rising inequality. The notable exception is Pakistan, where although poverty levels have declined, thanks largely to a spectacular growth in workers' remittances, human development has lagged behind badly. The contrast in this sphere between Pakistan on the one hand and Sri Lanka and Bangladesh on the other is quite stark. Sri Lanka has, of course, always been a leader in the field of human development in the region because of its singular emphasis on a welfare state since the early days, but in terms of rate of improvement, Bangladesh's performance has been the most spectacular. Its achievement has been based on the twin foundations of an active government, supported by increasing availability of resources made possible by steady growth, and a uniquely active role of the NGO community. Pakistan, in contrast, has been hamstrung in both respects—public expenditure on human development has been thoroughly inadequate in the face of frequent collapses in economic growth, and NGO activism has been one of the weakest in the region.

7. Challenges Lying Ahead

South Asia has overcome many challenges in the last fifty years, and achieved significant improvement in the living standards of the people, defying the dire predictions of many. It could be argued, though, that perhaps the region was unable to realize its full potential, and there is also no doubt that many more challenges lie ahead. Many of these challenges are common, but some matter more for some countries than for others.

The situation is perhaps the most challenging in Pakistan, where political uncertainty, weak governance, widespread terrorism, a high fertility rate, and a generally conservative attitude towards female education and female labour force participation combine to create an onerous set of constraints. Especially disconcerting is the fact that long-run growth potential is declining in Pakistan. It has been estimated that in the last fifty years Pakistan's steady annual GDP growth rate has fallen from 6 per cent to about 4.5 per cent (Lopez-Calix et al. 2012), which is much lower than the 7 per cent rate that the government considers necessary for gainfully absorbing a bulging young population (GOP 2011). This contrast between potential growth and warranted growth portends an ominous

---

[28] For a fuller analysis of the intergenerational transmission mechanism—in the specific context of Bangladesh—see Osmani (2017).

future for Pakistan, regardless of the political regime that comes to prevail, unless necessary structural reforms are undertaken immediately to reverse the decline in potential growth.[29]

Sri Lanka started its journey with the most favourable initial conditions, which have helped the country to maintain a fair rate of economic and social advancement despite prolonged and destructive ethnic conflicts, but for it to emerge fully from the legacies of the conflict and achieve its full potential still remains a huge challenge. A matter of concern here is the recent political backlash that has tilted the policy regime aggressively towards restrictive and inward-looking economic policies. It does not augur well that recent trade policy has rendered the country's import regime one of the most complex and protectionist in the world and that the consequent anti-export bias of the trade regime has seen the trade ratio plummet from 89 per cent of GDP in 2000 to just 48 per cent in 2016. The future success of Sri Lanka's economic performance will depend crucially on how well the politicians can combine the demands of populism with the needs of economic dynamism.

Nepal and Bhutan have found their own unique ways to overcome the inherent constraints of a landlocked economy that is dependent on a big neighbour. But excessive reliance on hydropower in Bhutan and on remittance in Nepal is creating a one-dimensional economy in each case, which is engendering a set of structural constraints that inhibit economic diversification and thereby limit the prospects of sustaining, let alone accelerating, the pace of socio-economic development.[30]

Bangladesh is perhaps the most favourably placed country within the region, and is most likely to be able to sustain a relatively rapid pace of socio-economic development in the coming decades. But in order to achieve its potential, the country will have to find ways of vastly improving its notoriously weak governance structure and lingering political uncertainty, which have led to stagnation in private investment in recent years.

In addition to these country-specific problems, the region as a whole also faces a set of common challenges: (a) a low skill-base, which is utterly inadequate in the face of the emerging challenges of global competition and technological upheaval; (b) rising inequality in multiple dimensions, which threatens to weaken the foundations of long-term growth, in addition to being unjust in itself; (c) excessive reliance on workers' remittances, which could jeopardize the sustainability of the region's economic achievements owing to growing uncertainty in the oil economies of the Middle-East, the rise of nationalistic sentiments in several industrialized economies, and the emergences of new suppliers of labour such as Vietnam, Cambodia, and Laos; (d) the slow pace in creating enough high-quality jobs, which not only constrains growth but also renders growth less

---

[29] See, Burki and Hasan (2013) for an insightful discussion of the kind of reforms needed.
[30] For a perceptive analysis of how excessive reliance on hydropower is creating serious structural imbalances for Bhutan, see World Bank (2015a).

Table 21.2 Correlates of economic growth in South Asia

	Investment rate		Trade ratio		Foreign aid		Foreign aid		Remittances	
	1966–1970	2011–2015	1966–1970	2011–2015	1981–1985	2011–2015	1981–1985	2011–2015	1981–1985	2011–2015
Bangladesh	11.5	28.3	21.1	45.7	5.9	1.3	35.8	5.1	2.7	9.1
Bhutan	na	57.4	na	101.0	11.7	7.7	24.1	12.6	na	0.8
Nepal	5.3	38.0	14.6	47.8	8.0	4.6	42.6	12.3	1.3	27.5
Pakistan	16.2	14.9	24.0	31.5	2.4	1.2	14.1	8.6	8.5	6.5
Sri Lanka	16.7	33.3	46.7	51.1	8.4	0.7	30.4	2.0	5.4	8.6
India	*16.5*	*35.9*	*1.2*	*3.5*	*0.8*	*0.1*	*3.9*	*0.4*	*1.2*	*3.5*

Source: Compiled by the author from the World Bank's World Development Indicators database.

effective in reducing poverty (Nayar et al. 2012); and (e) rapid urbanization, whose unique challenges none of the countries has yet to come to terms with. Furthermore, the global problem of climate change will have far-reaching implications for the living standards of the region's people, as might changes in global geopolitical alignments—with implications for trade flows and the flow of capital. The future trajectory of socio-economic development of the region will depend to a large extent on precisely how the political regimes respond to these emerging challenges.

Acknowledgements

The author is deeply grateful to Deepak Nayyar, an anonymous referee, and participants at two seminars in Hanoi and Shanghai for extremely valuable comments on earlier drafts of the chapter. The responsibility for any errors and shortcomings rests solely with the author.

References

ADB (2013). *Bhutan: Critical Development Constraints*. Manila: Asian Development Bank.

ADB (2014). 'Poverty Analysis (Summary)', Asian Development Bank, Manila, background paper for the Bhutan Country Partnership Strategy 2014–2018.

Ahmad, M., and R. Laporte (1989). *Public Enterprise in Pakistan: The Hidden Crisis in Economic Development*. Boulder, CO: Westview Press.

Asadullah, M.N., A. Savoia, and W. Mahmud (2014). 'Paths to Development: Is there a Bangladesh Surprise?', *World Development*, 62 (October): 138–54.

Athukorala, P., and S. Jayasuriya (1994). *Macroeconomic Policies, Crises, and Growth in Sri Lanka, 1969–90*. Washington, DC: World Bank.

Athukorala, P., and S. Rajapathirana (2000). *Liberalization and Industrial Transformation: Sri Lanka in International Perspective*. Oxford: Oxford University Press.

Burki, S.J. (1980). *State and Society in Pakistan 1971–77*. London: Macmillan.

Burki, S.J., and P. Hasan (2013). 'A Growth and Adjustment Strategy for Pakistan', World Bank, Islamabad, Policy Paper Series for Pakistan.

GOP (2011). *The Framework of Economic Growth*. Islamabad: Planning Commission, Government of Pakistan.

Gunatilaka, R., G. Wan, and S. Chatterjee (2009). *Poverty and Human Development in Sri Lanka*. Manila: Asian Development Bank.

Hasan, P. (2008). 'Pakistan'. In A. Chowdhury and W. Mahmud (eds) *Handbook on the South Asian Economies*. London: Edward Elgar.

Kelegama, S. (2008). 'Sri Lanka'. In A. Chowdhury and W. Mahmud (eds) *Handbook on the South Asian Economies*. London: Edward Elgar.

López-Cálix, J.R., C. Mejia, D. Newhouse, and C. Sobrado (2014). 'Pakistan Poverty Trends, Scenarios and Drivers', World Bank, Islamabad, Policy Paper Series for Pakistan.

López-Cálix, J.R., T.G. Srinivasan, and M. Waheed (2012). 'What Do We Know About Growth Patterns in Pakistan?', World Bank, Islamabad, Policy Paper Series for Pakistan.

Mahmud, W. (2004). 'Macroeconomic Management: From Stabilisation to Growth?', *Economic and Political Weekly*, 4(September): 4023–32.

Mahmud, W., and S.R. Osmani (2016). *The Theory and Practice of Microcredit*. London: Routledge.

Nayar, R., P. Gottret, P. Mitra, G. Betcherman, Y.M. Lee, I. Santos, M. Dahal, and M. Shrestha (2012). *More and Better Jobs for South Asia*. Washington, DC: World Bank.

NSB (2014). *Bhutan Poverty Assessment 2014*. Thimphu: National Statistical Bureau of the Royal Government of Bhutan and World Bank.

Osmani, S.R. (1994). 'Is there a Conflict between Growth and Welfarism: The Significance of the Sri Lanka Debate', *Development and Change*, 25(2): 387–421.

Osmani, S.R. (2009). 'Explaining Growth in South Asia'. In G. McMahon, H. Esfahani, and L. Squire (eds) *Diversity in Economic Growth: Global Insights and Explanations*. Cheltenham: Edward Elgar.

Osmani, S.R. (2017). 'Eradicating Poverty and Minimizing Inequality for Ensuring Shared Prosperity in Bangladesh', a background paper prepared for the Perspective Plan 2021–2041 of the Planning Commission of the Government of Bangladesh, Dhaka.

Osmani, S.R. (2018). 'Socio-economic Development in South Asia: The Past Fifty Years', World Institute of Development Economics Research, Helsinki, Working Paper No. 2018/105.

Osmani, S.R., and B.B. Bajracharya (2008). 'Nepal'. In A. Chowdhury and W. Mahmud (eds) *Handbook on the South Asian Economies*. London: Edward Elgar.

Osmani, S.R., B.B. Bajracharya, S. Tenzing, and T. Wangyal (2005). 'Macroeconomics of Poverty Reduction: The Case Study of Bhutan', a report prepared for the UNDP regional project on the Macroeconomics of Poverty Reduction, UNDP Regional Centre, Colombo.

Osmani, S.R., W. Mahmud, B. Sen, H. Dagdeviren, and A. Seth (2006). *The Macroeconomics of Poverty Reduction: The Case Study of Bangladesh*. Colombo: UNDP Regional Centre.

Osmani, S.R., S. Tenzing, and T. Wangyal (2008). 'Bhutan'. In A. Chowdhury and W. Mahmud (eds) *Handbook on the South Asian Economies*. London: Edward Elgar.

Pant, B.D., N.K. Joshi, and P. Rijal (eds) (2017). *Selected Essays on Nepali Economy*. Kathmandu: Institute for Integrated Development Studies.

RGOB (1999). *Vision 2020: A Vision for Peace, Prosperity and Happiness*. Thimphu: Planning Commission, Royal Government of Bhutan.

Sen, B., and Z. Ali (2017). 'Ending Extreme Poverty in Bangladesh: Trends, Drivers, and Policies'. In J. Devine, G.D. Wood, Z. Ali, and S. Alam (eds) *Extreme Poverty, Growth and Inequality in Bangladesh*. Rugby: Practical Action Publishing Ltd.

Uematsu, H., A.R. Shidiq, and S. Tiwari (2016). 'Trends and Drivers of Poverty Reduction in Nepal: A Historical Perspective', World Bank, Washington, DC, Policy Research Working Paper 7830.

World Bank (2013). *Bangladesh Poverty Assessment: Assessing a Decade of Progress in Reducing Poverty, 2000–2010*. Dhaka: World Bank.

World Bank (2014). *Kingdom of Bhutan: Green Growth Opportunities for Bhutan (Policy Note)*. Washington, DC: World Bank.

World Bank (2015a). *Hydropower Impact and Public Finance Reforms towards Economic Self-Reliance. Bhutan—Macroeconomic and Public Finance Policy Note*. Washington, DC: World Bank.

World Bank (2015b). *Sri Lanka: Ending Poverty and Promoting Shared Prosperity*. Washington, DC: World Bank.

World Bank (2016a). *Moving Up the Ladder: Poverty Reduction and Social Mobility in Nepal*. Kathmandu: World Bank.

World Bank (2016b). *Sri Lanka Poverty and Welfare: Recent Progress and Remaining Challenges*. Washington, DC: World Bank.

World Bank (2017). *Climbing Higher: Toward a Middle-Income Nepal*. Washington, DC: World Bank.

Index